THE GREAT RESISTANCE

Also by Carrie Gibson

El Norte:
The Epic and Forgotten Story of Hispanic North America

Empire's Crossroads:
A History of the Caribbean from Columbus to the Present Day

THE GREAT RESISTANCE

The 400-Year Fight to End Slavery in the Americas

CARRIE GIBSON

LONDON

First published in Great Britain in 2026 by Basic Books UK
An imprint of John Murray Press

1

Copyright © Carrie Gibson 2026

The right of Carrie Gibson to be identified as the Author of the Work has been asserted by her in accordance with the Copyright, Designs and Patents Act 1988.

All rights reserved. No part of this publication may be reproduced, stored in a retrieval system, or transmitted, in any form or by any means without the prior written permission of the publisher, nor be otherwise circulated in any form of binding or cover other than that in which it is published and without a similar condition being imposed on the subsequent purchaser.

A CIP catalogue record for this title is available from the British Library

Hardback ISBN 9781529363647
Trade Paperback ISBN 9781529363654
ebook ISBN 9781529363661

Typeset in Dante MT Pro

Printed and bound in Great Britain by Clays Ltd, Elcograf S.p.A.

John Murray Press policy is to use papers that are natural, renewable and recyclable products and made from wood grown in sustainable forests. The logging and manufacturing processes are expected to conform to the environmental regulations of the country of origin.

Carmelite House
50 Victoria Embankment
London EC4Y 0DZ

www.basicbooks.uk

John Murray Press, part of Hodder & Stoughton Limited
An Hachette UK company

The authorised representative in the EEA is Hachette Ireland,
8 Castlecourt Centre, Dublin 15, D15 XTP3, Ireland (email: info@hbgi.ie)

To freedom-seekers everywhere—past, present, and future

Contents

Maps	ix
Author's Note	xiii
Chapter 1: Overboard	1
Chapter 2: Landing	14
Chapter 3: Flight	23
Chapter 4: Alliances	34
Chapter 5: Plots	46
Chapter 6: Pirates	61
Chapter 7: Adjustments	72
Chapter 8: Expansion	79
Chapter 9: Hinterlands	92
Chapter 10: Overthrow	106
Chapter 11: Eruptions	122
Chapter 12: Codes	130
Chapter 13: Accelerations	139
Chapter 14: Connections	147
Chapter 15: Borders	163
Chapter 16: Poison	177
Chapter 17: Quills	197

Chapter 18: Revolutions	207
Chapter 19: Liberties	224
Chapter 20: Vengeance	241
Chapter 21: Escalations	252
Chapter 22: Openings	273
Chapter 23: Endings	294
Chapter 24: Royalty	305
Chapter 25: Opportunities	321
Chapter 26: Visions	338
Chapter 27: Decisions	359
Chapter 28: Safety	368
Chapter 29: Finale	382
Chapter 30: Liberation	399
Chapter 31: Lashings	419
Chapter 32: Repeat	438
Chapter 33: Reckoning	456
Chapter 34: Transformations	473
Chapter 35: Flowering	484
Epilogue: Beginnings	495
Acknowledgments	501
Timeline	505
Illustration Credits	515
Selected Bibliography	517
Notes	523
Index	611

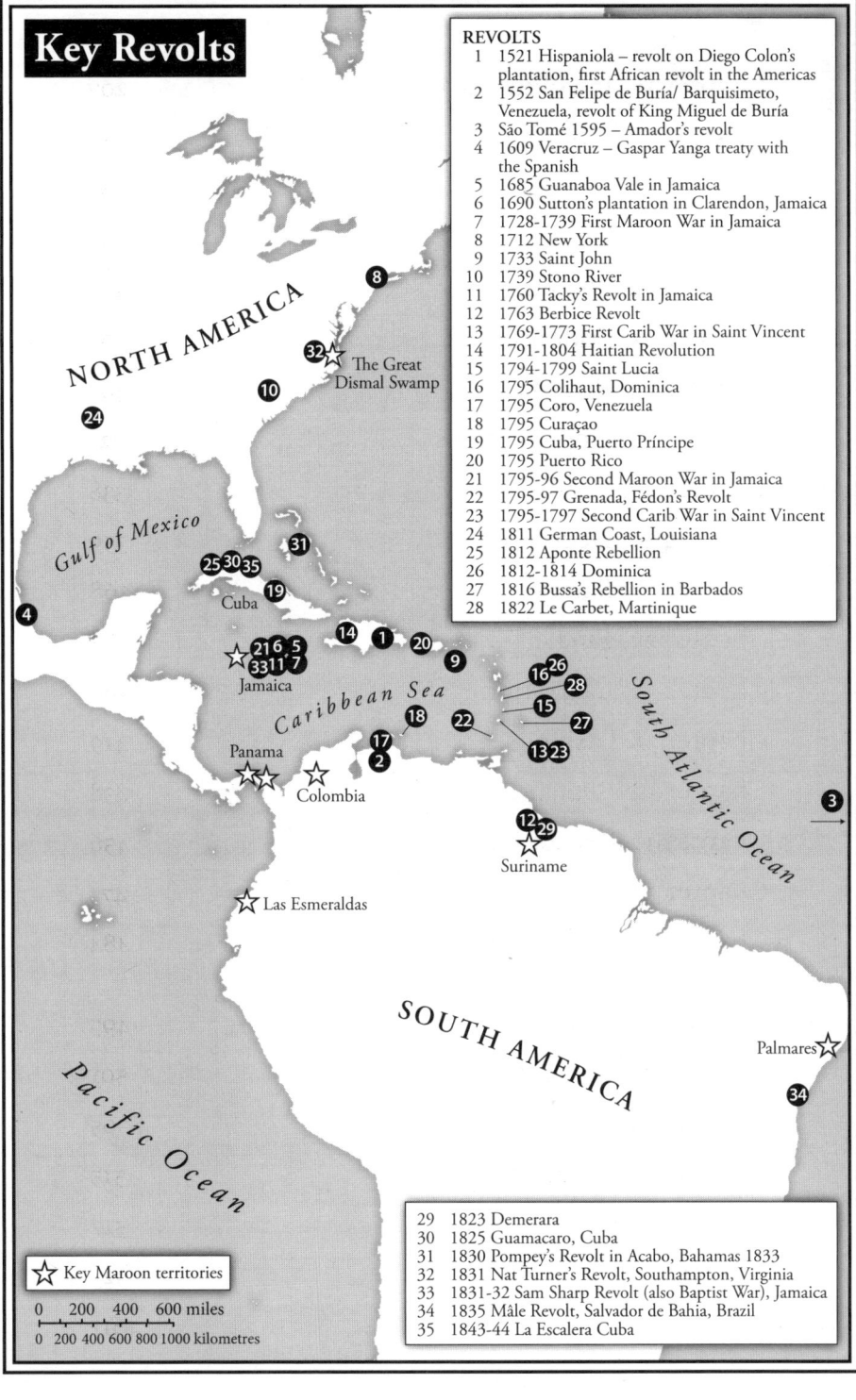

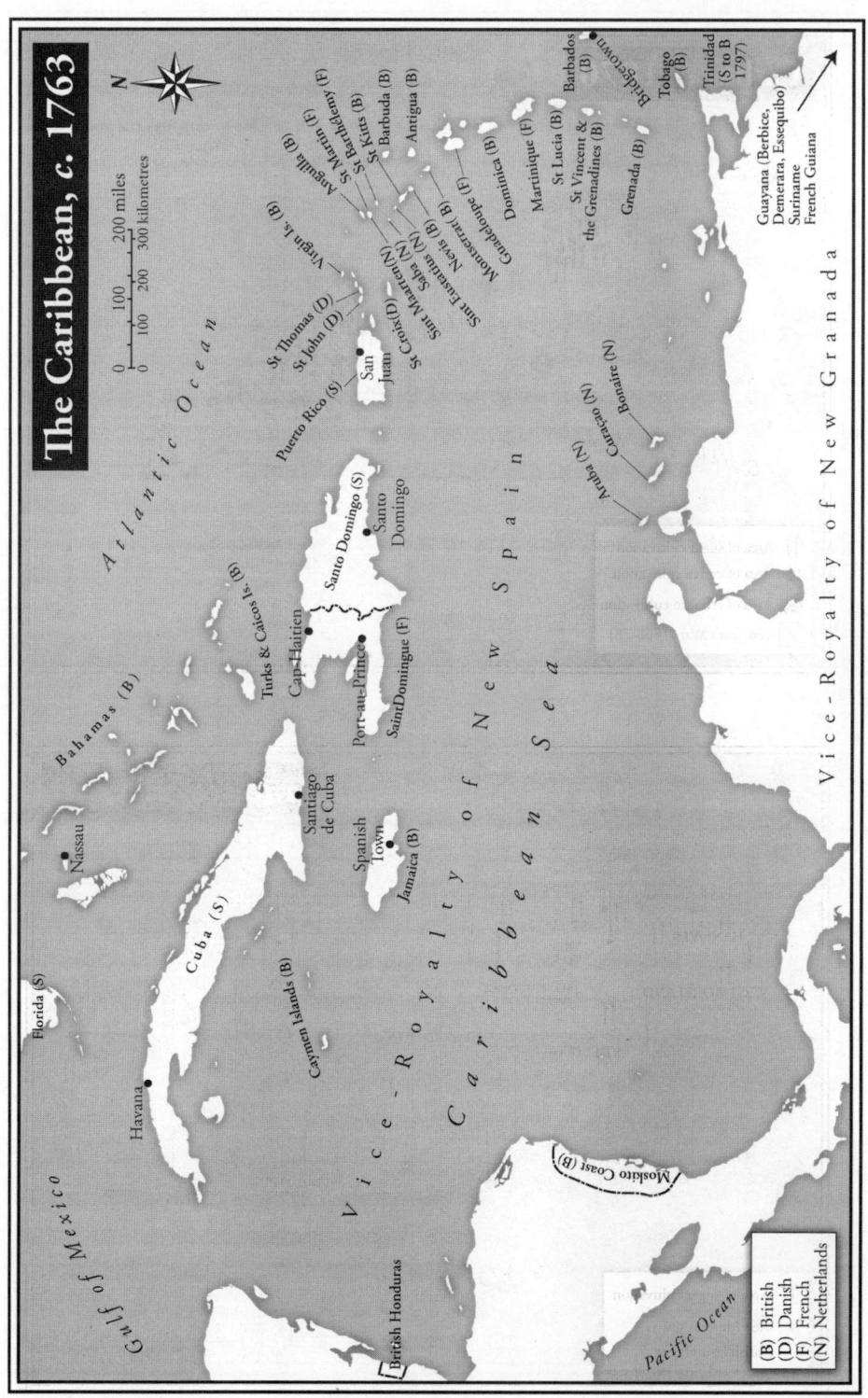

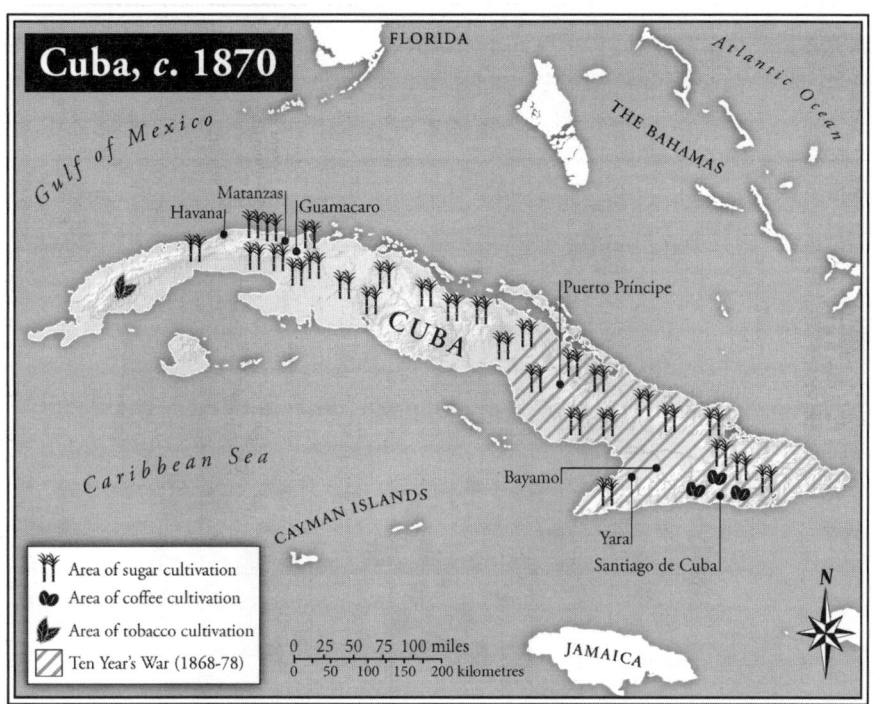

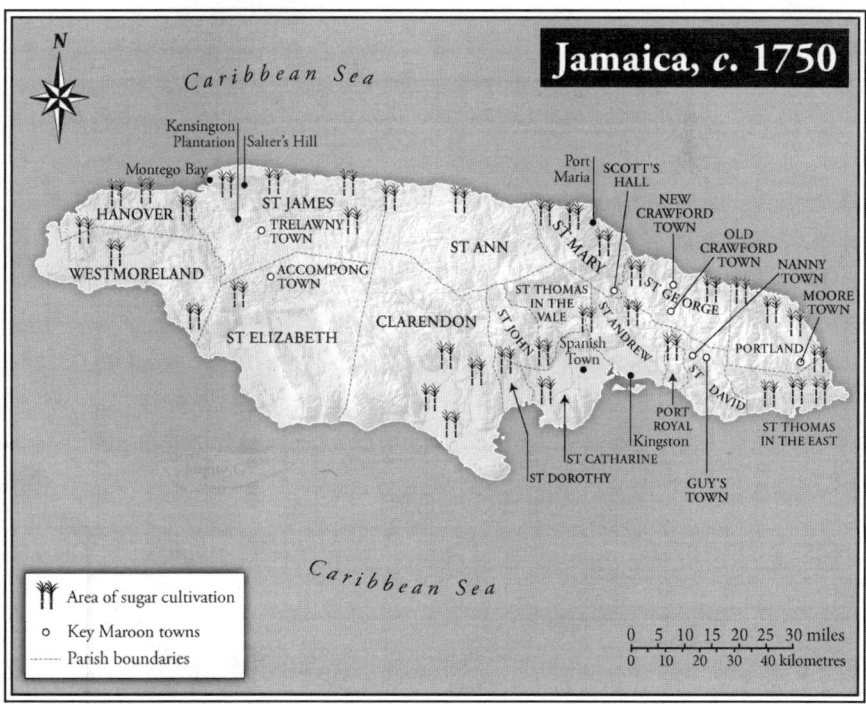

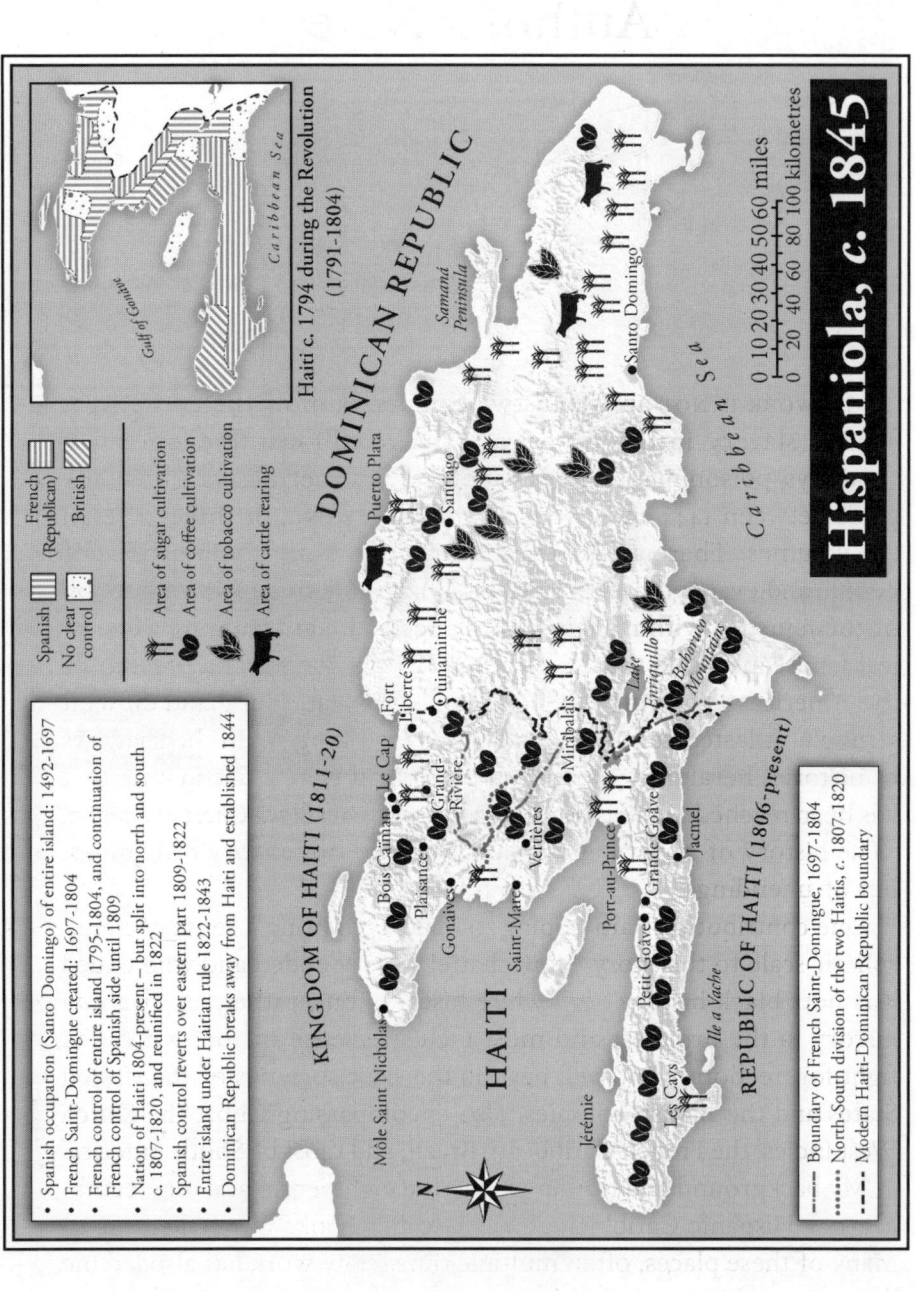

Author's Note

This work is not an exhaustive compendium of the entire fight against slavery in the Americas. The rebellions, freedom suits, runaways, poisonings, suicides, sabotage, and guerrilla wars that took place between 1444 and 1888 could not fit in two, or three, or even ten volumes. There are so many stories, so many combinations of people and events that it is virtually impossible to do even a fraction of them justice within a single book. Instead, I am painting a historical landscape—one that stretches the entire length and breadth of the Americas—to bring into full view what was a long and difficult struggle. It lasted centuries, and has for too long sat in the shadows of histories heralding "emancipation" as if it were a destination that has been reached. As Kris Manjapra puts it in his *Black Ghost of Empire*, "The history of slavery and emancipation is not a story of endings, but of unendings."[1]

One contribution I am hoping to make is to bring a sense of hemispheric scale to this story. How chattel slavery ended and who ended it is not "black history" or "white history" but, rather, an *American* history in the broadest and most inclusive sense of the word. The fight for freedom went well beyond the slave societies of the United States and the British colonies, also encompassing Cuba, the Dutch West Indies, the French Caribbean, Brazil, and most of South America.

My background and training are in the eighteenth- and nineteenth-century Hispanic Caribbean, and my other books have taken me to many of these places, often multiple times.[2] My work has also led me deep into archives—a vast bureaucratic warren, a maze of supporting documents of a system that took Africans from their continent and forced them to the Americas. These voluminous reams are also well known and deeply studied, in part because they contain data. The balance sheets, the ledgers, the ships' logs. The cotton bales counted, the sugar hogsheads shipped, the human cargo loaded on board.

While the bookkeepers tallied their sums and colonial officials filed reports, a much larger campaign was drawing battle lines across the hemisphere.[3] This war may not have unfolded in linear fashion across time or space, but the bloodshed seeped into the very fabric of life throughout the Americas. It was perhaps the largest, longest-running, and most diverse ongoing insurrection the world has ever known, and the responses to it shaped every nation in the Americas in meaningful—albeit sometimes overlooked—ways. That is the focus here: not the rise of Atlantic slavery and its barbaric conditions, but instead how the people enslaved by this system envisioned their freedom, and fought for it.

With this focus in mind, I have two main goals: first, to provide a wider vista to think about this shared history of the hemisphere, north and south, and its implications; second, to meditate on the meaning of freedom by tracing the thoughts and actions of those who were the least free, those who had to fight—and whose descendants continue to fight—to make abstract concepts of freedom concrete.

A number of notable studies and syntheses of abolition have been written, but much of this work has focused on the economic arguments of the viability of the plantation system or on the high-level politics that led to the ending of the slave trade and slavery by governments.[4] Slave rebellions—one constant through this whole period—were often shoved into the margins. Debates have arisen over the difference between slave societies—that is, places that depended on enslaved people to function—and societies with slavery. The academic consensus defines only five true slave societies: ancient Greece, ancient Rome, Brazil, the Caribbean, and the United States, while countries like Peru and Mexico were "societies with slaves."[5] To my mind, that distinction is a question of semantics: no place in the Americas escaped the consequences of the system that developed and implemented African slavery, so they were all societies touched in one way or another by enslavement. The story of the rise and fall of African slavery and its afterlife is one that connects the entire Western hemisphere. It is part of a wider shared history, which means the question of freedom must also be hemispheric in scope.

The criteria for a "slave society," the questions of commerce and capital, the involvement of Christian abolitionists, and the legislative debates in the United States and Britain are all parts in the story of the rise and fall of slavery, and they have been given leading roles in many histories of abolition. Earlier historians were reluctant to give the enslaved credit for their own emancipation for a variety of reasons, ranging from implicit notions of "white saviorhood" to the failure of rebellions to overthrow the entire system, with the very notable exception of Haiti.[6] What today might be called "white allyship" existed, but, as will be clearly seen throughout this book, these allies were unreliable and often held racist views. Many believed that black people should be freed because they were humans and Christians (or could become so) but at the same time deemed them unfit to become citizens or govern themselves—such contradictions cast whites not as "saviors" but as people who couldn't be fully trusted to understand freedom.* Indeed, as Tyler Stovall argues in his 2021 *White Freedom*, "Ideas of freedom in the modern world have been racialized. In particular, many have considered whiteness and white racial identity intrinsic to modern liberty."[7]

The Barbadian historian Sir Hilary Beckles observed more than 30 years ago that for too long many historians had misguidedly conceived of slave rebellions as "a lower species of political behavior, lacking in ideological cohesion, intellectual qualities and a philosophical direction."[8] This was, in part, because "emancipation was not conceived in terms of liberation from Europeans' power, values, and domination."[9] However, more recent work has considered the question in ways that diverge

---

* For the purposes of this project, "black" (as well as "white") will be lowercase. While acknowledging that capitalization is part of an effort to reclaim and identify positively a larger Black culture, in this book I have had to wrestle with how the word "black" became synonymous with "slave." This colonial era—and the development of scientific categorization during the Enlightenment—has left humanity with the reductive categories of black and white. Because this book is set in the time when these binaries were forged, I will keep the b lowercase, while completely accepting that in other contexts "Black" would be entirely preferable.

significantly from earlier historiography, not least in positioning the hundreds of rebellions that occurred from the sixteenth century to the dying days of the nineteenth as physical and psychological warfare.[10]

To say that slave rebellions "failed" is to miss the point. Rebellions, large and small, and other acts of resistance that were less dramatic but no less powerful, were a steady drumbeat through this fight for freedom, marking time through a long, difficult history. For the most part, measures by the enslaved were not successful in themselves, but taken together they made the entire system untenable. The story of slavery in the Americas has, for so long, been about oppression, not freedom. The perspective shifts when the many ways that people fought for what turned out to be a very imperfect freedom are placed in the center of this history. As Orlando Patterson, the sociologist and author of influential works on slavery and freedom, explains it: "Freedom was generated from the experience of slavery."[11]

Scholars of slavery and abolition have been prolific in recent years in examining these various forms of resistance in new ways, from legal battles to armed conflicts. A stream of monographs has cascaded into a vast sea of scholarship. Indeed, this book, which relies on such work, would be impossible to write without all the labors of historians—especially scholars of color around the world—who have stepped into the dark corners of the archives and brought to the light of public knowledge a raft of new names, events, and insights. Such work remains a challenge, however, in part because so many voices have been lost or, worse, were never recorded.[12] Some heroes are famous, but there are scores more—who remain anonymous—of the willing, the nameless dead with their heads on a pike or their bodies drawn and quartered. In recent years some of these stories have been recovered, the names repeated, the tales told.

Rebellions were only one path to freedom: Some sought manumission, or flight from a torturous situation, while others aimed to overthrow an entire system. For most of the centuries that human enslavement existed in the Americas, enslaved people used whatever opportunity became available to them, whether it was paying for freedom in sixteenth-century Cuba, setting up a runaway colony in eighteenth-century Jamaica, or campaigning in a black-owned newspaper for the end to slavery in the nineteenth-century United States.

Other routes were more problematic—some people gained their freedom as a reward for informing authorities about plans for a revolt or other subversive behavior, a potent reminder of the inescapable moral dilemmas the system of slavery produced, for enslaved and free alike.

The horrors of the Middle Passage and the cotton fields are well known. Less so is the story of the tireless fight for liberation across a vast, diverse area. This book is about that struggle and the complicated freedom found at the end of it. As historian Vincent Brown has pointed out, "If scholars were to emphasize the efforts of the enslaved more than the condition of slavery, we might at least tell richer stories about how the endeavors of the weakest and most abject have at times reshaped the world."[13]

History is often taught as a set of agreed facts or dates or things a person "ought" to know. However, what it really is, at its core, is a conversation. This book, I hope, will be a contribution to the current and ongoing dialogue about freedom that this particular chapter in the history of the Americas demands. Or to use the more precise words of the Trinidadian writer Earl Lovelace in his novel *Salt*:

> Four hundred years it take them to find out that you can't keep people in captivity. Four hundred years! And didn't happen just so. People had to revolt. People had to poison people. Port-of-Spain had to burn down. A hurricane had to hit the island. Haiti had to defeat Napoleon. People had to run away up the mountains. People had to fight. And then they agree, yes. We can't hold people in captivity here.
>
> But now they had another problem: it was not how to keep people in captivity. It was how to set people at liberty.[14]

Chapter 1

Overboard

The road to freedom is lined with bodies. Some of them lie in the darkest recesses of the sea, like the "hundred Men Slaves [who] jump'd over board" from the *Prince of Orange* during a balmy evening in March 1737, as the tropical sun inched toward the horizon. The crew tried to save them, but the men were "resolv'd to die, and sunk directly down," with at least 33 succeeding.

The ship's captain, Japhet Bird, had noticed a "great deal of Discontent" among his captives earlier that week, but believed, he wrote, "all our Troubles of this voyage was Over" as they neared the Caribbean island of Saint Kitts. However, the 360 people from Bonny (Nigeria) being forced across the Atlantic had their own ideas about Troubles. And so it was with "great Amazement" that Bird realized he had a mass suicide on his hands.

The crew sprang into panicked action and, as Bird later recounted, "it was with great Difficulty we sav'd so many as we did." This effort was spurred not by altruism but by profit. Some of those who were rescued, it was reported, "died since, but not [to] the Owners Loss" because they had been sold, presumably for a good price, "before any Discovery was made of the Injury the Salt Water had done to them." Bird was now "disconcerted" in his "Design of proceeding to Virginia with part of them."

Bird gave no acknowledgment of the dire conditions on the ship, or of the captives' terror of being taken into the unknown. Instead, he placed the blame on "one of [the Africans'] Countrymen," who had earlier come on board and, in a "joking manner," told them "they were first to have their Eyes put out, and then to be eaten."[1]

The fear of being taken to a land of cannibals was a persistent one.² Although Europeans are now better known for labeling other people "cannibals" when confronted with unknown cultures, at the time of the sailing of the *Prince of Orange*, many captives forced onto ships in West Africa believed they might well become the white man's supper. While Europeans may not have literally eaten Africans, they consumed them in unimaginable ways, and by the year the *Prince of Orange* incident took place, 1737, they had been doing so for nearly two centuries.³

⋘ • ⋙

T HE WORLD THAT gave rise to the *Prince of Orange* and its captives was thousands of years in the making. Only humans enslave their own, and the practice has been rife around the world—from Africa to Asia, Europe to the Americas—for millennia, from the Sumerians of 4000 BCE onward. But a particular change to this practice took place in ancient Greece. Slaves, for the most part, had been either captives of war or subjects of community-based servitude, punished for transgressions such as debt. Eventually, however, humans began to be bought and sold. Some historians believe this practice began in the final centuries BCE on the rocky, windswept island of Chios, in eastern Greece, near Turkey. Such purchases turned a slave into a possession, or property, that could be sold, an *andrapodon*.⁴ The English word for this would be "chattel," coming from the medieval Latin *capitale*, the root of the words "cattle" and "capital."⁵

Unlike enslaved Africans centuries later, the people purchased at this time were often physically similar to the buyers—slavery had not yet been racialized in the way it would be between Africa and the Americas. However, slaves had other markers of difference, such as foreign accents.⁶ To be a slave at this time, a person had to first be a "barbarian," that is to say, an outsider with no legal status. Such alienation was key, so the person could be put to work on the land or in a household, or be sent into battle, used in ritual sacrifice, exploited sexually, or exchanged commercially.⁷ Slavery, at its core, has always been about power.

However, within Greece, the social role of these alienated outsiders was crucial in the development of its democracy. Someone had to do the work while male citizens met to discuss political matters: The freedom of the *demos* was paid for by the labor of the enslaved. Indeed, the very machinery of democracy was oiled by them; in this period, slaves could also be owned by the state, working as clerks, police, and public laborers, and even overseeing treasury coinage.[8] Perhaps then it should be no surprise that a philosopher like Aristotle (384–322 BCE) claimed slavery was part of the human condition, his views still quoted millennia later: "Some are free men and others slaves by nature."[9] The entire system of slavery needed such illusions of difference to function, but even Aristotle was forced to accept slaves' humanity, saying, "There are some slaves who have the bodies of free men—as there are others who have a free man's soul."[10]

As Roman power grew in scale across Europe and North Africa, it absorbed the Greeks and embraced slavery, weaving it deeply into its society through the republican period and the later empire.[11] By the end of the first century BCE, around two million people were in a servile role on the Italian peninsula alone, out of a population of six million.[12] However, because Roman law considered slaves both chattel and human, manumission was an attainable goal and, unlike in Greece, it came with the promise of citizenship.[13] This also allowed Rome to expand its citizenry—by the end of the republican period, the majority of Romans plebs had some sort of slave ancestry.[14]

As the Roman Empire began to disintegrate in the late 400s CE and kingdoms formed across Western Europe, slavery lingered or morphed into serfdom and a peasantry, often little different from what had preceded them. For instance, there is evidence of significant slavery from Anglo-Saxon (c. 600–1000) into Norman times in England, during which around 9 percent of its population were recorded as "slaves."[15] However, in 1102, the Council of Westminster ruled to end the slave trade, such as it was.[16]

Islam, beginning in 610, had also become a powerful force, and extended into parts of the faltering Roman Empire, including much of the Iberian Peninsula and North Africa, under the Umayyad Caliphate (c. 661–750). It too would become involved in slavery, with Muslim slave traders working across continents, moving people east and west, north and south, with Europeans and sub-Saharan Africans taken to Islamic lands.[17] Part of this trade was fueled by African leaders in sub-Saharan kingdoms adopting Islam and then raiding their nonbelieving neighbors for captives. It was a system that presaged what was to come between Western Europe and Africa, though it had quite different attributes. The Quran accepted the existence of slavery, but it also acknowledged that slaves deserved to be treated well and, at some point, to be freed. Islam, therefore, recognized freedom, not slavery, as the natural state of humans.[18]

By the fourteenth century, some scholars in Western Europe had begun to revisit the ancient past. These humanists examined in earnest the remnants of Greece and Rome—much of which had been preserved by Islamic scholars—with an eye to what lessons could be learned about governance and tyranny.[19] Three Mediterranean city-states became key in bridging old ideas and new worlds: Venice, Genoa, and Florence. As these places grew and their trading networks expanded, so too did enslaved labor. Slave traders from these cities trafficked people from around the Black Sea.[20] These Slavic people were known in Latin as *sclavi*. As the centuries wore on, so did this word. The Latin root is evident in all the tangled branches that emerged: the French *esclave*, the Portuguese *escravo*, the Spanish *esclavo*, even the Dutch *slaaf*, and of course the English "slave."

By the 1200s, around 10 to 15 percent of Genoa's population of 20,000 were slaves, and some 10,000 men and women were sold in Florence between 1414 and 1423. However, with the rise of the Muslim Ottoman Empire and the fall of Constantinople in 1453, Slavic enslaved people were sent east, rather than west. Traders in Christian Europe would have to pivot in new directions.[21] When they did start to look south, they took an ancient practice and cast it into new lands.

This did not happen immediately—and it was certainly not an inevitability—but rather took shape over the course of the fifteenth century, alongside territorial expansion. The starting point of this process was, perhaps, the successful colonization of the Canary Islands in the early 1400s. The existence of this archipelago, around 60 miles (100 kilometers) off the coast of modern Morocco and around 1,000 miles (1,600 kilometers) south of Spain, was known in ancient times. Pliny the Elder referred to them as "the Fortunate islands" in his *Natural History* of 77 CE. There is some evidence of other Europeans—especially from the Balearic island of Majorca, a center of early cartography—trading in the Canaries before there were established settlements, often for a valuable dyestuff called orchil, or making slave raids on the native Guanche people.[22] Europeans justified this because the Guanches, who are thought to be related to the Berber peoples of North Africa, were not familiar with Christianity, so raiders used the idea of "just war" to enslave them, a practice adopted from the long-running Christian battle against Muslim states for the Iberian Peninsula. Over the course of the 1400s, Castile (Spain) and its European agents colonized all the islands, with Guanche people resisting them for almost a century, until the conquest of Tenerife in 1496, the final island to succumb. By then, thousands of Guanches had been either killed, through battle or disease, or enslaved.[23]

While Castile—then the dominant force in pre-consolidated Spain—focused on the Canary Islands, the Portuguese made inroads elsewhere. Around 1419, two Portuguese explorers, João Gonçalves Zarco and Tristão Vaz Teixeira, washed up after a storm on an islet they called Porto Santo, but they could see a much larger volcanic island in the distance. Although the pair were credited with this archipelago's discovery, it was more a reintroduction. These islands, located around 600 miles (1,000 kilometers) southwest of Lisbon, had also appeared on fourteenth-century maps.[24]

A volcano dominated the interior of the main island, with a peak of 6,100 feet (1,860 meters). Few parts of its craggy coastline could harbor a ship, but its valleys and hills were rich with woodlands. For this reason the island was named Madeira, which means "timber" in Portuguese.[25] The men saw the natural abundance, but they did not see any other people. They soon would, as Europeans wasted no time in arriving to seek whatever fortune might be available. By 1425, hundreds of axes were felling the thick forests of cedars and yews needed to make the chairs, tables, and beds that would adorn homes in Lisbon. Another uninhabited island chain 600 miles (1,000 kilometers) to the northwest, later named the Azores, was also colonized. Its land would be used to supply Portugal with wheat and grapes—both important crops, but not necessarily profitable ones. The plant that would bring riches was sown in the fertile volcanic soils of Madeira: sugarcane.[26]

While a welcome discovery, Madeira, with its forests and its sugar-growing potential, was not the prize some were seeking. That was gold, ideally the fabled rivers of it. This precious metal was believed to exist in Africa in the sort of abundance that only centuries of mythmaking could conjure. One of the more popular legends was that of Prester John, a Christian who travelled through Africa and possibly lived in Ethiopia and who, it was said, had access to this wealth.[27] His gold could be used, according to the thinking of the time, to help Christian kingdoms fight more powerful Muslim rivals. Portugal's Prince Henry, "the Navigator" (1394–1460), had long hoped for Prester John's aid, as would King João II (r. 1481–1495).[28] It was a seductive dream for a remote, relatively poor, and recently plague-ravaged corner of Western Europe in the early fifteenth century.

This desire to penetrate Africa was no doubt stoked by the Prester John legend, but also by knowledge of the very real Mansa Musa, the emperor of Mali who had made a lavish and famed pilgrimage to Mecca in the early fourteenth century. Such was his renown that he was depicted on the 1375 Catalan Atlas, one of the most important maps of its day. Musa is positioned in the middle of North Africa, resplendent in a gold-leaf crown, holding a golden scepter in his left hand and a large nugget of gold in his right, luring European fortune seekers.[29] Around this time, Mali was thought to be perhaps the richest place in the world.[30]

The question was how to get there, and by the 1430s, the Portuguese were making inroads. They were aided somewhat by new technologies that had arrived in Europe by the late 1200s, such as the navigational compass, first developed in China during the Han Dynasty (c. 202 BCE–220 CE). Ship design was changing too. The round-bottomed, square-sailed cogs that plied Mediterranean and Baltic waters were also used to explore the Atlantic, but they were joined in the 1400s by caravels, which were more streamlined and used lateen (triangular) sails, an innovation borrowed from Arab dhows. These helped Portuguese ships to more efficiently harness the trade winds and navigate variable currents.[31] However, they could not carry as much cargo. Other ships with more space emerged in the fifteenth century, including the carrack and, by the 1600s, the galleon, both of which had a rounded hull like a cog, but combined square and lateen sails on their multiple masts. These vessels could sail the Atlantic routes, had more space for cargo, and required smaller crews. As important, these ships had capacity for cannons and other artillery, and eventually captives.[32] They could go further, carry more, and inflict damage as necessary.

In 1434, the Portuguese explorer Gil Eanes connected these dots, aided no doubt by his participation in an earlier slaving expedition to capture Guanches on the island of Gran Canaria.[33] He managed to sail south of latitude 26° north—considered the "point of no return" by European mariners unfamiliar with the waters beyond it—and came back to tell the tale. He may have reached as far as Cape Bojador, on the coast of modern Western Sahara. Once safely back in Portugal, Eanes could relate details of the route. This hastened the understanding of the *volta do mar*, which involved sailing south toward the equator along the cool waters of the Canary current, but on the return heading northwest into the Atlantic, rather than hugging the coast, to harness the westerly winds that blow toward Portugal.[34]

Three more steps were to come: landing, meeting Africans, and attempting to trade. While the Portuguese had encountered North Africans—not least during their capture of Ceuta (Morocco) in 1415—what they would find in "Guinea," as they described sub-Saharan lands, they perceived to be of a different order.[35] In 1436, Afonso Gonçalves Baldaia led an expedition that landed around 200 miles (320 kilometers) south of Cape Bojador, with his European crew meeting Africans for the first time. According to the contemporary chronicler Gomes Eanes de Zurara, two young crew members were put ashore with horses they had brought with them and sent inland. They had managed to travel around 20 miles (seven leagues) when

> they found nineteen men all banded together without any other arms of offence or defence, but only assegais [spears]. And as soon as the youths saw them, they attacked them with great courage. But that unknown company, although so many in number, dared not meet them on the level, but rather for security retired to some rocks, whence they fought with the youths for a good space . . . And they kept on fighting until the sun began to give warning of night, on which account they went back to their ship.[36]

This hostile introduction proved no deterrent, and the Portuguese continued to explore the coastline. Europeans had arrived in sub-Saharan Africa, and soon Africans would start arriving in Europe. The first significant arrival was in 1444, on the southern tip of Portugal, in the Algarve, where the Bensafrim River runs into the Atlantic Ocean in the city of Lagos. A group of captives were marched from the ships' dank hulls into a late-summer dawn on August 8, and forced to await their fate.[37] Leading them was Gil Eanes, the man who had both gone on slaving missions and reached the west coast of Africa. Now he and a group of merchants had become slave traders, with a license from Prince Henry.

Six caravels had departed in June of 1444, heading straight to the Bay of Arguin and attacking the island communities along the shore, taking men, women, and children.[38] Such was the anticipation of their return to Portugal, according to Zurara, that "in a short time the news of their good fortune was well known, and all were much rejoiced at it."[39] The fortunes of the human cargo were rather different. One member of the expedition was forced to admit to Prince Henry that some of the 235 captives were ill and it might be better that they "be placed in that field which lies outside the city gate." There, on the edge of the city, the prince—who was on hand to witness events—took his royal fifth, as per his custom, of the human offering.[40]

Zurara described the Africans as a "marvellous sight; for amongst them were some white enough . . . others were less white like mulattoes; others again were as black as Ethiops [Ethiopians]." Yet he could not ignore their distress: "Some kept their heads low and their faces bathed in tears . . . Others stood groaning very dolorously, looking up to the height of heaven."[41]

The enslavers began to separate them, parents from children, husbands from wives, brothers from sisters. Their instincts immediately kicked in, as people resisted and struggled, with parents holding fast to their children. The entire partitioning became "very great toil" for the Portuguese, reported Zurara. After some struggle, Prince Henry was finally able to take away the finest "forty-six souls" that were his.

Those enslaved Africans enter this grim record on that August morning, but scant detail remains of their fate, except Zurara's claim that he later spotted the children and grandchildren of these captives in Lagos, "as good and true Christians as if they had directly descended . . . from those who were first baptised."[42]

From this point, Lagos and then Lisbon would eventually receive thousands of Africans, though this occurred unevenly. The Portuguese were still looking for gold. Taking captives was one way to try to turn a profit on an expensive voyage. By 1445 the Portuguese had made enough contact with coastal Africans to plant a small *feitoria*, or trading post, in the sandy soil of Arguin, a small island off the coast of modern Mauritania, near where Eanes and the others made their raids. This point lies about 300 miles (500 kilometers) west of Wadan (Ouadane), an important stopping point for the overland caravans that transported goods from North Africa to the kingdoms of the western coast. From there the Portuguese began to insert themselves into sub-Saharan African trade networks. For the remainder of the century, as the *feitoria* became established, around 1,000 captives a year were forced through it on their way to Portugal.[43]

News of Portuguese spread across Europe, reaching Rome. The papacy had followed these developments, interested in the prospect of salvation of souls, as well as the relationship of Christians with non-believers. In January 1455, Pope Nicholas V issued a papal bull permitting the king of Portugal to

> acquire provinces, islands, ports and seas, whatever kingdoms, duchy, principality, lordships, possessions and movable or immovable goods and whatever they have seized or possessed by invasion, conquest, purging, cleansing and subjugation from Saracens, pagans and other enemies of Christ, and reduction of their persons to perpetual servitude.[44]

While this text looks to modern eyes like permission to conquer and convert, some historians have argued that when understood in the context of its own times, it reflects deeper theological questions and concerns about the nature of sovereignty—of Europeans and Africans.[45] The answers would change as the centuries wore on, as Catholicism grappled with the implications of European expansion and the rise of the slave trade.

After the death of Nicholas V, the *Inter caetera* of Calixtus III in 1456 granted Portugal a monopoly over all African lands, as they were known at the time. These texts made such claims without, of course, any say from the Africans themselves, or even a clear sense of what sort of relationship between Portugal and "Guinea" would develop. At this point, Europeans had been mostly limited to exploring only small parts of the extensive coastline and had little idea about the societies they were encountering.[46]

By the middle of the fifteenth century, Castile had the Canaries, while the Portuguese had Madeira and the Azores, as well as the link to sub-Saharan West Africa. An ongoing rivalry between these two kingdoms was rectified by the 1479 Treaty of Alcáçovas, under which Portugal accepted Castile's sovereignty over the Canaries in exchange for recognition of its own monopoly trading claims to West Africa.[47]

Europeans in Africa soon developed a reputation, as Venetian sailor Alvise Cadamosto (or da Ca'da Mosto) discovered on a voyage on behalf of the Portuguese crown in 1455, sailing along the Senegal and Gambia Rivers, searching for gold. He was hoping to enter the Gambia River, but before his vessel could go far, seventeen canoes surrounded it and 150 men, who "appeared well-built, exceedingly black, and all clothed in white cotton shirts," began to shoot arrows at the Europeans. They retaliated with crossbows, and both sides eventually relented. Later, Cadamosto asked why they were met with such hostility when they were only looking to trade, and was told that "they firmly believed that we Christians ate human flesh, and that we only bought negroes to eat them: that for their part they did not want our friendship on any terms, but sought to slaughter us all, and to make a gift of our possessions to their lord."[48]

So nearly 200 years later, when the captives on the *Prince of Orange* spoke of their fear of being eaten, they were drawing from a very long history.

⊰ • ⊱

From Eanes's journey onward, Portuguese ships—later joined by those of other Europeans—over the course of the centuries ferried at least 12 million Africans to uncertain and terrifying futures, of whom 1.8 million died en route.⁴⁹ These grim numbers come after nearly four centuries of the slave trade, but in the 1450s such a scale of enterprise was unimaginable, to European and African alike. The system did not appear overnight. However, resistance to European captivity started with the earliest transports. The runaway slaves, the rebellions, the burning fields of cane would all follow, but some people simply tried to free themselves as soon as they could—in Africa if possible, but at sea if necessary.

Resistance was built into the system as it evolved, even after the slave trade spread up and down the coast. Sometimes it involved Africans in canoes firing arrows at ships; it could also be more personal, with a captive calling on a relative or ruler to negotiate with traders, to keep him or her safely on land. Other times, it might be an unnamed helper, breaking into a hold and setting captives free.⁵⁰

The struggle against the transatlantic slave trade started on African soil, though it inevitably moved to the sea. For those trapped on a vessel gliding through two planes of infinity, the endless sky above and the uncertain depths of the ocean below, options were limited: The freedom of the relentless celestial blue was out of reach, but that of the murky indigo ocean was only a leap away. Some captives believed there was a return home, or an afterlife beyond that water, while only death lay at the other end of the voyage. The choice was ever present; the terror could be extinguished by a quick decision. A space might open in the blink of an eye: a tired crew member not paying attention, a captain otherwise occupied with the female captives. People could hurl themselves into that opportunity, diving overboard, headfirst into the arms of the beautiful Mami Wata, hoping to be taken to eternal life in her kingdom under the waves.⁵¹

Others met death through illness or through violence inflicted by the crew, and some by their own action. In every one of these deaths is a story, but most of these stories disappeared with the person, to the dark and silent depths of the sea. Most could not be erased from the annals of history because they were never recorded in the first place.

The surviving slivers are jagged, written records produced by the pens of officials, sailors, or enslavers, in their diaries and reports. Onboard rebellions might merit mention, though usually far more space was allotted to observations about the weather, the voyage, and the natural world, or to remarks about the Africans they traded with, rather than to the condition of the captives. Some revolts were recorded, some captives who leapt overboard were counted. Sometimes the loss was too costly to be directly reported, or the unrest on the ship may have involved an angry or unwilling crew, causing problems for the captain.[52] There are entire worlds that will never be known. For all their painful similarities, no two voyages were identical, and no two enslaved people were alike.[53] Millions of stories will never be known, but the patterns persist, like ripples left in the wake of a rudder.

Those who remained watched as death came aboard in those overcrowded, filthy holds. Portuguese accounts in the seventeenth century describe Africans taken to Brazil as being depressed (or *banzando*) "which makes many of them die."[54] These sailors called their vessels *tumbeiros*, or coffin-bearers.[55] Sharks eager for a good meal followed a ship's stench, waiting for the dead or the desperate to be flung overboard.[56]

Captains and crews began to understand and adapt, knowing these voyages would be difficult, especially as the numbers grew. One account, by a French sailor in the late 1600s, recalled how captives would "fall into a deep melancholy and despair, and . . . refuse all sustenance." This forced him to take drastic measures, "to cause the teeth of those wretches to be broken, because they would not open their mouths, or be prevailed upon by any intreaties to feed themselves; and thus have forced some sustenance into their throat."[57]

Other grim adaptations were made. Larger ships were used to ferry more bodies. Nets went up on decks to stop those who would seek refuge underneath the waves.[58] Crew sizes were increased.[59] The crossing of the Atlantic became more routine, more formalized, more organized, more industrial. Its culmination was expressed in the most infamous image of the slave trade: the chart of the ship *Brooks*, built in 1781. The illustration of its hull, with the bodies of men, women, and children crammed together as every profitable inch was taken up with unimaginable suffering, shocked the public at the time. It still does. The *Brooks* remains a powerful symbol of the unbelievable realities of the slave trade.[60] It is, however, an image that tells only part of a much larger story. Not every slave ship started out like the *Brooks*, nor ended like it.

From an estimated 36,000 voyages between 1514 and 1864, there were at least 3,500 onboard rebellions.[61] Some of these would have organized on board among captives taken from different areas of Africa, who spoke a multitude of diverse languages and who had to find ways to communicate their plans.[62] The number of individual acts of resistance, such as refusing to eat or jumping overboard, was also significant. Such rebellions did not stop the ships from arriving, nor did they overturn the larger slave trade that was evolving. They did, however, make very clear that this deadly commerce was going to be fought at every level, including on African shores and at sea.

Chapter 2

Landing

THE INITIAL CAPTIVES from West Africa were taken to Portugal, and from there traded across the Iberian Peninsula, ending up in cities like Seville and Valencia through the latter decades of the fifteenth century. They would be forced aboard a ship from "Guinea"—as the Portuguese continued to call this area of Africa—stopping in Lisbon, which quickly became the hub of the slave trade, with a growing local black population. By 1486, the crown created the Casa dos Escravos de Lisboa (Lisbon Slave House) in the capital to process the captives, levy the appropriate taxes, and transport them onward. The Casa sat near the docks on the Tagus (Tejo) River, and by 1512 it was Portugal's only port of entry for Africans.[1]

A painting from the 1570s, the *Chafariz d'el Rey*, by an anonymous artist, shows what black Lisbon, slave and free, might have looked like, in a tableau of the area around the king's fountain, in the Alfama district, stretching downhill from the city's castle to the river. It is a lively scene, as black people mingle in the crowds, some selling goods. There are some women—probably enslaved—carrying water jugs on their heads. Black servants of unclear status ride horses, while others navigate the river by boat.[2] While it appears to depict Lisbon as a sixteenth-century boomtown, some art historians have suggested that the Flemish artist who painted it might have been criticizing, satirizing, or exoticizing Lisbon and its African population.[3]

The number of Africans in the capital was estimated at 10,000 by 1550, about 10 percent of the total population, among whom was a sizable number of free people of color.[4] They worked in a range of professions, from artisans to court musicians and painters, though laws restricted where they could go and what they could do, designating the places where black women—free or enslaved—were allowed to sell goods. Black people were also forced to use separate water fountains in Lisbon, a practice that would cross the Atlantic.[5]

Some of the Africans who remained in Lisbon ended up in the area known as the Mocambo Quarter, its name evoking the Kimbundu (Angolan) word for hideout.[6] Today it is known as Santa Catarina, poised on one of Lisbon's many hills, and it has a magnificent view of the city. Less than ten minutes' stroll from that overlook is the Rua do Poço dos Negros (Street of the Blacks' Pit), which looks like any other quiet Lisbon lane, with shops and busy cafes. Its name tells a different story, one of a time in the 1500s when the bodies of Africans who did not survive the voyage were tossed out with the rubbish, as they had been in Lagos. Such was the scale of this practice in Lisbon, in 1515 King Manuel I ordered that the *poço* serve as a burial ground because the people "brought from Guinea . . . are not buried as well as they should be."[7]

The Spanish kingdoms were also familiar with Africans in this period, mostly from North Africa. The long-running war between Christendom and Muslim states on the Iberian Peninsula created an equally long acceptance of both North Africans and slavery, with the enslaved being the nonbelievers. Religion was not the only factor behind enslavement, however, and there were other reasons, including capture in a conflict, kidnap for ransom by corsairs, and sometimes punishment for crimes.[8] However, some distinctions among enslaved people were made. A Moor (*moro*) was from a Muslim area, which could include North Africa, but an "Ethiopian," or "Ethiop," was considered a "black" Christian. To further complicate matters, white slaves (*esclavos blancos*), including Jewish people, were put in the same category as Moors, later including Guanches from the Canary Islands. Sub-Saharan Africans—many of them believed to be Wolof people from the Senegambia region of West Africa—became one more group in this mix.[9]

A woman named Johana, described in the records as black, may well have been one such Senegambian who followed the tortuous route from West Africa, via Lisbon, to Valencia. This is where she was living in the 1490s, and where she attempted to end her enslavement, after her enslaver Bernat Sorrell complained that she "poorly repaid" his alleged generosity. He was looking to sell her.[10]

In that period, Valencia was a part of the kingdom of Aragon and a bustling and productive Mediterranean port with influence that spread from the Balearic Sea to Naples and Sicily and beyond. It was situated northeast of the then-Muslim sultanate of Granada, and thus had a *mudejar* (free Muslim) population of about 30 to 40 percent. Slavery was not new to Valencia. Slavs and Muslims passed through its gates, later joined by North Africans and Guanches.[11] By the mid-1400s, the average human cargo on a trade vessel to Valencia was between 80 and 130 people, many of them Wolof and brought in by Florentine merchants via Portugal.[12] At least 3,000 sub-Saharan Africans were recorded as arriving in Valencia between 1479 and 1516, though revised estimates have pushed that number nearer to 5,000.[13] By the end of the fifteenth century, West Africans comprised some 40 percent of the city's slave population.[14]

Once a captive of any provenance reached Valencia, crown officials needed proof through testimony that the person had been enslaved appropriately, for instance taken in a "just war," before being sold. Selling a free person into slavery was considered a crime and concerns were raised that slave traders often lied about the source of their captives. However, Africans, and Canary Islanders, were often branded "infidels," which also rendered them suitable for enslavement or onward sale.[15]

By the 1490s, then, it would not have been a surprise to see a black woman like Johana working within Valencia's sturdy city walls, which enclosed a cluttered maze of churches, monasteries, convents, hospitals, schools, and administrative buildings, many of which were adorned with the best gilt altars, elaborate carvings, and detailed craftsmanship that Mediterranean trade fortunes could buy. In the heart of Valencia is the elaborate silk market, the Lonja de la Seda, whose construction started in 1483. The late Gothic design, including dramatic twisted columns and rich interior ornamentation, signaled the city's wealth, its trade having long moved past silk.[16] The area of narrow streets and small plazas around the Lonja would have been where servants, slaves, and free people encountered each other in the business of daily life.

In Valencia, an enslaved person had three possible routes to freedom (*libertat*). Some were freed by their enslaver, either through an oral statement in front of witnesses or in a will, though this freedom might come with strings attached, like paying a sum to the family or serving a few more years. Other enslaved people might receive a charter of freedom (*carta de libertat*), which was a document granting manumission usually after a slave paid for freedom.[17] The third route was redemption. This involved negotiating a price with the enslaver and then raising money to pay it, or similarly paying a ransom to the kidnapping corsair, a practice found among the Muslim community in Valencia.[18]

These bids for freedom could be confirmed or contested in the courts, and the question of Johana's redemption was what led to the inclusion of her case in the archives. In 1495, members of a black confraternity wanted to "redeem" her, or buy her out of slavery. This was a growing practice among the black Catholic community in Spain, and the funds were procured through a network of religious confraternities (*cofradías* or *hermandades* in Spanish). Black brotherhoods in Valencia had extensive roles in maintaining the community, functioning like mutual aid societies, with members assisting each other in times of illness, paying for funerals, lending money, and—crucially—buying the freedom of enslaved people. In Valencia, a black brotherhood was established by 1472, and its members could be seen in the city begging alms to raise money for legal freedom cases.[19]

At the point that the confraternity intervened, Johana had sabotaged Sorrell's efforts to sell her so effectively, he complained, according to his testimony, that "wherever they went, the slave represented herself so poorly that no one wanted to buy her."[20] Sorrell became so frustrated that he placed her in prison and began to organize her passage to the island of Ibiza, where she could be somebody else's problem. However, before that could take place, members of a black confraternity contacted Sorrell's broker, who was in charge of finding a buyer. Johana, too, had contacted the broker and told him "not to look for a buyer or a new owner for her because she could not and would not serve anyone."[21]

She told the broker that she would "seek out and secure the assistance of some black friends and relatives of hers in the city who would redeem her."[22] Those friends were confraternity members, including Anthoni Johan, an enslaved black man, one of two who were involved in her case. Anthoni wanted to free her because, according to the testimony, he was either her lover or her husband, and Johana had apparently given birth to their daughter.[23] Anthoni had the support of the confraternity, but they were short by 26 *lliures* of the sum needed to secure her freedom from a reluctant Sorrell. Anthoni was compelled to turn to his own enslaver—whose name he had been forced to take—and ask for the difference. He agreed, and so between the enslaver and the confraternity, Johana was redeemed from her captivity. But there was an unexpected price yet to be paid.

Five years later, the enslaver Johan decided to reclaim Johana, saying that he had not donated toward her ransom but had purchased her. Johana, in the meantime, had been running her own home and "work[ing] for her own benefit . . . [and] doing all those things that persons freed from servitude are accustomed to perform." During her five years of freedom, slavery had been hovering in the shadows, waiting to claim Johana once again. And once again, she had to fight. She filed for and was granted a *demande de libertat*.[24] From there Johana fades from the record, hopefully having faced no more challenges to her hard-won freedom. Other Johanas were not as fortunate. Only about two of these *demandes de libertat* were applied for each year between 1425 and 1520, with around 40 percent being successful.[25] Freedom for a former slave was always a place of negotiation, and never one of safety.

⊰⊱ • ⊱⊰

BY THE TIME of Johana's bid for freedom, the circuit connecting Iberia, West Africa, and the Atlantic island colonies had been vastly enlarged by Christopher Columbus's dramatic encounter in 1492 with the Americas, an entire hemisphere virtually unknown to Europeans.

Indeed, Columbus was, in a way, almost a perfect composite of this moment in Europe. He was allegedly Genoese by birth and married to Portuguese nobility. He was familiar with West Africa after travelling there, and had visited Madeira, Porto Santo, and even the Greek island of Chios, then under Genoese control, in 1475.[26] He expressed a fervent Catholicism, to the pleasure of the crowns of Castile and Aragon, though he may have been an even more devout believer in the myths of Marco Polo and the tales of Eastern riches that wound their way through European society in the fifteenth century.[27]

When he set out on his famed voyages, Columbus packed goods such as beads to trade, as he would have done for his trip to Guinea.[28] As he explored the islands of what Europeans would call the New World, he had to rethink his trade plan. His initial landing on Guanahaní, which Columbus later named San Salvador, in the Bahamas, was not what he had envisioned. It was not Cipango (Japan), the intended destination of his 1492 voyage, though he never admitted this. But neither was it Africa. If anything, perhaps, it was more like Madeira, or Spanish *Canaria*. The latter had provided a labor force of enslavable non-Christians, and Columbus felt this could be the case in these new islands. Given that he had not reached lands of spices and silks, captives were one way he could make money from this enterprise. The inhabitants of these unfamiliar places, at least as Columbus presented them, seemed ideal candidates for conversion (their own desires, of course, being somewhat different) or enslavement.[29]

Reports of these lands prompted more papal involvement on behalf of Castile and Portugal, resulting in the Treaty of Tordesillas in 1494, which confirmed Portuguese claims to West Africa, splitting the world into two spheres of influence along a line 370 leagues (around 1,185 nautical miles) to the west of the Cape Verde Islands. All the known lands west of the line were for the crowns of Castile and Aragon, while Portugal got everything east of that line, which included the entire west coast of Africa and the eastern part of what would be called Brazil.

Around the same time, the sugarcane planted in Madeira had yielded significant profits. The island had the ideal terrain and climate for the plant. However, the undulating topography meant that the crop could only be grown in small plots. That proved an inconvenience, though ultimately no barrier to the development of the sugar estates, known as *engenhos*, on the island. They could grow and process cane on the island before sending it for further refining in places like Flanders and England. As consumption of sugar increased, the Genoese financiers, who had been investing in sugar production in other parts of the

Mediterranean, redirected their capital to Madeira, and by 1500 the island was the leading sugar producer for Europe.

Money could buy the equipment for an *engenho*, but a combination of enslaved people and some free workers did the hard labor. From the earliest forest clearance, enslaved Guanches from the neighboring Canary Islands and some European *slavs* had been tasked with the transformation of Madeira.[30] West Africans joined them. The silence of forests was replaced by the grassy rustle of sugarcane, which quickly spread to the Canary Islands as well. Columbus may have been aware of this, and perhaps that is why he was said to have taken some cane stalks to plant with him on his second voyage in 1493.

If Valencia connected the Mediterranean to the new Afro-Atlantic world, then the city of Seville, on the Guadalquivir River, which runs into the Atlantic in southwestern Spain, linked the newly encountered lands of the Americas with Africa, the Atlantic islands, and Europe. In the wake of Columbus's four voyages, the Casa de Contratación was established in 1503 in Seville as an agency of the crown, overseeing and regulating trade, and taking the royal fifth (20 percent) of all imported goods. As the sixteenth century progressed, dockworkers unloaded increasing quantities of gold and silver from Spanish colonies in the Americas near the aptly named Torre de Oro, the golden tower. Other valuable and unfamiliar objects—spices, feathers, foods—from across the Americas were unloaded as well. A babel of languages could be heard in the streets, coming up from the riverside.

The Casa de Contratación was a brief walk from the river, near the grand Baroque cathedral built on the site of an earlier mosque. The Muslim past was not completely erased, as the scalloped arches and arabesque motifs of the mosque's stunning minaret attest, surviving today as the La Giralda bell tower. A few minutes' walk north is the commercial plaza of San Francisco, where the market for humans was in direct sight, near the port, the local political establishment, and even the church. Indeed, enslaved people could be purchased on the very steps of the cathedral.[31] African slavery had become part of Spain, accepted by crown and Church alike. By the mid-1500s, more than 6,000 enslaved people, including West Africans, were in Seville, comprising about 13.5 percent of the city's population.[32]

Seville's black community included both slave and free people, with many called *ladinos*, or Latinized—culturally assimilated and Spanish-speaking.[33] Those who were not so acclimatized were said to speak *media lengua* (half language), *guineo* ("Guinea," i.e., local African dialects), or *habla de negro* ("black speech").[34] Marriages took place along "color" lines, dark- or light-skinned tending to marry within the same group, even if they had different places of origin. Enslaved people tended to marry each other, and few official marriages occurred between slave and free. The Catholic Church permitted and even encouraged black people to wed, though many enslavers or employers of free servants preferred unmarried workers, in part because free married women would often leave their role to tend to their own domestic arrangements.[35]

A wall surrounded Seville, and much of black life took place beyond it. African and Afro-Hispanic people were allowed to meet in certain spaces, such as the plaza near the church of Santa Maria la Blanca, where they could dance and drum on Sundays and during religious festivals.[36] As was the case in Lisbon and Valencia, black people set up brotherhoods in Seville. The first known black confraternity in Spain is believed to have been established in Seville at some point in the late fourteenth century, dedicated to Our Lady of the Kings, with its celebration organized around Epiphany, on January 6. Although it predates the development of the European slave trade to Africa, records indicate that West Africans were in the city then, most likely linked to its earlier period under Muslim rule.[37]

Castile's legal system drew from Roman law, under which slavery was seen as a temporary condition and freedom as a human's natural state. This view was expressed in the *Siete Partidas* of King Alfonso X, which was compiled around 1265. These laws were influenced by the Roman code promulgated under the emperor Justinian, the *Corpus Juris Civilis*. The Iberian version formed the basis of slave law in Spain and in American lands that it claimed.[38] In the section on manumission the *Siete Partidas* declared that "all creatures of the world naturally love and desire liberty" and provided pathways out of enslavement.[39] As had been the case in Valencia, this often involved obtaining documents of emancipation (*cartas de ahorrías*) or being freed in an enslaver's will.[40] Under *coartación*—a word with its root in the verb *cortarse*, to cut something into pieces—a person could buy herself out of enslavement a piece at a time.⁴¹ However, until the debt to the enslaver was paid, the *coartado* faced the risk of being sold or transferred elsewhere.

The fifteenth century had witnessed the expansion of African slavery in Iberia. Now, this slavery would spread across the Atlantic and into the worlds Christopher Columbus had entered. The ships that ran between Lisbon and Senegambia would soon be redirected, taking Africans across the ocean to the Americas.

Chapter 3

Flight

It wasn't what Nicolás de Ovando had expected. The black slaves that were sent to the Caribbean island of Hispaniola—Spain's first colony in the Americas—should have been working but instead they were running away, aided by the local indigenous people. As governor, Ovando faced a serious enough problem with runaways that he complained to the crown in 1503 and requested a ban on the further import of such troublemakers. Fernando V noted Ovando's concerns about the enslaved Africans "that you say should not be sent there because [those] that were there had escaped," and agreed to prohibit further shipments.[1]

At this point, Spain was about a decade into its efforts to assert control over Hispaniola, Columbus having established the settlement of La Navidad there in 1492. That colony failed, but he tried again, having success with La Isabela in 1494, on the north coast. Columbus and his men brought their Old World beliefs and practices with them, fully expecting to find gold and other riches. In addition—or if other wealth failed to materialize—they could also enslave and sell the locals. They had done it in Guinea and the Canaries, and expected to do it in Hispaniola as well.

The Spanish called the indigenous people of Hispaniola *Taíno*, a mangling of the adjective *nitaíno*, meaning "noble" or "good" in their Arawak-based language.[2] But such "goodness" alone would not save them—they were not Christians, and were thus enslavable. So too were the "Caribs," the name the Spanish gave to the indigenous people on some of the neighboring islands who had managed to fend off their initial incursions. They were described as being actively hostile, and thus any fight against them was a "just war" and slaves taken would be legitimate. The vanquished were forced to grow food for their captors, work in gold mines, and dive for pearls; some were shipped off the island. At least 1,530 were taken to Spain while Columbus was still in charge of the colony, before he was forced to leave in chains in 1500 for his mismanagement.[3] Raids also continued on the nearby Bahamas islands, with numerous slaving expeditions putting some 40,000 to 50,000 Lucayan people in captivity by 1512.[4] According to one historian, there are records confirming that at least 70,000 indigenous people were enslaved between 1493 and 1542; however, because many others were not officially recorded and documents have been lost, some estimates range far higher, at between 250,000 and 500,000.[5]

The earliest years of this Spanish attack on the Caribbean resulted in many conflicts, and some powerful local chiefs, or caciques, resisted the Spanish in Hispaniola. At the time of Columbus's arrival, five main *cacicazgos* (kin-based communities) were believed to be on the island.[6] The Spanish crown granted settlers an *encomienda*, which was permission to extract tribute from people who lived on an area of land. In the case of Hispaniola, settlers had to make deals with the caciques, which might involve a chief paying tribute through labor of some sort, such as his people growing crops or mining gold. In exchange, their subjects received instruction in Christianity and protection from their enemies. Such an arrangement was not without precedent—it too was an Old World hangover. It was the basis of how land was reclaimed and people were treated during the Christian *Reconquista* of Iberia from Muslim rule. Although this system was supposed to protect those under it, in Hispaniola reports of abuses and exploitation soon filtered back to Spain, as did complaints of incompetency and corruption.

Alongside the rise of the encomienda were attempts to convert Hispaniola's people. The religious orders that were doing this work argued that once the Taínos had been baptized, they would become good Christians—which then raised the question of whether they could be slaves. In 1500, Queen Isabella declared indigenous enslavement illegal and freed all people she believed to be her subjects. However, news and policy moved slowly; letters could take months to arrive, if they did not blow away in a hurricane or during a shipwreck. It is therefore difficult to calculate who knew what when, or who was complying with what. The long intervals between correspondence, coupled with the lack of oversight, meant that legislation aimed at fixing a problem could instead appear contradictory or confusing. Sometimes it codified things that had already been taking place. In any case, in 1503, the policy shifted. Queen Isabella permitted the capture of "Carib" Indians, including people living on the coast of Colombia and Panama, who she was told were cannibals, and who resisted conversion.[7]

In addition to these changes, the dramatic introduction of European disease caused tens of thousands of deaths—and a shortage of labor. It is not entirely clear when enslaved people started arriving in Hispaniola directly from Africa; in theory they were supposed to come via Spain. Initially, people of African origin, free and enslaved, were on the early voyages from Spain to the Caribbean, but most would have been *ladino* slaves, who might have been born in Spain or had at least lived there and spoken Spanish. The first to come directly from Africa may have arrived as early as 1502.[8] Africans taken from that continent were called *bozal*, another term that was added to the developing lexicon of slavery. In any case, Ovando's request in 1503 shows not only that Africans were on the island, but that some were actively fighting their enslavement. Despite Ovando's plea, Fernando V approved 100 people going directly from Africa to work in his mines on Hispaniola in 1505 and added 50 more five years later.[9]

While the enslaved black population gradually expanded on the island, the overall concern of the religious orders was focused on the treatment of the Taínos. The *encomenderos*—men who had been granted an encomienda—were abusive, and the deaths could not be stopped. In 1512, the crown responded with the Laws of Burgos, which reiterated that indigenous people should not be enslaved, and called for their working and living conditions to be improved. To further address the issue, Dominican priests proposed that African slaves be brought to the island to work on the nascent sugar plantations, known as *ingenios*. The crop had grown well in the Canaries and Madeira, and now some colonists were eager to see if it would flourish under Hispaniola's tropical sun.

Bartolomé de las Casas, a Dominican friar known as the "protector of the Indians," agreed with this plan and recommended it to the

Spanish crown as a way to liberate Taínos from the encomienda, later writing that if he "could get a license from the King to bring a dozen Negro slaves from Castile, this would allow them to free the Indians."[10] The four Hieronymite friars appointed to govern the island from 1516 to 1519 also supported the idea.

Las Casas went to Spain in 1517 to make his case, both to stop the abuse of the indigenous people and to solve the labor problem. King Carlos I, who had become king of Spain in 1516, agreed and permitted the taking of 4,000 enslaved people across the Atlantic.[11] By that point, Spain needed workers beyond Hispaniola, having planted settlements in Puerto Rico (1508), Jamaica (1509), and Cuba (1511), all places where the native peoples resisted enslavement and, like their neighbors, were struggling in the face of European diseases as well.

Back in the urban centers of Spain, enslaved black people were a visible minority in a densely populated area. Official eyes were everywhere, and it was difficult to flee their captors or revolt. However, across these three islands there were no narrow Seville-style streets, but rather mountain ranges, coastal plains, lush hills, secret caves, and coastlines with hidden coves. While survival was never guaranteed, there was potential help from the Taínos and the possibility of an escape from slavery for anyone willing to take a risk on the uncertain future such flight would hold.

The slavery practiced in Europe had now crossed the Atlantic with the Spanish. Like the fields of sugarcane that were being planted, the practice of human bondage would take root in the Americas and grow to an unfathomable scale.

⊰• •⊱

The Spanish were not alone in their exploits. The Genoese, Venetians, Flemish, and others were part of the growing Atlantic project, as were the Portuguese. Portugal had been granted all points east of the Tordesillas boundary and were successfully sailing into uncharted waters. Portugal's crown had seen notable success when Bartolomeu Dias reached the Cape of Good Hope in 1488, and Vasco da Gama went beyond it in 1497, tracing a sea route to India. Another explorer,

Pedro Álvares Cabral, sailed south out of the Tagus River into the Atlantic in March 1500, heading, he thought, toward Asia. In late April his crew spotted land, having drifted further west than they had thought. Realizing it wasn't yet India, Álvares Cabral anchored and went ashore around modern Porto Seguro (in today's Bahia state in Brazil), calling it the Land of the True Cross (*Terra de Vera Cruz*) and claiming it for Portugal.[12] The Tupí-speaking people who lived along the coast were intrigued by these strange arrivals, with some reportedly joining in an Easter Sunday mass, the Portuguese having made an altar out of wood just for the occasion.[13] However pleasant the True Cross was, it was not the rich cities of India, so Álvares Cabral decided to continue his journey, this "Portuguese" land filed away to be further exploited another time. But it was clear something worth exploiting was there: The wooden altar was the clue.

This Land of the True Cross became a logging area, the forests rich with dyewood. The export of this commodity reached such a level within a decade or so that Europeans began to call this land Brasil, after the pau brasil (*Caesalpinia echinata*) they were cutting down and sending across the Atlantic—a commodity-centric name like the one that had been bestowed on Madeira. A small colony was planted, with an initial settlement called São Vicente (now south of modern São Paulo). The population started small and wasn't uniformly Portuguese. The crown granted private citizens permission to colonize and explore for Portugal in exchange for hereditary land rights, a system that could make use of eager French, Dutch, Genoese, and other Europeans.[14]

Few Europeans at this point ventured inland to discover who else was there. Initial efforts to enslave the coastal Tupís yielded poor results—most fled into the vast protection of the Amazon. European men tried other routes to secure a supply of labor, for instance marrying the daughters of indigenous leaders, hoping to create alliances.[15] They also traded with the Tupí, as they had done with others across the ocean in West Africa: metal tools, cloth, and guns for the wood. Demand grew, as did the need for a larger workforce. Relations with the Tupí soured, and Africans were brought over, entering the record, unevenly, by the 1520s, though at this point the scale was small.[16] Brazil, despite its wood, was not the focus of imperial or commercial attention just yet. Other developments in the Atlantic held the interest of slave traders far more than coastal Brazil.

⤛ • ⤜

Today it is called Cidade Velha, the Old City, but in 1462 it was known as Ribeira Grande (Great River). Now a sleepy village on the southern coast of the island of Santiago, it was once the earliest permanent European settlement on this arid volcanic archipelago of ten Atlantic islands that the Portuguese called Cabo Verde (Green Cape, today's Cape Verde). Small stone cottages are sprinkled throughout the quiet town. Nearby, grand ruins crumble into the earth, a former cathedral slowly decomposing. Some structures have survived, however. One church, Nossa Senhora do Rosário, has its roots in the final decade of the fifteenth century. It remains intact and open, a simple building, the tropical sun casting palm frond–shaped shadows on its plain white walls from the trees that surround it.

Overlooking the entire settlement is the fort São Felipe, perched on a hill behind the town. It offers a panoramic view of the dark sands of the empty bay. The fort's cannons remain pointing to the sea, as if they are ready to fire at a moment's notice on unwelcome vessels. From this vista, it's possible to look down toward the main square and just about see the *pelourinho*, the public whipping post. This might have been the first *pelourinho* outside of Portugal. It would not be the last. The pillar marked the general site of the slave market, where captives from Upper Guinea were sent before being dispatched to their fate in the Americas. An unknown few, however, slipped away, running into the interior of the island, searching for a different ending—the first runaways at the fault line of the Old and New Worlds.[17]

The Cape Verde islands sit around 1,000 miles (1,600 kilometers) south of the Canary Islands. The West African coast, crucially, lies about 350 miles (570 kilometers) away. At the time of the Portuguese arrival, the islands were thought to be unoccupied. That may have been because growing food was difficult. Settlers soon discovered that Iberian staples of wheat and grapes failed to thrive, and it was evident that colonization and profit on these islands would not follow the model of Madeira and the Azores.[18] By 1466 the few settlers there received royal permission to trade along the Upper Guinea coast; some tax exemptions were granted to help the struggling economy, with the stipulation that they could only sell goods produced in Cape Verde.[19] The crop that did flourish in Santiago was a type of cotton soon used to make a distinctive striped cloth. It became highly prized in West Africa. Such was the demand that cotton production spread to the neighboring island of Fogo, spurring its colonization.[20] Enslaved Africans were procured to do the growing, harvesting, processing, and weaving.

Success with cotton aside, it became clear that the islands' most lucrative trade would be in humans, thanks to their location. By the 1510s, enslavers from Spain were buying humans in Santiago from the Portuguese to take onward to Hispaniola. Indeed, the Hieronymite friars running Hispaniola specifically mentioned the islands, saying they wanted licenses "to fetch them from the Cape Verde Islands, or Guinea."[21]

As capital flowed in, other enterprises grew, such as breeding horses, grazing livestock, reprovisioning passing ships, and panning salt found in the neighboring islands, which were named Maio, Boavista, and, perhaps inevitably, Sal. But the sale of humans brought from Senegambia, Sierra Leone, and Guinea-Bissau dominated, and they were traded for cotton cloth. Thus, the island population of Santiago grew, and a new society began to take root.[22] It was large enough that by 1495 a black confraternity, Nossa Senhora do Rosário, was established at the church of the same name, in Ribeira Grande.

Further south, in the Gulf of Guinea, the Portuguese came upon another supposedly unpopulated island, which they called São Tomé. It was lush and rainy, where Santiago had been sandy and dry, being some 1,100 miles (1,800 kilometers) further south, almost on the equator. Near São Tomé were three other islands: Principe, Annobón, and Fernando Pó (Bioko), the latter having a small indigenous population. They all would receive attention from Portugal. The first settlement had been placed on São Tomé in 1486, but populating it proved to be a challenge.

Within a few years, King João II dispatched a few hundred Jewish children to the island. Their parents had been driven out of Spain in 1492 and sought refuge in Portugal. Rather than finding safety, the parents experienced the horror of watching the authorities take their children, forcibly baptize them, and ship them off to the fledgling colony, where a near-certain death from tropical disease or starvation awaited them.[23]

The Portuguese crown next devised a plan to give any settler who would go to São Tomé a female slave with whom he was encouraged to have children to populate the colony. Settlers would also be given enslaved workers to help them get established. Despite such inducements, few takers emerged, and the white European population remained small.[24] The resulting Afro-European *mestiço* population grew, as did the number of enslaved Africans being brought to the island. Indeed, by 1520, the crown permitted *mestiços* to hold public office as long as they were married and owned property.[25] By 1526, another black confraternity, also called Nossa Senhora do Rosário, was established there.[26]

Unlike the other islands, São Tomé, especially the north and northeast of the island, had good conditions for growing sugarcane. The system that had been worked out in Madeira was implemented here: Enslaved people were brought over, trees were cleared, cane planted, sugar *engenhos* built, and the harvest collected. From two plantations on the island in 1517, the number reached 60 by the middle of the century, with many large estates each enslaving between 150 and 300 people.[27] With so many slaves required for the sugar plantations, and given São Tomé's proximity to the coast, the island also became an entrepôt for captives taken to Brazil.[28] However, the island's population remained small, and the authorities could only do so much to stop the steady stream of people running into the mountainous hinterland or dense rainforest, far from the gaze or guns of officials. Already by 1535, complaints arose that "every day the bush is filled with runaway slaves and we are all terrified."[29]

◂◂ • ▸▸

In October 1526, the king (or *manikongo*) of Kongo, Afonso I (also Nzinga Mbemba, r. 1509–1542/43), was frustrated by the state of his kingdom and the pressures the Portuguese were putting on it. He wrote a letter to Portugal's King João III (r. 1521–1557) expressing his displeasure on a number of matters, but especially trade, telling him,

> Many of our people, for the avid desire which they have for the merchandise and objects of [your] Kingdoms which your people bring here, and so as to satisfy their rampant appetites, steal many of our free and protected people. And it has happened many times that they have stolen nobles and sons of nobles, and our own relatives, and have taken them to sell to the white men who are in our Kingdoms.[30]

Such dealings within his kingdom and among his subjects were a worrying turn for Afonso.[31] He was the second Christian king of Kongo, after his father, Nzinga a Nkuwu, who converted in 1491 and changed his name to João I, a nod to the reigning Portuguese monarch João II.[32] Using these Christian ties, people from Kongo were sent to Portugal to be educated or placed on diplomatic missions, and the two kingdoms built a relationship. By the time of Afonso's reign, Kongo had joined Ethiopia as another Catholic kingdom in Africa. In addition to the spiritual dimension, Christianity offered a political one, giving Kongo important connections to Catholic Europe, all the way to the papacy. It was a significant transformation, as was the arrival of Europeans and the developments in trade.

Indeed, from the small *feitoria* near Arguin, the Portuguese established a trading network along the coast, stretching from Senegambia to the kingdom of Kongo. A practice that Europeans called "slavery"—but that was very different from the form that was developing in the Americas—was widespread along the Atlantic coast of Africa. Generally speaking, there were multiple routes to enslavement in this part of the continent: Some people were captured after a conflict or kidnapped during a raid. Others were forced into slavery as a judicial punishment, while a number were pawned or sold by their families, in some cases to pay a debt. A range of experiences and potential outcomes existed, many of which were akin to servitude and most of which were misunderstood by Europeans.[33]

The men who arrived on ships from Europe in this era were initially limited in their ability to speak the local languages and had little knowledge about these unfamiliar societies. What they recorded in their journals and travel accounts must be read in this context. What they saw as "slavery" could actually have been other forms of servility or kin-based dependency.[34] Many slaves worked land in conditions little different from those of a free peasantry. Others had high-status roles, such as administrators and advisors.[35] Slaves were also considered to be loyal, especially as soldiers.[36] Opportunities for freedom existed in African slavery, such as manumission, and also self-ransom bought with money earned through paid work; female slaves could gain their freedom by marrying a free man. In some societies, bearing the master's child could also come with freedom.[37]

Commerce between Europeans and Africans was not straightforward. Europeans were always on the back foot; vastly outnumbered, they struggled with the tropical climate, often succumbing to unfamiliar diseases. There were also more logistical difficulties. For instance, European vessels could not navigate African rivers well and so could not make their way to places like the gold mines near the Volta River.[38] This helped Africans defend their coast, which meant the Europeans were also unable to go about raiding and trading with no restrictions. Their survival depended on relationships with African leaders and intermediaries, but those alliances were not always stable. Resistance sprang up along the coast—Portuguese sailors were run off or attacked, and fragile peace deals needed to be brokered on a regular basis.[39] Commercial interaction was regulated by local officials, who imposed duties and taxes, limits on what could be trafficked, and other trade rules.[40] The Portuguese quickly realized they were encountering diverse groups of people, who had different needs and interests, and with whom they entered into multiple rounds of negotiations as they learned about the complex cultural and economic ecosystem in West Africa.[41]

But the stakes—and profits—were high. The Portuguese traders came laden with copper *manillas* (rings or bracelets), cowrie shells, cloth, iron, beads, and weapons.[42] They were not always exchanged for humans, as the Portuguese sought other goods, not least their long-desired gold. Such was the initial volume of trade that they established a fort on the West African coast, which they named São Jorge da Mina (Saint George of the Mine, today's Elmina, Ghana), reflecting its location near a known mining area. It was finished in 1482, though not without a fight. The Akan king Kwamena Ansa explained to the Portuguese that they were putting the structure on a holy site, and they ended up going to battle to settle the matter, with Ansa ultimately relenting. From there, the Portuguese dispatched ever-larger quantities of gold to Portugal, while the Lower Guinea coast became known for its promise of riches, earning the name among Europeans of the Gold Coast, or *Costa da Mina*.[43]

Kongo's King Afonso understood the difficulties of dealing with the Portuguese, and the high social cost of trading with them. The traders were no longer referring to Africans as humans, but as *peça* (piece) or *cabeça* (head, like cattle), words that would also appear in his own letters.[44] It was a system, and his kingdom was now a vital cog in the transatlantic machine. He also realized that the kidnapping of nobility from other kingdoms was rupturing political alliances. His subjects and others were forced to raid deeper into the interior to find people to sell. Afonso knew the captives had a monetary value that would keep the Portuguese satisfied.[45]

Afonso's 1526 letter to João III was not his first complaint. He had written earlier to King Manuel (r. 1495–1521) to protest the bills that he was receiving from the Portuguese for many goods and services, including his children's education in Portugal, as well as guns, soldiers, and the transport of friars to Kongo so they could build churches and schools.[46] Not everything Afonso had received had been a gift, and payment was now due. As Manuel instructed, "The ships [sent to Kongo] should return full of slaves and other merchandises."[47]

While the Portuguese crown was eager to have a monopoly on this trade, both Manuel and João III expressed some reservations about what was taking place in West Africa and on the water. Manuel wrote to the pope to discuss the fact that many Africans died at sea without being baptized. He wanted to make sure they received this sacrament within six months of landing.[48] Similarly, João III wanted parts of the slave trade stopped because he was worried that at El Mina, captives traded to the Mandinka—people in parts of Mali, the Gambia, Senegal, and Guinea—might be converted to Islam.[49] But no one was yet calling for the whole enterprise to stop. Afonso, like other African leaders along the west coast, was left to find a way to protect his people and appease the growing appetites of the Portuguese.

Chapter 4

Alliances

In 1519 a cacique the Spanish called Enrique—sometimes known by the diminutive Enriquillo—decided it was time to return to his ancestral lands. He quit the Spanish encomienda of San Juan de la Maguana and took his wife and some followers to the Bahoruco Mountains, in the south of Hispaniola.[1] It is not entirely clear what drove him there, but some sort of upset ruptured his relationship with the Spanish.[2] His small party soon grew, as Africans and other indigenous people joined them, the numbers swelling to between 100 and 300.[3] The Spanish went to capture him, the first battle in a conflict that would last for nearly a decade.

A few years later, on Christmas Day 1521, some 20 enslaved Africans rebelled on the sugar plantation of Diego Columbus, the son of Christopher Columbus, who was also the governor of Hispaniola at the time. This "rebellion of the Blacks" was included in the 1547 *Historia General y Natural de las Indias*, by the chronicler Gonzalo Fernández de Oviedo, who observed, "It would be senseless that such a notorious thing was not written down."[4]

He recorded that the rebels were of "the Wolof language"—that is, Senegambian. When they left the estate, they "went to join at a certain place with as many others that were allied with them."[5] They moved west from the outskirts of Santo Domingo, not far from the banks of the Nigua River, raiding a cattle ranch before heading toward another sugar plantation as others joined them, eventually numbering around 100. The Spanish troops caught up with them around the mouth of the Nizao River.

As Oviedo related it, "In this first encounter fell some of the slaves but this did not prevent them from regrouping right away, throwing lots of stones, rods and darts, and with another greater yelling they met the second encounter with the Christian riders."

As the Spanish prepared to take a third pass at them, the Africans "turned their backs, fleeing through some rocks and crags that there were near where this defeating took place."[6] To Oviedo this was a "victory won," but given that some of the Africans managed to escape to the Bahoruco Mountains, where Enrique lived, it seems a premature verdict.[7]

Historians consider this the first African slave revolt in the Americas, and it bore the hallmarks of rebellions to come, taking place during a holiday when officials were distracted and slaves may have had time off, and occurring on a sugar plantation that had brutal conditions.

In the two decades after Governor Ovando's initial plea to stop sending black slaves, the number of Africans brought to Hispaniola rose, as did the problems, especially that of runaways. In the early period of colonization, the term *negro alzado* (insurgent black) appeared with some frequency, though it later gave way to *cimarrón*, which comes from a word meaning a wild or untamed animal, like a horse galloping into a forest, never to be seen again.[8] It initially applied to both Africans and indigenous people, though later it came to mean a runaway slave. Other languages developed terminology for these freedom-seekers, borrowing from the Spanish: *marron* in French and "maroon" in English, though the Dutch used *bosneger*, which roughly translates to "forest black."

Variants of this running away, or marronage, later developed. *Grand marronage* was a complete fleeing, with no return; *petit marronage*, on the other hand, involved an enslaved person departing for short periods and then coming back. Sometimes he or she might do so to highlight poor treatment and demand improved conditions, or see a friend or family member on a different plantation—though of course leaving brought with it the risk of punishment.[9] *Petit marronage* offered some fluidity, but each case was distinct.[10]

The ongoing issue of runaways, coupled with the Christmas rebellion of 1521, provoked a series of official reactions. Oviedo reported that the slaves who were caught were "punished as it was adequate to their daring and madness," but that was only the first step.[11] The Hispaniola *cabildo* (town council) quickly produced a slave code in 1522, the Ordenanzas de los negros (Ordinances on the blacks), in response to these events, with punishment aimed at the "Blacks of La Española island." Columbus says in his introduction to the Ordenanzas, "The Blacks and slaves that there are in this said island, without any fear and with devilish thoughts, have had the temerity and daring of committing many crimes and excesses . . . this last passed holiday of the Nativity of Our Redeemer, a certain number of them in quantity agreed to rebel and rebelled."[12]

The resulting ordinances reveal a colony struggling to keep order. The first of the 23 mandates that, within 20 days, "all the Blacks and Whites and Canarians that are slaves who currently wander rebel in this island, be forced to come back." Anyone refusing to do so would face the penalty of having a foot cut off, or even death by hanging, when captured. The fourth ordinance stipulated that neither "said Blacks nor slaves" could carry weapons. Number 8 mandated that a slave must not "unshackle loose or put out of imprisonment any slave belonging to somebody else without permission from his owner," again under threat of amputation or death.[13]

Later legislation continued to augment this code. As rebellions and acts of resistance were mounting, so too were the official efforts to control them. What's more, the conception of who was a slave was changing. While the 1522 code sometimes mentioned just black people, and other times, black, white, and Canarian slaves, the categories of "slave" and "black" were becoming conflated. While not all slaves were black at this point, within a few decades all blacks were slaves, unless noted otherwise. This linguistic eliding was complete in later ordinances; one from 1535 referred to a runaway as a "fleeing black" (*negro huido*), rather than a fleeing slave or a fleeing person.[14]

The paper trail in this period is one-sided, telling only a sliver of the story of Enrique and the Africans. The records do show, however, that eventually much of Hispaniola became dominated by rebel groups like Enrique's.[15] Over time, caciques known as Ciguayo, Murcia, Hernandillo el Tuerto, and Tamayo led their people in attacks on the Spanish.[16] The Taíno leaders had many advantages, perhaps most importantly an

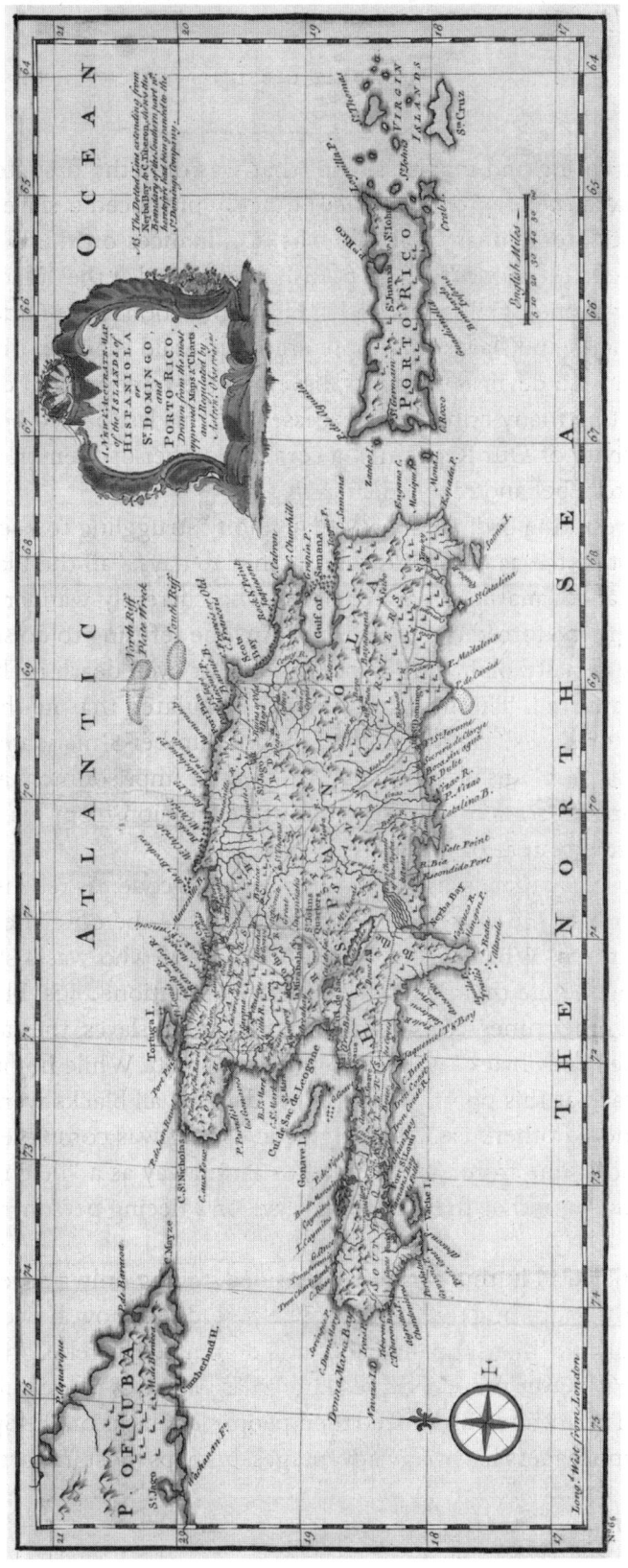

A British map of Hispaniola and Puerto Rico, dated 1767, by Emanuel Bowen, Royal Mapmaker to King George II

intimate knowledge of the difficult landscape around the mountains. Officials complained in a 1528 letter, "The rebels know the land, and thus they outwit the Spaniards."[17] But having been enslaved by the Spanish or forced into an encomienda, they also had a knowledge of their enemies and the sorts of tactics and weapons they might use.[18] The Spanish, realizing the implications of such resistance for their colonial project, threw money and manpower at the issue. At least three squadrons of 80 soldiers went out in 1528 to attack Enrique, but they were defeated. The Spanish took African and Amerindian slaves to help them, only to see them defect to the enemy.[19]

Enrique stayed in those mountains for another 14 years, starting with an estimated population of 300 and ending with one of around 4,000.[20] The attempt to control the runaways became a "war" to the Spanish, and a costly one. In another letter, officials noted with perhaps some understatement, "The expense of this war has been very great."[21]

It turned so costly that the Spanish began to look for a cheaper solution: a peace deal. This, too, would set a particular pattern. Some maroons could not be vanquished and so a resolution would have to come by other means. In this case, the religious orders stepped in, having kept a reasonably cordial relationship with Enrique. A deal was hammered out in 1528, but Enrique did not appear on the day of surrender. Instead, he launched another attack a few days later.[22]

In 1533, the crown sent in more troops. It also tried to lure Enrique through diplomacy, offering him a full pardon. Officials arranged a meeting, and Enrique finally agreed to a surrender in that year. He won land for his people with the status of "free town," or republic. In exchange, Enrique and his community were required to capture other runaways. As a show of his willingness to comply, Enrique turned in six black people to the authorities. The deal he brokered with the Spanish resulted in two measures that were replicated throughout Spanish America. The first was that indigenous people could negotiate with the Spanish for a "pueblo de Indios" (Indian town) and, rarely, a "pueblo de negros" for African maroons; the second was that they had to pay for their liberty by denying freedom to others.[23]

Enrique's new settlement was in Sabana Buey, to the southeast of the town of Azua, in the south of Hispaniola. Why Enrique ended the struggle is unknown, but he died soon after, in 1535, and it's impossible to say whether he believed this "free" town would be a secure home for future generations of his family. In the end, it was not. At some point in the 1540s, a group of African maroons attacked and destroyed Sabana Buey, perhaps in revenge for the initial six runaways who had been handed over. The survivors of Sabana Buey threw in their lot with the Spanish and continued to hunt for and spy on African maroons.[24]

From this point on, runaways and maroon communities were as much a part of the New World as the arrival of slave ships. The war for freedom had started. It would not end for more than 350 years.

⊰⊱ • ⊱⊰

It showed up as a mention, a brief line: "One night . . . it happened that some blacks set fire to Ginés's house on their own."[25] Today, that attack on the property of Ginés Doncel is recognized as the first slave revolt in mainland North America.

The ill-fated voyage of Lucas Vázquez de Ayllón, like so many events from this period, is like a jigsaw puzzle with missing pieces. What is known is that out of a total of around 600 people in six ships, only an unspecified "some" were enslaved Africans. Given, however, that Ayllón was trying—for the third time—to establish a colony, having mortgaged part of his sugar plantation in Puerto Plata, Hispaniola, to raise the money for the expedition, he would have brought slaves to do some of the work.[26]

Ayllón had made some of his wealth in the Bahamas, capturing 900 Lucayan people. His anticipated profits then fell short when about half of this human cargo died in holding pens.[27] He had been involved in the organization and funding of an earlier expedition to find more indigenous people to enslave, undertaken by Francisco Gordillo and Pedro de Quejo in 1521. The men landed in today's Winyah Bay, near Georgetown, South Carolina, about 60 miles (100 kilometers) north of Charleston. When they returned to Hispaniola, they had with them a young man, possibly from the Catawba people, whom they renamed Francisco de Chicora. Known as "El Chicorano," he was later taken to Spain. The tales he told of his homeland whetted Spanish appetites to know more.[28] By 1526, Ayllón was ready to see for himself, and went armed with a charter for settlement.

El Chicorano was on the expedition with Ayllón and his unknown quantity of slaves. His role was to lead them to his homeland, a place of fertile land and great riches, or so the Spanish had been told. They returned to Winyah Bay, a swaying sea of green cordgrass ushering them into the promised land along a waterway they called the River Jordan.

Whatever peace they may have experienced cruising those channels came to a halt when one ship was grounded upon entering the bay. The cassava and maize, livestock and horses they had so carefully loaded met a muddy end.[29] To make matters worse, soon afterward, El Chicorano and some of the other indigenous people on the expedition fled, disappearing into the forest.

August was a terrible time for such a predicament, the heat and humidity oppressive, dangerous storms frequent. In the salt and the sweat, Ayllón and the others assessed their situation, their guide now long gone, and the fabled promised land nowhere in sight. By September, after further reconnaissance, they decided to move south, trying to land again around today's Sapelo Sound, in coastal Georgia. The seagrass, the calm inland waterways, and the moss dangling from trees would now have looked familiar to them. They called the site San Miguel de Gualdape because they landed among the Guale people on September 29, the feast of Saint Michael the Archangel.

No doubt the enslaved people, who later estimates calculated to number around 100, were forced into action, their skills useful in the early days of establishing a new colony: felling trees for lumber; building livestock pens, homes, and a church; managing the animals that had survived the journey; and generally doing the actual work of settlement. However, the would-be settlers soon realized they had arrived too late to plant crops. They had to bargain with—or steal from—the Guale, which soon generated bad feelings. The air began to cool down; early autumn cold snaps brought temperatures not experienced in Hispaniola, a warning of the winter to come.[30] Ayllón soon took ill. By October 18 he was dead.

The surviving settlers fractured, with one faction supporting Ginés Doncel, who at one point imprisoned his rivals. Indigenous people attacked the Spaniards, adding to the stress and uncertainty. The disagreements escalated into more heated disputes.

One night in the middle of the confusion, some of the enslaved people set fire to Doncel's house, and possibly some of the buildings on his compound.[31] From there, the scant information trail that exists—a second-hand retelling—runs out.[32] By this point, the 600 or so people who had stepped on board in Hispaniola were down to around 150. The surviving settlers abandoned the colony and returned to the Caribbean. The fate of the enslaved fire-setters disappears from the record, but it is likely that some used the chaos as cover and fled, perhaps aided by the Guale.

The first known enslaved Africans in North America brought the first known revolt outside of the Caribbean, their actions reduced to a single line of history. But in the way these tales go, Ayllón's failure lived on: At least one 1529 map bestowed the area with the title "Land of Ayllón."

⋘ • ⋙

As more became known about the Americas, the grumbling from other European kingdoms grew louder: Why were these new worlds reserved for the Spanish and Portuguese? Even the Catholic French king François I (r. 1515–1547) was to have said: "The sun shines for me as for others; I should like to see the clause in Adam's will which excludes me from the apportioning of the world."[33]

One answer came in a roundabout way when a German priest named Martin Luther nailed his 95 Theses to the door of a church in Wittenberg, Germany, in 1514, calling into question the primacy of the Catholic Church. The subsequent Protestant Reformation reconfigured the religious landscape of Europe—but it also had consequential ramifications for the Americas. People across northern Europe turned their back on Catholicism, leading to religious wars and the establishment of Protestant denominations in France, the Netherlands, and Germany, with England officially splitting from Rome in 1534. The break with Catholicism brought with it a questioning of rights, power, liberties, and freedoms.[34] And that included who could go where and trade with whom. Ships with Protestant crews—that is, pirates, or "Lutheran corsairs," as the Spanish called them—ignored the papal treaties and crossed the Atlantic or sailed to West Africa. Indeed, so many French pirates were appearing in the Caribbean that one report described the sea around Puerto Rico as being "as full of French as [La] Rochelle."[35] In 1565 the Spanish chased a group of potential French Huguenot settlers out of Florida.[36] Portugal had to watch its back too. Other Europeans were arriving in Africa, muscling in on the trade there, including in humans. Along the Upper Guinea coast, the French arrived in the 1530s (Senegal), the English in the 1550s (Gambia), and then the Dutch and the English in the 1580s (Sierra Leone).[37]

Spain was forced to go on the offensive to defend its territories, while also attempting further colonization in the Americas. Spanish legal and ecclesiastical minds also continued to debate the question of who could be enslaved. A succession of Spanish legislation prohibited—in theory—the enslavement of indigenous people who were willing to accept Christianity and the Spanish crown. By 1537 a papal bull asserted the rationality of indigenous people in the Americas, forbidding their enslavement, but made no mention of Africans.[38] Similarly, Spain's "New Laws" of 1542 reiterated the prohibition of indigenous slavery and called for improvements in the treatment and working conditions of Amerindian people, but enslaved black people were not included. However, for enslaved Africans, even accepting Christian baptism would not make them free.[39]

This meant a willful disregard of the long connection to Christianity among some Africans, not least those in Ethiopia, where the religion dated back to the fourth century. Ethiopian and broader African Christianity, including the more recent conversion of the Kingdom of Kongo, was known in sixteenth-century Europe. However, the presence of Christianity in Africa was not the main concern of people bringing humans from that continent to the Americas—it was the evolving hunt for justifications for this practice. Some looked for a rationale in the Bible, where there was much to read about slavery. The question of freedom and escape from bondage is a theme that runs through the Old and New Testaments. Slavery appears here as both metaphor and actual state of being. The wages of sin are enslavement, as the story of the curse of Ham illustrates. In this tale in the Book of Genesis

(9:18–27), Ham sees his father, Noah, drunk and naked. Ham's brothers cover their father, but he does not. He then incurs the wrath of Noah, who declares, "Cursed be Canaan [the son of Ham]; a servant of servants shall he be unto his brethren," thus committing the descendants of Ham to slavery. From these rather ambiguous origins, the curse of Ham took on a life of its own in connection to Africans, in part because Canaan's descendants were said to have become Egyptians, and the taint extended from there to Ethiopia. The idea that Africans were doomed to this fate developed through the centuries as a convenient justification for their enslavement.[40]

Another critical factor tethered Christianity, blackness, and slavery: the idea of *limpieza de sangre* (*limpeza de sangue* in Portuguese)—"purity of blood," a concept very particular to Iberian Catholicism. This was related to the practice of the often-forced conversion of Jewish people (*conversos*) and North African Muslims (*moriscos*) who claimed they had adopted Catholicism, though official suspicion of such converts lingered. Initially, from around 1500 to the mid-1600s, these "new Christians" were denied permission to settle in the new American colonies for fear of a "corrupting" influence.

In contrast to these so-called new Christians, some free black people in Spain referred to themselves as "old Christians"—having been born to Christian parents—and were more successful in their applications to travel to the New World. A free black couple, Francisco González and his wife, Juana Rodriguez, petitioned the Casa de Contratación in Seville for permission to move from that city to Veracruz, Mexico, in 1569. In their application, they claimed they were "old Christians," which their witnesses verified in their statements. One described the couple as "blacks and of the caste of those of Guinea and not *Moriscos*," while another attested that they were "blacks of the caste of black Christians."[41] While the couple were successful in this case, life in a world with such categories was rife with contradiction, carrying within it forms of prejudice and racism recognizable to modern sensibilities. It held within it an underlying structure—blood and "caste"—that would become part of the developing racial language of the Americas.[42] In Spanish America, this would lead to the idea of *casta*. In theory, it was a hierarchy of three main "castes": Spanish, indigenous, and black. In practice, places like sixteenth-century Mexico had populations that provided multiple possibilities of combinations of the three, and so anxiety about "mixing" blood permeated colonial society. Such concerns could be found in a particular type of artwork of the time, mostly seen in New Spain (as Mexico was then called), known as *casta* paintings. They are often in a grid format, with each window depicting humans—usually a man, woman, and child—of varying "mixtures." One square might have a Spanish man, an indigenous woman, and their "mestizo" child, with a description usually provided underneath. Such works might have up to 12 or 16 panels, with every possible mixture, complete with a racial subcategory: *zambo, lobo, pardo, mulato, moreno, mestizo*. Genetics was not yet understood, and inevitably the physical appearance of people in colonial Spanish society did not always align with these sorts of images. However, blackness was at the bottom of the hierarchy, old Christian or not. By the late 1500s, the word "black," in reference to the skin color of Africans, had become more firmly associated with a set of ideas and institutions, including slavery, and was no longer simply a physical description.[43]

Throughout the first decades of the sixteenth century, the number of enslaved people brought to the Americas from Africa rose in dramatic stages as Spain continued to enlarge its territories, including the conquest of the México Empire in 1521. Around 20,000 Africans were transported to Spain's territories, including the Caribbean, New Spain, and Cartagena on the South American coast, in the period from 1526 to 1550. Over the next 25 years that number would double as settlement and demand grew, and then in the final quarter of the century it would more than quadruple, with around 150,000 captives taken to Spanish America by 1600.[44]

By the middle of the sixteenth century, the Dominican friar Bartolomé de las Casas realized the gravity of what he had said some 30 years earlier, recommending the use of Africans as slaves so the Amerindians could be saved. He could not ignore the world in motion around him, reflecting on it during a trip to Seville, where it would have been impossible to ignore the slaves for sale on the cathedral steps. He began to revise his opinion about Africans, and appears to have reread the accounts of Gomes Eanes de Zurara on the Portuguese exploits in Guinea, concluding that those early slaves were captured "absolutely unjustly." He wrote about it in his extensive *History of the Indies*, and about his own change of heart, saying he "was not aware of the unjust ways in which the Portuguese captured and made slaves of the blacks," but after he found out, he "would not have proposed it for all the world, because blacks were enslaved unjustly . . . exactly as the Indians had been."[45]

By the time he understood this, however, he must have also understood, with a sinking heart, that his about-face had come far too late.

Chapter 5

Plots

"It has been 10 years and more," said a 1546 complaint, "that [Diego de Ocampo] has been on the rise and killing many Spanish and doing very excessive damage." Ocampo and Sebastián Lemba, the two "captains" mentioned in this letter, had twice burned the sugar *ingenios* and cane fields of San Juan de la Maguana, on Hispaniola. Ocampo was near the settlement of La Vega, while Lemba was in the Bahoruco Mountains, "where Don Enrique, Indian, was." The Spanish were prepared to offer these maroons "life and freedom" to stop their revolt, and, as the letter went on to report, Ocampo had "come in peace, with which we have promised him life and liberty, and we plan to do the same in the name of Your Majesty with another one called Sebastián Lemba."[1] However, Lemba had no plans to surrender.

The overall situation on Hispaniola was tense. Governor Alonso López de Cerrato noted in a letter to the crown that "there were 12,000 Negroes on the island who could revolt at any time."[2] The locals in areas near maroon settlements—believed to total between 2,000 and 3,000 people—were worried. No one wanted to leave their house. Crops were being destroyed. Goods were being stolen. Settlers were giving up. The crown needed to send troops.[3] A few hundred maroons, perhaps up to 300, were in the mountains with Lemba, while Ocampo's party was closer to 40 or 50. López de Cerrato was now waging a campaign to eradicate these maroon communities.[4]

Officials believed that revolts and marronage were happening because they had *ladino*, or Europeanized slaves. They thus felt they needed more Africans, who were not familiar with the ways and language of the Spanish. As one island official had recommended in 1544:

"Going forward it would be advisable that there not be many *ladino* slaves born here, because these are a bad people (*nación*) very daring and badly inclined, and they are the ones that rebel . . . the *bozales* are not like that."[5] Officials would soon discover what the *bozales* were like.

Lemba was possibly from Kongo, though his provenance is not entirely clear. His name was a versatile word there: It marked a place, but it was also used to describe a mercantile group and a ritual between fathers and sons, and was associated with cults of healing and fertility.[6] There is no record of when Lemba arrived in Hispaniola or which ship brought him.

In a similar way, it's difficult to know what he thought when he arrived in Hispaniola, perhaps meeting other West Central Africans, watching the treatment of the Taíno, and taking stock of the Spanish. That he wanted out of the system is clear, but whether his vision of freedom stopped at the caves of Bahoruco or scanned the horizon for Africa isn't known.

Wherever he was from, Lemba could fight. The Spanish described him as "extremely able and very knowledgeable in the ways of war."[7] Lemba divided his fighters into small groups, sending them to raid rural settlements. In one raid Lemba took steel, iron, and an enslaved blacksmith to work with them. All of this suggests that he was aware of the sorts of weapons he would need, whether for self-protection or to drive the Spanish off the island.[8]

Another 1546 letter from the governor to Carlos V detailed the events of a significant battle, in which Spanish soldiers went into the mountains and killed some 100 people. It was combat with brutal consequences. "Of those who were caught," he wrote, "some were shot by arrows and others were burned, and others were tortured, and others were hanged, and others had their feet cut off and they were thrown off the island, and the women and some who were not guilty were expelled from the island so there could be no memory of them."[9] But such memories were not so easily extinguished.

Lemba's troops were eventually whittled down to just 20 men, but he stayed one step ahead of his enemies—until he did not. "The first one to lasso [dió una Lazada] him was a light-skinned black man, a slave of the *cabildo* [town council]," a later report recounted. "He was given his reward and freedom." As for Lemba, his "head was placed on the gate of this city [Santo Domingo]."[10]

That Lemba died at the hands of a slave who was also seeking his freedom but through very different means seems a cruel twist. But the colonial system that was being built, battle by battle, depended on such tactics. Offers of freedom kept the rumors and reports coming, and they brought willing soldiers as well.

The death of Lemba in 1549 seemed to elicit some confidence among the Spanish. "This matter of negro rebels has now been completely settled," they reported. The outcome "had been a great boon for the island and for the other [slaves] who now know they cannot rise up."[11] But the conditions were, in fact, ripe for far more rebellion. By the time of Lemba's death, the Spanish population on Hispaniola had reached around 4,500, with the enslaved population around five times that.[12] Places with such imbalances were appearing throughout the Americas, upsetting the precarious equilibrium that allowed for the social "tranquility" so ardently valued and constantly mentioned by the authorities. In Cuba, reports of runaways in 1536 claimed they were making common cause with the indigenous people and assaulting settlements like Trinidad. Earlier complaints were filed in Puerto Rico, in 1526, about the issue of runaways, and a more serious Afro-Indigenous revolt occurred, again involving Wolof people, in 1531.[13]

Running away and revolting were not the only options, as slaves in Spanish America also had access to the legal system, as they did in Spain. A 1540 *real cédula* (royal order) mandated that enslaved people who were contesting their status and claiming to be free had to be heard by the highest possible court in the colonies, the *audiencia*.[14] In addition, there was the continued possibility to buy one's freedom (*coartación*). As bureaucratic and cumbersome as these processes could be, they were successful for some people, and free black communities began to appear across Spanish America. For instance, the Cuban port of Havana was home to a sizable community by the 1560s, whose members comprised 10 to 15 percent of the city's overall free population.[15] However, other enslaved people decided to fight outside of the courts. Revolts continued—Cartagena in 1545, Honduras in 1548, Peru in 1553—and the maroon communities proliferated.

THE GREAT RESISTANCE

⋘ • ⋙

Draw a straight line south from Santo Domingo, across the blue of the Caribbean, and it hits Venezuela. These two places were connected by sea, by Spain, and by a certain spirit. By the time of the 1552 revolt in Venezuela led by Miguel de Buría, a runaway slave who called himself a king, the Spanish had been trying to colonize the coastline for around 30 years. They started on the offshore islands, where conquistadors discovered valuable pearls in the oyster beds near the islands of Margarita and Cubagua.[16]

They set up *rancherías de perlas* (pearl fisheries), first on Cubagua in 1516 and later on the larger Margarita. These *rancherías* consisted of small huts near the water, where indigenous people were forced to dive to sometimes dangerous depths to harvest pearls.[17] For a while the oyster beds were plentiful, and Cubagua alone had around 100 *rancherías* by the 1520s, but they dwindled in size and output over the course of the sixteenth century.

The workers were the first to disappear. The Spanish started with Guaquerí people from Margarita, and brought Lucayan people from the Bahamas and other Arawaks. By the mid-1520s, Africans had joined them on those pearling islands, with many initially brought from Santo Domingo.[18] Colonization on the mainland continued as well, as did the arrival of more slaves, including a young Miguel, who is believed to have been brought from Puerto Rico, possibly in the 1530s, though the exact year is unknown.

Miguel was described as *"muy ladino,"* so it seems likely he was born on Puerto Rico and grew up speaking Castilian. The watery oyster beds were not his fate; rather, the gold mines were. His enslavers were the Barrio family, and they were heavily involved in the quest for this precious metal.[19] Gold continued to guide Spanish expansion, the thirst for this metal seemingly unquenchable. Explorers soon found some in Venezuela—by 1551, gold had been discovered around 150 miles (240 kilometers) inland, in an area the Spanish named San Felipe de Buría. In 1552, the Barrio family established another new settlement, Nueva Segovia de Barquisimeto, nearby.

The hot, dirty work picking at rocks or panning in streams, hoping for a glimmer of ore, was done by at least 80 enslaved black and indigenous people, under the watchful eye of a Spanish overseer. One such supervisor pushed Miguel de Buría too far. Already exhausted by the labor and bristling at the constraints of his enslavement, Miguel found out one afternoon in 1553 that he was to be punished with a lashing.[20] The details are hazy, and perhaps this was not his first beating at the hands of this particular overseer, but it became his last. With a surge of rage, he picked up a nearby sword and began swinging it, using the ensuing uproar to escape.

There were plenty of wooded places to hide a short run from the settlements. Every night, Miguel came out, trying to communicate with the slaves left behind in the mines. Some followed him, around 20 in the end. A short time later, Miguel's maroons marched on the town and, as one account put it, "He took the lives of all those who had either beaten or abused him and his companions."[21] He warned the residents he would return to kill them all. More black and indigenous people joined Miguel, raising the number to around 180. They had enough people to create a small town and fortify it with defenses such as ditches. At that point, Miguel made himself king, and Guiomar, the mother of his son, queen. Such a move was in line with more general African traditions of power. Later testimony referred to him as a *"negro biáfra,"* which could link him to the area around modern Nigeria, Cameroon, or Gabón.[22] His self-proclaimed kingship raises the question of whether Miguel had a royal lineage, or if he picked up ideas about this from *bozal* slaves in Puerto Rico and Venezuela. Kingship was also a nod to the present, both to Spain's Carlos V and to local caciques in Venezuela, putting Miguel on a similar footing, allowing him to negotiate with the Spanish as the leader of his community.[23]

King Miguel also anointed one of his former mining colleagues as bishop and built a church in the runaway colony, or *palenque* (from the Spanish word for palisade or stockade). The *palenque* church was a clear indication of the role that Catholicism was expected to play, both in terms of personal faith and in establishing a community with roles and hierarchies that would be familiar to the Spanish. According to a later account by Padre Pedro Aguado, a Spanish Franciscan who arrived in 1561 and heard of the events second-hand, King Miguel had ordered his followers to "make houses where they could live, like men planning to remain in perpetuity."[24]

Miguel planned another attack on Barquisimeto, possibly in 1555, but it may have been earlier. In preparation, his people made lances and spears from their mining pans, while indigenous members of the group readied their arrows. They also put on war paint. Using the juice of the jagua (genipap) fruit, the Amerindian allies darkened their skin, rendering themselves a unified army of black fighters, ready to destroy the town and its oppressive industries.[25] They entered Barquisimeto with cries of *"Viva el rey Miguel,"* before setting fire to houses and charging the Spaniards scrambling to fight them.[26] The residents ended up asking the neighboring village of Tocuyo for backup. Help arrived under the command of Diego de Losada, who planned a surprise attack with about 50 men at the *palenque*. King Miguel was badly wounded and died. Everyone the Spanish managed to capture during that raid, including the queen and prince, was returned to slavery.[27]

Elsewhere in northern Venezuela, *cimarrones* continued to taunt the Spanish. In the Guajira Peninsula, to the northwest of Coro, were the escaped *"negros del Mariscal Castellanos,"* the black people enslaved by Miguel de Castellanos, a royal treasurer. Another official, Juan Bautista Nava, wrote to King Philip II in 1562, describing these maroons as having "put the land in such misfortune and hardship, killing and robbing, that it is unthinkable," before asking the king to "remedy it before there is no remedy" by sending in troops.[28]

The freedom-seekers were also causing other forms of economic havoc, with one 1575 royal decree agreeing to "wage war" on the *cimarrones* because they were making common cause with the northern European pirates who were arriving along the coast of *Tierra Firme* (mainland South America) to plunder and trade illicit goods.[29]

A contemporary chronicler, Juan de Castellanos, wrote Miguel into his epic late sixteenth-century *Elegía*, a poem recounting the "illustrious men" of the Indies (*Elegías de varones ilustres de Indias*) and enshrining into literary lore the events of King Miguel.

> Porque juraron rey solemnemente,
> Puestos en le lugar que les aplicó
> Aqueste fue Miguel, negro valiente,
> Criollo de San Juan de Puerto Rico;
>
> For they solemnly swore a king's oath
> Put in the place that applied to them
> This was Miguel, brave black man,
> Creole of San Juan, Puerto Rico;[30]

More than two centuries later, on his travels around South America in 1799, the Prussian naturalist Alexander von Humboldt visited the mining region of Buría and heard about the insurrection that took place nearly 250 years earlier. After King Miguel was killed, the people who escaped went to Nirgua, where they exchanged their loyalty to the Spanish king for a degree of freedom and autonomy. They were referred to as the monarch's "*Zamboes* of Nirgua," Humboldt wrote, using the term for an Afro-indigenous person. "The whole municipality is composed of men of colour . . . few families of Whites will inhabit a country where the system of government is so adverse to their pretensions; and the little town is called in derision *La república de Zambos y Mulatos*."[31] Derision aside, the significance of that community might have been lost on Humboldt, but it would not have been lost on the people of the town and on all those, slave and free, who knew the story of King Miguel. The king was long dead, but his memory lived on.

⋅⋅⋅ • ⋅⋅⋅

THE MAN IS unmissable. His skin is a darker brownish black than that of the *Mexica* people he shares the page with, his hair curly, theirs straight. He is dressed in red, and holding a red cross, a symbol of the Christianity which could not save him. His head hangs limp, straining the rope that ties him to a pole, his feet dangling above the ground. Below this grim scene, the scribe noted that in the year 1537 this man was one of "the blacks who wanted to rise up in Mexico City."[32]

The *Codex Telleriano-Remensis* is not the usual source for revolts by enslaved Africans, but this image leaps out of its pages. Works like this were crafted by Mexica *tlacuiloque*, or artist-scribes, in the sixteenth century, and it is possible that this unfortunate rebel may have been the first African to be depicted in the Americas, and also the first by the hand of an indigenous artist.[33] A few images of black people are scattered through the surviving codices, but this is the only one of a known, though unsuccessful, freedom-seeker.

In Mexico, by the 1530s, some 10,000 enslaved Africans were working in the mines and cultivating sugar, as well as doing jobs in urban settings such as domestic service or smithery. Over the next century, Mexico would become home to one of the most significant black communities in Spanish America, with the largest population of free black people and the second-largest enslaved population.[34] The authorities had dealt with maroons, but with such a large and growing slave population, they were also concerned about the prospect of revolts, like the one that was supposed to take place in Mexico City in 1537. This plot was to involve a group of enslaved workers and indigenous people around Mexico City who planned to murder the Spanish. They elected a king to lead them in their attack, to be on September 24, but before they could strike, the plot was revealed by one of the conspirators, perhaps fearing the consequences of it failing, or deciding to use the moment to pursue his own freedom. The records do not say who it was or if the person received any compensation.

Although the revolt did not come to fruition, it was enough to rattle the viceroy, Antonio de Mendoza. In his letter to the crown recounting events, he played down his initial concerns. "I was advised that the blacks had chosen a king and had reached agreement to kill all Spaniards and seize the land, and that the Indians were also involved," he wrote. "Since the news was brought to me by one of the Blacks, I did not give it much importance." But he had quickly sent spies to investigate the claims, and wasted little time making arrests. He then dispatched messengers to other areas with a high concentration of enslaved workers "so they would be forewarned and keep a close watch on the Blacks in those places." He also made an example of the rebels, sending some of them to the gallows. And one of them—perhaps the king-elect—continues to hang on the pages of a sixteenth-century codex.[35]

Mendoza did not attribute the plot to bad treatment or the existence of slavery, but rather to the fact that "the news from abroad is sent in more detail than is necessary and reaches the ears of the blacks and the Indians in its entirety."[36] Demand was always high for useful news, and there were circuits of communication, especially among Africans speaking languages other than Spanish, that officials were not able to infiltrate. But the real problem, to Mendoza, was the number of Africans. "If there were fewer blacks in this land, such plots would not be undertaken," he wrote, as his predecessor in Hispaniola had done 30 years earlier.[37]

Mendoza's successor, Luis de Velasco, made a similar appeal in 1553, claiming there were already around 20,000 enslaved people and that "this land is so full of negros and mestizos that they outnumber the Spaniards greatly" before telling the king that he "should order that they do not give so many licenses to send negros."[38] This situation had changed little by the time Velasco's son, also Luis de Velasco, became viceroy of New Spain in 1590.

In the years between the two Velascos, in around 1580, an enslaved man named Gaspar Yanga fled from the port city of Veracruz to the mountain peak of Cofre de Perote, around 100 miles (160 kilometers) to the northwest. There in the mountains, he and other runaways managed to establish a settlement, which was conveniently located near the Camino Real (royal road) that connected the sea to the capital, Mexico City. On that road, Yanga and his followers earned their reputation, raiding shipments of goods and allegedly kidnapping passengers, before retreating to their heavily fortified town.

The outline of this maroon leader's past is faint, like so many others. He was described as being from the "Bron" (Bran, Bramé) nation, roughly in Upper Guinea. Yanga (or Ñanga) arrived in the 1570s—the exact date is unknown—in Veracruz, then a key and thriving port city and point of entry for enslaved Africans. He may or may not have been of royal heritage, though at some point he took on the role of king in this maroon community.

By 1608, Viceroy Velasco was fed up with the raiding. At first, he tried sending the Franciscan priest Alonso de Benavides to live among the maroons and "reduce" them, by convincing them to live in a "legitimate" Christian town. Such a place, known as a *reducción*, would have put them under the watchful eye of the Spanish.[39] The attempt was not a success.

With God having failed, it was time for guns. Captain Pedro González de Herrera and his men were dispatched the following year, likely armed with the location of the *palenque* thanks to Benavides's time there.[40] For his *palenque* to survive for so long—nearly thirty years—Yanga must have had a network of informers and allies who would have sprung into action to warn him of what was coming.

In a grisly opening shot, some of Yanga's men raided a hacienda, where they came across two Spaniards. They asked them where González de Herrera was, and, when the men professed not to know, they attacked one with a sword, hitting him so hard it cracked his skull, whereupon the maroons killed him and allegedly "drank the blood of the unfortunate [man], holding it in their hands."[41] The Spanish Jesuit Juan Laurencio recorded the gruesome incident, though he was not there at the time. He may have heard about it later from the other Spaniard, whom the maroons kidnapped and took to the *palenque*, along with six indigenous women.[42] Laurencio was accompanying González de Herrera and at least 100 troops and 150 indigenous archers, though he himself "went with no weapons other than faith in God."[43]

One of Gaspar Yanga's men arrived back at the *palenque*, telling the others that the Spanish had been routed. Another followed, saying the Spanish were on their way to the town. While these conversations took place, women prayed in the *palenque*'s church. The candles were lit, and arrows were planted in the ground in front of the altar. Some of the women—including a few indigenous captives—were now scared and wanted to flee, but Yanga told them not to worry, they would have time.[44]

No sooner had Yanga reassured them than he could hear the clamor of the approaching troops. There was only one place left to go, further up into the hills, into the safety of the thicket and a barricaded fort. From there they could watch their 60 houses and plots of crops burn, as the Spanish set them on fire. The chilis, tobacco, cotton, corn, and sugarcane that had impressed Padre Laurencio enough for him to include them in his later account of events were now reduced to ash.

Yanga and his deputy, Francisco de la Matiza, an Angolan, went to greet their men and the new captives. He dictated a letter to the kidnapped Spaniard to take to González de Herrera. It was full, as Laurencio inevitably described, of "remarkable arrogance," for reminding the Spanish of their failure to apprehend him or his community.[45] He also sent some of his *yanguicos* to position themselves for an attack on the Spanish, behind large boulders. They did so, and successfully assaulted the troops when they arrived, in a skirmish known as the Battle of Peñol.

When the Spaniards finally made it to the town, the residents were gone. They rang the church bells and raised a standard. Some of them went into the church and pulled the arrows from the ground and blew out the still-burning candles.[46] Then they set the town on fire, while Laurencio observed that the houses had been "formed as if they were to remain in that place for ever." A house that was presumed to be Yanga's was torched as well. It was, Laurencio said, the place "where peace and war consultations were held," judging by the number of seats and benches it had.[47]

The Spanish waved a white flag, hoping to lure Yanga down from his hiding spot. He would not surrender, and skirmishes continued until Matiza was killed. At that point, his deputy now gone, Yanga sent the Spanish his conditions for peace in March 1608. He gave the crown 18 months to recognize their town, or they would go back to war.

At the top of the list was the demand for the continued freedom of everyone who had lived in the town before the previous September. Another condition was that no Spanish person could "have a house in or stay within the town" except on market days, when they could visit.[48]

As had been the case in Hispaniola, Yanga and his people had to capture runaways as part of the deal. There was also a clause that said they had to provide enslavers with their own people, slave or free, until runaways were captured. If they couldn't do that, they would have to give financial compensation, a version of a practice used in some of the slaving ports of Africa.[49]

The terms were agreed, and the first free black town in Mexico was created, receiving formal recognition in 1618. It was placed on land that belonged to the Riva de Neyra family. They donated it, they claimed, in gratitude for the crown's role in suppressing the long-running violence. It was named San Lorenzo de los Negros, though sometimes it was called San Lorenzo de Cerralvo—or just Yanga, as it is today.

Despite the arrangement, local landowners complained for decades about the maroons over a variety of issues, though there were no further raids by the Spanish.[50]

⋘ • ⋙

It is an arresting painting: Three men stand in the frame, an older one in the center, flanked by two younger ones. The gold dazzles the eye first. The man in the middle wears a nose ring in the shape of a thick crescent and has matching earrings. The other two are wearing similar earrings, but their noses are studded with gold piercings, including two long spikes descending from their nostrils. Their facial decoration, set off by the contrasting darkness of their skin, is luminous, initially drawing attention away from their ruffed collars and silk robes, and even the spears they hold. Perhaps it's fitting that the subjects of the painting shone in this way, as they were the gentlemen of Esmeraldas, the Spanish word for emeralds, but also the name of an area near the northern coast of Ecuador home to maroon communities.

At the time they were called "mulattos," a term also used to refer to people of Afro-European heritage, but these men were Afro-Indigenous, as their combination of dark skin and Amerindian decoration makes clear. These were not the usual subjects in 1599 for a portrait to be sent to the king.

In the upper-right corner of the painting is an inscription: "The doctor Juan del Barrio y Sepúlveda, Judge of the Royal Audience of Quito, had this [portrait] made at his own expense in the Year 1599, for His Majesty Philip [III]."[51] Barrio was in a celebratory mood. He had, to his mind, finally wrung some loyalty out of the long-recalcitrant maroons, and the portrait was painted to prove it. He commissioned an indigenous painter, Andrés Sánchez Galque, who was trained by priests in the European style. The men's names and ages are noted on the painting, and they are all referred to as "Don," a Spanish term signaling nobility and a mark of respect.[52]

In the center, looking at the viewer, is Don Francisco de Arobe, his short, curly hair flecked with gray, indicating his 56 years. To the left is his 22-year-old son, Don Pedro, and to the right 18-year-old Don Domingo, both keeping a respectful gaze on their father.

The story of the three dons started a long way from the highland city of Quito, where their portrait was painted. It began far to the north, in Nicaragua. In 1545, a ship heading along the Pacific from Nicaragua to Lima found itself tangled in the currents and winds around the equator. On board were enslaved people, including an African man named Andrés Mangache and an indigenous Nicaraguan woman whose name was not recorded. Some of the group jumped ship as soon as they reached land, running into the interior and establishing a maroon colony around San Mateo Bay, in northern Ecuador.

Another ship plying the same waters hit similar problems in 1553. It, too, had enslaved people on board, including a man possibly born in Senegal (though some accounts have him growing up in Tenerife, in the Canary Islands).[53] He had been captured by slave traders and taken to Spain, where he had lived for around 14 years. This man was enslaved by a merchant named Alonso de Yllescas (also Illescas), and from him received the same name. The enslaved Yllescas was working on his enslaver's vessel, travelling from Panama to Lima, when it was thrown off course in turbulent equatorial waters near Ecuador. Like Mangache, as soon as Yllescas could, he fled the ship, as did other Africans on board, seeking refuge inland.[54]

Africans were not limited to the Atlantic world—they were fast becoming part of the Pacific coast of Spanish America. By 1593, black people comprised more than half of the population of 12,790 in Lima, Peru.[55] Ongoing indigenous deaths from disease, coupled with the discovery of valuable silver mines, such as Potosí in 1545, increased the demand for enslaved African labor, men like Yllescas and Mangache. As Spanish colonization spread through the Americas—the Caribbean, North America, Venezuela, Peru—African slavery came with it, and left a long trail of resistance in its wake. The Pacific coast would be no different.

In Ecuador, Yllescas soon met the local Nigua people and married the daughter of a cacique, Chilnindauli, whom he apparently later killed, taking control of his land.[56] Such conquests enlarged the initial maroon settlement, as did the arrival of other runaways. They also illustrate the intense struggle to survive. There were rivals to defeat, territories to enlarge, alliances to make. Establishing maroon colonies took an extraordinary amount of work in an already nearly impossible situation. In the case of the Esmeraldas, the two maroon communities that evolved from those shipwrecks mostly stayed separate. Mangache went on to have two sons, Juan and Francisco, the latter taking the name Arobe. This is the Don Francisco in the center of the painting, clearly the leader of his community.

No doubt he inherited from his father the constant headache of the Spanish trying to cajole or attack his settlement. They believed there was more silver to find, as well as emeralds and other riches, and they knew the maroons were near an area that had a useful port—one that also was familiar with the English and Dutch ships that had started to arrive. The authorities wanted to get these communities under the crown's control, convert them to Christianity, and harness their labor.

In 1576, news reached Quito that Yllescas had helped some shipwrecked Spaniards, and officials thought this might provide an opportune moment to discuss their relationship, such as it was. They dispatched a priest who had been a soldier, Miguel Cabello de Balboa, to open negotiations with Yllescas.[57] Cabello had to wait for days before Yllescas appeared, eventually gliding up a river in a canoe.

The priest had a plan to win over the maroon leader. He brought with him a *real provisión*, a royal document that forgave Yllescas any past transgression and made him the "new and negro governor" of the area. It also made him a "Don." Yllescas knew how to play along. He offered his obedience to the king, as represented by the document and its royal seal, lifting it over his head.[58] However, Yllescas never returned to meet Cabello, and the mission was ultimately deemed a failure.

The Spanish did not give up.[59] The location was too valuable, and the rumors of riches seemed too real. The capture of the English pirate Richard Hawkins, near Atacames in 1594, renewed the drive to extract the loyalty of the maroons, at whatever cost. This time the effort was led by Juan del Barrio de Sepúlveda, who arrived in Quito in 1596. Barrio decided to send priests armed with lavish presents, including silks, beads, blankets, and foods like mutton for elaborate feasts.[60] Eventually, members of both communities were baptized, even as Spanish officials were emptying the coffers to make it happen.

Professions of loyalty followed, and this was the occasion that brought Don Francisco and his sons to Quito, along a mountainous route of some 250 miles (400 kilometers). It was worth marking the occasion, and Sánchez Galque got to work transforming Barrio's bureaucratic request into a masterpiece of South American art. Where Barrio saw proof of the "obedience" now given by "these barbarians," as he described them in an accompanying letter to the king, the artist saw something quite different: men of power and dignity. Sánchez Galque, an indigenous man himself, understood. He painted them in those rich, colorful silks and gleaming gold, both materials that a 1571 royal decree prohibited black people—slave or free—from wearing.[61] With his artist's eye, he saw men who were free in ways colonial officials could not comprehend.

Chapter 6

Pirates

A LITTLE PATCH OF land sits in the shadow cast by the forest of skyscrapers that is modern Panama City. Busy roads run past it on one side, and a flat, muddy bay is on the other. It's Panamá Viejo, Old Panama, the site of the former capital of a territory then called—not entirely fancifully—Castilla del Oro, or Golden Castile.

The Spanish had found gold in the earth of the isthmus that bridges the northern and southern continents, as well as pearls in its Pacific waters. Initially, the main port was on the north coast, at Nombre de Dios (Name of God), founded in 1510, but it was moved along the coast a decade later. Directly south, on the Gulf of Panamá, was another town, Nuestra Señora de la Asunción de Panamá (today's Panamá Viejo), built in 1519 on the site of an indigenous village. The early settlement was basic, with a few streets of houses, a church and convent, a port, administrative buildings, and a vista of a brown sea and heavy, water-laden clouds. Today it is a historic site, with most of the jagged ruins in a state of managed decay, though undoubtedly the skin-drenching humidity of the location remains much the same as it was then. The Spanish abandoned the site in 1671 after a devastating attack by the Welsh privateer Henry Morgan. The settlement moved to a more secure position further west along the coast, today's Panama City, but for more than 150 years, this town was one end of an imperial linchpin, with Nombre de Dios on the other.

Ships brough captives from Africa and the first reports of rebellion were as early as 1525.[1] Others took their chances in the dense jungle of the isthmus—with few Spanish settlers and troops, no one pursued them. With the continual importation of Africans, there were other uprisings, in 1530, 1533, and a much larger one in 1549, led by a man named Felipillo, who worked the fisheries of the Pearl Islands off the Pacific coast. Felipillo was the captain of a launch that took slaves out to make their dangerous dives. He convinced a group to flee into the interior, and they picked up more enslaved people from cattle ranches on the mainland. They were captured two years later, but now there was more *cimarrón* activity than the Spanish could suppress. By 1575, the number of maroons was estimated at 2,500, while in the area around the city of Panamá, 2,800 enslaved people worked in a variety of roles, including at ranches and orchards, in the pearl fisheries, and on the transport of goods between the two ports. There were around 800 Spanish or locally born creoles, and around 300 free people of color.[2]

Various groups and leaders emerged, including a man in the 1550s whom the Spanish called "the black king Bayano" (*el rey negro Bayano*). Bayano and his community of 1,200 people had numerous encounters with the Spanish.[3] His *palenque* was near Nombre de Dios, but inland and far enough away to require any Spanish militia to traverse the jungle, go up a mountain, and then breach a number of palisades to reach it. The maroons were kings of their hill, though starting in 1553 the governor made multiple attempts to knock them off it, and in the case of Bayano, eventually capturing him in 1556 and sending him to Spain.[4]

The Castilla del Oro, with its access to the Atlantic and South Seas, as the conquistador Vasco Núñez de Balboa saw in 1513 when he crossed the isthmus of Panama and was the first European to encounter the Pacific Ocean by land, was the place that brought the entire Spanish system together. Treasures from Peru, Bolivia, and, after 1565, the Philippines came via the Pacific to Panamá. They were unloaded and taken across the roughly 45-mile (75-kilometer) isthmus by mule train, and at Nombre de Dios loaded on to ships bound for Spain. By 1566, these sailings had been organized into the *flota*, or Spanish treasure fleet. These vast convoys left twice a year, with ships departing from Veracruz, Nombre de Dios, and Cartagena, meeting in Havana, and then sailing onward together to Spain. Ships bringing European goods, such as wine and wool, made the reverse voyage. The Panama mule trains bringing the silver of Peru and silks of Asia made for rich pickings, and the Spanish authorities were constantly trying to stop the maroons, who were able to appear out of the jungle, attack the convoys, and escape into their *palenques*.

This was the state of affairs that the English navigator Francis Drake sailed into in 1572.

⋖⋖ • ⋗⋗

Drake was no stranger to Spanish America. He was the cousin of the mariner and slave trader John Hawkins, and had joined him on an expedition to West Africa in 1567, where they had procured "between foure [sic] and five hundred Negros." They decided to sail their six ships to the Caribbean, "making our traffike with the Spaniards," though it was all contraband trade.[5] The merchants in Seville demanded a closed market for their wares, which took months to arrive in the Americas. This left intrepid smugglers like Drake plenty of time to hustle cloth, wine, and any number of other goods between shipments. This illicit trade also included human trafficking, as Drake experienced firsthand along the Colombian coast, where, he recounted, "the Spaniards resorted to us by night, and bought of us to the number of 200 Negros."[6] Smuggling was a reality of colonial life, and one that both corsairs and enterprising maroons could exploit.[7]

A storm in late July 1568 blew the English mariners off course; in September they tried to regroup in the port of San Juan de Ulúa, outside of Veracruz, Mexico. The Spanish initially granted them permission to anchor in the harbor and resupply, but at that time 13 ships of Spain's flota arrived, one carrying a new viceroy. Suspicious of the two English sea dogs, the Spanish turned on the men and nearly demolished their small fleet, leaving only two ships to limp home in 1569. Drake would not stay in England for long. Fueled by a desire for revenge, he returned to Caribbean waters in 1572.[8]

Three main maroon communities had formed in Panama by the time of Drake's arrival that summer: one near Panamá Viejo, whose members attacked along the trade route north; a second near Nombre de Dios; and a third, in the mountains, called Vallano (also Bayano).[9] The road connecting the two ports was a constant headache for the Spanish. One 1571 report noted that the *cimarrones* had "killed many persons, stolen a great quantity of merchandise and gold and silver."[10] There were also recurring complaints that the maroons would "carry negroes, men and women, into the wilds."[11] Overall, Panama was still largely indigenous, with the Spanish sprinkled on both coasts and the maroons in the interior. A letter from an official in Panamá to the Spanish crown in 1570, in discussing the Vallano *palenque*, warned, "The multitude of the blacks is increasing, and from everywhere many are joining them, and every day they become bolder."[12]

On this expedition Drake brought two of his brothers, John and Joseph, and around 70 others, according to a 1626 retelling.[13] In mid-July 1572 they entered a bay along the north coast of the isthmus, east of Nombre de Dios. His men started building a few small pinnace vessels, from which they could better conduct their raids. A short time later, they made their way toward Nombre de Dios, Drake's target. They stopped at the Isle of Pines, to the southeast of the port, and spotted some enslaved black people loading wood on to a Spanish frigate, who "gave us some particular understanding of the present state of the town."

The enslaved workers also warned Drake that Spanish troops were on alert, in part to "defend the town against the *Symerons* [*cimarrones*]." Drake took the informants and "set them a shoare upon the maine" so they could join the maroons "and gain their libertie if they would." At the very least, Drake hoped that in exchange for helping them flee, they would not tell anyone of his arrival.

Drake and his men continued in their four pinnaces, arriving in Nombre de Dios under the cover of darkness, at around 3:00 a.m. on July 29. However, an inbound vessel spotted them. Drake could hear the toll of the town bell and "noyse and cries of the people." He divided up his men and headed into the center, where they were greeted with a "jolly hot volley of shot." Drake managed to strong-arm his way into the governor's house, where he was greeted by "a huge heap of silver" in a storeroom. But then the news arrived from "one *Diego* a *Negro*" that the pinnaces were about to be taken by Spanish troops. Diego had earlier called out "to know whether they were Captaine *Drakes*? And upon answer received, continued intreating to be taken aboard," while bullets flew past him.[14]

Drake was not so lucky, as a shot wounded him and "he began to faint for want of blood." The men made a hasty retreat with their captain, taking refuge in a place they called the "Ile of Victuals," not far from Nombre de Dios, but out of sight of the Spanish. Diego was still with them, and as the men recovered, he shared "many other intelligences of importance" about the movement of the Spanish treasure fleet, telling them they could access the silver and gold "by means of the *Symerons*." He did add that he himself was not in the best standing with the maroons, and that "he had betrayed [them] divers times," though he offered no detail of what such betrayal might have been. However, Diego was confident that the name of Drake would stand the English in good stead with the maroon leaders.

Drake then decided to go to Cartagena in early August to trade, but found that the city had been warned not to let him enter, so he attacked vessels at sea instead, while some of his men made various raids elsewhere along the coast and waited for Drake's return. In the meantime, Drake's brother John went inland, where Diego directed him to the maroons. They held successful talks. Apparently, the maroons were delighted by the arrival of Drake "because they [knew] him to be an enemy to the *Spaniards*," and so they were ready to help. The maroons suggested a spot by the River Diego, on the coast but away from Nombre de Dios. From there, they travelled deeper into the interior and met another maroon community from the mountains.

The plan they agreed upon was to wait for the arrival of the Spanish Pacific fleet, still at sea and many months away. Drake's men built a hideout, naming it Fort Diego, on an island off the north coast and began to prepare while Drake sailed once again to Cartagena. When Drake returned in early December, however, the news was bleak. John Drake was dead, killed in November after a skirmish with a passing Spanish ship. Drake then watched his crew descend into illness, likely yellow fever, which also claimed the life of Drake's other brother, the younger Joseph, who died in Francis's arms.[15]

Finally, the maroons brought the news he was waiting for: In January 1573, the ships with silver had arrived, and the mule train would be leaving soon for Nombre de Dios. Drake conferred with maroon leaders, including one named Pedro Mandinga, whom he described as "our cheefe *Symeron*," to figure out their strategy. Mandinga's name suggests the leader's origins were in the Senegambia region, though from the surviving account it isn't clear which maroon colony he led, and there are scarce details about him.[16]

Soon they set out, "all fortie eight, of which eighteene onlye were English." The maroons remained in the majority, taking the English deep into the interior, marching for eight hours a day. The sailors were impressed at how adept the maroons were in managing the terrain, and how quickly they constructed shelters using palmetto or plantain leaves. After three days they stopped in a "Towne of their owne," presumably a *palenque*. It was in the woods, but near a river and on the side of a hill, protected by "a thicke mud wall of ten foot high." It had one main street and two smaller cross streets, where about 55 households "were kept so cleane and sweet that not only the house but the verie streets were verie pleasant to behold." The English found their hosts well dressed in "verie fine and fitly made" attire, and admired how they kept a continual watch on the town "to prevent the mischiefs which the *Spaniards* intend against them."

After a couple of days they continued, stopping again four days later. Pedro had something he wanted Drake to see: the two oceans. "The chiefest of these *Symerons* took our Captain by the hand and prayed him to follow him, if he was desirous to see at once the two Seas." They climbed steps carved into a tree, at the top of which was a lookout big enough for 10 people and affording views in both directions.

After this stop, they continued south, aiming to be within a day's journey of the Pacific coast. Reaching their spot, they sent a maroon into the capital to gather information about the timing of the mule train. The men took up positions in a grove not far from Venta Cruces (also Venta de Chagres or, as the English called it, Venta Cruz), a staging post where goods that had travelled up the Chagres River were put in a caravan to be transported across the isthmus. They hid deep in the long grass on either side of the route, aware that the mules in the front were carrying provisions, while the animals in the back had the treasure.

It would have been impossible not to hear the mule train coming, the noise cutting through the jungle during the cooler late hours of the night. They just had to be patient. But Robert Pike, one of Drake's men, could not be, "having drunken too much *Aqua vitae* without water." He lurched forth into the oncoming mules; one maroon swiftly pulled him down and tried to lie on top of him so the mounted Spanish guard would not spot them. But he did, and galloped off to warn the others. Upon hearing the hooves hit the hard ground, Drake knew their cover was blown. Pedro told Drake his options: to march back along the secret route they came on or to go forward into Venta Cruces and face the Spanish head-on. Drake chose the latter. Before doing so, he took a moment to "[ask] Pedro by name whether he would give his hand not to forsake him." Pedro replied he would rather "die at his foote than leave him to the Enemies."

Their commitment reaffirmed, the men readied for attack: Venta Cruces already had soldiers posted to defend it from maroons. Battle ensued, including the maroons taking out their bows "and in their manner of Country dance or leape, very lustily singing *Yó pehó, Yó pehó*." The Spanish officials' fears were coming true. Not only was "this coast so beset by such bold English corsairs," but now they were inland, setting Venta Cruces on fire, killing four soldiers and some mules, and wounding a Dominican friar. Without the crown's help, one of the Spaniards pleaded in a letter from Nombre de Dios, the colony was "as good as lost; the English will destroy it."[17] Officials echoed these sentiments, reporting, "This realm is at the present moment so terrified, and the spirits of all so disturbed."[18] What was especially upsetting was the alliance between the maroons and the English. Officials were concerned about "this league between the English and the negroes . . . because . . . the negroes will show them methods and means to accomplish any evil design they may wish to carry out and execute . . . It is indeed most lamentable that the English and negroes should have combined against us, for the blacks are numerous."[19]

Drake, Pedro, and their men had a long retreat ahead. They had managed to pillage "a quantity of clothing and merchandise" in Venta Cruces, according to a Spanish report, but that was all. They might have made away with some 80,000 pesos in gold and silver from the mule train "had not God by a miracle preserved it from them."[20] Mostly empty-handed, the men were forced to march many days, with Drake not wanting to stop in other *palenques*, leaving them "with hungry stomacks, much against the will of our *Symerons*."

While they had been away, however, the maroons who had stayed behind at the hideout had built "a little Towne" on the site. Drake would have to rethink his options there. A short time later, in March 1573, a French Huguenot ship under the command of Guillaume Le Testu arrived, apparently having spent the previous five weeks looking for Drake. Le Testu wanted to join Drake's mission.[21]

Together they decided to try another raid, this time from the north end of the mule train. They and their men travelled overland along the coast to Nombre de Dios, marching through the forest for days, led by maroons. As they neared the town, they were greeted by the sound of the arriving mules, and "the *Symerons* rejoyced exceedingly, as though there could not have befallen them a more joyful accident." They attacked the mule train, but Le Testu was injured by a retaliating Spaniard, and later captured. The rest of the men took as much as they could carry, running off to a nearby river to bury "about fifteen Tun of silver." However, they soon realized their escape pinnaces were nowhere to be found, their location possibly revealed to the Spanish by a confession extracted from Testu, who was later killed.[22] They quickly felled some trees and built a raft, with a "Sayle of a Bisket sacke." They set off on a choppy sea, and after about nine miles, they saw two of their pinnaces, which were safe. After briefly reuniting with the members of his crew who had stayed behind, Drake turned around that night to revisit the spot where the treasure was buried. Some of it had been dug up already by the Spanish, but they had missed 13 bars of silver and some gold. Drake brought that back, and then burned the pinnaces to give the iron used in them to the maroons.

Before he set off for England in their surviving frigate, Drake invited Pedro and "three of the chiefest" of the maroons who had helped them to choose a gift for their service. Pedro had taken a fancy to "a faire guilt Symeter (which had beene the late Kings of *France* [Henry II])" that Testu had given Drake. In exchange, Pedro gave Drake four ounces of gold as a token of his loyalty. There would have been no treasure without the maroons. Pedro knew this, and maybe the humiliation of the Spanish was compensation enough for the undoubted frustration of having to lead these men, who were clueless about the ways of the interior and who kept bungling their attacks. However these men might have felt about their months together, this had been a brief but critical moment in the connection between Old and New Worlds, Africans and Europeans.

Anglo-maroon relations would never be this good again.

⊰⊱ • ⊰⊱

Armed with the experience of the 1572–1573 expedition, Drake's shipmate John Oxenham returned to Panamá in 1576. Other English sailors had tried to re-create Drake's success in the intervening years but had been unable to secure the help of the maroons, which was crucial.[23] Oxenham's motivation for returning with a crew of 56 is unclear, but it may have had something to do with digging up the silver that they had hurriedly buried. It was, of course, long gone. Oxenham managed to enlist the maroons to help him find more, this time under a leader called Juan Vaquero. Oxenham's experience unfurled very differently, as he found himself recounting to the Spanish after his capture in 1577. His version of events, made under arrest, may not be wholly reliable, but it gives some idea of a growing maroon impatience with the English.

Oxenham told his inquisitors that he had come over after hearing that the maroons of Vallano were "rich in gold and silver." He wanted to barter with them using goods he had brought from England.[24] He said he soon encountered two maroons who agreed to trade with him, and who asked after Francis Drake. In Oxenham's version of events, he went inland to their *palenque*, but there was no gold or silver. While there, he also learned that the Spanish had found one of his frigates. He was low on options. The maroons told him that if he wanted food, he should burn the vessel he used to sail up the river to reach the *palenque* and give them its iron and nails and the hogsheads of salt he had on board. In exchange, they would guide him to the Pacific, where he could raid what he liked—on the condition that he kill any Spaniards he captured and share any takings.[25]

They raided the settlements in the Pearl Islands and attacked an incoming barque from Guayaquil, but when they returned to the mainland with their loot, the Spanish were waiting. The English had not followed Vaquero's instructions, and Spaniards who had escaped their grasp raised the alarm. Twelve English crew were killed in the resulting attack, and the others fled or were captured. What booty Oxenham and his men had taken was mostly recovered by the Spanish.

Later, Oxenham complained that the maroons "treated them very badly," making them live on bananas because "they had not killed the Spaniards they had captured" and had thus put the entire enterprise in peril. The maroons blamed Oxenham for forcing them to abandon their village to avoid Spanish attacks.[26] With few friends and no treasure, Oxenham was soon captured and sent to Peru. The Spanish then turned their attention to the maroons once more, wishing to eradicate them but realizing it was impossible. They tried with gun and pen, having issued an anti-maroon code in 1574 while also making raids throughout the decade.[27]

Eventually, maroon leaders met with officials in 1578 to agree to a truce, but it was more a process than an instant peace. Some maroon leaders were willing to surrender in exchange for their freedom, pardons, and grants of land.[28] Others were more hesitant. One Spaniard complained in a letter: "Having given great event of a desire for peace . . . the blacks of Vallano have failed of their promise and withdrawn and revolted."[29]

By 1585, however, peace deals with the maroons were mostly completed, right around the time that news arrived of Drake's return to the Caribbean. England was then at war with Spain, and over the course of less than a year, Drake captured Santiago in the Cape Verde islands and went on to sack Santo Domingo, Cartagena, and Saint Augustine, though he did not return to Nombre de Dios this time.

On his way back to England in 1586, he stopped at a settlement on the East Coast of North America, north of Spanish Florida, on an island called Roanoke, where a small English colony had been established the previous year. Seeing the dire state of the colony, he ferried the unhappy settlers back to England. English sailors were causing havoc at sea, but colonists were faring less well on land. Another attempt the following year to put a colony on Roanoke also failed. The ghostly word "Croatoan" (the name of a nearby island, now Hatteras Island) carved into a post was all that remained by 1590, with the fate of those settlers a still-unsolved mystery.

The Anglo-Spanish rivalry continued throughout the sixteenth century, and Drake returned once again, landing in Nombre de Dios in December 1595. He was not third-time lucky. The town was empty, the Spanish having relocated west, to Portobelo. All that was left in the old port was a handful of people and rotting ships in the bay. Nor were there any maroon allies.

The few maroons that did live nearby were in their settlement of Santiago del Príncipe. They were also members of a Spanish free black infantry, one that would not let the dreaded Drake succeed this time.[30] As the English came on land, the maroons blocked some of them from accessing water at a nearby river. Around this time, a man named Pedro Yalonga shot and killed one of Drake's officers. Yalonga, who described himself as a "black slave . . . [who] showed up with my arms to serve his majesty," used this assassination as part of a successful petition for freedom.[31]

In Nombre de Dios, very little was left to loot, so the English burned it down.[32] Drake's plan to go overland across the isthmus was looking far less promising, and in any case, the Spanish were ready for him. Over the previous two decades, the Spanish had extracted pledges from the maroons that they would not help pirates, in exchange for recognizing their freedom. They also cracked down on the number of enslaved people brought through Panama, requiring them to be registered while in transit. This reduced the number of slaves in Panama and the number of potential runaways who could swell maroon ranks.[33] Most of the conflict with the Spanish was over, as the maroons wouldn't risk their freedom to help the unreliable English. Drake died in January 1596 of the dysentery that had struck down many of his men. His final resting place was in Caribbean waters near Portobelo. The Spanish were, no doubt, relieved that he was finally dead, though it was not the end of piracy, nor of maroon activity for Panama or the rest of Spain's territories.

Chapter 7

Adjustments

ON A QUIET Sunday morning in July 1595, a slave named Amador burst into a mass at a church in the town of Trindade, a short distance outside the capital of São Tomé. He grabbed the chalice from the priest and drank some of its palm wine before ordering his accomplices to kill the officiating cleric, though one of Amador's deputies let him escape. From there, Amador led five or six men to the *engenho* of Pedro Álvares Freire, where they killed the owner and set fire to the sugar mill.[1] More *engenhos* would follow.

The São Tomé of Amador's time had been straddling two worlds, plantation colony and slave port, bridging Africa and the Americas, for nearly a century. As early as 1494, King João II boasted that the island could produce three times as much sugarcane as Madeira.[2] However, decades passed before the elements necessary for large-scale sugar production—settlers, slavers, machinery, financial capital—were assembled. By the 1590s, sugar *engenhos* could be found across the north of the island, with owners including the crown, the Catholic Church, and local officials and settlers, as well as some free people of color.

But many challenges remained. And although King João II perhaps was not wrong about the quantity of cane in São Tomé, the island's humidity meant the overall crop was of lower quality than what was produced in Madeira and, increasingly, in Brazil. By the 1570s, some planters had decided to move their operations in Brazilian soil.[3]

In addition, by the 1570s a significant maroon population was living in settlements called *macambas*, from the Kimbundu (Angolan) *mukambo*, meaning summit, but later also hideout.[4] The maroons on the island were known as the *Angolares,* a name based on their Angolan heritage, and had become a significant threat, forcing the Portuguese to wage an ongoing bush war against them, in an attempt to drive the freedom-seekers out of their mountain hideaways.[5] However, the maroons were able to survive in the forested hills, and continued to raid plantations and skirmish with the militia.

It is not clear if a specific incident inflamed Amador. Perhaps he had been planning an uprising for a while. The island's leaders were already distracted by a dispute between the bishop and the governor, which may have offered him a window in which to strike.

After that morning in the church, Amador and his deputies Lázaro and Domingos Preto saw their recruits rise quickly—an estimated 2,000 slaves soon joined his fight.[6] They set fire to the cane fields and the sugar *engenhos,* destroying 15 of them by July 11, two days after the initial attack on the church.[7] Another 30 sugar mills soon went up in flames, the number of destroyed *engenhos* rising to more than 60, leaving only 25 intact.[8]

By July 14, the authorities heard that Amador had made himself king of the island and freed all the slaves. Amador took 800 of the volunteers—some of them possibly maroons—and organized them into four units to surround the capital and fight the militia, though some 300 died in battle.[9] The militia lost only three or four soldiers and was able to drive the rebels back. However, they soon heard that Amador had plans to attack with reinforcements of 5,000 slaves, around half the island's slave population.[10]

The final battle commenced on the morning of July 28 and lasted four hours. It's not evident that Amador had managed to amass such a large number of troops, but the ones who did fight found themselves ultimately defeated by the militia, with 200 more killed. The following day, Amador fled into the forest, hoping to regroup. Someone betrayed him, however, for reasons that are unknown. Perhaps it was someone with a personal grudge, or a rival leader who had a different plan, or an enslaved person hoping to win freedom by bringing in the biggest trophy of all. The scant surviving accounts offer few clues.[11]

Once arrested, Amador was hanged and quartered on August 14, his mutilated body parts put on display as a reminder to any would-be liberating kings. His deputies, too, had their rebellion cut short by a hangman's noose, with one rebel, Duarte Amarroco, having his hands cut off first, an extra punishment for killing his enslaver.[12]

As the plantations recovered, other runaways fled to the mountains or even to nearby islands that still had no European presence, including Bioko and Annobón. There, they set up communities beyond the reach of the colonists.[13] São Tomé had barely recovered from the events of 1595 when, in 1599, the Dutch attempted to capture the island—a short-lived venture, as many on the expedition died of tropical illness within two weeks.[14] They did manage to land a second damaging blow to the island's sugar production before leaving, destroying almost half of the remaining *engenhos*, some of which had been rebuilt after the 1595 revolt.[15] But the brief foray by the Dutch was a sign of what was to come for the Portuguese.

<<• •>>

YEARS EARLIER, ANOTHER revolt had begun within the Spanish realm, this time in Europe, rather than the Americas: the Dutch Revolt. It is also known as the Eighty Years' War (1568–1648), a long-running conflict that took place in fits and starts between Habsburg Spain and its Low Countries (today's Netherlands, Belgium, and Luxembourg), also known as the Seventeen Provinces. A range of issues were at stake, not least religion, as Protestantism had taken hold in some of the provinces. The ascent of the devout Catholic Felipe II in 1555 as ruler of the Low Countries (and of Spain the following year) was a cause for concern. More generally, this region, which was part of the Holy Roman Empire, was already semiautonomous from the larger Spanish Empire, and internally it was a mix of diverse cultures and languages. Over the course of the next eight decades, the provinces would create or strengthen their own identities, and one outcome was the creation of the "United Provinces," in 1579, under the Union of Utrecht, which brought together a group of the northernmost provinces, including Holland and Zeeland, laying the basis for the Dutch Republic and bolstering the fight for independence from the Spanish.[16] Also aiding the Dutch was the money being made in the increased trade between the United Provinces and other parts of Europe, including England, the Baltic Sea, and the Mediterranean, and eventually the Americas, Africa, and Asia. Between 1598 and 1605, some 25 Dutch vessels went to West Africa, 20 to Brazil, and 150 to the Caribbean. They also sailed to the East Indies, with the Dutch setting up the East India Company (VOC) in 1602.[17]

Despite the growing maritime power of the Dutch in the 1500s and into the 1600s, the lands of the Americas remained in Iberian control, as did the slave trade. By the early seventeenth century, Portuguese slave traders mostly dominated the market, having pushed out rivals such as the Genoese.[18] The Spanish had relinquished any rights to the slave trade in West Africa by the Treaty of Alcáçovas in 1479, and so did not participate in significant numbers. However, between 1580 and 1640, Portugal and Spain were united in the Iberian Union, a time during which the slave trade boomed—around 500,000 Africans were forced across the Atlantic in those 60 years, nearly six times the 90,000 captives taken between 1520 and 1580.[19]

By the late 1590s, a system known as the *asiento de negros* had been developed, which was a contract, guaranteed by the Spanish crown, to allow a monopoly trade to bring a certain number of captives to parts of the Americas, such as the Caribbean and ports like Veracruz on the mainland. These contracts were auctioned, and Portuguese slave traders—often backed by merchants from across the Iberian Peninsula—were in an advantageous position during the Iberian Union to bid on and later profit from them.[20] This formalization regulated, controlled, and taxed the slave trade—in theory—but in practice smugglers, like Francis Drake and John Hawkins, worked in the shadows, as did their Dutch and French contemporaries.

⤛ • ⤜

As OTHER EUROPEAN kingdoms began to express their interest in both the Atlantic slave trade and the possibility of claiming overseas territories, closer to home ideas about "free soil" dominated. Under the legal principle of free soil, an Englishman, a Dutchman, or a Frenchman could not be a slave as long as he was standing in England, the Netherlands, or France. During the sixteenth century such people might be peasants, or indebted laborers, but they were ostensibly free. For enslaved people brought to Europe, this principle meant the possibility of some legal loopholes. In one case, an African man in 1495 was caught in Spain trying to reach the Pyrenees because he understood that once he was on French soil, he would be free.[21]

The French "freedom principle" dates to around 1315, with King Louis X saying France was the country of free men, though ideas about France's "free air" go back even further.[22] The belief that France did not have slavery was given life by author François de Belleforest, who wrote in 1570 that "the custom is such that not only the French, but foreigners arriving in French ports and crying '*France et liberté,*' are beyond the power of those that possess them."[23] A royal decree in 1571 confirmed this, declaring anyone stepping on French soil to be free. But the New World continued to disrupt the Old. In 1571, a slave trader from Normandy tried to sell his human cargo in Bordeaux, with the high court (in this case the regional *parlement*) ruling that "France, the mother of liberty, doesn't permit any slaves."[24]

Louis XIV (1643–1715) later ordered that individual slaves would have to petition the crown for recognition of their free status after arriving in France. By 1716, a new edict ruled that settlers and military officers could bring enslaved people to France with them in order to learn a trade or receive Catholic religious instruction without a loss of "property." However, if the enslaver failed to obtain permission from the colonial governor before departure or did not register the captive upon arrival, the slave could use those oversights to make a petition for freedom.[25]

In Great Britain, Britons "never will be slaves," according to the 1740 poem and later song, *Rule, Britannia!* But in the sixteenth century, the growing involvement of English pirates like Hawkins and Drake in the slave trade produced similar uncertainties about the freedom of black people. By 1596, there was a large enough black population in England that Queen Elizabeth I wrote an open letter to England's mayors complaining, "There are of late divers Blackmoores brought into the Realme, of which kinde of people there are all ready here to manie . . . Her Majesty's pleasure therefore ys, that those kinde of people should be sent forth of the lande."[26] She reiterated her call for deportation in 1601, in part because of a growing fear that black people were taking jobs from working English people, though even she brought them into court as entertainers and pages—as her father, Henry VIII, had done—despite her claim that most of them were "infidels."[27] The queen may also have been expressing a sort of anxiety about the slave trade, while giving permission to John Hawkins for his excursions to the West African coast.[28] Surviving records are not always clear about the legal status of black people in England, in part because common law did not recognize slavery.

Cases like the "black Ethiopian slave" purchased by a Portuguese physician in London show the complications of the categories of race and status that were developing both within England and in the larger Atlantic world. In 1578, a court heard that this unnamed African "utterly refuseth to carry and serve" Hector Novimies, who had bought the man from an English sailor. Novimies discovered that he did not have "any ordinarye remedie at and by the course of common Laws" in England. He asked the court to order the "Ethiopian" to serve him for life, or else force the sailor who sold the African to refund him the four pounds and ten shillings he paid, though the verdict is unknown.[29] But the refusal of the Ethiopian to work for the physician indicates an understanding on his part of the legal possibilities that could affirm his freedom. Although the concepts of enslavement and "unfree" labor were blurred in England, they would come into much sharper focus in the colonies.

An extra level of complexity existed for the Dutch, as they had been distant from the Mediterranean and its traditions of slavery until the Netherlands was brought into Spain's imperial fold. Some Dutch laws drew on Roman traditions, but others developed in the course of events, hewn by the Dutch Revolt as well as the rising involvement of the Dutch in the slave trade and plantation economy.[30] For instance, when ship captain Pieter van der Hagen brought a group of captive Africans to Middelburg in the province of Zeeland in 1596, the local authorities told him the group could not stay enslaved in the Netherlands. The Dutch, like their neighbors, held to the principle that they were a free people, a principle forged in the ongoing struggle with Spain and expressed in their 1581 declaration of independence. However, when Van der Hagen requested to take the ship and these "Moors," as he called them, to Portugal and on to the Caribbean, the national States-General (parliament) initially refused him permission, but later told him to "do as he pleased."[31]

The small African population in the Netherlands included enslaved and free people, though the numbers are not certain. Some of the slaves were the "property" of foreign merchants in cities such as Amsterdam. Indeed, a Portuguese Jewish cemetery in that city, Beth Haim, includes dozens of black people buried in the sixteenth and seventeenth centuries. Their skin color (*swarten*, *negros*) was usually noted, but not necessarily their legal status—and after 1617 no further occurrences of the word "slave" appeared in burial records, possibly to erase the traces of slavery on free Dutch soil.[32]

While the question of who was free might have seemed to be settled in some of these European kingdoms, the arrival of African slavery in the Americas would present challenges to these assumptions. What it meant to be free would require new definitions, laws, and ideas, and these would be steadily challenged by the people who had the least access to freedom.

Chapter 8

Expansion

After the *São João Bautista* left Luanda, Angola, at some point in the spring of 1619 with 350 captives on board, dozens of people fell ill. The deaths mounted while the ship was still thousands of miles from Veracruz. Nearing the Caribbean, the Portuguese captain of the vessel (which was also referred to as the *San Juan Bautista*) decided to stop in Jamaica. The cargo had to be partially unloaded, a Spanish account book later noted in a perfunctory paragraph, "including 24 slave boys he was forced to sell in Jamaica, where he had to refresh, for he had many sick aboard, and many had already died."[1]

Back underway, the troubles continued. Two English ships pulled near as the *São João Bautista* entered the Gulf of Mexico, their captains armed with letters of marque, which were royal licenses to capture any "enemy" ship, in this case that of Spain or Portugal, which were still united under the Iberian Union. Pinnaces rowed up, carrying English corsairs, who boarded the Portuguese vessel near Campeche. The two English captains demanded to look in the hold. They chose 30 humans each and sailed away.[2]

The *São João Bautista* straggled into Veracruz. Of the 36 ships recorded as having made the voyage between Angola and Veracruz from 1618 to 1622, the *São João Bautista* was the only one to be attacked by corsairs.[3] The surviving 147 captives were recorded in the ledger, accounting for the "8,657.875 pesos paid." The English had kidnapped 60 people, and at least 24 were sold in Jamaica, but that left more than 100 people unaccounted for, presumably they were the "many sick" who died on the voyage.

The privateers took their human loot and headed north. Captains John Jope and Daniel Elfrith set their course for the English colony of Jamestown, which had survived—barely—for just over a decade. The *White Lion* arrived a few days before the *Treasurer*, pulling into Point Comfort, where the James River meets the Chesapeake Bay.[4] Fort Algernourne sat at the tip, with the Jamestown colony further upstream. Planter John Rolfe met the *White Lion* and was not impressed by the cargo, as he noted in a letter: "He brought not any thing but 20. And odd Negros, which the Governor and Cape Marchant bought for victualle (whereof he was in greate need as he pretended) at the best and easyest rate they could."[5] Today Point Comfort—a place name of almost unbearable irony—is dominated by Fort Monroe, the construction of which started in 1819, two centuries on from the arrival of the *White Lion*. Now fishermen stand on the pier, hoping for a big catch, while tourists stroll along the beach looking at the gray-green waters, stopping to read the historical marker that explains how the first documented Africans in Virginia arrived.

There were most likely undocumented arrivals of Africans as well. A 1619 census believed to be from earlier that year, before the arrival of the *White Lion*, listed 32 "Negros in the service of severall planters."[6] The Africans on the *White Lion* certainly were not the first in North America. Other Africans could be found to the south, in the small Spanish colony of Saint Augustine, Florida, established in 1565. Although Spain claimed the Atlantic coast of North America and its hinterland, it had trouble keeping out European rivals. After the Spanish ran off a group of French Huguenots in Florida, they put a fortified settlement near the coast. Saint Augustine remained small; in 1600 it contained only around 500 people, with 27 enslaved, most in service to the crown.[7] Elsewhere in Spanish America, the enslaved population was far larger, with some 10,000 people in Hispaniola in 1606, around 4,000 to 5,000 in Havana by 1611, and 3,500 in Panama by around 1610.[8]

The *asiento* system of slaving contracts continued to deliver Africans, mostly at the hands of the Portuguese, in vessels such as the *São João Bautista*. The exploits of Drake and Hawkins had stoked English enthusiasm for piracy and settlement, which was further fueled by ongoing international conflict. This was the case with the two privateers who attacked the *São João Bautista*. John Jope obtained his letter of marque from the Dutch because England was temporarily in a truce with Spain. Similarly, Daniel Elfrith carried a letter from the Duke of Savoy.[9]

Enslaved people being taken across the Atlantic were at the mercy of the seas, but they were also human pawns in a larger geopolitical game. This situation would be exacerbated by long-running conflicts, such as the Thirty Years' War, which began in Europe in 1618, driven by the rise of Protestantism, ongoing rivalries, and territorial disputes. The English, French, and Dutch were pushing into Spanish America, and Spain did not have the resources to stop them.

Placing colonies on the northern coast of Florida was particularly difficult, with the settlement of Santa Elena (South Carolina) failing by 1586, due in part to attacks by Native Americans, disease, and poor planning. The English faced similar challenges, as the failure of the earlier Roanoke colony attests. However, the dream of the Americas persisted, and in 1606, King James I (r. 1603–1625) granted a group of merchants a charter, creating two companies to colonize Virginia, which they defined as being between latitude 34° and 45° north, roughly from Cape Fear, North Carolina, to the northern coast of Maine.[10] The following year, the fledgling colony of Jamestown was set among the marshy waters of the Chesapeake tributaries. It nearly failed due to poor crops and hostility from the Powhatan people. In those early years, the settlers had no enslaved Africans, and were also unable to harness indigenous labor. Settlers died in such significant numbers during the winter of 1609–1610 that the colony was on the verge of collapse.

As the English in Virginia struggled to establish their colony, one of the company's ships en route, the *Sea Venture*, was blown off course in July 1609. The storm spat it out onto a hook-shaped island that had been spotted a century before by the Spanish sailor Juan de Bermúdez—today's Bermuda. However, it had not been colonized by the Spanish, and this uninhabited archipelago of low-lying reefs soon became the next dot on England's Atlantic map, a waypoint at latitude 32° north for the ocean crossing.[11]

The situation started to improve in Virginia the following spring, and by 1612 experimentation with tobacco had begun. If the settlers couldn't find gold in the earth—which had been their initial hope—they would plant their riches. Tobacco was a recent discovery for Europeans, though its use dated back thousands of years for Amerindians. It was initially popularized by the Spanish, but the colonists of Virginia realized it could thrive in the area's soil and climate. The plant's dominance would present a paradox for King James I, who detested tobacco so much that he wrote a tract in 1604 denouncing the "vile custom of tobacco-taking." Little could he have foreseen that "so vile and stinking a custom" would make a success out of this scrappy English outpost.[12]

Bermuda, too, would see the arrival of more settlers, bolstered by a royal charter that allowed the Virginia Company to put a colony there in 1612, with many interested in plundering the passing Spanish treasure ships. It would, like Virginia, also turn to tobacco, relying by the 1620s on Amerindian captives and enslaved Africans for labor. Bermuda was successful enough with tobacco that it exported more than the Virginia colony until 1625.[13] Around the same time, in 1618, James I granted a charter allowing the creation of the Company of Adventurers to Guinea and Benin, to trade in Africa. While the surviving records give scant detail of its activities, the location implies at least some human trafficking.[14]

The captains of the two ships that had arrived in Point Comfort in 1619 were men of this expanding world of colonization and trade. They knew there was a market for enslaved Africans in this English colonial fringe, and this demand would only increase over time.

⊰• •⊱

THE WORLD THAT "20. And odd Negros" entered in Virginia was an indigenous one, surrounded by Algonquin-speaking communities. It was a different climate from the tropics, with cold seasons and hot ones, and the inescapable humidity of the low, boggy Jamestown site. The English in 1619 were finding their footing, and the population had reached around 1,200 people the year before.[15] Tobacco was thriving in the soil, and the colony's fortunes began to shift. For it to prosper, however, it would need more workers. Tobacco demanded it. Although any colony required an enormous amount of labor to survive—building homes and forts, growing food—tobacco was especially onerous. Clearing the land, planting seeds, growing, harvesting, and curing were all steps reliant on human hands.

Initially, most of the workers were not enslaved, nor, as had been the case in Spanish America, were they indigenous. There was nothing like the Spanish *encomienda* in Virginia, though indigenous people in some situations ended up in servitude or slavery. The colonists who answered the call of the Virginia Company, which had raised the funds for the expedition through the issuing of stock, were also responsible for the ensuing profits—or losses. They would have to do the work. The earliest colonists needed specialized workers, such as blacksmiths and carpenters, in addition to field hands.[16]

The initial settlers in 1607 came under seven-year work contracts, and while some people went back to England when these expired, others stayed and began working as tenant farmers. After 1616, when the Virginia Company was unable to pay dividends, it instead doled out land to people who had finished their contracts. This gave rise to a "headright" system, in which anyone who paid the passage of a person to Virginia would receive 50 acres.[17] Not everyone paying the passage wanted to go there, and so absentee landowners needed people to do the work for them, leading to the issuance of private indenture contracts. Such contracts usually stipulated the duration of the indenture, as well the terms, and the payment or "freedom dues" to be received at the end. The recruiting campaigns for potential workers that soon spread across England painted a picture of Virginia as a "very healthfull" land, as one pamphlet described it, somewhat overstating the delights of a place where unfamiliar diseases or animals could lead to quick death, and where there was the ever-present threat of violent indigenous resistance.[18] Despite the risks, the colony appealed for many reasons, not least because of the prospect of land ownership or a way to escape economic precarity in England, the English making up the majority of the early emigrants.

As English settlement continued, new colonies appeared in North America, including one at Plymouth, Massachusetts, in 1620 and one in Maryland in 1632, which also invested in tobacco. Although thousands of indentured servants arrived throughout the seventeenth century, not many Africans did. In the period up to 1670, an estimated 1,604 Africans were forced to disembark in these English colonies, though no doubt others went unrecorded.[19] By 1700, of the 100,000 people who had come to North America, somewhere between 70 and 85 percent used indenture contracts to fund their passage.[20]

As these colonies were taking shape during the seventeenth century, social hierarchies were more fluid and uncertain. Although a language of race was forming, it had not yet crystallized, and ambiguities would be clarified over the course of the century. Europeans and Africans lived in close quarters in hardscrabble 1630s Virginia, and the records attest to their proximity. Sometimes they made common cause together, such as the "six . . . servants and a negro of Mr Reginald's" who plotted in July 1640 to leave the estate of William Pierce. They took "shot and guns to accomplish their said purposes," and sailed away in a skiff on the Elizabeth River but were apprehended. The servants, including two Dutchmen, were all listed by full name in the proceedings, except for "Emanuel, the foresaid Negro." Emanuel and two others were to receive, among other punishments, 30 stripes of the lash, and were "to be burnt in the cheek with the letter R," branding them for life.[21]

Inevitably, intimate relations occurred as well, along with corresponding legal consequences. Early cases led to punishments for sex between English and Africans, such as that given to Hugh Davis in 1630, who was to be "soundly whipped" for "defiling his body in lying with a negro." Or a woman named Mary, described as "Mr Cornelius Lloyds negro Woman," and William Watts, who were required to "make penince service" in 1649 by "standing in a white sheete with a white Rodd in theire hands" in front of a chapel congregation. Mary Williamson, a woman who "hath Committed the filthy sin of fornication with William a negro belonging to William Basnett Squire," was fined 500 pounds of tobacco in 1681, while William was to receive 30 lashes.[22] Unlike the Spanish and Portuguese territories, where there was more social and sexual mixing (*mestizaje*) across white, black, and indigenous people, in English North America, the lines between these groups would become more rigid.

At this time, the word "negro" did not necessarily imply slave status, though black people were likely to be enslaved. One study, based on surviving 1660 estate inventories, found that the remaining term of service was noted next to the names of just under three-quarters of the 247 English workers listed, while this was the case for only two out of 64 people described as "negro," suggesting their terms may have been for life.[23]

At the same time, black people in Virginia had access to land, slaves, and the courts. One of the most often-cited cases is that of Anthony Johnson, a black man who may even have arrived in 1619.[24] By the 1650s he was free and owned at least a couple of enslaved people, who worked his 250 acres near Pungoteague Creek, on the Eastern Shore of Virginia, where there was a small free black community with a population of around 100 in the 1660s and 1670s.[25] However, in 1653, Johnson suffered a series of misfortunes, including a devastating fire on his plantation, which was followed by a number of legal challenges over taxes and, in 1655, one involving a servant who claimed he was not a slave. John Casor, described as "a Negro," said that "hee came into Virginia for seaven or Eight yeares (per Indenture)" and that Johnson "had kept him servant seaven years longer than hee ought." Johnson argued that he had never seen any proof of indenture and instead "hee had him [Casor] for life."[26] Johnson complained to the court that his neighbor Robert Parker had "most unjustly [kept] the said Negro [Casor] from Anthony Johnson his master," indicating that Casor had run away to Parker's and tried to claim his freedom there. In the end, the courts ordered Casor back to the Johnson household.[27]

Black, free, slave, servant: Identities still had some flexibility in English North America, some latitude for seeking and holding on to freedom. However, this fluidity was beginning to ebb. Although the court had ruled in Johnson's favor, when he died in 1670—after having moved to Somerset County, Maryland, a few years earlier—his land was to be "escheated," or reverted back to the crown, because "he was a Negroe and by consequence an alien."[28] His widow was able to renegotiate the lease on the Maryland tracts and keep them in the family. Seven years later, Johnson's grandson, John Johnson, purchased a parcel of land in Maryland and named it "Angola."[29]

By the time of Anthony Johnson's death, Virginia and Maryland were entering a new phase. Enthusiasm for indentureships was flagging. Indentured people had been around long enough for those in England to have heard the tales of hardship and exploitation from the returnees, or to have lost family members who had left for Virginia and died there. In addition, increased competition for the best plots of land arose, with some freed servants pushed into less fertile—or indeed more dangerous—territory at the frontier, or forced to continue in poorly paid service. The decline of servants became noticeable by the 1670s.[30] Between 1670 and 1700, the number of enslaved Africans arriving in the colonies increased nearly five-fold compared to the preceding period, to 8,400, with Virginia and Maryland taking almost 7,500 captives and the rest going to New England.[31] While this was a significant rise, Africans comprised only a small percentage of the overall nonindigenous population, around 10 percent in 1700.[32] However, by the 1690s slaves were outnumbering servants in many parts of Virginia and Maryland.[33]

From the 1660s onward, legislation began to make specific racial differentiations. For instance, a 1668 head tax demanded that free black women had to pay, but not free white women, because the former should not "be admitted to a full fruition of the exemptions and impunities of the English."[34] Another series of legislative acts passed from 1667 onward clarified that baptism would not negate the condition of slavery, and that any non-Christians who arrived by sea—that is, Africans—would be slaves for life, while indigenous people, who came by land, could not be, though they could be servants. One estimate of the population of Virginia in 1670 describes the colony as having "Forty thousand persons men women and Children of which there are Two Thousand black slaves, six thousand Christian servants," underscoring the distinction of white Christianity and the perpetual servitude reserved for the infidel.[35] This categorization of black people as "not Christians" contributed to their transformation into people without rights and eventually into "property."[36]

This is what "Fernando a Negro" discovered in his 1667 freedom suit against John Warner, with the records saying that he had been "pretending hee was a Christian." Fernando argued that he had been in England for many years, and so should be treated like "any other servant that came out of England accordinge to the custome of the Country," that is, not a slave. Fernando, as his name suggests, may have also spent time in Spanish America or on board a Portuguese ship. He seemed to understand at least one Iberian language. As part of his case, Fernando presented some papers in "Portugell or some other language which the Court could not understand" to prove his freedom. It was to no avail, however, and the court found "noe Cause wherefore he should be free but Judge him a slave for his life time."[37]

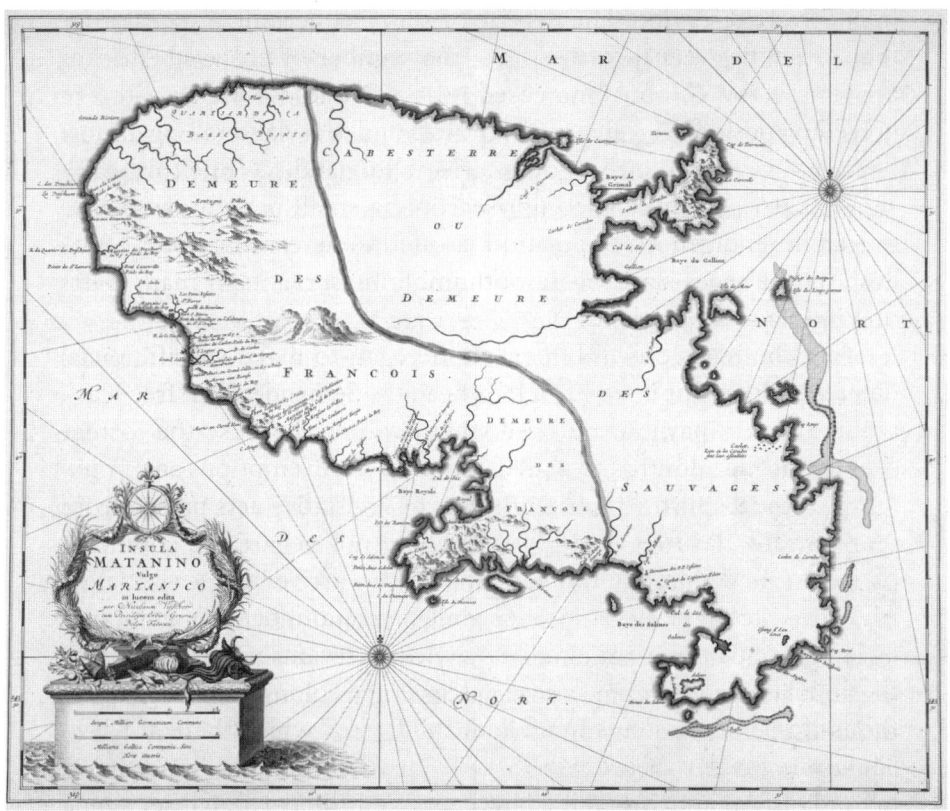

A Dutch map of Martinique circa 1680. The key in the bottom left, translated from Latin, reads "The Island of Matanino, commonly known as Martanico, published by Nicolaus Visscher with the Privilege of the Order: General of the Federation of the Belgians."

~~•~~

THE STORY OF Francisque Fabulé—a man later described as "a powerful black of extraordinary size [grandeur]"—is only a fragment, a glimpse of life in early colonial Martinique. The French had colonized that island in 1635, and some 30 years later Fabulé ran away and was leading a band of 400 to 500 maroons. Martinique is volcanic, with thick tropical forests that offer many ideal hiding spots, allowing hundreds of people to live scattered among the trees, taking refuge under the velvet green blanket that covers the island.

Such a large community of maroons inevitably came to the authorities' attention, not least because there were complaints of raids and theft. Such was the disruption that the French were willing to negotiate a treaty with Fabulé, in which he would keep his freedom and 1,000 pounds of valuable tobacco in exchange for stopping further disorder and not attracting any more maroons. As part of the deal, the existing maroons were not to be punished for running away, and Fabulé, in an unusual turn, went to live in the household of the island's governor, Robert de Clodoré, perhaps as a servant. Whatever his role, he was given a saber. This no doubt was a nod to Fabulé's military prowess, which Clodoré put to use, placing the former maroon leader in charge of a military unit of enslaved people to go to war against the English in the Caribbean in 1666–1667.

Around this time, Fabulé allegedly seduced a "young negress" in the household of Pierre le Comte and convinced her to stab her enslaver. Whether it actually might have been her idea is not clear, but Fabulé took the blame and the episode landed them both at the whipping post. Fabulé was not subdued—if anything, he was reinvigorated. By 1671, he had rounded up another band of maroons, this time 50 or so, and they began setting fires and pillaging. Officials were fed up and captured him, again. Fabulé was not killed, however. Rather, the island's supreme council decided to work him to death, sentencing him in 1671 to be a galley slave for life.[38]

Like the English in Virginia, the French in the Caribbean had moved from sea to land, from privateering to planting. They also created companies, like the Compagnie des îles d'Amérique, to obtain money and permission for colonization schemes, quickly claiming a clutch of islands, including Dominica in 1625, Martinique and Guadeloupe in 1635, and Grenada in 1650. They had to learn, as the Spanish did, that the rugged mountainous interior of these islands, coupled with a low European population, made the situation ripe for runaways. On islands with large surviving indigenous populations, enslaved people could find guides to the interior and allies against the French. But this was only one part of French exploration in the Americas. The other happened thousands of miles to the north, in the Saint Lawrence River valley, in what they called *Nouvelle France*, parts of which had been explored and claimed since 1534.

The Dutch, too, were coming to North American shores. After the English mariner Henry Hudson's successful navigation for the Dutch in 1609 of the river that would later bear his name, interest in the area grew, though for the next few years mostly fur traders arrived. By 1621, the Dutch had set up a West India Company (WIC), and in 1624 the colony of New Netherland was established on the lands of Algonquin-speaking Lenape peoples, roughly corresponding to parts of modern Long Island and Manhattan, stretching into New Jersey and Connecticut.

The Dutch involvement in slaving up to this point had been limited to raids on Iberian ships, not unlike the attack on the *São João Bautista*, and such human "prizes" were introduced into New Netherland as labor.[39] Like the "royal" slaves in Spanish America, who were property of the crown, the captives brought to New Netherland were "corporate slaves," owned by the WIC. In their case, these enslaved workers received housing, food, and clothing, as well as some legal rights, including access to the courts.[40] New Netherland was primarily a trading colony, so their work involved building infrastructure and growing provisions. They were also encouraged to marry and keep their families intact. One study counted 27 black marriages out of 441 that were recorded between 1639 and 1664.[41] These Africans were integrated, up to a point, into the New Netherland community, for instance learning the language and joining the Dutch Reformed Church—though conversion here would yield no path to freedom.[42]

In 1664, about 20 percent of the population of Dutch New Amsterdam was enslaved, compared to about 5 percent of the wider New Netherland colony's total population of 7,000 to 8,000 people.[43] Access to full freedom was limited, though there was a range of flexibility. For instance, in 1635 a group of slaves petitioned the WIC in Amsterdam to pay them wages.[44] In another often-cited case, enslaved people won what was called "half-freedom."[45]

In this instance, a group of 11 enslaved men who had helped the Dutch fight Kieft's War, a two-year battle against the Raritans (Lenape), petitioned for their freedom in 1644. These men—Paulo Angola, Big

Manuel, Little Manuel, Manuel de Gerrit de Reus, Simon Congo, Anthony Portugis, Gracia, Peter Santomee, Jan Francisco, Little Anthony, and Jan Fort Orange—had served, and now wanted their reward. The resulting act that freed them noted that the men had "been promised their freedom a long time ago." The claimants appealed to the Dutch desire to keep families together, because the resulting decree noted, "They are burdened with many children and if they continue in the service of the Company cannot support their wives and children." The WIC directive freed the wives as well, and said everyone should now "be able to earn their livelihood by farming the land manifested and granted to them." However, each man had to render to the WIC a tribute of "30 skepels of corn, wheat, peas, or beans, and one fat hog valued at 20 guilders." Far worse was the condition placed on each man's family: "His present children and his children yet to be born be bound and obliged to serve the West India Company as slaves."[46] Freedom became a dividing line between families. Half-freedom for some, full slavery for others.

English settlements had been inching nearer to New Netherland throughout this period. By the time of the Second Anglo-Dutch War (1665–1667), the English had been able to capture New Amsterdam without a fight, in 1664. This mostly maritime conflict was settled by the Treaty of Breda (1667), which ceded to England Dutch New Amsterdam, to be named New York. In exchange the English gave the Dutch the contested South American colony of Suriname.* In addition, the Dutch swept up a number of colonies in this period, including the Caribbean islands of Curaçao in 1634, Aruba, Bonaire, and Sint Eustatius in 1636, and Saba in 1640. The English, too, had added more Caribbean dots to their maps, with Saint Christopher (Kitts) in 1623, shared with the French, then Barbados in 1627, and Nevis in 1628, with more to come.

Even Sweden and Denmark muscled in. Under New Netherland company director Peter Minuit, Swedish settlers built Fort Christina in 1638, along the lower Delaware River, establishing the New Sweden colony. Other Swedes and Finns followed, coming to farm and trade

---

* The Dutch occupied New Amsterdam again briefly during the Third Anglo-Dutch War (1672–1674).

in furs. However, by 1655, the Dutch wanted the area back under their control and then-governor Peter Stuyvesant forced the Swedish to surrender the colony. In a similar way, Swedish attempts to join traders on the Gold Coast of Africa in the same period were later take over by the Dutch.

Denmark also looked to the Atlantic for economic opportunities and fared much better than Sweden. Its West India Company landed on the Caribbean island of Saint Thomas (today part of the US Virgin Islands) in 1671, later adding Saint John (1717) and Saint Croix (bought from France in 1733). The Danes, too, set up trading forts on the coast of today's Ghana, including Fort Frederiksborg. During their time in Africa, they sent at least 200 ships to the Americas, carrying more than 54,000 captives.[47] Although some indenture existed early on in Saint Thomas, by 1715 the work was done by 3,000 enslaved Africans, at 160 plantations and 32 sugar mills.[48]

By the middle of the 1600s, the Western Hemisphere was becoming a new world, with new people—welcome or not. It was indigenous, African, and European all at once, and while those categories would hold in some places, they would blur in others. Life, despite many hardships, went on. People fell in love, children came into the world, elders died. Old traditions might live on, but in different forms. Some corners of these vast lands would remain untouched by war and epidemics for a while yet, but the processes that had started two centuries earlier could no longer be stopped.

Chapter 9

Hinterlands

THE SCENE IS placid and inviting, with muted greens and browns. Palm trees frame the edges, and a large, watery sky stretches above. To the left is a white plastered church, browning a touch, perhaps due for a coat of paint. In front, people linger, their backs to the viewer, their forms hard to make out, except for the blackness of what little skin is showing. Most are fully clothed, as if it were autumn or spring in Europe, and not the endless summer of the tropical latitudes. A priest stands under the portico, the grayness of his cassock rendering him almost indistinguishable from the pillar he is next to, extending a white hand to a woman with her head covered. The five black people in the middle of the painting stand back, perhaps waiting to go into the church.

In the darkened foreground of the painting, a cobra eats a rabbit under the shade of the bushes, producing a rivulet of red that matches a pinecone-shaped bromeliad in bloom behind it. An armadillo walks past, taking little notice, while a nearby frog looks toward the church, also oblivious to the meal being had behind him.[1]

This was the artist Frans Post's vision of Brazil. Calm and orderly—except in the shadows, where the cobras wait to strike.

Post was a Dutch artist from Haarlem who travelled to Brazil at the behest of the governor, arriving in Pernambuco at age 25 in 1637. His paintings are among the earliest European depictions of Brazilian landscapes.[2] He had been invited as part of a larger West India Company (WIC) project that involved securing access to sugar. Because of the ongoing hostilities with the Iberian Union, the Dutch had difficulty sustaining a steady supply of valued commodities, including sugar. The Atlantic plantations were under Iberian control, as were the ones developing on the islands of Hispaniola, Puerto Rico, and Cuba. Brazil, too, began to see the establishment of sugar mills by the 1520s, perhaps an inevitability given the success of sugar in other Portuguese territories, including Madeira and São Tomé. Brazil had ideal conditions for the sweet grass to grow, with its rich, dark clay near the coastal rivers of the northwest, known as *massapé*.[3] But this was a relatively small area, so other planters moved inland, to the Recôncavo, a fertile area that surrounds the Bay of All Saints in Bahia.[4] Colonists in Brazil faced attacks from indigenous Tupí people, which hindered sugar production, though by 1570 some 60 *engenhos* had been established along the coast, mainly in Pernambuco and Bahia, a number that had more than doubled by 1585.[5] By the time the Dutch WIC turned its attention to Brazil, that colony's sugar plantations were producing around 960,000 *arrobas* (about 16,000 tons) a year.[6]

The Dutch WIC's opening move was an unsuccessful attack on the colonial capital of Salvador de Bahia in 1624. It had better results in Pernambuco, to the north, which it conquered in 1630 and would govern for more than two decades. Despite the inevitable disruptions brought by conflict, the sugar industry regained its equilibrium. The WIC was able to take many of the mills abandoned by fleeing Portuguese and sell them to investors.[7]

What was taking shape more broadly was the quest for wealth through new means. The English, French, and Dutch couldn't find the same gold or silver as Spain, but they were finding riches in commodities. The WIC understood this. Sugar in the Atlantic islands had been a multinational project, and so too would it be in Brazil, under governor Johan Maurits of Nassau (1636–1644). Dutch investors arrived, accompanied by other Europeans, including Genoese and Germans, though even by 1640 when residents and WIC employees reached around 13,000, they remained outnumbered by a Portuguese population of 25,000.[8] A small Jewish community was established as well, and Sinagoga Kahal Zur Israel remains as a testament to these times. It is the oldest surviving synagogue in the Americas, and its construction took place during this period. It sits on a street in Recife that is now called Rua do Bom Jesus, but street signs remind passersby that this was "Rua dos Judeus" (Road of the Jews) between 1636 and 1654, during the Dutch governorship.

Although some innovations in sugar technology were introduced in the 1600s, such as the development of a vertical roller to crush cane more efficiently, planting and processing remained difficult and dangerous work.[9] The cane was placed in the ground with hoes, and weeded and fertilized as it grew. The growing cycle was long, and harvests could stretch for months, with the cane cut by hand, under a relentless sun. The stalks had to be processed within 48 hours of being cut, and were then passed through rollers that squeezed out the juice—and also sometimes crushed unfortunate fingers and arms. These crushers were sometimes powered by wind, other times by oxen, and even at times by humans.

This process was followed by the inferno of the boiling house, where the juice from the cane was taken up to extreme temperatures so it could crystallize, moving along a series of caldrons as it was refined. From there the sugar was cured, and molasses—used in rum—was siphoned off. And still the sugar demanded more. If it was in its darker, *muscovado* state, it would be shipped to places like Amsterdam to be further refined, the dark stain of its production whitened to perfection, before being added to the sugar pots of the wealthy and expanding middle class in Europe.[10]

Planters required a small army of enslaved workers to produce their sugar, a labor-intensive and often dangerous process. Some *engenhos* had around 200 people, most of whom were employed in either growing or processing the crop in often specialized but repetitive roles; the assembly lines of the industrial revolution have their genesis in the sugar plantations of the Americas. Other enslaved workers ran the household and cultivated other foodstuffs to keep the entire enterprise going. The numerous paintings of Frans Post show a particular version of the Brazilian *engenhos*. As in his landscapes, Post depicts people in calm, unfettered settings, appearing to go about their work willingly, perhaps even cheerfully. There is no sign of an overseer's whip, no faces wincing in pain, no sweat beading on the foreheads of workers in the boiling house.

However, the sketches and paintings in a notebook belonging to a German WIC soldier in Brazil around the same time offer a more explicit tableau. In Zacharias Wagener's rendering of the slave market in Recife, the scene is anything but peaceful.[11] The market is ringed by two-story buildings, with four groupings of enslaved Africans within. Europeans buy, sell, or watch the proceedings, some from their balconies. The threat of violence is palpable. In the upper-left corner, a man holding a large stick looks like he is about to strike a group of four or five people sitting against the wall of a house. Elsewhere, a black body lies on the ground, possibly dead. Closer to the foreground, a man in elegant attire inspects the body of an African. The captive holds his arms over his head as the European reaches to poke him. It is both an everyday scene and an ongoing nightmare. This was not the work of a trained artist like Post, but rather of a soldier-adventurer-scientist, who was also interested in nature, using his notebooks to record the world around him, observing the cruel ecosystem of colonial life.

⋘ • ⋙

As the Dutch exerted their control over northeastern Brazil, they were also forging a relationship in Africa with the kingdom of Kongo, whose leaders expressed deep frustrations with the Portuguese. In 1643, King Garcia II of Kongo, early in his 20-year reign, wrote a letter to the Jesuit college in Luanda, stating his opposition to the growing slave trade. "Instead of gold and silver and other goods which function elsewhere as money, the trade and money are persons, who are not gold, nor cloth, but who are creatures."[12]

A couple of years earlier, in 1641, the Dutch had seized Luanda, following their capture of Portuguese Elmina in 1637. Dutch Brazil Governor Maurits had sent the expedition to Angola to secure a supply of Africans to work the sugar plantations that the WIC had acquired.[13] Kongo and the Dutch Republic became united in their animosity toward Portugal, building on the alliance they had formed during earlier trading encounters in the 1590s.[14] King Garcia II dispatched Dom Miguel de Castro to be his ambassador and meet with Governor Maurits in Olinda, in Dutch Brazil. Emissaries from Kongo travelled to Brazil, and some sailed on to Holland. They first arrived in Recife sometime around 1642. While they were there, another Dutch artist,

Albert Eckhout (1610–1665), who had also been invited to Brazil by the governor, did a series of paintings of the emissaries. The works showed the men wearing a mix of European and African items, such as traditional round *mpu* caps and wraps of heavy wool.[15] The diplomats arrived with presents for Maurits, including a gold necklace and a large silver basin that had been crafted in Peru, its use in this exchange testament to the currents of commerce in the seventeenth century.[16]

From Brazil, the envoys made their way to Holland, and there another striking set of portraits were painted, by the Dutch artist Jaspar Beckx, including one of Miguel de Castro and the two younger attendants in his entourage, Pedro Sunda and Diego Bemba.[17] In the main portrait, Castro gazes at the viewer with the calm expression of a man who knows his status as a representative of a powerful African and Christian kingdom. He is in full European dress, from an elegant black beaver hat embellished with a reddish-pink feather to the decorative baldric across his chest.[18] The two younger men gaze upward and inward, as if they are looking at Castro in the center. They wear similar outfits, of muted green doublets and stiff white collars. Bemba holds a small woven box, while Sunda cradles a much larger ivory tusk, both valuable gifts of material and symbolic value. On display across all three portraits is a level of wealth that could not be ignored. The beaver hat that Castro wears was given to him by the Dutch; in wearing it for the portrait, the exchange of gifts was committed to canvas.[19]

Other West Central African leaders continued to struggle in this period with the Portuguese, and considered the Dutch interference a potentially useful development. In 1626, the Portuguese had attempted to introduce a tax known as the *baculamento*. It was a tribute to be paid by kings and noblemen (*sobas*) who were loyal to the Portuguese crown, or at least professed to be in order to stave off attacks on their territory.[20] The ideal payment was in humans, the obvious currency to the Portuguese. By that point, Portuguese traders had marched onto their ships at least 90,000 captives from West Central Africa alone in just over a century (1513–1626).[21]

There were ways to avoid paying the tax, though they were costly. Queen Njinga (also spelled Nzinga), who ruled over the kingdoms of

Ndongo and Matamba (part of modern northern Angola), understood this and was willing to incur the cost. She defied the Portuguese and entered a war lasting some three decades against them. When the Dutch invaded Angola in 1641, she was quick to reach out, hoping to build an alliance, along with other, smaller local leaders, that would help drive the Portuguese out of her kingdoms. A treaty signed in Lisbon in 1643 with the Dutch should have returned Luanda to the Portuguese and stopped the fighting, but the conflict intensified in the years that followed.[22] Njinga and the WIC made a formal alliance in 1647, with the Dutch to receive half of any slaves she captured in return for supporting her fight against the Portuguese.[23] The following August, a new Portuguese governor, Salvador Correia da Sá, arrived in Africa from Rio de Janeiro with 900 men and proceeded to bombard Luanda, making a final push against the Dutch. The Dutch soon surrendered, but did so without informing Njinga.[24] The WIC left Angola, and Njinga was forced to resume her war against the Portuguese without them. She would not sign a peace treaty with Portugal until 1656.

King Garcia II continued to protest the high costs of any involvement with the Portuguese, keeping firm in his opposition to their taxes and system of enslavement. He took his dissatisfaction to the Vatican, writing about the Portuguese to Pope Innocent X in 1648: "Using the force of firearms, they kidnapped men and women, loaded them on ships, and sent them to Brazil to produce sugar, without being moved to pity by their weeping."[25] But it wasn't just the Portuguese. The Dutch had managed to transport about 13,000 captives from Luanda to Pernambuco between 1641 and 1650.[26]

African leaders like King Garcia II were continuing to protest expanding slave trade, but the machine was running, and it would take more than letters to the pope to stop it.

⋘ • ⋙

ALONG THE COBBLED streets of today's Olinda, on Brazil's northeast coast, only scant traces of the Dutch past can be seen. Its colorful single-story homes, 20 or so colonial churches in varying states of repair, and handicraft shops have turned it into a tourist destination. The African imprint is much more apparent, for Olinda is famed for its pre-Lenten carnival celebrations. The old town is home to musical groups that practice all year for the annual festivities, which pull in millions of visitors. At various hours of the day and night, the thumps of drumming, the singing, and the energetic sound of brass instruments warming up fill the air.

Elsewhere in the city, the church of Nossa Senhora do Rosário dos Homens Pretos de Olinda stands on the edge of the historic zone, its facade elegant but weary after centuries under the tropical sun, the white paint mottled with dirt and pollution. Unlike many of the other churches in the city, there is no tourism marker in front of it, despite its origins in the early seventeenth century and its place in Afro-Brazilian history. The confraternities, or *irmandades*, that existed in Portugal quickly spread to Brazil, with the brotherhoods establishing black churches. Olinda's was one of the earliest.

Nearby Recife, like Olinda, also lures visitors from around Brazil, and the vast Brazilian sky painted by Frans Post is now pierced by a forest of high-rise hotels and apartment buildings. Its carnival is also central to regional and national identity, and a large museum is devoted to this history. Known as the Paço do Frevo (*frevo* being the regional dance), it is housed in a gleaming-white neoclassical building that sits proudly on a square in Recife's old town. However, in that city one remnant from the Dutch period survives. About a 20-minute stroll south of the museum is the Fort of Five Points, a low structure facing the sea, where the Beberibe and Capibaribe Rivers run together. The fort was positioned near the point where ships could enter the gaps in the reefs (*Recife* is Portuguese for reef). Its rusted and weather-beaten cannons now point at parking lots and shops. But here, in January 1654, the Dutch surrendered to Portugal, relinquishing their Brazilian dream. They had done likewise in Luanda in 1648.

The years since the WIC capture of Angola had proven difficult for everyone involved, and there was a great deal of uncertainty in the wider European situation. The Peace of Westphalia had extinguished the fire lit by the torch of the Reformation. Some conflicts continued to smolder, including the one between the Dutch and Portuguese, though by 1648 the Dutch were free of Spanish rule, as the Portuguese had become in 1640. In 1645, the Portuguese in Brazil began what they called the War of Divine Liberty, to drive out the WIC. They fought alongside some free black allies, such as Henrique Dias, who led other freed men and maroons in the conflict. The leaders of the revolt against the Dutch also offered freedom to any enslaved person who served in the war, helping to swell their numbers. However, the actual manumission had to come through the enslaver rather than officials; many opted to keep their slaves in the sugar fields instead, well away from the possibility of freedom.[27]

While the Portuguese and Dutch were fighting, elsewhere in Brazil a new community had established itself, a place that could possibly undermine the entire European project in the colony. This was one scene Frans Post did not paint. He might not have known how to get to Palmares, though he most likely heard about its maroon community. The Dutch considered it dangerous enough that they sent a scout there.[28] Bartholomeus Lintz returned to tell officers that it was not one single site, but a few smaller ones, with what he estimated to be around six thousand people living across them, located about 60 miles (100 kilometers) inland from the coastal city of Maceió.[29]

Worried that the Africans they were bringing to work on the sugar plantations would want to flee to this maroon settlement, the WIC sent expeditions in 1643 and 1645, both failing to inflict much damage. On the second expedition, a Dutch Army lieutenant, Jürgens Reijmbach, kept a diary. In it, he described one of the larger towns of Palmares as being "half a mile long, its street six feet wide and running along a large swamp, tall trees alongside . . . There are 220 *casas* [homes], amid them a church, four smithies and a huge *casa de conselho* [town hall]." He was able to have a close look because the site had been temporarily abandoned in advance of his arrival.[30]

Palmares was a maroon community (*quilombo* in Portuguese), but on a vast scale. Its population would grow to more than 10,000 people living in numerous enclaves by 1640. Most of the freedom-seekers were Angolans, and they called their community Angola Pequena or Angola Janga (Little Angola). But it wasn't only Africans—some Amerindian people who had also suffered under the Portuguese lived among and aided them.

Palmares was originally founded in around 1605 by 40 enslaved men from "Guiné," though what was meant by "Guiné" was not exactly clear. It's likely that whoever they were, they had passed through Angola on their way to Brazil.[31] The colony's reputation was established by 1612.[32] The Portuguese authorities described Palmares as a *mocambo*, a military camp, though this may have been a willful misinterpretation of *macamba*, or community (the term comes from a Kimbundu word for friends, family, and relations). After all, if the colony was a military camp, a "just war" could be waged against it.[33]

Unlike the much smaller Caribbean territories, Brazil offered people fleeing slavery ample and fertile land well away from Portuguese settlements. Thus, maroons there did not steal or raid plantations for provisions with the same intensity as maroons elsewhere. Rather, the removal of enslaved people themselves—including, initially, enslaved women—was causing the issue, depriving planters of their labor. This was a problem the Portuguese were eager to rectify, having destroyed other large *quilombos* around this time, including three in Bahia (1632, 1636, 1646) and one in Rio (1650).[34]

Little is known about life in Palmares, though some contemporary sources provide a glimpse, albeit through a European lens. The Dutch officer Reijmbach mentioned in his diary a king who ruled "with iron justice," but that can be interpreted in a variety of ways.[35] Given that the colony's initial population was largely African, there is little doubt that some traditional social customs and political structures would have been used. At the same time, however, the maroons were deep in a new land, and that would have required adaptation.[36] What the balance of old customs and new looked like is impossible to say. The members of the community lived among the palm trees—hence its name—using the natural resources available to them to survive, including manioc and other crops grown on small plots of land, as well as fish and game.

More difficult is understanding less tangible aspects of everyday life: What did the colony sound like? Were people speaking in Kikongo or other Bantu languages? Was there drumming and singing? How did the food smell? What did people cook? Was daily life peaceful among the hilly green folds, or was there a steady thrum of anxiety about yet another attack?

Another later account described Palmares as a "Republic," and perhaps its size and organization meant it was viewed with admiration—and trepidation.[37] Even across the South Atlantic, Africans may have been aware of its existence.[38] The same account explained that some Portuguese residents who lived nearby, known as *colonos*, "had a secret confederation" with the leaders of Palmares, giving them "arms, gunpowder and bullets, clothes, goods from Europe and gifts from Portugal, in exchange for gold, silver, and money, which they brought back from what they stole [on raids], and some victualss."[39] Such behavior, of course, would have put the settlers at odds with the Portuguese authorities, who did not want runaway Africans to have access to weapons. Indeed, the early settlers of Palmares were quick to establish a militia to protect the area. But for the *colonos* living near the villages of Palmares, such pragmatic exchanges made sense in terms of protection against attacks or to secure access to trade in a remote area. The Portuguese authorities considered the *colonos* "lawless" and untrustworthy. The maroon leaders had their doubts too, and made them pay a tax, or tribute, to participate in the economic life of the community.[40]

A small runaway colony was one matter, but the autonomous society developing in Palmares posed a bigger threat. This was not only because of its size, scale, and organization, but because this free black community might offer white colonists a viable alternative to colonial governance, especially after decades of disruption under Dutch rule. The Dutch had failed to destroy any part of Palmares, and the Portuguese, back in control of northeast Brazil as of 1654, would similarly struggle in the decades ahead.

⤙ • ⤚

THE STOUT WALL that encloses the old city is a clue that Cartagena de Indias, founded in 1533 on the Caribbean coast of Colombia, was frequently attacked during its long history. Inside the walls, a pleasant maze of narrow streets contains colorful colonial houses turned into artisanal ice cream shops and expensive boutiques. The rest of Cartagena, where its actual population lives, spreads to the south, while the length of coast is no longer under siege by pirates but by the thousands of tourists who come to enjoy its beaches.

The city is full of foreigners and well-heeled Colombians seeking the sea, and not the city's storied past. One fact is particularly arresting: From Cartagena's founding until 1700, some 200,000 African captives were forced to disembark there; in comparison, around 10,000 did so in North America over the same period.[41] The tides of human misery would flow in different directions in the years ahead, but in the seventeenth century, this fortified Spanish city was known as an important crossroads for colonial expansion and the slave trade.

According to testimony from a trial in the early 1600s, it was common for Africans to arrive at the port "shouting that they had been born free and they [were] children of free parents and had come to a state of servitude."[42] They were aware that Spanish authorities struggled to know who was captured in a "just war" and, as this account pointed out, these Africans knew "how to proclaim their liberty."[43]

Most of the time, officials did not listen. Rather, thousands of Africans were disembarked and marched into one of 24 warehouses along the waterfront, or to a holding pen in a slave trader's yard, before being taken further into the beyond. All of this was in plain view of the residents, none of whom would have had to strain to hear people crying out for their liberty.[44] Captives were sent in many directions—some further into Nuevo Reino de Granada (New Kingdom of Granada, today's Colombia) to work in gold mines or on sugar plantations near the Pacific coast, others to Panama, Peru, Central America, and elsewhere in the Caribbean.

The walled city in the early 1600s was small, though it would grow as the port became a critical point in the treasure *flota*. The European population in the early seventeenth century was around 2,500, while the Africans numbered some 4,000, but not all of them were enslaved, and the population of free people of color was growing.[45] Many enslaved people were forced to labor in public works around the city. Even today, *Cartageneros* say the "blood of the slaves" is in the city's walls. Other slaves were tradespeople or domestic workers. There was a wide diversity among black people in South America in the 1600s, as they had been brought from many points along the West African coast, starting with Guinea, later reaching down to Angola. Priests at the time recorded dozens of languages being spoken.[46]

Cartagena, with so many of its people unfamiliar with Spanish ways, was also a worry for the Church, which was also keeping a close eye on the arrival of converted Jewish people, known as *conversos*, or New Christians. By 1610, the third tribunal of the Holy Office of the Inquisition in the Americas was established in Cartagena, forming a trinity with the other two, in Mexico and Lima. This one had a "denunciation window," a small portal with a grate that opened on the side of the building to what was the Calle de la Inquisición, where a person could profess the sins of others by dropping anonymous accusations. And some clearly did, because the Inquisition put around 400 people on trial between 1610 and 1660, with many coming from places like Cuba, within its larger jurisdiction. Some 16 percent of the defendants were black, and 11 percent recorded as enslaved. The church also fretted over African practices it did not understand—among them unfamiliar rituals and the use of herbs and talismans to cast "spells." Witchcraft was a common charge levelled at black people, usually women, free or enslaved, who used African medicinal and spiritual practices that the Catholic authorities deemed heretical.[47]

One such case was that of Paula de Eguiluz, who was tried three different times for witchcraft.[48] Eguiluz was born in the Caribbean and was living in Cuba, at the copper mines of El Cobre, near Santiago, on the east end of the island. She was described as well-dressed, and her enslaver granted her liberties, such as permission to visit friends in Havana, a considerable distance from El Cobre. She developed a reputation as a sorceress and was accused of killing a child by sucking its life out through its navel. From there, the other accusations piled up: She sold love potions, she could turn herself into a goat, she could vanish into thin air. In 1624, Eguiluz arrived, at the age of 33 for her first encounter with the Inquisition in Cartagena on the serious charge that she was a *bruja*, a witch who rejected God and followed the devil. In the trial, "she requested to declare her guilt." Her confessed, or perhaps invented, sins were many, including incest that involved "carnal knowledge" of two male relatives, though she admitted she did not know how they were related. She also told the inquisitors that she often believed her dreams were portents because they came true. Eventually she confessed that she had given her soul to the devil, "which she now regrets very much." She confirmed to the priests that she was a baptized Catholic, attended mass, and received holy communion, and she asked for forgiveness. In this instance the Inquisitor granted it. She survived her first round, but her punishment involved doing public penance, the infamous auto-da-fé, in the robe of a penitent, receiving 200 lashes, and serving a year in the city's hospitals.

This history of women like Eguiluz is traceable, even if the outlines are sometimes faint. Indeed, the Inquisition building is now the city's museum. Less easy to discern is the route of the enslaved who did not enter the records. They came in from the bay, in their coffles, forced under the arch that marks the southern entrance to the city. From there they turned left, walked to the customs house (*aduana*), and waited in the wide plaza in front of the colonnaded building. After the ship's captain paid tax on them, some were marched to the warehouses and holding pens, and others back to the plaza in front of the entrance. Now it's known as the Plaza de los Coches, but then it was the slave market. Today, one side of it is occupied by a row of sweets-sellers, who tend to their *dulcerías*, tables piled with sugar-laden concoctions, under the columns that line one side of the square. Not only do they sell popular confectionery made of the very product that wrought so much damage in the Americas, but most of them are *palenqueras*, or descendants from one of the most famous maroon colonies in the region: San Basilio de Palenque.

Of the many thousands who were shipped to Cartagena, hundreds ran off, hiding at first in the swamps not far from the city's wall, prompting the crown to issue a royal pardon in 1540 to all the "fugitive and rebellious slaves" in an attempt to lure them back, indicating that this was a significant problem.[49] One such rebel African was Benkos (also Domingo) Biohó, a captive thought to have been born in the Bissagos (or Bijagós) Islands off the coast of Guinea-Bissau. Much about the establishment of his *palenque* is lost to history, but it is thought to have begun around 1600, when he and some 30 others—including his wife and two children—rebelled and then fled into the swamps outside of Cartagena, fighting off a group of enslavers on their trail and establishing a settlement initially known as La Matuna, where he was referred to as their king.[50] Where his colony differs from many others is that it has been continuously occupied ever since.

* * *

Today the road to San Basilio de Palenque is easily travelled, winding out of Cartagena, over the Magdalena River, toward the Montes de María. Just over an hour's drive, about 30 miles (50 kilometers) from the city, is a small village. Single-story homes with corrugated roofs sit along unpaved roads, roosters peck at the ground, and farmers pass by on horses, sauntering through the humidity. This could be many places in Colombia, but other, similar towns with populations of about 5,000 don't have tourist vans and coaches parked at their edge. Palenque today has become an important site for visitors, with cultural spaces nestled among the houses that allow them to see what a traditional maroon dwelling was like and to hear about the African influences in religion, medicine, music, and language.[51] The last one is especially significant—Palenque sounds different from other places in Colombia, its Palenquero language retaining Bantu-influenced words and grammar, such as *burú* for money and *ngubá* for peanut (related to the English "goober").

Biohó himself is a presence in the town: A statue in the main plaza depicts him with his right arm held high, his mouth open in a cry for freedom. But Biohó had not been alone—Cartagena's hinterland was riddled with runaway colonies. In addition to San Basilio de Palenque, by the 1680s there were other powerful *palenques*, like Matudere, also in the Montes de María, and at least another nine along the Magdalena River.[52] However, Biohó looms large over this history, having intermittently fought the Spanish for well over a decade, until 1613, when they negotiated a settlement.[53] As part of the 1619 deal, the maroons could enter Cartagena, but any armed Spaniard could not enter the *palenque*. As one contemporary account described the situation: "Biohó went about [Cartagena] with such arrogance that on top of going around well dressed in the Spanish style, with sword and golden dagger, he acted as if he were some kind of great gentleman."[54] Six years later, the Spanish arrested him and betrayed their treaty, executing Biohó in a public hanging. His people fought on for decades, and a "legitimate" town was established in 1686—and by this point it had a population of around 3,000 people.[55] The leadership would inevitably change over the decades, but the name Biohó continued to be invoked, inspiring future generations of leaders in San Basilio de Palenque and elsewhere.

Chapter 10

Overthrow

Maroons were not just a problem for the Spanish and Portuguese, but for all the other European powers as they extended into the Americas, including the English. Where slavery went, resistance followed. Indeed, two runaways are even depicted on a 1657 map of the Caribbean island of Barbados.[1] This early rendering is slightly off kilter, as if the island has been tipped onto its side, its shape resembling a kidney bean rather than the island's actual teardrop form. Its western and southern coastlines have an orderly, if not neighborly, appearance, with names written next to tiny houses marking slivers of property: Carter, Patrick, Macock, Terrill, Stevens. These were the planters, the new landowners on the island—but not the only ones. In large, unmissable script, "The Ten Thousande Acres of Land which Belongeth to the Merchants of London" is written in the middle of the map.

Elsewhere, sharp-toothed sea monsters swim near the coast, while rather improbable camel-like creatures move goods on land, large boars frolic, and men on horseback gallop to the east and west. A man with a crown and dressed in a loincloth gazes directly at the viewer, representing perhaps an Amerindian leader. He must have been visiting from a neighboring island, because Barbados was allegedly "uninhabited" when the English arrived to settle it in 1627—though later evidence points to some Arawak activity before the arrival of Europeans. And then, in the upper left-hand corner of the map, wedged between a section of hills and a few lonely trees, two black men flee toward the coast, chased by a man on horseback, who appears to be firing a gun. Freedom-seekers were, literally, on the map in Barbados.

A British map of Barbados dated 1657 showing the location of plantation owners and roads. The missing text is estimated to say "A topographicall [Description and] Admeasurement [of the yland of] Barbados in t[he West Indyaes] with the Mrs. [Names of the Seuerall plantacons]"

The island of Barbados followed the pattern of the other English colonies, starting with tobacco and indentured labor before moving to sugar and enslaved Africans. This transition took place in the context of two crucial events. The first was a civil war in England (1642–1651), which included the beheading of King Charles I in 1649 and the subsequent establishment of a republic under Oliver Cromwell. This commonwealth lasted until his death in 1658, but not much beyond that; Charles II was restored to the English throne in 1660.[2]

The other crucial event was the collapse of Dutch Brazil in 1654. Very quickly, a few thousand people needed somewhere to go. The defeated WIC had to leave, and Jewish people, fearful of the return of the Catholic Inquisition under the Portuguese, did not want to linger. For some of them, Barbados was an obvious choice because it was under Protestant English rule. The island was also ideal for sugar, and there were planters eager and curious to learn about growing it.

Englishman Richard Ligon arrived in Barbados in 1647, two decades into its colonization. He recorded his three years on the island, providing a sketch of its early colonial society, including the contribution of the people who had come there from Brazil. He observed that "the great work of Sugar-making, was but newly practised by the inhabitants."³ Some planters had "gotten Plants from Fernambock [Pernambuco] in Brasill, and made tryall of them at the Barbados." After some trial and error the crop began to yield, and "about the time I left the Iland, which was in 1650 they were much better'd."⁴

In his account, Ligon uses the Spanish term *ingenio* (similar to the Portuguese *engenho*) to refer to what would later be called a "plantation" in English, in part because at the time "plantation" meant something closer to "colony"—for instance the "Plantation of Ulster" in Ireland—rather than the intensive and large-scale cotton farms in the nineteenth-century southern United States that the word came to represent.⁵

Initially, white indentured workers grew the crops of tobacco and cotton before the turn towards sugar and the increased arrival of African captives. However, even in the late 1640s, Ligon noted that African slaves were "more than double the numbers of the Christians" on the island.⁶ By the mid-1670s the white population—indentured and free—was 21,500, supported by 33,000 black enslaved people.⁷ In Barbados, as had been the case in Virginia, the indentured servants were portrayed as difficult and prone to taking recourse to the courts. Plots were also uncovered involving revolts or rebellions among the white servants in the 1630s and 1640s.⁸ Officials would continue to worry about the Irish—many of whom were forcibly sent over during the Cromwell era—and the Africans making common cause well into the 1680s.⁹ By then, however, the number of enslaved Africans had far surpassed that of indentured servants. Between the colony's founding in 1627 and 1700, an estimated 105,000 Africans were brought to Barbados, the majority coming after Ligon's time and mainly in English ships.¹⁰

But even while Ligon was in Barbados, he noted the presence of runaways, who often hid in the many caves dotting the island, some "extreamly large and Capacious." Here, he claimed, "the runaway Negres, often shelter themselves . . . for a long time and in the night range abroad the Countrey, and steale Pigs, Plantins, Potatoes, and Pullin, and bring it there; and feast all day, upon what they stole the night before."[11]

He mentioned that the runaways also "harbour themselves in Woods," though this option would soon disappear.[12] The trees on the 1657 map that represent forests were felled to make way for the fields and to provide fuel for the fire of the boiling houses. Barbados is mostly flat, with no mountains to which freedom-seekers could flee. The choices were limited.

Sometimes enslaved people chose the option of last resort. Ligon related an account of slave suicides on the plantation of a Colonel Walrond. Ligon interpreted these events as being related to the slaves' African spirituality, because, he explained, they believed in "a Resurrection, and that they shall go into their own Country again, and have their youth renewed . . . they make it an ordinary practice . . . to hang themselves." After three or four suicides on the Walrond plantation, the colonel made a macabre display of a severed head, which he

> set upon a pole a dozen foot high; and having done that, caused all his Negres to come forth, and march round about this head, and bid them look on it, whether this were not the head of such an one that hang'd himselfe. Which they acknowledging, he then told them, That they were in a main errour, in thinking they went into their own Countries, after they were dead; for, this mans head was here, as they all were witnesses of; and how was it possible, the body could go without a head. Being convinc'd by this sad, yet lively spectacle, they changed their opinions; and after that, no more hanged themselves.[13]

Amid such brutality, sugar production in Barbados soared, so much so that the nascent Brazilian industry lost its London market, dropping from 80 percent of imports in 1630 to 10 percent by 1690. This was due in part to England's Navigation Act of 1651, which established protectionist policies for the growing empire, requiring that only English ships could bring goods from its colonies to England.[14] However, some of the shift was also due to the success of sugarcane cultivation in Barbados—the tiny island was producing as much sugar as the much larger Brazil by 1670.[15]

Given that Africans outnumbered Europeans in Barbados from early on, observers like Ligon puzzled over why they didn't just take over—whether it was because they feared the guns of their enslavers or lacked access to them, as he suggested, or because they were from diverse parts of Africa and could not communicate with each other. They were also living under a system of surveillance, with overseers and enslavers watching their movements at work and at rest, with punishment in the stocks or by the whip an ever-present threat. By the 1650s, other observers had mentioned the existence of several rebellion plots, though how many of those were in the imagination of officials and overseers is difficult to say.[16]

However, in May 1675, such a plot nearly came to fruition when a conspiracy with a long fuse was almost lit.[17] In what might be considered the first published account (as opposed to official reports) of a slave rebellion in the English colonies, the 1676 anonymous pamphlet *Great Newes from the Barbados. Or, a True and Faithful Account of the Grand Conspiracy of the Negroes against the English* detailed the events.[18]

A woman called Anna, also known as Fortuna, or possibly Anna Fortuna, was enslaved by the family of Justice Gyles Hall. She worked as a personal servant to the mistress of the house. One day she overheard a young man, around the age of 18, working in the garden. He was speaking to another man from a neighboring plantation. Both were "Coromantee"—a colonial term meaning a person from the Gold Coast (Ghana), probably Akan.

She overheard the young man say, "boldly and plainly, He would have no hand in killing the Baccararoes [Buckras] or White Folks; And that he would tell his Master." Intrigued and possibly alarmed, Anna called over the fence to the young man to ask him what they were talking about. He told her that "it was a general Design amongst them the Cormantee Negro's, to kill all the Baccararoes or White People in the Island within a fortnight."

What went through Anna's mind is impossible to know. According to the anonymous author of *Great Newes*, she fretted that "so good people as her Master and Mistress were, should be destroyed," and felt compelled to tell them of the plot. Maybe that was the case. Maybe she sensed an opportunity, if not for freedom then for some sort of monetary reward. Maybe she was not Coromantee and worried what their revolt would mean for her own safety.

The authorities were quick to haul in the young man who had been working in the garden and extract a confession, made no doubt under duress and with the threat of violence looming. They heard that this plot was three years in the making, and the conspirators had kept it secret "even from the knowledge of their own Wifes," which is why, perhaps, Anna had not heard of it until the moment she passed by the garden. The plot's leaders were soon in front of justices eager to make an example of them. Seventeen people were found guilty and executed, with 11 of them beheaded and their bodies dragged through the streets of Speightstown and then burned, just to drive home the point. At least another five were said to have hanged themselves rather than go to trial.[19] Such a body count revealed the true level of the authorities' anxiety, and the lengths they were willing to go to send a message to any future plotters. Details of the rebels' plans came out during the trial, but how much was true and how much was in the fevered imaginations of colonial officials is a matter of speculation:

> Their grand design was to choose them a King, one Coffee an Ancient Gold-Coast Negro, who should have been Crowned the 12th June last past in a Chair of State exquisitely wrought and Carved after their Mode; with Bowes and Arrowes to be likewise carried in State before his Majesty their intended King: Trumpets to be made of Elephant Teeth and Gourdes to be sounded on several Hills to give Notice to their general Rising, with a full intention to fire the Sugar-Canes, and so run in and Cut their Masters the Planters Throats in their respective Plantations whereunto they did belong.[20]

Some of the condemned did not flinch at such charges. Officials tried to cajole one condemned man, who was not named, to confess. An enslaved man chained to him, named Tony—described as a "sturdy Rogue, a Jew's Negro"—implored him not to, saying, "Are there not enough of our country-men killed already?" The crowd weighed in, crying, "Tony, Sirrah, we shall see you fry bravely by and by." Undaunted, Tony replied: "If you Roast me today, you cannot Roast me tomorrow."

By the following month, Anna had been recommended for manumission, "sent in recompense of her eminent service in discovering the intended rebellion of the negroes."[21] Anna's story ends with her freedom, for which more than 20 people died.

In December 1683, the authorities were alarmed once again by reports of disturbances and the discovery of handwritten notices encouraging people to rebel, which one official dismissed as something "some foolish mischievous persons have scattered about . . . forgetting that negroes are not able to read." However, it was later determined that the notices might have been written by a slave, the use of English evidence that the plot involved collaboration between Africans and English-speaking creole slaves on the island. In the meantime, the alarm of mid-December was quelled and "four or five bold insolent blacks . . . were well whipped as an example." In addition, "one old negro" was "sentenced to be burnt alive" because he scared his enslaver "by saying of some Christians, who were beating negroes, that the negroes ere long would serve the Christians so."[22] Another rumor followed in 1686, this time alleging enslaved people were working with the Irish servants to "destroy all masters and mistresses."[23] Houses were searched, but no conspiracy was found, "only a discourse moved amongst some of them."[24]

Intelligence of a more serious conspiracy reached official ears in October 1692. How it was uncovered and the identity of the informant are obscured in the shadows of the past. The record picks up with two enslaved men named Ben and Sambo, who had been overheard discussing their supposedly "wicked design." They were arrested and jailed, and during this time another slave, Hammon, managed to see them and tell them not to reveal any information. Then the authorities got their hands on Hammon and promised to spare his life if he confessed. He did, naming himself, Ben, Sambo, and one other man, Samson, as the instigators of a rebellion. They were sentenced to starve to death on a gibbet, after which their heads were to be put on poles, bodies cut in quarters and burned. Samson was executed, and after four days on the gibbet, Ben and Sambo broke and agreed to talk. It was too late for Sambo, and he died soon after. Ben's confession—extracted under this torture—named many others, and officials rounded up 200 to 300 slaves.[25]

What Ben revealed appeared to be a complex, extensive plan that involved some three years of plotting, under an "oath of secrecy."[26] The rebels had apparently tried to put their designs into action at three earlier points, attempting and failing to take advantage of the distraction caused by English military expeditions to the nearby French islands in the Caribbean. One of the key differences between this plot and the one uncovered in 1675 is that the new one involved creole slaves who were born on the island. Many of them had elite roles such as grooms, blacksmiths, and carpenters, and thus had "more favour showne them by their Masters." This meant they lived and worked in proximity to their enslavers, rather than being more distant field hands. According to a report by the authorities, the conspirators came from at least 21 plantations, across many parishes. They had organized enough people to put together six regiments, four on foot and two on horses, which they allegedly planned to take from their enslavers.[27]

Over the course of a nearly two-week trial, authorities heard that the plot involved four or five of the "most capable and . . . most trusted" slaves, who were to go in the middle of the night and kill their enslavers, and then take supplies and arms and go to the next plantation and help the attack there. Then they would take the fort in Bridgetown and its stocks of munitions—having arranged for "four or five Irish" allies to get the guards drunk—before going on to "kill the governour and all the planters."[28]

From there, they would set up "a government of their own," in which they would "have enslaved all the black men and women to them and to have taken white women for wives," a claim which suggests that more than a little paranoia was creeping into the English interpretation of events, the only side of the story that was recorded.[29] According to officials' interpretation of Ben's confession, "After the conquest would be the most dangerous time as they could not have agreed upon a Government."[30] The authorities reiterated this belief, that internal division among the conspirators meant inevitable failure, with a subsequent report saying "that after the conquest over the White People they should have met a worse Enemy amongst themselves."[31]

However, the officials' subsequent actions revealed that these plans were not lightly dismissed. The officials were alarmed at what a close call this appeared to be. What followed was another round of the violence that was becoming as much a part of life in Barbados as the regular arrival of slaving vessels. Many more of the alleged leaders were killed in gruesome public executions, 96 in total, with four involving castration.[32]

At the end of October, the Barbados legislature passed a flurry of acts aimed at preventing further plots from materializing, including a law that offered manumission to anyone who informed on a conspiracy.[33] The government also compensated the enslavers for the loss of their "property" in the executions, with at least 42 people receiving payments between 1685 and 1688, some being paid in the very sugar the slaves produced, anywhere from 2,500 to 10,000 pounds.[34]

The governor, James Kendall, later reported to London that he had passed an act enabling him to raise 1,000 troops and 200 volunteers, should they need to suppress an uprising. "Our most dangerous enemies are our black slaves," he wrote. "The frequent alarms to prevent their devilish designs have caused such consternation and so much revealed our weakness that I shall not send so many men off the Island as I intended."[35]

⇤ • ⇥

The English colonies in North America continued to pick up momentum through the seventeenth century, buoyed by rising profits and ongoing settlement. Charles II, restored to the throne, was eager, like many of his supporters, to continue England's expansion in the Americas, partly to fund his spendthrift ways. In 1663, he granted a group of eight men, known as the Lords Proprietors, the charter for a new colony in North America, to be called Carolina, in honor of himself.

Such growth was aided by the Treaty of Madrid in 1670, which resolved the long-running border dispute between English and Spanish territories in North America, granting recognition of the British claims to Virginia. A new English settlement, Charles Town, was established that same year, on the west bank of the Ashley River, among the Kiawah people. A decade later it was moved across the river to Oyster Point, which was on higher ground and had deep water for a port. This would become Charleston, South Carolina. The Carolina colony also maintained a strong connection to Barbados, as some of the settlers and formerly indentured servants moved from there, bringing their enslaved Africans with them. The two colonies would trade, exchanging sugar and slaves for the wood of Carolina, in short supply on an island where the forests had been cleared. As the English spread throughout the colonies, they continued to need labor as well.

To supply them, Charles II granted a charter for the Royal African Company in 1672, declaring a monopoly over all English trade between the west coast of Africa, the Caribbean, and the North American colonies for 1,000 years.[36] In doing so, England, rather than just individual English merchants, officially joined the slave trade, as had other European kingdoms. The French crown also set up monopoly trading companies, with the *Compagnie française des Indes occidentales* (French West India Company) in 1664, *Compagnie du Sénégal* (Senegal Company) in 1673, and *Compagnie de Guinée* (Guinea Coast Company) in 1684. Similarly, Denmark established its own African trading company in 1659, as Sweden had done in 1649. Even Brandenburg-Prussia wanted to get in on the trade, with its Brandenburg African Company in 1682. Along with this, they all had trading forts dotted along the coast of West Africa.

The Royal African Company (RAC) quickly became a powerful force, being the most successful single institution to ply this deadly trade from 1672 until the early 1720s, transporting some 150,000 Africans. Portuguese ships would move more captives overall, but they were not organized into a single company.[37] The RAC also had a lucrative trade in gold from West Africa. So intertwined was the wealth of the nation and slavery in England that the country of Guinea lent its name to the English gold coin, first minted in 1663.* The going was so good

---

* The guinea was worth one pound, one shilling, and stayed in circulation until the early nineteenth century; the informal use of the word denoted twenty-one shillings until the decimalization of the British currency in 1971.

that the Royal African Company produced nearly 25,000 guineas a year between 1675 and 1688.[38]

European commerce with West Africa by the middle of the seventeenth century was robust. One contemporary chronicler, John Barbot, wrote with some detail in 1682 about the goods being offered by French, Dutch, and English traders to Africans. While he worked as a trader there, he observed:

> The French commonly compose their cargo for the Gold Coast trade ... of brandy mostly, white and red wine, ros solis, firelocks, muskets, flints, iron in bars, white and black contecarbe, red frize, looking-glasses, fine coral, sarsaparilla, bugles of sundry sorts and colours, and glass beads, powder, sheets, tobacco, taffeties, and many other sorts of silks wrought, as brocardels, velvets, etc. shirts, black-hats, linen, paper, laces of many sorts, beads, shot, lead, musket-balls, flints, callicoes, serges, stuffs, etc. besides the other goods for a true assortment, which they have commonly from Holland.
>
> The Dutch have Coesveld linen, sleysiger lywat, old sheets, Leyden serges, dyed indigo-blue, perpetuanas, green, blue, and purple. Konings-Kleederen, annabas, large and narrow, made at Haerlem [sic] ... copper pots, brass locks, brass trumpets, pewter, brass, and iron rings ... glass beads, of sundry colours and sizes ... iron bars, brass pins, long and short; brass bells, iron hammers, powder, muskets, cutlaces, cawris, chints, lead balls, and shot, of sundry sorts ... The English, besides many of the same goods above-mentioned, have tapseils broad and narrow, nicanees fine and coarse; many sorts of chints, or Indian callicoes printed, tallow, red painting colours; Canary wine ... China sattins, Barbadoes rum, or aqua-vitae, made from sugar, other strong waters, and spirits, beads of all sorts.[39]

In return the traders received some gold, and thousands of humans.

⋘ • ⋙

A FEW YEARS BEFORE his death in 1658 and while the English Commonwealth remained in power, Oliver Cromwell had managed to launch his "Western Design," which included an ill-fated attack on Hispaniola in April 1655. He hoped to take it—and eventually other territories—from Spain. Instead, in less than a month the English troops retreated, driven out by Spanish retaliation, illness, and a dwindling number of fit soldiers. From 7,000 men at the start, the English were left with around 2,000 who were in any condition to fight.[40]

By the time news of the defeat reached England in July, what was left of the expedition had turned its sights on the nearby island of Jamaica, arriving there in May 1655. The English would not encounter the same level of defense as existed in Hispaniola. The total population, estimated at the time to be 2,000, included Spanish, Portuguese, Africans, and indigenous inhabitants. Although Spain had claimed Jamaica, few settlers had gone there. Mostly, the island was used to provision ships crossing the Atlantic, including slave vessels. The Spanish population was small, only a few hundred, and the enslaved population had been put to work raising animals for food and staple crops for domestic consumption and trade.[41]

The English marched into the capital, Santiago de la Vega (today's Spanish Town), and immediately occupied it, finding that the residents had fled under the misapprehension that this was merely a pirate raid rather than an invasion. Within a week, a treaty of capitulation had been agreed between the English and Spanish.[42] But the transition was not smooth, and many residents refused to comply with the terms, including deportation to other Spanish colonies. The residents of Jamaica also knew the English troops were weak and had been routed in Hispaniola. A group of them decided to fight the English, while others left for neighboring Cuba.[43] The claims to the island were contested and sporadically fought over in the months to come, with some of the fiercest opponents of the English being the so-called Spanish Negroes, mostly maroons living in Jamaica's mountainous interior.[44] The Spanish had promised freedom to any enslaved person who helped fight off these Protestant invaders.[45]

In the Spanish era, runaway slave communities had become firmly planted in the deep hinterland forests, where they could make common cause with the surviving Arawak people. As had been the case in Panama and Colombia, the maroons were formidable foes. Jamaica had ideal conditions for hiding and living well away from Europeans. Its pocked limestone mountains provided some natural defense, while its forests and rivers offered sustenance. When the English arrived, they found records of at least four *palenques*.[46] With the defeat of the Spanish looming, these maroon communities needed to make decisions about the English. They aligned themselves with the Spanish, and guerrilla attacks continued. On two occasions, reinforcements from nearby Spanish territories were sent to Jamaica to take back the island, but those efforts failed.[47] Eventually, the English secured colony status for Jamaica from London and set up a functioning civil government by 1665.[48] The 1670 Treaty of Madrid recognized England's control of Jamaica, but only by Spain—the maroons were another matter.

Jamaica was proving difficult and unpopular, and the English settler population stayed low. The first census in 1662 counted 3,653 white inhabitants and around 702 "negroes."[49] It would grow soon enough, but one pressing order of business was to agree on what to do about the people in the hills. In February 1663, the deputy governor issued a proclamation guaranteeing some of the maroons their freedom: "Juan Luyola [also Juan de Bolas or Juan Lubolo, leader of Lluidas Vale, or today's Worthy Park] and the rest of the negroes of his Palenque, on account of their submission and services to the English, shall have grants of land and enjoy all the liberties and privileges of Englishmen but must bring up their children to the English tongue."

In an effort to end hostilities with all maroons, they extended this arrangement to the other settlements, declaring, "Other negroes in the mountains shall enjoy the same benefits, provided they submit within 14 days after receiving this notice." Then the English put Lubolo in charge, making him the "colonel of the black regiment of militia," and appointing him and others to be "magistrates over the negroes to decide all cases except those of life and death."[50]

However, other maroons turned down the terms, and Lubolo—who apparently had some enemies—was killed soon after in an ambush by another maroon community, led by Juan de Serras, of the "Varmahaly Negroes." The Varmahaly group would go on to be a great source of irritation for the English authorities.⁵¹ Two years later, in 1665, the English issued an order that "any servant or slave killing or bringing in one of those negroes shall be free; any Varmahaly negro bringing in one of his fellows shall be pardoned and set free; and any persons finding out the pallenque of said negroes, shall have and enjoy to their uses all the women, children, and plunder for their reward."⁵²

The attacks, unsurprisingly, kept coming. Throughout this period, more Africans did too. The number of slaves brought to Jamaica from 1659 to 1670 totaled 6,091, nearly double the recorded number brought under Spanish rule.⁵³ Although sugar had done well in Barbados, the landscape of Jamaica was more topographically diverse, and settlers initially cultivated a range of crops. Sugar was planted—a couple of surviving Spanish *ingenios* indicated its earlier cultivation—but so were tobacco, cotton, cocoa, and even a little indigo. Most of these would later be overtaken by sugar, but in this early period, the agriculture was diversified.⁵⁴

In 1670, orders were issued to stop the "outlying negroes, commonly called the Vermahaly Negroes who have committed murders, robberies, and other outrages on his Majesty's subjects."⁵⁵ The Varmahaly *palenque* was never found, and that of Lubolo eventually disappeared. Some maroons fled further into the hills, others joined groups elsewhere. By the end of the 1600s, two significant communities had formed. In the east (windward), one group lived among the rainy, steep slopes of the Blue Mountains, while to the west (leeward) another community lived among the pockmarked karstic hills and valleys north of Montego Bay that the English called "Cockpit Country."⁵⁶ The Windward maroons had links to the older communities of runaways and surviving indigenous people, while the Leeward maroons in Cockpit Country were almost all runaways from the plantations that were being set up across the island.⁵⁷

Because of the strong maroon presence, the English settlement of Jamaica was never going to be straightforward. As they brought in more Africans, they also had to contend with an increasing number of slave rebellions, such as the one in July 1685, when "all Widow Grey's negroes at Guanaboa rose in rebellion."

Late July and early August are in the middle of the Caribbean rainy season, the air thick and humid, the pressure sometimes dropping as hurricanes roll in. In this stormy time, the enslaved people on Widow Grey's plantation, about 22 miles (36 kilometers) west of today's Kingston, rose up. The rebellion started when some people from the Grey and other plantations attacked a house where, according to Lieutenant-Governor Hender Molesworth's report, "there were five and twenty good arms." They "broke through the walls and killed one man." While the widow fled, the rebels grabbed the guns, and they took hold of the neighboring plantation of Major Price. Molesworth claimed the aim of the group, which he estimated to be around 150 people, was "to be masters of all Guanaboa, and have a thousand more negroes to join them." He thought they might have managed this, too, had one enslaved man belonging to Widow Grey not run in the opposite direction and alerted the authorities.

Molesworth sent 70 soldiers and declared martial law, but "the negroes then chose an advantageous hill full of craggy rocks and stumps of trees, where the horse could not possibly approach them." Soldiers who tried to go on foot were shot at, while the group dispersed into two or three parties and headed for the mountains to the north.

As an English report explained, the rebels chose "such inaccessible mountains and rocks for their refuge that it [was] only with the greatest difficulty" that their pursuers were able to catch up with them. Nevertheless, the English managed to "capture about thirty, kill seven outright, and force in about fifty." At a Council of War meeting, it was agreed that one Captain Davis, "with his Indians," would "follow the track of the negroes as well as a beagle follows the fresh scent of a hare." Davis intended "to destroy them all in less than two months . . . and not leave them till he has rendered them incapable of further mischief."[58]

Further mischief, however, would follow.

English officials were still hunting some of the rebels in November, offering rewards for the killing or capture of any of the runaways, including ten pounds for "the negro Cophy," [also Cuffee or Coffee] five pounds for any of his deputies, and two pounds for any other accomplice.[59] The following April, the "killing of the rebel negro Coffee" was reported and someone earned ten pounds.[60] The uprising at Widow Grey's was not the only one; at least five serious revolts occurred between 1673 and 1690, leaving a few planters and far more slaves dead.[61]

The last decade of the century would see another significant rebellion, also in the summer at the end of the harvest period, and possibly on the same day—July 31—as the one at Widow Grey's five years earlier. Some 500 enslaved people, many from the Gold Coast, rose up on Sutton's plantation in Clarendon, "in the mountains of the middle of the Island," to the west of Guanaboa. As on many of the estates developing across the Caribbean, the ratio of enslaved to free was in the slaves' favor, in this case around 90 to 1. When the initial group began their revolt, few people were available to stop them. The rebels were able to seize around 50 muskets, kill a white overseer, and set at least one house on fire before marching to another plantation, though according to a later report, "the slaves therein would not join them." The militia eventually arrived, but hundreds of enslaved people had fled. Some 200 people, including women and children, surrendered, but 200 more remained at large in the mountains, leaving the governor, the Earl of Inchiquin, to observe: "I am afraid that so many will be left as to be a great danger to the mountain plantations." He was also concerned about the large disparity in the numbers of slave and free, writing in his report on the matter: "There were but six or seven whites in that plantation to five hundred negroes, and that is the usual proportion in the Island, which cannot but be a great danger."[62]

Chapter 11

Eruptions

HER NAME WAS unknown, her description unrecorded, apart from the fact that she had a pipe. Like a few of the other "one hundred and thirty five negroes" on a vessel anchored about two miles off the coast of Guinea in August 1682, this woman was having a smoke.[1] The fact of the pipe was not unusual, as the enslaved people were "being allowed by the M'r [Master] to take tobacco." They were supposed to do this in the open air, however, and not between decks, "for fear of mischiefe that may ensue thereby."[2]

Two crew members spotted this woman with her pipe just moments before they were "all blowne into the seas" by an explosion. Second mate John Leyton, who survived the blast and floated on a piece of wood for hours until he was rescued, later told an English Admiralty Court that he remembered carpenter Nathaniel Mills saying he did "see a negro woman betweene deck of the ship who had fire with her which he did take to be a pipe of tobacco lighted which he had got." Apparently Mills "did observe that she did fling the same pipe lighted from her which . . . he really believed did fall into the hole of the said Shippe where the powder was and instantly the shippe thereupon was blowne up."

The name of the vessel, unlike that of the woman, was recorded: the *Dorothy*. It had set off from Tilbury Docks outside London in November 1681 in pursuit of "negroe slaves and gold and Elephants teeth." They had some obvious success in finding human cargo. Because the vessel was destroyed and did not return, an inquest was ordered, in which it was never considered that this woman, who threw her flame into the powder storage between decks, quite possibly knew exactly what she was doing, and had been willing to blow everyone up in order to save herself and her fellow captives from their fate.[3]

⋘ • ⋙

A FEW YEARS LATER, in 1684, Lourenço da Silva Mendonça threw his pipe into a different sort of powder keg. No known portraits of Mendonça have survived, though he was one of the earliest abolitionists from Africa, who took his fight on behalf of others to one of the highest powers in Europe, the pope.

Mendonça was a member of the Ndongo royal family in Pungo-Andongo, a part of what was then the kingdom of Kongo. In 1684 he launched a criminal case at the Vatican over the legality of the entire Atlantic slavery system. This should have brought a level of recognition that lasted well beyond his lifetime, but the trial was buried deep in archives until its exhumation in 2022.[4] Mendonça was "requesting justice," according to the paperwork from the papal office of Propaganda Fide (Propagation of the Faith), which handled the suit. The entire wretched practice of slavery as it existed in the Atlantic, from ship to shore, was, he argued, "against any Divine or Human law."[5]

But Mendonça's journey from Kongo to Rome was anything but straightforward. Indeed, what he was forced to endure only gave him more ammunition. In 1671, the Portuguese forced Mendonça, along with the royal family of Pungo-Andongo, out of their kingdom, and they arrived in Brazil the next year.[6] At the root of the animosity between Mendonça's uncle, King João Hari II, and the Portuguese was the unpopular tribute, or *baculamento* tax, which was paid in captives and which had existed by that time for at least a generation. Mendonça would have been aware of its payment, perhaps watching humans rounded up and put on ships. He also would have listened to the family debates about not paying it, and ultimately seen the stiff penalty they were charged for their attempt to stop. In addition to opposing the tax, João Hari II wanted to wrest back commercial power for the kingdom, and to do so had blocked the trade in enslaved people in 1668.[7] This angered the Portuguese, and they attacked, causing friction and infighting among the nobility, further destabilizing Pungo-Andongo.

Mendonça was likely in his early twenties by that point, and much of his life would have been shaped by the interaction of his family and neighbors with the Portuguese.[8] He spoke the language, and he used a European name, at least in these official contexts. His family were powerful elites—until they were exiles. They were, however, not enslaved, unlike many of the people he would meet in Brazil. There, he would see the other side of the trade taking place in his homeland.

By the late 1600s a significant population of enslaved Africans lived in Brazil, boosted by the earlier Dutch involvement, with some 130,000 captives arriving between 1600 and 1700, around 50,000 from West Central Africa.[9] Alongside the enslaved population was a small but growing number of free people of color. While the majority of captives were forced into servitude, a few were able to gain their freedom—often symbolized by a certificate, or *carta de alforria*—through a process similar to Spanish *coartación*.

Additionally, some enslaved people, known as *negros de ganho*, were permitted to work part of the time for wages. They were allowed to save some of the money, which many put toward buying their freedom, although inevitably the process took years. They did jobs such as carrying messages, hunting, or working with mules or herds, as well as jobs on ships or as coachmen. Others gained their liberty through some sort of militia or military service, for instance during the war against the Dutch in the 1640s. However, in Brazil it was usually the enslaver's prerogative, rather than the crown's, whether to grant freedom after participation in a conflict.[10] Freedom was limited, expensive, and contingent on the willingness of those in power. In addition, all African-descended people, free or enslaved, were forced to endure discrimination at the bottom of Brazil's social hierarchy.

Mendonça was not alone when he arrived in Brazil; 15 other family members were in his group, and some were dispatched to other parts of the colony. His first stop was Salvador, Bahia, then the colonial capital of Brazil, which had been established in 1549. Given the connections between Pungo-Andongo and Brazil, Mendonça and his family might have had some idea of what it would be like. At the very least, they would have quickly learned that they could communicate with many people—and not just in Portuguese but in Kimbundu, because a large number of enslaved Mbundu people were from their southern part of Kongo.[11] By the time of Mendonça's arrival, Africans already outnumbered Europeans two to one in the Bahia region.[12] Mendonça would have arrived to hear familiar intonations of his native language on the other side of the ocean. Salvador, a city on a cliff, was stuffed with forts and churches by the late seventeenth century. The Bay of All Saints that it overlooks provided a peaceful vista when its tranquility was not ruptured by the noisy arrival of ships, or by the crack of leather on skin at the central whipping post, the *pelourinho*.

Mendonça and the other exiled royals made contact with their Mbundu people, and the Portuguese officials fretted that these new arrivals might conspire with the Africans against them.[13] Around the same time that Mendonça and his family arrived, Salvador's city council had asked for the crown's support in destroying the maroon colony of Palmares, "so these enemies can be obliterated."[14] While the connection is tenuous, especially because Palmares was quite a distance from Salvador, there was evidence among the documents of the Portuguese Overseas Council that some of the Kimbundu speakers in Palmares appeared to know of Mendonça's arrival, though whether he visited is unclear.[15]

As significant as the Africans in the runaway *quilombo* might have been, the connections that Mendonça forged with the Catholic black brotherhoods, or *irmandades*, in Salvador were crucial in what was to come. By this point these brotherhoods had continued to grow in Brazil, and in Salvador they had a significant presence, with at least six black and five *pardo* (Afro-European) brotherhoods in existence by the start of the eighteenth century.[16]

Mendonça appears to have had a busy time in Salvador during his first 18 months in Brazil, before a short stay in Rio de Janeiro. In August 1673, Mendonça left for Portugal. Certainly, by the time he arrived in Europe there would have been a sizable black community for him to join in Lisbon. He headed instead to the convent of Vilar de Frades, in Braga, Portugal. Three of his brothers were in the same city, although at different monasteries. He also would have met other Africans there, as this monastery had been receiving students from Kongo, as well as indigenous Brazilians, since the 1530s, nearly 150 years before Mendonça's stay.[17]

Although Mendonça's exact movements are hard to trace, he probably stayed there from 1673 to 1676–1677, studying law and theology, both of which would serve him in the years ahead. After that, he moved to Lisbon and was living there by 1681.[18] In Lisbon, he connected once again with black confraternities. Now, with his legal training and his brotherhood contacts, Mendonça turned to the problem of slavery. Being familiar with the confraternities, he would have known about the 1526 constitution (*compromisso*) that was first issued in São Tomé—as it was the home of the first Brotherhood of the Rosary in Africa—stipulating that it should have the same privileges as those in Lisbon. One key component in this constitution was that all enslaved members could gain their freedom, as well as challenge anyone who was seeking to prevent it, and the brotherhoods had lawyers at hand to do that work. Beyond the legal rights enshrined in the document, it also embodied the idea that freedom was not an individual struggle but a collective effort, an idea that would later resonate through Mendonça's case.[19]

Mendonça threw himself into this work, becoming the attorney general (procurator) for the confraternities of Our Lady of the Rosary of Black Men by 1681. This was in addition to the role he had earlier acquired as a legal representative for black people in Portugal, Spain (Castile), and Brazil, which involved dealing with freedom petitions and lobbying for the liberation of Africans within Iberia and later in Rome.[20]

From this place, a lived triangulation of Africa, Brazil, and Portugal, Mendonça started his long journey to Rome. Among his papers was a letter from Lisbon dated February 15, 1681, that described him as a *homen pardo*. This term, *pardo*, would go on to mean of mixed heritage, but at this time and in this context, it signified someone born free.[21] Now Mendonça was trying to ensure no one would be born a slave.

He was forced to make a stop in Madrid to get a supporting letter for his trip to the Vatican, because the Portuguese prince regent was unable to grant it. In Toledo, Mendonça then waited 18 months for an appointment to a similar legal role for the confraternities of the Rosary of Our Lady of the Star of Black Men in that city and Lisbon. Now his work had a truly international dimension, encompassing brotherhoods in the Americas, along with ones in Africa, Asia, and Europe.[22]

Mendonça had his own profound experiences of exile and of witnessing the destruction of Pungo-Andongo, and as the legal representative for a much larger black world, he had an expanded understanding of the quest for freedom. Mendonça had plenty of personal reasons to attack the Portuguese, but now he was looking beyond his family and to the supreme court of Christendom. He wanted to make sure the pope understood how the entire system of colonial slavery had brought them and other Africans—as well as Amerindians and "New Christians" who had been forced to abandon their Judaism—to this point.

The documentation was extensive, gathered over the years building up to this moment, and was filed in three groups: Mendonça's case; the responses from authorities and enslavers in Spain, Portugal, Italy, and Brazil; and the petitions and writings from confraternities and other interested groups, including from some women.[23] The case began on March 6, 1684, and would last two years, with Mendonça going to the Vatican numerous times. In the dock were Italy (such as it existed then), Spain, and Portugal, as well as enslavers in Spain, Portugal, and Brazil. Unlike the occasional lone cry into the darkness of a priest concerned about the horrors of the slave trade, Mendonça's charges would have been impossible for Pope Innocent XI to brush aside.

Mendonça laid out his case, perhaps in a style that does not align with the flow of modern court cases, but one that involved making arguments and providing evidence all the same. First of all, he explained, Europeans were capturing Africans and selling them like cattle; human beings were being hunted like animals and treated as such, especially in the practice of selling children—and Christian merchants were lying to officials when they claimed that some African groups at war with each other practiced cannibalism and that the merchants were thus "saving" them.[24] He went into great detail about "the cruelties practiced in the Indies against the Blacks and the unjustified methods used to enslave them, from which results the loss of countless Souls."[25]

Beyond this, he claimed four crucial types of law were being broken: human, natural, divine, and civil. What he argued regarding human law was akin to a modern discussion of human rights—that enslavement violated a person's humanity and dignity. In terms of natural law, he drew from the idea that God the creator wanted all humans to have a good life and be treated equally. Mendonça contended that divine or canon law involved respecting the dignity of others, especially as followers of Christianity. And with regard to civil law, the people involved in the slave trade lacked a duty of care toward the enslaved, and were not acting in accordance with existing codes or rules about the treatment of Africans.[26] Humans, all of them, deserved equal treatment, argued Mendonça, who said "the colour of Black and white people is an accident of nature," pointing to the fact that such difference as a basis for enslavement could not be found in the Bible.[27]

The remedy for this state of affairs was to end the slave trade and the practice of slavery.

The black confraternities from the Americas also weighed in, citing suffering and abuses. Six groups in Salvador organized a complaint, and one member, Paschoal Dias, a freed Angolan in that city, travelled to Rome to deliver their memorandum.[28] They spoke openly of "the miserable state in which all the Black Christians of this city and all the other cities of this Kingdom of America are."[29] They, too, wanted to see an end to the system, and they were willing to negotiate what this might look like. At the very least, they wanted freedom in the future and that "the children born from Christian slaves should not remain slaves; so that in the purchase everyone will know they are buying only the life of the present man or woman."[30] As a way to transition the system, Mendonça and the confraternities referred to France's law regarding indentured servants (*engagés*), which the country's parliament passed in 1663. As with similar indenture legislation elsewhere, it allowed emigrants to go to the colonies on a contract of a set number of years, after which they would be freed.[31]

The initial Vatican response to the case was positive, and the pope called on Spain and Portugal to stop being cruel to enslaved Africans. Portuguese authorities rebutted by claiming that they couldn't tell the difference between the Africans supposedly captured in a "just war" and those who were Christian. They also pointed out that Portugal's King Pedro II opposed any "unjust" enslavement of Africans on false pretenses, although whatever his feelings about slavery might have been, the king took no active measures to end it or, for that matter, to forgo the 20 percent tax that was levied on enslaved people bought "legally."[32]

The Spanish crown under Carlos II also professed a desire to do away with slavery, but he was overruled by advisers. Portuguese officials pledged that conditions on board the ships would be improved and that any governor or merchant who committed abuses against the enslaved would be "punished."[33]

The Vatican adjourned the case in 1686, but not without being confronted by a new question that took in the broad sweep of humanity, not just Christians: not the question of who could be enslaved, but whether any human should be forced to suffer in this way.[34] The legal fight was far from over. The pope had accepted some of the ideas that this African abolitionist had presented. Spain and Portugal were told to change their behavior. Portugal passed legislation in the aftermath of the case attempting to prohibit the abuse of enslaved Africans, but it was, inevitably, subject to interpretation.[35]

At any rate, events had already surpassed Portugal and Spain—and even the Vatican. The Dutch and English were in Africa and the Americas, and they didn't care what the Vatican or an African noble thought about their actions. The battle on this new Protestant front would require different tactics. But for Mendonça, what was taking place under the slave trade were crimes against human law, crimes against humanity. In his fight against slavery, Mendonça anticipated the contemporary struggle for human rights.[36]

Chapter 12

Codes

THE RECOMMENDATION LETTER that Mendonça carried with him on his journey to Rome bore a version of the coat of arms of the Propaganda Fide, which depicted two keys and a skull, encircled by writing in Castilian that said: *Morir es lo mas cierto*. "Death is certain." The second part of this well-known saying, "the hour is not," had been removed. To Mendonça it was clear why. Death was everywhere, at all times, for his fellow Africans.[1] Despite his best efforts, this living death would continue for millions.

Around the time Mendonça was making his case to the Vatican, the French crown under Louis XIV (r. 1643–1715) turned its attention to the question of slavery in its colonies, the answer coming in the form of the Code Noir of 1685. Although France's colonial enterprise had begun with some indentured labor, which was referenced in Mendonça's case, that system eventually petered out, as it had done in the English colonies. The French, like other Europeans, moved to using Africans. That practice, coupled with the taking of indigenous lands, meant French colonists also experienced revolts from native and imported slaves, as every other European power had done. However, as the title implies, the "Black Code" was intended for one group of people.

Emerging alongside colonial plantations and the rising numbers of enslaved Africans were growing anxieties. At the root of these concerns was not the question of who could be enslaved, but rather the question of who could be free. In trying to distinguish free from slave, all the European colonies enacted or passed local ordinances that limited what the enslaved could do. Spanish America continued to use the thirteenth-century laws of the *Siete Partidas*, which gave enslaved people some pathways to freedom and also legal recourse to challenge abuse, but France, England, and Holland had no such precedent to follow. Spain, and to a lesser extent Portugal, fashioned its approach to slavery, at least initially, in the context of the long-running war against Muslim states in the *Reconquista*.[2] The Christian countries of northern Europe, meanwhile, had fought among themselves. Despite the varying legal debate over who could be a slave and how slaves should be treated, all eventually converged on a formulation that black meant African, and that meant enslavable. The French called it the Black Code, not the Slave Code.

France's foothold in the Americas was now firm. The economic experiments that started with French pirates were productive and profitable. France had also moved into the African trade, with French ships bringing more than 7,000 captives to the Caribbean between 1670 and 1685, at least half from the Senegambia region.[3] France had claimed and was profiting from a significant collection of island colonies, including Martinique and Guadeloupe (1635), Saint Martin (divided with the Dutch by treaty, 1648), Saint Barthélemy (1648), Saint Lucia (c. 1650), Saint-Domingue (ratified by treaty in 1697), and the South American littoral of Cayenne (French Guiana, 1643).[4]

The Code Noir would try to regulate the treatment of enslaved and free black people across France's lands.[5] However, its first article targeted Jewish people as "enemies of Christianity," commanding them "to be gone within three months" after the code was issued. From there, the focus was on black people. The code required all enslaved people who were brought to France's colonies to be baptized Catholic. It stipulated that the enslaved have Sundays and holy days off; their enslavers had to feed them and look after their health; and families under the same enslaver were not to be sold separately. And while Article XLII allowed enslaved people to be chained together or "beaten with rods and straps," it prohibited "torturing them or mutilating any limb," however that rule might be interpreted.

What the articles attempted to control indicate the kinds of issues that worried the authorities. Sex rated high, or at least its regulation through marriage. Article IX stipulated that free men who had one or more children "during concubinage with their slaves, together with their master who accepted it," would be fined 2,000 pounds of sugar. If the father was the master himself, not only did he have to pay the fine, but "the slave and the children [would] be removed . . . never to gain their freedom." However, that was only in the case of a married man. An unmarried enslaver "should then marry according to the accepted rites of the Church." The enslaved woman would then become free, and the children of this union would be "free and legitimate," and for a while this offered some enslaved women a route to freedom.

Enslavers could not stop slaves from marrying, but if two married people had different owners, any children followed their mother and became the property of her enslaver. If a male slave married a free woman, the children would be free, like their mother, and vice versa, if the mother was enslaved but the father free. Every combination was considered, every interaction had its corresponding rule.

French officials also fretted about marronage and rebellion. Again, much detail went into the code, down to the "large sticks" that an enslaved person was prohibited from carrying in Article XV. A number of points addressed the issue of slave autonomy. In addition to bans on weapons, slaves from different enslavers were prohibited from gathering "under the pretext of a wedding or other excuse." There were to be no meetings, under pain of lashing, in "major roads or isolated locations." Frequent offenders could even face death. Any slave who struck an enslaver or member of his family would "be punished by death." Runaways faced particularly painful castigations, according to Article XXXVII: Someone who had been gone for a month, it read, "shall have his ears cut off and shall be branded with a *fleur de lys* on one shoulder." The second offense would lead to his hamstring being cut and the other shoulder branded. The third time caught, a runaway would be stopped by death.

And finally, the penultimate article, LIX, granted "to freed (*affranchis*) slaves the same rights, privileges and immunities that are enjoyed by freeborn persons." The gulf between this rhetoric and the lived reality in the islands was apparent at the time, and as the free black community grew, so too would its calls for true equality.

While the Code Noir strove to be comprehensive, it was not the first attempt in the Americas to codify the question of slave treatment. That came from Barbados, no doubt as a consequence of the ongoing and unsettling attempts by Africans to run away and resist their enslavement. In 1661, the colony's assembly adopted an act "for the better ordering and governing of Negroes."[6] It, too, articulated a fear about enslaved people meeting, having weapons, or running away, and its clauses mostly focused on this. The act prohibited people from leaving plantations on Sundays and holidays without permission. Clause 5 ordered overseers to check their plantation's "Negroe houses" for runaways twice a week. Every two weeks, the same houses were to be searched for "clubs wooden swords or other mischievous weapons." Sugar was used as both a fine and a reward, for slaves lost and returned.[7] The act was updated after the uncovered conspiracy of 1675 with provisions to further "restrain the wanderings and meetings of Negroes at all times," and prohibited the beating of drums or blowing of shells.[8] In 1688, the assembly brought in a new Act for the Governing of Negroes, though its concerns echoed that of its predecessor.[9] Its preamble expressed a clear frustration—and subtext of worry—declaring:

> Negroes and other Slaves brought unto the People of this Island . . . are of barbarous, wild, and salvage [sic] Natures . . . wholly unqualified, to be governed by the Laws, Customs and Practices of our Nations. It therefore becoming absolutely necessary, that such other Constitutions, Laws and Orders should be in this Island framed and enacted for the good regulating and ordering of them, as may both restrain the Disorders, Rapines and Inhumanities to which they are naturally prone and inclined.

Similarly, Virginia found itself forced to constantly rewrite its rules, to adapt them to circumstances on the ground. A 1640 ordinance prohibited black people from bearing arms. In 1661, a law stipulated that the "negro womens [sic] children [were] to serve according to the conditions of the mother."[10] This was followed in 1667 by an act confirming that "the conferring of baptism doth not alter the condition of the person as to his bondage or Freedom."[11] Christianity would provide no route out of slavery; the promised land would have to come in the afterlife. In 1680, Virginia passed an "act for preventing Negroes Insurrections" to stifle any further plots, officials having already been unnerved by the white-led Bacon's Rebellion in 1676. That conflict, initially triggered by Native American raids, turned into a short-lived war between elite Virginians and a group of disaffected colonists, which had indentured servants and enslaved people among its ranks. It was suppressed the following year—though not before the rebels burned down Jamestown in September 1676.[12] The 1680 act declared, "The frequent meeting of considerable numbers of negroe slaves under pretence of feasts and burials is judged of dangerous consequence." It went on to prohibit "any negroe or other slave" to carry arms, leave his enslaver's property without permission, or "lye hid and lurking in obscure places."[13] The Dutch joined the English and French in creating laws and codes in the late 1600s, including a law prohibiting marriage between blacks and whites.[14]

Even though slavery reduced humans to the status of "property," the laws that colonists created to govern them forced everyone to confront slaves' humanity, even if they were unwilling to admit it.[15] While a rhetorical effort was made to strip all enslaved beings of their humanness and equate them with beasts, there simply was no escape from the reality of the personhood of every single captive brought to or born in the Americas.

Not all colonists were insensitive to these contradictions and hypocrisies, though what they were able or willing to do about them was limited. Some Protestant groups began to question the entire enterprise, including the Quakers, many of whom had settled in the Americas. That sect's founder, George Fox, called for slaves to be freed after a term of service, prompted by a 1671 trip to Barbados.[16] Indeed, Quakers on that island soon found themselves scrutinized by the authorities because they were bringing enslaved people to their religious services. By 1676, "An Act to Prevent the People called Quakers, from bringing Negroes to their Meeting" had been introduced.[17]

In North America, a group of Quakers drew up a protest letter in 1688, known as the Germantown Petition, which criticized human trafficking and addressed the ways blackness and slavery were becoming intertwined, saying: "Now tho they are black, we can not conceive there is more liberty to have them slaves, as it is to have other white ones . . . have these negers not as much right to fight for their freedom, as you have to keep them slaves?"[18] Nonetheless, the Quaker founder of Pennsylvania, William Penn, had already given up any sort of fight to limit the terms of slavery. The colony of Pennsylvania, like the others, depended too much on it.[19] Noble sentiments gave way to economic realities, and even gradual measures of abolition remained a century away in Pennsylvania.

⋘ • ⋙

WHILE WHITE QUAKERS were pondering slavery in North America, the residents of Palmares in Brazil were preparing yet again to defend their freedom by force. The Portuguese had reached the limit of their patience. Captives fled to Palmares, while its residents continued to make raids and participate in contraband trade with some Portuguese settlers. Officials had been trying to destroy the colony on a regular basis since 1672, sending in armed expeditions every year or so, leading to a complaint in 1681 that "our campaigns have not had the slightest effect on the Negroes of Palmares . . . who seem invincible."[20] By 1677 the entire area held at least 10 towns or enclaves.[21]

By this point, a leader known as Ganga Zumba was in charge, his title possibly based on the Bantu term *nganga a nzumbi*, meaning priest or spiritual leader.[22] One report, from a member of a failed expedition in 1676–1677, described him as king, and gave details of his domain. He lived in a place believed by the Portuguese to be called *Macoco*—apparently named for a monkey (*macaco*) that had died on that spot—which also functioned as the capital, and had about 1,500 houses. According to the report, Ganga Zumba lived in "a palatial residence, [with] *casas* for members of his families, and is assisted by guards and officials who have, by custom, *casas* which approach those of royalty." His own household was large, and he reportedly had three wives, "one mulatto and two *crioulas* [native black] women."[23] Ganga Zumba, to European observers, appeared to be "treated with all respect due a Monarch . . . they address him as Majesty."[24]

By the 1670s, the inhabitants of Palmares would have included a significant creole (*crioulo*) Afro-Brazilian population, though captive Africans continued to arrive. However, Ganga Zumba and the leaders of the smaller *mocambo* settlements were all Africans, which meant that, to some degree, their political structures probably incorporated many African traditions. The diversity within the communities caused no significant divisions, especially in dealing with the Portuguese.[25]

After the failure of 1676–1677, Ganga Zumba sued for peace, as he had done before, whenever a new Portuguese governor arrived in Pernambuco determined to destroy Palmares. The resulting agreement this time allowed Palmares and the Portuguese to continue to trade, as well as ensuring "the liberty of those born in Palmares," and securing the release of a group of *palmarista* captives.[26] However, the question of Palmares's territorial limits was not settled and, within a few years, tensions resurfaced as colonists encroached on maroon land. In 1679, a new leader emerged, known as Zumbi, the nephew of Ganga Zumba, who killed his uncle and succeeded him. Zumbi was ready to take on the Portuguese, tearing up the treaty and returning to battle. Portuguese chroniclers described Zumbi training his soldiers to be "very handy in the use of all arms."[27] Indeed, six more colonial expeditions went in, and limped back out, between 1680 and 1688, the Portuguese hemorrhaging men and money.[28] Even Pope Innocent XI, in the wake of Mendonça's case, instructed Jesuit Antonio Vieira to take "the blessing of Christ to Palmares" in 1689, though the priest opted not to go.[29]

It took an epic final push, involving a band of frontiersmen composed of some Portuguese and some Portuguese-Amerindians, who lived near São Paulo and were skilled in the sort of rural conflict that destroying Palmares would require. A regiment of these *paulistas* arrived in 1692, though nearly 200 died and another 200 deserted along the way. In the end, the Portuguese used around 6,000 troops.[30]

The urgency had been intensified by the discovery of gold to the south, in 1693, in an area that would bear its geological future in its name, *Minas Gerais* (General Mines). The presence of maroon *quilombos* was a threat to this enterprise. Palmares had to be destroyed, lest the enslaved people who were going to be sent into the gold mines try to go there instead.

Over a couple of years the paulistas managed to eliminate many of the smaller *mocambos,* driving their inhabitants into one central location. By February 1694, the end was in sight. The fighting was now hand-to-hand, culminating in a six-week siege. Zumbi persisted, but the Portuguese caught him in the end.

For the Portuguese, Zumbi, like the entire Palmares settlement, had to be made an example of. The following year, on November 20, he was executed, and his severed head was taken to Recife to be put on display, in part "to kill the legend of his immortality."[31] That legend never died. In other tellings of this story, Zumbi leapt off a precipice, avoided the rocks below, and escaped, keeping the story of Palmares and its near century of freedom alive. Today in Brazil, November 20 marks the *Dia Nacional de Zumbi e da Consciência Negra* (the National Day of Zumbi and Black Consciousness).

⋖ • ⋗

Building these slave societies required the creation of several fictions—such as the "good treatment" demanded by the slave codes—which were backed up with whips and guns, physical assault, sexual abuse, and the mental anguish that this system demanded. The biggest story, the largest fiction, was that somehow one group of people could be free and another not, and yet they could be yoked together under a banner of political "freedom." The English philosopher John Locke, in talking about freedom as a natural right, used a particularly telling example: a slave's suicide. He wrote, "It is in his power, by resisting the will of his master, to draw on himself the death he desires."[32] Locke was ostensibly, or at least philosophically, opposed to slavery, at least political slavery, as he wrote in his *Two Treatises of Government* (1689): "Slavery is so vile and miserable an estate of man, and so directly opposite to the generous temper and courage of our nation; that it is hardly to be conceived that an Englishman, much less a gentleman, should plead for it." However, on a personal level Locke was deeply embedded in the English colonial project, and intimately involved with the establishment of Carolina. As secretary to Anthony Ashley Cooper, one of the Lords Proprietors, Locke helped craft the colony's 1665 charter.[33] Locke was also a shareholder in the Royal African Company, and supported the "just war" rationale for slavery.[34] Freedom, as was already clear to anyone who had had it "given" to them, was conditional and subject to the sorts of contradictions espoused by thinkers like Locke.

Richard Ligon saw a more grounded example of freedom among the free black people he encountered in mid-seventeenth-century Barbados. Those people, he explained, wore "upon the small of one of their legs, the badge of their freedome; which is a small peece of silver, or tinne, as big as the stale of a spoone; which comes round about the leg; and by reason of smoothnes, and lightnes, is no impediment to their going."[35]

So fragile was their freedom, they felt compelled to wear a symbol of it at all times.

Chapter 13

Accelerations

THE CAPTIVES ON board the *Clare* knew what lay ahead. In 1729, more than two centuries into this trade, there was no mystery about what was beyond the water. Slavery was now firmly entrenched in the Americas, and its captives were forced into every area of colonial life: on country estates, in urban households, in the dockyards and aboard ships, or below the earth, mining gold.

In the case of the *Clare,* it left West Africa, destined for the bustling colony of South Carolina, where fortunes were being created by the rice that could be grown in its marshy lowlands. By 1740, that colony exported 90,000 barrels of rice, worth £220,000, or around £60 million today.[1] As the decades of the eighteenth century progressed, the colonies prospered. Virginia and Maryland would harvest 10 times the amount of tobacco in 1770 as they had in 1700, from 20 million to 220 million pounds.[2] Further south, the gold rush in Brazil was proving profitable, while since the 1500s the number of sugar *engenhos* had increased six-fold, to 146 by 1710, well on its way to 855 by the end of the nineteenth century.[3]

Of all the commodities produced in the Americas, sugar would end up being the most valuable throughout the 1700s.[4] By the 1770s, the annual net profit of the British West Indian colonies could be estimated at £3 million, or £685 million in today's money, though other estimates range higher.[5] The wealth generated on the sugar plantations of the Caribbean—although it fluctuated as the sugar market did—provided the means for their owners to fund lavish lives in Britain. It also allowed them to enter politics and form the West India lobby to protect their own interests.[6]

Refiners and merchants processed and sold the sugar, earning profits in Britain while also forming a long chain of commodities that reached from Africa to the Americas to Europe. Textiles, guns, and other manufactured goods were traded in Africa or taken to the colonies. The long human trafficking voyages required provisions like salted cod, and the ships required sails, ropes, nets, and iron wares such as coffles and chains. The very building of the ships themselves required small armies of craftsmen and laborers. The trade among three continents created an entire economic ecosystem.

The eighteenth century had opened with the War of the Spanish Succession, triggered in 1701 by the death of the Habsburg king Carlos II, who had no heir. It was resolved in 1714 by the ascension of the Bourbons to the Spanish throne, with the crowning of Felipe V. The peace treaties that brokered the end to what had turned into a continental conflict also granted Great Britain—now including Scotland under the Acts of Union of 1707—the lucrative *asiento* slaving contract. This meant that Britain had a monopoly contract to take thousands of enslaved people to Spanish America. The South Sea Company would fulfill it. This was one of the factors in the company's rising stock price, which created a financial bubble that burst a few years later, to the ruin of many investors. But this was not quite the same pain as that suffered by the 36,000 captives who disembarked from company ships between 1714 and 1750, arriving after nightmarish voyages in Spanish America and the Caribbean, mostly Rio de la Plata and Jamaica.[7] The Royal African Company earlier lost its monopoly, but it still managed to deliver some 13,000 captives in the same period. Overall, the 3,000 voyages made on all ships sailing under the British flag—not just the South Sea or Royal African companies—resulted in the total trafficking of an estimated 760,000 humans between 1714 and 1750.[8]

The slave trade could generate enormous profits. In one ten-year period, from 1783 to 1793, the value of some 850 slaving voyages on Liverpool ships alone was around £15 million. Sometimes voyages could have returns of 100 percent, other times they could sink without a trace.[9] But the entire enterprise of slavery, be it slave ships at sea or plantations on land, came with risk—crops could fail, ships could wreck or disappear. Much of the wealth that was generated from this complex enterprise was not in cash, but instead bound up in debt. The system relied on credit, mortgages, and promissory notes. Bankruptcies were not uncommon. The development of an insurance trade, with Lloyd's of London being one of the earliest and best-known houses, led to the creation of financial products to cover the loss of or damage to slave ships and their human cargo.[10] Multiply this sketch of the eighteenth-century British Atlantic economy across the other European powers and their colonies in the Americas, and the profits were almost incalculable, as was the suffering that begat them.

A life of enslavement was to be the lot of the captives on board the *Clare*, until events took a different turn. The ship "was not got 10 Leagues [30 miles] on her Way," sailing south from Cape Coast Castle (Ghana), where the captives had embarked, when, catching the crew unawares, "the Negroes rose and [made] themselves Master of the Gunpowder and Fire Arms."

There are no details in the records about how this uprising was planned and carried out, whether the captives had plotted as they waited in the fort, or acted on a quick decision, one person seizing just the right pause, grasping a sliver of opportunity. The crew were forced to flee in a longboat to Cape Coast Castle, while the captives ran the galley ashore and "made their Escape."[11]

This extraordinary absconding scarcely received a mention in the newspapers of the time, such news mostly reserved for private or commercial correspondence.[12] Such losses, by revolt or worse, death on board, were one of the trade's grimmest realities. Another 197 voyages took place in 1729, the same year as the *Clare*, embarking 60,000 people in Africa but only delivering just under 51,500 to their destinations. The losses of 15 percent on average were marked in a ledger somewhere, with the names of the dead usually unrecorded.[13]

The captives on the *Clare* avoided the fate of millions of others and were able to save themselves. Only a few could manage such an escape, but as those aboard the *Clare* showed, it was possible—and it was expected that they would try. By the 1700s, ship captains had their ideas and stereotypes about who was liable to rebel, for instance people from the Gold Coast (Akan and Coromantee), Aja (Ewe) people brought from the Bight of Benin, and Ibibio people from Bonny (Nigeria).[14]

Far from being isolated incidents, these rebellions happened on around one in ten ships. Some historians have argued that this rate of escape went some way toward reducing interest on the part of potential investors, and thus reduced the overall volume of slave ships.[15] Indeed, those rebels may have, through their direct actions and the indirect consequences of onboard rebellions, saved countless others from being forced across the ocean over the four centuries of the slave trade.[16]

Ship captains often forced captives to work on the ships that carried them across the Atlantic, cooking, cleaning the decks, helping to make repairs, and even participating in the actual sailing.[17] Some captains were enslavers themselves and took their captives to sea with them. Maritime work led to some enslaved people becoming ship pilots, a vital task on vessels that could run aground or crash into reefs because the cartography remained incomplete. Such work required knowledge of local waterways, tides, and currents, and because of this, it came with some level of compensation.[18] Some pilots were able to carve out a degree of autonomy, though they continued to be forced to live under the category of "slave." The presence of an enslaved person at the helm of a ship inverted the existing hierarchies and often caused white sailors to grumble, though they usually conceded the black sailors' competence at avoiding hazards and disasters.[19] The maritime world was also one in which information and news moved from the ship decks to the docks, and black sailors were important conduits. For a few, the seas represented freedom, a place to enjoy what limited liberties they had been granted. Free black people had been travelling the Atlantic with Europeans since the earliest Spanish explorers and conquistadors set sail.[20] They also found opportunity on the pirate ships that plied the waters. The feared pirate Blackbeard, who terrorized the North American coast, had 60 black sailors in his crew of 100 at the time of his death in 1718.[21]

Other captives might have better chances in port, such as the 16-year-old Quoshey (or Quashey from Kwasi, an Akan name meaning "born on Sunday") who absconded from Captain Edward Archer while in Bell Wharf in Shadwell, London, on Christmas Day, 1700, wearing "a Plush Cap with black fur, a dark Wastcoat, a speckled Shirt, [and], old

Callamanca Breeches." The newspaper advertisement offered a one guinea reward for his return and identified Quoshey as "belonging" to Archer, and having E.A. "branded on his left Breast."[22] Quoshey was able to use the Christmas holiday to his advantage, fleeing like an urban maroon to one of the free black communities in East or South London, not far from the docks but where perhaps he could elude his captors and establish an autonomous life for himself on land.

<< • >>

REVOLTS AND CONSPIRACIES were not limited to slave ships and plantations but also became part of the fabric of urban life, as the inhabitants of the growing town of New York discovered in 1712. The Dutch by this time had been long gone from New Amsterdam, and in their place increasing numbers of English arrived, along with Africans. Between 1600 and 1700 around 1,500 captives were recorded as arriving in New York, but between 1700 and 1800, the number of captives arriving from Africa rose to at least 5,700, with some 3,300 more coming through the inter-American trade, via places like Jamaica and Barbados.[23] The city was also developing as a hub of commerce and finance, so many merchants involved in various aspect of the slave trade would eventually be located there.

Most Africans who arrived in New York were not destined to stay there but were sent on to New England or elsewhere. By 1712, the city and colony of New York had a population of around 5,300 white and 1,000 black people.[24] The black community, though numerically small, reflected the growing diversity of the people forced into this trade: Some people were locally born creoles; others were from the West Indies, West Africa, and the Malagasy (East Africa). Those from Spanish America were sometimes called "Spanish Indians." The New York governor at the time reported that he had "received petitions from several of these Spanish Indians . . . representing to me that they were free men subjects to the King of Spain." These petitions were probably of little avail, because being an indigeous American was no safeguard against enslavement in New York, though by 1706 the colony's assembly clarified that "negroes only shall be slaves."[25] Most of the black population was enslaved, and after the events of 1712, the path to freedom would be strewn with even more obstacles.

As enslaved people worked in New York, officials worried about their proximity to each other.[26] This was not a plantation society, with large stretches of land and rural isolation, but it was also not the recognizable urban crush of later years. Rather, like many places along the North Atlantic coast, it was a small colonial city with a few basic roads leading to a fort on the edge of a waterway, with farms further out, and an indigenous hinterland. Here, some enslaved people stayed in the town, with skilled workers employed in jobs such as carpentry or sail-making, and others working in domestic or agricultural settings in and around New York.[27] However, in 1702 an act "For the Regulating of Slaves" was introduced, followed in 1708 by "An Act for Preventing the Conspiracy of Slaves." This legislation came after an enslaved Native American named Sam and his black wife were executed for murdering their enslaver, William Hallett, and his family on Long Island. Although the violence did not spread beyond the seven people killed, two other black men were also executed in connection with the crime, and it remains unknown whether this was part of a larger conspiracy. Whatever the case, the authorities were concerned enough to enact legislation.[28] By 1711, rumors circulated that some of the recent Coromantee (Akan) and Mina (Popo or Papa) arrivals from the Bight of Benin were ready to revolt in response to their harsh treatment, though for the moment all was quiet.

April 6, 1712, started like any other Sunday, with the city's residents going to church and returning to their homes. Once it had grown dark, the spring day cooling with the setting of the sun, a group of plotters slipped away to a nearby orchard in the East Ward of the city, and by midnight around 25 people had gathered.[29] Unlike their counterparts on many of the Caribbean islands, enslaved people in New York were not in the majority. They were outnumbered by the Europeans, so those gathering that night made a point of arming themselves well, bringing to the meeting place rifles, pistols, swords, daggers, and any other weapons they could lay their hands on.

The arms were distributed as the conspirators huddled under the bare trees. A free black man called Peter the Doctor performed a ceremony, giving the plotters "a powder to rub on their Cloths which make them so confident," after they had sworn their loyalty to each other "by Sucking ye blood of each Others hands." Both actions probably had some connection to Akan military practices, such as using a substance called *hyire*—a white clay believed to bring a layer of supernatural protection to warriors going into battle.[30]

By around 2:00 a.m., they were ready. Cuffee, an Akan man enslaved by baker Peter Vantilborough, struck first. He approached his enslaver's bakery, a block from City Hall, set an outhouse on fire, and then returned to the orchard. They waited for the blaze to grow and for people to come and put it out. The public soon stirred, roused by a ringing bell in the fort.

After a good crowd had assembled to douse the flames, the rebels attacked. As a later report described it, they "stood prepared . . . to kill everybody that approached to put [the fire] out."[31] They fired on the assembled people, and then they charged. At least nine people were killed in the subsequent commotion.

News quickly reached the governor, and troops were dispatched, while the rebels withdrew to the woods near the "Negro Burial Ground" on the northern edge of the city, a place they anticipated whites would either be reluctant to enter or not be familiar with.[32] However, within 24 hours most of the rebels—and many others—had been rounded up, with some 70 people arrested, except for six of the rebels, who killed themselves rather than submit.[33] The militia kept hunting until all the organizers were found. The legislation of 1708 was clear: A slave found guilty of involvement in a conspiracy would be executed. The enslaver of a rebel, however, would receive financial compensation.[34]

An obvious question is missing from the testimony at the subsequent hearing: Why did they rebel when the odds against them were so terrible? No clear hiding places existed, such as the caves of Hispaniola or the mountains of Jamaica. If the rebels had plans to retreat into the woods, aided by Native Americans, there was no indication of this, and they were captured nearby. It's possible that some of them were so recently arrived, they did not have time to become familiar with the area.³⁵ Given that many of the white people who were attacked or killed were prominent in this colonial community, as well as being enslavers themselves, perhaps it was a revenge-suicide mission. Governor Robert Hunter later wrote in a report that the slaves "had resolved to revenge themselves, for some hard usage, they apprehended to have received from their masters (for I can find no other cause)."³⁶

The trial began within a week, while the public hysteria lasted longer. The jury identified 14 people as being involved, including Cuffee, who lit the fire, though he later turned crown's witness, as did a man named Dick. In the final tally 39 were indicted for murder or as accessories to it, and another four for assault with intent to kill.³⁷

The sentences handed down to 20 people in the weeks that followed were brutal, torturous deaths. Some were broken on a wheel, left to die in chains, burnt alive, or hanged. They were referred to only by their given names: two men named Caesar, Claus, Tom Furnis, Hannibal, Kitto, Mingo, three men named Quaco, Quasi, Robin, Sam, a woman named Abigail, Titus, Toby, and three men named Tom.³⁸

Another woman who had been arrested, known as Sarah, avoided the noose because she was pregnant. However, she was forced to spend the rest of her pregnancy in jail, causing the governor to later make the case for her pardon, saying that "she is since delivered, but in a woeful condition ever since . . . and . . . has suffer'd more than death by her long imprisonment."³⁹

The entire episode further panicked the white colonists. A curfew was established for any black person over the age of 14, with a lashing as punishment for those who broke it. It became more difficult to manumit a slave, with the requirement of a £200 deposit, which was often many times the actual price of the person. Freed people could not own real estate after 1712, and any person who entertained slaves or sold them alcohol could be fined, with free black people receiving double the penalty. These rules were crafted to limit the number of free black people in New York, and to keep them away from the enslaved.⁴⁰

The governor who oversaw this trial and its aftermath, Robert Hunter, would take up the governorship of Jamaica in 1727. There, he would face a similarly determined and far more practiced adversary: the maroons.

Chapter 14

Connections

GOVERNOR HUNTER STRUGGLED after his arrival in Jamaica. Here, the white population was tiny compared to the enslaved, and the maroon settlements were sizable. While New York easily attracted white settlers, Jamaica presented more challenges to would-be planters and estate managers. Hunter wrote of their struggles in 1730, saying, "Of late there has been many depredations and violencys committed upon the frontier settlements to the great discouragement of new setlers." He was referring to people around Port Antonio, on Jamaica's north coast, who had to contend with the Windward maroons living in the nearby Blue Mountains.

Maroons weren't Hunter's only challenge. He also told the Council of Trade and Plantations they needed a method of "better regulating slaves and rendering free negros and mulattos more usefull." He complained that "the number of free mulattos, and free negros daly increase, and their houses and habitations are often times receptacles of rebellious, and runaway slaves." What's more, free people were arming the runaways, "which may prove of pernitious consequence to the Island."[1] Population figures from this time in the parish of Saint Andrew, in the south of the island, give a snapshot of the situation: white people, 477; free people of color, 34; enslaved workers, 7,220.[2]

Some aspects of the maroons' strategy may have caught Hunter off guard. Not only was the topography of Jamaica diverse and difficult, the connections between the island and its neighbors and their ever-changing political alliances posed challenges. For instance, in a July 1730 report, Hunter enclosed information about a man who had been to Panama and claimed he was told there were "30,000 rebellious negroes in Jamaica, and that they had written to the Governor of Caicas [sic], (? Carracas) [sic] offering to put the island into the possession of the King of Spain, if he would grant them their freedom."[3] The following year, Spanish neighbors surfaced again, with Hunter writing that "a negro woman ... who has been some years with the rebels confirms the account we had of their correspondence with the Spaniards of Cuba."[4]

Between 1665, when the English gained control of Jamaica, and 1730, some 250,000 Africans had been brought to the colony, though many were sent onward. Of those who remained in Jamaica, there were significant numbers of Coromantees from the Gold Coast, as well as people from the Bight of Benin and Dahomey.[5] The maroons naturally benefited from such a dramatic increase in the African population, and the communities that had taken shape in the 1600s under the Arawak and earliest Africans brought by the Spanish were now sizable enough forces to pose a legitimate threat. However, not every runaway wanted to join the maroons, nor was every enslaved person necessarily welcome. A considerable degree of diversity existed among Africans, too often misunderstood and misrepresented by the authorities. Maroons were trying to protect their freedom, but they were also creating a new world from the old, building on cultures like Akan or Angolan, sometimes leading to conflict among themselves.[6]

Today, visitors scamper on the beach and cruise ships pull into the port of Montego Bay, but the hills of Cockpit Country remain well away from most tourist trails. Even now, the road to Accompong is winding, its coordinates still not accurately mapped on GPS. Here, nestled in the green carpet of the cockpits, one group of self-emancipated people created a community and became known as the Leeward maroons.

They elected a man named Cudjoe in the 1730s to lead them. He was born sometime around 1700 and may have been the son of the 1675 rebel leader Cudjoe, meaning he would have been born into marronage and not captivity.[7] His British adversaries later described him as a "bold, skilful and enterprising man."[8] He had four leaders under his command, with two possibly being his brothers, though the kinship may have been symbolic: Accompong and Johnny. Also aiding him were Cuffee and Quao. Such Akan "day" names—Cudjoe (Monday), Quao (Thursday), Cuffee (Friday)—indicate Coromantee/

Gold Coast heritage.[9] Cudjoe's maroons were considered more "African" than other maroons in their political, cultural, and military practices, in part exemplified by his strong centralized leadership. He also required runaways from other African ethnicities to assimilate, and there were conflicts with larger, non-Akan groups, some of which were eventually incorporated—sometimes by conquest—into this maroon community. Cudjoe also required that his followers use English by the 1730s, though colonial records claim they used their own "Wild Negro Court Language" for rituals.[10] Life in the maroon settlement was traditional in the sense that the men were warriors and hunters, while the women for the most part farmed and cooked, and Cudjoe was thought to have a number of wives.[11]

Cudjoe and his fellow maroons had an intimate knowledge of their unique landscape, which they could use to their advantage to lure in militias, ambush them, and escape before the soldiers could get their bearings.[12] Finding their towns was an immense physical challenge: up hills, through forests, along rivers, into valleys, caves, and gorges. The maroons used conch shells and a curved instrument known as an *abeng*, fashioned from a cow horn, that gives a low, mellow sound, to communicate and make noise, calling out and taunting the soldiers, using sound to lead militias astray and exacerbate their dislocation. Maroons could also blend in with the slaves when needed, for instance at a Sunday market, and obtain necessities, including gunpowder and shot, by trading with locals.[13] So great were the difficulties in suppressing them that Governor Hunter brought in Miskito Amerindians from coastal Honduras, along with their dogs, to track down the maroons, as well as 800 British regulars from Gibraltar in 1731 to supplement the roughly 200 troops on the island and the militia.[14]

But Cudjoe and his people were only half of Hunter's problems. In the northeast of the island the Windward (eastern) maroons were spread among three main villages in today's Portland Parish, all named after powerful priestesses of obeah, spiritual practices based on African traditions: Nanny, Diana, and Molly. In general, the Windward maroons drew from their indigenous predecessors, and were arranged more like a confederacy, with no single person in charge.[15] Among the many people associated with the Windward communities, Nanny was perhaps the most famous.

Nanny is everywhere in Jamaica. Her face—firmly set, eyes staring into the distance as if she is about to enter battle—is printed on 500-dollar notes in the island's currency.[16] She is the only official female national hero of Jamaica. For someone whose spirit looms large, very little was recorded about her life in official documents, though oral sources run far wider and deeper.[17] Only four mentions of Nanny appear in the archival records, which are complicated by the fact that her name itself was commonly used by other people, since it is an anglicized version of the Ashanti words *nana*, meaning leader or respected female elder, and *ni*, meaning "first mother."[18]

In one version of events, Nanny is an obeah woman, or priestess, who exits the story early after being killed in 1733 by an enslaved man named Cuffee, who was rewarded for this.[19] She reappears in 1735, when she was said to be involved in killing three white men and an escaped Ibo slave named Cupid. In these skirmishes with the British her legend was forged. She was thought to have supernatural powers, such as being able to catch or deflect enemy bullets and shoot them back, as well as exceptional tactical skills.[20] She appears again in 1739, in the memoirs of a British soldier involved in later peace negotiations, this time mentioned as an obeah woman.[21]

Nanny was not the only Windward captain—she was joined by Cuffee, Kishee, and Quao, their names also pointing to Akan heritage.[22] The Windward maroons were able to use the ridges and folds of the Blue Mountains in the east to their advantage, but, as Hunter's letters illustrate, the British wanted to develop the northeast coast, so these communities were under more pressure from the militia than the Leeward maroons. Hunter tried to rout both groups, but his militia was no match for them. Not only did the maroons have a deeper knowledge of the island, but many of them may have been warriors in Africa and so were excellent soldiers. For every British gain, there were human losses not only in the form of casualties but also in the defection of so-called baggage Negroes, who assisted the British in their attacks. Even offers of freedom to any slave who captured or killed a maroon yielded few bodies.[23]

By March 1732, the British had taken the maroon village of Nanny Town, but with the ongoing defections of black soldiers, the high cost of these expeditions, and the general military incompetence, they could not keep up the momentum. Some of the maroons from the besieged enclave joined the nearby settlement of Guy's Town, while others scattered. However, by 1733, the maroons managed to take back Nanny Town.[24] According to one report, Nanny Town was guarded by "300 men all armed with guns . . . their present head is call'd Cuffee, and he is distinguish'd by wearing a silver-lac'd hatt [sic] and a small sword, no other daring to wear the like." Guy's Town was described as having "a great deal of open ground around it, in which is plenty of coco, sugar canes, plantains, mellons, yams, corn, hog and poultry. The number of men is about 200, and a greater number of women."

These two towns were forced into an uneasy alliance, driven by the constant encroachment of the British. They cooperated, but relations soured when the British torched Nanny Town in 1734, driving its inhabitants to take refuge in Guy's Town.[25] After this point, the groups further splintered. Nanny and some of her followers moved eight miles to the east, while other bands of fighters from Nanny Town and Guy's Town marched west, through 100 miles of mountains, toward Cudjoe and the Leeward maroons around Accompong Town. Cudjoe, however, was hesitant to accept them, not wanting to be drawn into their conflict.[26] At one point, he is said to have gestured toward some nearby graves, telling his new arrivals that "people were buried whom he executed for murdering white men contrary to his orders."[27] Despite his misgivings, he let his fellow maroons stay. They left a few months later, still managing to evade the British troops that pursued them.[28]

Governor Hunter died in 1734, with the maroon situation unresolved. A successor, Edward Trelawny, arrived in 1738, determined to put an end to the ongoing and costly war. Trelawny, along with John Guthrie, a militia colonel and planter, pushed for a treaty. The governor later wrote: "Indeed I am persuaded myself by what I have seen of the country, and it is the universal opinion of those that have been the oftenest out on parties and the most acquainted with it, that it is impossible to reduce the rebels by force." He put the blame on the "thick woods, craggy mountains and stony precipices," but he knew there were many other factors, not least an outnumbered white population battling skilled soldiers.[29] Fighting continued, wearing down both sides. By the following February, Colonel Guthrie told the governor "we are now masters of Cudjoe town," though that was a bit of an exaggeration.[30] Cudjoe had, however, agreed to talks—though he held the cards.

The negotiations were at a place of his choosing, near what would become known as Trelawny Town (today's Flagstaff), about 15 miles (25 kilometers) inland from Montego Bay. The talks lasted 10 days, resulting in a treaty on March 1, 1739. In the British version of events, Cudjoe "threw himself to the ground, embracing Guthrie's legs, kissing his feet, and asking his pardon," with the other maroons following suit.[31] An 1803 account by Robert Charles Dallas, who was born more than a decade after these events, contains an etching based on the author's description, in which a short and stocky Cudjoe grips his gun, his body tight and coiled, looking warily at the tall, elegant Guthrie, who is extending his hand in a gesture of peace. One of Cudjoe's lieutenants stands nearby with his back to the viewer, presumably keeping watch for a British ambush or other trickery.[32]

What Cudjoe thought isn't known, though he, too, must have been tired of the years of attacks. What he looked like or what symbolism his actions held cannot be gleaned from the writings of a colonial official of this era or from subsequent artistic interpretations. However, reading backward from the treaty, we can see that the status of his people was paramount. The treaty granted them "a perfect state of freedom and liberty," and any runaway who had been with them less than two years was also permitted to stay, or to return to their enslaver with a full pardon. The treaty also protected their land, giving them 1,500 acres. They were allowed to grow food, raise animals, and hunt, and could bring some of their commodities to market, so long as they had the correct licenses. They could manage their own justice, except in capital cases, which the colonial judiciary would hear under terms "equal to those of other free negroes."[33]

Peace. Land. Autonomy. Freedom. If this treaty can be read as a maroon text, despite being written by the British, these are its themes. Unlike maroon communities in the Spanish territories, which sometimes were pushed into being "reduced" or relocated near cities, this is a different outcome, one in which the maroons fought to stay apart, on their own land, protected by the forests and cockpits, away from the white people, free to make their own lives.

The governor was pleased. These terms were so favorable, Trelawny wrote, that "I do not believe they will ever revolt as it cannot be their interest to do it, they receiving greater advantages than we do by the agreement." However, he later added this qualification: "But I offer as my opinion that we are not so entirely to trust to our agreement with them as not to be upon our guard against any treachery."[34]

The treachery worked both ways. One stipulation in the agreement required the maroons, like others before them, to assist the whites in fighting external foes and any other internal rebel slaves, as well as to catch and return any future runaways. The price of freedom in these slave societies continued to be someone else's captivity.

The terms of the deal were not met with universal satisfaction, and some members of Cudjoe's community tried to organize a revolt with slaves on nearby plantations. Cudjoe himself quashed the plot and sent four of the conspirators to the governor for punishment. Two were hanged, and two were transported off the island.[35] More plots followed, with some enslaved people angered that this avenue of escape was now closed to them and irritated that these rebels had ultimately been rewarded for their transgressions. As the governor continued to hear rumors, he came down hard on any alleged conspirators, killing them as he deemed necessary.[36]

On the east side of the island, the remaining Windward maroons had carried on fighting, and Trelawny wanted them subdued as well. Now that the Leeward maroons under Cudjoe had pledged their support, they helped the governor force the Windward communities into a corner.[37] One Windward leader, Quao, soon signed a treaty, on June 30, 1739, mostly similar in spirit to Cudjoe's but with key differences. In some versions of these events, Nanny was still the main leader but she didn't trust the British and didn't want to sign the treaty.[38] At any rate, Quao put his X on the paper. The treaty does not say clearly that Quao's community could live in freedom, as the deal with the Leeward maroons does. Rather, it says, "Four white men shall constantly live and reside with them in their town." Other measures required them to help "suppress and destroy . . . rebellious Negroes," fight any invader, and return runaways. The community, it said, would "be in Subjection to his Excellency the Governor," and Quao had to appear before him at least once a year.[39] They also had to turn over to the authorities any runaways who had joined them in the previous three years.[40] The Windward maroons paid a steeper price for their relative freedom than Cudjoe and the Leeward maroons had. However, despite the unwanted oversight, they still managed to eke out their autonomy.

The final trace of Nanny came in the aftermath of this treaty, her name appearing in a 1740 "Land Patent" addressed to her. During the conflict with the Windward maroons, after the British took and destroyed Nanny Town, they seized the lands around it, which became property of the crown. Officials now wanted white settlers or free people of color to live there to help prevent the establishment of maroon communities, but Nanny managed to acquire this land anyway, through unrecorded machinations.[41] The grant gives "the said Nanny and the people residing with her and heirs . . . a certain parcel of land containing 500 acres," and this became New Nanny Town (renamed Moore Town in 1760), beginning about nine miles (15 kilometers) south of Port Antonio and stretching into the mountains.[42]

Over time, the poor quality of the soil, along with infighting, caused the Windward maroons to disperse over a wider area, where they more often came into contact—and occasionally conflict—with the growing number of white settlers. The maroons remained in two areas after the treaties. On the Leeward side, the main settlements were Trelawny Town (today's Flagstaff, also Maroon Town), named in honor of the treaty, and Accompong, which lies about 18 miles (30 kilometers) south of Trelawny Town and deeper in the cockpits. On the Windward side, maroons lived in the recently established Crawford Town, and in New Nanny Town, the site of Nanny's 500-acre grant.[43] Later on, a maroon group that had been based at Crawford Town broke up and settled other townships, including Scott's Hall; Saint Mary Parish, in 1749; and New Crawford Town, in 1756, which later became Charles Town, situated near the north coast, where the Blue Mountains meet the sea.[44]

For the moment, there was peace. Autonomy and independence remained precarious, but both maroon communities were now enmeshed in the political and legal systems of the island. Their rebellious spirit was not extinguished, but it would not reignite for another two decades.

⊰• ⊱

THE SOLDIERS AT Frederiksvaern, which overlooked the placid blue waters of Coral Bay on Denmark's island of Saint John, paid little heed to the knock on the door. It came early in the morning on November 23, 1733, when some slaves were delivering firewood needed for that day's cooking. But this was no regular delivery. Seven enslaved men—Thoma, Printz van Juff, King Claes, Kanta, Juni, Prince, and Apinda—quickly pulled out weapons and killed the soldiers. They fired the fort's cannon, signaling that the rebellion was starting.[45] But they missed one soldier: a man named John Gabriel feigned his death, and once the rebels left he fled to alert the authorities.[46]

Saint John (also Sankt Jan) had endured a series of hardships, including drought, flooding, a hurricane that July, and subsequent crop failure. It was a difficult place in the best of times, the cacti dotting the island testament to its aridity and heat. The island was Denmark's second Caribbean colony (today part of the US Virgin Islands), obtained in 1718, following Danish settlement in Saint Thomas in 1671. Saint John is a forested, hilly island, and what parts were suitable for sugarcane were soon planted with the crop, taking up the little available fertile land. Few Europeans wanted to live there, and the white population was small. Most of the work—including overseeing and driving slaves—on the island's 106 plantations was done by Africans. The difficulties of the previous few years meant many enslaved people were leaving plantations and trying to survive—or at the very least find nourishment—in the woods. Such was the level of marronage that the governor, Philip Gardelin, tried to enact a slave code in 1733, which called for harsh punishment for absconding. This only stoked resentment further.[47]

This dot of 20 square miles (52 square kilometers) was then under the control of the Danish West India Company, which also had forts in Africa, including Christiansborg on the Gold Coast, in modern southern Ghana.[48] Thus, the roots of the Saint John revolt were in Africa, and in many ways this was an African revolt, like others in the early eighteenth-century Caribbean.[49] The people involved in the uprising were the Akan-speaking Akwamu—also called "Amina" at the time—whose kingdom stretched along the coast of present-day Ghana and Togo. The Danish West Indies was the point of disembarkation for some 17,000 captives between 1700 and 1733.[50] The uprising also coincided with the 1733 Danish purchase from France of the island of Saint Croix, to the south of Denmark's other two islands.

When the cannon rang out that November morning, the news ricocheted around the island. White people grabbed their guns and headed to Frederiksvaern, where they were ambushed by around 80 Africans. Within 24 hours of taking the fort, the rebel band had attacked nearby plantations, killing a number of planters and seizing much-needed weaponry and supplies. By November 26, Danish troops arrived to subdue the rebels, entering what would become a protracted conflict. Before long, the British were also forced to pay attention. The governor of British Saint Christopher (Saint Kitts), William Mathew, said of the situation, "The Danes at present hardly have possession." Indeed, the governor of Saint Thomas had reached out to him for help, and Mathew relayed to London his annoyance that someone from Saint Kitts had gone to the Danes' aid despite Mathew's orders to the contrary, and had suffered for it. "The negroes have killd one if not both his sons, and two or three more of his company, and beaten them off," he wrote.[51] Fearing the rebellion could quickly spread, the British continued to monitor the situation, especially because their island of Tortola was only a few miles northeast and a short sail from Saint John.

The rebels worked their way around the island, destroying houses and plantations, taking provisions, and keeping the whites at bay. Officials estimated that the band consisted of 43 men, led by a man called King Claes.[52] This may have been a conservative guess, but since there was a slave population of at least 1,200 on the island, clearly many African and creole slaves did not join the rebels.[53] The leaders of the revolt were Akwamu nobles, imprisoned and taken captive when their kingdom suffered a defeat around 1730.[54] The politics of their kingdom came with them, as did their fighting prowess. This background helps explain why most of the creole slaves stayed away from the revolt. Other Africans remained wary too.

One conflict that occurred on Saint John prior to the revolt illustrates the internal tensions among enslaved people, in this case between the Akwamu and the Loango, as they were called, from West Central Africa. There was an incident at a Coral Bay plantation in which a particular *bomba*, or head slave, who was Loango, ordered an Akwamu subordinate to whip another slave. That person refused, stoking hostility between the two groups and potentially starting the revolt.[55] Certainly, whatever nomenclature Europeans used, Africans defined themselves in their own terms, and that did not always mean alliances. This moment also illustrates the dynamic that emerged within the context of the slave society, pitting enslaved people against each other, or free black people against slaves. Indeed, some of the small free community on the island joined Europeans in suppressing the rebellion.[56]

As later recounted, King Claes and his followers wanted to establish an Akwamu kingdom on the island, which also meant enslaving people outside their own group, another probable cause for the reluctance of other Africans and creoles to join. However, this interpretation of the rebels' intent could also have reflected the European perspective of these events.[57]

As the months wore on and planters began to abandon the island, the Danish, like the governors in Jamaica and elsewhere, realized that the best way to end this standoff was by treaty. But attempts to broker a deal failed, in part because King Claes didn't trust the Danish overtures. Instead, the rebels attacked the north side of the island.[58]

In April 1734, French troops arrived at the request of the Danes, bringing 220 men to subdue the rebellion. Other enslaved people on the island were forced into helping them. As the members of the expedition tried to capture or kill the rebels, news reached them that some of the Africans were going to kill themselves.

According to island lore, there was a mass leap, maybe 20, maybe 100 or more bodies flying through the air, over the Ram Head cliffs, plunging to their deaths in the green-blue waters around Saint John. Other endings were equally grim. A young African boy named January, who survived the rebellion, told officials in May 1734 that 10 men and three women "had six guns to kill themselves with," which they did in the east, near Brown Bay.[59] Either way, many rebels took their own lives rather than suffering capture once again. Discovered among the bodies in one group suicide was a woman named Breffu, who the colonial officials assumed was a man but were shocked to find was a woman.⁶⁰ Breffu was believed to have killed the Van Stell family and planter Pieter Krøyer and his wife. Other rebels were taken prisoner and put on trial, with at least five alleged leaders executed. Six months later, the rebellion was over, but marronage and unrest continued.

The island of Saint John today is covered with ruins of sugar mills, scattered in all parts, the remains of conical windmills serving as gravestones of a sort, marking this living history of death. The remnants of the boiling houses and the plantation homes are now crumbling, ferns growing in their crevices, the salty wind slowly eroding the stones. Some are marked as historic sites, others are in worse condition, decaying near the beaches where tourists snorkel, not far from the point where King Claes and his followers perhaps hoped to re-create a bit of Africa or, in a way, finish the war that resulted in their arrival in this strange island. Or, at the very least, grasp at something like freedom.

⋘ • ⋙

THE PLAN WAS perfect. A ball was to be held at the Dunbar mansion in Antigua's capital, Saint John's, to mark the ninth anniversary of the coronation of George II, on the evening of October 11, 1736. Tomboy, a master carpenter, was in charge of setting up the seating, so it would have been easy for him to lay the gunpowder for blowing up not only the governor, but all the island's great and good. Once the explosion was heard, other men could take to the harbor and seize the fort and ships, while the rest could set the hated cane fields ablaze. Then the island could be turned over to Court, the rightful king.⁶¹

Oaths, possibly in the Ashanti style, had been taken across the island, the loyalty of others sealed with rum, the blood of cockerels, and the dirt from graves. Promises were made to kill the whites and be loyal to Court and the conspiracy's leaders. Overseeing this planning was an Akan priest named Quaco (or Quawcoo). A war dance was held the Sunday before, as was done in Africa when Ashanti kings declared war on an enemy.⁶²

Then the governor's son fell ill, and the ball had to be postponed. But rumors had begun to circulate that the slaves were up to something, and the planters were jittery. Judge Robert Arbuthnot decided to investigate.

The planters of Antigua knew all about the events on the island of Saint John, only 200 miles (320 kilometers) to the east. Larger than its neighbor, Antigua had enough fertile soil, wind, and sun for the cultivation of sugar, leading to its settlement by the British in 1632. Among the earliest arrivals in its handsome harbors was Christopher Codrington, the son of a successful Barbadian planter. He set up his plantation, the fancifully named "Betty's Hope," in 1674 in the fertile east of the island, and later at least five more.[63] Today, Betty's Hope is a historical site, the restored windmills once used to power sugar refining still driven by the steady wind that blows across the island, the former scale of the operation evident in the multiple surviving outbuildings.

Antigua's landscape has nothing like Jamaica's Cockpit Country or Blue Mountains. Runaways were more limited in their options, many of them taking refuge on Boggy Peak, the highest point in the Shekerley Mountains, which rises some 1,300 feet (400 meters) above sea level.[64] The island is also close to many others, and some people fled by canoe to hide among the Carib or Kalinago people in Dominica.

Threats of revolts also existed well before the plan to liven up the coronation ball in 1736. Christopher Codrington, the son of the founder of Betty's Hope and governor of the Leeward Islands (Antigua, Barbuda, Montserrat, Saint Kitts, Nevis, Anguilla, and the Virgin Islands), received a late Christmas surprise in 1701. He was told that on December 27, "about 15 new Calamantee [Coromantee] negroe men belonging to Major Martin came upon his chamber door . . . and with their knives and bills barbarously murthered him." They cut off his head, which was found later "in the grass, where they had washed it with rum, and triumphed over it."[65]

Codrington blamed the events on Martin, writing to the Council of Trade and Plantations, "I'm afraid he [Martin] was guilty of some unusual act of severity, or rather some indignity toward the Corramantes." He praised the Coromantees, saying they were "not only the best and most faithful of our slaves, but are really all born Heroes." He went on:

> There is a difference between them and all the other negroes beyond what 'tis possible for your Lordships to conceive . . . not a man of them but will stand to be cut to pieces without a sigh or groan, grateful and obedient to a kind master, but implacably revengeful when ill-treated. My Father, who had studied the genius and temper of all kinds of negroes 45 years with a very nice observation, would say, Noe man deserved a Corramante that would not treat him like a Friend rather than a Slave, and all my Corramantes preserve that love and veneration for him that they constantly visit his grave, make their libations upon it, hold up their hands to Heaven with violent lamentations, and promise when they have done working for his son they will come to him and be his faithful slaves in the other world.[66]

Such beliefs about the supposed affections of the enslaved for their captors, coupled with the low number of runaways in Antigua, led to a degree of complacency among planters and officials.[67] However, another plot was uncovered in 1729, on the plantation of Nathaniel Crump, who sat on the Antigua council. The enslaved men who were accused of organizing the plot to kill Crump and "Cutt off every White Inhabitant" were examined in front of the council. An enslaved man named Tom gave testimony that would lead to the death of four others—three burned alive and one hanged and quartered—while securing for himself manumission and an annuity of £10.[68]

Nonetheless, by the 1730s, runaways and revolts were not in the forefront of planters' minds in Antigua, given other problems: sugar prices declining, cane-eating bugs infesting the fields, and an earthquake in 1735.[69] When times were difficult, enslaved workers were the first to feel the pain, through the loss of extra rations or the exhaustion of being driven even harder, or the anger and frustration of an enslaver with a shorter fuse than usual. King Claes and the others had tasted this bitterness in Saint John. Now the slaves on Antigua were experiencing it.

During his investigation following the cancelled celebration to honor George II, Judge Arbuthnot was alarmed about an exchange he heard between an enslaved cooper named Jack and his enslaver's sister, referring to the coronation of a man named Court at a recent ceremony among some of the slaves. The sister teased Jack, asking him if Court was his king, to which Jack responded: "Court is King and I am to be one of his Generals."[70] It was all a joke, Jack insisted when asked about the exchange.

Arbuthnot's investigation unleashed rumors that a plan was in place to kill the white colonists and set up a kingdom under the leadership of Court (also known as Tackey, the Akan word for "chief" and a common name in records across the region; in Antigua he is today known as Prince Klaas). Court was one of the thousands of Coromantees in the British islands, and the judge discovered that he was one of the purported ringleaders and, more worrying to the white community, that he had long held a privileged position in Thomas Kerby's household.

Court was believed to be about 35, having been taken to Antigua at around the age of 10. His enslaver, Kerby, who was the speaker of the Antigua Assembly, thought highly of him, telling the investigators that he was "incapable of any bad Design . . . and had Always behaved like a Faithfull Slave and lived very well, besides which he was under no Temptation, for that he had Offer'd him his freedom."[71] His fellow slaves admired him as well, and "he had for many Years covertly assumed among his Countrymen, the Title of King."[72]

Perhaps Court did not trust Kerby's promise of later freedom, or he wanted it now, or he wanted others to be free. Whatever the reason, he was moved to fight for liberation. Court was an excellent strategist. He realized that the Coromantees could not execute their plan in isolation, so he brought in Tomboy, a creole slave and master carpenter. The men then recruited Scipio and Tony, who had overseer roles among the slaves, and four more craftsmen: Hercules, Jack, Ned, and Fortune. There were also two drivers, Secundi and Jacko.[73]

These men were rounded up in the investigation and told to explain themselves at trials. Tomboy and the others participated in the war dance, but later accounts claimed they said they did not want a kingdom, but a "creole commonwealth." According to the testimony, *"Court* amused and flattered by all with being King of the island but the *Creoles* had resolved unknown to him and his *Coramantees*, to settle a *Commonwealth* and to make Slaves of the *Coramantees*, and Negroes of other Nations, and to destroy *Court*."[74]

Whatever their vision of a world without the whites—kingdom or commonwealth, united or riven—Court, Tomboy, and 10 others were killed.[75] The entire island felt the ramifications as well-known and skilled men—drivers, coopers, carpenters—were executed or deported off the island. By April, a total of 88 men had been put to death, about a third of them African.[76] As one island resident wrote in a letter, "The Burning of Negroes, hanging them on Gibbets alive, Racking them upon the wheel, &c. takes up almost all our Time . . . I am almost dead with watching and warding."[77] This had been a revolt of the elite slaves, and an alliance of African and creole, chilling officials on the island and further away—at least 23 reports of the investigation into the conspiracy were published in North American newspapers.[78] Arbuthnot also castigated the enslavers for being lax and allowing their captives too many liberties.[79]

But it should have been quite clear by now: The British had created an Afro-Caribbean world on these islands, one in which black people were a significant majority. Antigua in 1734 was nearly 87 percent black, mostly enslaved.[80] The numbers were in their favor. If anything, a conspiracy, if not an outright revolt, had been overdue—and not only in Antigua.

Chapter 15

Borders

On a stretch of US Highway 17 that runs between Savannah, Georgia, and Charleston, South Carolina, a historical marker sits just south of a branch of Wallace Creek.[1] It stands alone, surrounded by yellowing grass on the shoulder of the four-lane road, making it easy to miss, but it has not been entirely overlooked. A small bouquet of artificial flowers is tied to the front, the purples and greens of plastic blooms faded but resilient under the South Carolina sun. The small sign tells of a group of slaves who "marched south toward promised freedom in Spanish Florida, waving flags, beating drums, and shouting 'Liberty!'" This was the short-lived Stono Rebellion of 1739, named for the nearby Stono River, one of the many Lowcountry waterways that fed the agricultural dreams of colonial Carolina settlers. The rebels couldn't have known it at the time, but Stono would be one of the largest revolts ever to take place in what became the United States.

Today, the name "Stono" is used on new housing subdivisions. Modest homes, power lines, billboards, convenience stores, and strip malls edge into what were once farms and fields. And yet it is a place that still compels a person, nearly 300 years later, to lay flowers that will not wilt. The rebels' drumbeats echo underneath the din of the traffic.

Soon after the rebels set out in the direction of neighboring Spanish Florida in the early hours of Sunday, September 9, according to a surviving report, they had "two Drums beating" while they were "pursuing all the white people they met with."[2] This report, "An Account of the Negroe Insurrection in South Carolina," was compiled months after the event, and the Stono Rebellion is shrouded in as much conjecture as verifiable facts.

Mentioned in this report is a man known as Jemmy, identified as the captain and as an Angolan. Nothing more is said about him, so it is difficult to know his motivations, but he likely would have heard at some point how, years earlier, Spain's Carlos II had granted freedom to any runaways from the English colonies.

Spain had long claimed Florida as its own, an area reaching from the peninsula's southern tip to the fortified city of Saint Augustine and up to the Chesapeake Bay. However, Spain did not have the military manpower or sufficient settlers to fend off its rivals. Florida was still on the margins of its empire. The English succeeded along the coastline where the French incursions had failed, first with Jamestown in Virginia in 1607, later with Charles Town (Charleston) in Carolina in 1670, and then, creeping south, with Georgia in 1733.

There were inevitable skirmishes and retaliations, with Britain using Native American allies to attack Spain's territory. At the same time, Spanish officials in Florida encountered enslaved people fleeing the British settlements and, unsure what to do with them, wrote to Madrid seeking advice.[3] Rather than force them to return or take them into captivity, the Spanish decided on another response: In 1693, the king offered liberty to anyone who reached Florida, in exchange for loyalty and conversion to Catholicism.[4]

Officials in South Carolina had been struggling with runaways and maroons from the colony's beginning. In 1711, the Commons House of Assembly heard that there were "several Negroes runaway from their Masters & keep out, arm'd, robbing & plundering houses & Plantations & putting ye Inhabitants of this province in great fear and terrour."[5] The following year, the assembly passed an act "for the better ordering and governing of negroes," which imposed harsher penalties for running away, including death. Before long the new law was leading to complaints: Too many slaves were being executed, and paying compensation to enslavers who had lost their "property" was draining the treasury.[6]

Enslaved people continued to flee, despite the risks, seeking freedom, albeit an inconsistent one, in Florida. In 1729, the governor of

Florida, Antonio de Benavides, sold a handful of runaways, arguing that Britain and Spain were at peace and thus the 1693 edict did not hold. After the resumption of hostilities, the previous policy was resurrected and enslaved people were freed and inducted into the militia. In 1738, another governor, Manuel de Montiano, ordered the establishment of a new town, Gracia Real de Santa Teresa de Mose, which would become home to around 100 freed people. It was two miles north of Saint Augustine, on Mose Creek, and thus helped to create a buffer against the English.[7] The policy of sanctuary continued, as Captain Caleb Davis found out when a group of up to 19 of his slaves ran for freedom in 1738. The *Account of the Negroe Insurrection* mentions this, noting that "certain Negroes" belonging to Davis "escaped to *Augustine* and were received there." When British officials attempted to recover those and another 50 freedom-seekers, Montiano "showed his Orders from the Court of Spain, by which he was to receive all Run away Negroes."[8] Perhaps the community of Mose was too recently established for Jemmy to know of it specifically, but there is little doubt he knew what lay in Florida.

The Stono Rebellion began on a Sunday, the allotted day of rest. This was one of the last Sundays before a new Security Act was to go into effect, requiring all white men to carry firearms to their places of worship. A gun might seem unnecessary for a visit to the house of the Lord, but nervous whites knew that their captives had Sundays off and were concerned about what they might get up to on their one day of rest.

The year up to that point had been difficult. Great swathes of Charles Town's populace suffered yellow fever in the humid days of late summer, after smallpox had devastated the city the previous year. To further dampen the mood, the perfidious Spanish were causing trouble again; the opening shots of the War of Jenkins' Ear would come soon. In addition, news of the maroon treaty in the fellow British colony Jamaica, published in July 1739, was circulating around Charles Town.[9]

It may have been a normal Sunday for some enslaved people. Many had the day off, and were resting or tending to their provision gardens, but a few might have been working on a drainage system for the North

Branch of the Stono River. Enslaved people were often put to work on public projects, and that sometimes involved laboring on Sundays.[10]

Elsewhere, rice fields had overtaken the small farms, cattle ranches, and lumber operations that had been the backbone of the Carolina economy, pushing it towards the production of a single commodity. September and October were the harvest months for rice, involving long hours and backbreaking work.[11] Cultivating rice was labor-intensive, and so the ships continued to arrive from Africa and the Caribbean. The growth of the enslaved population in South Carolina was dramatic, reaching around 39,000 by 1740, having been around 4,000 in 1709.[12]

Many of the African arrivals were listed as "Angolan"—nearly 60 percent between 1735 and 1739 alone.[13] Many, however, might have been from elsewhere in West Central Africa, such as the Kingdom of Kongo, which had experienced a series of civil wars between 1680 and 1740, contributing to the number of captives sent to the coast.[14] Their Kongo heritage would have meant three important things in relation to Stono. First, they may have been able to understand some Spanish and been aware of the potential for freedom in Florida—indeed, the report on the insurrection described them as "brought from the Kingdom of Angola in Africa, [where] many of these speak Portugueze (which Language is as near Spanish as Scotch is to English)." Second, they were also likely baptized Roman Catholic, which was also a factor in their knowing about "the good reception of the Negros at [St] Augustine."[15] Third, given the ongoing wars in Kongo, some of the captives may have been trained warriors who knew how to use guns and modern weaponry.

Whatever their background and connection to each other might have been, a group of about 20 men came together early that Sunday. They were soon on the move, making their first stop, where "they surprized a Warehouse belonging to Mr Hutchenson" and killed two shopkeepers. They took whatever arms and gunpowder they could find and "next they plundered and burnt Mr Godfrey's house, and killed him, his Daughter and Son," before ransacking the place.[16] They then started their march along the Pons Pons Road, which would lead them to Saint Augustine, stopping at Wallace's Tavern. There, they spared the owner's life, "for he was a good Man and kind to his Slaves," but plundered the tavern all the same.[17] According to "An Account of the

Negroe Insurrection," the rebels' numbers swelled as they travelled, burning down houses, killing white people, and taking goods. Many joined freely, while others were goaded into participating.

By chance, Lieutenant Governor William Bull, travelling with four others, spotted the men making their way south that morning and alerted other white colonists.[18] Then the freedom-seekers stopped, possibly near the Jacksonboro Ferry, which crossed the Edisto River. According to a later account, "Sixty, some say a hundred" of them "halted in a field; and set to dancing, Singing and beating Drums, to draw more Negroes to them, thinking they were now victorious over the whole Province."[19]

Early September is still hot in the Lowcountry, and the men, having marched 10 miles, were probably thirsty and tired. While the reported "dancing" may seem counterproductive in that late-afternoon heat, it was anything but frivolous. British colonists unfamiliar with African cultures of war would not have understood that dancing in this situation was akin to drilling. It was preparation, a warmup for what lay ahead.[20] A war dance.

One hundred militia members caught up with the rebels at their resting stop, a battle ensued, and the militia prevailed. In the end, some 40 rebels and 20 whites died.[21] Some of the rebels fled, though around 30 were found a week or so later, and many of them faced immediate execution.

No news of the events of that Sunday was printed in the *South Carolina Gazette*, though word blazed through the colony. A ranger's report from the following week mentioned, "As we were going down the River, we met a Trading Boat going to Fort Augusta, the People on board her told us the Negroes in Carolina had raised up in Arms and killed about forty White People."[22] The news eventually moved north, first to Boston and then across the Atlantic, with the anonymous "Account of the Negroe Insurrection" appearing in London newspapers by March 1740. A few more of the rebels managed to avoid the Native American rangers the British sent after them, perhaps making it to Saint Augustine, though it's more likely they ended up living as maroons in the impenetrable areas of the Lowcountry swamps. In 1742, three years after the event, the *South Carolina Gazette* reported that "one of the Ringleaders of the last Negro Insurrection (belonging to Mr Henry Williamson) was lately seized in Cotaw Swamp, by two Negro Fellows that ran away from Mr Grimke, who brought him to Stono, where he immediately was hang'd."[23]

That the newspaper felt confident to report this final turn of events indicates a belief that the threat was gone. The colony had moved on. By 1740 officials in South Carolina had amended the slave code in the hope of preventing a repeat. It further restricted the movement of enslaved people, the shadow of Stono hanging over the legislation. Section 36 stipulated

> that all due care be taken to restrain the wanderings and meetings of negroes and other slaves, at all times, and more especially on Saturday nights, Sundays and other holidays, and their using and carrying wooden swords, and other mischievous and dangerous weapons, or using or keeping of drums, horns, or other loud instruments, which may call together or give sign or notice to one another of their wicked designs and purposes.[24]

The following year, 1741, a duty was levied on the import of new slaves—but black people already outnumbered whites two to one.[25]

Stono was not only a local uprising but a product of a reordered world, in which Britain, Kongo, Spain, and others were part of an ever-shifting mix. The town of Mose played an important role as the War of Jenkins' Ear spread to land. A British expedition to Spanish Florida resulted in the capture of two smaller forts in January 1740. The free black militia helped defend Saint Augustine with such fierce fighting that the British referred to the encounter as "Bloody Mose." However, for protection the residents of Mose were forced into the walled confines of Saint Augustine, where they would end up staying for nearly two decades. Starting around 1752, part of Mose was rebuilt, and the free black population was urged to return to it by the governor, Fulgencio García de Solís, who wanted them living outside the city's walls. Understanding the meaning of García's action, many refused. Eventually, Mose had enough residents to survive until Florida was ceded to the British in 1763, when the Spanish evacuated the residents of Florida to Cuba, bringing this particular path to freedom to a close and sending the descendants of Carolina runaways into unknown futures in the Caribbean.[26]

⋘ • ⋙

THE STONO REBELLION had an impact on the young neighboring colony of Georgia, established in 1733. Indeed, James Oglethorpe, the colony's founder, is suspected to be the author of the "Account of the Negroe Insurrection in South Carolina," writing it to warn settlers in Georgia of the dangers of slavery.[27] The colony had started in a very different way than Carolina. Georgia was founded for debtors, a place to give the impoverished a new life, as Oglethorpe, an enthusiastic social reformer, saw it. Such industrious people, he thought, would not need to use slave labor.

Oglethorpe had chosen the site for the Georgia colony, named after George II, in 1730, near the Savannah and Altamaha Rivers. He presented it as a potential buffer zone against Spanish Florida, and a royal charter followed in 1732. He tried to stay resolute in his stance on slavery, though he and the colony's Board of Trustees in London were not opposed to it in theory. Rather, they did not think it was compatible with their aims for the colonists. In addition, given Georgia's location between slave-holding Carolina and the freedom offered to runaways in Spanish Florida, permitting slavery in the new colony could further exacerbate regional tensions, in part because some of the enslaved people might end up fighting on the side of the Spanish in the likely event of an attack on the English.

However, pressure grew from within Georgia, as some settlers looked at the profits being made in South Carolina, while the planters in that colony eyed the potential of Georgia's lands. A campaign to introduce slavery within Georgia formed by the end of the 1730s. The arguments included the unfounded claim that white servants were lazy and unproductive because English people were not adapted for the hot climate, unlike the Africans, who labored in the rice fields of South Carolina. It was "utterly impracticable," wrote one supporter of slavery, that the colony could prosper without the introduction of enslaved workers.[28] The campaigners pressured the trustees, while also taking their case to the British Parliament. Oglethorpe had left Georgia in 1743, though he remained a trustee. However, his influence was not enough to stop the board from relenting—in part because the members recognized that they could do little to enforce a complete ban or stop the human trafficking from South Carolina—and slavery was permitted from January 1, 1751.[29]

Around the same time the royal charter came through for Georgia, Oglethorpe was also appointed a subgovernor for the Royal African Company. The RAC had shifted in both its operations and purpose by then, looking to diversify from the slave trade and into more "civilizing" forms of commerce.[30] Oglethorpe was not being inconsistent, to his mind, by opposing slavery in Georgia while joining the RAC. Later on in this role, he also became acquainted with the unusual case of Ayuba Suleiman Diallo, or, as he was known at the time, Job, the Son of Solomon, or Job Ben Solomon.

Unlike the many millions of Africans transported across the Atlantic whose past was eradicated by the voyage, Job was memorialized in a portrait, which is displayed in the National Portrait Gallery in London. The painting, by William Hoare, was used as the basis for a frontispiece etching for the 1734 account of Diallo's life as written by Thomas Bluett, *Some Memoirs of the Life of Job, the Son of Solomon, the High Priest of Boonda in Africa*. Diallo looks like a priest or a wise man in the painting, his head covered by a white turban, his gaze and smile peaceful, and his red Quran hanging around his neck as a symbol of his devotion.[31]

Diallo's calmness bears little trace of the tumultuous years that led him to this point. Bluett encountered Diallo in Kent County, near Delaware Bay, Maryland, after hearing about a black man who was apprehended and jailed for not having the correct papers to enter the area. Bluett "had heard of Job, [and] went with several Gentlemen to the Goaler's House, being a Tavern, and desired to see him. He was brought into the Tavern to us, but could not speak one Word of English."[32] Diallo eventually got them to understand the words "Allah" and "Mahommed," and that, along with his refusal of a glass of wine, made Bluett and the others realize he was Muslim. They soon sought out an "old Negroe Man" who could speak the "Jalloff" (Wolof) language to translate Diallo's story.

According to this account, Diallo was born to a prominent family in the Muslim kingdom of Futa, around today's Senegal and Gambia. He was thought to be around 31 or 32 by the time he arrived in North America. In February 1730, Diallo's father had sent him to trade with an English ship near the Gambia River and "to sell two Negroes, and to buy Paper and some other Necessaries," but warned him not to go beyond the river because the Mandinka people there were their enemies at that time. Diallo was not pleased with the English goods and so disobeyed his father, crossed the river, and traded the humans for "some Cows." He stopped on his way home at the "House of an old Acquaintance." Because it was quite hot that day, he took off his weapons—a sword with a gold handle, a gold knife, and a quiver of arrows—while he refreshed himself. A "Company of Mandingos" passed by and abducted him before he could grab his sword. They also kidnapped his interpreter, and "shaved their Heads and Beards, which Job and his Man resented as the highest Indignity" because the Mandinkas wanted "to make them appear like Slaves taken in War."

But more was to come.

The two men were sold to the same English ship anchored in the river, leaving Diallo to convince Captain Pike, who commanded the vessel, "that he was the same Person that came to trade with him a few Days before." Despite promises that Diallo's father could come redeem the two men, the ship pushed out to sea, and they were brought to Annapolis, Maryland, as slaves.

Diallo was quickly sold and put to work in a tobacco field, but he was not "used to such Labour . . . [and] every Day shewed more and more Uneasiness under this Exercise." Eventually he became ill, and his enslaver sent him to tend cattle instead. He passed his time going into the woods to pray, isolated by his faith and his lack of English. Diallo believed that at some point he would "meet with some lucky Accident, to divert or abate his Grief," and so he left, walking through the woods where he had prayed, destination unknown. When he arrived at Delaware Bay he was picked up because he was "not known" in the county. He was languishing in jail when Bluett befriended him.

Soon thereafter, Diallo wrote a letter in Arabic to his father, hoping Captain Pike might take it back to Africa. Pike, however, was already at sea, and instead the letter fell into the hands of James Oglethorpe, who was preparing to leave London for Georgia, because of his RAC connections. He was immediately impressed by Diallo's literacy, despite not being able to read the letter until it was translated, and quickly worked to get him out of bondage. In March 1733 Diallo and Bluett left Annapolis for England, and during the voyage the African "had learned so much of our Language, that he was able to understand most of what we said." Upon arrival, they discovered that Oglethorpe had already left for Georgia. Diallo remained concerned that the efforts to free him were not entirely transparent, and "he feared they would either sell him again as a Slave, or . . . expect an unreasonable Ransom for him." Eventually, the necessary amount was raised among Bluett's associates and Diallo was promised that he could return home.

In the meantime, Diallo met many of the great and good of English society. As Bluett recounted, "He was soon clothed in a rich silk Dress," before being presented at court, an African royal among the English aristocracy, where he received "a rich Gold Watch" from Queen Caroline. It seemed to Bluett that Diallo believed "most of the Gentlemen that conversed with him frequently will remember many Instances of his Ingenuity." Bluett recounted the portrait-sitting with William Hoare, which Diallo initially resisted because such depictions were not in accordance with the teachings of Islam. "We assured him," Bluett wrote, "that we never worshipped any Picture, and that we wanted his for no other End but to keep us in mind of him." After he consented, he asked the artist to depict him in his traditional dress, to which Hoare responded that he couldn't draw that unless he could see it. Not missing a beat, Diallo answered, "If you can't draw a Dress you never saw, why do some of you Painters presume to draw God, whom no one ever saw?"

Bluett had grown fond of Diallo, saying that he had "solid Judgment, a ready Memory, and a clear Head." Diallo also had an outsize helping of luck. Not only did he return home in 1733 to his family, including two wives and four children, but he now had a job with the Royal African Company, which furnished his passage.[33]

THE GREAT RESISTANCE

⋘ • ⋙

Although the largest enslaved populations were in the Southern colonies of British North America, cities in the North, including New York, continued to reckon with slavery. Nearly 30 years after the revolt of 1712, another situation involving enslaved people and arson arose. This time, there was a series of fires, which an increasingly alarmed public began to blame on black people in the city, though there was little evidence. The only concrete fact was that 13 buildings had caught fire over the end of the winter and into the spring of 1741, and slaves, along with free black people and white allies, were suspected.

The governor's house within Fort George went up in flames first, on March 18. The lieutenant-governor said in the immediate aftermath that it must have been caused by some repair work being done on the gutters, and that it was an accident. Then, on March 25, the house of Captain Peter Warren burned, followed by Van Zant's storehouse on April 1. Three days later a stable belonging to Jacobus Quick went up in flames, and then the house of Ben Thomas. Those with long memories observed that two of the 10 fires broke out on March 25 and April 6, the exact days of similar blazes during the revolt of 1712. Speculation started to turn into accusation.[34]

If anything was more frightening than the prospect of a fire in a world constructed of wood, it was the idea that the flames were lit by the slaves who had done the building. Fire was a potent, symbolic weapon. The fire at the fort was no accident, the city began to believe. The residents of this growing imperial port would have heard the news from Antigua and Jamaica, Saint John, and Stono. They knew that where slavery existed, so did the threat: "Kill all the whites."[35]

The free black and enslaved populations were no doubt bracing themselves for what was to come. The flames were frightening, but the greater terror for them would be blame and punishment. Cuffee Philipse learned this as he was dragged to jail from his enslaver's house, "borne upon the people's shoulders," after he was spotted leaping out of Frederick Philipse's burning storehouse on April 6, as others were trying to douse the flames.[36]

New York now had imaginary and possibly real plotters on its streets, with officials eventually rounding up some 200 suspects, like Billy, called "Will" in the records.[37] He was described at his arrest as being "very expert at Plots," having been forced from Antigua after turning informant regarding the events there in 1736.[38] Three people he named had burned at the stake on that island; his own life spared, he was sold on to New York. His reputation appeared to precede him, and whispers spread that he had also participated in the Saint John uprising of 1733.

Now, Billy was languishing in the cold basement prison of the city hall, waiting to be told what the charges against him were this time. He tried again to protect his life by confessing that he was guilty and offering to tell the authorities more after he was pardoned. The chance never came. Officialdom no longer trusted him, and he could no longer avoid the stake, a punishment reserved mostly for alleged instigators of slave uprisings. Apparently, as the flames licked at his feet, he tried to shift the blame onto two white soldiers and two "Papists" (Catholics), and also gave some other names. He did protect his prison mate Pedro—but Pedro had already told investigators that Billy had advised him to lie in his confession.[39]

These fires coincided with an ongoing investigation into a robbery at Robert Hogg's shop in late February, which proved to be the initial spark to the entire conspiracy blaze.[40] An enslaved man named Caesar committed the theft, aided by another man, Prince. Caesar buried the money and objects he stole in the cellar of a tavern owned by John and Sarah Hughson, who were known for fencing goods stolen by enslaved people.[41] Caesar then returned the next morning to see a lodger, a "Newfoundland Irish beauty" named Margaret Sorubiero, also known as Peggy Kerry. She was 21 and a "prostitute to negroes," as the records put it, and had just given birth to their child.[42] Once the theft was reported, Caesar was apprehended and the investigation into the case began. Then, on March 18, the first fire broke out, followed by several others.

By April 22, a grand jury had been assembled and was listening to the testimony of a 16-year-old indentured servant named Mary Burton, who worked for the Hughsons, and who tied the two series of events together. She said that Caesar and Prince had brought the looted goods to the house. Despite an initial reluctance to speak about the fires, she later told the jury that Caesar, Prince, and another man, Cuffee, had frequently spoken of burning down the fort, and that "when all this was done, Caesar should be governor, and Hughson, her master, should be king." She added that she had seen 20 to 30 black people gathering at the tavern. This evidence was "most astonishing" to the jury.[43] The crown had its case.

The next day they hauled in Peggy Kerry, who was already implicated in the theft. At first, she was steadfast in her refusal to cooperate, despite offers of a pardon. She did, however, speak to a prison mate, perhaps in a moment of exhaustion or weakness, through a hole in her cell door. Arthur Price immediately understood the value of their conversation and reported it to the court.[44] She folded, naming another seven men, including Caesar, who were involved in the alleged plot.

Caesar and Prince soon faced their charges for theft, to which they pleaded "not guilty," but really they were on trial for setting the fires, and justice was not a consideration where slaves were concerned. Their execution was to be by hanging, with Caesar in chains.

In the end, whiteness could not save Kerry, nor could her confession. She and the Hughsons were executed for their part in organizing the supposed conspiracy, to which many of the witnesses had attested.[45] Then, a man named John Ury, a private tutor who had not been in the city for very long but had been seen at Hughson's tavern, was implicated, and later executed. He was alleged to be a Catholic priest, possibly in the service of the Spanish, and priests were illegal in 1740s Protestant English New York, meaning he could face a punishment of death.[46] Now, the entire trial and investigation was moving into "popish plot" territory, which some of the apprehended suspects had claimed in their testimony. The paranoia knew no limits, and the imprisoned slaves told similar versions of the same story, hoping it would keep them alive.

A 16-year-old named Sandy was the first to turn for the prosecution, followed by a man he named, Fortune, who in turn named others. Two men, Quack and Cuffee Philipse, were awaiting execution by fire on the wooden stakes, where they "shewed great terror in their countenances," before agreeing to talk. But it was too late. Quack said the whole thing had been Hughson's idea; Cuffee reaffirmed this. It was all duly noted, but to no avail. The sheriff told the court officials that "carrying the negros back [to jail] would be impracticable." What he meant was that the impatient crowd now assembled wanted to see these so-called conspirators killed by the same weapon they had used against the town: fire. Better to keep the mob happy, and so the men were killed.[47] The public was calling for blood, needing to witness violence to confirm their own security. The subsequent trials were never about justice, but rather about understanding what took place, and doling out punishment for transgressions real and imagined. On it went, for six months. In the end, some 172 people, including 20 whites, were hauled in for questioning.[48] Out of these, 13 black men were burned at the stake; 21 black and white people were hanged; and 84 men and women sent onward, mostly to the Caribbean.[49] After this, far fewer West Indian slaves were brought to New York—they were believed to have played a key part in this alleged plot.[50] Officials may have been able to douse the fires of this particular conspiracy, but others would ignite in British North America, with or without the help of West Indians.

Chapter 16

Poison

IF ALL THE fears of white planters could have been bundled up into one person, he might have been Makandal: An African. A healer. A herbalist who had a way with poisonous plants. A maroon. Even his name held magic, being the Kikongo word for amulet or charm.[1] François Makandal (also Mackandal or Macandal) was all that and more, and while the precise details of his legend have been subject to debate, there is no contesting the importance of the mythology about him. As one anonymous colonist in Saint-Domingue wrote in a June 24, 1758, letter: "The number of people he [Makandal] caused to die . . . is incalculable."[2]

This plantocracy version of Makandal's story can also be seen in the writings of Médéric Louis Élie Moreau de Saint-Méry, a Martinique-born lawyer and administrator, best known for his multiple volumes on French colonial law and writings about Hispaniola. In his time, the island was divided into French Saint-Domingue in the west and Spanish Santo Domingo in the east. French buccaneers spent much of the seventeenth century hiding and plundering along the northwest coast of Hispaniola, eventually realizing more money could be made farming tobacco and sugar. France's hold on that third of the island was secured by the Treaty of Rijswijk in 1697, and Saint-Domingue soon ascended to the top of the colonial hierarchy as France's "jewel" of the Caribbean. Sugar played a large part in this, but coffee and indigo also benefited from the versatile topography of Saint-Domingue.

Slave ships began to arrive in significant numbers by the 1720s, hitting a peak in the 1780s. An estimated 690,000 Africans arrived in Saint-Domingue in the century after it was ceded to France, many from West Central Africa and the Bight of Benin, the majority carried under a French flag.³ By 1778, the value of Saint-Domingue's exports to France, along with the smaller contributions of its other colonies, was nearly 180 million *livres tournois* annually, nearly three times the 60 million *livres tournois* they were worth in 1749.⁴

France, too, had created an African world in the Caribbean, and nowhere as dramatically as in Saint-Domingue, where the enslaved population would grow to be seven times as large as the population of the white and free people of color combined by the end of the century. With such an imbalance and with a mountainous landscape, the island offered numerous opportunities for marronage, of both the *grand* variety, where people fled never to be seen again, and the *petit*, where they returned to a plantation after a short absence. Like the rulers of other European colonies, French colonial administrators sent in troops—known as the *maréchaussée*—to track down the maroon groups, but the French rarely negotiated. Some maroons persisted, like those in Le Maniel, a community in the southern mountains near the border with Santo Domingo, despite French and Spanish officials trying to drive them out.⁵ However, French officials' tolerance of *petit marronage* allowed for the forging of maroon and slave connections across the island, as people gathered for religious ceremonies or dances, building networks that were useful at the time and would become vital in the future.⁶

In Moreau de Saint-Méry's telling—which came some 30 years after Makandal's death—this famous maroon was born in Africa but survived the Middle Passage to end up on the estate of Lenormand de Mézy, in Limbé, in the north of Saint-Domingue, where sugarcane dominated. Other accounts mention Makandal's use of Arabic words such as "Allah," with one report saying he used "words that seemed to come from the Turkish [Arabic] language," suggesting he was from a Muslim part of Africa.⁷ Makandal lost one of his hands working in the plantation's sugar mill and was put to work tending livestock before he finally ran away. In another version of the story, he and his enslaver fought over a young black woman, leading Makandal to receive 50 lashes of the whip and leave soon thereafter.⁸

Once he was a maroon, his full powers were on display, according to Moreau de Saint-Méry: "He became famous for his use of poison, which spread terror among the blacks and made all of them obey him."[9] As part of Makandal's work, he created objects known as fetishes or gris-gris, amulets made with symbolic ingredients, such as particular herbs and fragments of bones. Such talismans blended Africa and the Americas, bringing together old and new practices, beliefs, and objects. Indeed, the word *macandal* comes from two possible Kongo roots, *mak(w)onda* (amulet) or *makanda* (a packet of something wrapped in a leaf).[10]

Like fire, poison was a constant concern for colonial societies. Many unfortunate events were blamed on poison—the unexpected death of an enslaver or a slave, a spate of local deaths due to a virus or other disease, or problems on the plantation such as ill livestock or bad harvests. Enslaved people also worried about dangerous potions, because they could be used to settle disputes or end romantic rivalries. In addition, the creation of the fetishes, with their bits of bone, dirt, plants, and other objects, also unnerved enslavers and colonists. They did not understand the practice and considered it to be heretical, though sometimes incense or holy water, both common in Catholicism, were used in the making of a gris-gris.[11] Another account, from 1787, described Makandal as carrying a stick made from the wood of an orange tree that had carved upon it "a small figure of a man who, when touched a little at the base of the head, moved its eyes and lips and seemed to come to life." Apparently, the little man was an oracle, foretelling deaths with certainty.[12] Such were Makandal's reputed powers that "at the slightest sign from him, people died."[13]

Moreau de Saint-Méry wrote that Makandal had "agents all over the colony" who would assist him with his "vast plan" to overthrow the whites.[14] The reality of his situation is more difficult to ascertain. In his 18 years as a maroon, Makandal would have relied on a network of people, but it is difficult to establish how big his community was, and what his role as leader entailed.[15] What is clear is that he was connected to small traders, known as *pacotilleurs*, who sold goods to the enslaved community. Through these sellers, Makandal had a means of distributing what officials called his "supposedly magical packets," his herbs and potions, around the area. In doing this, he made connections with enslaved and free people alike.[16] For all of this, the authorities deemed him a threat—and wanted to see him dead. An official document from 1758 claimed that Makandal was somehow responsible—either directly or through this network—for a staggering 6,000 deaths over the previous three years.[17] In the months leading up to his capture, at least 18 other people—12 enslaved and six free—were arrested on charges relating to poison, such as its possession or alleged misuse.[18]

Makandal's eventual arrest came after a night during which he went to a dance on the Dufresne plantation, where he began to drink and "found himself deprived of reason."[19] He was sleeping in a slave hut when he was arrested by two white men who had been informed of his whereabouts by a slave. They left him under the guard of two other servants, who later fell asleep. Relying on physical rather than supernatural powers, Makandal climbed out of a window, but the noise woke his guards and the plantation's dogs, and he was soon recaptured.[20]

After his arrest, the author of the June 1758 letter claimed that Makandal "had discovered three types of poisons, some of which are so dangerous and violent that dogs who were given them by doctors and surgeons died immediately."[21] Another report, commissioned by the French government, claimed, "The trial of François Macandal and his accomplices . . . clearly proves that the *nègres* in their superstitious practices successively move on to all [kinds of] crime," though there was no evidence except the existence of gris-gris and other talismans.[22]

On January 20, 1758, the council of Le Cap condemned Makandal to death at the stake, wearing a sign declaring him a SEDUCER, PROFANER, POISONER.[23] His alleged crimes were many, including emancipating himself, using poisons and instructing others how to administer them, and, not least of all, conceiving "the hellish project of eliminating everyone in Saint-Domingue who was not black."[24] Furthermore, according to Moreau de Saint-Méry, Makandal had sworn he would not die at the hands of the French but that, should he be caught by the whites, he would turn into a mosquito to escape—more proof of his dark arts. What happened next was nearly as dramatic. His stake was prepared in front of the church in Le Cap. But "the stake to which he was chained was rotten, and his violent movements . . . pulled out the metal ring and he tumbled out of the fire. The blacks cried out, "*Macandal sauvé*

[Macandal saved]."²⁵ The guards then tied him to a plank and tried again, but the faithful did not believe their eyes, and many remained convinced "that the execution did not kill him."²⁶

The unnamed planter who wrote his June 1758 letter recounted the "general dismay" Makandal caused. The author noted that "since this execution, four or five have been burned every month," by his count 24 people, mostly slaves, over the latest poisoning scare.²⁷ According to other accounts, some white residents believed Makandal and his allies were behind a plot to poison the water supply in all the houses in the city of Le Cap. Then, as people became panicked, they would flee into the countryside, where they would be massacred.²⁸ The letter-writer who witnessed Makandal's death complained, "We tremble to go to each other's houses, and we do not know who to trust, it being impossible to do without the service of these wretches [slaves]."²⁹

Some historians contend that this alleged plot actually existed and that it was an opening maneuver of another sort of rebellion—not a local response to bad treatment, or the establishment of a community in the forest, but an organized, intricate plan to upend the system of slavery on Saint-Domingue.³⁰ That Makandal survives in the collective imagination of Haiti today attests to the power of the vision that has been attributed to him.³¹

The question of poison, however, went beyond Makandal. The French had long prohibited the use of poisons as unfamiliar plants or concoctions were often understood to be at the time, and traditional healing practices were likewise restricted or banned. While all colonial enslavers were anxious about the possibility of poisoning plots in general, other, more local, even personal, concerns existed, such as an enslaver's fear that one of his captives might try to hasten his death by putting something toxic in his food.

In one case, in the year before Makandal's death, a servant in Saint-Domingue named Médor was arrested for poisoning his enslaver to obtain his freedom. In the subsequent testimony, Médor claimed that the only way to stop these poisonings was for enslavers to stop promising slaves their estate would free them after their death. Médor said in his confession that "if he named all the slave poisoners and criminals he would never finish, since they are on all the plantations."³² Poison was another weapon in the arsenal available to enslaved people, and the idea of these deadly concoctions brewed up terror without requiring an actual potion.

⋘ • ⋙

It started with a simple request for some bullets. That in itself was not unusual, but the entreaty came from a slave. In early December 1759 on the Danish island of Saint Croix, an enslaved man named Cudjoe noticed two white men molding bullets on Søren Bagge's plantation.[33] One of the men, Benjamin, refused when Cudjoe explained why he wanted them. The other man, Matthias, handed over a dozen when Benjamin wasn't looking. Benjamin later mentioned the exchange to another white man, Peter, and when they next saw Cudjoe they threatened him. Cudjoe replied: "You look out that some of your heads won't lie at your feet pretty soon," claiming Peter would be killed first.[34]

Cudjoe was soon arrested. Accusations began to fly, and Engelbret Hesselberg, a judge, later wrote about them in a report to the crown. The authorities were quick to bring in a man named Quamina, who was apparently Cudjoe's "own blood brother." He said that Cudjoe had "proposed an uprising in his presence."[35] Cudjoe then confessed and pointed at a free black man, William Davis. Rather than confess, Davis slit his throat in prison. He survived into the next day, but after more efforts to extract information, Davis that evening "tore the bandage from his neck . . . and swore that if they cut him up piece by piece and roasted [him] on the fire, he would nevertheless confess nothing."[36] He died the following day.

Hesselberg never got to the bottom of it, despite the stream of testimony, writing, "It is impossible from the hearings that have been held to learn with full certainty who was the first author of this plot . . . since no one would acknowledge having started it."[37]

To complicate matters, two people were named who had been involved in the 1736 plot in Antigua. George Foot and Sam Hector (also called Quaw) had turned informant about that plot and been deported to Saint Croix. Now they were implicated in this one, with Hesselberg believing Hector might have been the lead instigator, because he was literate and "he was always practiced in the art." He also knew that

Hector had saved his own life by testifying against his father, who was hanged in Antigua.[38]

From multiple witnesses, Hesselberg heard how the alleged conspirators were going to use the distraction of Christmas celebrations to kill their enslavers, and then take one of the island's forts to secure weapons before setting the plantations on fire, "killing and burning all whites who collected to put out the fire." After that, they would storm the island capital of Christiansted. That was the story from those who testified, including details of the oath of secrecy they had taken. One suspect, George, described how they were asked to "put a piece of earth in the mouth" and say, "By Jesus, I will." Apparently, the oath was administered by Davis's wife, who explained, after she was arrested, that this was the "most binding oath" they could make, taking "earth from a dead Negro's grave," mixing it with water, and drinking it.[39] Maybe that was the truth, or maybe Davis's wife knew the sort of tantalizing tale that colonial officials expected to hear. She was later released. Of the 89 people rounded up, 59 were acquitted, 10 were sent off the island, and a few escaped and remained at large. Thirteen faced the stake, the wheel, and the gibbet. Some were "first pinched with hot tongs," with two being "hanged by the legs in a gallows, and a dog likewise, by the neck between them." Sam Hector, who never managed to escape the taint of rebellion, stayed alive for 42 hours on a gibbet before dying.[40]

Quamina, however, was rewarded for his confessions. He received his "letter of freedom" and some money, both of which "were presented to him publicly in the presence of the prisoners and many other Negroes."[41] He was made an example of, in the hope that more people would continue to report these alleged plots, rather than gain the freedom that only came through death.

From a conversation about a few bullets to death on the gallows in a matter of days: The merest whiff of conspiracy was enough to spark a full panic. Even mere thoughts of freedom seemed to lead to the flames of the stake. Hesselberg blamed the mistreatment of the enslaved for the plotting, which was a common excuse. He also pointed to the demographic imbalance common in the Caribbean. In 1758, there were 1,690 white people and 11,807 black, mostly enslaved, on Saint Croix.[42]

But in an introduction to his report, aware of the gruesome punishments he would detail at the end, Hesselberg observed, "The greater part of the slaves on the colonies as recently developed as St Croix are free-born [in Africa], and have therefore just as good claim to their freedom as we have to ours . . . what wonder then that such persons seek freedom."[43]

⋘ • ⋙

News of the events in Saint Croix no doubt reached Jamaica, but the lone guard on patrol at Fort Haldane in the northeastern town of Port Maria was unprepared for a slave rebellion in the early morning of April 8, 1760, when nearly one hundred Africans entered the fort and took arms and gunpowder.[44] The rebels left, their weapons now secured, and headed across Saint Mary's Parish, raiding and setting fires as they went. Officials were quick to name Tacky as ringleader, a Coromantee who was described as having "been a chief in Guiney."[45] Although this would become known as "Tacky's Revolt," the uprising was the work of more than one person, and it was far more than a revolt. Historians have recently argued that it was a war—taking place within the larger Seven Years' War (1756–1763)—and as such could encompass a larger landscape and seascape of Africa and the Americas, sailors and slaves, officials, soldiers, free people, plantation owners, Amerindian scouts, and maroons.[46] In short, the entirety of the colonial world was knotted into this conflict.[47] Tacky's Revolt—like many others that had come before and would come after—was not a small, local eruption, easily snuffed out. Rather, this resistance was akin to a multisite, decentralized guerrilla war, not against a particular king or ruler, but against a social and economic system. The more that system grew, the more the fighting and these sorts of conflicts intensified, as they did that April in Jamaica.

Tacky and his soldiers continued their raids on some of the plantations. Saint Mary's was a zone dominated by sugar production, with a small white population and a much larger African one, with many recent arrivals, some of whom quickly joined the rebels. Although maroons are rightfully given credit for their skillful use of a complicated landscape, such as the one in Jamaica, enslaved people like Tacky also had to learn the contours and secrets of the topography in case the moment should arise to exploit them. The rebels raided plantations, taking what they needed and sparing some lives. A few days later, now numbering around 400, they went into the forest to plot their next move. There, they had what was later described as a "celebration," but, as had been the case in Stono, it was not a victory party. It was a time to eat, drink, and rest to prepare for the battles ahead.[48]

As in Nanny's rebellion decades earlier, the supernatural played a role. Obeah practitioners were involved in administering oaths to the new recruits, as well as helping to protect Tacky. Word of his supposed invincibility soon spread. The rebels continued to fare well, using the forests to their benefit, outmaneuvering British soldiers. The authorities declared martial law and mobilized whomever they could, eventually blocking main routes and driving Tacky deeper into the forest, away from the plantations. They also called in the maroons, as part of the deal they had struck. Maroons from Scott's Hall and Crawford Town were soon in the forests, which they knew as well as, if not better than, the rebels.[49]

About five days into the insurgency, Tacky was injured. With his supernatural protection pierced, morale started to fall. On April 14, the maroons faced the rebels again, with Lieutenant Davy from Scott's Hall pursuing Tacky and shooting him dead as they were running. The first phase of the conflict was over. Some of the rebel slaves were captured by the maroons and the British, while others killed themselves. The maroons, meanwhile, cut the ears off the dead, 17 pairs as proof to the British of their assistance.[50] In the case of Tacky, however, his entire head was the trophy, and it was carried to Spanish Town and placed atop a pole. Not long after, someone stole it, possibly to take it to a more respectable final resting place.[51]

The Royal Navy brought soldiers and provisions to the island, also providing a shipboard holding space for the growing number of people who were arrested.[52] In May, the interrogations and executions began, as well as the rumors. According to one story, this was to have been one of many uprisings to murder all the white people, and it would have happened earlier but Tacky had gotten drunk and bungled the timing. Before the officials had time to investigate the veracity of this claim, news arrived from Saint Thomas of a conspiracy there, then another revolt erupted in Jamaica's Westmoreland Parish, some 120 miles (190 kilometers) west of Saint Mary's.

Events took a new turn with the attacks in Westmoreland, with its many sugar plantations and a far denser population than Saint Mary's.[53] This became the second front, the continuation of battle. It started with an attack on the Masemure estate and soon moved across many of the plantations in a systematic fashion—with the rebels securing weapons, taking followers, and killing white colonists.[54] Leading the revolt was Wager (also known as Apongo), a West African military leader who had had dealings with the British at Cape Coast Castle, on the Gold Coast, before being captured and enslaved. He had the dangerous combination of knowledge and a desire for vengeance.[55] With that sort of background, he was a formidable foe. Within a day, attacks were made on plantations near the Hanover mountains, where these rebels had their hideout, with an advantageous vista of the plantations below.[56]

Troops from the 49th Regiment of Foot, the local militia, and the Royal Navy stepped up their efforts. The island was now far more fortified than it had been, owing in part to the ongoing Seven Years' War. Its theater of war extended to the Caribbean, and Jamaica was a strategic spot. At least 16 warships were assigned to the island, with 3,700 men, and at least another 7,500 fit to serve on land, mostly in the militia. There were also the maroons.[57] Despite the rebels' small numbers and bad odds, their knowledge of the terrain meant that the British would have to use more guerrilla and scorched-earth tactics, rather than fight their enemy on the battlefield. Ultimately, the British had to starve the rebels out of the forests, while also dissuading any more enslaved people from joining them.[58]

By July, Wager was captured, having earlier been wounded. His band of 80 or so rebels were becoming exhausted, and had been fighting among themselves about strategy and tactics. Wager hung in chains for three days, and then was burned alive.[59] After this there were sporadic raids, but no more mass uprisings like the one that had started with Tacky. The official end of the rebellion was announced in October 1761, more than a year after its outbreak. The total dead numbered around 60 whites, 60 free people of color, and 300 to 400 rebels, some in battle and others by suicide, with another 100 executed and some 500 sent to British Honduras.[60]

The rebels might have been stopped, but their spirits were not flagging. In 1765 an enslaved man known as Blackwall, or Abruco, who had been acquitted in relation to the events of 1760, was implicated in an attack by fellow Coromantees on the Whitehall estate in Saint Mary's.[61] Some enslaved people employed other forms of revolt, liberating themselves by sea, including by stolen canoe, and sailing to Cuba. Nearly 100 people fled to that neighboring island between 1765 and 1767, hoping to be granted liberty by the Spanish monarch, like the Stono rebels who had marched from South Carolina to Florida.[62]

News of the ongoing unrest spread beyond the island, drawing the attention of an increasingly concerned public in Britain. A growing print culture made it difficult to be ignorant of the situation in the West India colonies. Early abolitionists, still a small group at this point, in Britain could add the potential for revolt to the growing list of reasons why slavery needed to end.

In Jamaica, social control tightened, on both slaves and free people of color, circumscribing movement, prohibiting gatherings, and criminalizing obeah practices, making them punishable by death or deportation. Free people of color had to officially register their status, and renew its certification annually. In addition, they were told to wear a blue cross on their right shoulder, called the "Badge of Freedom," to differentiate themselves from the enslaved.[63]

Any maroon or slave who brought in a rebel received a reward, including manumission, but also money and medals. Some rewarded slaves were given a silver medal with the words "Freedom for being Honest" engraved on one side, and "By the Country" on the other.[64] Planters clamored for compensation to offset their "property" losses, as well as damage incurred to their estates during the conflict. Military regiments were stationed permanently and defenses were reinforced. Fewer Coromantees from the Gold Coast were taken to Jamaica, and by 1780, the number of creole slaves on the island surpassed that of African captives.[65]

The British authorities in Jamaica prevailed for the time being, but the "spirit of rebellion" had not been extinguished.

⊰⊰ • ⊱⊱

His name was Oroonoko. He was a Coromantee prince and fierce warrior who was "adorned with a native beauty so transcending . . . that he struck an awe and reverence."[66] He was in love with Imoinda, the daughter of one of his generals, who was as beautiful as he was handsome. Their lives became upended after Imoinda was sold into slavery while Oroonoko was away fighting. Upon his return, he was tricked by the captain of an English vessel and also enslaved.

When the ship he was on arrived in Suriname, at some point in the 1660s, he was quickly sold, and his enslaver renamed him Caesar. As fate would have it, Imoinda was in Suriname as well, on the same plantation, having been renamed Clemene. Their enslaver permitted them to marry, and Oroonoko intensified his campaign for freedom. The prince's frustration mounted, leading him to ask, "Why . . . should we be slaves to an unknown people? Have they vanquished us nobly in fight?"

He decided to lead the exodus of a group of slaves, some of whom recognized his royal identity and became loyal followers. They would leave and set up a new colony, until they could seize a ship and return home, and "if they died in the attempt it would be more brave than to live in perpetual slavery."[67] They tried to escape, but the planters and authorities caught up with them and Oroonoko and his deputy, Tuscan, eventually surrendered. Before they knew what was happening, they were tied to a post and whipped. Oroonoko tried to betray no emotion, except "a woe and revenge from his eyes, that darted fire."[68] The now heavily pregnant Imoinda was taken into confinement and did not see the whipping.

Once he had recovered, Oroonoko decided to try a different plan. It was clear there was no escape, so he would kill Imoinda and then his enemies, before taking his own life and joining her. He committed the first murder in the woods, staying with Imoinda's body in the deepest grip of grief until his enslaver came to look for him. At that point, "he ripped up his own belly, and took his bowels." But Tuscan, who also arrived, tried to rescue him, and a surgeon was sent for. The governor soon heard of these developments with the troublesome prince, and wanted him dead. Oroonoko was dragged to the stake. He asked for a pipe of tobacco, which he smoked "as if nothing had touched him," while the executioner "cut off his members and threw them into the fire," followed by his ears and nose, and one arm. He kept smoking. When the other arm was severed, he dropped the pipe and died, after which he was cut into quarters.[69]

Oroonoko was many things, but he was not a real person. Rather, he was the creation of Aphra Behn. This Restoration-era writer was rare in her time, in part because few women made a living by their pen in the seventeenth century. But it was also unusual that Behn had travelled to Suriname, probably at some point in the early 1660s. Her experiences there inspired the novel *Oroonoko, or the History of the Royal Slave*, published in 1688.[70]

Suriname at this point was still on the fringes of Britain's nascent colonial empire, on what was then called the "Wild Coast," although it would not be connected to Britain for long. The colony was traded to the Dutch in exchange for New Netherland (New York) in 1667. Suriname had an unsteady start, with planters attempting and often failing to survive the tropics, seeking sugar fortunes along the Suriname River, hemmed in by the sea to the north and dense jungles to the south.

While there was no actual Oroonoko, Behn may well have seen a Coromantee prince when she was there. There would certainly have been Africans working in the fields, even at this early point. The novel became popular and was adapted for the stage in London. It was ahead of its time in presenting the moral dilemmas that the system of slavery presented, especially as there was not a white abolitionist movement in England at the time. Jump forward nearly a century, and the novel and play enjoyed renewed interest in the 1760s, just as the abolitionist movement was stirring.[71] The public was by now more familiar with a figure like Oroonoko, as the newspapers had been carrying stories of slave revolts for decades. Indeed, an equally dramatic uprising broke out in 1763, in the Dutch territory of Berbice (today's Guyana)—and its events were true.

Seventy-five years after Behn introduced the fictional Oroonoko to the world, in neighboring Berbice, directly west of Suriname, a man named Coffij was very real to the Dutch authorities. Berbice was another narrow colony, established around 1627. From its coast it wound inland, along the sinews of the Berbice River. The Dutch probably felt some familiarity with the low, flat coastal plain of this region of South America, parts of which resemble the Low Countries. Canals and sluices control the waters of the lowlands, where most of the population lives, but the palm trees and tropical foliage are a reminder that this isn't Holland. Berbice was similar to Suriname in that Europeans began to creep inland from the sea, but they could only go so far, with its hinterland being difficult for settlers to survive. At the time of Coffij's arrival in 1762, the colony was controlled by the Company of Berbice (Sociëteit van Berbice), operating under the auspices of the Dutch Republic.[72]

Neighboring Suriname was home to an increasing number of maroon communities, the dense jungles offering numerous locations for people who wanted to establish lives far from Europeans. Like maroons in other colonies, they sometimes had to broker peace treaties with the European authorities—in this case the Dutch; for instance, the Okanisi (also Ndyuka) maroons signed a treaty in 1760, as did the Samaaka (or Saramaka) maroons in 1762, both parties probably aware of similar arrangements made between maroons and the English in Jamaica. Officials in Berbice also made treaties with the Amerindians, requiring them to return or kill runaways; it was an attempt to limit marronage, but it also created an alliance that would prove advantageous in the summer of 1763.

During the rainy season of 1762, the slaves on the plantation called Goed Land en Goed Fortuin used the temporary absence of their enslaver to flee in the hopes of finding their own good land and fortune.[73] The work on this estate, already difficult, had been rendered nearly unbearable by disease and food shortages. That July, a group of 26 enslaved people, led by the *bomba* Adam, first slaughtered and ate some cow, then raided the plantation house, taking provisions and arms before fleeing by canoe along the river. They managed to stay away from the few Dutch soldiers stationed in this remote spot, but in early August their fortunes turned, and half the group were killed or captured. The survivors fled deeper into the woods, though Adam was eventually caught and killed. Only two survivors remained, an

Amerindian woman named Antoinette and a man named Coffij, who was going to be executed for his part in the events. Taking a drink of rum before he was forced to depart this world, he told the officials that what they had failed to do, "others would soon carry out."[74] Little could he have known that it would be through the actions of a namesake.

The following year opened with similar unrest, as the governor, Wolfert Simon van Hoogenheim, heard reports of attacks and desertions at plantations on the Canje River, which flowed into the Berbice. Then, at the end of February, he faced an even larger uprising of people at four plantations located about 25 miles upriver from New Amsterdam and Fort Nassau, the hub of the colony. The initial attack was on a Sunday, probably for strategic reasons, and during the dry season, which brought the rebels some advantages in navigating the forests and jungles. Within a short time, panicked—and vastly outnumbered—planters and settlers fled, some by canoe, others to neighboring plantations. Emerging out of the chaos was another Coffij, who led the revolt. He was soon identified by the authorities as Coffij van Lelienburg, from the Lelienburg plantation. His lieutenant was Accara, also possibly an Amina (Coromantee) from the Gold Coast.[75]

The white colonists continued to flee, unwilling or unable to fight the rebels, making the journey to the coast and trying to leave by ship. The rebels were soon able to base themselves at Fort Nassau. Other Europeans ended up hostages to the rebels, and were either later killing them, punishing them, or putting them to work.[76] Governor van Hoogenheim watched as potential soldiers fled. He sent for help from Suriname, but the hundred or so soldiers that came would not be enough. Coffij and Accara were quick to send messages to the governor, explaining that this uprising was in response to bad treatment and naming the abusive enslavers. They also said that they had not been receiving "what was their due," though they did not specify what that meant.[77]

In April, a letter from Coffij and Accara to the governor contained a surprise. Referring to themselves as Coffij, Governor of the *Neegers van de Berbice*, and Captain Accara, they laid out a new vision. Coffij and his people wanted half the colony. They would keep the upper half, and the Dutch could take the lower. And while they made clear they would not be slaves, they told the governor that the "blacks you have on your ships can be your slaves."[78] The meaning of this statement is not entirely clear; possibly they were proposing that theirs would be a land of freedom, while those enslaved people who did not join their cause could stay as Dutch slaves. But apparently they intended to make money, like the white colonists, carrying on the plantation model, growing sugar and other crops. This would be no maroon colony, but rather, a black state.

Coffij asked for a meeting so they could discuss this offer, but it was not forthcoming. His comment about the remaining slaves points to what may have been his undoing, as not all enslaved people had joined them. West India Company slaves in Berbice, many of whom had been creole for generations, were wary.[79] They did not want to be freed only to find themselves forced to serve these Africans, in a traditional Amina/Coromantee style. Some, however, found themselves coerced into participation as the rebels attacked plantations. It is also not entirely clear how well Coffij articulated his vision to his followers, because rifts began to emerge. Confidence in his leadership waned, and some in his ranks did not want to negotiate with the Dutch.

The Dutch were not having much luck either. Some of the troops who had come to help ended up mutinying and ultimately joining the rebels. The rebels shot 28 of the mutineers, but kept the rest of the 41 who absconded.[80]

It was a difficult rainy season. Van Hoogenheim waited on reinforcements from Holland, though he continued to use the services of Amerindians in attacking the rebels when possible. He and Coffij exchanged correspondence in late summer, with Coffij discussing negotiations again in August, this time reframing his demands to keep four WIC plantations—though this was mostly the same area under discussion—and telling the governor "the rest is for you."[81] The correspondence continued, with Van Hoogenheim stalling for time. Then, in startling news, Coffij shot himself. He had lost the confidence of his people and a rival named Atta had taken charge.[82]

Reports of the rebellion finally reached Amsterdam, and reinforcements were dispatched, setting off in October 1763. In the meantime, Atta began to craft his vision. It resembled a traditional maroon colony rather than an independent state. In the end, the combination of reinforcements from Holland and the reliability and skill of the

Amerindian allies gave the Dutch the advantage. Hundreds of rebels began to return to their enslavers, forced out of hiding by exhaustion and hunger. The conditions under Atta must have been extremely difficult for them to surrender and face potential death and almost certain slavery. Atta was caught the following April, in 1764. His death assured, the Dutch captured the other leaders.[83]

The enslaved men forced to be executioners had a grim summer that year: One hundred twenty men and four women were condemned to death. The rebellion was over, but the colony never completely recovered, economically or socially. The Dutch government eventually stepped in, taking it over in 1795.[84]

Coffij's vision was never realized, but it spoke to possibilities beyond marronage. A black state, economically independent and on a level footing with the whites. If the system could not be overturned, then at least some people could live in dignity and cultivate their patch of freedom.

⋘ • ⋙

THE REVOLTS INITIATED by Tacky and Coffij took place as the Seven Years' War raged in the background. In North America, that conflict started slightly earlier, with the French and Indian war of 1754, before turning into a global conflict by 1756 with theaters of war in the Caribbean, West Africa, India, and Europe. When it came to an end in 1763, Britain dominated North America and the Caribbean, having taken the French colonies of Canada, Dominica, Grenada, Saint Vincent and the Grenadines, and Tobago, while also receiving Spanish Florida in exchange for the Cuban port of Havana, which it had occupied in 1762.

The growth of the European colonies and their clear value at that point, along with the hundreds of thousands of Africans required to run them, exacerbated an unresolved problem. The issue of freedom was knocking on Europe's door, and no one wanted to answer. From 1700 to 1763, the year the Seven Years' War ended, nearly 3 million people had been taken from Africa, 2.5 million of them disembarking at ports throughout the Americas.[85] But other people from Africa or of African descent had been born in or taken to France, Britain, and Holland, countries that had long proclaimed their soil to be free. This claim clearly could not be made about their colonies.

In 1759, the French Supreme Court upheld the notion that setting foot on French soil would free a slave.[86] The earlier royal edict of 1716 stated that owners could bring their slaves to France and take them back to the colonies, so long as they made clear that the stay was temporary.[87] But it was not possible for a person to return to France and keep an enslaved person in that status permanently. France found itself continually adapting its law as the African population of its colonies grew. In 1724, it went so far as to update the 1685 French *Code Noir* for its Louisiana territory, making even more severe restrictions. Some 7,000 Africans had been taken to New Orleans between 1718 and 1735, doubling the population.[88] Colonial officials there found themselves dealing with problems like runaways. Now these problems would fall to Spain, which took over France's vast Louisiana territory in a 1762 *pacte de famille*, between the Bourbon crowns of both kingdoms, intended to keep it out of British hands.

In 1777, another royal decree, known as the *Police des Noirs*, was issued to address metropolitan fears about a rising free black population within France. The minister of the marine, Antoine de Sartine, had complained, "The public houses are infected, the colors mingle together; the blood degenerates." He was also concerned about the sorts of ideas black people were carrying across the Atlantic. To counter such fears, the government implemented a full ban on any people of color, including free people, being brought to mainland France.[89] However, such broad legislation would prove extremely difficult to enforce.[90]

In 1761, the Marquis de Pombal, Portugal's first minister, introduced legislation under which an enslaved person who arrived in the country would be set free and not forced to return to the colonies as a slave. This was followed by a 1773 law that freed enslaved people in Portugal. The marquis also prohibited the introduction of new slaves into Portugal and its North Atlantic islands. However, none of these changes applied to Brazil or the African colonies.[91] The matter at hand wasn't "free soil," as it was in France, but rather an unwelcome disruption of the social order. The question of whether a "civilized" Enlightenment city such as Lisbon, rebuilt after a devastating earthquake in 1755, should have enslaved people in its public spaces was more a concern about appearances than about the rights of enslaved people. The law also reflected worries that urban male slaves, *moços de servir* ("service boys"), were underemployed, rendering them not only idle but, in the imagination of the white public, potentially dangerous.[92]

However limited the Portuguese legislation might have been, a crack had appeared. Black Catholic confraternities in Portugal helped secure freedom for enslaved people who arrived there after 1761. Such was the volume of applications for manumission that the law had to be amended to exclude enslaved sailors registered on ships' lists, because "it would be a blow to navigation . . . if the slaves who make up the crew of these ships became free as soon as they arrived."[93] This change came at a time when the Portuguese were still in control of around 40 percent of the transatlantic slave trade.[94] The new law did not apply in Brazil: That colony would see the implementation of different measures meant to improve the harsh conditions of slavery, though whether they were enacted and to what degree is impossible to measure.[95]

Britain was experiencing challenges over its free soil as well. By the mid-1700s, the population of enslaved and free black people within Britain had reached 14,000 to 20,000.[96] Enslavers sometimes brought their domestic servants to Britain with them—indeed, many West Indian plantation owners did not live in the colonies—but the captives were considered legal property and thus could not be freed simply by setting foot in Britain.[97] However, the legal position was not entirely clear, being covered by common law rather than codified legislation. Enslaved servants who managed to run away and join black communities challenged the system with their actions. Hundreds of advertisements were placed by angered enslavers in newspapers across Britain looking for freedom-seekers.[98] In addition, by the 1760s a small but growing number of voices in the white community began speaking out against the treatment of humans as property. Prominent among them was Granville Sharp, who published a pamphlet in 1769 entitled "A Representation of the Injustice and Dangerous Tendency of Tolerating Slavery, or Admitting the Least Claim of Private Property in the Persons of Men in England," which argued, "No man therefore, of whatever estate or condition that he be, can lawfully be detained in England as a slave, because we have no law, whereby a man may be condemned to slavery, without his own consent."[99] In that same year, a notice in the *Edinburgh Advertiser* called for the return of "An American black boy, named James, about 15 years of age, with short curled hair, speaks remarkable good English, and is very artful, had on when he went away, a brown suit of cloaths with white metal buttons, and black stocking breeches. As he also carried off some shirts and silk stockings of his master's, which, in all probability, he may offer to sale."[100]

Young men like James would be forced to flee for some time yet, but in only a few years Sharp would come across a court case that would change the legal landscape of Britain over the question of who was free.

Chapter 17

Quills

Just inside the main body of the elegant Christopher Wren–designed Saint James's Piccadilly, in London, a sturdy baptismal font stands to one side. Attributed to Grinling Gibbons and installed around 1686, the font survived the bombings of the Second World War, its solid marble now showing the smoothness of age. It tells the story of creation, Adam, Eve, and the serpent wrapped around its base, while the bowl features a depiction of the baptism of Christ on the front, and Noah's Ark along the side. On the back is a more obscure biblical tale, the story of Saint Philip's baptism of the eunuch of Candace.

In this story (Acts 8:26–40), an angel directed Philip to leave Jerusalem and head toward Gaza. Along the way, Philip saw the chariot of the "Candace," or queen, of Ethiopia. Among her entourage was a eunuch, her treasurer, who happened to be reading the Prophet Isaiah. Philip, moved by the spirit, ran to him and "preached unto him Jesus." As they went along the road, they spotted a pool of water, and the eunuch said: "See, here is water; what doth hinder me to be baptized?" Philip performed the sacrament on the spot, and "when they were come up out of the water, the Spirit of the Lord caught away Philip, that the eunuch saw him no more: and he went on his way rejoicing."[1] That scene completes the font, Saint Philip sprinkling water on the eunuch's head as the chariot waits.

Of all the baptismal fonts in all the churches of London, this is the one that a 15-year-old African boy named Quobna Ottobah Cugoano stepped up to on August 20, 1773, to receive his baptism. Whether or not he was already well-versed enough in the Bible to know that story, and to recognize that the Europeanized figures in the carving had an

African dimension, his baptism that day wove together these strands of people and place—Africa, the Americas, and Europe.[2]

The previous few years had been eventful for the young Cugoano. He had lived among his Fante people on the Gold Coast (Ghana) until he was 13, when he was kidnapped and sold into slavery. He landed in Grenada, which was one of the islands recently ceded by France to Britain after the Seven Years' War. In 1772, his enslaver, Alexander Campbell, brought him to England. It was an auspicious time for an arrival, coming at around the same time as the *Somerset* legal decision of June 22.[3]

This case came in front of the Chief Justice of the King's Bench, Lord Mansfield, after an enslaved man named James Somerset had fled while in England. He was recaptured, and his enslaver, Charles Stewart, tried to ship him to Jamaica. Somerset invoked the writ of habeas corpus to secure his freedom in court. White abolitionists heard about this case, and it was quickly picked up by Granville Sharp, who understood its potential. Somerset had been taken from Massachusetts to England in 1769 by Stewart, a customs official. Somerset ran away and was caught in November 1771. Stewart wanted to send him to Jamaica, but Somerset understood that he could claim freedom in England, and he was determined to try.

The ruling came down in Somerset's favor: An enslaver could not force a slave to leave England against his or her will. In his oral opinion, Mansfield said, "Whatever inconveniences, therefore, may follow from a decision, I cannot say this case is allowed or approved by the law of England; and therefore the black must be discharged."[4]

The impact was immediate. "Several Negroes were in court yesterday, to hear the event of a cause so interesting to their tribe," the *Morning Chronicle* reported. "And after the judgment of the court was known, [they] bowed with profound respect to the Judges, and shaking each other by the hand, congratulated themselves upon the recovery of the rights of human nature."[5]

Mansfield had significant personal connections to this case. He was the great-uncle of a young woman named Dido Elizabeth Belle, whose mother, Maria Bell(e), was African, and whose father, John Lindsay, was a Royal Navy officer and Mansfield's nephew.[6] Belle grew up in Mansfield's home in Kenwood House, on Hampstead Heath, in

London, which was not the usual fate for mixed-heritage children born out of wedlock.

Mansfield's decision helped lift the legal fog around slavery in Britain, even though the judgement didn't ban the practice outright. Rather, the ruling said a enslaver could not seize a slave and remove him from England against his will, and the slave could invoke habeas corpus.[7] However, the judgement was soon understood to be the abolition of slavery in England, and Scotland followed suit. However, the overseas colonies, inevitably, did not—so some enslaved people decided to take themselves to England. Newspapers in British North American colonies saw the number of advertisements looking for runaways believed to have gone to sea triple in the immediate years after the decision.[8]

Whatever his thoughts on these legal questions, Cugoano's first concern was staying free. Being baptized and taking the name John Stuart (or Stewart) was one step, as he recalled 14 years later, writing "I was advised by some good people to get myself baptized, that I might not be carried away and sold again."[9] *Somerset* may have been a legal reality, but enslaved and free black people were all too aware of the fragility of any promises of freedom.

Cugoano found work as a servant, living among the well-connected in the Pall Mall home of the artists Maria and Richard Cosway, less than 10 minutes by foot from Saint James's. The only surviving glimpse of Cugoano is in Richard's 1784 engraving of the couple, in which Cugoano is serving them grapes from the side, his head tilted downward but his smile evident.

In his time there, Cugoano became involved in the growing abolitionist movement among both black and white communities, for instance helping to secure, along with another black man, William Green, the release of Harry Demane. This enslaved man was due to be sent to the West Indies in 1786, and the other two brought in Sharp to help prevent the forced deportation.[10] The following year, Cugoano published *Thoughts and Sentiments on the Evil and Wicked Traffic of the Slavery and Commerce of the Human Species*, which appeared in French in 1788.[11] "What is required, is evidently the incumbent duty of all men of enlightened understanding, and of every man that has any claim or affinity to the name of Christian, that the base treatment which the African Slaves undergo, ought to be abolished," Cugoano insisted.[12]

In his book, Cugoano mentioned the work of Ukawsaw Gronniosaw, a fellow African who ended up in England. He wrote the *Narrative of the Most Remarkable Particulars in the Life of James Albert Ukawsaw Gronniosaw, an African Prince, as Related by Himself* in 1772, which ran through multiple editions. Cugoano described Gronniosaw as being "in a very poor state" but insisted that "he would not have given his faith in the Christian religion, in exchange for all the kingdoms of Africa."[13] Whereas Cugoano wrote about the evils of slavery as a system in his work, Gronniosaw mostly recounted his experiences, which, as one of the earliest slave narratives published in English, would have been of great interest to the public.

Gronniosaw started by discussing his childhood in Africa. He claimed to be the son of the king of Zaara, in Bournou (northeast Nigeria) and to have been raised Muslim. He was tricked into slavery, being told that he "should see houses with wings to them, walk upon the sea, and should also see white folks."[14] The disturbing reality soon sank in as Gronniosaw found himself aboard a ship bound for Barbados, sold to a man who later took him to New York. This man, he wrote, "dressed me in his livery, and was very good to me." After that he was sold to Theodorus Jacobus Frelinghuysen, a Dutch Reformed clergyman, who freed Gronniosaw upon his death, in 1747.[15] Much of Gronniosaw's account is about his discovery of and conversion to Christianity, which began in earnest while he was in the Frelinghuysen household, where he also learned to read and write. He continued living with the Frelinghuysen family for a number of years, "'til they died . . . When it quite pleased God to take them to himself, I was left quite destitute, without a friend in the world."[16]

Gronniosaw decided to leave for England, particularly desirous to go to Kidderminster, which had been home to the Calvinist preacher Richard Baker. To earn money for his trip, he first joined a privateering mission as a cook, ending up in battle with French ships near Saint-Domingue, though he was swindled out of his prize money by an unscrupulous lender after that expedition. Next, Gronniosaw enlisted in New York as part of the 28th Regiment of the Foot, bound for Martinique via Barbados during the Seven Years' War, eventually landing in Havana. He secured passage to England on a prison ship, and finally arrived in Portsmouth around the end of 1762. His experience in England started badly, and he was quickly cheated out of what little money he had.[17] He made his way to London and connected with the prominent Methodist preacher George Whitefield, who helped him.

Whitefield, for his part, was an enslaver who owned plantations in Georgia. However, he was famous as a minister who lobbied for the better treatment of slaves—though not for the end of the system that tortured them. He had established the Bethesda Orphan House, near Savannah, buying the land for it around 1739, but was frustrated by the poverty of the colony and the limited funds for the orphanage. He campaigned for the introduction of slavery there to improve its economy. Whitefield bought a plantation of 4,000 acres and eventually 50 enslaved people produced an income for the orphanage.[18] At the same time, he called for the better treatment of slaves, by which he meant their instruction in and conversion to Christianity. His was a particularly dexterous—but by no means unique—display of the moral gymnastics required to both own slaves and also champion their inclusion in Christianity.

Gronniosaw left for Holland, spending a year there, but returned to England to marry an English weaver named Betty. The couple and their children lived in financial precarity, and this may have been one impetus for publishing a book. At the end of the account, the family arrives in Kidderminster, where both parents find work, and Gronniosaw concludes, "Thus far the Lord has brought me on."[19]

Christianity features in many of the narratives by formerly enslaved people in the late eighteenth century, the conversion story running alongside the struggle for bodily freedom. Putting aside the personal and spiritual dimension of faith, invoking Protestant Christianity was vital for securing patrons and the assistance of white abolitionists, most of whom were members of Protestant denominations, such as the Quakers.

The year after Gronniosaw's work was published, a review of the poems of Phillis Wheatley appeared in *The London Magazine*. Wheatley was an enslaved woman in Massachusetts who arrived in Boston on the *Phillis*, for which she was named, in 1761, as a child of about seven. She lived in the household of John and Susanne Wheatley, who bought her around the time of the ninth anniversary of the death of their own daughter, Sarah. They were believed to have treated her well and they allowed her to receive an education.[20]

Her education facilitated the development of a literary talent that soon came to international attention. This first arrived in 1770, when she wrote an elegiac poem upon the death of Reverend Whitefield, which was published in the *Boston News-Letter*, attracting both local and international acclaim.[21] However, Phillis was not able to find a publisher for more of her work in Boston, so she and the Wheatleys began to look to London, where the publication of *Poems on Various Subjects, Religious and Moral* was eventually secured.

Wheatley's health had been poor over the previous year, but in May 1773 she left Boston for London, accompanied by John Wheatley's son, Nathaniel. Such was the interest in her poetry that newspapers in Boston and New York reported on her trip. She attracted the notice of Selina Hastings, Countess of Huntingdon, who was deeply involved with Reverend Whitefield—later inheriting his plantation—and his branch of Methodism. Wheatley was aware of Huntingdon's influence, and sent her a copy of the Whitefield elegy, opening a correspondence between them. Due to the countess's ill health, she and Wheatley would not meet in person, though that did not hinder Huntingdon from becoming Wheatley's patron, as she had done with other black writers, including Gronniosaw.[22] As a patron, Huntingdon would have doubtless been cheered by the glowing review of Wheatley's poems in the September edition of *The London Magazine*, whose editors could not "suppress [their] admiration of talents so vigorous and lively," though they tempered their praise by saying that the poems in themselves "display no astonishing power of genius," their merit coming from the fact that they were written by "a young untutored African."[23]

The frontispiece of the book labels Phillis a "negro servant" rather than a slave. London in the post-*Somerset* era would have been a complicated place to bring enslaved people, as they were technically free. Wheatley and her enslavers must have been aware of this, especially because one of the people who showed her around the city was the abolitionist Granville Sharp.[24] However, she returned to Boston and slavery, though a short time later, the Wheatley family freed her.

The image of Wheatley on the frontispiece shows her dressed plainly, her hair covered by a ribboned cap. Her eyes look upward, as she holds a quill, her paper and inkpot in front of her. She is captured in the midst of her creative process, or perhaps the upward gaze was also meant to signify her faith. She is shown in profile, too busy writing poems to look back at the viewer. However, she is constrained in an oval, and around her neck is a dark string, a subtle symbolic representation of the slave's collar.[25] Included in her volume is a short but pointed verse about her condition, "On Being Brought from Africa to America":

> 'Twas mercy brought me from my *Pagan* land
> Taught my benighted soul to understand
> That there's a God, there's a *Saviour* too:
> Once I redemption neither fought nor knew.
> Some view our sable race with scornful eye,
> "Their colour is a diabolic die"
> Remember, *Christians*, *Negroes*, black as *Cain*,
> May be refin'd and join th' angelic train.[26]

This work is very much in conversation with that of other African writers, like Gronniosaw and Cugoano, who used Christianity as a way to express belonging in the white world in which they found themselves. Even Cugoano, critical as he was of slavery, cast his experience as a deliverance to Christianity, writing, "Whatever evil intentions and bad motives those insidious robbers had in carrying me away from my native country and friends, I trust, was what the Lord intended for my good."[27]

While Cugoano was settling into London and Wheatley was promoting her book, Ignatius Sancho was tending his grocery shop.[28] Sancho had been in the city since the 1730s. He was born around 1729, on a slave ship sailing between Guinea and Cartagena, ending up in England in the home of three unmarried sisters in Greenwich. They treated him badly, but during his time there he made the acquaintance of the Duke and Duchess of Montagu in nearby Blackheath who educated him. Sancho eventually joined their household.[29] The duke had died by this time, but Sancho was a paid butler to the duchess until her death.[30] He later ran a grocery store funded by an annuity he received from the Montagu family. He maintained connections and correspondence with many people in literary circles, and was considered to be a talented writer and musician. He was also a property owner, which meant that he was one of the earliest men of African origin to vote in Britain, casting his ballot in the 1774 and 1780 general elections.[31]

Thomas Gainsborough painted a portrait of Sancho in 1768, an engraving of which was printed on the frontispiece of his collected letters, which were published by an admirer in 1782, two years after his death. Like Wheatley's portrait, Sancho's is constrained in an oval. He shows a hint of rotundness—he was plagued by gout—and is dressed in an elegant red waistcoat.

Sancho and Wheatley did not meet when she was in London in 1773, but he was familiar with her work. In one letter, he said her poems "do credit to nature—and put art—merely as art—to the blush." But he was also aware of the hypocrisy of the white people who would publish and lavish praise on the poems, while perpetuating the system that put Wheatley in captivity: "These good great folks—all know—and perhaps admired—nay, praised Genius in bondage—and then, like the Priests and the Levites in sacred writ, passed by—not one good Samaritan amongst them."[32]

Like Wheatley and Cugoano, Sancho was forced to reckon with his Africanness and the legacy of slavery in the context of Christian salvation. To invoke the Christian, Protestant God was to participate in the dominant discourse, of which Sancho would have been well aware. He wrote in another letter, "Let us ... look into ourselves—and by a critical examination of the past events of our lives, fairly confess what mercies we have received—what God in his goodness hath done for us."[33]

While it is not clear that Cugoano and Sancho ever met, around the same time, another man arrived in London who would write the most famous work of the three, Olaudah Equiano, who published *The Interesting Narrative of the Life of Olaudah Equiano; or Gustavus Vassa, The African, Written By Himself*, in 1789.[34] Equiano and Cugoano did know of each other and collaborated on letters to newspapers, and perhaps even on Cugoano's manuscript. Equiano also occasionally worshiped at Saint James's Piccadilly.[35] Equiano's story starts with a mystery. In his book, he claims to have been born an Igbo, in West Africa. However, his 1759 baptismal certificate from Saint Margaret's Church, Westminster, from when he was around 12, says he was born in Carolina, as does a later ship record from an Arctic expedition in which he participated.[36] Both stories are plausible.

After his kidnapping from Africa, as he wrote in his narrative, he was transported to Barbados and then Virginia. While in North America, he was bought by Lieutenant Michael Henry Pascal, given the name Gustavus Vassa, and brought to England. The next period of his life was spent on the seas with the Royal Navy as Pascal's enslaved servant. On his return to England, he was baptized. This sacrament may have secured his spiritual freedom, but not his physical one.

To Equiano's shock, Pascal sold him to another captain, James Doran, in 1762. "I had never once supposed, in all my dreams about freedom," he wrote, "that he [Pascal] would think of detaining me any longer than I wished."[37] A while later, he was sold again in Montserrat, to Robert King, a Quaker, who allowed him to work as an assistant and clerk.[38] While enslaved by King, Equiano went to Philadelphia, and during his visit to the city, he noticed a crowd gathered at a church to watch George Whitefield preach. Equiano recalled, "I had often heard of this gentleman, and had wished to see and hear him," presumably unaware of the preacher's slaves in Georgia.[39] He was struck by Whitefield's style, observing, "I saw this pious man exhorting the people with the greatest fervour . . . sweating as much as I ever did while in slavery on Montserrat beach."[40]

Equiano bought his freedom in 1766, at the age of 19, paying for it with the money he earned doing a bit of side work, returning to what he called "my original free African state."[41] But keeping that freedom was a challenge.

While he was on a stop in Savannah, Georgia, at a friend's house, a patrol came by at around 9:00 p.m. and "drank some punch with us" before telling Equiano that he had to go back to the watchhouse with them because "all negroes who had light in their houses after nine o'clock were to be taken into custody, and either pay some dollars or be flogged."[42] Equiano's friend was enslaved, so the men could not take him without his enslaver's permission, but they could take Equiano. He passed the night at the watchhouse and observed as "these imposing ruffians flogged a negro-man and woman."[43] Equiano, they made clear, was next. He questioned their right to do this, because he was a free man. Tempers began to rise, when "one of them, more humane than the rest, said that as I was a free man they could not justify stripping me by law."⁴⁴ Equiano was able to send for a doctor he knew in the city, and his release was secured.

However, before he could get out of Savannah, two white men tried to kidnap him, claiming they had been looking for him. Equiano was wise to such maneuvers and "told them to be still and keep off for I had seen those kinds of tricks played upon other free blacks."⁴⁵ Freedom, as Equiano already knew, required constant vigilance.

Equiano travelled and worked on ships in the years that followed, calling in and out of London. At some point after the *Somerset* decision, he mentioned securing a habeas corpus writ to help an enslaved acquaintance claim his liberty in England and avoid being deported. He also asked Sharp to assist in the case, but he was not able to help in this instance, in part because the ship had already left, with the enslaved man aboard. Equiano later learned that the man had been "flogged most unmercifully" upon arrival in Saint Kitts.⁴⁶ A scheming captain could find ways around *Somerset*, to which free people like Equiano were forced to bear witness.

Around this time, Equiano began to have profound and disturbing dreams, leading him to fully embrace the Christian faith in which he had been baptized more than a decade earlier. At one point, he wrote, "it pleased God to direct me to a house where there was an old sea-faring man, who experienced much of the love of God shed abroad in his heart. He began to discourse with me; and, as I desired to love the Lord, his conversation rejoiced me greatly."⁴⁷

By 1777, Equiano had settled in London on a more permanent basis, and he became increasingly involved with the campaign to end the slave trade. He married and had a family, and his book quickly became a bestseller. Cugoano's work, more of a jeremiad in tone, had failed to attract reviews, but Equiano's *Narrative* ran into multiple editions and was translated into Dutch (1790), German (1792), and Russian (1794).

The years between the publication of Gronniosaw's and Equiano's works had seen a rising sentiment in segments of the British public against the slave trade. The grim realities of the trade had been hinted at, hidden away in letters, reports, and colonial correspondence, but now there was little excuse for the reading public not to be well aware of its horrors.

Mansa Musa, who reigned over the Mali Empire, was thought to be the richest man of his time, and this is illustrated on the 1375 Catalan Atlas by his holding an orb of gold.

A sixteenth-century painting depicting residents of Lisbon, Portugal—including members of the city's black population—around the King's Fountain (Chafariz d'el Rey).

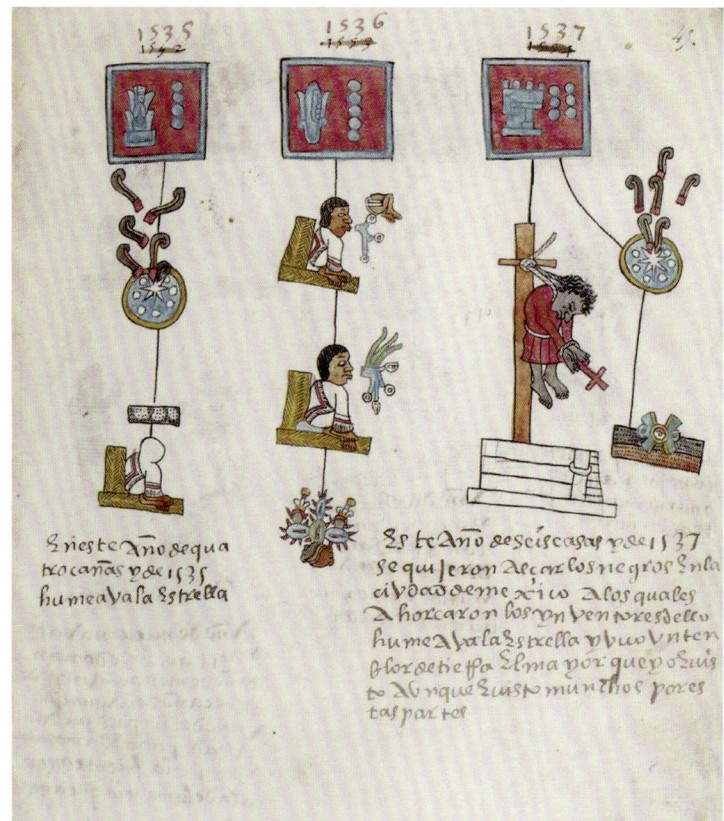

This page from the sixteenth-century *Codex Telleriano-Remensis* shows the hanging of a black man who may have been an enslaved rebel leader.

Miguel de Castro was an emissary for King Garcia II of Kongo. The painting, by Jaspar Beckx, was completed around 1643 when Castro was on a mission to Holland.

Dutch painter Frans Post painted *View of the Jesuit church at Olinda, Brazil* around 1665. He had been invited to travel to Brazil in 1637 by the governor of the short-lived Dutch colony Pernambuco, and he stayed for about seven years. His works mostly show a bucolic tropical landscape, largely devoid of the horrors of slavery taking place around him.

German-born Dutch West India Company soldier Zacharias Wagener recorded his time in Brazil with sketches and watercolors in his journals. His rendering of the slave market in Recife, Brazil, in the 1630s showed some of the violence and terror.

A statue of rebel leader Benkos Biohó in the main square of San Basilio de Palenque, Colombia.

A statue of Zumbi in Salvador, Brazil. He led the *quilombo* of Palmares to fight against the Portuguese in the 1690s. Although the Portuguese ultimately destroyed Palmares, Zumbi remains a hero and an important symbol of resistance.

A British etching from 1803 depicting the treaty between Jamaican maroon leader Cudjoe and the British in 1739.

Images of two of Jamaica's national heroes, maroon leader Nanny and Samuel Sharpe, who led the Baptist Revolt of 1831–32, adorn the country's $500 note.

A portrait of Ayuba Suleiman Diallo, who managed to escape slavery after being kidnapped and taken to Maryland in the 1730s.

Toussaint Louverture was a former slave who helped secure the freedom of enslaved people in the French colony of Saint-Domingue. He was briefly governor of the island before Napoleon Bonaparte had him arrested and imprisoned in France, where he died in 1803.

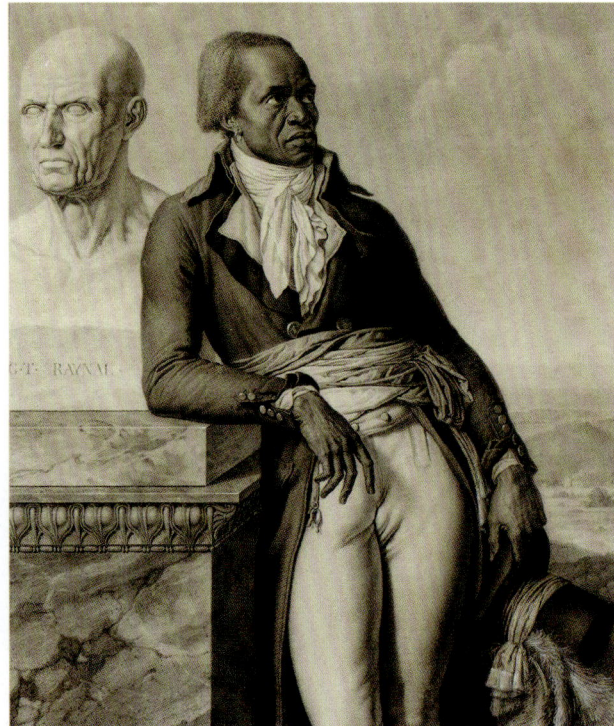

Former slave and soldier Jean-Baptiste Belley was selected as a commissioner from the French colony of Saint-Domingue to tell the French Assembly in 1794 that slavery had been abolished on the island.

Abolitionist Olaudah Equiano wrote about his experiences being enslaved in his 1789 *The Interesting Narrative of the Life of Olaudah Equiano*, which was printed in many editions and was translated into multiple languages.

Boston-based poet Phillis Wheatley won great acclaim on both sides of the Atlantic for her verse.

A version of the 1773 treaty talks ending the hostilities between the Black Caribs of the Caribbean island of Saint Vincent and the British crown, painted by Italian artist Agostino Brunias, who had been commissioned by the island's governor Sir William Young.

Another work by Agostino Brunias shows Black Carib "paramount chief" Joseph Chatoyer with his wives in Saint Vincent.

Elizabeth Freeman, also known as "Mumbet," filed an important freedom suit in Massachusetts in 1781.

The "Mulâtresse Solitude" was a legendary figure who fought while heavily pregnant against reenslavement in Guadeloupe in 1802.

Chapter 18

Revolutions

Today, the best way up Dorsetshire Hill is in a taxi, the road being winding and, at times, seemingly vertical. Where forests once were, luxury homes now look out past Kingstown, Saint Vincent, and out over the deep blue waters of the Caribbean to the Grenadines in the distance. The top of the hill affords vistas of the surrounding mountains. The peak of La Soufrière reaches just over 4,000 feet (1,200 meters), so Dorsetshire Hill is by no means the tallest on the island, but it's high enough to have a large cellular phone tower and various satellite dishes placed there. Next to these is a much smaller obelisk, set on a small tiled base, with a sign in front. It is a memorial to Joseph Chatoyer, the paramount chief of the island's Black Caribs, a role he had assumed by 1768, and one he still held when he died after more than 25 years of fighting the British. The story of Chatoyer and Britain's colonial authorities spans a particular period of turmoil, upheaval, and war, between Britain and its colonial subjects who did not want to submit.

Saint Vincent, along with Grenada, Dominica, and Tobago, were known to the British as the Ceded Islands, coming into the imperial fold as part of the Treaty of Paris in 1763.[1] Moving from south to north, it's possible to leapfrog along three of the islands: from Tobago to Grenada, and then to Saint Vincent. Dominica, however, is sandwiched by the French territories of Martinique to the south and Guadeloupe to the north.

All of the islands are volcanic in origin, with rugged interiors and dense forests, though Tobago lacks an active volcano. Whether British- or French-controlled, they were places of ongoing resistance by

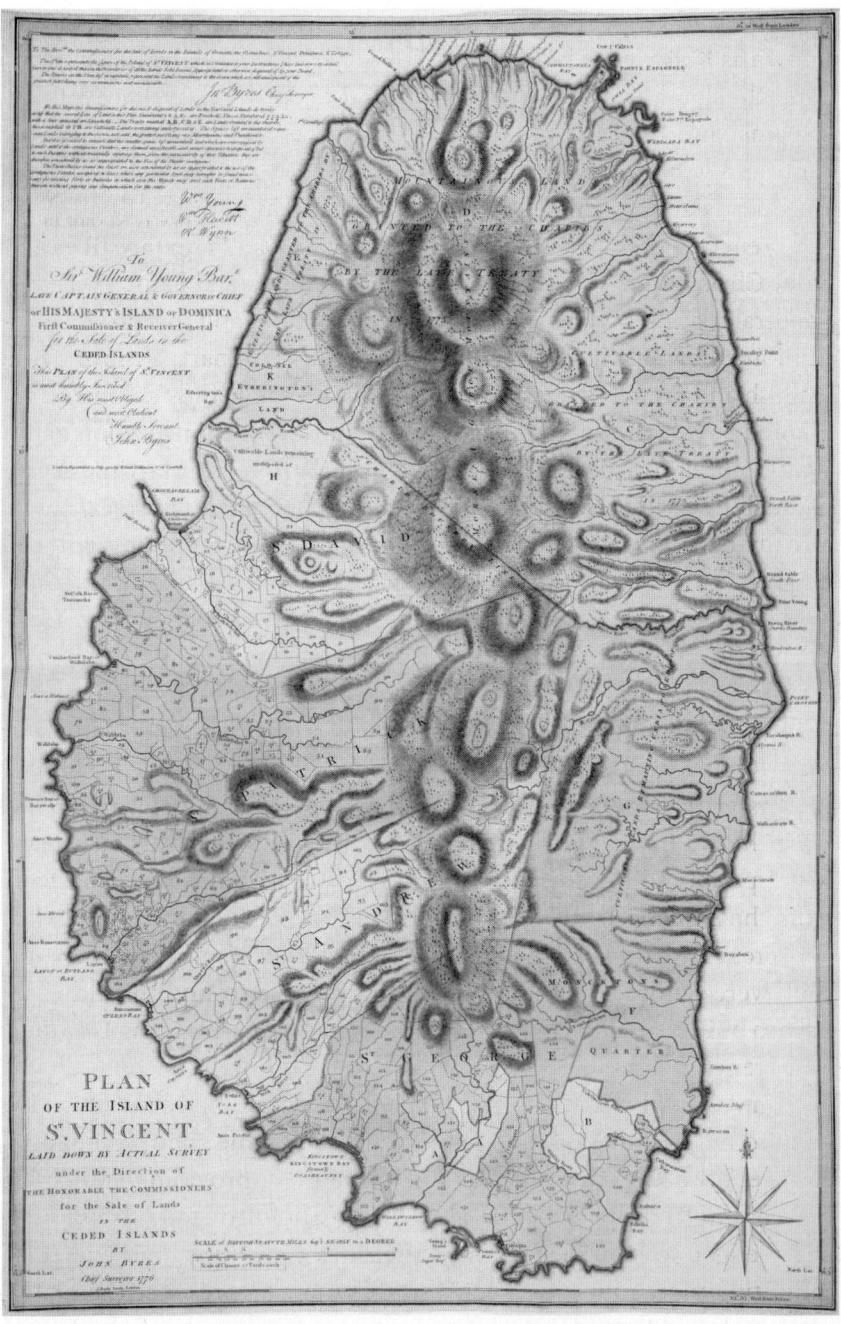

A British map of Saint Vincent from 1776 by John Byres, Chief Surveyor of the Ceded and Neutral Islands

the Amerindian people that Europeans called "Carib" but today are known as Kalinago. The Kalinago knew the secrets of the rich interiors of each island, the mountain peaks and deep ravines, the rivers and streams, and how the islands were connected to each other by currents and winds. They could put all this knowledge to use in keeping Europeans at bay. Agreements had been made with the English and the French in the previous century to do just that: The 1660 Treaty of Saint Christopher was meant to leave Dominica and Saint Vincent as "neutral islands," without European occupation, and this promise was reinforced by another treaty in 1668. This was, in part, a move by the English and French to avoid attacks and raids while they colonized and planted sugar on neighboring islands.[2] But before long, colonization would creep into Dominica. French planters from Martinique and Guadeloupe would steal over to that island to cut down trees, having already exhausted their own forests, eventually competing with the English for rights to cut wood. Runaway Africans also took refuge there. The worlds of sugar and slavery were encroaching on Dominica.[3] By the 1690s, the earliest planters began to arrive. Unusually for the Caribbean, the first plantation was established by a free black man, Jeannot Rolle, who came from Martinique, bringing slaves with him. Rolle managed to obtain permission from one of the Kalinago leaders to live there and continue logging. He had prior experience with the Kalinagos during their trading expeditions to Martinique. More people followed, and by 1715, poor smallholders and servants from the French islands were arriving in Dominica. In the 1730s, British and French officials tried to enforce the earlier neutrality treaty, but they were ignored, as they were again in 1751. Around this time, the French built a small fort near Roseau, seemingly formalizing Dominica as a French possession.[4]

Saint Vincent was feeling similar pressure, and its Kalinago leaders tried to negotiate another treaty in 1719. This time they were willing to accept the king of France as their sovereign, providing French settlers did not take their land. They also wanted to learn to use arms and pledged to help in any conflict with "the negroes their enemies," indicating there may have been a sizable maroon presence there. This pledge also indicated a desire to be treated as equals of the French subjects on the island, and not like the slaves.[5]

At the time of the Treaty of Paris 1763, 5,000 settlers, both white and free people of color, 1,400 Kalinagos, and 17,000 enslaved lived in various combinations across Dominica, Saint Vincent, Tobago, and Saint Lucia, a neighboring island that was restored to French rule.[6] In general, these planters mostly had modest farms, growing smaller-scale crops like coffee and cocoa, rather than sugarcane, though that would come soon enough.

Tobago is a small, thin island, with an interior of lush, low mountains, some of which could harbor maroon communities. Indeed, some of the Africans brought there decided to seek their freedom in the remaining uncleared forests. Others took more drastic measures, such as an African named Sandy—believed to be Coromantee—who killed his owner in 1770.[7] He and six others then attacked a military post and burned estates and cane fields, gathering followers as they set fires across the island. It took the arrival of troops from Barbados to quash this rebellion, and eight people were later captured. Sandy, however, never was.[8]

Despite other outbreaks of violence and unrest—there were instances in 1771, 1773, and 1774—the British pushed ahead with settling Tobago. They divided it and began planting, with 77 estates in place by 1776. Within a decade, the island produced 1,200 tons of sugar, in addition to 1.5 million pounds of cotton, and 5,000 pounds of indigo—all done by the hands of more than 3,000 enslaved workers. The settler population remained low, and the black-to-white ratio was around 20 to 1.[9]

The British saw the same opportunity in Saint Vincent as they had seen in Tobago, but in trying to transform it into a sugar colony, they sowed the seeds of their war against Joseph Chatoyer. Little is known of Chatoyer's earlier life, but he enters the record around the time the Commission for the Sale of Lands in the Ceded Islands began to carve up Saint Vincent, in 1764. In charge of this body was Sir William Young, who would end up being one of Chatoyer's adversaries.

Young died in 1788, and his son, also named William, published his father's papers in 1795, in part to continue to publicize the islands but also to build up the legend of the "Black Caribs," whom Chatoyer led.[10] In Young's telling, the genesis of the Black Caribs was a slave ship that had wrecked on the nearby Grenadine island of Bequia. That island has an arid climate, and the Africans struggled to survive, until the Kalinago, referred to in this account as "Red Charaibs," (though also called "Yellow Caribs" in other sources) came to their aid.

Then, according to Young, the Africans "soon proved restive and indolent servants" to the Kalinago, and their relationship descended into violence, with the Africans killing the people who had helped them survive. When they fled into the mountains, they found more former slaves who had run away from neighboring islands. They united to become the "Black Charaibs," who numbered around 5,000, and drove the remaining Red Charaibs off their land, causing them to seek aid from the French in Martinique.[11] The reality, no doubt, was more complex.

This dramatic story served a particularly useful purpose: It established the Black Caribs as maroons, descendants of slaves with no true claim to the land, unlike the "Red" Kalinago.[12] Such an argument facilitated the taking of their land. If Chatoyer and his community were Black Caribs, then to British officials they were not indigenous but instead "fugitive Negroes."[13] The introduction to Young's account says as much: "The Charaibs have been regarded by some persons in Great Britain as an independent nation, the original and rightful possessors of the island of St. Vincent's . . . The Charaibs, it is contended by others, had no original right in the soil of the country, but that the right was directly conferred from the British crown, under which they swore allegiance."[14]

The British might have desired to parcel out land as soon as possible, but they were forced to face the reality that the Kalinago and the French had agreed on a relationship in the early 1700s, an arrangement similar to the one that had evolved in Dominica. French settlers had appeared on Saint Vincent, too, trading and growing crops on smallholdings. African maroons had taken refuge there as well. By the time it was ceded to the British in 1763—with no warning from the French to the local population—some 1,300 French settlers and 3,400 slaves had been living alongside a few hundred "Yellow Caribs," and 5,000 "Black Caribs," more or less amicably.[15] Now the British had arrived, ready to add Saint Vincent to their existing collection of sugar islands and using the story of the Black Caribs to justify the land grab.

At first, the Black Caribs tried diplomacy with the British. William Young attempted to fob them off by offering to pay them and relocate them to another part of the island, well aware that they lived in an area ideal for sugar. They met with the Commissioners for the Sale of Lands, who later reported that these Black Caribs were willing to be subjects to the king. But Chatoyer, as "paramount" leader, asked them in 1768: "'*Quel roi?*'—what king was this, of Great Britain?—They would listen to the governor of Martinique, and no other."[16]

Further attempts to negotiate stalled. The land commissioners called on London to take more forceful action in October 1771, saying that "all treaty and negociation [sic] . . . will be fruitless."[17] The planter lobby in London went a step further, demanding that the Black Caribs be jettisoned to "any unoccupied tract of 10,000 acres of wood land, upon any part of the coast of Africa."[18]

By April 1772, the British agreed that force—or at least the threat of it—was necessary against the Black Caribs. The expedition would be led by Major General William Dalrymple, and by the summer troops were being sent to the island, though two New York battalions were delayed in Bermuda after their ship was struck by a storm.[19] The Black Caribs watched the arrival of the soldiers, who eventually totaled around 1,100, and began making preparations for what seemed inevitable.[20] The British invited them once more, in September, to submit, but they refused.

By the end of the month, official battle had commenced, with both regular troops and island militia encountering a "vigorous opposition" to their attacks near Black Carib settlements, including a number of ambushes.[21] Saint Vincent, with its high volcanic peak and densely forested interior, presented a significant challenge to British troops, especially those with little or no experience in the Caribbean. Attempts in November to attack from the sea fared somewhat better, after a shaky start when one of the five British vessels trying to approach the large Black Carib community of Grand Sable, on the east side of the island, ran aground. The British regained their footing and managed to drive the Caribs out of the settlement.[22] But then the rainy season set in, complicating the conflict, while tropical disease took out many British troops, helping the Caribs.

This was not an isolated colonial skirmish dragging through the months—by this point it had attracted public attention in Britain and other colonies in the Americas, coming up in debates in the House of Commons in London, with some arguing that the Black Caribs should not be attacked.[23] The fighting attracted notice in British and colonial newspapers, and a later parliamentary inquiry would declare the expedition unjust.[24] The conflict continued to inch along, delayed by winter rains. By January 1773, the British troops were attempting to advance once again, but were repeatedly outmaneuvered by the Caribs, who could work the island's interior to their advantage. British troops were dropping—some 72 British soldiers had died in the fighting, along with 110 from disease, with 80 wounded and 428 sick.[25] In early February, two Carib leaders appeared at a British camp to discuss a possible ceasefire. Within a few days, a group of 26 Caribs met with Dalrymple to sign a treaty.[26] Like the deal brokered in Jamaica, this one required the Black Caribs to swear their loyalty not to the French *roi*, but to George III, and in exchange they would retain some of their land. They did, however, have to allow roads to be built through other parts of the island. They would not be relocated off the island—an idea popular with settlers—but their territory would be moved, freeing up 4,000 acres of prime sugarcane land. And, inevitably, the agreement stipulated that "runaway slaves in the possession of the Charibbs, [were] to be delivered up." It would be a capital crime to help or harbor any runaways.[27] The deal served, for the moment.

⇐ • ⇒

Most maroon and indigenous leaders lived lives and fought battles that were rarely captured by an artist's brush. Chatoyer, however, appears in two portraits, both done by an Italian painter in service to British aims.

For Agostino Brunias, the invitation must have been a fascinating one. The senior William Young asked the artist to come to the islands and paint them. Brunias's background was in composing portraits and painting scenes for people on the "Grand Tour" of Europe. He later moved to London, creating both architectural designs and decorative ones, such as friezes, for stately homes.[28] This would be a very different challenge. In his work in the Ceded Islands, he excelled in portraying the idealized, happy scene. There are no horrors of the plantation in his Caribbean. No lash, no violence. Instead, he depicted the islands as a place of elegantly dressed ladies and gentlemen, of varying white and brown skin tones, going about their business in places like a linen market in Dominica (c. 1780). In this well-known image, free people of color and whites buy goods from black sellers in the bustling marketplace. Slaves are depicted, but not on auction blocks or in chains, but rather just going about their work.[29] In his paintings of more rural settings, enslaved people dance or engage in a friendly cudgeling match (stick fight). His work presented an ideal form of colonial life for distribution, to lure investors into the Caribbean dream. They also, quite pointedly, reflected an idea that was gaining traction around this time: amelioration.[30] This was the belief that treating enslaved people well would naturally increase the slave population, and thus the importation of slaves could be done away with. This is part of Brunias's vision. The enslaved people have decent clothes, they look happy, they are dancing, and the message is clear. A little investment made in the right manner could go a long way on this island. Brunias himself bought into this vision, settling in Dominica permanently in 1784, and remaining there until he died in 1796.[31]

The Ceded Islands of Agostino Brunias were a long way from the experience of Ottobah Cugoano, who had been taken there in the late 1760s or early 1770s, escaping by 1772. Cugoano had vivid recollections of his brief time in Grenada, calling it "the most dreadful scene of misery and cruelty." For something as simple as eating a piece of the sugarcane that they grew, doubtless out of a desperate hunger, "some [slaves] were cruelly lashed, or struck over the face to knock their teeth out."[32]

Brunias's two paintings that include Chatoyer offer subtle differences in messaging. The first is his 1773 *Sir William Young Conducting a Treaty with the Black Caribs on the Island of St Vincent*. The scene is orderly and calm, even thoughtful. Guns are lying on the grass in the foreground, signaling that the conflict is over and the discussion is peaceful. To the right, the British are in full uniform, their red coats and white breeches unmarked by sweat or stains. One official is seated but holding out his hand, while others consult papers, presumably maps and the treaty. On the left is a group of Black Caribs, with Chatoyer presented as the tallest, holding his chin and thinking deeply as the treaty is read out by a British officer.

Unlike the Jamaican maroons, who were depicted in rough British dress of ragged shirts and trousers, the Black Caribs are in loincloths, their hair in headwraps. Their bodies are athletic, dark, and muscular, while the British look pale and flabby. The setting behind the maroons is the unknowable interior, the foliage all shades of greens, while the British are framed by their tents, the temporary architecture of an ordered world. This tableau is presented as an almost mythical scene, with people so far outside of what would have been considered "civilized" in this period in terms of their dress and demeanor. The British public would have no choice but to believe that the colonial officials were the ones bringing order to the island, rather than the ones who inflicted the opposite, and that the now-defeated Black Caribs would melt into the forests, back into the legend out of which they had emerged.[33]

The other work is of Chatoyer himself, a painting called *Chatoyer the Chief of the Black Charaibes in St. Vincent with His Five Wives*. In this work, his wives are depicted wearing just a cloth around their waists, with three of them hauling loads on their backs in traditional woven baskets (*pegals*). Another wife has fallen on the ground, possibly because of her basket's weight. The fifth wife holds an infant, an expression of exhaustion on her face.[34] Chatoyer, meanwhile, puffs his pipe and watches them, resting his right hand on a sword. As in the other work, he is wearing a turban and a loincloth, and is fit and muscular: a handsome tyrant, a polygamous savage who treats his wives like slaves and so should not deserve sympathy from the British public. True to Brunias's style, it is not a violent scene, but it is one of his few works that carry an undercurrent of distress, for which he lays the blame at Chatoyer's feet. It was a form of visual propaganda, another weapon for the British arsenal. But it was only part of the story. Chatoyer was not done with the British.

⃸ • ⇾

While British authorities in the Ceded Islands were dealing with the Black Caribs and maroons, officials further north were contending with the rumblings of another rebellion—this time among white colonists in the 13 North American colonies. They were aggrieved at the high price they were forced to pay for the costly Seven Years' War and were vocal in their protests about the steady stream of taxes that had been flowing out of the colonies throughout the 1760s. They shouted about the unfairness of it, about how they were the slaves. For instance, one former slave owner from Pennsylvania, John Dickinson, wrote in a 1768 pamphlet, "*We are taxed* without our own consent, expressed by ourselves or our representatives. *We* are therefore SLAVES."[35] Such was the mood of grievance emanating from the North American colonies that the London writer Samuel Johnson, a critic of the growing rebellion, was moved to ask: "How is it that we hear the loudest yelps for liberty among the drivers of negroes?"[36]

It is a sharp rhetorical line, cutting to the quick of this period's core hypocrisy. By the time Johnson wrote it, in 1775, the war for American independence was well on its way, and the conflict had already claimed its first victim, an Afro-Indigenous man. Five years earlier, at the "Boston Massacre," when the British fired on a mob in that city, they killed five people, the first of whom was Crispus Attucks, believed to have had an African father and a Native American mother. Attucks is thought to have been born into slavery, and may have acquired his freedom before he lost his life and became the first martyr to the cause of independence on March 5, 1770. That Attucks was involved in the mob does not necessarily come as a surprise—enslaved and free people of color were watching events closely, trying to work out what those events might mean for them. It was a tumultuous time: the 1773 Boston Tea Party, the protests and boycotts in response to the Intolerable Acts used to punish the Massachusetts colonists for their defiance, the Battles of Lexington and Concord in 1775, the speeches, the pamphlets, and the war of words between colony and crown. But the contradictions were apparent. Thomas Jefferson recognized the situation in which he and the other rebels found themselves. In his first draft of the Declaration of Independence, Jefferson attempted to place the blame for slavery at England's door, writing that George III

> has waged cruel war against human nature itself, violating its most sacred rights of life and liberty in the persons of a distant people who never offended him, captivating and carrying them into slavery in another hemisphere, or to incur miserable death in their transportation thither . . . Determined to keep open a market where men should be bought and sold, he has prostituted his negative for suppressing every legislative attempt to prohibit or restrain this execrable commerce.[37]

This paragraph was edited out of the final version of the declaration under pressure from Jefferson's fellow Southern slaveholders, who did not want to draw attention to that "execrable commerce."[38] The contradiction would simply have to be borne: "We hold these truths to be self-evident, that all men are created equal," the final 1776 version read. There was no place for slavery in a document about freedom.

Enslaved people in households and fields, cities and countryside, heard these words—"freedom," "liberty"—and then found out that they were not meant for them. Free people of color soon butted up against the reality of the document, too, perhaps initially hopeful that they would be counted as "men." Though Jefferson did not use the qualifier "white," it was obvious that the rebellion was under the control of white men.

The 13 colonies differed in many ways from the West Indian ones, but a crucial difference was the ratio of black to white, enslaved to free. At around the time Dr. Johnson made his famous quip, about 500,000 black people, mostly enslaved, were spread out from Florida—under British control since 1763—to New England, among some 2 million white settlers.[39] The majority of black people were in the Southern colonies, as their economies were increasingly monopolized by agriculture, especially tobacco and rice—king cotton would arrive later. By around 1770, 187,000 enslaved people lived in Virginia, up from 27,000 in 1720; similarly in South Carolina, the number reached 82,000, having been around 12,000 some 50 years earlier.[40] Although the free white population outnumbered the enslaved, the ghosts of slave revolts past continued to stalk the imaginations of the elite men leading the rebel colonists, some of whom—like George Washington—were enslavers themselves.

But the fighting power of black people was nonetheless apparent, however dangerous the quest for collective freedom may have been. In response to a growing colonial militia in Virginia, in November 1775 John Murray, the Earl of Dunmore and governor of the colony, offered freedom to enslaved people who would fight for the crown, a move that immediately attracted at least 1,000 slaves, as well as a few white servants. It was a move that also alarmed white colonists prepared to fight for the rebels, some of whom feared a slave rebellion could seriously disrupt the independence struggle.[41]

News of the revolt in the 13 colonies quickly spread to Jamaica, where planters received their own lesson about freedom in July 1776 after a plot was uncovered that was planned to start in Hanover, an area in the northwest part of the island with one of the highest black-to-white ratios, at 25 to 1. The Hanover conspirators might have been inspired by a combination of factors: the events in North America and the talk of freedom that surrounded those events, as well as the disruption of food supplies that resulted from the conflict. However, the plans were uncovered at the last minute after a suspected plotter was spotted in suspicious proximity to his enslavers' pistols. Forty-eight people were promptly arrested, with more to come.[42]

What made this conspiracy shocking to the white community is that it involved elite slaves, such as drivers and craftsmen, and was organized by creole Afro-Caribbeans, though it also included Coromantees and Eboes. Even maroons were contemplating cooperating with the rebels this time. Cudjoe and his Trelawny maroons were increasingly annoyed with the planters, who were using their own rangers to catch runaways and thus depriving them of income.[43] Timing had been key, with the governor observing that the plotters knew Britain troops were engaged elsewhere and so the slaves "would not have a better opportunity of seizing the Country to themselves."[44]

Some colonists blamed themselves for being too loose-lipped about events in North America. "We have I am afraid been too careless of Expressions, especially when the topic of American rebellion has been by the Disaffected amongst us, dwelt upon and brandished with strains of Virtuous Heroism," wrote one Jamaican in the aftermath of the uncovered conspiracy.⁴⁵ By the end of the subsequent investigation and tribunal, 17 people charged with participation in the plot were executed, 45 shipped off the island, 11 flogged, and 62 others acquitted.⁴⁶

For enslaved people in the North American colonies, fleeing behind British lines proved a more attractive—and perhaps safer—option than using the chaos of conflict to mount a separate uprising. Some of the men would go on to join Dunmore's Royal Ethiopian Regiment, whose soldiers wore white sashes that said LIBERTY TO SLAVES as they went into battle against the rebels in Virginia. But the war also presented an opportunity to simply flee. Some estimates put the number of black people who left the Southern states—be it to fight or simply to escape slavery—at around 30,000 in Virginia, 20,000 in South Carolina, and 15,000 in Georgia, though others say the total for all colonies was at most 20,000, with around 12,000 being from the south.⁴⁷

Washington and the Continental Congress eventually had to respond. By 1777, enslaved and free black people could enlist in the Connecticut militia, and this move was followed by a similar one in New Hampshire. In 1778, Rhode Island raised an all-black regiment, the 1st Rhode Island. Of the initial 130 volunteers, at least 87 were enslaved, though they gained their freedom by enlisting.⁴⁸ The Southern colonies were more hesitant about using black troops. South Carolina considered raising a black regiment, but then decided against it. North Carolina allowed the participation of free black men in the military, as did Maryland.⁴⁹ In Virginia, around 40 percent of the black people who joined the rebels helped at sea rather than on land.⁵⁰ Some enslavers were able to send their captives in their place to fight. In the end, an estimated 5,000 black soldiers fought on the side of the rebels in the Revolutionary War, mostly in all-black units under white officers, with many in noncombatant roles such as servants or grooms.⁵¹ On the front line or not, these men were betting on freedom under this new republic, taking active choices to join this fight, with many proving their loyalty and staying on for the duration of the conflict. At the very least, those who were enslaved might be able to secure their own freedom. Others dared to hope that an independent nation might consider ending the practice of slavery altogether.⁵²

The British commander Henry Clinton retaliated against the growing number of black troops in the Continental Army with his 1779 Philipsburg Proclamation, which further extended the promise of freedom to any enslaved person involved in any military duties on the British side, not just combat, allowing women, who could serve in auxiliary roles, to join and bring their children. Indeed, he went so far as to promise "freedom and a farm," to black recruits, telling them they would receive land belonging to the defeated rebels.[53]

For the British, this engagement with enslaved volunteers would also influence the later foundation of the West India Regiments, which would be installed across that region between 1795 and 1807 and constitute the largest slave army (becoming a free black army from 1807 to 1833) among European powers in the Americas.[54] Britain had already put some enslaved men, alongside free black soldiers, into battle in other regiments, including during the occupation of Havana in 1762, the earlier War of Jenkins' Ear, and the battles against the Jamaican maroons in the 1730s.[55] The British hoped to fill the ranks with free black volunteers, but many men steered clear, perhaps concerned about the implications on their freedom. This ultimately meant the government decided to buy many of its soldiers and, in doing so, become one of the largest enslavers of the time, spending nearly £1 million on 13,000 enslaved people to fill its ranks between 1795 and 1808.[56]

Other European powers, most notably Spain, had long organized free and enslaved black men to fill militia posts. Military service could be a route to freedom, but it could also instill loyalty on the part of the former slave. In Cuba, by 1760, for instance, the Spanish military had 2,493 soldiers of color, both black (*moreno*) and Afro-European (*pardo*).[57] A similar situation developed in nearby French Saint-Domingue, where a sizable militia of free people of color was established. They soon mobilized when France entered the American Revolution in 1778 on the side of the colonies. The Chasseurs Volontaires drew its members from the free colored militia in Saint-Domingue. While the troops were not white, the top officers were, and of the 700 troops ready to fight the British, three-quarters were free people of color. Upon arrival in Georgia, the regiment was assigned mostly to trench digging and other auxiliary work until the British launched a surprise attack on September 24, 1779, and the Chasseurs managed to drive them back.[58]

Whichever side free and enslaved people decided to enlist on, their participation in the American Revolution constituted a mobilization of black people—including those who came to the rebels' aid, like the Chasseurs Volontaires—on a scale not seen before within the slave societies of the Americas. In some ways, it was the largest slave rebellion yet.[59] But once the conflict was over, they would face great uncertainties, whether in an old empire or a new republic.

In the meantime, another front had opened in North America. Black people, enslaved and free, began to make petitions, and many of these would chip away at the system, carving out new and different pathways toward freedom. Some of them had started on the eve of the Revolution, such as a petition by a group describing themselves as "many Slaves," though it was signed by only one, "Felix," in January 1773. The group petitioned the governor, council, and court of Massachusetts "to take their unhappy State and Condition under your wise and just Consideration."[60] They used religion to appeal to their audience, arguing that in their condition it was impossible "to keep all [God's] Commandments." Their plaintive cry was clear: "We have no Property! We have no Wives! No Children! We have no City! No Country."[61] They used the petition to assert that if they gained their freedom, they would be "discreet, sober, honest, and industrious" Christian members of society.[62] They followed up again, in April, this time including more signatures and taking a firmer tone, referring to themselves as "fellow-men."[63]

In 1779, a group of 20 "natives of Africa" in Portsmouth, New Hampshire, petitioned for their liberty, saying, "Freedom is an inherent right of the human species."[64] Another group petitioned the Connecticut General Assembly, and Pomp, an enslaved man in Norwalk, petitioned for his freedom on the basis that his enslaver had deserted to the British—and he won.[65] The following year the free Afro-Indigenous sea captain Paul Cuffe and his brother, John, made their case to the court in Dartmouth, Massachusetts, that they should be exempt from paying taxes because as both Native American and African they did not receive political representation. Instead of receiving the vote, the men ended up in jail for refusing to pay their taxes, though they were able to secure their release.[66] Undeterred, a short time later, the two men, now joined by others, issued a petition along similar lines, saying "Contrary to the invenerable [sic] custom and Practices of the Country we have been & are taxed both in our Poles and that small Pittance of Estate . . . we are not allowed in voting in the town meetings in—nor to Choose an officer of neither."[67] This time they had more success, and by 1783 Massachusetts dropped racial restrictions on voting.

Around the same time, also in Massachusetts, Elizabeth Freeman brought a successful freedom suit (*Brom and Bett v. Ashley*), which opened the way for some degree of emancipation in that state. Freeman, also called Mum Bett or Mumbet, was born into slavery in New York around 1744. She was enslaved by Pieter Hogeboom, and later by his son-in-law, Colonel John Ashley, in Berkshire County, Massachusetts. Freeman was still with the Ashleys in 1781 when she decided to file a freedom suit, arguing that her state of enslavement violated the new Massachusetts Constitution. She, like many hundreds of others, was using this period, so full of the talk of freedom, to press for her own.[68]

With the help of the prominent local lawyer Theodore Sedgwick, and the inclusion of another case, that of her fellow slave Brom, she was successful. After the trial, Freeman moved into the Sedgwick household and was the family's head servant for 27 years.[69] The youngest daughter of the family, Catharine Maria Sedgwick, was one of the most popular writers of her time, and many years later, in 1853, she produced a brief account of Freeman's life. In Sedgwick's telling, Freeman was at a village meeting house in Sheffield, Massachusetts, when she heard the Declaration of Independence read out loud. The next day she arrived at the office of Sedgwick's father and told him: "I heard that paper read yesterday, that says all men are born equal and that every man has a right to freedom. I am not a dumb *critter*; won't the law give me my freedom?"[70]

Such cases could only address the issue of bodily freedom and rights—they did not confront the other side of slavery, the profits New England businesses were reaping from the slave trade or related commerce. Shipbuilding and the direct slave trade—especially in Rhode Island, where nearly 1,000 slaving voyages began—were tied to the trade, as were the ancillary industries, not least finance.[71] Farmers supplied the sugar-producing colonies with products such as wheat, corn, livestock, and lumber, and such exports continued to rise after independence, though now merchants also traded with the French and Spanish territories. Crops from New England fields ended up on voyages destined for Africa, while on the way back, sugar and molasses from the West Indies flowed north, making New England a hub of rum production. In 1770, Massachusetts and Rhode Island distillers produced nearly 3 million gallons of rum with the imported molasses. Much of this popular spirit went abroad on ships bound for Africa, giving New England merchants a valuable ware to sell in exchange for humans.[72] The courts could hear petitions and lawsuits, but the system of slavery was deeply entrenched in many facets of Northern life, and this would change little with independence.

But in some places white communities were taking small—though considered radical for their time—steps toward ending bondage, and the idea of human property.[73] A few states started to enact gradual emancipation laws while the revolution was still underway. Vermont was technically the first. In its 1777 constitution Vermont declared its own independence, and it would not join the United States until 1791. The same document banned slavery for any man over the age of 21 and women over 19, but there was little enforcement and there were plenty of loopholes, including the practice of redesignating slaves as "servants." Pennsylvania was next, in 1780, though its measures were also limited. They required manumitted people to compensate their former enslavers with a period of unpaid labor, and they allowed children to remain in bondage until they were 18. Rhode Island and Connecticut passed similar measures in 1784; children born to enslaved women after the enactment of the legislation would not be freed until the age of 18 for women and 21 for men in Rhode Island and 25 in Connecticut. Massachusetts—despite its many petitions and lawsuits—and New Hampshire lingered in a gray area, never explicitly ending slavery. In the case of Massachusetts, freedom suits, including that of Elizabeth Freeman, led to judicial abolition, with the courts ruling that slavery was incompatible with the state's 1780 constitution, but there were no clear guidelines about how that would be implemented.[74] Black people in those two states may have been in bondage, paid servants, or both at different points.[75] Such unevenness—both within particular locations and inside families—meant the North was a long way from being a land of freedom.

Chapter 19

Liberties

WITH FREEDOM WON and the new United States of America created, the promise of liberty was now delivered, but the cleavages were clear from the start. In article 1, section 2, the nation's new Constitution called for anyone who was not free, Native American, or serving an indenture contract to be counted as "three-fifths of all other Persons"—an obvious reference to the enslaved population. But this was not initially about their personhood—to enslavers they were property who would never have voting rights. This clause was about the political power of the Southern enslavers. They understood that, in terms of population, if enslaved people were not counted, slave-holding states would have fewer representatives in Congress. Northern politicians were outraged by the demand to include slaves, pointing out the obvious hypocrisy of counting enslaved people as part of the population and yet treating them as "property." However, there were enough Southerners to stall the Constitutional Convention in 1787, so a compromise had to be found. If all people, including enslaved workers, were counted in the population, Southern states would have more seats, and if free-only population were, then Northern states would. Deciding to count slaves as "three-fifths" meant they would have roughly the same representation, and subsequent taxation.

The clause also served as a painful reminder to all enslaved people of their place in this new nation, though without the text ever using the word "slave."[1] James Madison, a slave owner, used Federalist Paper No. 54 to defend this arrangement, writing:

> Let the case of the slaves be considered, as it is in truth, a peculiar one. Let the compromising expedient of the Constitution be mutually adopted, which regards them as inhabitants, but as debased by servitude below the equal level of free inhabitants, which regards the slave as divested of two fifths of the man . . . We have hitherto proceeded on the idea that representation related to persons only, and not at all to property. But is it a just idea? Government is instituted no less for protection of the property, than of the persons, of individuals. The one as well as the other, therefore, may be considered as represented by those who are charged with the government.[2]

Significantly, however, the importation of slaves would be banned throughout the nation in 20 years' time. Again, without using the word "slave," article 1, section 9, clause 1 of the Constitution stipulates that "the migration or importation of such Persons as any of the States now existing shall think proper to admit" would be prohibited after 1808.[3] One factor behind the decision was a growing belief on the part of some Southerners that more Africans would not be necessary because the population of enslaved people would be self-perpetuating by then.[4] And, they hoped, the slaves would be under tight control. Section 8 of the Constitution called for the state militias "to execute the Laws of the Union, suppress insurrections and repel invasions."[5] To clarify the matter, the 1791 Bill of Rights listed the right of citizens to bear arms as its second amendment, in order to keep a "well-regulated" militia that would be "necessary to the security of the free state," presumably capable of putting down a slave revolt should that be necessary.

For the black soldiers who had invested their hopes of liberty in a British victory, their freedom looked threatened. Article 7 of the 1783 Treaty of Paris promised the return of "negroes" and other "property" to the victors. As a result, many black people—including some who had fought for the British—ended up being enslaved "property" once again. Some were also taken by white loyalists who were leaving for other parts of the British Empire.

Other former slaves held on to their liberty and joined the thousands of people whom the British evacuated, including 3,000 who were listed in the British Army commander-in-chief Sir Guy Carleton's "Book of Negroes." Despite the protests of George Washington and others that the now-free people should be handed over, Carleton and fellow British officers evacuated many of the former slaves.[6] That included one Harry Washington, from Washington's Mount Vernon plantation. Even people enslaved by the first president of the United States had followed what they had hoped would be a path to true freedom.[7]

In total, around 60,000 white and free black loyalists, along with 15,000 enslaved people, left the 13 colonies.[8] Around half of all the loyalists went to Canada, including some 3,000 free black people. Many of those who went to Canada were sent to Nova Scotia, where they faced a brutal introduction to the Canadian climate. They had no money, and were forced to fight to get the land that the British had promised them. During the hard winter of 1789, one visitor noted that black people were forced to sell their clothing and blankets to buy flour, and others "fell down dead in the streets from hunger."[9]

As a former French and now British territory since 1763, Canada did permit slavery throughout, but its roughly 3,000 enslaved people, including those recently brought by white loyalists, were a small fraction of the population.[10] In 1793, Upper Canada (modern Ontario) passed a gradual emancipation law similar to those of some of the states in New England.[11] The Canadian act prohibited the further importation of enslaved people; children born after the date of enactment would gain their freedom when they reached the age of 25, and their children would be born free.

Canada presented a difficult life for the first black people who arrived from the new United States. Most were impoverished, with few resources or friends to help them. Some began to feel they had no choice but to go elsewhere, opting for London or even the West Indies, although the slavery there could put their freedom at greater risk.

A significant number of black and white loyalists went to the Bahamas, which Britain had claimed but had made only sporadic attempts to settle from the 1650s onward. The archipelago of low-lying islands supported mostly small-scale farming and fishing at this time, in part because of its rocky soil. The indigenous population had mostly been killed by disease and earlier Spanish slaving raids. The majority of the small European and African population lived in Nassau on New

Providence island, and the rest were scattered across six other islands. However, with the arrival of white loyalist slaveholders from the Southern states, the Bahamas was quickly transformed into a plantation society. The numbers were significant—1,600 whites and 5,700 enslaved and free black people arrived, causing the white population to double and the black population to triple by 1790.[12] The existing settlements boomed, and people began to spread on to other islands.

White and free black communities quickly came up against each other, one group wishing to expand slavery and the other trying to protect hard-won freedom. Black refugees seeking a place of safety would see increasing threats to their liberty and be forced to prove their freedom. Free black people were being pushed into indentured servitude, and a 1784 Negro Act gave magistrates permission to examine anyone's manumission papers, thus putting a heavy legal burden on black people. Stepping into the fraught environment was the man who had set the entire process in motion: Lord Dunmore, the former British governor of Virginia, who was appointed governor of the Bahamas in 1787. Now he had to confront these issues immediately.[13] He set up a special agency, called the Negro Court, to hear the claims of black loyalists, which angered slave owners. There had been long-simmering tensions between the black loyalists and whites who were trying to coerce the black population into work, despite the fact that they were free. The former slaves had come this far, and many were prepared to carry on fighting to defend the freedom they had been promised—a freedom they also expected Dunmore, of all people, to uphold.[14]

In November 1787, free black people on Abaco island began a serious revolt, with Dunmore reporting that "members of the outlying negroes went about with muskets and fixed bayonets, robbing and plundering," and that "the white inhabitants had collected themselves in a body, and having come up with the negroes had killed, wounded and taken most of them prisoners, three of the latter they immediately executed."[15]

Although he set up the Negro Court to hear the grievances of the black loyalists, Dunmore ultimately fell in line with the planters. He put in place an even more restrictive act that made proving freedom increasingly difficult for free black people. In November of 1787 the island legislature passed an act stipulating that officials could "examine the manumissions or passes of any Negro, Mulatto, Muskee, or Indian pretending to be free." Should they be found lacking evidence, they could be jailed and later sold, with the money going to the public treasury.[16] With such a burden of proof on the black loyalists, the Negro Court experienced a flurry of cases. In one hearing, a man named Thomas Smith had to face a white claimant who said he was Smith's owner. These were the sorts of claims that had so many black people in a state of anger and anxiety. In Smith's case, he was found to be free and "acquitted from all obligation of slavery and servitude."[17] The American Revolution may have been over, but the fight for freedom seemed to be a war without end for the formerly enslaved, loyalist or not.

Others decided to try their luck in Britain. Around 7,000 black and white loyalists arrived in London, many of them having never set foot in England before. Black people had their freedom secured there because of the *Somerset* ruling of 1772, but little else was certain. London was a difficult city then, and hundreds of thousands of people were eking out the barest of existences. For newly arrived black people from North America, the challenge was intensified, since most of them were already impoverished, having been enslaved prior to the war.

While there was a black community to connect with in the city, constant prejudice also emanated from white people, and employment—to say nothing of fair pay—was not guaranteed. Even after *Somerset*, black people could find themselves in service positions little different from slavery.[18] Most of the new arrivals remained underemployed, struggling to survive in the East End of London, along the docklands, in places like Deptford, where the lodging was cheap and the ships offered potential work.

Some tried to access the relief available from the Loyalist Claims Commission, while others were practically pushed into it by greedy landlords, and the commissioners brushed many of them aside, treating some of the former soldiers only recently arrived in an unfamiliar land as little more than scammers. Other commissioners believed that being freed and allowed to come to England was reward enough.[19]

Such was the extent of black poverty that in 1786 a philanthropist named Jonas Hanway convinced other prominent men to set up a Committee for the Relief of the Black Poor.[20] It distributed food, opened a hospital to tend to the ill, and provided temporary lodging.[21] Having such a large, unemployed, and poor black population was untenable for the city's authorities. Black people were already being blamed for the city's crime, and the idea began to circulate of sending them to Africa. Britain had a foothold in Sierra Leone, on the West Coast. Abolitionists were soon on board with the idea, including Granville Sharp. They would create a "Province of Freedom," using land belonging to the Mende, Temne, and other West African peoples.[22] And this land of freedom would be surrounded by the ports of the still-bustling slave trade. Between 1780 and 1790 alone, Europeans embarked some 750,000 Africans, with the three leading traders being Great Britain, France, and Portugal.[23]

To Sharp's mind, it was a chance for these freed black people to seek their fortunes and govern themselves. It could offer, according to the scheme's instigator, Henry Smeathman, "a sanctuary for the oppressed people of colour."[24] The first fleet left in February 1787 but had a three-week delay in Plymouth after sailing into a gale. By May, 377 settlers stepped ashore in Sierra Leone.[25]

At first, even Olaudah Equiano got behind the plan, though he ended up embroiled in a row with the navy over the waste and corruption he observed as Commissary of Stores for the scheme, causing him to quit and later write: "Thus ended my part of the long-talked-of expedition to Sierra Leone; an expedition which, however unfortunate in the event, was humane and politic in its design."[26]

Life in the initial settlement of Granville Town was a struggle, and these free people found themselves surrounded by slave traders, once again put in a position where their own freedom was at risk.[27] However, the struggling colony would soon get a boost: Some 1,000 free black people from Nova Scotia were quitting the freezing climes of Canada. In 1792, they set sail south, under the newly formed Sierra Leone Company.

⋘ • ⋙

L<small>EAVING THE COAST</small> of West Africa on September 6, 1781, with 440 captives and 17 crew on board, the captain of the *Zong*, Luke Collingwood, was bound for Jamaica. But as he approached that island in late November, he made a navigational error, and when he spotted land, he believed it to be Hispaniola, not Jamaica.[28] The crew then sailed west, not realizing their mistake, adding weeks to the voyage time. By this point, many on board had fallen ill—including Collingwood—and 60 enslaved people and seven members of the crew were already dead. Many more were barely alive, owing in part to the scarcity of drinking water. By the end of November the crew decided that "part of the slaves should be destroyed to save the rest," and 54 women and children were thrown to their deaths under the cover of night. They were followed by 42 men two days later, and another 38 people a short time after that. Finally, 10 more Africans decided to jump to their end, retaining what little choice they had in the dire situation.[29] The ship arrived in Jamaica in late December, with more dead—possibly 30—on board. Collingwood died a short time later.[30]

One of the invisible threads that held together the transatlantic slave trade was insurance. These humans were considered property and, like other property, could be insured as cargo. This meant that the ship's owner, and by extension the captain, could receive compensation for any captives that died en route to their destination.

There were limits to what the insurance underwriters would cover on a slave ship. In the case of the *Zong*, the insurers refused to pay out because they believed the deaths of the captives who had been thrown overboard did not fall under what was covered by the policy, and that is why the case eventually came to the public's attention. The Liverpool shipowner William Gregson went to court on behalf of his slaving syndicate against the insurer Thomas Gilbert in 1783. The court report summarized *Gregson v. Gilbert* as "an action on a policy of insurance, to recover the value of certain slaves thrown overboard for want of water."[31] This was not a murder trial—it was a fight over an insurance payout.

One of the judges presiding over the trial was Lord Mansfield, who had issued the *Somerset* decision a decade earlier. In the first hearing, in March 1783, a jury found in favor of the owners, ordering the insurers to pay £30 for each dead captive, as agreed in their contract.[32] The insurers appealed, and the case went to trial again in May 1783 in front of the Court of King's Bench.

The defense argued that they could not verify what happened because the ship's logbook had long been missing, though Gregson claimed the papers were with Collingwood when he died in Jamaica. They never spoke to the obvious witnesses—the surviving Africans—but instead to the surviving crew for testimony, though none appeared in court. Crew member James Kelsall's account would come in a written statement, and the only witness summoned to appear in person was a passenger, Robert Stubbs.[33]

The point of contention had a gruesome simplicity: Was the murder of some 150 Africans due to "necessity" over a lack water, or was this a ploy to defraud the insurers? To the shipowners, the Africans were, first of all, "property," though they later claimed that this "property" was actually planning a revolt, and so the killings had to take place or else "all the blacks would have killed all the whites."[34] Lord Mansfield, seemingly on the side of the slave traders, weighed in, saying that, in the earlier March hearing, "the matter left to the jury, was whether it [the massacre] was from necessity: for they had no doubt (though it shocks one very much) that the case of the slaves was the same as if horses had been thrown overboard."[35] The sufferings of the victims were seemingly given no place in the courtroom. However, the insurers' lawyers later capitalized on this point, bringing up the question of murder and the brutality of what took place. Ultimately, their argument rested on the navigation error that led to the ship's distress. Since the losses were due to human mistakes, they were not covered under the insurance policy. They claimed that the crew's motive was to "saddle a bad market upon the underwriters instead of the owners."[36]

During the course of the second trial, it was revealed that the 38 final murder victims had been killed after it had rained, the presence of rainwater now casting grave doubt on the "necessity" question. The judges ordered a new trial, but there is no sign that it ever took place, nor any clear reason why not.[37] The merchants of death carried on, the machinery of the slave trade still far from dismantled.

Although the *Zong* trial delivered no justice, abolitionists could use it as a painful example of why the slave trade needed to end.[38] Equiano had been in touch with Sharp as soon as he heard about the case. Sharp attended the trials, and advised the insurers' lawyers. He was hoping for the case to require a retrial, one that could bring in murder charges and turn into a larger human rights case, though this failed to happen.[39] However, Sharp and Equiano helped stoke the fires of public outrage as people learned about the sorts of atrocities taking place on the ships that regularly departed from Liverpool's harbor.[40] Ottobah Cugoano brought up the trial in his book, recounting his horror at the events that transpired. He wrote:

> Their argument was, that the slaves were to be considered the same as horses; and their plea for throwing them into the sea was nothing better than it might be more necessary to throw them overboard to lighten their vessel than goods of greater value . . . These poor creatures, it seems, were tied two and two together when they were thrown into the sea, lest some of them might swim a little for the last gasp of air, and, with the animation of their approaching exit, breath[e] their souls away to the gracious Father of spirits.[41]

The trial took place around the time that the American Revolution was ending, and much about its aftermath had yet to be decided. Cugoano observed in *Thoughts and Sentiments*, "Since the last war, some mitigation of slavery has been obtained in some respective districts of America, though not in proportion to their own vaunted claims of freedom."[42]

The *Zong* trial and the end of the Revolutionary War also overlapped with a June 1783 petition from the Religious Society of Friends in London (Quakers) exhorting Parliament to abolish the slave trade.[43] Sharp, already involved in freedom cases, became one of the leading proponents of this growing abolitionist movement. By 1787, Sharp and other abolitionists established the Society for Effecting the Abolition of the Slave Trade (SEAST). The corresponding black abolitionist group, the "Sons of Africa," counted Cugoano and Equiano among their members.[44]

But full freedom, much less *equality*, was not part of the SEAST vision. Its initial goal was to ameliorate the condition of slaves, rather than to abolish the entire system. No singular strain of white antislavery existed at this early juncture—different groups were involved for their own reasons, and their aims were not uniform. Ending the trade was the goal for some, with the idea that the surviving slaves would be better treated if no more could be imported from Africa. For others, the introduction of enslaved people to Christianity was key. Some thought that with conversion and the amelioration of conditions, eventually the entire practice would come to an end.[45]

The only abolitionists expressing a clear, ringing vision of absolute freedom and emancipation were black people. Cugoano proposed "that a total abolition of slavery should be made and proclaimed; and that an universal emancipation of slaves should begin from the date thereof."[46] He wanted to see the end of the entire system, saying, "The whole business of slavery is an evil of the first magnitude."[47] He was referring to each element of the business, from the seller of glass beads to trade in Africa to the insurers in London to the salt-fish merchant selling food to feed the captives to the overseers forcing enslaved people to whip their fellow slaves to the "master" raping his female "property" to the sugar in teacups and the tobacco in pipes in the drawing rooms of London and Bordeaux.

Many white abolitionists may not have realized at that point how many strands of society were knotted up with slavery, but a reasonable starting point for them was to end the trade, and so SEAST put Thomas Clarkson and the member of parliament (MP) William Wilberforce to work making the case for its abolition. Wilberforce was friends with the prime minister, William Pitt the Younger, who had developed a sympathy with the abolitionists' cause.[48] He could see that, owing to a boom in French sugar in the Caribbean, the slave trade was becoming less beneficial to Britain. For instance, Saint-Domingue alone had produced 87,000 tons of sugar in 1787, compared with Jamaica's 49,000. Saint-Domingue plantations averaged a profit of 8 to 12 percent, while Jamaica's netted 4 percent in the 1780s.[49] With the shifting Caribbean market and with the loss of the 13 North American colonies, imperial attention began to focus elsewhere, such as on India.

Indeed, if Britain were to abandon the slave trade, according to Pitt's calculation, it could undermine the French colonies, because they depended on the British slave trade to supplement their own. Without those extra captives in tropical fields, islands like Saint-Domingue would falter. Pitt was also concerned about the profitability of the trade to Britain and interested in the possibilities of Indian sugar, and in 1788 he commissioned a report.[50] A debate took place in Parliament the following spring, in 1789. Nothing changed beyond that, in part because the West Indian planters' lobby continued to wield significant power. However, the public mood in Britain was shifting. Dissenting sects like the Baptists and the Methodists shored up the abolitionists' numbers. Geographically, there was momentum in this early campaign from all over Britain, especially among mill workers in Manchester, whose cloths had become an important commodity in the triangular trade. A national push to send petitions to Parliament netted an estimated 60,000 signatures in 1788.[51] The abolitionist movement also mobilized women, who made donations and spoke out against the trade, bringing them into public political life.[52]

Equiano's *Interesting Narrative* appeared around two weeks before the 1789 debate in Parliament, giving MPs time to read it.[53] It was the secret weapon the movement needed, with its detailed retelling of the horrors of the Middle Passage, and the inhuman treatment of enslaved people. Both Equiano's and Cugoano's works also showed the public how slavery reached into so many corners of life. That debate was not successful in securing a bill, but it did raise public awareness of the abolitionist cause. More concrete results, however, would be nearly two decades away.

Britain, of course, was not the world, and it could do nothing to control the movement of slave ships under other flags. The eighteenth century had been mostly a rising tide of human misery in this regard, with hundreds of thousands more captives being moved at the end of the century than at the beginning. The system that European powers had created looked almost unstoppable, but a new front was about to open that would radically disrupt it.

⇜ • ⇝

On the evening of October 22, 1789, the Société des Amis des Noirs (Society of Friends of the Blacks) held a dinner in Paris with some special guests. In attendance was the British abolitionist Thomas Clarkson, and alongside him were two free men of color from the French colony of Saint-Domingue, Julien Raimond and Vincent Ogé.[54]

The Amis des Noirs had been set up the previous year. It was a small abolitionist group and had nowhere near the swell of public support that SEAST did in Britain.⁵⁵ Although the interest was small, the interested were powerful and connected people, such as the journalist Jacques Pierre Brissot, who moved in intellectual circles and also abolitionist ones, making contact with people in Britain. Brissot would also become deeply involved in the French Revolution, the opening shots of which had been fired a few months previously, with the storming of the Bastille on July 14 and the promulgation of the Declaration of the Rights of Man and of the Citizen that same year. The powerful planter and merchant lobby realized that such events, coupled with the establishment of the Amis des Noirs, were counter to their interests, so they set up the Club Massiac—named after the hotel where the meetings took place—in 1789.

Throughout the eighteenth century, French Enlightenment intellectuals, known as the *philosophes*, had given thought to the question of slavery amid the larger issues of rights and governance, while after the losses of the Seven Years' War, a group of French political economists known as the physiocrats aimed to reform France's empire and make agricultural production more efficient and prosperous.⁵⁶ Thinkers across Europe had turned their attention to more scientific inquiries. Systems of classification were developed in the 1700s, such as the taxonomies invented by the Swedish botanist Carl Linnaeus. Humans soon followed plants as subjects of these taxonomic schemes. Terms like "quadroon" (one-quarter black) and "octoroon" (one-eighth) circulated widely in the French colonies. Science was taking over from religion the question of difference and reorganizing it into categories of "race." Such was the interest in racial types that the Bordeaux Royal Academy of Sciences offered the following question in its 1741 prize competition: "What is the physical cause of the Negro's color, the quality of [the Negro's] hair, and the degeneration of both [Negro hair and skin]?" However, the essays submitted were deemed of poor quality and not "scientific" enough, and the prize was not awarded.⁵⁷

Many aspects of French society had been under scrutiny after the Seven Years' War. France had suffered the loss of its territory in North America, but had held on to what would become the most valuable colony in the West Indies, Saint-Domingue, as well as Martinique, Guadeloupe, half of Saint Martin, and Saint Barthélemy, giving it influence and power within the region, though not on the mainland after the loss of Canada and the ceding of Louisiana to Spain.

Between the end of the Seven Years' War in 1763 and the start of the French Revolution in 1789, at least 400,000 Africans disembarked in Saint-Domingue.[58] Leading thinkers, such as the Baron de Montesquieu, had been increasingly vocal in their critique of slavery—Montesquieu called it "unnatural"—but had not demanded the abolition of the trade. Having served as the president of the appeals court of Bordeaux, a city intimately tied to colonial commerce, Montesquieu would have been especially aware of the enormity of the system.[59] Of course, slavery also remained a metaphor for white oppression, most famously enshrined in the lines of the Genevan philosopher Jean-Jacques Rousseau's *The Social Contract* (1762): "Man is born free and everywhere he is in chains."

The men who gathered at the Amis des Noirs dinner that October night in 1789 had much to discuss. Only a short time before, in September, a group of free people of color in Paris had issued their demands to the National Assembly, saying that "the creole freedmen, as well as their children and posterity, must enjoy the same rights, rank, prerogatives, freedoms, and privileges as the other colonists."[60] And yet, they wanted these rights on an island where they were surrounded by enslaved people.

Raimond and Ogé represented this paradox of the Saint-Domingue society. They were both *gens de couleur*—born free, with one African grandparent—but they were also enslavers. Ogé was one of the richest men of color on the island, much of his wealth generated through coffee, as the crop thrived in the cooler altitude of the island's mountainous interior. Raimond had fields of indigo, later adding cotton, and owned at least 100 slaves.[61]

They were both members of the larger free black population (*nègres libres*), which numbered around 30,000 in the colony. Another 30,000 people on the island were white, and that number included the colonial authorities, the clergy, the large sugarplanters, and the *petits blancs*, or poorer white people. Raimond and Ogé, and other free people of color, were tired of being treated as second-class citizens because of their African ancestry. They were richer than many of the white colonists, but their wealth could not buy them access to the privileges those people enjoyed. This problem was quite separate from the issue of slavery, on which their fortunes also rested. At this juncture, the fight for equality was not the same as the one for emancipation.

Ogé had in mind as an example of the discrimination he faced the growing use of the word *affranchis* (freed person) on the island, which means freed-person or ex-slave—rather than *gens de couleur*—and so it was a linguistic reminder that somewhere in Ogé's family tree, a slave or two could be found, thus keeping him in his social place. In 1770s Saint-Domingue, demands to prove manumission or freedom were increasingly required. A judge in Le Cap—Cap Français, where Ogé lived—said that free people of color needed to wear "a *cockade* or a piece of red ribbon on their head" so that officials would be able to easily identify them. Raimond, who had moved to France in 1784 in part to fight for reforms, called these sorts of measures "a humiliation."[62]

Ogé had not initially come to France to campaign, as Raimond had, but rather to iron out some creases in his business dealings, as his fortunes had experienced significant fluctuations.[63] But while he was there in 1789, the world around him was changing. In August a slave revolt had broken out in Martinique. While news of the storming of the Bastille had not yet reached the island, rumors circulated that the king of France had freed the slaves and that local officials were hiding the news from them. An anonymous letter from "the *Nègres*," dated August 28, 1789, says as much: "We know we are free and that you are aware that rebellious people are resisting the orders of the king. Well, remember that we *nègres* are numerous, and we want to die for this liberty." Writing after the unrest had been suppressed, an official described the scene: "*Nègres*, armed with the tools that they used to cut sugarcane, refused to work, saying loudly they were free," after which they fled into the volcanic hills above Saint-Pierre.[64]

What's more, a letter from this period, signed by the "Entire Nation of Black Slaves" in Martinique, makes clear that enslaved people knew that free men like Ogé were fighting a different battle. It states:

> We have just learned with extreme desperation that the mulattos, far from taking care of their enslaved mothers, brothers, and sisters, have dared claim that we do not deserve to enjoy, as they do, the

benefits that come from peace and liberty . . . It is not jealousy that forced us to complain about the mulattos, but the harshness they have shown in creating a plan of liberty only for themselves, when we are all of the same family.[65]

In September Ogé spoke to the Club Massiac in Paris, attempting to highlight their commonality, calling himself a "property owner from Le Cap," and appealing to the white members that they must come together "to avoid the disaster that threatens us." All the free people needed to unite—white and black—otherwise, he said, "blood will flow, our property will be invaded, the fruits of our labor destroyed, and our homes burned." Ogé knew the island well, but his scare tactics were too efficient. The white planters denied him membership in the group, despite his intention of presenting himself as an ally who was looking out for the interests of all property holders.[66]

After this rejection, he later met with other free people of color back in Saint-Domingue; many were artisans and people of humbler means, but they were in agreement about what to do. They called themselves the Colons Américains (American Colonists), purposely avoiding a name that used any racial category, and began the process of obtaining representation in the National Assembly. They believed the 1789 Declaration of the Rights of Man should include them.[67] At this point Raimond joined them. From there, the Colons began to make common cause with the Amis de Noirs, which led the two enslavers to a dinner table in Paris with abolitionists that October evening.

The Colons were unsuccessful in obtaining seats in the National Assembly, and Ogé began to think about returning to Saint-Domingue and bringing some of his fellow members with him. The plan fell apart after Club Massiac members—who had been keeping a close eye on Ogé—leaned on the ship captain to cancel the chartered voyage. They were convinced that he was planning some sort of uprising.[68]

The pressure was growing in Saint-Domingue as well, as worried whites were barring free people of color from participating in elections of representatives to the National Assembly in Paris. A group in Grand-Rivière retaliated, petitioning the local assembly in the north in November 1789. They pointed to their role in protecting the colony, including "when slaves who had deserted had to be brought back," before getting to the heart of their claim. The white community, they said, was going "so far as to deform the precious right to freedom bestowed on us by our magnanimous sovereignty. These fathers treat us like slaves."[69] Rejected, they continued to build their own group, electing two commissioners, one of whom was Jean-Baptiste Chavannes.

Chavannes was a military version of Ogé. He also had only one African grandparent and was a coffee planter, but he served in the free colored militia as a sergeant.[70] That military service was part of this group's claim to equality on the island. They defended it, they captured the runaways, and they fought the invaders. But still, they were denied the right to vote.

By March 1790, the National Assembly simply chose to ignore the issue of who could participate in parish assemblies to select representatives to go to Paris, which was of great concern to Chavannes, Ogé, and Raimond. It was left up to each colony, which meant that free people of color had no recourse if they were excluded.[71]

By the time Ogé returned to Saint-Domingue that October, the mood was tense. He very quickly got in contact with Chavannes, whose group continued to press for their rights. They wrote to the governor and the Provincial Assembly on the island, demanding the right to vote in upcoming elections because they were qualified to do so as wealthy free men.[72] The governor refused their request, and on October 28 they gathered about 300 free men of color around the northern Grande-Rivière district, while the city sent 600 militia members and volunteers to stop them. Chavannes had been pressuring Ogé to consider bringing slaves into the picture, but he had resisted the idea.[73]

Ogé, Chavannes, and the assembled men prevailed in their skirmish on the first night, and so the Provincial Assembly stepped in with 1,500 soldiers. The two men, along with some of their supporters, fled into the mountains of Spanish Santo Domingo. Ogé asked for asylum, but he was arrested instead, as were the 23 other men who had come with him.[74] After some debate, Spanish officials decided to extradite Ogé and cooperate with the French. They were also eager to avoid any similar sort of disturbance among the free people of color in Santo Domingo.[75] The men were hauled in for questioning by a prosecutor from the royal court in Le Cap.[76] During the interrogation, Ogé produced a letter, likely taken from the soldiers who had come to arrest him, from the Provincial Assembly, saying Ogé's "destructive plans are only too well known" and instructing the recipient of the letter "to do everything necessary to arrest him." After revealing this, Ogé told the examiner, "You see perfectly well that I have nothing more to lose."[77]

The execution of Ogé and Chavannes took place in February 1791. They were both broken on the wheel and tortured in front of the cathedral of Le Cap for all to see. The sentence stipulated that they be killed "on the side [of the main square] opposite the one used for the execution of whites" where they would "have their arms, shins, thighs, and pelvis broken while alive on a scaffold."[78] Their heads were put on pikes—as if they were rebel slaves or maroon leaders—as a warning to any would-be free black plotters of the dangers of pushing the limits of their liberty.[79]

The next stage of this battle would come from people who had no freedom to lose.

Chapter 20

Vengeance

People living in the north of Saint-Domingue woke up on August 23, 1791, to the smoky, sweet scent of smoldering sugarcane. Earlier that month, a group of enslaved people in the north had held secret meetings, led by a man known as Boukman, who may have been deported from Jamaica.[1] Accounts differ as to the genesis and sequence of events. Some say a voudou ceremony was held in the woods near a place called Bois Caïman on August 14, where the attack was planned. The ceremony may have involved the blood sacrifice of a pig and the swearing of an oath of loyalty. It might have happened a week later. Others say that it was raining, that there were prayers and drumming, with a blow on a conch shell signaling the start of the attacks.[2]

However the uprising was planned, once it actually began the night of August 22, there would be no stopping it for a very long time. And on this island, it would leave a trail of blood. The 500,000 enslaved creoles and Africans on Saint-Domingue knew change was afoot in France and on the island. They had heard about the events in Paris and, closer to home, the execution of Vicente Ogé. A sizable contingent of slaves decided that this was the moment to leap, to make the first blow in the fight for emancipation, starting a battle that would continue for 13 years. The smoke signals they sent that August morning would be read far and wide.[3]

That the revolt began in the north of the island is no surprise. Its fertile plains were home to at least 200 large sugar plantations. There were also some cotton fields and indigo farms, along with around 2,000 coffee plantations scattered throughout the mountains that rose up from the coast.[4] And Cap-Français, or Le Cap, the port city through which humans entered and all these products exited, was a tactical and symbolic target.

Within a month almost all the sugar works and some 1,200 of the 2,000 coffee plantations in the north were in ruins.[5] More significantly, the number of slaves on the march continued to rise, from around 1,000 at the beginning of the revolt to 20,000 only a fortnight later. By some estimates there were possibly around 80,000 in revolt by November 1791.[6] Some of the Africans in Saint-Domingue were recent arrivals, with many from Kongo, possibly trained soldiers from the conflicts in Africa that had left them in captivity, and ready to fight.[7]

This wasn't so much about the ideals of the French Revolution coming to the island as it was about enslaved people in the north seizing an opportune moment. Throughout 1791 and 1792, there were multiple conflicts at play—including whites against free people of color, republicans against royalists, and enslaved people against the island's military forces. This was not yet a singular struggle for emancipation from slavery. It was a confusing time, and the only consistency was the belief that freedom lay ahead: Some rebels were found with the 1789 Declaration of the Rights of Man and of the Citizen on them, others said the king had given them three days of rest but the planters were hiding this news.[8] Whatever their motivation, thousands of people were tearing through the north of the island, the fury of decades now unleashed.

One plantation manager, writing only a few weeks after the revolt started, had to inform his employer that his cane fields had been reduced to ash. "Monsieur, I save myself wounded, with only the shirt on my back, having lost in an instant the fruit of nine years of work on your plantations." The force of such destruction, the manager mused, came from somewhere beyond his comprehension. "There is a motor that powers them and that keeps powering them," he wrote, "and that we cannot come to know."[9]

By December, at least 2,000 to 3,000 men were under the command of the former slaves Georges Biassou and Jean-François Papillon, with the rest fighting in smaller bands with local leaders.[10] Both men had been coachmen, roles of responsibility with proximity to planters. Boukman, too, may have been a coachman, as was Toussaint Bredà, a former slave who would later adopt the surname Louverture. For the moment Louverture was serving as Biassou's secretary—the two

A French map showing the 1733 arrival of the Marquis de Fayet at Cap François, now Cap-Haïtien, in Haiti

men had had a long friendship.[11] Unlike the other three, Boukman was killed early on in battle, his head placed on a stake in a square in Le Cap. If that was meant as a warning, it was paid little heed.[12]

Around November 1791, a group of commissioners arrived in Saint-Domingue bearing a decree of general amnesty for colonists involved in political acts relating to the French Revolution. They had departed France before news of the revolt could reach them, so they had no idea what was taking place on the island. They also brought with them a decree concerning free people of color, which overturned earlier ones of May and October 1791. The earlier decrees were supposed to grant some equal rights, calling all free men "citizens" and integrating segregated militia units.[13] Now, the political status of free non-white men in the colonies was to be determined by the local assemblies. In Saint-Domingue, there was little chance of the hostile assembly granting free men of color the same rights as whites, so this measure all but erased their earlier gains.[14]

Biassou and Jean-François (he was customarily referred to by his first name) decided to use the moment to end the rebellion, or at least their participation in it, with an amnesty for the rebel slaves. In a letter to the commissioners, the two men wrote, "We must tell you that you do not understand the nature of our position . . . in ordering us each to return to our own homes, you are demanding something both impossible and dangerous . . . A hundred thousand men are in arms; we make up 80 percent of this population . . . the consequences can be deadly if we do not approach this operation with the greatest caution."[15]

They said they would end the conflict if certain conditions were met. The first was freedom for rebel leaders, followed by amnesty for the rest—at this juncture, Jean-François and Biassou did not think general emancipation was practicable, and it was important that the rebel leaders be able to influence and control those slaves under their command. They also wanted the use of the whip banned. The Colonial Assembly denied these requests.[16]

So by the start of 1792, the two generals were on the march again, this time capturing areas near the border with Santo Domingo and, in the case of Biassou, freeing his own mother, Diana, who worked at a hospital.[17] Louverture had been building up his own forces, with around 600 men under him, while still reporting to Biassou; he was promoted to general by the end of that year.[18] The men were so successful in the north that a steady stream of people was crossing the border to the Spanish side to escape the fighting or seek refuge, with Spanish officials observing, "The Blacks traverse the entire frontier pursuing familiars of Mulattos, free Blacks, and Whites that they encounter."[19] Fighting had intensified in the south and west of the island as well, with plantation-owning whites and free people of color arming slaves in some areas, while in others groups of rebel slaves controlled small areas. The entire colony was now engulfed in fighting.[20] One of the key leaders in the south was André Rigaud, an *homme de couleur* who had been trained as a goldsmith in Bordeaux before returning to the island. Like Louverture, he would become a key player in what was to come.

In France—convulsed by the vicissitudes of its own political upheaval—the events in Saint-Domingue demanded the National Assembly's attention. Its members decided to overturn the previous ruling regarding *gens de couleur*, issuing a decree in April 1792 that free men of color and whites would have equal political rights. Now there was only slave and free. Some assembly members and abolitionists concluded that the only way to end the revolt in Saint-Domingue was to placate the free people of color so they would ally with the republican whites.[21] They also dispatched another 6,000 French troops to assist.²² Along with the soldiers, the revolutionary government in Paris sent three new civil commissioners, Légér-Félicité Sonthonax and Étienne Polverel, who were known to have antislavery sentiments, and Jean-Antoine Ailhaud, who left the mission shortly after their arrival in September 1792 on a ship named *America*.²³

That same month, the French Republic was declared. Sonthonax had supported the French Revolution and was a Jacobin. But however committed he was to equality in France, liberating the slaves was not his initial mission. Indeed, his first challenge was resolving the clashes between republicans and royalists.²⁴ He was able to lean on free people of color for support, wanting to both implement racial equality between them and the whites and also enlist their help in suppressing royalist uprisings. He scrapped the Colonial Assembly and set up an "Intermediary Commission," for which he selected six white men and six free men of color.²⁵

Early the next year, on January 21, 1793, France's Louis XVI was executed. While the revolution was clearly taking control in France, other monarchies watched with alarm, especially Britain and Spain. By March, Spain had declared war against France, and soon thereafter, so did Britain. The three nations by now had long histories of using the Caribbean as a theater of war, having done so in the Seven Years' War and the American Revolution. The French Revolutionary Wars would be no different.

In Spanish Santo Domingo, Governor Joaquín García had been alarmed by the early success of the slave rebellion in 1791, as well as the requests for assistance from the French governor Philibert François Rouxel de Blanchelande. Although Spanish Santo Domingo had a much smaller population than and less than one-tenth the number of enslaved people of Saint-Domingue, Blanchelande raised the specter of a spreading revolt. "After the defeat of the French," he wrote, "the Spanish could have the same luck."²⁶ García watched in the intervening years as the slave rebellion raged and refugees crossed the border, and now the French had cut off their king's head.

The Spanish were not the only ones who were uncertain about this new French Republic. The rebel slaves were unsure whether to trust it. As far as they understood, Sonthonax and the *gens de couleur* would have them back on the plantations. García was able to exploit this situation, and he decided to mobilize three white and two black (*moreno*) militia companies.[27] They would take back the island, which had been Spain's for more than 200 years before part of it was ceded to the French in 1697. As part of this plan, he offered an alliance with Biassou, Papillon, and some of the other rebel leaders. Louverture went to Santo Domingo as well, joining his comrades in June 1793. This time he was able carve out his own rank, as a colonel, eventually leading 4,000 men.[28]

There were obvious practical considerations to this deal—the Spanish could provide arms and other support, and made promises of freedom and land at the end. But an undercurrent of shared royalism also animated it, a belief in the figure of a benevolent king—with the colonial officials as the enemy. Indeed, upon hearing the news of the death of Louis XVI, Biassou lamented the loss of the "best King on the earth."[29] The king of Spain may have seemed a safer bet than the French republicans, at least at this juncture, and so the rebel leaders became the "Black Auxiliaries of Carlos IV."[30] Louverture, too, flew his royalist flag while he made tremendous gains in the north.

On August 29, 1793, he decided to reintroduce himself to the public in a proclamation:

> I am Toussaint Louverture, you have perhaps heard my name. You are aware, brothers, that I have undertaken vengeance, and that I want freedom and equality to reign in Saint-Domingue. I have been working since the beginning to bring it into existence so as to establish the happiness of us all.

He signed it with his adopted name, Louverture, which means "the opening" (*l'ouverture*), describing himself as "general of the Armies of the King, for the Public Good." Although Louverture was known as one of the rebel leaders, and now was fighting on behalf of Spain, he was also signaling his rise and his own vision.[31]

Although his rise was singular, his background was like that of so many thousands of his fellow former slaves. His parents were of Allada origin (modern Benin), and he grew up learning their Fon language, as well as their botanical and medicinal knowledge, which allowed him to become known as a healer before he was a general.[32] He worked as a coachman and assistant for the manager of the Brèda estate, and was formally emancipated at some point by 1776.[33] After that, he was a free black man and part of a small community compared with the more powerful *gens de couleur*. As a free man, he purchased at least one slave and, while leasing his son-in-law's coffee plantation, oversaw 13 others—one of whom, intriguingly, may have been a young Jean-Jacques Dessalines, who would later become one of his trusted generals.[34] Like many others on the island, he straddled these multiple worlds, until the opening provided by the 1791 rebellion.

On the same August day that Louverture made his proclamation, Sonthonax declared the abolition of slavery in the north of the colony after a public gathering of some 15,000 people in Le Cap five days earlier voiced its support for the measure.[35] This move came on the heels of a revolt in Le Cap in May over the new governor and the plundering and burning of the city in June. Sonthonax's emancipation decree—only intended for the north of the colony at this point—was part of his attempt to regain order.

Despite the promises of freedom, Louverture was unmoved. He had been working off the battlefield to end slavery, presenting plans that involved full emancipation to both French and Spanish officials, but had found neither receptive.[36] He and the other leaders stayed with Spain—by this point they had around 10,000 soldiers under their command.[37]

Then, in the autumn of 1793, the situation became even more complicated when the British arrived.

White Saint-Domingue planters, some of whom were exiled in Jamaica, began to consider reaching out to the British. A group of French planters in London did so, offering to pledge their allegiance to the king and in exchange for protection, as well as relief from debt repayments. In addition, many wanted to believe that the Republic was only temporary, and the French monarchy would be restored, as would the old order.[38] It was a fatal error.

In Britain, abolitionists and planters alike were following the news from Saint-Domingue. A few months before the August 1791 revolt, in May, William Wilberforce had introduced a motion in Parliament on the abolition of the slave trade. It was defeated by 163 to 88, with the anti-abolitionists arguing that it would bring economic devastation.[39] By the time the news of Saint-Domingue reached Britain, the proslavery West India Committee tried to blame abolitionists for the uprising.[40] Thomas Clarkson hit back with a 1792 pamphlet saying the real cause was ultimately slavery itself, writing, "We cannot keep people in a state of subjection to us, who acknowledge no obligation whatever to serve us, but by breaking their spirits and treating them as creatures of another species."[41]

The popular sentiment against the slave trade continued to grow, and national petitions for another motion attracted some 400,000 signatures.[42] In addition, a 1791 pamphlet by the Baptist minister William Fox exhorted people to abstain from West Indian products, sparking a national conversation about boycotting sugar. "The laws of our country may indeed prohibit us the sugar-cane unless we will receive it through the medium of slavery," he wrote. "They may hold it to our lips, steeped in the blood of our fellow-creatures; but they cannot compel us to accept the loathsome potion." Fox wanted to see the end of the slave trade and of the use of slaves in the production of sugar, desiring a product "unconnected with slavery, and unpolluted with blood."[43]

In the spring of 1792, another vote on the slave trade was held in the House of Commons. Wilberforce moved the proposition "that the trade carried on by British subjects, for the purpose of obtaining Slaves on the coast of Africa, ought to be abolished." During the debate, the Home Secretary, Henry Dundas, proposed an amendment to make it a gradual abolition of the trade. To his mind, time had to be given to increase the enslaved population locally, ideally through good treatment. With a stable enough population, British planters would not need the slave trade, even if other nations continued in it. He argued, "This trade must be ultimately abolished, but by *moderate* measures, which shall not invade this property of individuals, nor shock too suddenly the prejudices of our West India Islands."[44] To this end, he introduced his amendment to the motion: "That the Slave Trade ought *gradually* to be abolished."[45]

Prime Minister Pitt weighed in with his support, saying, "However we may differ as to the time and manner of it, we are agreed in the abolition itself . . . the point now in dispute between us, is, a difference merely as to the period of time."⁴⁶ The measure passed the House of Commons by 230 to 85, only to be blocked by the House of Lords. When Pitt referred to time in his speech, or indeed when Dundas made his plea for gradual measures, they could not have envisioned it taking 15 more years for this matter to be resolved. Wilberforce persisted in his struggle, but with the onset of the French Revolutionary wars in 1792, attention inevitably pivoted away from slavery.

Except, of course, in the West Indies. Certainly, for planters and officials in Jamaica, an island with a similar black majority and history of rebellions, Saint-Domingue looked like a warning that should be heeded. It was also an opportunity to take control of a very valuable sugar island, even if this motivation was never explicitly stated. Dundas later defended Britain's intervention, claiming it was "a war for security."⁴⁷ That is what the French planters were seeking, and to this end they swore their allegiance to George III early in 1793. By September, 600 British troops had arrived in Jérémie, a city in Saint-Domingue which lay less than a day's sail from Jamaica. They were greeted with cries of "Long live the English!" That town quickly capitulated, as did the key naval port of Môle Saint-Nicolas, also on the west coast.⁴⁸ Ultimately, the entire expedition would cost the lives of 15,000 troops.⁴⁹

The western part of Saint-Domingue had a large population of free people of color, many of whom were prosperous landowners who wanted to keep their plantations running. They also wanted to keep their hard-won equality with whites, but that was quickly eroded as part of the deal—under the terms of the capitulation, they would enjoy the same rights "given to this class" in the British colonies, certainly not equality. They could thus save their plantations by returning to second-class status.⁵⁰

By the end of 1793, Sonthonax found himself squeezed on both sides—thousands of rebels were attacking from Spanish Santo Domingo, the British were arriving in the west, and the royalists were continuing their fight. Despite there now being tens of thousands of free people in the north who could fight, Sonthonax and Polverel had to work hard to gain recruits to the republican cause, while trying to convince others to stay and work on plantations rather than flee. It was an increasingly impossible situation. Sonthonax decided to extend abolition to the south and west, building on his earlier emancipation of slaves in the north, all of which was done independently of the National Convention in France. He also went beyond the boundary of much of the discussion at the time, which mostly argued for gradual abolition measures. There was no time to spare on the ground in Saint-Domingue. As he declared in August, "The French Republic wants all men to be free and equal with no color distinctions . . . a new order of things will be born, and the old slavery will disappear."[51]

As part of that new order, a black soldier began preparing to go to Paris. Jean-Baptiste Belley was a striking Senegalese army officer who had been sold into slavery but eventually bought his freedom and rose to prominence in the free black community in Le Cap. He had been involved in the black militia and quickly formed an alliance with Sonthonax. Belley was one of a trio of commissioners—the second was white and the third of mixed-heritage—selected to tell the National Convention the news: Slavery had been abolished in Saint-Domingue. The men set off for Paris, running a gauntlet of hostility, first on the ship, which was full of white exiles fleeing to the United States. Then, while in Philadelphia, Belley was attacked by a mob of people—including royalist refugees—who came aboard the ship and robbed him of all his goods and papers, while demanding that he remove his tricolor cockade, claiming that a black man should not be allowed to wear one.[52]

The trio eventually arrived at the National Convention and were accepted as delegates for the northern province of Saint-Domingue.[53] The following day they informed the body that slavery was finished on the island. A law to end it throughout the Republic's other colonies passed on the spot, with slavery abolished on February 4, 1794.

Belley made a passionate speech to the members of the Convention about his childhood as a slave and his path to freedom, using the rhetoric of the revolution to reaffirm his place in this new order. "It is the tricolour that has called us to our liberty," he told the gathering, and he made clear that he would fight for it with every drop of blood in his body.[54] He stayed on in Paris as a delegate—the first black man to be one—and was later commemorated in a 1797 painting by Anne-Louis Girodet de Roussy-Trioson, *Portrait of Citizen Jean-Baptiste Belley*. It is an arresting depiction, Belley's muscular body leaning next to a bust of the prominent Enlightenment antislavery writer Abbé de Raynal.

Belley's face is turned, his eyes look toward the sky. He appears both relaxed and powerful, dressed in the appropriate style for a member of the National Convention, with a gold hoop in his right ear. The white bust of Raynal contrasts quite purposely with Belley's dark skin, the artist perhaps hopefully anticipating a world of black and white equality.

While Belley was in France, Toussaint Louverture was trying to work out his next step. By July 1794, Louverture had decided to join the French republicans. His relations with Biassou, Papillon, and Spanish officials soured as they continued to disagree over strategy. The emancipation of the French side was also undoubtedly a factor, despite Louverture's wariness of the republicans.[55] Sonthonax and the republicans had been mostly reduced to controlling parts of Le Cap and Port-de-Paix in the north, and they would certainly welcome Louverture's help. The British were holding firm in the south and west of Saint-Domingue, and they managed to pick up the French islands of Martinique, Saint Lucia, and Guadeloupe in their wider Caribbean campaign. The light of emancipation was surrounded by the darkening menace of re-enslavement.

Louverture began to organize a talented coterie around him, among them Henry Christophe and Jean-Jacques Dessalines. Beyond the military, Louverture had many connections, including through his Catholic faith. From the prerevolutionary days, he would also have known about the maroon secret societies, including the man and myth of Makandal. Later on, Louverture would use both the Afro-Catholic syncretic practices of voudou and references to Makandal, such as appearing or disappearing quickly as if by magic, to build a mystical presence among the public. To some, Louverture was Makandal reborn.[56]

Sonthonax had promised a new order of things. Louverture was going to make it happen.

Chapter 21

Escalations

SAINT-DOMINGUE WAS NOT the only island on fire. By the 1790s, the entire Caribbean basin was on high alert. While Louverture and Sonthonax recalibrated and prepared for the next series of challenges—and they would come, one after the other—the region responded. It was as if the struggle in Saint-Domingue were a volcanic explosion and now the hot ash and glowing embers were falling on its neighbors, igniting more blazes. The year 1795 would be a particularly heated one, a time of feverish conflict. Historians argue over whether this was a direct result of the slave revolt in Saint-Domingue, but that question misses the larger point: There was no putting the lava back into the volcano.

Spanish officials around the Caribbean had already managed to curb the importation of slaves from any of the French islands but had less success blocking the news and rumors that were making their way across the Gulf of Mexico and into North America, to places like Pointe Coupée.[1] This small, flat rural settlement sits 100 miles upriver from New Orleans, along the Mississippi. It might have seemed thousands of miles away from the upheaval in Saint-Domingue, but ideas were travelling in ever wider circuits.

Pointe Coupée had been French territory until it was ceded, as part of Louisiana, to Spain in 1762 to keep it out of British hands. The Spanish struggled to assert authority over the French community in the lower part of the territory, including New Orleans. The area mostly coinciding with the modern state of Louisiana had been one hub of French operations, including the establishment of many plantations. The Spanish, certainly no strangers to slavery, absorbed this part of its empire as if it were another Caribbean island. Upper Louisiana, further north along the Mississippi, presented problems for a variety of different reasons, including the lack of interested Spanish settlers and ongoing Native American attacks.

The small plantations along the river near Pointe Coupée (or Punta Cortada to the Spanish) were diversified, growing tobacco, indigo, and cotton, among other crops, but not yet sugar on a large scale. It was an ideal spot, nestled between the Mississippi and an oxbow lake, and 512 free people and 1,492 slaves were living there in 1788.[2] The majority of the slave population at this time was African, not creole.[3] There were only a few Spanish soldiers posted in a dilapidated fort.[4] These factors no doubt played a part in the formation—and uncovering—of an earlier conspiracy in July 1791, ahead of events in Saint-Domingue. In that case, the alleged plot had been organized by enslaved people mostly of Mina (Gold Coast) origin who had been taken to Pointe Coupée. Their plan allegedly involved raiding the settlement store for supplies, then turning on the white settlers and massacring them. Before they could carry it out, word of the plot reached officials, and they rounded up suspects to interrogate.[5] Ultimately, 17 slaves were sent to New Orleans to be tried, which they were in 1792. The alleged rebels managed to win an acquittal, thanks in part to a Mina man, Antonio Cofi Mina, who had been free for about 15 years and who served as their translator. He possibly advised them on their defense, which was to argue that they were ignorant of any rebellion plans. After the prisoners were released, the Spanish governor, Baron de Carondelet, decreed that planters should treat slaves in a more "humane" manner, and provide them with better food and clothing.[6] Conditions, however, did not improve, and anger among the enslaved soon resurfaced.

The spring of 1795 brought new plans for an uprising in Pointe Coupée, to be held shortly before April 12.[7] This time, Governor Carondelet initially believed that this talk of slave rebellion was really the work of white French planters plotting to overthrow him. He was unpopular, and three attempts to oust him had already been made.[8] But what was happening on his watch was something very different from the alleged plot of 1791.

The information about the April plot came from two enslaved people, Juan Bautista Herrera and María Luisa.[9] It was corroborated by the testimony of Jean Baptiste Riché, who claimed that two indigenous women from the Tunica nation, Françoise and Madeleine, "had warned him that they [the slaves] were going to kill all the whites except young women and girls, whom they wanted to make their slaves." Their plan, according to the women, was to set fire to a cabin on the property of Julien Poydras and then attack the whites who came to douse the blaze."[10] When Françoise was brought before the authorities, she told them that she had spoken to an enslaved man named César, who had explained that "a letter had come from the government addressed to the commandant that gave the slaves their freedom and that he hid the letter. But although he didn't want to give them their freedom, they were going to take it themselves by killing all the whites."[11]

Suspected participants were rounded up—a significant number of them belonged to the enslaver Julien Poydras, who happened to be away from his plantation.[12] These included Antoine Sarrasin (also Sarazin), who lived on that estate and whom Françoise directly named in her statement. In his confession, he told officials that another of the leaders, Jean Baptiste, "had come to his tent," where they discussed "giving freedom to the slaves." Sarrasin also told officials that two months previously, two mulatto men on a riverboat bound for Natchez "had told them that all the slaves were all free by the King."[13]

In their search to find out the extent of the plan, officials in New Orleans brought in for questioning Antonio Cofi Mina, who had been the translator for the 1791 defendants. He relied on his own defense strategy, pleading ignorance of any plans in Pointe Coupée.[14] The Spanish administrators accused him of knowing about the plot but not reporting it. Now fully suspicious of him and his motives, they banished Mina to Havana.[15]

Three white men were also arrested in connection with the conspiracy, confirming Carondelet's fears about a "Jacobin" overthrow in Louisiana. The conspirators were planning an uprising along with another group upriver in Natchez. One of the whites was a German tailor named George Rockemborgh (also Roquemborg), who had allegedly written a pamphlet about liberty to distribute among enslaved people.[16] Another white man, Joseph Bouyaval, was said to have read news of the revolution in France to some people and was found to have a copy of the Declaration of the Rights of Man.[17] These two were sentenced to six years' imprisonment, while the other white conspirator was banished. The rest of the 60 people in prison by May were free black or enslaved. This time they were not mostly Mina, but instead a mix of creole and African. Twenty-three people were hanged and decapitated, with Sarrasin among them. Four of the heads were placed along the road to Pointe Coupée, while eight others were put on display elsewhere, with two in New Orleans and six in regional towns like Baton Rouge.[18]

In the aftermath, Carondelet continued to issue proclamations to improve the treatment of slaves, but such policies were a step behind in a world where revolution was on the march, and the promise of freedom seemed so near.[19]

Mainland South America, too, would feel the reverberations. In Venezuela, an uprising began on May 10, 1795, at the El Socorro plantation in the mountains, near the north coast city of Coro.[20] It spread to neighboring plantations, and some 170 people, including Amerindians, joined in. The rebels, under the leadership of José Leonardo Chirino, attacked Coro two days later, but were defeated.[21] Some tried to flee in the aftermath, but others were caught and killed. Chirino managed to elude capture until the middle of August. All the while, the Spanish authorities in Venezuela, like their counterparts in Louisiana, would have had their ears tuned for any mention of events in France or Saint-Domingue.

Chirino was a free man, of Afro-Amerindian origin (*zambo*), though he was married to an enslaved woman. He worked a plot of land and had a good relationship with José Tellería, who was his wife's enslaver. Apparently Chirino was trusted enough to have joined Tellería on trips to nearby Curaçao and further afield to Saint-Domingue.[22] Travelling there in the 1790s, it would have been impossible for Chirino to not know what was taking place. When he returned from trips, he shared news of France and Saint-Domingue with the people he lived among in the mountains, ultimately inspiring the uprising.

Around the time of Chirino's insurrection, another leader emerged, José Caridad González. He had been enslaved in Curaçao and fled to Coro, winning his freedom and joining other maroons.[23] The runaways settled in the mountains near Coro and in the city, in an area called Curazaíto (formerly named Guinea), where González and other freed people, known as *luangos*, lived.[24] González initially answered the authorities' call to arms to defend Coro, but they were suspicious of him and the other *luangos*, in part because González had been in a number of legal disputes. These suspicions spilled over into later investigations of the uprising. González was exonerated but was forced into service on Spanish ships. When Chirino was caught, he was quickly executed.[25]

Cuba was also affected by events in the summer of 1795. Thousands of people fleeing Saint-Domingue were arriving on that island, despite officials' wariness of anyone associated with the French. But Cuba was one of the largest and nearest places of refuge for royalists, especially the southern city of Santiago de Cuba, a short sail from some of Saint-Domingue's ports. In the south of Cuba, the nearby copper-mining *cobreros* had started claiming in 1788 that they were no longer the king's slaves and that he had freed them. This came around the time that the crown ordered the better treatment of slaves. However, the calls for freedom continued to intensify, and some *cobreros* decided to run away.[26]

A *cobrero* named Romualdo, who was 25, became involved in a rebellion in July 1795 on a hacienda called Cuatro Compañeros, in Puerto Príncipe (today's Camagüey), about 220 miles (350 kilometers) north of Santiago. The other enslaved man involved was called Joseph el Francés, possibly from Saint-Domingue, as his name suggests. The farm was small, with seven enslaved people. When the owner, Don Serapio Recio y Miranda, came home on July 6, he found the men agitated. Romualdo pulled out a machete and told Recio, "The whites should soon see how the blacks should be treated." Recio went to get his weapons, but Joseph already had them, and cried out: "No one has a master now; we are all free."[27] The men failed to set the house on fire but hit the stunned Recio with a chair. That night they tried to gain recruits from neighboring plantations, but they made a tactical error in leaving Recio unguarded while they did so. He soon alerted the authorities, and the men were captured.

In Bayamo, a town in the *oriente* of about 20,000 people, and similar in size to Santiago at the time, another conspiracy was uncovered in August. This plot was closely related to another event of 1795: Spain issued a royal decree known as the *cédula de gracias al sacar*, which allowed free people of mixed white and Amerindian (*mestizo*) or white and African (*pardo, mulatto*) heritage to purchase or petition to obtain privileges that had previously been exclusively for white people, such as administrative posts, access to universities, and marriage into a white family.[28]

Their plan involved the rebels, mostly free men of color, gathering outside Bayamo and then marching together into the town. They would use their militia connections to attract new military contingents along the way, helping to increase their numbers before presenting themselves to officials, at which point they would demand that officials implement this *cédula*. The plotters had heard about the decree, but it had not been brought into effect in Cuba, and they believed officials were keeping it a secret. They also planned to make demands about dropping a sales tax and having access to land. Their plans were interrupted, as officials heard about the plot. One of the alleged ringleaders claimed it was a joke that got out of hand. The authorities were not laughing, however, and questioned the conspirators, asking them if they had been influenced to demand greater equality by what was taking place in Saint-Domingue.[29]

In Puerto Rico, an attempt at a rebellion was quickly suppressed around October, in Aguadilla, on the island's west coast. Rattled, Governor Rámon de Castro implemented measures to prevent people from Saint-Domingue entering Puerto Rico, and to keep out printed material or any kind of dangerous propaganda.[30]

In a final blow for Spanish imperial officials worried about the designs of revolutionary France as well as the rebellion in Saint-Domingue, Spain ceded its oldest colony, Santo Domingo—the eastern side of Hispaniola, whose leaders had spent the previous four years worrying about events on the French side—to the French Republic. Under the 1795 Peace of Basel that brought the War of the Pyrenees to a close in Europe, the island would be united, but this time under French rule. As part of the deal, the Black Auxiliaries, which Biassou and Jean-François were still leading, would be disbanded. In fact, the generals would have to depart the island as well, after being told their presence was not "compatible" with the change of regime. They left for Cuba in 1795. Toussaint Louverture had changed sides just in time.[31]

⊰⊷ • ⊶⊱

THE SPANISH COLONIES were not the only ones to become tangled up in events in the Caribbean. The Dutch, too, would find themselves challenged in Europe and in the colonies. France occupied the Dutch Republic in 1795, which was renamed the Batavian Republic. Although France had abolished slavery in its colonies, this did not extend to the ones that were under Dutch control. Enslaved people on the island of Curaçao responded to these dramatic changes in their own way, possibly aided by the rebels from the earlier uprising in nearby Coro, Venezuela.

Curaçao, with its arid climate, had never developed a plantation economy. Rather, it grew wealthy through its port, especially serving as an entrepôt for slaves transported from Africa and redistributed across the Caribbean. The local slave population numbered 12,864 in 1789, with a white population of 4,410 and 3,714 free people of color.[32] Some enslaved people grew food for the island, while many others were urban slaves working in the capital.

There had been minor revolts before on Curaçao, but what occurred in the summer of 1795 was by far the most significant. The influence of world events was clear; the rebels no doubt knew all the news—port cities were hubs of gossip. Curaçao ships were often found at anchor in southern Saint-Domingue.[33] Although the De Knip (also known as Kenepa) plantation where the uprising started was in the less populated north, the island was small and information travelled quickly.

On August 17, around 50 enslaved people on the De Knip plantation went on strike. As the plantation bell tolled, a group of slaves gathered in front of the estate house, framed by a backdrop of scrubby green-and-brown hills, and told enslaver Caspar van Uytrecht they were not going to work for him any longer. He told them to take it up with the governor.[34] So, under the leadership of Tula Rigaud and Bazjan (Bastiaan) Carpata, they left to do just that.

They did not burn down the plantation house, or kill Uytrecht or anyone else. Initially, they walked out, releasing slaves in the plantation's prison, or "dungeon," and moving to other nearby farms to gather more protesters. The initial 50 rebels swelled to 2,000, a significant percentage of the slave population. They gathered by the coast, near the Santa Krus (Santa Cruz) plantation, where they took an oath and drank *awa di huramentu*, a potion that included rum and a bit of ground-up animal horn.[35] The next day the rebels marched to the capital, picking up more people at the plantations along the way. Then things turned more violent, as the militias—white, "coloured" (mulatto), and free black—moved in, and armed skirmishes began.[36]

The rebels remained hopeful. Tula used the surname of "Rigaud," possibly to signify a connection to Saint-Domingue—he claimed to be in contact with the general André Rigaud, at that point in charge of the south and west of that island. The rebels believed that Rigaud would come to their aid, too.[37] Along with Tula was a man also named Toussaint, who apparently told officials in French: "We are here to win or die."[38]

Tula had taken a more conciliatory tone. A local Catholic priest who had been sent to convince the slaves to go back to work claimed Tula told him, "We do not want to do anybody harm but we seek our freedom, the French blacks have been given their freedom, Holland has been taken over by the French, hence we too must be free."[39] When the priest asked him if he had any message for the Dutch, Tula said: "We want nothing more than our freedom."[40]

Eventually the combined force of the island's militias overpowered them. Curaçao is low-lying, with few mountains and water supplies, so marronage was almost impossible.[41] In September executions began, and by September 22 all the key leaders had been rounded up and subjected to long and arduous interrogations. In the end, 26 people were executed and an estimated 200 rebels died in battle.[42] In early October, more sentences were handed down: Tula and Bazjan were put on a crossed pole, their bones broken, their faces burned, then decapitated, with their heads placed on pikes. Bazjan had extra punishment doled out—he was forced to watch Tula undergo all of that before experiencing the hell of it himself.[43]

⤎ • ⤏

THE BRITISH, MEANWHILE, were fighting on multiple fronts, against France in Europe and the Caribbean, and now, in 1795, once more against the Black Caribs in Saint Vincent. The Black Caribs had never been satisfied with the 1773 treaty, and they had made overtures to the French during the American Revolution, inviting them to occupy the island and drive out the British. France was happy to oblige, and it also found similar welcome in the other Ceded Islands of Grenada, Tobago, and Dominica. French forces stayed on all of them until 1783, when the Treaty of Paris forced France to relinquish Grenada and Dominica to Britain, but allowed it to keep Tobago. The previous treaty between the Black Caribs and the British was reaffirmed in 1784. The return of the British echoed their first occupation in 1763, with officials determined to control the "unruly" factions on the island, including French Catholic landowners, the Black Caribs, and other free people of color. They stripped away rights and privileges these groups had enjoyed under the French, and old animosities resumed. The intervening years brought increasing development of sugar plantations and constant land-clearing near the Carib settlements, which further irritated the Black Caribs. Amid the ongoing revolutions in France and Saint-Domingue, the Black Caribs began to establish connections with revolutionary French officials in the Caribbean. The British government on Saint Vincent felt worried enough about this contact to try to extract pledges of loyalty from the Black Caribs in 1793.[44]

Nearby Guadeloupe was under the governorship of Victor Hugues, a Jacobin like Sonthonax, who arrived in the Caribbean in 1794. He was ready to implement the abolition of slavery in France's other island colonies, but first he had to drive the British out of Guadeloupe, which they had invaded that same year. French forces also took back Saint Lucia and Saint Martin.[45] Hugues was not only willing to give the Black Caribs arms and support, he believed they could help defeat the British in Saint Vincent as well. Hugues addressed the residents of Saint Vincent in a proclamation, saying, "Behold your chains forged and imposed by the hands of the tyrannical English! . . . Fall on these despots, extirpate them from your country, and restore yourselves, your wives and children to the inheritance of your fathers."[46]

Joseph Chatoyer, still in command as the Black Caribs' principal leader and strategist, had been planning an uprising for some time, set to start in early March 1795. The Black Caribs and French-speaking free people of color started donning the cockades of the French Revolution, at one point setting upon the estate of a Madame La Croix, whom they reviled for her support of the British. As they were sacking the estate, members of the Saint Vincent militia arrived to chase them out.[47] By March 10, reports appeared of estates and cane fields consumed by flames, though the rebels were being careful to target the British, following Hugues's suggestion to "attack, exterminate all the English; but allow the French to support you."[48]

Another chief, Duvallé, who was Chatoyer's brother, along with French whites, free people of color, and a few enslaved people, joined Chatoyer, with their numbers growing to 450 by the end of March.[49] However, many enslaved people on British plantations did not join the rebellion, as they were wary of the Black Caribs and distrustful of the French.

Chatoyer scored early victories with the taking of Chateaubelair, on the west of the island, before working his way toward Dorsetshire Hill, with its vistas above the Kingstown harbor, from where he could drive the British into the sea.[50] However, the British governor had requested reinforcements and some had now arrived.

March 14 would start with a violent dawn, as Chatoyer used a saber given to him by the British years before to kill three British prisoners they had taken earlier.[51] The British decided to make a raid that night, taking the nearly 400 Black Caribs and their French allies on Dorsetshire Hill by surprise. With more than 100 men, including militia members, sailors, and even some armed slaves, the British struck at around 1:00 a.m. One party went up the side of the hill, to divert attention, while the others went straight up the steep slope. When it was over, 21 Black Caribs and French were dead, and one of the militia officers had taken the top prize—he had killed Chatoyer.[52]

The death of Chatoyer caused the Black Caribs to retreat in shock and grief, but they did not surrender. Hugues implored Duvallé and the other Black Caribs to continue the fight, but in the immediate aftermath they retreated to their settlements. The British, despite their victory, would need more troops to secure the island, and so decided to arm 200 slaves.⁵³ A few days later, Black Caribs and French allies were plundering estates and burning cane fields. By April more reinforcements arrived for the British. The plan to pursue the Black Caribs in the forests and root them out of their camps, an already difficult job, was made more complicated by the arrival of the rainy season. The governor, James Seton, decided to arm even more slaves, around 500, who were known as loyal rangers and put under his son's command. They began making successful attacks on Black Carib villages, burning their houses and destroying provision grounds.⁵⁴ Yet by May, the Black Caribs and French had recaptured Dorsetshire Hill. The two sides continued to fight, with many skirmishes but no decisive battle. The casualty count mounted, with one particularly vicious battle in early January 1796 leading to the loss of 400 British troops, forcing them to wait for General Ralph Abercromby and more reinforcements.⁵⁵

Abercromby arrived in the Caribbean in March 1796 with a force of 17,000 men, though his first order of business was not to put down the uprising in Saint Vincent but rather to recapture Saint Lucia, which had been going back and forth between the British and French since 1762. By the time of the French Revolution, it was France's colony, and its estates used enslaved labor to produce sugar, coffee, cotton, and cocoa.⁵⁶ With the onset of the revolution, the white population split between royalist and republican, as had happened elsewhere in the French Caribbean. By 1791 enslaved people—who numbered around 18,000—were planning revolts and demanding their freedom, and by 1793 some had abandoned the plantations.⁵⁷

When the British entered the French Revolutionary wars in the Caribbean, attacking Saint Lucia was one of their objectives, which they achieved in the spring of 1794, after capturing nearby Martinique. The conquest of Saint Lucia, such as it was, involved taking the main fort, known as Morne Fortuné, near the main town of Castries, along the northwest coast. The other defense fortifications or outposts remained in French hands, which were increasingly republican.⁵⁸ Attacks on the British continued, and the situation intensified after France's abolition decree began to circulate in 1794, bringing more black people, slave and free, into what was turning into a war, fought by the people who called themselves *l'armée français au bois*—the French army in the woods—while the British referred to them by the more derogatory term "brigands."⁵⁹ Saint Lucia, like its neighbors, is volcanic, giving it steep mountains and valleys, with deep forests that were virtually unknown to the British and not yet mapped.⁶⁰ In January 1795, around 70 members of the Black Carolina Corps—comprised of black loyalists—who were in Martinique were sent to Saint Lucia to chase the insurgents from one of their key mountain posts. They failed, and the attempt cost the lives of 14 soldiers.⁶¹

This was the situation Abercromby sailed into in the spring of 1796. He quickly recaptured the Morne Fortuné citadel, with around 11,000 troops, forcing a surrender by the end of May.⁶² That, however, did not amount to a full capitulation of the island—the black soldiers in the garrison managed to elude the British plans for deportation and fled into the woods to regroup. Many of the black insurgents—thought to number around 6,000—turned to guerrilla tactics, outmaneuvering the British throughout 1796 with successful ambushes and ongoing destruction of plantation property, while the British retaliated by targeting provision grounds.⁶³

In the summer of 1796, General John Moore tried to penetrate the island's interior, a mission that nearly killed him after he contracted yellow fever while on the expedition. Many of the British troops stationed in the fort were also dying of the illness—up to 600 a month.⁶⁴ Moore's misguided attempt to offer pardons to the insurgents went ignored, as did his hopes that now-free people would return to plantations and slavery. He lobbied for the better treatment of slaves, but given the reality of French abolition, the British did not win any converts.⁶⁵ Moore later wrote in a report to Abercromby, "The Negroes in the island are to a man attached to the French cause; neither hanging, threats, or money would obtain for me any intelligence from them."⁶⁶ He was doubting the possibility—or even desirability—of prevailing, writing, "If we keep Saint Lucia, it must be by the greatest accident; my situation is irksome to a degree."⁶⁷ Indeed, Moore was faced with an enemy unwavering in its aims: to get rid of the slave-driving British and live in freedom under the French Republic.

Moore began to consider negotiation. The British reached out to Jean-Louis Marin Pedre, a Saint Lucian and former brigand commander, who spoke English and French, and had also been involved with the Saint Vincent Caribs. The rebels rejected the British terms—not least because one provision was that anyone who had left a plantation would have to return and resume life as a slave.⁶⁸

Hostilities started again in early 1797, beginning with an attack in January at a guard post in Praslin, on the east side of the island, killing 15 British soldiers. British retaliation left 12 insurgents dead and further battle looming. General Moore had another round of yellow fever and was sent back to Britain. His replacement, Colonel James Drummond, took up the fight with more success, with his troops killing a key leader, Stanislaus, in October 1797, lowering rebel morale.⁶⁹ He was willing to make a more generous offer to the insurgents, hoping to both bring the conflict to a close and restart the plantation economy. His terms included not punishing any free people native to the island who participated, and not enslaving any of the former slaves who fought the British. Instead, they would form a regiment for the British to be sent to Africa, which some accepted. By the time Drummond's successor, Brigadier General George Prevost, arrived on the island in 1798, the conflict was winding down. By the following year, Prevost expressed his confidence that the few insurgents left in the woods would be dealt with, by either capture or death, and later that year the conflict was over. The island was back in British hands—and slavery was reinstituted.⁷⁰

Some years earlier, during the conflict in Saint Lucia, General Abercromby had left that island for Saint Vincent, ready to finish off the Black Caribs. He arrived in early June 1796 with 4,000 men. Their first target was a 1,200-foot (365-meter) ridge and military post in the hills to the east of Kingstown known as the Vigie, which had been the scene of a violent clash the previous June. The British had earlier captured the Vigie, but it was back under Black Carib and French control by January 1796.⁷¹ Abercromby sent all 4,000 men, in six columns, to the Vigie, where they began their assault on June 10. There were around 700 Black Caribs and French to defend the spot, and they saw little option but to surrender. About 500 did so, but another 200 fled into the forests.⁷² The French would be sent off the island, and the enslaved back to the plantations. But the Black Caribs would not be allowed to simply return to their land. The British wanted them off the island, even entertaining Abercromby's idea of deporting the 5,000-strong community to Saint-Domingue.⁷³ First, though, the Black Caribs had to agree to the surrender, as their French allies had. To hasten this, British troops began to attack Carib settlements, destroying their canoes and provision grounds, leaving them with few options for survival.[74]

By June 15, three chiefs—Desfon, Jack Gordon, and Baptise—were ready for talks. Like Chatoyer in the 1773 negotiations, they wanted to keep their lands. This time, however, there was no accommodation. Wanting to rid themselves of a troublesome population, the British told the Black Caribs they were going to be sent off the island because they were guilty "of numerous acts of Treachery, Murder and Treason."[75]

By July 18, Chatoyer's son—also called Chatoyer—officially surrendered, addressing his people and telling them, "Have we power to continue the war? No, we have not the power."[76] He apparently changed his mind, leading a group of around 300 people deep into the forest, clearly ignoring British plans for deportation, having earlier said in his address, "You may do as you please, I can only be accountable for my family and myself."[77] Hostilities resumed, and 3,000 troops, including 500 black rangers, were ordered to drive the Black Caribs out.[78] In addition to the armed skirmishes, the British troops began to round up prisoners, including women and children. By November 1796, one later dispatch from island officials claimed, "The number of Charaibs now in our possession is about 4,700—any that remain are very inconsiderable," before asserting that it was a "matter of the greatest importance to these Islands that the whole of that Country should be inhabited as soon as possible" by British settlers.[79]

At first the Black Caribs were taken to the nearby Grenadine islet of Baliceaux, around five miles southeast of Bequia, the island where the mythology of the Black Caribs began. Baliceaux was so dry that drinking water had to be brought over from Saint Vincent. Despite its obvious unsuitability, over the course of the winter of 1796 more people were taken to the island, with a recorded 4,633 Black Caribs and 102 "Yellow" Caribs by February 1797 being held on the tiny rock. The crowded conditions soon gave rise to the spread of deadly diseases, which ravaged the population.[80]

Abercromby decided to send the survivors to the remote island of Roatán, off the coast of Honduras, "if there is a Spanish War." Absent a war, he gave orders to "land them upon Santo Domingo when the Spanish have given it up—perhaps the Island [sic] of Samaná would be a good spot."[81] In the end, the British opted for Roatán, some 1,700 miles northwest of Saint Vincent. By the time they arrived that April, the Caribs' numbers were down to 2,026—meaning thousands had perished in a matter of months.[82] Some of the survivors would be forced to move again later, this time to coastal Honduras, where they became known as the Garifuna and where many of their descendants live to this day.

In addition to Saint Vincent and Saint Lucia, the British faced unrest in Dominica, another of the Ceded Islands, in 1795. Maroon resistance had persisted there since the British took over the island. There was a serious incident in 1791 involving a plot driven in part by rumors that enslaved people were supposed to now receive three days, rather than one and a half, to work their own provision grounds—not dissimilar to what was being said in Saint-Domingue around the same time.[83]

The following year, 1792, unrest in the neighboring French colonies had driven some whites to nearby Dominica. By 1794, with the French abolition of slavery, Dominica—sandwiched between Guadeloupe and Martinique—was literally in the middle, causing concern to Governor John Orde. Having intercepted correspondence from Jacobins in the Caribbean offering support to the maroons of Dominica, who were led by a man named Pharcell, Orde attempted a preemptive peace treaty, modeled on the Jamaican ones of 1739. He offered Pharcell and his hundred or so maroons amnesty and land if they would work as mountain rangers, capturing runaways.[84] The agreement came in useful when a small uprising occurred in Colihaut in May 1795, led by francophone smallholders and supported by some slaves.[85] It was intended to coincide with the arrival of French troops at Pagua Bay, on the opposite side of the island.[86] Rebels in Colihaut joined the newly arrived French, and freedom was offered to any enslaved person who wanted to join them, though many were uncertain and did not. Some black people thought they had more to gain by helping to repel foreign invaders. It was a short conflict, one of many in 1795. The British killed or captured the rebels, bringing it to a close by the end of June.[87]

Events on Grenada, south of Saint Vincent and north of Tobago, were even more complicated. An uprising in March 1795—news of which reached Saint Vincent just as Chatoyer had been about to make his attack on the British—grew into a two-year conflict, later known as Fédon's rebellion, after the free Afro-French planter Julien Fédon, who led it. It involved enslaved people—some estimates say as many as 7,000—but was led by Fédon and French-speaking coffee planters and smallholders who, simmering with resentment, wanted to be rid of the British.[88]

A Protestant Scottish planter, Ninian Home, had become the island's lieutenant governor in 1793, a cause for concern on an island where most of the residents professed to be Catholic. The unease was soon followed by anger as French law was replaced by British, and Catholics were increasingly ostracized. As part of this change, the fragile rights that free people of color had clawed from the French, among them the right to hold civil or military office and to buy more land, were now undone by the British.[89]

Planters in Grenada knew of the rebellion in Saint-Domingue, as well as struggles against the British in Saint Vincent and Saint Lucia. Fédon began plotting at his plantation, Belvedere, high in a mountain valley, and sufficiently distant from the capital, Saint George's, on the south coast.

In early 1795 Fédon dispatched two delegates to make contact with the French in Guadeloupe. They came back as officers in the Revolutionary Army, with Fédon now named the commandant general.[90] In some ways, what took place after this was a smaller-scale—though no less dramatic—replication of the situation in Saint-Domingue at the same time: a white French population of 1,500, split between royalist and republican, 3,000 free people of color wanting equality with whites, 1,500 British troops and settlers, and a majority enslaved population of 30,000, many of whom were recent arrivals living on British plantations. French white and free colored planters were also enslavers, and Fédon had 83 slaves by the 1780s.[91] Indeed, the enslaved people on his estate were put to work shoring up the defenses around the plantation, and perhaps catching a glimpse of Fédon's growing weapons stockpiles. He brought in some of his most trusted slaves at the earliest planning stages of the revolt, aware that their cooperation—and their silence—would be crucial for success.[92]

By the evening of March 2, the rebellion was underway after the rebels sacked Grenville, a village in the east, with others attacking the town of Gouyave, on the island's western coast.⁹³ Hundreds of enslaved people joined in and began to set fire to estates.⁹⁴

While suspicious of French activity in this period, the British were blindsided by the assault. Lieutenant-Governor Home was on his estate at the time, and tried quickly to return to Saint George's but was captured by rebels, along with four others. On March 4, Fédon's representatives arrived in the capital with demands that the island be surrendered to him.⁹⁵ The president of the council and acting governor, Kenneth McKenzie, rejected the offer and instead said he would give amnesty to rebels who quit the rebellion, so long as they had not killed anyone, and a handsome reward of £40 for every insurgent killed or captured.⁹⁶ Fédon, however, as a French republican, represented freedom, and because of this gained many more willing to fight with him. While the number of enslaved people who sided with Fédon was significant, others chose not to participate, or were unable to escape to do so. Some did remain loyal to the British, who later on in the conflict would create a corps of slave rangers, as they had done in Saint Vincent.

Still others hid, uncertain about what was taking place. One planter and militia soldier, Samuel Cary, discovered people hiding among the cane on an abandoned plantation, who came "running to us from different Bushes and Canepieces & informed us that the enemy had been there two days before."⁹⁷ Would-be maroons used the confusion to slip away to the mountains.⁹⁸

Fédon sent a second flag of truce a couple of days later, along with a letter signed by Home and a threat to kill the captured men if the British attacked Belvedere, but McKenzie did not relent, despite the gravity of the situation. He had only around 200 regular troops in the garrison and the island militia to call upon, against a slave army of possibly thousands. His requests for help were met with several hundred regular troops from Barbados and Martinique, which Britain still occupied, and then-Spanish Trinidad also contributed (only to be thanked with the British capture of the island in 1797).⁹⁹

By mid-March the British had moved to the interior, attacking Fédon's plantation and nearby main rebel camp, which they did again in early April. The fighting there turned into hand-to-hand combat. The casualties continued to rise, and Fédon's brother, Jean, was killed.¹⁰⁰ Fédon also contributed to the body count, keeping his side of the threat: He ordered the white hostages killed—48 people shot—one by one.[101]

As the rainy season set in, so did disease, wiping out troops by the hundreds. In August of 1795, another black ranger corps was set up, comprising 300 men.[102] By late summer, after months of guerrilla skirmishes, Fédon began a campaign to take Grenada and make a final push against the British, capturing Gouyave in the west, and much of the east, with ease. The British troops were all but confined to the fort at Saint George's by the end of 1795, waiting for reinforcements. The island was nearly under Fédon's full control, but it was also in tatters. Plantations were in ruins, crops were destroyed. Much of the cattle and livestock had been used up to feed Fédon's troops. While some of the formerly enslaved continued to fight, others began to focus on growing food and preserving their provision grounds.[103]

In February 1796, Fédon captured Mount Saint Eloi, on the edge of the capital.[104] The British began to retaliate in March, and by May the bulk of the reinforcements had arrived, 5,000 troops, followed in June by General Abercromby. Britain now had the advantage, and the soldiers pushed into the countryside, seeking out rebel camps. By June 18 the last camp was captured, and British troops had taken back the island.[105] Fédon and a handful of rebels fled deep into the mountains. The rebellion was among the most destructive of this time: Some 7,000 slaves and 1,000 white Europeans and free people of color died over the course of the conflict, while another 400 rebels were shipped to Honduras and their land was confiscated by the British.[106]

Some accounts say Fédon died trying to flee, the evidence being an upturned canoe found floating in the waters between Grenada and Trinidad. Other stories say Fédon fled to Cuba or Trinidad and was biding his time, waiting to lead another rebellion against the British.[107]

Throughout this period, the maroons of Jamaica were watching—and 1795 would be a significant year for them too. News not only of Saint-Domingue but of the Ceded Islands was travelling through all levels of Jamaican society, including to the Leeward maroons in Trelawny Town, now the largest maroon community on the island.[108]

The Windward maroons had access to the coast, and so could easily forge connections with Saint-Domingue, Jamaica's nearest eastern neighbor, by this point occupied by British troops.[109] Misinformation blew through the island, including a rumor that the rebels in Saint-Domingue or French republican troops—whose ships were making privateering raids off the coast of Jamaica—were going to invade the island and rally the slaves to their cause.[110]

However, no sources point to the maroons receiving arms or willing volunteers from the French islands, unlike what was taking place in Saint Vincent and Grenada. While Jamaica chattered with such speculation, the real issue for the Trelawny maroons was land. They wanted more than the initial 1,500 acres granted in the 1739 treaty.[111] But they also intensely disliked the new and unpopular superintendent, Thomas Craskell.[112] Tempers turned into blows after an enslaved man employed at the penal workhouse flogged two Trelawny Town maroons who were in there for allegedly stealing a pig. As it turned out, the flogger had been a runaway whom the two maroons had earlier captured.[113] This sort of public humiliation was insulting to the maroons.[114]

By July 13, 1795, news of the tense situation reached the capital. Governor Alexander Lindsay, Earl of Balcarres, decided to make an example of the maroons and use this opportunity to break their power, as well as ensure they could never have an alliance with the French. He declared martial law and ordered militia units to search for arms in slave huts.[115] On July 29 he recalled troops who had been dispatched to Saint-Domingue. A short time later, around Saint Ann's Bay, on the north of the island, he met with Trelawny leaders who were on their way to the capital to discuss their grievances. Balcarres accused them of plotting with the French and had them arrested and imprisoned for insubordination. He followed this by demanding all maroons come and submit themselves to the British government.[116]

This was no deterrent to people with a long history of fighting the British, and the Trelawny maroons were quick to retaliate, at first torching their village before the British could and sending those who could not fight to hide in their emergency provision grounds. Full conflict followed, with the maroons successfully ambushing British regular and militia troops, initially killing 34. Maroon snipers spent the following month adding to the death toll, pushing it up to 70, while the maroons themselves suffered no casualties.[117]

On the Windward side of the island, the maroons were refusing to pledge their loyalty, as Balcarres was demanding, but had not yet engaged in battle to either help the British or join the Trelawny maroons. Balcarres began to target Leeward maroon provision grounds to threaten the entire community with the prospect of starvation.[118] The maroons turned to the enslaved people on nearby plantations, finding some willing recruits but having to use more forceful measures to get others to help.[119] In one case, an enslaved man named Abraham said he had been taken by three maroons while he and some others were working in the woods; they had threatened him with decapitation but also offered him freedom. Abraham said in a later account that the maroons insisted they go with them and promised that "when they got the better of the Backra's [Buckra, the whites] . . . they should live very easy and should have their freedom."[120] However, there was a long memory among the enslaved when it came to trusting the people who had captured them and returned them to the plantations.

As the conflict intensified, so did the lack of food, and the maroons were forced to increase their raids on plantations. By the end of the year, about 60 people surrendered, driven in part by hunger. That was not enough for Balcarres, and in the middle of December he brought in the feared Cuban "chasseurs" and their fearsome hunting dogs to chase the maroons out of the forests.[121]

By January 1796, around 500 people had surrendered and been sent up to the coast from Montego Bay. Until this point, the Accompong maroons and the Windward maroons had stayed out of the conflict. However, the Accompong maroons were now willing to help the British, perhaps to secure their own precarious position. The maroons of Charles Town and Nanny Town in the east, for their part, refused to obey any orders from the governor.[122]

By March only a handful of Trelawny maroons were left fighting, and Balcarres proclaimed the war over. From there, the British decided that any rebel who had been caught or had surrendered after an initial negotiation deadline of January 1 would be shipped away from Jamaica. The punitive first destination for some 600 of them was the frigid province of Nova Scotia.[123]

⤝ • ⤞

Louisiana, Venezuela, Cuba, Curaçao, Puerto Rico, Saint Vincent, Dominica, Grenada, and Jamaica: All of these places faced upheaval, rebellion, war, and violence in 1795. Even if Saint-Domingue was not invoked in every case or the connection made explicit, it provided the backdrop to that explosive year in the Caribbean. The outcomes were varied, and most involved enslaved people being forced to continue in bondage while the world around them spoke of freedom and equality.

Chapter 22

Openings

"My only objective," Toussaint Louverture wrote in 1795, "is the unity and happiness of all my republican brothers."[1] It was a straightforward aim that Louverture expressed in his letter to the island governor Étienne Laveaux, but one that both men knew would be difficult to achieve. Laveaux, an army officer, was temporarily in charge of Saint-Domingue after Sonthonax and Polverel had been recalled to France. Laveaux admired Louverture, later calling him "the Spartacus predicted by Raynal, whose destiny was to avenge all the outrages committed against his race."[2] He had also been involved in trying to lure Louverture to the French side, making the successful case for the republicans.[3] Now the two men surveyed the considerable challenges ahead of them.

Louverture had quickly proved his value to the French, ridding the north of Spanish control through successful attacks on his erstwhile allies Jean-François and Biassou until they left the island once the 1795 Treaty of Basel went into effect. Dislodging the British, however, would not go as smoothly. Although the British were not on a very steady footing, they held on to Port-au-Prince while facing both disease and defeat at the hands of André Rigaud, who had attacked them in the south in 1794.[4] In the summer of 1795, British troops began to push inland from Port-au-Prince, to an area around the town of Mirebalais. Louverture took it back after a brief battle, but the British returned to attack in September and drove him out—Louverture told his troops to burn the plantations as they retreated.[5]

Equally troublesome was keeping the plantation economy in motion. This had been a concern for Sonthonax and Polverel, not least because any abandoned land became the property of the state. In theory, Sonthonax devised a system that would pay the newly freed workers (*cultivateurs*) one-quarter of the sale of the sugar or coffee crop. In practice, strict regulations emerged to bind people to the land—anyone who left the plantations without permission could be charged as a vagrant or be marched back to work by soldiers.[6] To the former slaves, the new system bore some striking similarities to the old one.

Polverel, who had been in charge of the south and west of the island before his recall to France, had promised land to the ex-slaves in the early days of the revolt, but he soon revoked that pledge, saying in a February 1794 decree: "The land does not belong to you. It belongs to those who purchased it . . ." He outlined a plan later that year, trying to convince the now-free cultivators to keep the island's prosperity alive. He told them, "No one has the right to force you to work a single day if you don't want to. You are completely free." The only thing they did own was their labor, and Polverel explained, "The portion assigned to you in the revenues of the land will be given to you only in compensation for your work." He initially set that portion at one-third, but that, of course, was based on the assumption that they would want to work six days a week, as they had under slavery. He also argued that because they would receive a share from the plantations, they would "need [their] provision grounds less than ever," informing them that their gardens—of practical and symbolic importance—would have to be reduced in size.[7] Louverture joined in the campaign, saying in one 1795 proclamation that workers had 24 hours to "return to pursue all forms of agricultural labor in the plantations to which they are dependent," threatening, "Every lazy and errant man will be arrested to be punished by the law."[8] As part of his productivity drive, Louverture believed it necessary to invite planters to return to their coffee or sugar estates. He seemed to be designing a plantation regime underpinned by compulsory labor, which forced him to continually make the case to the workers that this was not the return of slavery.

This question of work became another front for Louverture and Laveaux. Sometimes it would be an actual battle—the same people who overthrew plantation slavery were not going to submit to an estate unreceptive to their demands, and intermittent local uprisings broke out. In one 1795 incident Louverture ended up with a bullet in his leg during a workers' rebellion on a northern plantation in Marmelade.[9] Such divisions among the newly free only added to the challenges, and he knew he must unite the workers behind him, while goading them into work they did not want to do. But plantation revolts continued, as did marronage. Louverture understood that all black freedom was fragile—but he believed stability and profit across the island would be the safest way to secure everyone's future. To many, however, freedom and prosperity appeared to be at odds with each other.

While Louverture was dealing with the cultivators and continuing to push against the British, Sonthonax returned to the colony in 1796, reappointed as a commissioner, alongside Philippe Rose Roume de Saint-Laurent, who had had the role in 1791. With them was another commissioner, Julien Raimond, the *homme de couleur* activist, who was finally returning home after a decade in France.[10]

Sonthonax would not be back for long—later that year he was elected as the island's representative to the National Assembly, along with Laveaux. The two men would have to leave for Paris. Sonthonax, however, was bothered by the ongoing unrest among plantation workers and decided to delay his departure—indeed both black and white residents begged him not to go.[11] Over the following months, his differences with Louverture became clearer. For instance, Sonthonax did not approve of Louverture welcoming back the planters with open arms, because he considered them to be hostile to the French Revolution. Ultimately, it was the loyalty of the workers—the true source of power—that they both wanted. Sonthonax remained very popular because of his association with abolition. Cries of "Long live Sonthonax!" from the *cultivateurs* were common.[12] While Sonthonax was no supporter of slavery, in private he was disdainful of black people, including Louverture. In one letter he described the general as "a thick-headed man, as lowly as his first occupation as a slave herdsman," adding, "He normally speaks kreyol and barely understands the French language."[13]

Louverture had grown impatient waiting for Sonthonax to depart, and in August 1797 he wrote a letter signed by many of his generals prodding him to leave and "tell France what you have seen," which he judiciously did shortly thereafter. However, once in Paris, Sonthonax publicly criticized Louverture, calling him a tyrant and claiming he was an enemy of the Republic.[14] In addition, a faction of angry Saint-Domingue planters had managed to increase their presence in the French parliament, where they decried the emancipation decree. By the end of 1797, Louverture was drawn into these Paris debates, writing to the five-member governing directory to contest the criticism directed at him. He claimed that exiled planters had crafted, with their allies in the United States and the British West Indies, "a resolution, unequivocal and carefully constructed, for the restoration of slavery." He continued, asking, "Could men who have once enjoyed the benefits of liberty look on calmly while it is taken from them? . . . But no, the hand that has broken our chains will not subject us to them again."[15]

On Saint-Domingue, Raimond, only recently returned, submitted to Louverture, who had been made commander-in-chief of the island in May 1797. Saint-Domingue was now mostly Louverture's. There was just the question of regaining the south and west from the British.

By 1798, at least 6,000 of Saint-Domingue's fighters were trying to root out Britain's troops, who, with their white and free colored allies, proved difficult to dislodge. The British held on to Port-au-Prince and Môle Saint-Nicolas, though they were losing ground under continual attacks from Louverture and Rigaud. Britain's General Thomas Maitland arrived that year, just in time to watch as slaves on British estates fled to join the free black troops. The free colored allies—still deprived of equality—also began to sour on Britain, and some joined the republicans.[16] It was time for Britain to pull out. Some 60,000 soldiers had been sent to the various theaters of the Caribbean over the previous four years.[17] Saint-Domingue would not be one of their victories.

Into this complex situation entered Gabriel-Marie-Théodore-Joseph d'Hédouville, a French commissioner armed with orders to get the island back under control and curb the growing powers of Louverture and Rigaud. Knowing this would be difficult and concerned about the reception he might receive, he chose to sail into Santo Domingo, on the east of the island, rather than straight into Le Cap.[18] General Maitland understood how he could use this to his advantage, playing

Louverture and Hédouville off each other by promising each man he would be the only person involved in negotiations. Hédouville warned Louverture that the British general was "manifestly trying to sow the seeds of division" between them.[19] Louverture agreed, while concealing the fact that he was about to reach a settlement with Maitland.

In the end, Maitland peacefully evacuated and received in exchange an amnesty for Britain's planter allies. Any black soldiers who fought for the British would also be permitted to remain, and no property was to be destroyed. The deal arranged, Maitland led the retreat, with a few embittered planters following him, as they departed that summer.[20]

He also left with a secret trade deal. Despite Britain and France being at war, the British would end their blockade of Saint-Domingue so they could resume trade. In return, Louverture would not do anything to encourage an uprising among the slaves of Jamaica. British merchants were eager to buy sugar and coffee from Saint-Domingue. Now they would have a way to do so.[21] The deal with Britain didn't stay secret for long, and mentions of "a treaty with Toussaint" began to appear in the press, with one paper saying, "We cannot but applaud the address with which General Maitland has executed this important business."[22]

The British gone, the trade deal secured, Louverture turned to face Hédouville, who had brought fellow counterrevolutionary officers who expressed their bitterness about emancipation, apparently repeating slogans like "The cultivator was unworthy of the freedom he enjoyed."[23] However, Hédouville had too few troops with him to challenge Louverture, so for the time being Louverture continued to hold the real power, but even he was becoming increasingly suspicious of France's government.

Hédouville soon made a significant mistake, attempting to rejuvenate the island's fortunes by forcing cultivators to sign three-year contracts with plantations, ideally working for their former enslavers. Workers began to voice their concerns—for some, this was now too close to the slavery they had only just defeated. To make matters worse, Hédouville angered Louverture's adopted nephew, Moïse. One of Louverture's most trusted generals, Moïse was in charge of a garrison in Fort-Liberté, near Le Cap. In October 1798 Hédouville decided to put a different officer in charge of the fort, a move that led to unrest. Later, he claimed Moïse was organizing the cultivators to do something seditious. Louverture shot to his nephew's defense, ordering Hédouville's arrest. Faced with thousands of troops, Hédouville had little choice but to flee Le Cap on October 23, along with the officers who had come with him, their mission to wrest control from Louverture a failure.[24]

A November 1798 edition of the British Sunday newspaper *The Observer* published one line about Saint-Domingue in that week's international roundup, which read: "The negro French General, Toussaint, is the undisputed possessor of the entire of St. Domingo."[25] While it may have looked that way from Britain, on the ground in Saint-Domingue Louverture had one more enemy to face: his former friend André Rigaud.

Rigaud had fought on the Republic's side since 1792 in the south, which was especially crucial when the British began their invasion. He had been able to call upon the *gens de couleur* community to shore up his position, though they remained vastly outnumbered by the former slaves. Now, in the aftermath of that conflict, Louverture quickly realized the extent of Rigaud's power in the south and the danger it posed to his quest for island unity. Rigaud had acquired a great deal of autonomy over the years and pursued his own policies. While he, too, wanted the plantations to return to profitability, he enacted some different schemes, the main one involving the renting of confiscated land to private citizens. Usually only the already wealthy could invest in these enterprises, while the former slaves were ordered to work on them, so that left him—like Louverture—with unhappy *cultivateurs*. He also had to contend with maroons living in the mountains near Port-au-Prince who were refusing to submit to his or the French regime.[26]

Despite the similar challenges and shared victories, ultimately Rigaud refused to submit to Louverture, who, as commander-in-chief, was his superior. Hédouville had tried to sow division between the two, seemingly siding with Rigaud. In addition, longer-running tensions existed between Louverture and the free colored community of which Rigaud was a member.[27]

Their differences had become irreconcilable by 1799, and on June 18, Rigaud sent 4,000 men to attack Petit and Grand Goâve, towns on the southern peninsula that Louverture demanded be under his command, as a way of refusing him. Revolts followed in Le Cap, Môle Saint-Nicolas, and elsewhere, in a brief conflict known as the War of the South (1799–1800). Louverture's retaliation was fierce—the rebellions were put down and alleged conspirators were executed. Although it was clear he had enemies, he still had the most troops—45,000 to Rigaud's 15,000. In July 1800, Rigaud relented and abandoned the fight, fleeing to France. The previous month, an emissary from France, now under the control of First Consul Napoleon Bonaparte, had confirmed Louverture's role as "general-in-chief."[28]

Before the battle with Rigaud began, Louverture had also been trying to extend his economic reach, this time pivoting toward the slaving nation to the north. He wrote to the US president John Adams (1797–1801) about its "Quasi-War" with France that started in 1798, which prohibited French ships from entering US ports. He invited the United States to have a separate relationship with Saint-Domingue, and assured him that US ships would not be attacked.[29] The offer gained support, and in 1799 Congress approved a revised version of the French Embargo Act of June 1798, with a new provision for reopening trade with "any persons, claiming, and exercising command and authority, in any island, port or place, belonging to the French Republic."[30] Its detractors were quick to call it "Toussaint's Clause."[31] In exchange, Louverture had to promise the US that French ships from anywhere else would be turned away. Saying in public he would do that was almost akin to declaring independence, but he assured the US consul general, Edward Stevens, that their ships would be safe. And they were: Over the course of the following year, of the 1,800 ships that came into Saint-Domingue's harbors, only 15 were French. And these US vessels weren't just taking away sugar—they were also bringing guns and munitions, though not always legally, because an arms embargo with France and its colonies was still in place.[32]

This was quite a state of affairs for the slaveholding United States to be drawn into. It was now buying goods from and selling guns to a black general with 30,000 freed slaves under his control. Southern members of Congress had voiced their concerns about the possibility of Louverture declaring independence and the ramifications of a free black state only a short distance from the US. Indeed, Adams's inner circle also believed that Louverture might do so, and that if independence did come about, the US should support it.[33] Ultimately, Congress looked at the potential "mine of gold" in profits to be realized on the island, and approved the measure in the House by 55 to 37, including some Southerners who had been persuaded that the commercial trade potential outweighed their concerns.[34]

Planters and merchant ships continued to arrive, stirring the island's economy back to life, but Louverture's entire project remained fragile. Whether he needed independence to guarantee it, or whether the French government would refuse to give him the autonomy he desired to forge the free, prosperous future he could see in his mind, was yet to be determined.

Worried about potential retaliation from France, Louverture now directed his attention to the former Spanish side of the island. Technically under French control since 1795, with Roume as its chief official, its day-to-day operations were still handled by Spanish administrators. Its ports were wide open for any of his enemies to sneak into and catch him unawares, and so Louverture was compelled to bring the eastern side of the island under his control.

In addition, he wanted the languishing estates there to contribute to overall productivity and extend cultivation in an area nearly twice as large as Saint-Domingue. While haciendas existed in Santo Domingo, there was no plantation economy comparable to the French side's. Rather than competing in sugar or coffee, the Spanish side mainly exported valuable cowhides to its richer neighbor.

The issue of slavery was also unresolved in the east. Louverture claimed that people from the French side were being sold into slavery in Santo Domingo, complaining to Roume that many of the Spaniards were involved in this "despicable trafficking."[35] Under Spain's rule, Santo Domingo had an enslaved population of 30,000 at the time of the 1795 handover, and how the 1794 emancipation decree would be applied was unclear. Louverture pressured Roume to put the eastern side of the island under his control, while also receiving instructions from the French minister of the navy in November 1800 to "not undertake anything."[36]

Louverture ultimately ignored these orders and marched an army of 10,000 into the capital, Santo Domingo, on January 26, 1801. He faced some Spanish troops on the way, but they were quickly dispatched, and he implored the enslaved people there to fight with him and be freed.[37] When he arrived in the capital, he was greeted by a festive delegation, with music and all the appropriate fanfare—not the entrance he or Governor García would have expected less than a decade earlier. The remaining Spanish administrators, having long delayed their departure, considered this the opportune moment to leave.[38]

In the meantime, Bonaparte was developing a new colonial policy, with different rules for different colonies, rather than one that applied to all of them.[39] Louverture saw how this could mean the return of slavery in other parts of France's empire, threatening the supposedly universal principles of liberty and equality. He decided to ensure the liberty of Saint-Domingue in writing, convening a constitutional assembly in February 1801. Included in the assembly was Julien Raimond, two other *gens de couleur*, and seven white representatives. Moïse had been elected as well, but he refused to join—the growing tensions between him and Toussaint would soon reach a breaking point—and no other former slaves were involved.[40]

The Constitution was promulgated on July 8, 1801, with article 3 proclaiming: "There cannot exist slaves on this territory, servitude is therein forever abolished. All men are born, live and die free and French."[41] For the first time in the Americas, the abolition of slavery was enshrined in a written constitution. However, many of its other provisions were of a less emancipatory nature. It decreed the island Catholic, despite the long tradition of voudou, and limited the freedoms of workers, all of which would only further fuel resentment.

Louverture had enacted reforms in 1800 and 1801, with stricter labor laws, attempting to apply a military-style discipline to agriculture. The cultivators faced punishment for failing to work; they paid fines or were imprisoned for leaving plantations without permission; and they were no longer permitted to buy or sell small plots of land, a way that some poor workers were able to gain property.[42] The murmurs became louder: Louverture was bringing back slavery. At the same time, his plan was working: By 1801 coffee production would reach about two-thirds of its pre-1798 level, and sugar production around one-third in 1802.[43] But Louverture was extracting this success by squeezing the loyalty of the very people who had enabled his rise to power.

The concern about agriculture had a prominent place in the new constitution, with article 14 saying the colony "cannot suffer the least disruption in the works of its cultivation."[44] This section outlined a paternalistic vision, not unlike the one that had existed under slavery: Each plantation would be a "family," with the owner as the "father," and "each cultivator and each worker" would be "a member of that family." This was followed by an article that said, "The introduction of cultivators . . . shall take place," meaning that the government was going to import more workers, potentially from Africa.[45]

As a final touch, article 28 stated that Louverture—"upon the wishes of the grateful inhabitants"—would be governor of the colony "for the remainder of his glorious life," with the power to choose his successor.[46]

Now the document had to be sent to France, though Louverture was warned that it would most likely be interpreted as a declaration of independence.[47] He might have worried how the islanders felt about it too, including his nephew, Moïse.

Moïse was an "agricultural inspector" in the north, as General Dessalines was in the south and west. Both men were seeing the result of Louverture's increasingly draconian measures. Moïse had chosen not to participate in the constitutional assembly, and had been distressed by its provisions concerning the cultivators.[48] In October 1801, a number of uprisings erupted in the north, and some rebels briefly captured the town of Plaisance and killed 300 white colonists. Dessalines and Christophe quickly helped Louverture put this rebellion down.[49] Louverture then blamed his nephew, claiming he was the "soul and leader" of the unrest. Moïse denied it. Louverture remained so unconvinced, he had Moïse executed in November. In the aftermath, Louverture warned the public that this would be "the fate of all who imitate [Moïse]."[50]

In France, Bonaparte's advisers recommended that a mission be sent to the island to overturn what, according to one adviser, was a "state of rebellion against the Republic."[51] Bonaparte drew up plans, putting the expedition under the leadership of General Charles Leclerc, who was also his brother-in-law. The plan involved Leclerc recruiting Louverture's enemies, including Rigaud and Alexandre Pétion, an ally of Rigaud in the War of the South.

Once on the island, they were to round up Louverture and his generals. If they cooperated, they would be exiled; if not, they would be killed. Any other black military officers would be deported.[52] After that, Leclerc could restore the island to what it had been—a rich, productive slave colony. Bonaparte was no stranger to the money that could be made in the West Indies: The family of his wife Josephine owned a plantation, *La Pagerie*, in Martinique. They also had holdings in Saint-Domingue, which had collapsed during the initial stages of the conflict. However, when Josephine heard Louverture was inviting planters to return, she wrote to him directly in 1798, while Bonaparte was in Egypt, and asked for his help. He provided it, and soon her family were making profits again. As a means of thanking him, she had his sons, who were studying in Paris, over to dine a number of times.[53] Such goodwill on the part of Josephine and her husband had been worn away by the events of the subsequent few years, especially the unauthorized invasion of Santo Domingo and the creation of an island constitution. By 1802 Bonaparte's feelings about Louverture were decidedly darker. In a letter to Leclerc, he wrote: "Rid us of these gilded negroes, and we will have nothing more to wish for."[54]

Bonaparte made his case for the expedition in terms of its being a crusade against "black barbarism," no doubt cheered on by the planter lobby. The French foreign minister, Charles Maurice de Talleyrand-Périgord, echoed these sentiments, telling the British diplomats that it was "in the interest of civilization in general to destroy the new Algiers that is being organized in the center of America."[55]

Such talk was coupled with rumors that France was not going to enforce the 1794 abolition of slavery in the colonies that were to be returned to it under the 1802 Treaty of Amiens, which was being drawn up to end the latest round of conflict among European powers, including Britain and France. Indeed, in Martinique, slavery had never been abolished, because it was under foreign occupation. The island had been under British control since 1794, which left the slave regime uninterrupted. Now, upon being returned to France, it would stay that way.

Although Louverture tried to dismiss the rumors flying around the island during 1801, he also began quietly preparing his 30,000 regular troops for a seemingly inevitable French invasion.[56] He would be aided by the arms that continued to arrive from US merchants. The previous embargo had now expired and the new president, Thomas Jefferson (1801–1809), chose not to renew it.[57]

Louverture's instincts had been correct. Leclerc reached Saint-Domingue in late January 1802 with some 50 ships, 22,000 soldiers, and 20,000 sailors.[58] On board with him were Louverture's sons, Isaac and Placide, carrying a letter from Napoleon. The correspondence informed Louverture that Leclerc would now run the colony. Louverture's constitution would no longer be necessary. "While concluding many good things," Bonaparte wrote, it "contains some that are contrary to the dignity and sovereignty of the French people, of which St-Domingue forms only a portion."[59]

Christophe, in charge of Le Cap, refused to let Leclerc's troops enter, on Louverture's orders. Leclerc decided to invade, dropping soldiers on either side of the city so they could surround it. Christophe had earlier threatened Leclerc, "You will enter the town of Le Cap only once it has been reduced to ashes," and so fulfilled that promise, giving orders to set it alight.[60]

Now Louverture was clear: French troops were here to "put us back into slavery."[61] He wrote to Dessalines a few days after the torching of Le Cap, saying, "We have no other resource than destruction and flames . . . Tear up the roads with shot, throw corpses and horses into all the fountains; burn and annihilate everything, in order that those who have come to reduce us to slavery may have before their eyes the image of hell which they deserve."[62]

Open battle began, with some troops fighting the French, while others—especially in the south—quickly surrendered or even joined Leclerc's troops, reflecting wavering support for Louverture.[63] Leclerc would need the help, as—despite his avoiding the rainy season—disease quickly began to wipe out his troops, many of whom had no experience in the West Indies. Not long after the conflict erupted, Leclerc had at least 2,000 ill soldiers. He also had poor provisioning and struggled to get the supplies he needed.[64] Despite these early challenges, Leclerc was successful in the south and gained territory.

Dessalines, meanwhile, retreated from the port of Saint-Marc, where he torched the town, including his own home.[65] Christophe had managed to control parts of the north, and Louverture's troops continued to put up a stiff fight. In April, however, Christophe began talks with Leclerc about a surrender. It was a surprising move, no doubt welcomed by Leclerc, but a severe blow to Louverture. Christophe might have been uncertain of victory with Louverture, or perhaps he had been growing tired of his autocratic ways before the war. In a secret correspondence, Leclerc told Christophe, "If it is your intention to submit to the Republic, think on the essential service you could render her by furnishing the means to secure the person of General Toussaint."[66] Christophe wavered, asking for guarantees that slavery would not return, and Leclerc promised him it would not.[67] For his part, Louverture was running out of options, and so he too opened discussions with Leclerc soon after.

The two generals met in Le Cap, accompanied by Dessalines, Christophe, and hundreds of Louverture's honor guards. Louverture agreed to retire, keeping his rank, as part of the negotiations.[68] However, such was Louverture's suspicion of Leclerc that he ate only a tiny slice of cheese at the lavish lunch held in celebration of the deal.[69]

But retirement was not enough. Bonaparte and Leclerc wanted Louverture off the island, believing his continued presence posed a threat to order. Indeed, the generals may have surrendered, but Leclerc still had to contend with a few officers who had not, who they believed were in contact with Louverture and inciting cultivators to revolt.[70]

In June, some of Leclerc's officers set a trap for Louverture, luring him on the pretext of a meeting about suppressing local banditry, and then arresting him and taking his sword.[71] Louverture, his wife, Suzanne, their sons, and other family members were put on a ship to exile in France.[72] Louverture would die there, in a cold prison cell in the Jura Mountains, separated from his family, in April 1803, at the age of 59. Before he was forced off the island, never to return, he fired a parting shot: "In overthrowing me," he said, "you have cut down in Saint-Domingue only the trunk of the tree of the liberty of the blacks; it will grow back from the roots, because they are deep and numerous."[73]

In this he was correct. For a time Dessalines and Christophe cooperated with Leclerc, helping to suppress local insurgent rebellions throughout the summer of 1802. By then, they would have heard the news of the legislation in France that passed in May, relating to the Treaty of Amiens. The first article was clear, saying, "Slavery will be maintained in accordance with the laws and regulations prior to 1789" for the colonies being returned to France under the treaty, as well as French colonies elsewhere. Article 3 provided for the resumption of "the trade in Blacks and their importation in the said colonies."[74]

It was as if the emancipation of 1794 had never happened. Indeed, Bonaparte's colonial minister, Denis Decrès, wrote, "I want slaves in our colonies. Liberty is a food for which the stomachs of the negroes are not yet prepared." Soon after, a ban was enacted on any soldier of color entering France without government permission, followed by one on all people of color—anyone who ignored it would be arrested.[75]

By October 1802, the black and free colored generals turned on Leclerc. Alexandre Pétion and Augustin Clerveaux joined rebels outside of Le Cap rather than suppressing them. Christophe followed, and in the port of Gonaïves, north of Port-au-Prince, Dessalines did too. The retaliation against Leclerc and Bonaparte began in earnest. Leclerc told Bonaparte they needed to kill the rebels in the mountains—not only anyone who had been a soldier but women too, sparing "only children under twelve years of age." To Leclerc's mind, the colony would need to start again, after the memory of freedom had been wiped away.[76] But he would not live to see it, succumbing to illness and dying, like thousands of his troops, in November.

General Donatien Marie Joseph de Vimeur de Rochambeau would take charge, bringing in his particularly brutal ways, importing more of the Cuban tracking dogs to chase and maul insurgents. By this point, the black officers' resolve was unshakable, and they were able to unite with rebel leaders in what they called *l'armée indigène* (the native army), with Dessalines in command. Internal conflicts between the generals and the rebel leaders continued, but they weren't sufficient to impede the final push against Rochambeau, whose army was seriously weakened by defections and disease. Troops had been dying by the thousands, and their reinforcements—some 80,000 men in total had been sent there—were faring no better.[77] Dessalines and his men—and increasingly women—continued to attack and ambush. In addition, Britain and France were squaring up for another conflict in Europe, and British ships in the Caribbean arrived to block the harbor in Le Cap. By November 1803, Dessalines was able to lead a devastating attack at Vertières, where Rochambeau was now surrounded and outnumbered. He surrendered, leaving some 50,000 dead French troops in his wake.[78]

Rochambeau and his remaining troops left in December, and on January 1, 1804, Dessalines's new declaration of independence was read before a crowd in Gonaïves. In it, Dessalines made clear that the new nation of Haiti—a name taken from the island's indigenous name Ayti—must "forever ensure liberty's reign in the country of our birth; we must take any hope of re-enslaving us away from the inhumane government that for so long kept us in the most humiliating stagnation." The vision was clear: "In the end we must live independent or die."[79]

This resolve would be reflected in the second article of the 1805 constitution. Haitians would always be free. Dessalines also tried to kill the deep-seated distrust between black and *gens de couleur*, declaring in article 14, "Haitians will henceforth only be known generically as Blacks."[80] Dessalines kept himself at the head of this project, the first independent black nation in the Americas not only to be a beacon of full liberty, but to be governed by the very people who had been enslaved by the previous system.

However, there was no formal recognition from France of Haiti's independence. Napoleon could return at any time, meaning that Dessalines was forced to look to the future while also watching his back. He kept 20,000 troops on active duty, ready to fight France should it dare to try.[81]

In such a climate of uncertainty, the French could use misinformation and rumor as weapons: News of a massacre of white residents in Haiti began to circulate. One white eyewitness, who managed later to escape, recounted the violent events in the city of Jérémie in early March 1804, claiming he saw "upwards of four hundred white men, quite naked, dragged forcibly on the rough stones." He described his experience of watching the massacre from an upstairs window: "I saw blood gushing out of the inflicted wounds. I could see no longer; I fainted and fell."[82] It is hard to say exactly what happened, since there are no firm figures, and contemporary accounts sometimes inflated the numbers beyond the actual white population, claiming for example that 3,000 were murdered in Le Cap, when only 1,700 white people had remained there.[83] Other whites fled to nearby Cuba, the United States, and France, further spreading their versions of events. To Dessalines, it had been the French who had perpetrated the true atrocities, the "drowning, suffocating, assassinating, hanging, and shooting of more than 60,000 of our brethren under the inhuman Government of Le Clerc and Rochambeau."[84]

The massacre episode proved useful for a humiliated France, and Napoleon could use it to paint a portrait of a bloodthirsty Dessalines. Some—including France's enemies, such as Britain—were not so quick to believe the reports. The Scottish newspaper *Caledonian Mercury* described the accounts in French newspapers as "very exaggerated," because it was "the policy of Bonaparte to make the State of Saint Domingo an object of horror in the eyes of France, and of all the other nations—to efface the memory of the frightful scenes which he caused to be acted there."[85]

Haiti's new leader stood his ground in an April 1804 proclamation, asking, "Of what consequence to me is the opinion which contemporary and future generations will pronounce upon my conduct?" Dessalines reminded his audience that it was the French who had committed "the massacre of the entire population of this Island," and claimed, "I have been faithful to the promise which I made to you when I took up arms against tyranny, and whilst the last spark of life remains in me I shall keep my oath: *Never again shall a colonist or an European set his foot upon this territory with the title of master or proprietor.*" He expressed no regret for his determination to keep Haiti free: "Yes, I have saved my country," he said. "I have avenged America."[86]

⤛ • ⤜

THE FIGHT AGAINST re-enslavement was not limited to Haiti—this challenge also fell to Guadeloupe, situated to the southeast of its larger neighbor.[87] In June 1794, Victor Hugues brought news of the National Convention's abolition of slavery to a Guadeloupe occupied by British troops. These forces were part of the same British West Indian expedition that had arrived in the Ceded Islands, and had also attacked—and successfully occupied—Martinique, while faring less well in Saint-Domingue.

Earlier unrest and uprisings had rocked Guadeloupe as news of the French Revolution and the uprising in Saint-Domingue crossed the seas, but now Hugues could harness the energy of the newly freed by enlisting them in his war against the British and the island royalists who supported them. By the end of 1794, he was successful. Britain surrendered and the island was under republican rule.

From there, attention turned to keeping the island profitable, as had been the case in Saint-Domingue. Guadeloupe's agriculture was a mix of private plantations and ones appropriated by the government, and Hugues needed the newly free people to cultivate coffee, sugar, and cotton; however, unlike Saint-Domingue, there was not enough surplus to pay them a share of the crops. He needed cultivators to work on their former plantations, incentivized by laws and proclamations, and other more desperate measures. In one case he proposed that managers goad people to work, waking them early in the morning and appealing to the patriotic struggle by leading them to the fields while singing the "Marseillaise." Such an approach had few takers, and people continued to stream from the plantations into the island's towns, and output plummeted.[88]

In 1797, the cultivators in the northern part of Basse-Terre, one of Guadeloupe's two main islands, turned on Hugues, declaring they wanted to "slit the throats of all the whites and make [themselves] masters of the country."[89] This did not come to pass, but it was a clear expression of frustration with the republican regime. Hugues left his post as commissioner in 1798, and his replacement, General Edme Étienne Borne Desfourneaux, was greeted with small insurrections across the island in reaction to the rumors that he was going to reinstitute slavery.[90]

As the new century dawned and news of Saint-Domingue and France continued to circulate in Guadeloupe, the public mood was uncertain. Some formerly enslaved people started to put their papers in order, using the island's bureaucrats to notarize their freedom, preparing for the worst.[91] They knew Bonaparte had supporters in France and in the colonies for a return to slavery. As one pamphlet from a pro-slavery Guadeloupean explained it: "It's easy to conceive what the sentiments of the blacks must have been when they first heard the flattering words *you are free* . . . They took shadow for reality and had only vague and indeterminate ideas about the meaning of their new existence."[92] If anyone was vague about that meaning, it certainly was not the former slaves.

The next governor, Admiral Jean-Baptiste Raymond de Lacrosse, who had previously been governor in 1792, was welcomed back in 1801 as a republican liberator hero. However, warm feelings cooled quickly after it became clear that he had come with a different mission this time. He soon had an uprising of black and *gens de couleur* soldiers on his hands.[93] Lacrosse had instituted a number of unpopular policies, such as inviting émigré planters back and arresting members of the military he believed were plotting against him. He also angered the *cultivateurs*. They were now receiving some pay, but the administrators he brought in to oversee the payment system were taking a cut. People continued to leave estates, and Lacrosse tried to force them back, but many were not willing.

One plantation manager reported that a worker named Arselle had left his plantation and joined a "company of artillery workers." When the manager ordered him back to the fields, Arselle replied that "he was free and French and had a profession that he had always had the right to pursue." Angered, the manager grabbed him by the collar, and Arselle pulled out a dagger and stabbed himself six times, dying the next day.[94]

The rebellion against Lacrosse started when he tried to arrest a popular officer, a *homme de couleur* named Magloire Pélage, in October 1801. The situation escalated, and soon black troops were arresting white ones. Attempts to negotiate broke down, and a short time later Lacrosse was put on a ship off the island, though he would return the following year. While this was happening, Lacrosse's aide-de-camp, a *homme de couleur* named Louis Delgrès decided to join Pélage and the other insurgents.[95]

The news of the Treaty of Amiens and its implications also brought fear and anxiety to Guadeloupe. Pélage had managed to keep the island under his control by reassuring Bonaparte of the island's loyalty, but he could do little to prevent growing suspicion about France's designs, especially after news of the Leclerc expedition to Saint-Domingue reached the island. Division and distrust grew among his troops, and between black soldiers and *gens de couleur*. Delgrès, now in charge of Fort Saint-Charles, accepted French authority but wanted firmer guarantees of the preservation of equality.[96] However, he and other soldiers were not pleased by Pélage's attempts to keep cultivators on the land by further restricting their movements. Such were the tensions that in December 1801, 600 armed *cultivateurs* from outside the capital marched into Pointe-à-Pitre. Pélage sent his officers rather than his troops to deal with the mob, because he was afraid the latter would defect and join the workers.[97] Months of unrest followed, and General Antoine Richepanse was dispatched with nearly 3,500 soldiers to the island. He promptly disarmed and deported some "rebel" black soldiers, while others saw the direction things were heading and escaped into the woods to regroup. Delgrès had changed his mind about the French authorities, deciding to fight them. He had a growing band of supporters, which included soldiers, some whites, and angry *culitvateurs*. In 1802 he issued a proclamation addressed "to the entire universe," saying, "The maxims of even the most atrocious tyranny have been surpassed today."[98] The fight to preserve freedom in Guadeloupe had begun.

With the battle cry of *Vivre libre ou mourir* (Live free or die), Delgrès and his followers faced the French troops led by Richepanse and Pélage on May 10, 1802, and into the days that followed, as battles took place across the island—including in the streets—with cultivators using their machetes, pikes, and whatever else they had to hand.[99]

Women also joined the insurgents, fighting on the front lines and singing the "Marseillaise" while hauling ammunition to the soldiers.[100] Little detail is known about them, but one woman, "the mulâtress Solitude," was recorded by name in an account published 50 years after the conflict. She was described as an "evil genius" (*mauvais génie*) who "let burst forth, on every occasion, her hatred and fury."[101] She was from somewhere near the capital but ended up in Basse-Terre, in one of the rebel camps. The camp had around 80 prisoners, and the rebels were debating the future of their captives. Solitude apparently kept rabbits, and when one tried to escape, "she picked up a knife, pursued it, pierced it, and held it up in front of the prisoners," saying to them, "Here is how I will treat you when the time comes!"[102] She would later be captured and sentenced to execution after French troops attacked the camp, by which point she was heavily pregnant. She managed to get a stay of execution until the baby was born that November, but then she was killed.[103]

Despite the efforts of fighters like Solitude, the insurgents were soon on the defensive and nearly surrounded, as some 3,500 French troops attacked by land and sea. Within a few weeks, they were closing in on Delgrès and bombarding Fort Saint-Charles. Delgrès took some of the insurgents north, into a tactical position near the foothills of the Soufrière volcano, while another general took a group to the capital, setting fires as they went and rallying more recruits.[104] On May 28, French troops marched toward the small town of Matouba, on the southern slope of Soufrière. Delgrès was aware of their advance. He and his men had earlier made a decision that they would rather die than surrender. As the French approached, they surrounded themselves with gunpowder, shouting, "No slavery! Long live death!" before igniting a giant blast and killing at least 500.[105] That was the turning point for the insurrection, although others would keep fighting until French troops had the colony back under control—aided by widespread arrests and executions—by the end of 1802. At least 10,000 people were executed or deported during or after this struggle.[106] Once-freed people were forced back to the plantations, while some managed to produce the necessary papers to prove their free status. But for all people of color on the island, the brief moment in which they enjoyed an expansion of their rights—though never really full freedom or equality—had expired.

Victor Hugues, the official who had brought news of emancipation to the Caribbean, was now tasked with the reinstatement of slavery in French Guiana, where he was appointed governor in 1802.[107] Indeed, over the next 30 years, the slave ships returned, bringing around 45,000 people to the French Caribbean colonies—Martinique, Guadeloupe, Guiana, and Saint Martin. France's first full abolition of 1794 was now a distant dream, except for the existence of Haiti, which was living proof of what had taken place between 1791 and 1802.[108]

The turbulent first few years of the nineteenth century ushered in profound changes in the Americas, especially the establishment of Haiti as a beacon of freedom in a sea of slavery. Other developments were significant too, not least Jefferson's purchase of the vast Louisiana territory in 1803 from a defeated Bonaparte, which would soon exacerbate the question of free and slave states as the US expanded to the west.

In the end, the universal principles of *liberté, égalité, fraternité* of the French Revolution proved to be an illusion in the Caribbean. The French Revolution is often credited for "inspiring" the events in Saint-Domingue, but it did not inspire the enslaved—it betrayed them. Through every twist and turn of the 13-year struggle, responsibility fell back on the people with the least access to freedom to continue to define and grasp for it. The Haitian Revolution has been described as "being unthinkable even as it happened."[109] The very audacity of the attempt meant that Haitians would spend the next century and beyond paying for their freedom.

Chapter 23

Endings

IN 1803, A slave ship called into Savannah, Georgia. On board were captives, mostly Igbo people (from modern Nigeria). About seventy-five of them were sold to the enslavers John Couper and Thomas Spalding, then taken aboard a smaller vessel, where they were shoved below deck. Their destination was a place near Saint Simon's Island, and as the boat was winding its way through Dunbar Creek, a few managed to free themselves. A struggle ensued, during which the enslavers might have been driven into the water, leaving no one at the helm, because at some point during the fight, the vessel ran aground.

According to the later testimony of a white overseer on a nearby plantation, the fleeing captives "took to the marsh," succumbing to the dark, brackish water.[1] The boat was wrecked, the others drowned. In different tellings, they walked into the water, singing; or they even walked *on* the water, back to Africa.[2] But there is one more account, passed from person to person. In this retelling, the Igbo didn't drown, but soared, taking to the sky.[3]

The spot between land, sea, and sky where it might have happened is elusive. There is one marker planted in Old Stables Corner, in the center of Saint Simon's, near a busy main road and surrounded by strip malls. There is another, a dot on Google maps, where there are no roads. Getting close requires a short drive to where a quiet street ends, just past a water treatment plant. Invisible, the location is somewhere across the way, on the western side of the creek, impossible to reach without a boat. Just beyond, the landing can be glimpsed over the velvety browns and greens of the marsh grass. There, the Igbos could take their legendary flight into the silent freedom of the skies, leaving the pain of this cruel and violent world behind.

⋘ • ⋙

GABRIEL AND HIS men were going to carry a white silk flag saying DEATH OR LIBERTY and march to Richmond, Virginia, but torrential summer rain interrupted them.[4] Despite months of planning, they could not control the possibility of an August storm. But Gabriel's dream of freedom had already been washed away: Two men reported the plot that morning, well before the first drops fell. Until that last moment, Gabriel, an enslaved blacksmith on the Thomas Prosser plantation, believed it could work. There would be enough people to march, hundreds had pledged to help him. Plus, the local militia had not been patrolling much lately and their arms were in the city's storehouse, so they would be caught unprepared. The other craftsmen, the free white ones, would join his cry for liberty and equality, because they too were suffering at the hands of the merchants.

All of these elements made sense individually; together, they added up to a fatal miscalculation.

Gabriel began to make plans in the spring of 1800, well after France had declared emancipation in 1794, and a couple of years before that decree was withdrawn. The unrest in the Caribbean had spilled north, and officials in all the US ports eyed people fleeing Saint-Domingue with increased suspicion, or sought to keep them out entirely. They could not suppress the news—given that the US had made a trade deal with General Louverture in 1799—nor could they ignore the possibility that Saint-Domingue might inspire enslaved people within the US.

Richmond at this time was a growing port, but it had not yet reached its later prominence as a hub of the internal slave trade. In 1800, its population was around 6,000, with 2,400 enslaved and 600 free black people.[5] Similarly, by 1800 the state overall had gone from being majority white to being just more than half black, both free and slave.[6] Gabriel was, like his closest accomplices, an urban slave, and a skilled, literate blacksmith. In this period, no legal barriers in Virginia prevented slaves from learning to read and write.[7]

On the Prosser tobacco plantation, Gabriel was one of 48 enslaved adults, and Prosser was one of the largest enslavers in Henrico County.[8] As a blacksmith, Gabriel was often hired out to neighbors or people in the city, which gave him the sort of mobility that was nearly impossible for people who labored in the fields. This came with risks, however, such as being underpaid by employers or overcharged by merchants for raw materials.[9] Such unfair dealings rankled Gabriel and other enslaved craftsmen.[10] They no doubt complained about this when they met, using their relative freedom to socialize when possible. One day, Gabriel was chatting with other hired-out slaves, including a man named Sam Byrd Jr., who was seeking recruits for a plot to "kill the white people."[11] Gabriel quickly became interested.

Perhaps the Yoruban deity Ogun, the blacksmith warrior god, whispered in his ear—or his namesake, Gabriel the archangel—giving him a message of freedom to take to his community.* Maybe it was also auspicious that he was born in 1776, a child slave in a new land of freedom. Whatever the impulse, Gabriel was well situated to join Byrd and ultimately take charge, utilizing the prominent position blacksmiths had in slave societies.

His ferocity was already established after a dispute the previous year with a white neighbor, over a stolen pig.[12] Gabriel bit the man's ear off, but managed to skirt the gallows through a technicality known as the "benefit of clergy," an English legal privilege dating back to the Middle Ages, initially intended for clerics but eventually extended to lay people in the North American colonies. It allowed a person convicted of a crime to avoid capital punishment. In Gabriel's case, it meant he was spared execution this time but would not be in the future. Instead, his left hand was branded, a reminder that next time he would receive no reprieve.[13]

People described Gabriel as an imposing man, over six feet tall, with scars on his head and some missing teeth, a fellow, as one acquaintance later put it, "of courage and intellect above his rank in life."[14] Gabriel, as a literate, mobile person, would have undoubtedly been

---

* Ogun remains a popular orisha (god or spirit) in Cuban *santería*, his colors black and green, while in Brazilian *candomblé* they include blue and white, and he is syncretized with Saint George, the slayer of dragons.

aware of the uprisings in Saint-Domingue and elsewhere, as well as of earlier rumors that had peppered the farms in the Richmond area.[15] He began to plan on "freeing the Negroes from slavery" and shared his ideas with his brothers, Solomon and Martin,[16] and with a young man of around 18 called Ben, who was also a slave on the plantation. Ben would be a key witness to what happened next.

They planned to gather by the brook near the Prosser plantation, and from there, one group would stand guard at the bridge between the city and the plantation; the other would march to Richmond, set fires in the Rocketts warehouse district; and another would use arms stashed at a local tavern to attack the whites when they came to put out the blaze. After that, some men would secure more weapons from the state's armory.[17] Then the whites would have no choice but to "agree to their freedom."[18]

By the summer of 1800, many black tradespeople were aware of the conspiracy. Some who travelled to nearby towns, like Charlottesville and Petersburg, continued to enlist others.[19] In quiet moments, they fashioned their weaponry, taking the metal from scythes and turning it into swords, as much a symbolic act as a practical one.[20] They also sought much-needed powder for what guns they could acquire, while continuing to whisper to potential recruits.[21]

Gabriel was organizing his revolt at a time of great domestic disquietude. The presidential election of 1800 had heightened the tensions between the Democratic-Republicans (also called Republicans) and the Federalists, with the former donning the French tricolor and the latter black cockades. One Federalist tactic was to terrify the public with allusions to the abolition of slavery, which, they claimed, the Republicans would enact should they take power. There was talk of division, of possible civil war.[22] One conspirator, Ben Woolfolk, later claimed that Gabriel's plan was to kill "all the Whites" except Quakers and Methodists, who were "conceived to be friendly to liberty," and any French because they were potential allies.[23] Indeed, two Frenchmen were supposedly involved.[24]

As the summer wore on, Gabriel gathered at least 500 recruits.[25] Such a high estimate indicates the level of interest, but also the ability of the recruits to meet and plan away from white eyes, utilizing urban spaces, like the blacksmith's forge, or remote but well-known gathering spots, like the brook from which they were going to set off (today's Upham Brook[26]).

A date was agreed: August 30. But the one thing they couldn't plan was the weather. The clouds gathered that Saturday. Rumors of a possible uprising reached the governor's ears by the eve of the plot. As the storm unleashed its fury—later described as "one of the most extraordinary falls of rain ever known in our country"—Gabriel and his inner circle decided to postpone until the following night, not realizing that two enslaved men on the neighboring Sheppard plantation, Pharoah and Tom, had reported the plot many hours earlier.[27] Any direct connection they might have had with the plans is unclear.[28] Equally murky is their reason for alerting the authorities, especially because there was no guarantee of reward. Perhaps it was the threat of a bloody and violent reprisal from both white and black—one witness later claimed, "The blacks were determined to Kill every black who should not aid . . . them in the Insurrection."[29]

With the rumors now confirmed, Richmond officials had placed guards at the prison, the capital, and the ammunition magazine by Saturday afternoon.[30] The torrential rain that followed could not wash away the anxiety in the air, and mounted patrols began to search the area. Despite more talk that the plotters would now try on Sunday, the city remained quiet, but uneasy.

The governor of Virginia, the future United States president James Monroe, wanted to proceed with caution, uncertain if this was just the product of overheated imaginations, or if a group of rebels was lying in wait. He did not want white fear whipped up, nor did he want to have to pay the bill for rolling out the entire militia. The troops began to round up potential informers and conspirators, looking to get to the truth of the matter, eventually concluding that the threat had been real. By September 9, Monroe wrote to fellow Virginian Thomas Jefferson that he hoped "the danger is passed."[31]

Soon, the local jail, at that time shared by Richmond and Henrico counties, could not hold all the suspects who had been rounded up.[32] The militia stepped up patrols while interrogations began. They brought in young Ben, from Prosser's plantation, who would testify against Gabriel and many of the others. Over the course of the investigation, Ben spoke in 36 of the 58 trials—all of which were held in a court of "oyer and terminer" (hear and determine), which was often used in criminal cases and was comprised of a panel of judges and no jury. In the trials that involved Ben's testimony, 21 people were executed—out of a total of 26 killed—two transported, two pardoned, and 11 acquitted.[33]

Gabriel managed to stay at large while others were painfully forced to reveal the details of his plot. Monroe called for Gabriel's capture, offering $300, with notices appearing in local newspapers.[34] While Gabriel was still in hiding, his brother, Solomon, confessed that Gabriel "was the person who influenced me to join him and the others in order to (as he said) conquer the white people and possess ourselves of their property."[35]

As the executions mounted, Monroe wrote to Jefferson, calling the event "the most serious and formidable conspiracy we have ever known of the kind." Monroe asked Jefferson's advice on "where to arrest the hand of the Executioner"—that is, how many people he should permit to die—because his mind was not clear about "whether mercy or severity is the better policy in this case."[36] Jefferson replied, "Where a familiarity with slavery, and a possibility of danger from that quarter prepare the general mind for some severities, there is a strong sentiment that there has been hanging enough," before cautioning that "the other states & the world at large will for ever condemn us if we indulge a principle of revenge, or go one step beyond absolute necessity."[37] What constituted absolute necessity remained opened to interpretation.

In the meantime, Gabriel was on board the *Mary*, sailing south down the Elizabeth River toward Norfolk. By September 23, the lingering suspicion of a crew member about the black man who had boarded without papers was confirmed: It was Gabriel. He was arrested, and a few days later he was jailed back in Richmond.[38]

The politics of the time followed the case, with Federalists claiming that the Republicans were "exciting our negros to cut our throats."[39] Indeed, the mention of the two French plotters led the Federalists to attempt to associate Jefferson with the dangers of the French Revolution, not least the radical Jacobins.[40] The events of Saint-Domingue would have been more pertinent, but they received no mention from the witnesses associated with the case. However, during the trials some mention was made of "French people of colour, originally from Guadalupe [sic]."[41]

By early October, Gabriel himself was in the dock. He had earlier refused to confess anything, and in the courtroom he did not speak, but instead listened to the testimony of others, some of whom perhaps he had thought were on his side.[42] Ben was a witness in this case too, telling the judges that Gabriel wanted to kill Thomas Prosser and some of the other plantation owners before going into Richmond, "where they would kill every body," break into the treasury, and divide the money. "If the White people agreed to their freedom they would then hoist a White flag and he [Gabriel] would dine and drink with the merchants of the City."[43]

The truth of Gabriel's plan would ultimately go to the gallows with him and 25 others. His vision of freedom was never fully explained, but instead was left to be pieced together through the words of informers and officials. The enslavers, in the meantime, received more than $11,000 for their loss of "property."[44] Virginia, like other Southern states, had compensation laws dating back to the colonial era that reimbursed enslavers for the execution or banishment of convicted slaves.[45]

In addition, five Richmond men pooled their money to pay to free Ben, while Pharoah and Tom also gained their freedom and an annuity, though there had been no legal guarantee at any point that the three men would be manumitted for their actions.[46] Only a few years later, in 1806, Virginia would require any manumitted slaves to leave the state within the year or face losing their freedom.

Today Interstate 95 cuts through the center of Richmond. It would take an eagle eye to notice from a car speeding along an overpass a small patch of green below. Nothing in that quick blur would indicate that this was once the site of the city's gallows, on the edge of town. It was also a black burial ground until around 1816, before decades of development paved over that history. It has been more recently restored as the Shockoe Bottom African Burial Ground, now part of the city's historical Slave Trail. On the edge of the site's parking lot, near a few information markers, is a makeshift altar with a number of offerings—an apple, some pebbles, a few pennies, and a bare wreath. These objects are placed around an engraved stone that reads, HERE LIES THE HERO GABRIEL NOT FORGOTTEN.

Gabriel lived on in the minds of Virginians in the months and years following his execution. When Governor Monroe addressed the Virginia Assembly in December 1800 to explain what had happened and assure the public that the "danger of the crisis had passed," he momentarily puzzled over the events.[47] "It seemed strange," he said, "that the slaves should embark in this novel and unexampled enterprise of their own accord. Their treatment has been more favorable since the revolution." But that very same revolution—coupled with the one in France—had made it clearer than ever that slavery could not exist in a place that had ostensibly been built on the values of freedom. Freedom would have to be redefined, or slavery would have to end. Monroe conceded, "What has happened may occur again at any time, with more fatal consequences."[48] Slave rebellions were part of the system that the colonists had created, and they would continue to be so until that system was dismantled. In the meantime, the ghosts of the gallows would stalk the public imagination. A column in the *Virginia Gazette & General Advertiser* that same December praised Monroe for preventing in Virginia "the dreadful scenes, which have been realized in the rich cities and fertile plains of St. Domingo."[49]

⊰⊱ • ⊰⊱

THE BRITISH PUBLIC had been watching the events in the Caribbean closely, both in their own island colonies and during the dramatic transformation of Saint-Domingue into Haiti. The years since William Wilberforce's 1792 defeat in Parliament had been exhausting for Britain, with the onset of the Napoleonic Wars and the corresponding West India campaign, with its costly victories and losses, including the withdrawal from Saint-Domingue. Throughout this time Wilberforce and fellow abolitionists continued to fight against the slave trade, and by 1806 the winds appeared more favorable to their cause.

The public mood had been buoyed by the resounding naval victory over France in the Battle of Trafalgar in 1805, which reaffirmed

British supremacy at sea.[50] The demise of French Saint-Domingue as a major competitor brought a boon to the British Caribbean islands, with Jamaica now dominating sugar and coffee exports.[51] The establishment of Haiti was seen as separate from the question of the slave trade. Nearly all white abolitionists wanted an immediate end to the trade, but a gradual end to slavery itself. What happened in Saint-Domingue was an instructive lesson for them about the "dangers" of instant liberation. However, it was also a compelling example of why the slave trade needed to end; some abolitionists argued that the large recently arrived African population had been a critical factor in the events of 1791.

There were also some domestic aspects to the support for the abolition of the slave trade. The abolitionist movement was a way for British working people to give voice to their own feelings about work and struggle during the transformative Industrial Revolution. The power of the West India lobby was waning, too. By the early 1800s, the reading public had been exposed to a steady stream over at least 20 years of writing and campaigning about the horrors of slavery and the slave trade.[52] The fight against the slave trade allowed some political and religious leaders to occupy a moral high ground, one that would later have far-reaching diplomatic ramifications.[53]

In 1806, Wilberforce and his allies scored a partial victory with the passage of the Foreign Slave Trade Abolition Bill, which prohibited British traders from taking captives into foreign-held territories. This legislation curbed Britain's existing slave trade and opened the way for its full abolition, which would include the British colonies, with the Act for the Abolition of the Slave Trade in early 1807. Wilberforce and the abolitionists delayed the final motion until after the upcoming general election in late 1806, in the hope that the public would pressure their MPs or vote for ones who were abolitionists. The strategy succeeded, and the bill passed the House of Commons on February 23, 1807, with a resounding 283 in favor and only 16 against.[54] British ships would now stop human trafficking—but there were at least 700,000 people still in bondage in Britain's Caribbean colonies.[55]

Around the same time that Britain abolished its role in the slave trade, the United States banned participation by its citizens in the international slave trade. Slavery itself, however, remained fully in place. The 1807 Act to Prohibit the Importation of Slaves was the fulfilment of the provision set 20 years earlier, in article 1, section 9, clause 1 of the US Constitution permitting the "migration or importation of any such persons as any of the states now existing shall think proper to admit." It also built on 1803 legislation prohibiting the importation of any "negro, mulatto, or other person of color" into the country.[56] This had been a response to concerns about internal order during the events of Saint-Domingue, when thousands of white people, often with their slaves, fled to the US, along with free people of color looking to escape. This law more or less ended the slave trade in most of the states, though in that same year, South Carolina went in the other direction and reopened its slave trade. After the 1807 ban, the port of Charleston would become one of the most important in the domestic slave trade, which would intensify in the aftermath of the termination of international trafficking. Enslaved people could, and increasingly would, be moved from the upper to the lower South as the cotton regime took hold.

Around this time, New York and New Jersey joined the other Northern states in introducing gradual emancipation measures. In New York, enslaved children born after July 4, 1799, would be freed after reaching the age of 25 for women and 28 for men. In New Jersey, the provisions were similar—children born to an enslaved mother after July 4, 1804, would be freed from bondage after reaching the age of 21 for women and 25 for men.[57]

The Southern states marched headlong in the opposite direction, increasingly rescinding any laws or practices that gave access to freedom, such as manumission, which had been legal in Virginia. By the time the 1807 legislation on the slave trade passed, the number of captives brought to the United States—mostly to South Carolina—had risen precipitously, totaling 70,000 between 1783 and 1807, with more than half coming in the final five years of the slave trade.[58]

Such behavior was not unprecedented. The Danish saw a similar increase in trafficking after passing a law in 1792 that abolished the slave trade in their Caribbean islands, which was to take effect in 1803. This made the Danes—who are often overlooked in the story of abolition—the first European power to abolish the slave trade.

This happened in part because the Danes had only a small part of the slaving market, and it was seen as not profitable while also becoming increasingly politically unpopular. The Danish government had been watching the British debate on abolition in 1792 and believed the bill would pass, though it did not. Over the Danes' transition period from 1792 to 1803, around 9,500 Africans were taken to many parts of the Caribbean, including the Danish islands, with nearly half (4,500) trafficked in the final two years.[59]

Ultimately, the efforts of Britain, the United States, and Denmark had only a limited effect on the problem. The Portuguese, Spanish, Dutch, and French traffickers who remained active in the trade—as well as smugglers—took some 650,000 captives across the Atlantic in the decade after 1808, and nearly 2 million more in the years beyond.[60]

Absalom Jones understood the challenges ahead when he stepped up to the pulpit at Saint Thomas's African Episcopal Church in Philadelphia on January 1, 1808. "Dear land of our ancestors! thou shalt no more be stained with the blood of thy children shed by British and American hands," he said in his sermon of thanksgiving. Despite the law prohibiting the importation of enslaved Africans into the United States, Jones knew that any freedom for black people in the US was fragile, and implored his congregation to conduct themselves "in such a manner as to furnish no cause of regret to the deliverers of our nation, for their kindness to us." While doing so, he said, they must continue to pray for "our legislatures to pass laws, to ameliorate the condition of our brethren who are still in bondage," including instructing them in Christian doctrine so "they may become, even while they are the slaves of men, the freedmen of the Lord."[61]

Chapter 24

Royalty

It was clear that this was no ordinary letter that Doña Josefa Giralt received at her home in San Juan, Puerto Rico, in early January 1812. Upon reading it, she began to cry and tore it up on the spot, but not before uttering out loud some of its contents. Two of her enslaved workers, Jacinto and Fermín, listened closely. The letter was from her son, Don Ramón Power y Giralt, in Spain. He thought that the abolition of slavery was going to take effect soon, and wrote to his mother to say that, should this happen, she must be the first to free her slaves.[1]

Power y Giralt was in Spain as a delegate to the Cortes de Cádiz, an attempt to hammer out a constitution during the political upheaval of the Peninsular War (1807–1814) triggered by Napoleon Bonaparte's invasion of the Iberian Peninsula in 1807. Months earlier, Bonaparte met with Spanish officials to sign the secret Treaty of Fontainebleau, a plan for France and Spain—who were then allies—to invade Portugal and divide control of it. French troops marched across Sapin to Portugal in October 1807 and occupied Lisbon by the end of November. However, the events did not go as Spain had expected, as Bonaparte had other ideas. By May 1808, he gathered some 60,000 French troops in Bayonne, near the border, to march into Spain. He then forced the abdication of Spain's Carlos IV in favor of his son, Fernando VII, before deciding to exile Fernando and place his own brother, Joseph, on the Spanish throne as José I.

British troops arrived in 1808 to help defend their long-standing ally, Portugal, and eventually their erstwhile enemy, Spain. The conflict would rage across Portugal and Spain for the next six years, and it would also trigger a political crisis throughout Spanish America.[2]

In Spain, supporters of the crown organized themselves into provincial juntas comprised of local elites and officials that deferred to the *junta suprema central* in Madrid. This *junta central* would exercise sovereignty in Spain and in the overseas colonies in the name of Fernando VII, and in so doing form a resistance to Bonaparte's rule.[3] However, the *junta central* did not stay in Madrid for long, moving first to Seville and then, in 1810, to Cádiz, a southern port protected by British ships patrolling from nearby Gibraltar, as French troops continued to advance south.

In Cádiz, a Council of the Regency took charge, and decided to call a *cortes*, a representative legislative assembly, to draw up a constitution as a sort of road map to the future for Spain and Spanish America. It was, in a way, a response to Bonaparte's July 1808 Bayonne Constitution, under which he intended to rule Spain. Such a document was the first of its kind for Spain, which had been operating under the precepts of absolutist rule; now, in Cádiz, the Cortes was crafting a more representative model of governance.[4]

While this was taking place in Spain, juntas also appeared across Spanish America, and while ostensibly in support of Spain, for the moment, these bodies were also places of debate and discussion about long-standing grievances, among them the irritation many powerful locally born creoles felt upon seeing Spaniards placed in key offices and posts. In some places, however, calls for independence from Spain came swiftly, such as the one issued by Father Miguel Hidalgo in Dolores, Mexico, on September 16, 1810. In that same year, the Spanish American territories were invited to send delegates (*diputados*) to the Cortes, with the body's membership fully aware that these colonies were more populous and prosperous than Spain and their continued alliance was needed.

In this context, wedged between an occupied Spain and an unclear future for Spanish America, the question of slavery in Spain's empire was placed on the discussion table. Slavery and the slave trade were impossible to ignore. Haiti had thrown off the entire system, while Britain, the US, and Denmark had ceased their participation in the international trade. With the exception of Haiti, however, no one had ended the *practice* of slavery, and that included all of Spanish America. Domingo García Quintana, a deputy representing Lugo, Galicia, was first to raise the prospect of the abolition of the practice to the Cortes, on January

9, 1811, by proposing to "banish for ever even the memory of slavery" and suggesting that enslaved people have a representative in the Cortes on their behalf while this was undertaken. A delegate from Venezuela, Esteban Palacios, gave a swift reply: "I approve of it [abolition] as a lover of humanity; but as a lover of political order, I disapprove."[5]

The issue surfaced again toward the end of March. By this point, a powerful planter from Cuba, Andrés de Jaúregui, had arrived in Cádiz, with two slaves in tow, in addition to his secretary and three other servants.[6] He had missed the earlier call for abolition, but was on hand to hear the Mexican priest José Miguel Guridi y Alcocer lay out an extensive plan to end the slave trade and enact gradual emancipation. However, all that is recorded in the main diary of events is that Guridi y Alcocer "presented some propositions relating to the wellbeing of America," which were shuffled off to the constitutional committee.[7] These were debated in private, Jaúregui understanding well that eager ears—perhaps even those of the slaves he brought with him—would be listening with great attention.

Guridi y Alcocer's words would soon surface in public and in that March 26, 1811, session he outlined the complete dismantling of the slave system, in stages. It would start with the end of Spain's participation in the slave trade, while existing slaves would stay in that condition until they could buy or otherwise obtain their freedom (a measure included to appease the enslavers), but with treatment and pay like those of a paid servant. However, the children of slaves would no longer inherit slavery as a condition, and the system would eventually come to an end.[8]

The question of slavery continued to reappear in the Cortes, this time brought to the floor a few weeks later, on April 2, 1811, by Agustín de Argüelles, a Spanish delegate from the northern city of Oviedo and the leader of the liberal faction in the Cortes.[9] Argüelles read out a proposition that the Cortes "declare the abolition of torture," and then "that the Congress decree that this infamous [slave] traffic be abolished for ever," and report this decree to their British allies as quickly as possible.[10] Argüelles had been living in London in 1807, serving as a spy for Spain, when he watched from the public gallery as the House of Lords moved its second reading of the Bill for the Abolition of the Slave Trade.[11] By 1811, Argüelles was more than simply inspired by William Wilberforce; he was in active talks with British diplomats in Spain, including Henry Wellesley, the ambassador, who was eager to use the moment to bring up the slave trade. This was part of larger diplomatic machinations, as Spain was now reliant on Britain's help. The immediate revolts in Spain in 1808 against Bonaparte's rule had given Britain cause to aid Spain against France. The Peninsular War had rearranged European alliances, and now Britain's involvement—led by Wellesley's brother Arthur, the future Duke of Wellington—was crucial for defeating Bonaparte on the Iberian Peninsula.[12]

Some delegates remained unconvinced by Argüelles, as the shadow of Haiti fell across the proceedings. Even he was not in favor of full and immediate abolition. "The terms in which [the proposal] is conceived show that it does not deal with the manumission of slaves from the American possessions," Argüelles said in his own defense, adding that that matter required "the greatest circumspection, in view of the painful example which occurred in St Domingo."[13]

This time, Jaúregui spoke on the record. He claimed in his speech that his own "principles and feelings" were similar to those of Argüelles, before going on to demand, again, that these debates about "so delicate a business" be held in secret. He, too, was stalked by Haiti, its revolution uncomfortably close to Cuba, reminding the audience of "the imprudent conduct of the National Assembly of France, and of the sad, most fatal results it produced." He wanted no record of another discussion about abolition printed in the *Diario de Córtes*, "to avoid the consequences that otherwise are to be feared." However, some members rebutted his call for secrecy and even printed, along with that day's proceedings, the earlier proposals from Guridi y Alcocer.[14] The entire world could read about his plan, but that was all they would do: The Cortes did not put any form of abolition in the 1812 Constitution.[15]

However, in general this constitution was considered liberal for some of its other provisions, including ending the Inquisition; enfranchising all men, including those with no property qualifications, except those of African origin;* and limiting the powers of the king.[16] None of this

---

* The Cortes excluded black people completely from the resulting constitution. Even free black people were not given voting rights, though indigenous men would be permitted to vote under the 1812 Constitution.

was to Fernando VII's liking, and in 1813, when he was returned to the throne after his six years of imprisonment at the Château de Valençay, south of Paris, he ripped up the document.

The debate about slavery became known in the colonies, as Jaúregui had feared, and in some places the news took on a life of its own. People like Jacinto and Fermín, the enslaved men in the Power y Giralt household in Puerto Rico, had heard the words "slavery" and "abolished" in January 1812, as Don Ramón relayed news of the Cortes debate to his mother in his letter. The two men left the house that morning, and quickly passed along the news, stopping to tell other enslaved people, including Romualdo and Margarita, who told another enslaved man, Antonio. However, Antonio claimed he had already heard the news from Marcial, whose enslaver, María Gertrudis de la Puente, also had a son in Spain who had hinted at similar developments in his correspondence.[17]

In addition, a carpenter named Benito and two brothers, Francisco and Antonio Nobo, who were members of the crew on the brig *El Cazador* that arrived in San Juan from Spain in January 1812, had, according to a later report by the authorities, spread in this city the false rumor that the Cortes had granted liberty to slaves.[18] In the village of El Roble, which lies to the south of San Juan, Antonio Charboniel told people that "the slaves were already free" during the celebrations for Three Kings' Day (January 6).[19] The news reached the western coast of the island, rounding the tip toward Aguadilla. Juan Evangelista, an enslaved man, even claimed he had heard of someone being imprisoned in that town for *not* freeing their slaves.[20]

However, another enslaved woman, Carolina, reacted differently to the news; she told her enslaver, Madame Morín, that the slaves were organizing an uprising.[21] The officials were alerted, and military troops were rolled out, followed by a spate of arrests, with more than 26 people rounded up and at least 11 given between 50 and 80 lashes.[22] Juan Agapito del Rosario was injured while attempting to resist arrest in nearby Guaynabo, and Juan Luis, a slave of Don Gregoria Sandoval, was charged with "propagating the seditious species of freedom."[23] The majority of people thrown into the *real carcel* (royal prison) were enslaved, but some free people, such as "the free mulatto" Miguel García, were also arrested for taking part in the dissemination of this news.

Testimony was taken and punishments were distributed, though this time no heads were put on pikes. Charboniel was sentenced to 50 lashes, while Jacinto and Fermín were pardoned because officials thought their intentions were not seditious. Another group of slaves, including "the mulatto" Juan Luis, Antonio de Castro, Josef Púa, and Juan Evangelista, were considered a threat and deported "for the greater safety of the faithful inhabitants of this island."[24]

Writing about this moment at the end of January 1812, when this spark of hope had been thoroughly snuffed out, Governor Salvador Meléndez indicated that his measures were necessary, given what was going on in the region, observing that it had been "an evil of great significance in the Antilles to have seen the black Christopher become the King of Haiti."[25]

Cuba, too, had been buffeted by the strong winds of rumor. Around the same time that news of freedom was blazing through Puerto Rico, a black man sauntered through the streets of Havana in a smart military uniform, claiming he was Jean-François, who had fought alongside Toussaint Louverture for Spain before the latter joined the French.[26] Jean-François had been in Cuba before going to Cádiz, Spain, in 1796, but his brief time on the island had made an impression on the locals, which was part of the reason authorities directed him to Spain, where he was reported to have died in 1805.[27] More than a decade later, he—or an impersonator—was back. A lot had changed in Cuba since Jean-François's departure for Spain.

Before the disruption of the Peninsular War, Spain, under Carlos III and Carlos IV, had enacted a number of imperial reforms, one of which was allowing more "free trade" in slaves (*comercio libre de negros*) in what had been a monopoly economy controlled by the crown. This meant that after 1789, foreign merchants were permitted to come to otherwise closed Spanish American ports if they were selling humans. Spaniards themselves also became more actively involved in the trade. The timing was fortuitous, as the events in Saint-Domingue made clear a short time later. Certainly, Cuba's leading planters, such as Andrés de Jaúregui, understood that France's loss in Saint-Domingue was their gain. The Cuban economy had previously been dominated by defense and ship provisioning, but the large, fertile island had plenty of land for sugarcane. It just needed labor.

Soon, the era known as the "second slavery" was underway in Cuba.[28] The changes were dramatic. In 1774 there were 44,333 enslaved people on the island—by 1810 the number reached 217,000. Alongside this increase was a growing population of free people of color, up from 30,847 to 108,600, meaning white people were now in the minority in a larger population of 600,000.[29]

As this change was taking place, Cuba, like all of Spain's colonies during the upheaval of the Peninsular War, debated its own future. Ultimately, powerful officials and creole families chose to stay the course with Spain, unlike much of South America, where independence movements had begun. There were many factors behind this, primary among them the fear of slave revolts and the desire to have access to the military resources of Spain. Even people in favor of independence worried about the possibility that it could be subsumed by a rebellion. Cuba sat near Saint-Domingue, and Cubans had witnessed the arrival of thousands of people fleeing that conflict, so they understood the risks. Cuba's captain-general, the Marques de Someruelos, had Haiti on his mind when he wrote to the Cortes on May 27, 1811, asking it to take into consideration the island's "loyal inhabitants" and "allay all fear of seeing a repetition in it [Cuba] of the catastrophe of its neighbor, Santo Domingo, now dominated by those who were formerly slaves there."[30] Cuba became known as *siempre fiel*, the ever-faithful isle, even if what bound it to Spain was more fear than loyalty.

This was the state of affairs when the man who claimed to be Jean-François walked through Havana in January 1812. Two other free men of color, Estanislao Aguilar and Juan Bautista Lisundia, joined him in March, and they made their way into the countryside, stopping at a sugar plantation called Trinidad. A Havana grandee, Nicolás Peñalver, was its owner. The men strode over to the huts where the slaves lived and read a proclamation to them, in French. It had been sent, they said, by the king of Haiti.[31]

The men did another reading at the Peñas Altas plantation. A short time later, fire ripped through its fields and buildings. The men pushed on to their next stop, the Santa Ana plantation, but it would be their last. They were captured by a party already waiting to intercept them.

Within a few weeks, the head of "Jean-François" would be displayed on a stake in front of Peñas Altas, though before his death, he claimed that he was Juan Barbier and not the former soldier-hero. His identity in life and death remains a mystery.[32] Reports of unrest flowed into the capital, coming from other parts of the island, far from Havana: Puerto Príncipe (Camagüey) in the center, and Bayamo and Holguín to the south and east.[33]

Alleged participants continued to be rounded up for interrogation, or worse. Soon, the name of Jose Antonio Aponte y Ulabarra surfaced. Like Gabriel on the Prosser estate in Virginia only a few years earlier, Aponte had had previous experience with the authorities. In 1800, he had been suspected of stealing from Havana's weapons arsenal, and the following January he was forced to step down as a captain in the *moreno* (black) militia, after serving for more than 20 years.[34] Unlike Gabriel, however, Aponte was a free man.

Aponte and the impersonator of Jean-François had been seen together at the house of another black militia member, Clemente Chacón, who later testified that Aponte had been sent by "Cristoval [Christophe] king of Santo Domingo . . . to entice free blacks and slaves of this island to achieve the independence of the latter."[35] Aponte was also said to have been the author of a public declaration nailed to the governor's residence in mid-March that read: "I order you at the sound of the drum and trumpet to be ready and without fear to destroy this empire of tyranny." It was crafted with enough vagueness—and no direct mention of slavery—that it could have referred to the French, or been a call for the island's independence.[36] It was not, however, interpreted that way.

The authorities soon arrived at Aponte's home and did a search so thorough that they found a strange book in a wooden box buried deep inside a trunk full of clothing. They had no words for this object, resorting to the lackluster description of *libro de pinturas* (book of paintings). It was unlike any book they had ever seen, filled with Biblical and historical images, with many black faces, as well as cutout bits of paper and handwritten words. It was more a multipage sprawling collage than a tidy sketchbook. Far from seeing it as a work of art, the authorities believed it to be the master plan for a conspiracy. No, Aponte told officials when they arrested him, they had it all wrong: His creation was meant for the king of Spain. But the officials remained unconvinced.

Aponte's *libro* has been lost in the intervening years—misplaced in an archive at best, destroyed at worst. All that is known about it is what Aponte and others said in their subsequent testimony, and even that would have been filtered and paraphrased by the Spanish scribe. The missing *libro* is a colossal loss, as it was a visual and tactile version of one man's past and present and, possibly, his vision of a fair and equitable future. The surviving descriptions render the book as a kind of historical record, blending contemporary times and distant history, lands near and far. For instance, one of the *pinturas* depicted Diogenes the Cynic. In the image, Diogenes is outsmarting a Spanish king from his jar in ancient Greece. The king, however, is Rey Don Rodrigo, the last king of the Goths (r. 710–711 CE), and Diogenes was believed to have spent some time as a slave. The message, once decoded, is easier to make out, but Aponte assured the Spaniards during his testimony that Diogenes's prowess was only due to the protection of the goddess Isis.[37]

Such complex layers of knowledge and meaning were nearly incomprehensible to the Spanish officials. There were Egyptian gods, but also Aponte's grandfather, Joaquín, who had served in the *moreno* militia and fought during the British attack on Havana in 1762, along with other free black soldiers.[38] Although Aponte was likely trying to express his family's history of service, officials were concerned by military depictions, including those of installations like the Castillo del Morro fort, which looked like they could be part of an attack plan. The investigators would not, or could not, entertain the possibility that Aponte may have been trying to communicate something about the service of black people in the militia and their place in Cuban society.

Officials called in witnesses to testify and explain some of these meanings, including Chacón, who claimed Aponte had earlier put Henry Christophe in one of his images, and written below *cúmplase lo mandado* ("execute what is ordered").[39] Another witness explained that he knew "there was a black King that José Antonio Aponte had painted" who was called "Henry the First, king of Haiti." This image, Aponte later told officials, he copied from another black man at the

Havana docks, and added that he had destroyed any likenesses of Haiti's revolutionary leaders when he learned they were illegal.[40]

Aponte was not unique in wanting images of Haitian leaders. In 1805, the crown in Portugal heard about how the "Portrait of Dessalinas [sic], Emperor of the Blacks of the Island of S. Domingos, [was] ripped from the chests of some manumitted *cabras* [dark-skinned mulattos]." The men wearing these medallions in Rio de Janeiro, the author of the report pointed out, "were employed in the troops of the city's militia, where I saw them skillfully handling artillery."[41] Haiti was proving talismanic—and troubling—from its inception.

The authorities searched Aponte's house again and listed on the subsequent inventory his books as well as "an effigy of General Washington."[42] Perhaps this was because of Aponte's admiration for Washington's ability as a general, something he understood given his own experience in the American Revolution's Pensacola campaign, led by Bernardo de Gálvez and involving troops from Havana. Aponte had also been part of a black militia battalion that successfully obtained a British surrender on New Providence Island, Bahamas, in 1782. In another drawing, Aponte depicted "the ships transporting the companies of blacks that landed at eight in the morning" on that island and were successful in securing the "enemy's capitulation."[43] While illustrating both events he had heard about and events from his own life, Aponte was also positioning himself in a larger sense between two worlds—that of the old European empires and that of the potential represented by the American Revolution, though its promises of freedom continued to fall short.

The authorities eventually interrogated Aponte about his work, a three-day ordeal with officials demanding explanations for each of the 72 images in the book.[44] They saw black faces they felt should have been white, they read intent where Aponte said there was none, and they failed to accept that Aponte was telling his version of black history, from Genesis through classical Greece and Rome to the medieval legend of Prester John in Ethiopia, the American Revolution, and the establishment of Haiti. Even the Ethiopian eunuch—from the same Biblical story which was represented on the London baptismal font of Ottobah Cugoano—was found in those pages.[45]

The interrogators asked Aponte over and over how he knew certain things (he had read about them, he said, as they could see from what was on his shelves) and why he chose to compose the images the way he did. To this question he replied: "For Reasons of history, like everything else in the book."[46] He, in turn, reminded them that this book was for the king. But neither the king nor history could save him. On April 9, Aponte was hanged, his head put on a pole in a cage and placed on a corner in his neighborhood. Clemente Chacón and his son were also hanged that day.[47]

Toward the end of Aponte's trial, a small piece of paper was found on the ground in the prison fortress of La Cabaña, where all the suspects had been held and interrogated. On it was an image of Henry Christophe.[48]

◂◂ • ▸▸

THE KING OF Haiti was becoming a public preoccupation for both enslaved and enslaver around the region. Who was the ex-slave now calling himself royalty? Henry Christophe: military commander and fellow avenger with Dessalines. Yet the journey to his coronation had been strewn with obstacles.

Dessalines had not lasted long. He had been crowned emperor, a move that was not popular, and his rivals, led by fellow general Alexandre Pétion, killed him.[49] A new constitution heavily influenced by Pétion was issued in 1806, making Haiti a republic. Haiti, at independence, reverted to the boundaries of Saint-Domingue. The Spanish side, which had been transferred to the French in 1795, returned to Spanish colonial rule after a revolt by its elites in its War of Reconquest (Guerra de la Reconquista) of 1808–09.

The new Senate chose Christophe as president, though it would wield the legislative power, and it was dominated by members from the south and west, while Christophe's base was the north.[50] Unhappy with this arrangement, Christophe gathered his troops, telling them, "Your general does not want to compromise with the enemies of liberty." By early 1807 he had some 18,000 soldiers preparing to do battle against the new republic.⁵¹ Pétion and Christophe fought each other in a brief civil war, which ended in a stalemate. Christophe took control of the north, as well as the western ports of Gonaïves and Saint-Marc and the fertile Artibonite Valley in the center of the island, while Pétion would take Port-au-Prince and the rest of the south and west.⁵² In 1811 Christophe proclaimed his realm a kingdom, crowning himself that June. In the south, Pétion had re-established a republic.

This was the situation on the island as Aponte was creating his images of black kings, including Haiti's. Monarchy continued to have resonance—the cries of "the king has freed us" had been uttered at some point or another around the entire region.

In Haiti, the political crisis was existential. Christophe had crowned himself the successor to Dessalines, but titles could only go so far. The real issue was how to secure Haiti from future occupation or enslavement. Whoever was in charge needed to keep social control and raise money to ensure this did not happen. Here, too, Christophe and Pétion differed. Both understood that their success rested on the profitability of trade and agriculture. Christophe wanted to continue with plantations, forcing people to work the land. Pétion, however, began to move away from this model and allow more smallholdings. Although they faced similar challenges, their methods diverged significantly.

Christophe did not skimp on his vision for the Kingdom of Haiti. He established all the accoutrements of royalty, including a nobility of some 85 members, a royal coat of arms, and a coronation covered in the foreign press. There were the lavish royal tours of his kingdom, a gilded state carriage, the court's elegant fashion, and a grand palace. Such spending would ultimately be more than Christophe could afford, personally and politically.⁵³

Christophe arranged his economy in a similar way to Louverture and Dessalines, retaining the plantations but also using the heavy hand of the military to keep people working on them. Sugar and coffee would pay for freedom, but someone still had to grow and harvest it. Along with this, there were other unpopular measures, such as limiting how much land members of the public could privately hold.⁵⁴ The following year, in 1812, Christophe issued a 750-page, nine-volume *Code Henry*, which covered all aspects of life in the kingdom, such as law and the military—and inevitably agriculture. The land use outlined in the code was, in parts, quite similar to what had preceded it, such as granting farmers a quarter of the harvest as pay. According to the Code, workers would be tied to the land and could face arrest as a vagabond if they were found away from their plantation. The code even stipulated working hours of sunrise to sunset, with breaks for breakfast and around noon, at the hottest part of the day.[55]

Throughout this period, Haiti served as a beacon of freedom for the enslaved, as a specter of destruction for planters, and as something in between for white abolitionists trying to make sense of it all. Some British abolitionists liked to use Christophe as an example of "enlightened" or "civilized" freedom.[56] Christophe corresponded on a regular basis with some of the British abolitionists, including Thomas Clarkson. In these letters he sometimes expressed anxiety about the French returning to the island. Their control of the east bothered him, as did the resumption of Spanish rule. Such instability and the continuing colonial occupation—be it by France or Spain—meant that enemies could have easy access to the island, which was a constant concern. In one 1818 letter, Christophe wrote to Clarkson: "I repeat that I must have the positive assurance that England will recognize our independence, or will take some equivalent step such as promising that the French will undertake no expedition to blockade our ports and harass our territory, and also that Spain will not be permitted to cede her part of this island to our enemies."[57]

The British were drawn to Christophe, perhaps because of his connection to the abolitionists, or perhaps because of his respect for certain British systems, including educational methods. He brought over teachers trained in the Lancasterian model, which was designed for large class sizes across a range of ages and abilities.[58] Indeed, the larger British public was familiar enough with Henry that his eventual death in 1820 would be the subject of a hit play, *The Death of Christophe—King of Hayti*.[59] Before then a portrait of the king, painted by the British artist Richard Evans, would hang at the 1818 Royal Academy Exhibition to positive reviews.[60] The work shows Christophe in a relaxed but commanding pose, standing with his hand on a sword by his side. By contrast, most depictions of Christophe in the popular press in Britain and Europe mocked his pretensions to royalty.

Christophe also had a secret weapon—the pen of Baron de Vastey. Born Pompée Valentin Vastey, the baron was an Afro-European, free-born, wealthy, educated man who was involved in the Haitian Revolution and ultimately allied with Christophe. He was a brilliant writer and propagandist, and carried on a war of words against slavery and also against their rival, Pétion.[61] To Vastey, the republican system was not to be trusted, because France, he said, "told us, we were all brethren, and all equal in the sight of God, and the Republic, yet while making this profession with their lips, they meditated in their hearts the horrible design of either reducing us to slavery, or, if that was found impractical, totally exterminating us."[62] The memory of 1802 was still vivid.

Vastey's writings travelled well beyond Haiti, telling the world what King Henry could do. Christophe also brought Prince Saunders, a prominent African American from New England, into his retinue. Saunders was involved in colonization schemes that sent willing black people from the United States to Africa, and he was also in touch with British abolitionists. He personally delivered Christophe's correspondence to them. He published *Haytian Papers* during a stay in London, bringing the many policies of the Kingdom of Haiti to wider public attention.[63] He became a popular enough figure to hold a ball in London attended by then-US ambassador John Quincy Adams, who would become president in 1825.[64]

Pétion, now fully in charge of the south and west of the island as a constitutional republic, created a society of smallholders by parceling out land to soldiers as payment and allowing people to buy plots. However, he, too, could not resist the allure of power, and decided to issue a new constitution in 1816. In it, he was made president for life.[65] This was more ammunition for Vastey, who decried it as a "sham constitution" before imploring Haitians in the south to "destroy this demagoguery, which tends to dishonor and demean you in the eyes of nations."[66]

While Vastey was no fan of Pétion, the president had his admirers, including Venezuela's independence leader Simón Bolívar, who took refuge for a short time in southern Haiti in 1816. While there, he received arms from Pétion and had the opportunity to regroup for the next phase of his own independence struggle. Bolívar wrote to

Pétion, flattering him and calling him the "the father of all the true republicans."[67] The Haitian general made his wishes clear in a reply, saying: "You know, General, my feelings for what you are determined to defend and for you personally. You must be aware of how much I wish to see those who still suffer under slavery escape from it."[68]

These two competing systems in Haiti were alike in one crucial way: underestimating their respective publics. The coerced-labor model in the north faced the sort of resistance that had frustrated Louverture and Dessalines. People did not want to be forced to work on plantations. Southern smallholders were more content, but the economy there struggled. In both north and south, some people tried to opt out of the system. Haitian *cultivateurs* had to vote with their feet, and some sought freedom away from political projects that had harnessed their labor but given them little in return.[69] It was, in a way, an extension of marronage.[70] It was also an expression of the freedom for which they had fought and for which thousands had died.

Pétion died of natural causes in March 1818, and another general, Jean-Pierre Boyer, became the president of the south. Later that same year, during an August storm, lightning struck Christophe's citadel in the north, causing a fire and killing dozens of soldiers, including Christophe's brother-in-law. It was an ominous portent.[71] Christophe knew his allies in the south were few, and he was concerned about Boyer's designs, including a possible invasion of the north. Christophe's attempts to plan his retaliation were hampered by an illness, possibly a stroke, in August 1820, which left him physically weakened. Rather than carry on in this diminished state, he shot himself a couple of months later.

A Swedish sea captain who had led an expedition to the kingdom of Haiti, hoping to profit from being of service to Christophe, was on hand to witness the aftermath of the king's death. He watched as "four bayonets were run into the back" of Christophe's son, the crown prince Jacques-Victor, who was only 16. The leaders of the anti-Christophe insurrection also came after Vastey, who pleaded to be allowed to exile himself but was "hit with an axe in the head, and still showed signs of life" the following day, though he soon died.[72] Henry's wife and daughters escaped to Europe, and spent time in Britain, where they used their contacts to secure a temporary refuge.

The deaths of Pétion and Christophe closed an early but formative chapter for Haiti. Two tangible legacies from Christophe have survived the turbulent centuries since his rule. The first is his grand Italianate palace, Sans-Souci ("without worry"), about 12 miles (20 kilometers) south of Le Cap. It is poised on a hill of vibrant green, its remains indicating it was as elaborate as any European royal residence. Once a symbol of wealth and power, it now lies in ruins, its elegant arches crumbling. A long, steep walk from the palace is the imposing Citadelle Laferrière, the largest fort in the Americas. Unlike the palace, it is in reasonable repair. It is perched high on the Bonnet à l'Evêque mountain, almost above the clouds, keeping a silent vigil, constantly scanning the horizon for invaders.

Chapter 25

Opportunities

THE EVENTS IN Spain and Cuba began to have ripple effects in the United States. The French invasion of Spain in 1808 had triggered the Cuban authorities in that year to force anyone who was "French"—that is, any person who fled Saint-Domingue during the fighting—to vacate Cuba. Some refugees had been living there for a decade or more. Many pressed the United States to let them in with their slaves, despite the 1807 ban on bringing foreign slaves into the country. Congress agreed in a near-unanimous vote in 1809 to make an exception for these refugees if they were going to Louisiana, which was then a territory and would not become a state until 1812.[1] This was an obvious place for many of those forced out of Cuba, as Louisiana had long-standing connections to both the French and Spanish Caribbean, having previously been a French territory (1682–1762, 1801–1803) and a Spanish one (1762–1801).

Because of this exemption, more than 3,000 enslaved people landed in Louisiana, along with another 3,000 free people of color.[2] In total, 9,059 people entered New Orleans, mostly from Cuba, between May 1809 and January 1810.[3] This was in addition to the 10,000 or so who had already left Saint-Domingue for the US over the course of the 1790s. Of the group who arrived between 1809 and 1810, 3,226 were listed as "slaves," though slavery had been abolished in Saint-Domingue in 1794 and never reinstated.[4] Some enslavers no doubt used the uncertainty of the time and an initial move to slaveholding Cuba to keep those "property" rights intact. An enslaved person might have feared the consequences of declaring their status to suspicious officials, especially if they had no documentation to support the claim.[5] However, for some, the change in territory offered an opportunity to use the US courts to clarify their status and perhaps obtain this elusive freedom. In one study of 31 freedom suits coming from this group, 11 won, 11 lost, and the ruling in the remainder of the cases is unknown. Not all of those suits were made in Louisiana—indeed, those fought in Pennsylvania were more likely to result in a win, but each state could make and amend restrictions on freedom throughout this period.[6]

However, only a small group brought suits; other enslaved people arriving in Louisiana from Cuba had to resort to extralegal measures in reaching for their liberty. Some simply used the opportunity to run away, such as an enslaved man named Dominique who had been born in Saint-Domingue and "lately arrived [in Louisiana] from St Jago [Santiago de Cuba], about 18 years of age," according to the runaway notices in *Le Courrier de la Louisiane*. He had "some scars on his breast," according to the announcement, and when he fled he was wearing "a yellow nankeen jacket and pantaloons nearly worn out," with a handkerchief tied around his head. He had on him "a bundle of dry goods which he had for sale," and which would come in handy in paying for his journey to self-emancipation, if he managed it.[7]

A much larger grasp at freedom took place in 1811 about 30 miles (50 kilometers) upriver from New Orleans, along a stretch of land between the Mississippi River and Lake Pontchartrain, an area known as the German Coast, named for its settlers in the early French colonial period. The land was now divided into long, narrow neighboring plots that stretched between the river's levee to the south and the foreboding swamps to the north, with most of the 3,840 enslaved people in the area forced into the brutal work of planting and processing cane.[8] Sugar had taken root here, nourished by the rich alluvial soil and the heat of the long summers.

The plotters decided to strike on a cold night, right at the beginning of the Mardi Gras season, which started after Three Kings' Day, on January 6. Three of them—Charles Deslondes; Komina (also Quamana), an African on the estate of James Brown; and Harry Kenner, a carpenter at the Kenner and Henderson plantation about 20 miles (30 kilometers) east—had met the night before at Manuel Andry's Woodland plantation, in today's LaPlace, Louisiana. They likely gathered in one of the slave cabins. The main Andry house faced the river, with a porch running the length of the front, while the enslaved workers lived at the back of the property.

Charles Deslondes knew the place well. He worked for Andry, possibly as his driver.[9] Such a role gave Deslondes power over some 80 slaves—despite being one himself—as well as privileges, such as greater freedom of movement. Deslondes was described as a light-skinned man, and he may have been born just down the road from the Deslondes plantation, where he appears on an inventory in 1793, listed as being 16 years old.[10] All of these factors meant Deslondes's own life was deeply rooted in this area, with its river and fields of cane, and quite possibly in the white Deslondes family. That family merged with Andry's when Manuel's son, Gilbert, married Marie Marcelite Deslondes.

Such intimate ties could have meant Charles Deslondes was a trusted part of the system, a person seemingly removed from whispered plots to burn the cane fields and kill the whites. In fact, he was the architect of what was called the German Coast uprising, later considered to be the largest slave revolt in the United States, though at this point Louisiana was still a territory.

That January night, Deslondes, Komina, and Harry finalized their strategy. Deslondes believed they would find weapons somewhere in the Andry house, given that Manuel and Gilbert were prominent members of the local militia. In the final hours of January 8, 1811, they began their search, a torrential winter downpour proving no deterrent. Andry and his son were asleep in their beds when a group of rebels entered and began to look all over the house for weapons, eventually entering Andry's room. With no other way out, Andry fought them, ending up with a few cuts before fleeing the house. Gilbert, however, was not so fortunate: He was hacked to death. Andry ran to his small launch and crossed the river for safety, making his way to another plantation to find help.[11]

Rather than chasing after him, the rebels resumed their hunt for weapons, perhaps not realizing that he would be able to seek assistance. After the men found some gun stores and even militia uniforms, they moved on, with Deslondes leading on horseback through the driving rain. They moved at a slow pace, searching each property they passed for much-needed firearms. The larger plan was to march to

New Orleans, a journey of two days, where slaves in the city would join them.[12] Around 25 of them made their way through the puddles that formed on the River Road. As night gave way to morning, more joined, having spent hours in nervous anticipation. Planters and their families, warned by slaves who were not participating, had started to flee.

The men marched, now beating drums, waving flags, and setting fires as they travelled. Soon they reached the François Trépagnier plantation. Deslondes had an enslaved girlfriend there. She remains unnamed in the records, leaving no indication of her role in the plot, except to be the reason for Deslondes's frequent visits and possibly making it a place where he was able to discuss these matters with others. Trépagnier decided to stay put and wait for the rebels upstairs, his gun loaded and ready. Perhaps he heard the drums before he saw the crowd. Death came quickly as the axes fell upon him.[13]

By the morning of January 9, the news, as well as panicked planters, arrived at the gates of New Orleans. One witness recalled that it felt like the city was about to experience "a miniature representation of the horrors of St Domingo."[14] Officials started to pull together troops, but many at that moment were in West Florida, the site of ongoing tensions with Spain, which still controlled that territory; only 30 regular troops remained in the city, along with two companies of volunteer militia. These were dispatched to face the rebels, while a small group of sailors were also armed, as the weather was too severe for them to go by boat.[15]

Deslondes and the others continued their march southeast toward New Orleans, passing plantations that lined the road, now abandoned. More freedom-seekers joined, as did maroons who lived in the nearby cypress swamp.[16] They moved along the main river road, their numbers swelling to at least 100, although by some counts the total grew to 500.

They reached Harry Kenner, who brought even more recruits. They continued to march, covering some 20 miles that day. Eventually they needed to rest—and to find more weapons. Entering New Orleans was not going to be as easy as raiding an abandoned plantation; officials had instituted a curfew and blocked a route into the city via Bayou Bridge.[17] The population of New Orleans, at this time, was divided roughly into thirds, with 4,507 white residents, 3,332 free people of color, and 4,386 enslaved people; across all these groups, there would have been people who had direct experience of Saint-Domingue.[18]

The army's initial attempt to attack the "brigands," as the planters called them, took place near today's city of Kenner.[19] But as the troops began their charge, they found no one to battle. The rebel slaves had made a strategic retreat, hoping to confuse the planters. However, Deslondes and the others soon found themselves under a surprise attack from the rear, led by Andry, who had organized a militia from plantations on the West Bank of the river.[20] The rebels opened fire but soon ran out of ammunition. Bodies began to drop, and 40 or so rebels made for the swamp, including Deslondes. Others, among them Komina, were captured, a death sentence in itself.[21]

The militia, now emboldened, headed for the swamp, taking Native American trackers and dogs with them. The animals found Deslondes on January 12 and dragged him to a group of planters. After a summary trial, they killed him, cutting off his hands, shooting him, and then roasting his body.[22] Other reprisals were equally violent and bloody. Some rebels had to endure interrogation first. A tribunal was set up on the the nearby Destrehan estate, with another 20 rebels tried in New Orleans.

In the end, at least 66 freedom-seekers in addition to Deslondes were killed, with at least 20 dying during the fighting and 45 executed afterwards.[23] They had come from more than 20 different plantations, a mixture of African and creole, sharing a vision with Deslondes. The involvement of people from many estates suggests that the uprising involved a detailed level of planning, but little is known about its mechanics or rationale. The planters, of course, described the rebels as bandits out to cause trouble and destroy property, and were unable to admit to themselves that the very system they upheld had caused the rebellion against it.

In a sign of the resulting paranoia, officials stuck the heads of the dead slaves on poles and placed them at intervals along the River Road. Their flesh was left to decompose in public, the rot of the plantation system on grisly display. Normality, such as it was at the time, resumed. Some of the "missing" rebels presumably joined the maroons, while others snuck back to their plantations, hoping to evade notice of their participation. The enslavers whose captives were killed received $300 for each one from the federal government—Louisiana was not yet a state.²⁴ The plantations never saw such a revolt again, and Louisiana was quickly ushered into statehood. Talk of numerous conspiracies—real or imagined—as well as smaller acts of resistance, continued there and everywhere slavery existed, but there was never another uprising of this scale within the United States.

The Andry house weathered the storm of 1811 and still stands today, until recently as a museum devoted to the Louisiana creole jazz trombonist Kid Ory, who was born on its grounds some 70 years later. In 2024, a nonprofit called the Descendants Project acquired the site for a museum focusing on the 1811 uprising.²⁵ The Destrehan plantation, where some of the interrogations were held, also remains intact, sitting by the river, an elegant two-story French colonial house with wraparound porches, framed by live oaks. It became the property of the Mexican Oil Company in 1914, and later of Amoco, until local citizens succeeded in having it returned to the public in the 1970s and subsequently restored.²⁶ Today, visitors can read and hear about its place in the German Coast rebellion, as it is now a stop on the 1811 Slave Revolt trail that stretches along the river. However, the entire stretch of US Highway 61 South is dominated by the petrochemical industry, with so many pipes carrying what is extracted from the bayous that they are forced to go up and over the road, forming futuristic overpasses for chemicals only. This is, not surprisingly, a "cancer alley," one of the areas with the highest rates of that disease in the United States. The plantations of Deslondes's world gave way to the petroleum pipelines of today, the toxins of a painful past and present simmering beneath the earth.²⁷

⋖⋅•⋅⋗

For the British, the years after ending the slave trade in 1808 brought a number of challenges across the Caribbean, especially on the long-troublesome island of Dominica. An earlier revolt in 1802 on that island pushed British officials towards declaring in 1807 that all enslaved members of its West India Regiments were to be free.

The revolt involved a group of soldiers who were part of the 8th West India Regiment, stationed in the north of the island, at the Cabrits Garrison, part of the slave-built Fort Shirley, which sits in the valley of a hilly peninsula overlooking the placid waters of Prince Rupert Bay. Some of the enslaved soldiers at that time were put to work tending the governor's fields or clearing brush—tasks more associated with plantation slaves than with soldiers, and they were well aware of the difference. This led to teasing by some of the local enslaved workers, who told the soldiers that it looked like they were on their way to the plantation rather than the platoon. The low status of these assignments, coupled with the grueling task of clearing a nearby swamp, stoked anger among the ranks in the spring of 1802. On April 9, the African members of the regiment mutinied. They surrounded the officers' quarters in the fort and launched their attack, killing three and imprisoning the others. They took over the garrison in short order, but their victory did not last long.[28] The enslaved creole soldiers did not join them, but decided to use the opportunity to flee, swimming into the bay or securing canoes to escape.

The following morning, four British warships sailed into the bay, coincidentally coming from Antigua for supplies. The mutineers fired on them from the fort, doing little to deter the vessels and instead alerting them to the situation. By April 12, the governor, Colonel Andrew Cochrane-Johnstone, arrived with reinforcements. At first, when confronted, the Africans declared their loyalty to the king, but when given orders to drop their arms, they instead fired on the other soldiers. The war was a brief one. At least 60 members of the 8th West India Regiment were killed, and it is estimated that around 100 men died in total, while others were imprisoned on HMS *Magnificent* in the harbor. Thirty-four of those prisoners would hang. However, their deaths helped open the way for the liberation of at least 10,000 slave-soldiers who became free with the passing of the Mutiny Act of 1807.[29] The soldiers freed in 1807 would go on to fight for a British Empire at war on many fronts, including in the Caribbean against slave rebellions in British territories. In Dominica, that took the form of renewed conflict with the maroons.[30]

By 1812, there had been years of skirmish with the maroons, who wanted to undermine sugar production. At this point, Dominica had about 24,000 slaves, 1,500 free people of color, 800 whites, and at least 800 maroons, about half of them women, scattered in settlements in remote parts of the volcanic island.[31] The local leaders included Jacko, who had spent more than three decades fighting the British on the island.[32] These years saw a number of sporadic battles, pushing matters toward an inevitable showdown. The British destroyed a few maroon camps, such as the one run by Chief Elephant, but other raids were less successful, leaving troops exhausted in vertiginous mountain forests, with no maroons in sight.

To further complicate matters, in June 1812, the young United States declared war on Great Britain, a conflict known as the War of 1812, fought mainly near the Great Lakes, on the Eastern Seaboard, and in the Gulf of Mexico. Although the reasons for the war were not related to slavery, it would make a difference in the lives of thousands of enslaved people, especially in Virginia and Maryland. A new conflict with the British might just mean a possible path to freedom, as it had during the Revolutionary War. It was also potentially an opportunity for enslaved people to rise up themselves.

A few months earlier, on April 2, two justices of the peace in Montgomery County, Virginia, heard the confession of an enslaved man named Tom. He told the justices—the surviving account is a transcript written by them, and not his direct speech—that he had murdered his enslaver, John Smith, on March 23, claiming he had been "instigated thereto by a woman of the property of said Smith by the name of Celia."[33] As they questioned him, the justices asked if other slaves were "disposed to rise in order to kill their masters," and received an affirmative answer. Apparently, a "conjurer" by the name of Goomer would protect people who killed their enslavers. In Tom's case, "a negro man Jack . . . told me to kill my master; that I could not be hurt for it, and that Goomer would conjure me clear, and that when they got fixed they intended to rise and kill the white people."[34] Tom told the justices that on the appointed day he was supposed to have killed John Smith, but "he could not." He and Celia "had further conversation about it Sunday night," though he did not elaborate. Whatever they decided, he murdered Smith the following day. He then returned to the house, and Celia "told him to take a horse and clear himself," which he did, riding to Franklin, where he met "a negro woman of a Mr. Hall." He told her his story, and added that there would soon be an uprising, to which she replied "they could not rise too soon for her, as she had rather be in hell than where she was."[35]

While there were myriad reasons to revolt, the timing was key. According to Tom, "the negroes in the neighborhood said that these British people was about to rise against this Country, and that they intended to rise sometime in next May."[36] The justices were curious, asking Tom how he heard about the possible British attacks. He replied that "it was heard from the poor people in the neighborhood, and by hearing the newspapers read."[37]

It is unclear how Tom was caught, and if he possibly thought that telling officials of the plot would somehow ameliorate his sentence. He may also have been leading them astray or protecting some people by naming others. The inquisitors took the information at face value and concluded, "A spirit of rebellion is very obvious in this country."[38] In the weeks that followed, the militias in Virginia readied themselves for a conflict—one that might involve fighting the British and suppressing a slave revolt.

Meanwhile, in Dominica, some 75 enslaved people on the Castle Bruce plantation left en masse to join the maroons in July 1812.[39] Such maroon activity was the most serious challenge awaiting the new governor, George Robert Ainslie, who was appointed in April 1813. Ainslie was hostile toward the maroons from the beginning. He and the planters were aware that the maroons lured enslaved people away from the plantations and that their goal had long been to uproot and destroy the entire slavery system on the island.

At first, Ainslie offered a pardon in exchange for surrender—which meant a return of the maroons to their "owners," an untenable idea to people who had spent years if not decades out of bondage. Such was the mounting level of distrust that one maroon leader shot the slave who had been sent as a messenger.[40] The next bearers of an amnesty offer—a Kalinago soldier in the 4th West India Regiment and a white soldier named McFarlane—were also shot, and their hearts were torn out and placed on poles at the entrance of one of the maroon camps.[41] Ainslie got the message.

The governor's opening retaliation was a $1,000 bounty on the head of one of the leaders, Quashee (also Quashie). Not to be outdone, Quashee replied by offering $2,000 for the head of Ainslie.[42] Then, a hurricane pummeled the island on July 23, 1813, destroying most of the capital, Roseau. Just over a month later, on August 25, another storm barreled through, causing more floods and landslides, further damaging an already battered landscape.[43] Everyone was weakened by this double blow, especially the maroons. They would have to replant their crops and rebuild their defenses, all in the face of a rising threat. This was the ideal time for Ainslie to strike.

By February 1814 an expedition was underway, and Ainslie had declared martial law.[44] His strategy was to push the maroons further inland, to the most inhospitable parts of the island, where they would starve—or surrender. This was all the more effective in a hurricane-torn landscape. News of these events reached the abolitionists and the press in Britain, with *The Times* of London calling it a "most sanguinary warfare" by spring.[45] Ainslie was recalled to London to explain himself. However, because of the disruption to shipping caused by the war with the United States, he was stuck on the island until late November 1814, allowing him to witness the bloody finale.[46]

Jacko, the oldest chief, fell on July 12, after he was ambushed and shot by a slave ranger, John Le Villoux, who was later given his freedom for this action.[47] Others who were captured would face trial, often followed by flogging, deportation—or death. Trials ran through 1814, with some heard under courts-martial. Those took place in the Market House, which sat between the market square and the bay in the capital, rather than the courthouse, which had been destroyed by the earlier hurricanes.[48] The word "trial" is something of a misnomer for these hearings; there was no jury of peers, or even a lawyer for the accused. The guilt often already presumed.

Not only maroons were in the dock. Some enslaved people had used this moment to press for their own freedom. This was the case on the Hillsborough estate, where a series of events had left many of its slaves facing trial in 1814.[49] Hillsborough's owner lived in Britain, and the property was managed by an overseer. Its legal counsel was an attorney named William Bremner, a Scot who had come to the island as a doctor and who wrote about this period in an unpublished memoir.

The incident in Hillsborough began with the death of an enslaved man named Frank on the morning of January 5. Other slaves said he was flogged to death by the manager, and a group of 20 left the estate to walk to the capital, about eight miles away, and lodge a complaint with the governor. Upon hearing their grievance, Ainslie told them to get back to work. Bremner echoed the governor's words. He had not been on the estate at the time of Frank's death, later writing that Frank had been killed not by plantation violence but by an illness for which he was given "a dose of salts" the day before.

Frustrated and angry, the group left the capital and headed for the woods. The next morning, when Bremner arrived at Hillsborough, he discovered that they had not returned. He sent the slave driver and some others to warn the missing slaves that they should come back. The runaways appeared around seven that evening, with Bremner promising leniency in exchange for the name of the ringleader. Instead, Bremner later recalled, they told him "with great clamour, if I punished one I must punish all." He grabbed a woman named Sarah, whom he believed to be "at the bottom of the plot," and the rest fled once more. Two more joined them later that night.

Bremner now turned to the governor for help, and ordered an enslaved man named Peter, whom he called "one of the most shrewd slaves on the estate," to guide them to where the runaways were hiding. Bremner later wrote that since Peter's wife was one of the runaways, he believed Peter would know where they had gone. However, Bremner suspected that Peter was misleading them after they arrived at a spot with no one there. Peter "pretended the runaways must have decamped a short time before," and Bremner grew angry.

After two more days of searching, Peter finally confessed that he knew where the group was but would not tell until the murderous overseer was fired. After that, he replied to all further questions with the chilling answer "Your time is done now." Peter was sent into confinement, and soon after that, a runaway woman named Candau appeared and claimed that Peter had instigated the plot from the beginning.

Peter thus found himself on trial in January 1814, for the second time. He had been tried a few years earlier for setting the plantation's sugar works on fire but was acquitted for lack of evidence. He later admitted his guilt, according to Bremner, but was allowed to keep working on the plantation. This time, Peter protested his innocence, saying, "I left the runaways telling them the manager said they must come home. They said they would not until the manager left the estate." The judges believed him and decided that he should be employed as a guide to the maroon camps, but the governor dramatically overruled this, demanding that Peter be killed and his "head be cut off and put on a pike in the market place." It was, and his rotting corpse was taken to the plantation and put on display as a lesson. The same day, the runaways returned, presumably including Peter's widow.

But that was not the end for the slaves on the Hillsborough estate. The following week, Sarah, whom Bremner had suspected of being the ringleader, was put on trial, along with Dick, Hetty, Penny, Placet, and Daniel, all of whom were charged with having "absented themselves from their duty" after Frank's death.

Dick told the judges that they had left the estate because its manager had ignored Frank's complaint of being unwell and instead flogged him, forcing him back into the fields. The six defendants escaped death, but faced the horrific punishment of the lash the following morning. Dick and Daniel were to get 100, Sarah 50, and the others 50 lashes each.

When he finally reached London in the summer of 1815, Ainslie failed to convince his superiors of the necessity of such costly and brutal methods, and his next posting was to the chilly island of Cape Breton, Canada.[50] When the casualties of Ainslie's policies were tallied up, they included another 577 people. Eighteen maroons were killed in the forest, 188 were captured (68 of whom were children), and seven surrendered. Another 153 enslaved people were jailed or punished for various infractions but were not believed to be part of a maroon camp. More than 200 others surrendered on the spot and were sent back to their plantations.[51]

In justifying his violent tactics, Ainslie had earlier described the maroons as having been an "imperium in imperio," a state within a state, for more than 30 years. But some people in Great Britain did not see this as a reason to kill or capture the maroons. On the contrary, one article in *Scots Magazine* described the situation this way: "Scarcely a day passes that Maroon women and children, and runaway slaves, are not brought for trial and punishment. Many of the former declare they were born in the woods, and never saw a white man until the moment of their apprehension."⁵² And when they did, the only world some of them had known came to a swift, brutal end. By December 1814, the camps had been destroyed.

The blood of that year was never fully washed away. Today, a small but elaborate red-orange wrought iron canopy stands in the center of the old Market Square of Roseau. It once covered a drinking fountain, which was installed in 1872 to celebrate the arrival of piped water on the island, built on the site of an old well. But by this point the residents had long believed the well water to be contaminated. As a historical marker explains: "On one particular day [in 1814] there were so many executions that the well was never used again *'from the belief that it was defiled with the blood of these unfortunate people'*" (italics in original). Ainslie may have run off the maroons and their leaders, but their stories continued to circulate, forming the very lifeblood of the island.

Thousands of miles away from the violence on that small island, along the coast of the United States, the British were pursuing a very different policy during the War of 1812: The military was offering freedom to enslaved people, rather than re-enslaving the self-liberated, as they had done in the Caribbean. Tom and Celia and the others named in that report by the two justices in Montgomery County, Virginia, were correct. Not only would the British soon attack; they would disrupt slavery in the Chesapeake Bay, much as Lord Dunmore had done in Virginia in 1775 at the start of the American Revolution. Enslaved people were offering to work for the British as scouts, spies, messengers, guides, soldiers, and in other roles during the conflict, knowing that the British could grant them freedom.⁵³ Military activity did not arrive in the Chesapeake until 1813, as most of the earlier conflict had taken place along the US-Canadian border. Once it did arrive, regular reports cited runaways joining the British, as well as talk of insurrection and conspiracies. Some 400,000 people were enslaved around the Chesapeake in Maryland and Virginia during this period, a sizable population that, coupled with British firepower, was potentially lethal.⁵⁴

Rumors ricocheted in all directions. A possible insurrection in Gloucester, Virginia, was suppressed, with 10 arrested.⁵⁵ Another report claimed "upwards of one hundred negroes have effected their escape."⁵⁶ Canoes were particularly useful for slipping out to British ships. One letter writer fretted, "Not only every white person but almost every negro has a canoe. We have lost twenty-eight negro men lately."⁵⁷ Angry enslavers found themselves sailing out to British vessels, waving a flag of truce and demanding their "property" back, or financial compensation. In these cases, the British would let the enslavers speak to the runaways and try to convince them to return, always to no avail.⁵⁸ Now, in addition to watching for British attacks, enslavers had to keep an eye out for absconders and militias forced into night patrols with nervous and trigger-happy troops.⁵⁹

When the British landed on Kent Island in the bay, they found immediate recruits who "became pilots for them in plundering," as they also did in Lynnhaven Bay.⁶⁰ A letter from a US military officer to the governor of Virginia concluded: "I am confident that unless some vigorous measures are adopted and a sufficient force allowed us, this whole peninsula will be stripped of its most valuable personal property."⁶¹ Then the British vice admiral Alexander Cochrane upped the ante, issuing a proclamation on April 2, 1814, welcoming anyone "disposed to emigrate." They would "have their choice of either entering into His Majesty's Sea or Land Forces, or of being sent as FREE Settlers to the British Possessions in North America or the West Indies."⁶² What had started as a local response to the particular situation of the Chesapeake area was now official policy, coming at exactly the same time that Governor Ainslie was pursuing the maroons of Dominica, looking to strip them of their freedom.

The US now had to reconsider the policy of keeping black troops out of the federal militia; some states, including New York, had started to open their militias to black recruits, because they needed additional soldiers during the War of 1812. The Navy, too, had black sailors participating in battles at sea and on the Great Lakes.⁶³ But Cochrane's policy provided the British enough labor to build a fortified camp on Tangier Island, near the Potomac, as well as to create a black unit of some 200 now-free men, similar to Lord Dunmore's Ethiopian Regiment in 1775.⁶⁴ One report noted that the British were "training to make soldiers at the Camp on the [Tangier] Island seven hundred negroes; the negro women and children were sent to Bermuda and Halifax."⁶⁵ Battle reports had increasing appearances of black troops in "full uniform" who had taken the British up on their offer.

Some of them ended up in the advance unit involved with the burning of Washington, DC, and the White House, on August 24, an attack that saw enslaved people greeting them as they marched, asking to enlist in exchange for their freedom.[66] A short time later, in September 1814, the British fleet sailed out, taking its free black soldiers into uncertain waters.[67] By the end of the war, the British were left with somewhere between 3,000 and 5,000 freed people. Some 2,000 were abandoned to the cold of Halifax, Nova Scotia. Like the black loyalists 30 years before, they had been left with few resources and little more than a difficult struggle ahead.[68] Around 150 people were sent to Trinidad, including women and children, forming the basis of a community that would grow to around 800 free "refugees" from the US and members from disbanded black military units. They were given land, mostly in the south of the island, which they could farm. They formed six "company villages" and became known as the "Merikins."[69]

The war was technically over with the December 24, 1814, signing of the Treaty of Ghent, which restored US-British relations. However, news of the treaty travelled slowly back to the US. While the war with Britain was being waged further north, General Andrew Jackson was bringing another conflict, the ongoing war against the Creek people over the Mississippi territory, to an end with the Battle of Horseshoe Bend on March 27, 1814. He also had Florida—now back under Spanish control since 1783—in his sights, looking to drive the Spanish out. He knew that Spain relied in part on enslaved and freed people in Florida and former slaves from Georgia who had escaped to help with their defenses.[70]

Near the end of the War of 1812, the British, with black and Native American allies, built a rudimentary fortification in an area known as Prospect Bluff in 1814, on the Apalachicola River in Florida, about 15 miles inland from the Gulf of Mexico. It was intended to serve as a recruiting point on the Gulf, but with the end of the war a short time later, the British abandoned it, leaving a community of free black people—along with leftover ammunition. The fortification soon became known as "Negro Fort," and as word of its existence spread, it became a destination for freedom-seekers from as far away as Mississippi, Tennessee, and even Virginia, growing to around 500 to 700 people.[71] At its helm were three skilled carpenters: Garçon, who was referred to as a "French slave"; Cyrus; and Prince, possibly from Africa.[72] Under their leadership, military displays continued, housing was built, and corn was planted—but their future, like that of most maroons, was tenuous.

Andrew Jackson began moving east in late 1814, and on November 7 he launched a successful attack on Pensacola, seizing Spanish forts. The British were also there, using Fort Barrancas with Spanish permission. Before they retreated, the British blew up their powder so the fort would be unusable. At the same time, a British squadron was sailing into the Gulf of Mexico, preparing to attack and gain control of the Mississippi River. General Jackson then turned back, heading west to New Orleans, where he began to gather recruits, including free colored militias and enslaved people, to help fortify and defend the city.[73] Jackson mounted a victorious defense on January 8, 1815, some two weeks after the Treaty of Ghent had been signed. From there, Jackson strode onto the national stage as a war hero.

He still had unfinished business in Florida, both with the Spanish who controlled it and with the black and Native American people who inhabited it, especially those at Prospect Bluff. It was an ideal spot in many ways—set back enough to be hidden by forests, but near enough to the river for easy transportation. The contested borderlands of Florida were fertile ground for maroons to make allies and lay claim to freedom, taking advantage of the tumult of the 1810s and the willingness of Native Americans to help them.

By 1816 Jackson was writing to the Spanish governor to complain about the threat the fort at Prospect Bluff posed to Georgia, searching for a pretext to invade and bring all of Florida under US control. He threatened that if the fort's occupants were "not put down by the Spanish Authority," he would be compelled "in self Defence to destroy them."[74] Having heard, in June, a rumor that some of the inhabitants—whom he and others referred to as "banditti"—had left to go on raids for supplies, Jackson sent two ships up the Apalachicola River on July 27, 1816. Before the residents could mount a defense, one of the gunboats made a direct hit on an open magazine of gunpowder, which exploded and killed at least 200 people and left 70 more injured. The dream of Negro Fort lay in ashes.

That objective accomplished, Jackson's next task was to go after the Seminoles. Their name was a corruption of the Spanish *cimarrón*, or maroon, earlier applied to Lower Creek people in Florida, as well as other Native American people who had ended up there through war or displacement. This also included Afro-descended people enslaved by the Seminoles, given to them by the British earlier but occupying a gray area in terms of their status as "property." Now their community expanded to include the runaways who joined them, positioning themselves in a vassal-like relationship.[75]

The surviving maroons who fled Prospect Bluff headed for Seminole villages deep in Central Florida. Their pursuit by Jackson would become the first of three conflicts known as the Seminole Wars. Jackson—himself an enslaver—would prove a determined adversary, intent on driving the maroons out, along with the Spanish, and ready to bring Florida into the Southern slavery fold. In 1818 he led more than 2,000 troops toward maroon settlements around the Suwannee River, to the east of the now-destroyed Prospect Bluff, and deep into Seminole lands.[76] The attacks on the maroons put Seminole and Creek leadership in a difficult position, and they repeatedly claimed that they were not harboring any runaways.[77] The maroons found themselves on the move across Florida, trying to avoid further assault.

By 1819, Spain had capitulated to US pressure, and in 1821, the Adams-Onís Treaty was ratified, making Florida a territory of the United States. Its new governor was General Jackson, who continued his campaign against the Seminoles, looking to remove them completely. Some Seminoles decided to flee, using trade alliances with Cubans and Bahamians to escape to those islands. Others continued to fight.[78] Eventually, a treaty was brokered between US officials and Seminole and maroon leaders. The 1823 Treaty of Moultrie Creek established a Seminole reservation in central Florida, which included the maroons, but under the terms of the agreement, the US took the best of the Seminole lands.[79] It brought a temporary peace, but one as fragile as the maroons' freedom.

Chapter 26

Visions

NANNY GRIGG WAS certain that freedom was coming to Barbados. That's what they were saying in Britain—she had read it in the newspapers. Plus, as officials later heard, "her Master was very uneasy at it," which was all the more proof. Grigg spread the word to the other slaves on the Simmons estate: They would be free on New Year's Day, 1816. But January 1 came and went without emancipation. Grigg persisted and told the others "they were all damned fools to work."[1] Every night, Grigg and others across the plantations of Saint Philip Parish fell asleep with a restless anticipation. As the weeks wore on, it was becoming clear that enslaved people were going to have to make their own emancipation real. Grigg was clear, telling others that they needed to "set fire, as that was the way they did in Saint Domingo."[2]

What Grigg had interpreted as a portent of freedom, parliamentarians in London and planters in Barbados understood as the Imperial Registry Bill of 1815, which had been drafted in response to the confusion over a register for slaves in Trinidad a few years earlier. Planters were worried that the bill, which sought to prevent smuggling by registering slaves to a territory so they could not be moved, might pave the way for emancipation. Enslavers considered the bill an attempt by abolitionists in Parliament to intervene in the affairs of each island—hence the concerned looks that Grigg had noticed. In London, the bill was supported by William Wilberforce, whose name was well known throughout Barbados after the ending of the transatlantic slave trade in 1808. The legislation's reception among planters in Barbados was predictably hostile, and the island's House of Assembly rejected it. Other important news in 1815 that would have been in the papers was the signing of the Final Act of the Congress of Vienna, which brought peace to Europe following Napoleon's capture. Britain had put the abolition of the international slave trade by other European powers on its agenda, to their surprise and annoyance. France grudgingly acquiesced to banning its slave trade in 1815, as did Spain and Portugal in 1817, and the Dutch in 1818, but these agreements were only words—compliance would come much later.[3]

While Nanny Grigg and others believed the end of slavery might be in sight, the reality of its continuance caused mounting anger about that unfulfilled promise and tipped the island into its most serious insurrection in more than a century. The frustration was not sudden; the pressure had been building. Since the establishment of Haiti in 1804 and the British abolition of the slave trade, enslaved people in Barbados had been pushing ever harder against the system. More slaves were running away, others were refusing to work.

Captured freedom-seekers were forced to wait for their punishment in Bridgetown's infamous "Cage," a temporary prison of wire and wood that faced the bustling thoroughfare of Broad Street and the busy wharf. People passed it day and night, perhaps even speeding up their steps to avoid looking at the occupants or inhaling its notorious stench. Sailors, hucksters selling their wares, enslaved and free black people going about their business strode past while the captured awaited trial or return to an estate. The original occupants of the first Cage, built in the mid-1600s, had been badly behaved sailors, but "troublesome" slaves soon supplanted them.[4] Between 1811 and 1816, at least 200 enslaved runaways had been captured, with dozens crammed into the Cage at a time. They usually had their clothing taken away so that they could be identified by their various scars.[5]

Many of those absconding or charged with "insubordination" were so-called elite slaves, with important roles on the sugar plantations. While often in regular contact with planters or overseers by day, many of them made their own plans by night.[6]

The news of the Imperial Registry Bill, however it was interpreted, arrived on the island at an uneasy juncture, as rumors of a promised freedom were gaining momentum. An enslaved man named Daniel, at the River plantation, was stopped one evening in late March

1816 by a free man of color, Cain Davis, who "asked him if he had heard the good news." Daniel had not, so Davis told him that "the Negroes were all to be free—that the Queen and Mr. Wilberforce had sent out to have them all freed, but that the Inhabitants of the Island were against it."[7] Other versions of this story claimed the king had purchased them all, with the intention of setting them free, but the planters and authorities were hiding this news.[8] For his part, Davis said, he was willing to join the fight, especially because some of his children were still in bondage.[9]

By this point, the island's slave population was around 77,000, far surpassing the combined free population of less than 20,000, mostly white.[10] Many enslaved people lived in family-based "villages" within a plantation, and some also had provision grounds, growing crops such as corn, yams, and ginger. The extra food was sold by street hucksters, and the system allowed enslaved people to earn extra money and have some autonomy. It also provided mobility, and enslaved people could be in contact with each other without oversight as they went to market or worked on their patch of land. Slaves were also permitted to have dances on weekends and holidays, allowing more points of contact away from the eyes of white people.[11] Good Friday 1816 was such an occasion, and a dance at the River estate allowed Cain Davis, another free man named Sarjeant, an enslaved ranger from Bailey's estate named Bussa (also Busso or Bussoe), and a driver named Jackey from the Simmons estate to meet. While others danced, the music muffled the sound of their conversation. These men were in the final stages of making Nanny Grigg's prediction come true.[12]

Jackey was one of the key coordinators, and he and fellow conspirators managed to keep their plans quiet while eliciting the tacit support of others.[13] Bussa, whose name would later be used in association with the revolt, also emerged as a leader, though little is known about him except that he was African-born—something now rare on an island where more than 90 percent of the enslaved people were creole.[14] The Bailey estate had a number of participants later named by witnesses, including King Wiltshire, a carpenter; Dick Bailey, a mason; a man named Johnny, who was the standard-bearer; and a cooper named Johnny Cooper.[15]

The crack of a whip at around eight thirty on Easter Sunday night was the signal to start at the plantations of Bussa and Jackey in Saint Philip Parish in the southeast of the island. First, they would take guns and horses from the estates, then set fires. After that, they would turn the windmills toward the wind as a signal for others to begin.[16] Before long on that calm Easter night, the rustling of cane in the wind was replaced by a crackling sound, the sweet, grassy smoke spreading to some 70 estates, mostly in the island's southeast, though later there were reports of unrest in Saint Lucy, the island's northernmost parish.

Saint Philip was a long way from the capital, Bridgetown, buying the rebels some time. News of the unrest did not reach the city until the early hours of Easter Monday, by which point the rebellion was spreading as quickly as the winds could take the flames. The military response involved 600 regulars—which included black troops—and 250 militia, but they would not arrive in Saint Philip until that afternoon.[17]

A military detachment led by Col Edward Codd marched on Bailey's estate, including 150 members of the black 1st West India Regiment, whom the rebels greeted with "three cheers," believing the soldiers would join their struggle. As one witness later explained, "the insurgents did not think our men would fight against black men." But they did—though the soldiers' thoughts and feelings about it remain unrecorded. Two of the regiment's soldiers died in the subsequent fighting.[18]

Also during this battle, a soldier took an extraordinary flag, perhaps borne by Johnny, the standard-bearer.[19] Surviving sketches of that flag show images that would have confused the officials who found it, like the *libro de pinturas* discovered among the possessions of José Antonio Aponte in Cuba a few years prior. Three main images adorn the flag. On the left is a red-coated British soldier. Toward the center is a black man dressed like a wealthy gentleman in a hat and blue frock coat, and below him a black man in similar attire with his arm around a black woman in a flowing white dress. On the right side, a white woman sits on a lion, presumably Britannia, the warrior symbol of Britain. Also depicted are ships, guns, axes, and a crown. There is writing, too, including the slogan HAPPINESS FOR EVER REMAINS WITH ENDAVOURANCE [sic] under the black couple, ENDAVOURANCE FOR

EVER under the dapper man, and in larger writing at the bottom, GOD ALWAYS SAVES ENDAVOURANCE. The warship and the crown are obvious nods to the power of George III, a visual evocation of the belief that the king would free them or indeed already had.[20] It is an arresting image, not one that evokes Haiti or the destruction of whites on the island, but rather one that places free black loyal subjects at the heart of Britain's vast imperial world, between Britannia in the left corner and warships sailing off the right-hand side.

Such a vision was not shared by the white colonists, and the military put the rebellion down on April 16, killing at least 50 enslaved fighters in battle—including Bussa—and summarily executing 70 others. Another 300 people were rounded up for trial. The troops also began to destroy slave quarters, attempting to drive any remaining rebels out of hiding and take what authorities claimed had been looted.[21] A few days later, however, an amnesty was offered to any rebels who had not been captured or who returned to their plantations within the next five days.[22] The 300 facing trial received no such reprieve. Their trials dragged on as the clouds swelled, the dry months giving way to the rainy season. At the end of the first round, 111 enslaved people and three of the four captured free people of color were sentenced to find their freedom at the end of a gallows. Another 124 fighters were deported to British Honduras to join the Black Caribs from Saint Vincent.[23]

Colonel Edward Codd, who led the retaliation against the rebels, wrote to the governor a few weeks later. After making "many enquires," he came to this conclusion: "The chief cause to which this unfortunate calamity is to be attributed is the general opinion, which has pervaded the minds of those misguided people, since the proposed Introduction of the Registry Bill, that their Emancipation was devised by the British Parliament and this idea seems to have been conveyed by mischievous persons."[24]

The Barbados Assembly appointed a select committee to investigate, which came to a similar conclusion. However, in nearly every examination, they asked enslaved people and free witnesses if the slaves had been mistreated, and received only answers in the negative. Some planters used their examination to explain just how well their slaves lived—as if a daily ration of salt-fish and Sundays off could substitute for full liberty. Codd had earlier asked some of the captives similar questions, noting in his later report, "They maintained however to me, that the Island belonged to them, and not to the white man, whom they proposed to destroy."[25]

The rebellion was over, and the mood was low. One letter from June 1816 noted, "The disposition of the slaves in general is very bad; they are sullen and sulky and seem to cherish feelings of deep revenge. We hold the West Indies by a very precarious tenure, that of military strength."[26] Even with that power, the resistance continued. The *Barbados Gazette* was peppered with ads and notices to this effect. As 1816 drew to a close, one article provided a *"LIST of NEGROES in the CAGE"* as of December 28: Robert Rowlston, Abraham, Fanny Ann, Jenny, Betty Grace, Aubah, Nelson, Nanny Barnes, George, Sarah, Charles, Sharper.[27] All of them had been punished for various infractions. A few weeks earlier, an advertisement offered a reward of five pounds for the capture of

> Molly, a mulatto woman, about 5 feet 9 inches high, 48 years old, supposed to be harboured by Sam, at Mount Poyer . . . Philly, a yellow-skin woman, 5 feet 9 inches high, about 21 years old, square shoulders, a little bow-legged; supposed to be harboured by her husband Joe Lewis, who says she shall not come home, and . . . Jessy, a yellow-skin Man, 5 feet 10 or 11 inches high, 22 years old, square shouldered, bow-legged, and surly down look . . . The man Jessy may wish to pass himself as free.[28]

Others, like Jessy, would have had to pass themselves off as free for a while yet. But the struggle of Bussa, Nanny Grigg, and their fellow rebels had not been in vain. The year 1816 was a turning point in Barbados as well as in London, as the news of the rebellion and its suppression reached Parliament and abolitionist ears. Those forced to continue under slavery counted on their "endavourance" to make it to the end, however long it took.

⋘ • ⋙

THE REVOLT IN Barbados took place at a time of intense political debate in Britain. The abolition of the slave trade continued to maintain public interest—popular abolitionist pressure in the form of 1,370 petitions containing hundreds of thousands of signatures forced British politicians to insist on the issue of the slave trade being included in the Congress of Vienna and resulting Treaty of Paris.[29] But the Napoleonic Wars had been costly, and Britain now faced financial chaos and growing public hostility toward Parliament. Significant moments of rioting and violence occurred in these years, including a mass meeting held at Spa Fields, in Islington, London, on December 2, 1816. An earlier meeting on November 15 ended peacefully, but the Prince Regent refused to receive the resulting petition calling for parliamentary reform, and so a second meeting was organized—this time with the aim of igniting a mass uprising, if not a revolution. The Spa Fields riot didn't go quite that far, but it caused plenty of damage, with shots exchanged, windows broken, and people descending on Newgate Prison and the Tower of London. The fracas was eventually subdued, but it only further stoked public desire for change.

The organizers of the Spa Fields meetings were "Spenceans," followers of Thomas Spence, a bookseller and political radical with a vision of expansive land reform in Britain. Spence wanted the fair distribution and common ownership of land, believing that as long as land was held as private property, inequality and injustice would continue to flourish. Inevitably, the government spied upon and sometimes imprisoned him and his followers—including a Jamaica-born man named Robert Wedderburn.

Wedderburn was born in Westmoreland Parish in 1762, the year after Jamaica was rocked by Tacky's Revolt. He was the son of James Wedderburn, a wealthy, successful sugar planter from whom, Robert later wrote, he "received no benefit in the world."[30] His mother, Rosanna, was enslaved by James and endured multiple pregnancies before being sold. However, she managed to negotiate Robert's freedom, and his manumission paperwork was completed around the time he was two.[31] "To the present hour," he wrote in a later account of his life, *The Horrors of Slavery*, "while I think of the treatment of my mother, my blood boils in my veins."[32] It continued to boil throughout his life. His Jamaican childhood was marred by scenes of brutality and violence. On one occasion, he saw his mother "stretched on the ground, tied hands and feet, and flogged in the most indecent manner, though pregnant at the same time."[33]

Wedderburn was raised mostly by his grandmother, a woman called "Talkee Amy," although she too remained enslaved. She was well-known in Kingston, and worked the docks selling "cheese, checks, chintz, milk, gingerbread, &c" for her enslaver, as well as being a trusted smuggler.[34] However, even she was stalked by the lash. At around the age of 70, Robert's "poor old grandmother was flogged for a witch by her master," who blamed her for laying an obeah spell on the family's disastrous trading voyage and for "having bewitched the vessel."[35]

Around 1778, at age 16, Robert Wedderburn joined the Royal Navy, and later settled in London, married, and started a family, eking out a precarious living as a journeyman tailor. He started moving in radical working-class political circles, where he met Spence. Wedderburn then joined other acolytes in the Society of Spencean Philanthropists, entering the lively world of preaching as a Unitarian minister and pamphleteering during the chaotic and exhilarating years of the late Georgian era in London. However interested he was in the plight of the working poor in Britain—among whom he counted himself—he was never far from his West Indian roots. Inspired by Spence, Wedderburn articulated his own transatlantic vision, connecting the worlds of inequality and poverty, both of which he inhabited.

In October 1817, then 55, Wedderburn published a short-lived newspaper called *The Axe Laid to the Root, or a Fatal Blow to the Oppressors, Being an Address to the Planters and Negroes of the Island of Jamaica*. It only ran to six issues, but in them Wedderburn attempted to speak to both enslaved and enslaver. In the first edition, he exhorted the enslaved: "Convince the world you are rational beings, follow not the example of St Domingo." Yet, a few pages later, he warned the enslavers, "Prepare for flight, ye planters, for the fate of St Domingo awaits you."[36] Such mirror images held one shared object in their reflection: land. Rational beings would use the land to survive, to create a just world, while the merchants of misery would lose the very soil that had yielded so many bitter riches.

Land being central to Wedderburn's vision, he wrote that the slaves had to focus on keeping it, even when they were free: "Without that, freedom is not worth possessing; for if you once give up the possession of your lands, your oppressors will have the power to starve you to death."[37] As a small child raised by enslaved women, in a world of plantations, Wedderburn would have known that the provision grounds in Jamaica were one of the few places where slaves could exist with autonomy. As was the case in Barbados, enslaved people in Jamaica used these parcels of land, often where nothing more valuable could grow, to plant extra food like yams and cassava to eat or sell, providing necessary nourishment in difficult times and much-needed money at others. It was a breathing space, away from the plantation, a connection to the existence of other lives, other possibilities. Wedderburn's attraction to Spence's reforms made sense: Spenceans had subsistence agriculture at the heart of their plan for Britain.[38] Land would be held in common, with limits on what a person could individually accumulate, rooting out the evils of private property.[39]

Land reform also had a biblical dimension for Wedderburn, a Unitarian minister, as it had for Spence, and they drew from Old Testament ideas in Leviticus 25:10, where God commands Moses: "And you shall consecrate the fiftieth year, and proclaim liberty throughout all the land to all its inhabitants. It shall be a Jubilee for you; and each of you shall return to his possession, and each of you shall return to his family."[40]

A jubilee was meant to restore land to its original owners and cancel any debts. Slaves and any bonded servants would also be freed. The jubilee was also meant to be a fallow year for the land, as well as a year of no work for the people.[41] Through such jubilees, the use of land could be radically transformed, leading to justice, self-sufficiency, and freedom—in Britain and in the West Indies.

The Jamaican influence on Wedderburn's political thinking came to the fore in *The Axe Laid to the Root*—as when he declared, "I am a West-Indian, a lover of liberty."[42] He expressed his ideas about land and liberty in a series of letters, published in the newspaper, between himself and Elizabeth Campbell, a Jamaican landowner and enslaver, who Wedderburn hints was both of Windward maroon origin and possibly his half-sister. She was also a convert to Spencean thought, causing some historians to argue that Campbell was Wedderburn's creation, or that he based her on a real person but used the imagined correspondence as a rhetorical device.⁴³ In an earlier round of letters, Campbell discussed the manumission of Wedderburn's mother and brother, who had been bought by her family, as well as the freeing of her other slaves. Wedderburn wrote in issue number 4 of *The Axe* that he had been "struck with wonder and astonishment, when John, our brother, described to me your manner and action when you went to your drawer and took the record and presented it to him, saying, here, John, take your freedom."⁴⁴ Campbell also wrote about ceding her land, thus giving form to Wedderburn's transatlantic visions, bringing together the maroons, freedom, and land.

Jamaica's maroons were of particular interest to him, though he had to sidestep the nature of their treaties with the British and their relationship to enslaved people, especially their role as slave catchers. He also had to overlook their intermittent raids on plantations for supplies and their participation in the contraband economy. Rather, he fell under the sway of a near-utopian ideal, of being free in body and rid of the poisons of private property. Through *The Axe* he was able to bring their world, as he understood it, to a wider public, most of whom would have little idea about places like Accompong. The horrors of slavery were well-known to the British public; but the possibility that the West Indies could provide a way toward a fairer future for British and Caribbean people alike was new and radical.

In early 1818, Wedderburn set up a chapel on Archer Street, in Soho, London, and completed his Unitarian ordination. This may have, in a roundabout way, allowed him to put Spencean meetings under the protection afforded to religious dissenters.⁴⁵ The government, anxious during a time of so much social unrest, had long been sending spies to his services. The following year, in the aftermath of a hostile split with other Spenceans, Wedderburn set up a new chapel, in Hopkins Street, also in Soho.⁴⁶ He and others debated the matters of the day, often coming close to the flames of sedition or blasphemy. A spy reported that at a meeting on the night of August 9, 1819, the questions at hand were "Can it be murder to kill a tyrant?" and "Has a slave an inherent right to slay his master, who refuses him liberty?" The whole room answered the second question in the affirmative, to which Wedderburn replied, "Well Gentlemen I can now write home and tell the Slaves to murder their Masters as soon as they please."⁴⁷

Wedderburn may have been thinking about Jamaica, Barbados, or even Saint-Domingue, but as he and the others in the heated debate that August night would find out, Demerara would be the next battlefield.

⋘ • ⋙

From the air, the endless forests that stretch away from the northern coast of South America have an ocean-like appearance. However, this vast, dense area on the ground proved difficult and deadly for those who tried to settle in the interior throughout the eighteenth century. Rather than go deep and work their way out, the Dutch, British, and French stuck to the coast, usually along the thin strip of land between the wide rivers that run into the brown waters of the Atlantic. Here they planted their sugarcane—hugging close to the shore and utilizing parts of the waterways creating two known as Demerara and Essequibo, both part of today's nation of Guyana. Formerly a Dutch territory, the colony of Demerara was planted along the Atlantic, and its development followed the river of the same name inland, leaving a trail of plantations alongside the waterway's rich soil. Similarly, Essequibo shared its name with the mighty river that fed its plantations, many of them huddled on the sizable inlet islands.

Like Wedderburn's Jamaica, Demerara-Essequibo, under British control since 1803 and unified in 1812, would have been familiar to the highest echelons of British society, as would the wealth produced on its plantations. John Gladstone, father of William, who became prime minister in 1868, owned a plantation called Success and was an enslaver on a vast scale, with 1,300 slaves in Demerara alone, making a fortune in cotton and sugar.[48] And in Demerara, on his plantation, another deadly revolt erupted in 1823.

Because the colony's growth had come later than that of places like Jamaica or Barbados, about half of its 77,000 enslaved people in 1823 were African-born, living with 3,500 whites and 2,500 free people of color.[49] Two other populations shared the land: the indigenous people, who lived deep in the hinterland, and the maroon colonies that dated back to the earliest attempts to establish plantations in this part of South America.

John Smith, a white Englishman, arrived in Demerara in 1817 on behalf of the London Missionary Society, which had been sending clergy since 1808.[50] Baptism, marriage, and church attendance of slaves had been permitted mostly in Catholic Spanish and Portuguese America, but since the end of the slave trade, nonconformist English denominations had been having some success in gaining permission to go to the British West Indies, though under the wary and increasingly irritated watch of planters and officials. They felt these naive interlopers understood nothing about their world, and were carrying with them potentially incendiary messages of salvation.[51] In addition, the missionaries were teaching slaves to read and write, and the enslavers knew that might be the next step toward the slaves' freedom and their own oblivion.

Such was the tense atmosphere of Demerara around the time of Smith's arrival. Long-running friction had existed between the missionaries and officials over the question of working on Sundays, as many enslaved people often did, sometimes as paid labor. This was increasingly important at a time of economic stress, which Demerara was experiencing. The Sabbath for many was no longer a day of rest or even a day to tend to provision grounds, and this would become a heated issue between the missionaries and officials. However, some people still guarded their Sundays and attended church services.[52]

In May 1823, an old order from 1811 was recirculated, presumably this time for enforcement, stating that slaves could be denied passes to leave plantations to attend Sunday worship, and that they should not be allowed to simply leave without permission. In addition, it recommended that an overseer or other white person attend church as well, to hear what was being preached. It caused a ripple of confusion and uncertainty at the time, but within a few weeks enslaved people were attending services as they previously had.[53]

Only a few months earlier, in March, Parliament had debated legislation to ameliorate conditions for enslaved people and possibly enact policies that would lead to gradual emancipation. This, perhaps inevitably, turned into a rumor that the slaves had been freed.[54] One enslaved man, Jack Gladstone, spent weeks trying to find out if this was true. Jack was a cooper on the Success plantation. He was around 30 years old, and a striking man, described as being over six feet tall, handsome,

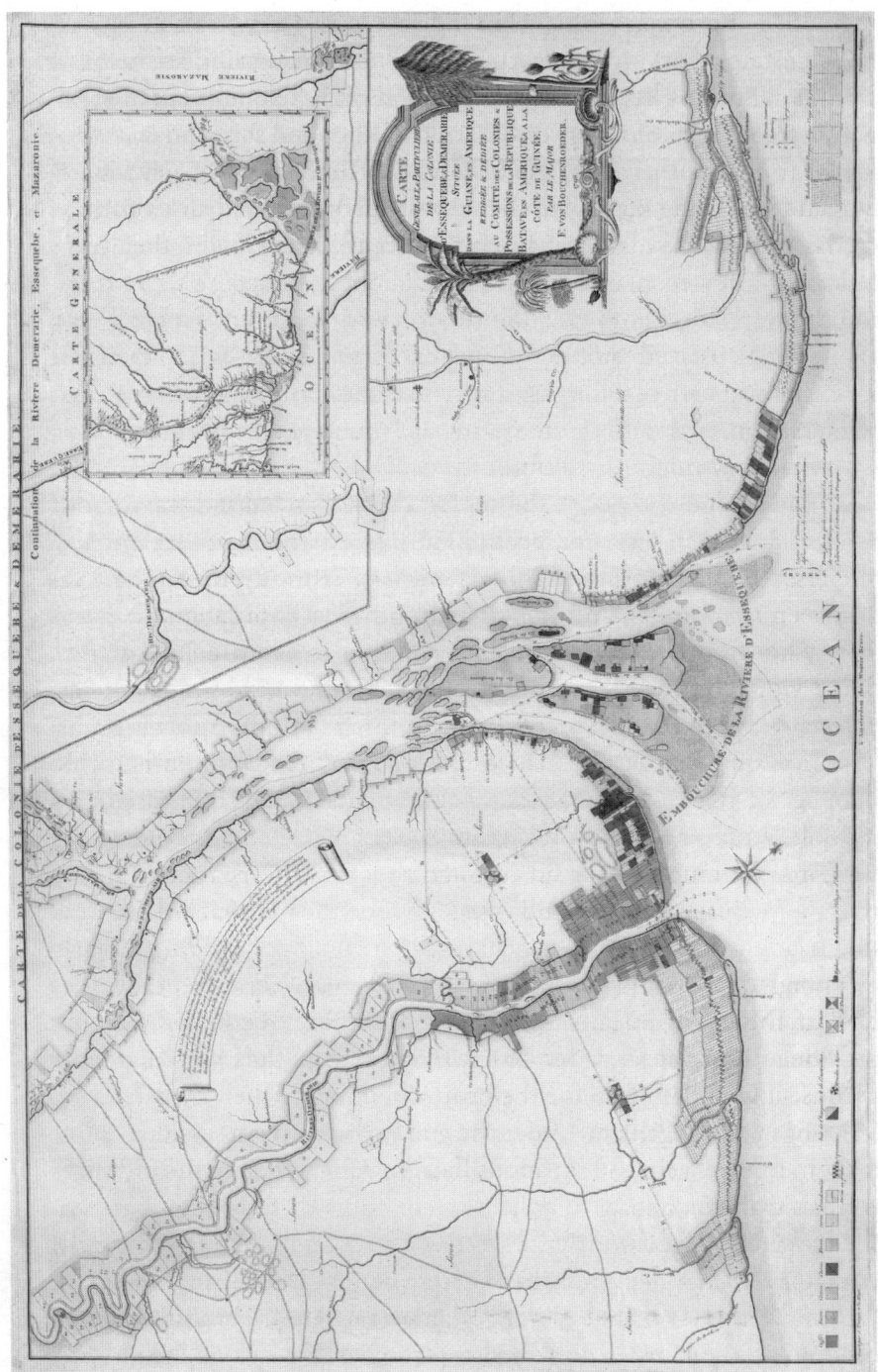

A Dutch map of the colony of Essequibo and Demerara by Friedrich von Bouchenroeder, published in Amsterdam in 1795.

and with a "European nose."[55] His father, Quamina, was also enslaved on the estate, working as a carpenter, while also serving as the head deacon at Smith's Bethel Chapel on the Le Resouvenir plantation.[56]

The freedom rumor was discussed by father and son, and Jack continued to press others for details, trying to find out what news from England was being kept from them. More people joined Jack's conversation, using Sunday chapel as a safe place to discuss what they were hearing.[57] They even asked John Smith about it, but he told them the rumors were false. However, Smith took what Quamina had told him about what enslaved people were saying seriously enough to mention it to the overseer of Success. The white community began its own conversation, trying to figure out what the slaves thought they knew, and what they might do about it.[58]

By early August, Jack had the confirmation he needed. It came from Susana, a woman Jack had been involved with but who became the mistress of John Hamilton, the overseer of Le Resouvenir.[59] Hamilton had been fired and, as he was preparing to leave, Susana asked him to buy her freedom and that of her children. He refused, telling her that it would be a waste of money because they would soon be free.[60] Susana relayed this to Jack soon after, during a Sunday morning conversation outside Bethel Chapel. She added that Hamilton had told her "he did not think [freedom] would be given to us, unless all the sensible people went by force about it."[61]

Word continued to spread through the plantations along the east coast, an area along the Atlantic shore beyond the main city of Georgetown. Jack and some others started to figure out how this might work, by taking up arms and herding white people together to get the attention of the governor and finally demand their freedom. Quamina cautioned that they needed to make sure no whites were harmed, because it would undermine their cause and lead to their own deaths.[62] Meetings were organized under the guise of catechism sessions. More talk emerged: Caches of weapons had been located, and the maroons were said to be coming to help.[63]

Finally, on August 17, 1823, a Sunday afternoon, Jack and others finished their plans, but even at this juncture there was disagreement about the timing. Some wanted to wait; others wanted to try bargaining. One brought up the fate of the slaves in Barbados. But Jack and the others were firm. They would fire guns as a signal the next night, and then go for the plantation managers and stick them in the stocks and take their weapons.[64] Later that night, Quamina tried to convince Jack to delay and, when he refused, tried to send word to people not to rise up on Monday night, but it was too late—and too many people knew.[65]

Early the next day, an enslaved man named Joe told the owner of the Le Reduit plantation that there was going to be an uprising. The enslaver spread an alert through nearby plantations on his way to see Governor John Murray. The governor, too, gave rushed orders and by that afternoon Jack and Quamina were arrested. As they were being taken to Georgetown, a group of slaves ambushed the arresting party and freed the prisoners. Rather than run into the bush, Jack, Quamina, and the band of rescuers escorted the overseers back to Success. Once there, the overseers and others were locked up in the house, and ammunition was secured. The revolt had begun.[66]

On a post-dinner walk, Smith and his wife heard cries for help from the manager at Le Resouvenir. The peacefulness of their usual evening stroll was shattered by a group of some 50 slaves waving cutlasses and calling for "our rights."[67] Governor Murray, too, had an eventful Monday night: On his way back from a meeting with planters, about 40 rebels blocked his way on a bridge. Upon seeing Murray, they cried out, "We have them!" Murray asked them what they wanted, and they answered, "Our rights."[68] He attempted to explain that what they had understood as a declaration of their freedom was actually a set of instructions for their better treatment. They told Murray that they were fed up, and that they knew the king had freed them. The governor tried to get the group, which had swelled to around 200 during this exchange, to put down their arms and negotiate, but they refused. Murray and his party decided to flee the scene before it turned violent.[69] Once safely in Georgetown, he organized the militia. Although he had about 1,000 men, including Amerindian allies, assembled on land and sea, he knew that if the maroons showed up or if the revolt spread west into Essequibo, the uprising might be impossible to put down.[70]

The rebels' plan appeared to be working—freedom-seekers raided plantations and put overseers in the hated stocks that so many slaves had endured as punishment. They grabbed their overseers' guns, and those who didn't have one used swords, knives, or anything they could lay their hands on. As in so many revolts that had come before this one, the rage built up over years erupted, and the rebels attacked the plantations. New recruits joined, some unaware of the plans until the moment the rebels descended on their estates. In this way, within a short time thousands were in revolt, with the potential to raise another 12,000 in the area along the east coast alone.[71]

The militia and regular troops went on the attack, and the governor declared martial law. However, they remained outnumbered. Arriving at the plantation Bachelor's Adventure, a group of soldiers found themselves surrounded by what one officer estimated to be 4,000 enslaved fighters, holding whatever weapons they had to hand, including muskets. The officers decided to call a truce on the spot, and negotiate with the rebel leaders, including Jack Gladstone, who was there. The officers tried to order the rebels back to their plantations, using the martial law proclamation, but Jack and the others refused. A battle began that would leave around 200 rebels dead.[72]

The governor needed to stop the revolt from intensifying and spreading, so he issued another proclamation, threatening to cancel any proposed amelioration measures—including a ban on flogging women—that the government had been considering if the rebellion didn't stop. He followed this with another, saying the rebels would be pardoned if they put down their weapons and went back to their plantations. Some began to take up his offer, fearful of the consequences of the rebellion failing. This helped to fracture the unity of the rebels, and ultimately allowed the military to restore "order" to the colony after a few weeks.[73] More deaths would come through summary trials and the resulting executions. And this time a white man would be in the dock: John Smith. Even before the revolt had been suppressed, officials and planters were laying blame at the missionary's door.

Quamina and Jack managed to stay at large for a few days, with Jack ultimately captured on September 6. Shortly after that, Quamina was found. He had earlier told another slave that no white man was going to take him alive, and indeed he was killed by the arrow of an indigenous tracker. But his body was taken to Success and put on a gibbet for all to see.[74]

The trials continued, and officials heard differing testimony. Some witnesses spoke of plans to burn down the colony, kill all the whites, and make Quamina their king.[75] Others claimed that the missionaries had told the slaves that they were free, and that they were going to march along the east coast and burn the plantations down, as well as the capital, Georgetown. The flames would be a signal for the enslaved people in neighboring Essequibo to join them.[76]

The timing, as it was related by people under interrogation, was also unclear. Some witnesses said the rebellion was in response to the recent news from Britain regarding Parliament's debate earlier that year over better conditions for the enslaved, which some believed might bring emancipation, while others claimed the planning had been going on for more than a year. Indeed, there had been rumors—and arrests—around an alleged conspiracy in December 1820.[77] This was followed by a spate of fires in 1822 in buildings in the capital and at two plantations, suggesting that officials may have willfully ignored the signs of what was to come.[78]

In the end, 72 enslaved people were tried and 51 executed, with three acquittals. Of those killed, 10 were decapitated and had their heads stuck on poles. Those who were not executed were flogged. More than 225 slaves had been killed or wounded in the fighting.[79]

Jack, however, managed to avoid the fate of his father, though he did endure a long interrogation. He explained that he and Quamina had heard "of our freedom being come out," and this had been confirmed by others. They continued to find out more, but it had become evident that they would have to take action, though in his testimony he denied having a gun and told officials, "We were desirous that no injury should be done to any of the whites."[80]

He added that John Smith had known about the plan, that Quamina had gone to see him and he had said, "Now that we had begun, we must go on with it." However, in Jack's telling, Smith wanted the slaves to postpone the rebellion. By the end of his testimony, he laid the blame on Smith, saying, "Had there been no Methodists on the East Coast, there would have been no revolt."[81] Whatever Jack may have felt about Smith, this was clearly a tactic to shift the burden of guilt and perhaps avoid the gibbet, which he did. Murray had not wanted to make a martyr of him with an execution, and so Jack was banished to Saint Lucia.[82]

Jack was not the only one whose testimony involved Smith: His name came up repeatedly, though with many others claiming the missionary had no knowledge of the plot.[83] It was finally Smith's turn to go to trial, under court-martial, on October 13, 1823. After nearly a month of testimony, Smith was found guilty of complicity, although not of inciting rebellion. He was inevitably going to be found guilty of something, with the animus of the entire white population against him. Not willing to accept that enslaved people needed no instigation to rise up, officials and planters blamed Smith. The verdict was enough for a death sentence. Although he was granted a reprieve, the news of it arrived too late, and he died in prison, suffering from "pulmonary consumption," on February 6, 1824.[84]

The uprising in Demerara was a critical battle in the war to end slavery. The news was met by a metropolitan uproar in London.[85] The public reaction was one of increasing horror, and now a white, Christian missionary had been sacrificed in the struggle over slavery. The events in Demerara brought a surge of momentum to the abolitionist movement, including the London Anti-Slavery Society, which Thomas Clarkson had set up in 1823.[86] At the same time, many abolitionists were beginning to reckon with the fact that while they were debating the merits of gradual or immediate abolition, it was becoming quite clear that enslaved people in the British colonies were not the passive victims they often had been presented as. They were moving closer to seizing freedom with their own hands. The white English abolitionist Elizabeth Heyrick understood this, chiding the movement's leadership in her 1824 pamphlet *Immediate, Not Gradual Abolition*. She observed, "It is no marvel that *slave holders* should cry out against immediate emancipation . . . 'Insurrection of all the blacks—massacre of all the whites,' are the bugbears which have been constantly conjured up to deter the British Parliament from all interference between the master and his slave." That was to be expected. But she decried the fact "that the *abolitionists* should have caught the infection;—should be panic struck . . . that they . . . should swallow the bait, so manifestly laid to draw them aside from their great object; that they should be so credulous." To Heyrick, writing this in the context of the Demerara revolt, there was a clear answer: immediate abolition. As proof for her argument, she brought up Haiti, saying, "The conduct of the emancipated slaves for thirty years subsequent to that event . . . is a complete refutation of all the elaborate arguments which have been artfully advanced to discredit the design of *immediate* emancipation."[87] The pamphlet caused a stir, and the overall momentum of the events and debates of 1824 carried into the 1826 election, with parliamentary candidates forced to make their positions on abolition clear.

Before the revolt in Demerara erupted, Robert Wedderburn had been facing a crisis of his own. It didn't take long for officials to build up a dossier that they could use to charge him with sedition and blasphemy. Wedderburn was arrested in November 1819, only a few months after the Peterloo Massacre, during which cavalry charged on 60,000 peaceful protesters amassed in Manchester, injuring hundreds and killing at least 18, leaving the public horrified and the government jittery. It was a particularly bad moment to be in his position. By February the following year, he was convicted of blasphemous libel and sentenced to a jail term, which he began in May 1820.[88]

While he was imprisoned, Wilberforce came to see him, encouraging him to continue contributing to the abolitionist fight. The result was *The Horrors of Slavery*.[89] The book was published in 1824, when attention had returned to the question of abolition in the aftermath of Demerara. Wedderburn dedicated it to Wilberforce, writing, "When in prison, for conscience-sake, at Dorchester, you visited me, and you gave me—your advice, for which I am still your debtor."[90] The work is a mixture of autobiography and an attack on planters, including his father. It also features the reprinting of a war of words from the weekly *Bell's Life in London* between Wedderburn and his paternal half-brother, Andrew Colvile, who denied all his claims.

The years after the book's publication were difficult for Wedderburn. He no longer occupied a central place in radical politics, and he was further reduced to the difficult margins of London life, becoming associated with a couple of printers who also dabbled in pornography. In 1830, he returned to prison for 12 months on charges of keeping a "disorderly" house, most likely meaning a brothel.[91] During this incarceration he put pen to paper once more. Only a few years earlier, in *The Horrors of Slavery*, he had written that he was proud of his outspoken nature, a familial inheritance from his mother, Rosanna: "I glory in her rebellious disposition, and which I have inherited from her."[92] But by the time this final tract was published, his disposition seems to have dissipated; or perhaps it was a final pragmatic gasp.[93]

His *Address to Lord Brougham and Vaux* (1831) came at a time when Britain was on the brink of enacting gradual abolition, and once again parliamentary and public attention were turned to these debates, as well as other wider social ones. Henry Brougham, the addressee, was appointed Lord Chancellor in January 1831, and he was seen as a reformer on the question of abolition and colonial policy. However, in the aftermath of Demerara, even he understood that something significant had shifted, and he was involved in the founding with Clarkson, of the London Anti-Slavery Society, whose original name was the Society for the Mitigation and Gradual Abolition of Slavery Throughout the British Dominions.[94] So perhaps Wedderburn, in his own way, was appealing to Brougham's gradualism. Wedderburn's creativity and intellectual dexterity remain present in the *Address*, but he also shows a willingness to compromise on how to build the road to freedom.

He starts with a brief introduction of his life, before moving on to slavery, saying—in a surprising turn—that "the conditions of the slaves were far superior to European labourers," and telling Brougham that "in a state of slavery, there is no seizing for rent or taxes, no casting into prison for debt, no starving families obligated to destroy themselves, or their offspring for want of provisions." Not that Wedderburn was romanticizing slavery—he was most likely trying to appeal to his reader by signaling his understanding of this particular line of argument. Given that he was writing from prison, it's possible he was also reflecting on the often-painful trajectory of his own life, and that of the working poor. He mentioned poverty in Britain throughout the letter, calling more than once for charity to begin at home and not on the plantations of the West Indies.[95] He likely didn't trust an abolitionist movement that had not signed on to the Spencean precepts of common land, and wanted to somehow ensure that freed people would not be prey to the cruel ravages of the marketplace, as he himself had been.[96]

Instead of a dramatic second "St Domingo," Wedderburn's vision of emancipation blurred, creating a world where enslaved people found their freedom gradually, but were also given rights. In such a state, a slave could "demand his release" when he could afford to buy his freedom, or have the right to "choose another owner." Enslaved people would also be able to give evidence, sit as jurors, and have an extra day of rest in addition to the Sabbath.

However, land, even in this version, remained central. The way for enslaved people to pay for their freedom, in his plan, was through saving money, rearing livestock, and growing crops that could be sold, which would mean "a man and his wife would be enabled to purchase their own children." Again, the provision grounds of his youth returned. He told Brougham that on these plots slaves could grow corn, yams, coffee, ginger, pimento, and even sugar and cotton, and that it would be all theirs to live off and sell.

Wedderburn wrote the *Address* only a few years before his death, in the winter of 1834–1835. Although he died in London, the Jamaica of his youth was always present in his mind. He was never able to quit his self-imposed exile, as he wrote in *The Horrors of Slavery*: "I should have gone back to Jamaica, had I not been fearful of the planters; for such is their hatred of any one having black blood in his veins and who dares to think and act as a free man, that they would most certainly have trumped up some charge against me, and hung me."[97] But London was relentless in its challenges. He lost the support of other radicals, his earlier Spencean dream fallen by the wayside of public opinion, and was left to live out his final years in obscurity and poverty. The land, however, remained his endpoint. The potential of those provision grounds never left him, the knowledge of the maroons buried deep within. There was never any going back to Jamaica, but he never stopped carrying the island inside himself, the vision of freedom sustaining him.

Chapter 27

Decisions

THE JUDGES WERE perplexed, writing in their sentence for Denmark Vesey, "It is difficult to imagine what *infatuation* could have prompted you to attempt an enterprize so wild and visionary. You were a free man; were comparatively wealthy . . . You had, therefore, much to risk, and little to gain. From your age and experience, you *ought* to have known, that success was impracticable."[1]

Denmark Vesey knew all of this. He also knew how difficult it was to be a free black man in a city at the epicenter of the slaveholding South. He knew what it was like to win his freedom but see his children continue to bear the burden of their enslavement.[2] He knew what it was like to see slaves coming into the port and being sold at the market as he went about his daily life. He had lived in this liminal world, with one hand on freedom and the other reaching out to those in bondage. Now, with this sentence of death in 1822, his 22 years of freedom were at an end.

Captain Joseph Vesey first bought Denmark in 1781. He was born around 1767, possibly on the island of Saint Thomas, then a Danish colony. If he was born in Africa, it may have been on the Gold Coast—he was later described as "Coromantee"—where Danish slave ships trawled for human cargo before sailing to the Caribbean. Denmark was initially called Telemaque—enslavers like Captain Vesey were fond of bestowing classical names on their captives, an allusion to ancient Greece and a taunting reminder of their low status. The original Telemaque, or Telemachus, comes from Homer's *Odyssey*, the son of Odysseus and Penelope, who goes to search for his father—a cruel name for a young man forcibly taken from his own family.

Captain Vesey, who had been born in Bermuda and worked as a captain on ships going between South Carolina and the Caribbean, participated in human trafficking within the West Indies at least twice, taking Africans from Saint Thomas to Saint-Domingue in the early 1780s, when it was still a French colony. Vesey first encountered the 14-year-old boy in Saint Thomas, purchasing him and then selling him in Saint-Domingue, where he was likely just old enough to be sent into the hell of the cane fields. Soon the boy was having "epileptic fits," and was dispatched to the port of Cap-Français to be returned to Vesey as "defective." When the captain arrived again in April 1782, he was surprised by the news, as the boy had displayed no issues on the voyage from Saint Thomas. The fits stopped and Vesey decided to keep him, having earlier noted his shrewd intelligence. Young Telemaque continued to serve Vesey, at sea and eventually on land when he settled in Charleston in 1783.

Many years later, in 1799, the gods intervened. When he was around the age of thirty-three, Telemaque bought a ticket for a local lottery—and won. The $1,500 was more than enough to pay the Veseys $600 for his freedom and set himself up as a carpenter; that year was the last year he spent as an enslaved man. He took the name Denmark Vesey, keeping his association with Captain Vesey in his surname, with his first name perhaps a nod to the island of Saint Thomas or to the linguistic evolution of "Telemaque" as pronounced in South Carolina.[3]

Charleston was no easy place for this newly emancipated man. The free black community was small, though the city was majority black. By 1822, Charleston had a population of 10,653 white people and 14,127 black, most of whom were enslaved.[4] For a free black man like Vesey, there were restrictions on what work he could do, even the type of clothing he could wear. He may have no longer been a slave, but he certainly did not live in full freedom. His first wife, Beck, had been enslaved, meaning at least three of his subsequent children were as well. It's unclear whether he had enough to buy their freedom, or tried to and was refused, but his desire to stay in contact with them would have been a powerful reason for remaining in Charleston when he could have moved to the far larger freed communities in the North.[5] He may have had other partners and children, but in 1821 he was married again, to Susan, who was listed as being free, though she had been born into slavery. She took his surname, indicating that they were both free and could have their marriage solemnized in the church.[6] The couple may have been free, but Vesey's children were not. One foot in, one foot out—the heartache of living in such a cruel and challenging situation might have been one of the forces compelling Vesey to eventually take action.

In the early nineteenth century, South Carolina had turned to lucrative cotton-growing. The state's slave population soared by more than 100,000 people between 1800 and 1820.[7] With this development came increased pressure from white churches, especially the Methodists, over the question of slaves' religious instruction, similar to what was taking place in Demerara. By the early 1800s, enslaved and free black people were attending church, with ministers trying to convince planters that it would help stabilize the social order, not undermine it. As the numbers grew, however, so did divisions between the white ministry and free black congregants. This led to the incorporation of Charleston's first African Methodist Episcopal (AME) Church in 1818, initially located in Philadelphia Alley (also referred to as Cow Alley), named in honor of that city's financial contribution to rebuild Charleston after an earlier fire. The members of the new church met under the watchful eye of city authorities, who were often spotted in its pews, listening with full attention to the lessons of the Sunday sermon. Matters took a violent turn in the summer of 1818, when a delegation from the parent AME Church in Philadelphia came to Charleston and 140 people were arrested. Relations between white authorities and black congregants soured, and officials began harassing black congregations.[8]

The following year, Vesey and others would have followed the national debate concerning Missouri: Would this section of the former Louisiana Territory enter the Union as a slave state, or free? The result was the Missouri Compromise of 1820, prohibiting any expansion of slavery north of latitude 36°30' north, with Missouri becoming a slave state while Maine entered the Union as a free state, keeping the nation in balance for the moment. The gradual emancipation laws introduced in Northern states meant that fewer people were being held in bondage there. Slavery also had been prohibited in lands north of the

Ohio River valley under the Northwest Ordinance of 1787. Free people and white abolitionists did not want to see the spread of enslavement as Western territories were organized into states. The lower South, meanwhile, was turning in the opposite direction.

Vesey and others also followed news about Haiti in the newspapers. The island remained of great interest in Charleston, in part because a significant population connected to the Saint-Domingue refugees from the revolutionary period lived there. But there was also intense curiosity among black and white alike about the state of affairs in the independent post-slavery nation.

Since the time of Alexandre Pétion and Henry Christophe, Haiti had attracted black migrants from the other slaveholding parts of the Americas. This continued under Haiti's new president, Jean-Pierre Boyer. One notice in an 1821 edition of the *Washington Gazette*, regarding the "Haytian company of Maryland," reported that Boyer had been "charmed to hear that the descendants of the African, form the project of coming here and of carrying their industry into a free country."[9] Having briefly experienced the island under slavery, Vesey now watched as fellow free black people were going to live under the rule of people who had delivered themselves from bondage.

By the end of 1821, another intriguing item appeared in the newspapers: The South Carolina state legislature was discussing a bill that would permit a small number of slaves to be granted their freedom, provided they leave the state. This was in response to an 1820 law prohibiting future emancipation. One report explained that the bill in the South Carolina Senate had been intended "to emancipate the slaves whose owners have petitioned, on security being given that they shall leave the State. The whole number applied for is less than 45, and consists chiefly of women and children."[10] Just as reports about the Slave Registry Bill in Barbados turned into cries of "the king has freed us," so too did this news gain in strength and meaning as it circulated around Charleston. Vesey would have read about it. Before long, some—including Vesey—were saying that the legislature had, in fact, freed the slaves, but white people were keeping this news from them.[11] This was the multilayered backdrop against which events unfurled during the late spring of 1822.

On the evening of Saturday, May 22, two enslaved men, Peter Prioleau and William Paul, were down on the wharf, near the fish market. Prioleau had been puzzling over an unusual flag on a nearby vessel when Paul approached him and they discussed the ship briefly. Paul then changed the conversation, saying, "Many of us are determined to right ourselves! . . . We are determined to shake off our bondage," and invited Prioleau to join them. He declined, explaining that he was "grateful to [his] master for his kindness and wished no change," and left quickly. However, the conversation weighed on him, and Prioleau went to see his friend William Penceel, a free man, who encouraged Prioleau to tell his enslaver, John Prioleau, once he had returned from a business trip on May 30. Peter Prioleau did exactly that, and within a few hours, the city council convened to hear his version of events.[12]

William Paul was soon brought in for interrogation, but he denied any knowledge of a plot. The assembled officials planned to imprison him in the guardhouse, before transferring him to solitary confinement at the infamous city workhouse the next day. That night, faced with a number of prospects, none of them promising, Paul gave officials the names of Mingo Harth and Peter Poyas, and said the AME congregation was involved.[13] Officials took him to the workhouse anyway, "with the hope of further disclosures."[14] Harth and Poyas were brought in, but, according to the later report, "these fellows behaved with so much composure and coolness, and treated the charge, alledged [sic] against them with so much levity" that they were dismissed.[15]

The next development came a couple of weeks later, on Sunday, June 9, when the enslaved blacksmith George Wilson met fellow slaves Joe La Roche and Rolla Bennett, who ran the governor's household. La Roche approached Wilson after AME church services that morning, asking to meet, and the three men gathered that night. La Roche and Rolla told Wilson that a revolt was going to take place the next Sunday, June 16, at midnight, and if he didn't want to participate, he should "go out of town" to avoid being hurt. Wilson tried to convince them that he was going to tell his enslaver, but Rolla said of the plan, "'Tis gone too far now to be stopped." Wilson grappled with the information for days, ultimately deciding on Friday, June 14, to report it to the authorities.[16]

Now officials had a separate, unconnected confirmation of what Peter Prioleau had said at the end of May, and enough to reinforce their suspicions about the veracity of a plot. However, the governor, Thomas Bennett, had trouble accepting the news because Rolla was his slave. He would soon find out that two more of his men—Batteau and Ned—were among the plotters.[17] The militia was assembled on the evening of Sunday, June 16, the night they believed the revolt was to erupt, but nothing took place.

Officials continued rounding up suspects. When Joe La Roche was called as a witness a few days later, he told the assembled men that Rolla had asked him to "join with him in slaying the whites." According to Joe, Rolla had told him that "some white men said our Congress had set us free, and that our white people here would not let us be so." Joe claimed he told Rolla that the Bible prohibited such violence, at which Rolla laughed and told him, "St Domingo and Africa will assist us to get our liberty if we only make the motion here first."[18]

Joe also mentioned an earlier encounter with Vesey, who had asked him if he was satisfied in his "present situation" and brought up the fable of Hercules and the Wagoner, the moral of which was "Heaven helps those who help themselves." Vesey drove the point home, telling him what Rolla had insisted: They were free, and "a large army from St. Domingo and Africa were coming" to help them.[19]

The arrests of Joe La Roche, Rolla Bennett, and others were followed by two rounds of hearings, from June 19 to August 8. The Charleston Court of Magistrates and Freeholders, consisting of two judges and three to five "freeholders" (white property owners), heard the testimony in private to avoid a public spectacle. And while some of the slaves were given legal counsel and there was some cross-examination, the hearings could not be considered fair. The manner in which they were conducted was criticized, prompting the magistrates to defend themselves in the official report on the hearings, published in October 1822. In it, the authors invoked both the Antigua Conspiracy of 1736 and the New York Conspiracy of 1741, pointing out that the hearings in both of those cases were held privately. By citing these cases, they were placing Vesey in a long genealogy of conspiracies and revolts.[20] The report also conjured up the ghosts of 1739 through the inclusion of portions of the 1740 "Negro Act," which was passed after the devastating Stono Rebellion.[21]

Contradictions emerged over many points in the trials during those heavy, humid summer days. One witness, Robert Harth, who spoke in the case of Peter Poyas, another alleged organizer, said he was told that on the Fourth of July "the whites are going to create a false alarm of fire, and every black that comes out will be killed in order to thin them," in part because "they have a knowledge of an army from St Domingo."[22] The subsequent court documents considered Vesey the leader, but not all the witnesses named him as such.[23] Vesey had apparently told some of his men to make weapons stores and hide a number of pikes, yet none ever materialized. Some 6,600 slaves from the countryside and nearby James Island were going to help them; others said 9,000 slaves.[24] There may or may not have been a letter sent to "St Domingo." The conspirators were going to set fires and then kill the whites who came to put them out. And then, according to later prison testimony from Rolla, "as soon as they could get the money from the Banks, and the goods from the stores, they should hoist sail for Saint Domingo."[25]

Many things did not add up. Certainly, all of this being mediated through a white legal system further obscured the truth. If the white interrogators or the black witnesses had a vendetta against Vesey, it does not come out in the surviving records. However, on June 22, Vesey was arrested and imprisoned, his hearing taking place five days later. The magistrates heard from William Paul that Vesey "said he would not like to have a white man in his presence—that he had a great hatred for the whites."[26] According to a witness called Frank Ferguson, Vesey had said "that the negroes' situation was so bad that he did not know how they could endure it and was astonished that they did not rise and fend for themselves."[27] In the official report, a paragraph after the testimony described how Vesey sat in the room listening to the witnesses, "with his eyes fixed on the floor." He apparently cross-examined some of them, but this was not recorded, nor was his address to the court in which he pleaded his innocence and claimed the testimonies were due "to the great hatred which he alleged the blacks had against him." In a final dramatic flourish, the report noted that when he received his death sentence, "the tears trickled down his cheeks."[28]

Whether or not he cried at his sentencing—or whether he was present at all—by June 28, six men were slated to be executed: Vesey, Peter Poyas, Jesse Blackwood, and Rolla, Batteau, and Ned Bennett.

In the predawn hours of July 2, the six men were taken from their cells. They were transported to Blake's Lands, at the edge of the city, about two miles away.[29] Black and white people lined the route in those early hours, watching the men make their way, waiting for the gruesome spectacle.[30] The dream of freedom was killed once again, the social order reaffirmed. After their execution, their heads were not put on pikes, but their bodies were given to doctors for "dissection."[31]

That, however, was not the end of the matter. The executioner stayed busy. Another 82 people were rounded up in those sticky July weeks, a total of 131 arrests.[32] Twenty-nine more men joined Vesey for a total of 35 killed.[33] Another 32—including Sandy Vesey, Denmark's son—were sold out of the state or the country. A white mob also attacked the AME church, and it was later demolished.[34]

The Vesey conspiracy of 1822 has been the subject of a long-running debate over whether it was the product of fevered, paranoid white imaginings brought to life by coerced black testimony and embellished in the later transcripts, or truly a plan only days from fruition.[35] Whatever the truth—and historical consensus and public memory lean toward its veracity—Vesey's plot connected a number of points across maps of slave and free, from South Carolina to the Missouri territory to Haiti, offering another glimpse into the dynamics among the free and the enslaved: the way the church could be put to use (wittingly or not), the way Vesey could read a newspaper and tell others what he learned, the way a simple rumor could alert a militia and cause 35 necks to snap in a matter of weeks.

Denmark Vesey became the figurehead of this conspiracy, and his name was seen in newspapers up and down the country. It was either the story of a danger avoided or that of an innocent victim of a corrupt Southern regime, depending on the reader. Whether Vesey was the instigator or not, his life was testimony to the difficulty of being a free black man in a land shackled by chattel slavery.

Charleston swept in new policies to prevent this happening again, including the 1822 Negro Seamen Act, which put any ship with black sailors under quarantine, and permitted officials to board any vessel and make arrests as needed.[36] There could be no loose talk, no rumors of Haitian invasions, or pending freedom. But trying to stifle the circulation of information in a port city was akin to trying to stop the daily rise and fall of the Lowcountry tidal creeks that surrounded Charleston.

The next time hundreds of people gathered around the name of Denmark Vesey it was to bring a version of him back to life. A statue in his honor was unveiled in a Charleston park in February 2014, the product of a 20-year struggle, with critics decrying Vesey's violent intentions and calling him a "terrorist."[37] Perhaps the contentious nature of this memorial is the reason it is placed three miles north of the cobbled streets and carriage rides of the historic district.

Vesey stands instead amid the elegant suburban landscaping of the city's Hampton Park. He is on a plinth in the middle of a tidy brick circle, ringed by low bushes and flowers. The front and back of the statue's base are covered in dense text, telling the story of the foiled revolt, though the engraving and typeface make it difficult to read under the glare of the South Carolina summer sun. He is wearing a coat and long trousers, a period cravat covering his neck, while carrying a Bible in one hand and a bag of carpenter's tools and his hat in the other. He looks off in the distance, perhaps toward the Haiti that lived in his memory. Or maybe he is thinking of what was behind him. At the other end of the park sits the campus of The Citadel, the military college that grew out of the Municipal Guard, a full-time corps of 150 soldiers set up in the aftermath of the events of 1822 to make sure such a conspiracy could never come to fruition.

Chapter 28

Safety

HAITI MAY HAVE been a beacon of liberty for many, but it faced a number of challenges in its first decades. Initially split into the north and south of Christophe and Pétion, Haiti was now united under Jean-Pierre Boyer, a military general who had fought alongside Dessalines and the others for independence, though he, like Pétion, had come over on the Le Clerc expedition to fight for France and later changed sides. Boyer's reunification of Haiti may have brought the young nation together, but he continued to face the same problem that had perplexed his predecessors: keeping the nation prosperous and thus free. Armies were not cheap, and Boyer was anxious about Spanish Santo Domingo.

The eastern side of the island had gone from unification with the west under Toussaint Louverture in 1801 to French rule from 1804 to 1809, after which it had returned to Spain's empire, during the period known as *España boba* ("Foolish Spain"). Frustrated residents started to consider independence; some were in favor of joining forces with neighboring Haiti, others—mostly creole elites around the capital—looked to Simón Bolívar in South America. After his sojourn in Pétion's Republic of Haiti, Bolívar returned to Venezuela in 1816 and in 1819 created Gran Colombia, a federation carved out of the old Viceroyalty of New Granada, before defeating the Spanish in 1821. In 1830 Gran Colombia would dissolve and become the nations of Venezuela, Colombia, Panama, and Ecuador.

Despite being hundreds of miles away, some of the creoles in Santo Domingo wanted to have an alliance with Gran Colombia as a way of securing independence from Spain and maintaining white creole power. Boyer, watching this, had other ideas.

Tensions erupted on November 15, 1821, when people in Dajabón and Monte Cristi, near the border with Haiti, raised the blue-and-red Haitian flag and declared their desire to join their neighbor. Support for an alliance with Boyer soon spread in the north and along the border, including the important agricultural city of Santiago de los Caballeros. Two weeks later, on December 1, elites in the capital, Santo Domingo, called for the creation of the *Estado independiente de la parte española de Haiti*, and continued to press for inclusion in Gran Colombia.

The division and uncertainty in Santo Domingo worried Boyer, always vigilant about the possibility of France's return. In addition, slavery had not been completely eradicated on the Spanish side of the island. Armed with both existential fears and abolitionist aims, Boyer marched thousands of troops into Santo Domingo on February 9, 1822. Outnumbered, the creole elites could offer no resistance, and Santo Domingo was consolidated into Haiti. The local leadership handed Boyer the keys to the city, which he refused, saying he had not come as a conqueror but "as a father, a brother, and a friend." Slavery was then abolished across the island.[1]

If Haiti was already a beacon of freedom, now it shone even brighter because its constitution of 1816 was now in effect for the entire island. In addition to general emancipation, article 44 of that document established the island's "free soil" policy, which decreed that "all Indians, Africans, and their descendants" would become Haitians with full rights as citizens after a year's residency.[2] Haiti was now an obvious place for people throughout the Caribbean region to flee from slavery, and the number of arrivals rose after unification, with people coming from around the Caribbean, including Jamaica, the Turks and Caicos, and the Bahamas.[3] Haiti was also a place where enslaved people were freed on the spot if their slave ship was captured and brought in, a policy adopted as early as 1810 under Henry Christophe, and continued under Boyer.[4]

Free black people in the United States imagined the sorts of liberties they might find amid Haiti's lush, tropical splendor. Thousands of people had arrived from cities like Boston and New York since 1817, but under Boyer such immigration was gaining momentum.[5] In 1824, Loring Daniel Dewey, a white abolitionist Presbyterian minister and president of the New York branch of the American Colonization

Society, published *Correspondence Relative to the Emigration to Hayti, of the Free People of Colour, in the United States*, which included letters between him and Boyer.

Such emigration was not exactly a new idea. Thomas Jefferson had mentioned this possibility to James Monroe as early as 1801, in the aftermath of Gabriel's conspiracy in Virginia, as the two corresponded over the question of where to deport convicted enslaved people. Jefferson wrote, "The most promising portion of them [the West Indies] is the island of St. Domingo, where the blacks are established into a sovereignty de facto, & have organised themselves under regular laws & government." He wrote those words when Louverture was still in charge, but more than 20 years later he continued to mention Haiti in this context, writing in 1824, "In the plan sketched in the *Notes on Virginia* no particular place of asylum was specified; because it was thought possible that, in the revolutionary state of America, then commenced, events might open to us some one within practicable distance. This has now happened. St. Domingo is become independent, and with a population of that colour only; and, if the public papers are to be credited, their Chief offers to pay their passage, to receive them as free citizens, and to provide them employment."[6]

The American Colonization Society (ACS) had been set up in 1817 to promote the emigration of free black people and freed slaves to Africa, attempting to appeal to people in the North and South. It immediately aroused suspicion among abolitionists, since Southern enslavers were members. Some in the free black community were vocal in their outrage over what they saw as little more than a plan "to get rid of the free colored people," as one critic described it.[7] For others, the lure of a new life in Africa was strong. In the early 1820s, the ACS wanted to establish a settlement on the west coast of Africa, near Sierra Leone, where the British had been sending free black people and maroons since the 1780s.[8]

The ACS site ended up to the south of Sierra Leone, on the coast where the Saint Paul and Mesuardo Rivers run into the sea, an area known as Cape Mesuardo. By 1822—after forcing the local Dei people to hand over land—it had established a settlement soon to be called called Monrovia, named after James Monroe, who was then US president and an enslaver. Eventually, Monrovia would become the capital of the colony, which was named Liberia, from the Latin verb *liberare*, to set free.[9]

The first years were difficult and deadly, as dozens died from unfamiliar tropical ailments, and tensions arose with the Dei people. The colony struggled, and the emigration numbers stayed low, though over the next 40 years some 16,000 black people from the United States would leave for Liberia. Among them, on an 1833 voyage of the *Hercules*, was Susan Vesey, Denmark's widow, 45 years old and more than a decade removed from the terrible summer of 1822. She travelled with her two children, Diana and John Anthony, and his wife, Eliza.[10]

Haiti, however, offered advantages over Liberia as a destination for emigrants from the United States, not least proximity. Haitians and black people in the US had a shared history of displacement and enslavement. Many abolitionists felt the success of migrants in Haiti could have far more potential to strengthen the case against slavery in the US than a distant colony in Africa.[11]

However, the ACS was less eager to consider Haiti, in part under pressure from Southern enslavers. Some of its members felt the island was "too near for the safety of our Southern brethren."[12] Dewey then decided to create a different body to facilitate a Haiti scheme, the Society for Promoting the Emigration of Free Persons of Colour to Hayti.[13] Boyer wrote to Dewey, "My heart and my arms have been open to greet, in this land of true liberty, those men upon whom a fatal destiny rests in a manner so cruel."[14] Anyone who wanted land would be given it, according to Boyer, and migrants could keep their own language and religion.[15] Included in Dewey's *Correspondence* was a copy of a letter from Baptist minister Thomas Paul, originally printed in Boston's *Columbian Sentinel*. Paul had been living on the island for a few months and extolled its "beautiful scenery" and "verdant mountains," while reminding readers that it was "a country possessing an enterprising population of several hundred thousands of active and brave men, who are determined to live free or die gloriously in the defence of freedom."[16]

The *National Intelligencer* reported on a meeting in Richmond, Virginia, in the summer of 1824, where "many of the most respectable free men of color" in the city gathered to discuss the correspondence between Dewey and Boyer. They unanimously resolved that the meeting offer "lasting gratitude to that government for the offer of asylum where we can enjoy liberty, a blessing so precious to man." Above this item was another report on a similar meeting in Baltimore to set up an emigration society.[17] The idea of passage to Haiti proved immediately popular, and an estimated 13,000 people left the US for the island between 1824 and 1827.[18]

Immigrants alone, however, would not solve Haiti's economic problems. Many African Americans arrived to find that their imagined tropical utopia was actually a place where the work was hard, the conditions difficult, and the politics complicated. The vision of Haiti as a place of freedom and safety did not dim, but life on the ground challenged those hopes and expectations. It was an island with a complex relationship to the world, and to itself. There were also cultural differences, not least language, with the island being French- and Kreyol-speaking. Many ended up returning to the United States after only a few years.

Boyer was disappointed that many of the immigrants did not take up the offer of land and instead came as tradespeople—such as barbers or shoemakers—setting up in the towns. He was hoping the settlers would want to work the land and help restore Haiti's agrarian fortunes. Nor did the emigration scheme bring him any closer to official recognition from the United States, another of his aims.[19]

Boyer believed that foreign recognition and trade were necessary for Haiti's survival. However, official recognition by France was going to be costly. In a deal that was unpopular with the Haitian public—though one made under the threat of attack or blockade by French warships cruising near Port-au-Prince—Boyer agreed in 1825 on a price of 150 million francs as an indemnity in exchange for recognition. The payments, sometimes in coffee beans picked by increasingly bitter workers, were the beginning of a long and punishing debt cycle with France that stretched well into the twentieth century.[20]

Like Haitian leaders before him, Boyer was forced to put some of his high-minded ideals to the side in the pursuit of agricultural output to fund this costly ransom. In 1826 he issued what would become a much hated and mostly unenforceable *Code Rural*. It tried to curb the liberties of the farmers, tying them to land and not allowing them to move, undermining mobility, and creating a second-class citizenry.[21] But the tradition of marronage had not ended when Haiti won its independence, and instead it became a way for the now-free peasantry to resist such exploitative measures. Maroons in Haiti continued to exercise their liberty by squatting on land, putting themselves as far from the reach of officials and tax collectors as possible, seeking alternatives to a system tied to capitalist markets, and, in doing so, creating a "counter-plantation" system that had self-sufficiency at its core.[22] Slavery might have been over, but there was still military and political domination to contest. Autonomy and land, however small the plot, were part of freedom, even if political leaders had other priorities or designs. This is what Robert Wedderburn had been arguing a decade earlier in London when he invoked Jamaica and land, and no doubt many of Haiti's maroons would have agreed with him. They may have been free people on paper, but protecting freedom required the continued subversion of a system trying to suppress them in other ways.

Boyer, like all of Haiti's leaders, had to reconcile the desires of the people he governed with a mostly hostile world. He understood that freedom had a price—but deciding to pay for it with the indemnity agreement and with profits wrung out of reforms brought by the *Code Rural* created a noose that would slowly strangle him.

⋘ • ⋙

THE UPHEAVAL CAUSED by the 1808 coup in Spain had raised questions across the empire, and they were increasingly answered with the word "liberty." Many of Spain's colonies had declared their independence around 1810 and had secured it by 1824, after bruising civil wars between rebels and royalists. As part of this conflict, the republicans had to grapple with the question of slavery. Spain had been forced to abandon the slave trade in 1817, in the aftermath of the Congress of Vienna, though this was ignored for decades as thousands of captives would continue to arrive in the surviving colonies of Cuba and Puerto Rico.

The emerging republics were quick to turn their back on the slave trade, mindful that British recognition—and valuable commerce—depended on it. Liberal republicans wanted to be seen as modern, moving away from imperial practices such as slavery. In addition, slaves and free people of color had been crucial in the independence struggle.[23]

The earliest call for total abolition came from Mexico. Padre Miguel Hidalgo is given credit for initiating the independence movement, along with a band of supporters that eventually numbered 80,000, with his "Grito de Dolores" in a small town about 200 miles (320 kilometers) north of the capital, in September 1810. He was also clear about his desire to end slavery, and issued a *bando* (decree) a month later, which called for the immediate freeing of Mexico's 10,000 slaves, on pain of capital punishment and the confiscation of all the goods of any enslaver who did not comply. Hidalgo's actions, however, were only the opening shots of Mexico's independence war, and by early the following year he was killed. Mexico began its long struggle against Spain, and another two decades passed before Hidalgo's call for abolition was enshrined in a constitutional document. However, a limited abolition briefly appeared during the short-lived Mexican Empire established in the aftermath of independence in 1821. The importation of foreign slaves was banned, and any enslaved person who was born in Mexico was freed. But that regime fell in 1823.[24]

Chile, like Mexico, also endured a long fight against Spain after declaring independence in 1810 but not securing it for another eight years. It established a National Congress that would govern during this time, and slavery came up for discussion in 1811, when one member of the congress proposed gradual emancipation measures, known as "free womb" (*libertad de vientres*) laws, inspired by Pennsylvania's 1780 Act for the Gradual Abolition of Slavery. In Chile, this meant any child born to an enslaved mother after October 11, 1811, would be free. Other proposals included a ban on any foreign slaves being brought into Chile and the freeing after six months of any captive who had been in transit to another country.[25] Chile had never developed the plantation economy of places like Cuba and had a slave population of around 10,000 at the time this legislation was approved.

In Argentina, then part of the Viceroyalty of the Río de la Plata (United Provinces of the Río de la Plata from 1816), the slave trade had been significant during the final decades of Spanish rule. An estimated 45,000 captives had passed through Buenos Aires between 1750 and 1810, with some remaining in the city and others forced elsewhere along the Río de la Plata. Another 15,000 went through Montevideo, and an enslaved population of about 30,000 people lived throughout the United Provinces, with half in Buenos Aires.[26] Independence leaders recognized that they would need the support of all black people, free and enslaved, in their fight against Spain. However, they had to balance that with their interests in maintaining the property rights of the wealthier and more powerful segments of the population. The Constituent Assembly banned the slave trade in April 1812, then passed a "free womb" law in January 1813, but with more restrictions than Chile's. Children born to an enslaved mother in the United Provinces after the legislation was enacted would be known as *libertos*, an intermediate status between full slavery and full freedom. The *libertos* would be kept working for their enslaver until the age of 20, with no pay until the age of 15, and then some pay for the remaining five years. The legislation also banned the importation of foreign captives.[27]

In Venezuela, Simón Bolívar attempted to make good on his 1816 promise to Haiti's President Pétion, that he had "proclaimed the absolute liberty of the slaves" in his country. He offered freedom to anyone willing to fight for independence, but such a move attracted criticism and noncompliance from the elites.[28] Although Bolívar said it was "madness that a revolution for liberty should try to maintain slavery," even he didn't free his own slaves in one swoop.[29] He offered them liberty in exchange for military service in 1814—before his exile in Haiti—and about 15 accepted. However, not until 1821 did he unconditionally free the rest, over 100 people.[30] And by 1825, some 138,000 people, or 4.75 percent of the population, remained enslaved throughout the territory of Gran Colombia.[31]

In 1821, the first Constitution of the Republic of Colombia spoke of "equality," and the Law of July 21 that year banished the slave trade and importation of captives, but required children born to slaves to work for their mother's owners until they were 18, under a "tutelage" system that functioned as compensation to the enslavers.[32] The law also stipulated that manumission juntas be set up to buy "deserving" people out of slavery—and thus compensate their enslavers—with money raised from an inheritance tax, though very few towns collected enough money to free a significant number of people. At the same time, enslaved people could still be bought and sold within Gran Colombia, but not trafficked out.[33]

Despite the unevenness of this abolition, Bolívar continued to express his admiration of Pétion and Haiti. A decade after his exile there, Bolívar said in his preface to the draft 1826 constitution of the new nation of Bolivia (previously known as Charcas or Upper Peru but now renamed in his honor) that Haiti was a model, explaining: "I have taken for Bolivia the Executive of the most democratic republic in the world." He went on to praise the Haitian system as devised by Pétion, saying, "A president for life, with the power to choose his successor, is the most sublime inspiration in the republican system."[34] He also brought up the 4,700 enslaved people of Bolivia in the draft, freeing "all those who until now have been Slaves." However, a "special law" would determine how much compensation would be paid to enslavers. Delegates were quick to amend the text to say that such freed slaves were now "citizens," but that they could not "abandon the house of their former masters," leaving life little changed for the remaining slaves. They would have to compensate their "masters" with their labor.[35]

For all his talk, Bolívar did not invite Haiti to his gathering of independent nations at the Congress of Panama in 1826; its potential inclusion was the subject of heated discussion in the United States. This led one Haitian to ask, "Did Bolívar, as head of state, capitulate to the demands of the deputies of the American Union who refused to sit with black and yellow deputies of our country?"[36]

In Peru, a place with nearly 90,000 slaves in 1812, the question of abolition did not surface until the independence struggle was nearly over in 1821. The Argentine independence leader José de San Martín ran the Spanish out of Lima and declared Peru's independence. He also made a number of promises, decreeing that the slave trade would be abolished; enlisted slaves who fought for independence would get their liberty; and anyone born after July 28, 1821, would be free.[37] Bolívar met with San Martín at a conference called in Guayaquil in July 1822, but the two men could not agree on the best way forward to independence, in part because San Martín was in favor of a constitutional monarchy and Bolívar was not.[38] A couple of years later, San Martín, with his hold on Peru tenuous and his enemies closing in, stepped down, allowing Bolívar to complete Peruvian independence, which he did by 1826. However, San Martín's departure closed the door on full abolition. Bolívar wanted to put some measures toward emancipation in the 1826 constitution of Peru, but these were rejected on the grounds that abolishing slavery would hinder agricultural recovery. Despite San Martín's proclamations of 1821, and despite their participation in the independence struggle, enslaved people in Peru were left in an uncertain position as the new nation took form.[39]

Throughout this period of constitutions and civil wars in the Spanish colonies, free and enslaved black people had vital roles in the independence struggles, making up impressive troop numbers, at points comprising 30 to 40 percent of soldiers—often far higher than their percentage of the population in these parts of Spanish America.[40] Their participation proved crucial for the success of independence struggles, but it was also crucial to enslaved people who believed that, if they survived battle and completed an agreed term of military service to either republicans or royalists—and such terms varied by colony—they would receive their freedom. However, their willingness to enlist on the side of independence was far from guaranteed, owing in part to a long royalist tradition among enslaved people.[41] Both republicans and royalists across the region wanted and needed the fighting power of the slaves—and not just in battle but in all the auxiliary roles and jobs surrounding the logistics of warfare. Bolívar understood this, which is why he made at least partial abolition a component of his strategy in Venezuela. However, he also understood the recalcitrance of enslavers. He eventually bowed to pressure for compensation, and agreed that the state should pay for each enslaved recruit. In addition, by the 1820s, an enslaver in Gran Colombia could take back a slave who was not in active service.[42]

Argentina saw hundreds of slaves join the fight for independence after 1810, alongside free people of color. In the Banda Oriental (today's Uruguay) some local military leaders were offering freedom to enslaved recruits, though this was not a uniform policy. By 1813, the military was also assembling or increasing black and *pardo* ("brown") units through conscription and compulsory "purchase"—that is, paying the enslaver, which became a way to take enslaved people from the Spanish and royalists and put them in the independence army. In some cases, enslavers backing the rebels "donated" their enslaved workers.[43]

Formerly enslaved soldiers were especially crucial for San Martín as he assembled his Army of the Andes in the Argentine province of Cuyo. His goal was to have 10,000 slaves among his troops. He didn't manage that, but in the end around 1,500 of his 4,000 soldiers were former slaves. They set off in early January 1817 to cross difficult and dangerous passes through the Andes Mountains, before joining up with the Chilean general Bernardo O'Higgins to take the Spanish forces by surprise, one of the key victories in the larger independence struggle.[44] When San Martín turned his attention to the liberation of Peru in 1822, he was able to conscript more than 4,000 slaves who had belonged to royalists.[45] Bolívar, when he took up the reins in Peru, had an army of 8,000, with about half of them *pardo* or black, helping him win the decisive battle in 1824 at Ayacucho.[46]

Fighting was not the only avenue to emancipation. The chaos unleashed by war also allowed others to flee from their bondage amid conflict. Many women used their relationships with soldiers as grounds for claiming freedom, with their returning partners supporting their cases. Some even followed the army or tried to fight. A woman named Juliana García from the Banda Oriental went to the courts in Buenos Aires to secure her freedom and that of her three children based on her enslaved husband's military service and her own willingness to follow him and attach herself to the army through its grueling campaigns between 1811 and 1815 in Montevideo and Upper Peru. She stated in her case, "The *patria* [nation] owes me for my sufferings of more than four years." But her contribution was not considered combat, and she and at least two of her children remained enslaved.

Another woman, Josefa Tenorio, asked San Martín for her freedom in Peru on the basis that she had dressed as a man and offered herself for combat. "Having heard the rumor that the enemy was trying to re-enslave the *patria* once again," she explained, "I dressed myself as a man and ran at once to the barracks to receive my orders." At the time, she was given a flag to carry but did not see combat. Freedom, she said, was "the only thing that I crave," but her military service was not considered sufficient grounds to be freed.[47]

As these republics emerged, they espoused a legal equality across all free people and universal male suffrage, in contrast to the United

States, where this was mostly limited to white men. In the republics, free men of color were able to vote, and some held electoral offices.[48] There was an implicit understanding that independence had been won because of the shared efforts of indigenous, mestizo, black, and *pardo*. Indeed, such alliances may have been the deciding factor. And yet the question of what the resulting nations would look like was far from straightforward, and long-lasting hangovers from the social stratification of the colonial era remained. In some places, rumors and fears of "caste" (*casta*), or race, wars persisted, especially involving powerful free *pardos*.[49] Two of the most infamous cases had taken place right in the heart of Venezuela's independence movement. Bolívar himself feared what he called a *pardocracia*—brown rule—in part because the *pardo* population was, at around 400,000, twice that of the white population in Venezuela. Indeed, Bolívar even worried that his old ally, Haiti, might help ignite a race war. He was well aware that the 1821 constitution had not fully ended slavery and so did not live up to his promise to Pétion. Concerns that Haiti might try to incite Afro-Colombians to revolt were heightened when a Haitian diplomat arrived in 1824 to establish a relationship with Gran Colombia, which was ultimately rejected over fears that this would give European nations cause to avoid the new republic.[50]

Bolívar had been wary of *pardos* in part because some of them had fought on the royalist side in the earlier stages of the independence struggle, but also because of their numbers and their demands for equality. However, thousands came to join Bolívar, including the *pardo* general Manuel Piar. Piar was a successful military leader, but Bolívar had him executed in 1817 over concerns that he was both gaining too much power and also developing an uncomfortably close relationship with Haiti. Bolívar had been trying to consolidate his control over the military, which Piar resisted, causing their relationship to deteriorate. When another *pardo* officer claimed Piar was planning an insurrection against the whites, Bolívar used this against him, despite there being no evidence, arresting Piar and sentencing him to death by firing squad.[51]

In 1824, Bolívar's fear of *pardocracia* returned with the rise of another prominent *pardo* general, José Padilla, a popular hero of the independence struggle who was the son of a black man from Saint-Domingue and an indigenous Wayúu mother.[52] Padilla issued a broadside in

November 1824, declaring that he would fight "anyone who tries to lower my class and degrade my person." He aired his grievances against members of the white elite, like Bolívar, who had consistently denied him the pay and promotions he was due, and responded to rumors about his personal life.[53] To Bolívar, Padilla's complaint was proof that "legal equality is not enough for the spirit the people have, as they want absolute equality, in the public and the domestic areas alike; and next they will want *pardocracia* . . . in order to then exterminate the privileged class."[54] The following year, Padilla was elected as a senator, representing the Magdalena region in the north—the Caribbean coast had a large non-white population—and Bolívar changed his tune, now praising the general and trying to avoid antagonizing the *pardo* community.[55] Gran Colombia at this time was having a number of internal problems, and Bolívar needed the support of regional leaders, including Padilla, but by 1827 some of Bolívar's supporters began to mobilize against him. Padilla backed Francisco José de Paula Santander, a fellow war hero and vice president of Gran Colombia who was leading a faction against Bolívar's plan to increase his own power and in support of the 1821 constitution. There were rumors that Padilla was now arming black and *pardo* people around Cartagena, and by April 1828 the situation had escalated to the point that Padilla was arrested. Charged with organizing a race war, he was tried and sentenced to death, shot and then displayed on the gallows on October 2.[56]

The specter of slave rebellion had given way during the independence struggle to a broader, more inchoate idea of race, or *casta*, war, and rumors and fears similar to those that existed in Gran Colombia could be found throughout the new republics. This complicated the ideas of equality that were espoused in the various constitutions of these new nations, and also overshadowed the fact that in most of the new republics, the practice of slavery had not been abolished.

In the immediate aftermath of achieving independence, only Chile and the then-united Federal Republic of Central America established full abolition, in 1823 and 1825 respectively. In Chile, a law was introduced in the Senate in June 1823 for full and unconditional emancipation, with no indemnity to enslavers. It was passed and was included in Chile's 1823 constitution. However, other legislation was quickly added afterward that called for now-freed people who were not in an "honest occupation," or were unable to work, to remain under their former enslavers, who would now be their patrons. It also required all freed slaves to register with the police. Despite these social controls, Chile remained the first South American republic to fully abolish the practice of slavery.[57] In the case of Central America, its leaders had followed the 1821 decree in Mexico that banned the slave trade and freed anyone born on Mexican soil. After the end of the Mexican Empire in 1823, the republic split from Mexico but kept the measures in place, adding a decree that no person could be born a slave. Those provisions stayed in place in the nations that emerged in the 1820s and 1830s from that republic (Guatemala, Nicaragua, Honduras, El Salvador, and Costa Rica), more or less ending slavery, though not as clearly as Chile's constitution.[58]

As for the rest of the new republics, they would continue to debate whether slaves were "prepared" for their freedom, and grapple with the question of "property" rights of slaveholders. Those still enslaved in newly liberated nations continued to seek alternative routes to freedom: running away, petitioning, or using the courts. There was no escaping the fact that although these wars had been fought for political freedom, the ornate rhetoric of independence turned out to be hollow. When Simón Bolívar rallied his troops for battle in 1824 by saying, "You are going to complete the greatest task that heaven has been able to entrust to man, that of saving the entire world from slavery," he wasn't actually talking about the enslaved among them.[59]

Chapter 29

Finale

THEATERGOERS IN NEW YORK braved torrential rain on the evening of September 26, 1831, to attend the opening of *The Gladiator*, a play by Robert Montgomery Bird at the Park Theatre.[1] Over five acts, Bird tells the story of the Roman slave Spartacus and his epic struggle for freedom. In one scene at the end of Act II, with the audience no doubt anticipating the revolt, Spartacus calls his fellow slaves to action: "Ho, slaves, arise! It is your hour to kill! Kill and spare not—For wrath and liberty!—Freedom for bondmen—freedom and revenge!"

For Bird, the timing was uncanny. He had finished the work in the spring, and so could not have foreseen what was to come that summer. But he wrote the play with the abolitionist audiences of Philadelphia, where he lived, in mind. Indeed, when it opened there a month after its success in New York, Bird noted in his diary that "the jam of visitors was tremendous; hundreds returning without being able to get seats or stands."[2] However, like many white abolition sympathizers, he was ambivalent about black people, harboring a fearful hostility about the very real threat of slave violence—not unlike the subject of his play—remarking in his diary, "I had sooner live among bedbugs than negroes." He reflected in that same diary entry, of August 27, on the events in Virginia earlier that week, writing, "If they had but a Spartacus among them to . . . lead them on in the Crusade of Massacre, what a blessed example might they not give to the world of the excellence of slavery! What a field of interest to the play writers of posterity! Some day we shall have it, and future generations will perhaps remember the horrors of Haiti as a farce compared with the tragedies of our own happy land!"[3]

Maybe Nat Turner wasn't a Spartacus to Bird, but at the same time that the New York actors were rehearsing their staged revolt, Turner was taking part in a real one deep in the Virginia countryside.

It started well before the night of Sunday, August 21, 1831, with months of planning during the late hours and quiet nights of Southampton County, a remote spot near the border with North Carolina, some 75 miles south of Richmond and 60 miles west of Norfolk. Saint Luke's Parish, where the revolt took place, had 339 slaveholding households.[4] Nat Turner had lived his entire life under the wide sky of this parish, like many of the slaves there and most of the men who would assist them in their uprising. There were deep familial ties, and corresponding animosities. They knew each other, they knew each other's enslavers.[5] Turner was clear about where he wanted to strike, and which houses they would visit. He had been moved around the extended Turner family, and possibly hired out at points, before ending up, in 1830, in the household of Joseph Travis, a Turner relative by marriage.[6] The Travis home—where Turner's trusted deputy Hark Moore was also enslaved—would be the starting point.

The Sunday afternoon before the attack, Turner met with his small band of rebels—Hark Moore, Sam Francis, Nelson Edwards, Henry Porter, and two late recruits, Will Francis and Jack Reese—to discuss final preparations. They ate roasted pig and melon, and, with the exception of teetotaler Turner, drank brandy. They decided that "neither age nor sex was to be spared" as they made their way from house to house later that night.[7] Turner understood that gossip and rumor could undermine any plot, especially one with these aims, so he kept it limited to this very small circle. However, he probably expected that with the killing of white families, their slaves would join the rebels as they went along.[8] "'Twas my object," Turner later said, "to carry terror and devastation wherever we went."[9]

The men moved across the countryside starting around 10:00 p.m. that Sunday, heading back to the Travis house. The family was out, and the men came in to gather axes and other weapons before going to the estate's cider press. They returned a few hours later, and now the family was home and in bed. They entered the house, and Turner and Will entered Travis's bedroom. Turner decided that he "must spill the first blood," but the room was dark and his hatchet only skimmed Travis's head. Now, startled awake, Travis lurched at the men, but Will landed a blow of the axe and killed him, and then this wife. Three children were also murdered, one an infant that Will and Henry returned to kill when they realized it had been left alive in its crib. They decapitated the child and put it in the fire, sending a message of terror to whoever would find the bodies in that house. Turner took the Travis household's guns and marched on, next killing Salathiel Francis, taking horses and arms before going to the Reese plantation, where Jack was enslaved, finding only the mistress and her son. They too were murdered, and their horses and arms were taken. By sunrise, the group had reached the Turner plantation, where they set upon the family, who were already awake and had started their day.[10]

Up to this point, Turner and his men had been able to move unimpeded, but as day broke, their trail of devastation was discovered. The panic spread as quickly as the attacks did, as neighbors ran from house to house and also alerted the authorities. At around 9:00 a.m., a group of volunteers grabbed guns and went on the hunt for Turner.[11] By then the rebels had grown in number as they moved through the countryside, and they would ultimately kill 55 people, including women and children.[12]

Turner's ultimate plan was to take all the weapons he had gathered and head to the county seat of Jerusalem (today's Courtland), which he and his men would storm. By the time they were three miles south of town, they numbered at least 40 men.[13] But enough militia and volunteers were now assembled to stop them. Turner and some of the others managed to retreat and quarter together that night, but by Tuesday, August 23, it was clear the revolt was over. Turner fled, eluding capture for the time being.

After many arrests, more than 100 witnesses were rounded up to testify.[14] The cases for the court of oyer and terminer ran into November. Magistrates heard the trials of 43 slaves, finding 30 guilty, with 12 sentenced to transportation, and 18 to be hanged. Four free black men were also tried, with one found guilty and hanged.[15]

Throughout this period Turner hid, though he was almost in plain sight, staying in a nearby field rather than joining the maroons in the Great Dismal Swamp, about 20 miles to the east.[16] Instead, he created a "cave" in the ground near a tree, where he could not be detected, though he was forced to make raids on farms to find food. Eventually, a slave named Red Nelson alerted authorities that he had seen Turner in the woods but was afraid and ran from him.[17] The entire region was still on edge, and reports appeared of vigilante violence being committed against black people beyond Southampton County, attempting to thwart the efforts of would-be imitators, real or imagined.[18] The public was told to be on the lookout for Turner, who was described as being "5 feet six or 8 inches high" and knock-kneed, with broad shoulders, "broad flat feet," and "very thin" hair. He carried the indelible marks of life in slavery such as an injury from "a blow" that left a knot on his right arm, near his wrist, and a scar on his temple, supposedly "produced by the kick of a mule."[19]

Turner was finally captured on October 30.[20] As he was being held that afternoon, a crowd of people gathered, and he spoke to them, talking of his visions and his motives, though nothing of what he said was recorded.[21] The following morning he was taken to the courthouse in Jerusalem, where two magistrates interrogated him for hours. It is not clear whether his lawyer, Thomas R. Gray, was in the courthouse. At some point later that afternoon or in the early evening, Gray came to the jail where he and Turner agreed to speak the following day. They proceeded to discuss the events at length in his jail cell, and over the course of three days they finished what later would be published as *The Confessions of Nat Turner*.[22] On Saturday morning, November 5, Turner was called to trial and pleaded "not guilty" in front of 10 magistrates. It did not take them long to pass a sentence of death by hanging, scheduled for the following Friday.[23]

Confessions is an unusual record of a slave revolt, as rebels were rarely accorded the opportunity to tell their story. Of course, this version was mediated through a white narrator, and told when the shadow of the gallows was falling across Turner's short life. All the same, it offers rare expression of the interior world of a person forced to endure the silences of enslavement. How much was misunderstood or embellished by Gray, or how much of Turner's authentic voice comes through, is impossible to tell. Gray had been involved in the preceding trials and cases, gathering information and writing about them in local newspapers, and some of that may have gone into the *Confessions*.

In the testimony, there is no talk of Haiti, or Denmark Vesey, or, even closer to home, Gabriel Prosser—who was awaiting his execution on October 2, 1800, when Turner was born.[24] There are, however, many Biblical references. At the time, this was used as evidence of Turner's delusions. Even Gray described him, at the end of *Confessions*, as "a complete fanatic." However, read closely, Turner's confession can be seen as a man's search, through faith and signs, for a way out of a difficult and unjust world.[25]

The work starts with Turner recalling his early life, bringing up a moment at the age of three or four when his mother told him he "surely would be a prophet," because he was speaking with confidence about something that had happened before his birth. His parents continued to tell him that he was "intended for some great purpose."[26] He was clearly intelligent: he claimed that he could not remember when he learned to read and write, but recalled that as a small child he was shown a book to keep him from crying and "began spelling the names of different objects—this was a source of wonder to all in the neighbourhood."[27]

Religion was one avenue where such talent could be nurtured in a world that would deny young Nat so much. He decided that "to be great, I must appear so," and for many years kept to himself, focusing on the Bible, especially Luke 12:31, which he mentions in *Confessions* as his inspiration: "Seek ye the kingdom of Heaven and all things shall be added unto you."[28] He prayed continually. This was at a time, around 1824, when he was placed under a new overseer, which caused him to flee into the woods for 30 days. Turner returned, "to the astonishment of the negroes on the plantation." Turner's father had escaped long before, and everyone believed his son had followed in those footsteps.[29] The Holy Spirit had commanded him to come back, Turner said, citing Luke 12:47: "For he who knoweth his Master's will, and doeth it not, shall be beaten with many stripes," a particularly resonant verse for a slave, especially one who was beaten in 1828 for saying that black people should be free and would be one day. This whipping does not appear in *Confessions*, though Gray knew about it through other testimony.[30]

Turner continued to be guided by signs and visions, including one after his return, when he saw "white spirits and black spirits engaged in battle, and the sun was darkened—the thunder rolled in the Heavens, and blood flowed in streams." The darkened sun was more than a vision—he had seen it during a solar eclipse on February 12, 1831. After that, he knew what to do: "I should arise and prepare myself, and slay my enemies with their own weapons."[31]

He began to confide his plans to Henry, Hark, Nelson, and Sam. They would strike on July 4, taking advantage of the distraction of the holiday while also making a point about its supposed celebration of freedom. However, they could not agree what to do, and "many were the plans formed and rejected" by the group. Turner fell ill, and July 4 came and went. Then a few weeks later "the sign appeared again." Although it is not spelled out in *Confessions*, strange atmospheric conditions occurred between August 12 and 15, resulting at one point, according to newspaper reports, in a sun that looked greenish, before turning white, then yellow, then green once again. A black spot on the sun was visible to the naked eye. This unusual celestial display was rounded off by a red-tinted sunset. This was later attributed to volcanic dust, and there were reports of dramatic skies along the Atlantic coast and beyond.[32] If Turner was waiting for an external sign, this one was unmissable. A few days later, the conspirators had their Saturday afternoon feast and headed to the Travis house.

As Robert Bird complained to his diary, Turner was no Spartacus, but his story contains no less drama than Bird's play. While Spartacus led thousands, Turner carried the suffering of his community within himself. To be a slave in rural Virginia, or anywhere else, was to not only know your own pain but to bear witness to that of others. In *Confessions*, Turner mentions the moment he asked Will why he joined them, and the young man told him that "his life was worth no more than others, and his liberty as dear to him." Turner asked him if he planned to obtain that liberty, and Will said "he would, or loose [sic] his life."[33]

Turner's parents were ultimately right about their son's destiny. The memory of Nat's brief, bloody struggle for freedom continues to live on.

The entire blood-soaked affair attracted national attention, not only the events themselves but also the context in which they took place. The abolitionist mood had shifted in the years between the Vesey conspiracy of 1822 and the events of August 1831, with segments of the public moving away from the idea of gradual measures of abolition and pushing harder for the immediate end of slavery. This more forceful tone was most evident in the writings of David Walker, a black man who was born free in North Carolina but eventually moved to Boston, though he spent some time between 1817 and 1821 living in Charleston. As a fellow free man active in the AME Church, he might have crossed paths—if not conversed at length—with Denmark Vesey.[34] In 1829, Walker published *Appeal to the Coloured Citizens of the World*. It caused a stir in the North and the South, and among free and enslaved black people, as its radical contents were disseminated and debated.

Walker did not mince words in the tract, opening with this observation: "We, (coloured people of these United States,) are the most degraded, wretched, and abject set of beings that ever lived since the world began."[35] The work took aim at a number of targets, but the hypocrisy of Christianity in the United States especially draws Walker's ire: "O Americans! Americans!! I call God—I call angels—I call men, to witness, that your DESTRUCTION *is at hand*, and will be speedily consummated unless you REPENT."[36] He was also a critic of colonization schemes, writing: "This country is as much ours as it is the whites, whether they will admit it now or not." To Walker, colonization was a "trick" to get rid of free black people and secure "the perpetuation of slavery in this country forever."[37]

As the *Appeal* travelled in the cargoes of sympathetic sailors on voyages to the Southern states, it caused an uproar. So immediate was its impact that laws were passed against its circulation in Georgia and Louisiana. Georgian officials were panicked that this material might incite slaves to revolt, and the state offered a reward for the capture of Walker: $10,000 alive and $1,000 dead. A group of enslavers offered $3,000 for his severed head. In the end, Walker died in 1830, at around the age of 33. The cause was tuberculosis, though with such bounties on his head there was a lingering suspicion that he had been poisoned.[38]

In the same year that Walker's *Appeal* appeared, the abolitionist William Lloyd Garrison turned up the intensity of the white abolition debate, making a clear call for immediate emancipation. In September 1829, he wrote in the newspaper *Genius of Universal Emancipation*, "I am convinced, on mature reflection, that no valid excuse can be given for the continuance of the evil [of slavery] a single hour," adding, "The slaves are entitled to immediate and complete emancipation."[39] He would go on to set up his own newspaper, *The Liberator*, and continue his campaign. He, like many other abolitionists, would disavow the violence displayed in Turner's revolt, though they used it to bolster their case for immediate emancipation to avoid future uprisings.[40]

A literate man, Turner would have been aware of some or all of this. However, in his preface to *Confessions*, Gray makes a point of saying, "The insurrection in this county was entirely local"—that is, not something swept in by the winds blowing in from the North.[41] Turner makes no direct mention of any events outside the ones in Southampton County, his only inspiration direct from God.

When the Virginia legislature met in the autumn of 1831, this case inevitably dominated their attention. There had been some earlier discussion over a proposition that the state move toward a plan of gradual slave emancipation followed by a colonization scheme to remove free people. The events in Southampton quickly shut down any such potential talk, and the subject would not be revisited for decades.[42]

⋘ • ⋙

NAT TURNER'S REVOLT, though shocking to Virginia and the United States, was only the opening act for what happened after Christmas that year in Jamaica. Christmas was a highlight of the year on the island because enslaved people were given extra days off for their Junkanoo celebrations. In 1831 Christmas fell on a Sunday, which should have meant an extra day's holiday—however, authorities announced only a three-day Junkanoo, rather than the expected four.[43] Anticipating some pushback, the governor, Somerset Lowry-Corry (Second Earl of Belmore), mustered the local militias.

There had been some disputes and unrest in the run-up to Christmas. At the Salt Spring estate, near Montego Bay, the lawyer William Grignon beat an enslaved woman for allegedly stealing sugarcane after her husband, a plantation driver, refused to enact the punishment. Grignon was chased off the plantation by some enslaved people, and a ruckus ensued. Arrests were made, and the militia was called out, but no one was punished.[44]

The sugar industry was going through a rough patch, and many of the plantations were failing, with numerous bankruptcies. At the same time, enslavers' complaints about the push for emancipation legislation made enslaved people believe they were on the cusp of freedom, if not actually free already. This was the case not only in Jamaica but also across the British Caribbean colonies. The rumors reached such a pitch that an official circular from the colonial secretary was issued in 1831 saying that freedom had not been granted and that enslaved people should return to their duties.[45]

There was also a growing awareness across the islands of the legislative changes that had taken place, and what rights—such as they were—could be claimed. The previous year, in 1830, a revolt broke out on Exuma Island, Bahamas, a thin, flat strip of coral limestone. It had a small settlement that included the Rolle plantation, where 254 enslaved people had been growing cotton. As cotton was faltering there, along with John Rolle's fortunes, he was forced to let some of his enslaved people live with limited supervision. He was an absentee planter and could only afford one overseer.[46]

Rolle wanted to transfer some of his slaves to another plantation in Trinidad, but he did not do so before a law was passed by Parliament in 1825 that prohibited moving slaves between colonial territories. He continued to petition the government about this problem, and soon his slaves heard about it. An attempt to move some of them within the Bahamas in 1828–1829 necessitated bringing in the military and using force. A few years later, Rolle's lawyer hatched another plan to send 77 people to nearby Cat Island, with only three days' notice. This was enough time for the enslaved workers to flee into the bush, with a man named Pompey emerging as their leader. Pompey seized one of Rolle's boats and, with 43 others who did not want to be moved, sailed north to Nassau to put their case to the governor.[47] Before they could do that, they were chased by a sloop, picked up, jailed, and severely flogged, without the governor being aware. When he finally heard the case, he ruled in favor of Pompey, and they returned to Exuma, where they were greeted with such exuberance that there were fears it could tip into a revolt. Enslaved people were refusing to work, and soldiers were sent in, with one official reporting that the slaves "understood they were to be free." Officials gave Pompey 39 lashes to make it clear they were not.[48] Despite the punishment, Pompey had won a significant battle. He and his followers did not have to leave against their will.[49] The Bahamas incident was just one more push against the system, another attack coming from the colonies. What happened in Jamaica took this to the next level.

Protestant missionaries had come to Jamaica, as they had to Demerara and other colonies. Jamaican planters were wary, as those in Demerara had been, not only because the missionaries pressured the authorities to allow the enslaved to mix with free people during worship, but also because they wanted to educate the slaves so they could read the Bible. While some hoped these measures would be considered good treatment and result in better "behavior" among the slaves, others worried about where such liberties might lead.

One person who became heavily involved with the missionaries was Samuel Sharpe, who was enslaved on the Cooper's Hill estate. However, as a Baptist deacon, he had a great deal of mobility due to his religious duties.[50] A contemporary described Sharpe as having "intellectual and oratorical powers above the common order . . . I was amazed both at the power and freedom with which he spoke."[51] Sharpe took his speaking skills around Montego Bay and throughout Saint James Parish, allowing him to connect and meet secretly with people with a greater degree of flexibility than many other enslaved Jamaicans.

Sharpe had been following the news and knew that Parliament was debating abolition again. Like many other enslaved people, he believed the king had freed them, but that they were not being told. "I know we are free," he told some of his fellow plotters. "I have read it in the English papers."[52] Another rumor circulated the planters were going to take Jamaica from British control and join United States, ensuring that they would never be free.[53]

Sharpe had a radical plan, reckoning that the best way to gain freedom was for the slaves to stop working: a strike. If the planters wanted them to go back to the fields, they would have to pay them, like the free people they were. Violence, Sharpe told them, had to be kept to a minimum. If they were attacked, they could retaliate and damage property, but they should not hurt people or the cane fields. According to his logic, if they could get the planters to relent, they would no longer be slaves, but free laborers, and they would finally have the freedom long denied to them. Word spread through the north of the island, aided by Sharpe's religious networks and his own mobility. His plans reached an estimated 100 plantations, which meant the ears of some 20,000 enslaved workers and potential recruits. They would strike during the Christmas holiday.[54]

On Christmas morning 1831, after seven o'clock prayers, Sharpe told one member of the congregation that if the minister asked whether they intend to work after Christmas, they should tell him, "No—that you know very well that you are free, and that you won't work for any body unless you get paid for it."[55] Later that day, Sharpe and his inner circle met to finalize their plans. Everything remained calm, though the authorities had been keeping an eye on Sharpe, whose name had surfaced as rumors of an uprising circulated around the northwest part of the island.[56]

Two days later, on December 27, some of the rebels gathered in the foothills of Cockpit Country above Montego Bay for the dedication of a new Baptist chapel at Salter's Hill. During that event, Reverend William Knibb made a point of preaching about obedience, having heard the night before reports from another minister that people were saying the king had freed the slaves. He told the congregation: "What you have been told is false—false as hell can make it."[57] The mood quickly shifted among the congregation: Now, some thought, even the ministers were lying to them.[58] Freedom would have to be taken. Within a few hours, that taking began.

The Kensington Estate was the first to go, its hillside flames some 1,660 feet (500 meters) above Montego Bay becoming a sign that the uprising had begun.[59] Other estates responded, and cane fields, plantation houses, and outbuildings burned, pumping smoke into the night sky. At least six plantations were ablaze by 10:00 p.m.[60] By the next day, people had put their tools down—those fields that were not burning were not being worked either. As was the case in other rebellions, some slaves warned their enslavers about what was to come, others used the chaos to run away rather than participate, and some fled with their enslavers. The following night, there were more flames, and by December 28, news had reached the capital, Spanish Town.

On New Year's Day, some 200 troops arrived in Montego Bay to reinforce the disorganized militia, some of whose volunteers were refusing to go into the hills to put out the fires or confront the rebels.[61] Soon there were captives and confessions, and a bounty of $300 was placed on Sharpe's head.[62] Still the fires burned, and more enslaved people felt emboldened to join the rebels. The number of fighters swelled into the thousands.[63] All the planters' nightmares were coming true. Jamaica was going to be the next "St. Domingo."

The military, while outnumbered, had their special reserve troops: the maroons. The Leeward maroons in Accompong were only a few miles from the Kensington estate and the locus of the unrest. In making his plans, Sharpe was aware of the maroons' loyalty to their treaty with the British, and he knew they would be on the military's side unless they could be convinced otherwise. Right after Christmas, he dispatched two of his trusted men, Peter Douglas and John Williams, to take a gift to Colonel White of the Accompong maroons. Instead of receiving the emissaries and accepting their gift, the maroons captured Douglas and Williams and handed them over to the authorities. The two men were later executed.[64] The maroons ended up helping the British troops find the rebels who were hiding in the precipitous hills. In January, around a hundred Windward maroons from Moore Town and Charles Town were also brought in to help.[65]

The conflict led to extrajudicial killings, facilitated by the declaration of martial law. Executions on the spot became routine. Any action could be construed as a sign of guilt. Heads on pikes once again lined thoroughfares. During this time, around 3,000 of the rebels managed to secure themselves on Greenwich Hill, where they built a stone wall and stockpiled food and weapons, though eventually they had to flee as the military advanced.[66] By late January, the momentum was faltering, and the fighting was coming to an end. Sharpe, however, was still in hiding. It is not clear if he willingly surrendered or if he was betrayed, but by February it was over. At least 344 people were executed in the aftermath of the rebellion, adding to the 200 or so who were killed during the conflict. "The gibbet erected in the public square in the centre of the town was seldom without occupants, during the day, for many weeks," Henry Bleby, a Methodist minister, recalled in his 1853 account of the revolt.[67] Having arrived in Jamaica in 1831, Bleby was swept up in these events, and claimed to have spoken to Sharpe in jail while he was awaiting his death sentence.[68]

Sharpe later told Bleby the fires were not part of his plan, and when "he saw the first incendiary fire break out, and then another, and another . . . he knew that his whole plan was rendered abortive; for now the 'buckras' would shoot and murder the people without mercy."[69] Sharpe would also face the gallows, and his hanging came on May 23, 1832. "He learnt from his Bible, that the whites had no more right to hold black people in slavery, than the black people had to make the white people slaves," Bleby wrote, recalling Sharpe's words. And he accepted the cost of failure: "I would rather die upon yonder gallows than live in slavery."[70]

A March 1832 report claimed that 207 properties had been damaged and that £175,000 had been spent on the military operation, but the total damages were more than £1.1 million—an astonishing sum for the era.[71] Within Jamaica, the planters turned on the missionaries—including Bleby, who was tarred by an angry mob.[72] The chapel at Salter's Hill was destroyed by the militia, and other frenzied crowds set upon at least a dozen more.[73]

The so-called Baptist War in Jamaica galvanized abolitionist sentiment in Britain, and news of this came at the end of a year during which another significant event had occurred: the publication in 1831 of the first slave narrative by a woman, *The History of Mary Prince*. It ran through three editions in that year alone.[74] The book gives a painfully detailed and graphic account of Prince's time as a slave, and—like many of the growing number of slave narratives—it was mediated by a white person, in this case Susanna Strickland, a writer and member of the Anti-Slavery Society in London, who wrote the manuscript. Women were becoming increasingly vocal in the abolition movement, with many calling for an immediate end to slavery. The travails of Mary Prince armed them with more ammunition, and gave further impetus to action, drawing on the horrors recounted in the book.

Prince's difficult life started in Bermuda, where she was born in 1788. She later went to Turks and Caicos, doing unbearably hard, hot work in the salt pans, before ending up in Antigua. Throughout the book, she details the routine beatings and lashings she suffered at the hands of her enslavers, and the many contradictions and cruelties of her world.

She ended up enslaved by the Wood family, living in Antigua at first and then travelling with them to England in 1828. Upon arriving in London and making contact with abolitionists, she discovered that she was free in England. However, should she return with her current enslavers to Antigua to be united with her free husband, Daniel James, she could not take her freedom with her: another of the system's incongruities manifested in one person's life. She stayed in England, and became a paid servant for Thomas Pringle, the secretary of the Anti-Slavery Society.[75]

At the end of her narrative, Prince fulminates:

I am often much vexed, and I feel great sorrow when I hear some people in this country say, that the slaves do not need better usage, and do not want to be free. They believe the foreign people [West Indian planters], who deceive them, and say slaves are happy. I say, Not so. How can slaves be happy when they have the halter round their neck and the whip upon their back? . . . I will say the truth to English people who may read this history . . . I have been a slave myself—I know what slaves feel—I can tell by myself what other slaves feel, and by what they have told me. The man that says slaves be quite happy in slavery—that they don't want to be free—that man is either ignorant or a lying person. I never heard a slave say so.[76]

By 1830, members of the Anti-Slavery Society were beginning to call for an immediate end to slavery in the British colonies, as Garrison and others were doing in the US. To the British reformers, it was clear after reading about Prince's travails and hearing about the events in Jamaica that gradual measures would not work. The abolitionists were pleased with the slaves' enthusiastic reception of Christianity, which rendered them now "fit"—to white, metropolitan eyes—for freedom.[77]

As these debates were taking place, Britain continued to struggle with economic problems, including in the West Indian colonies, which were no longer as profitable to tax or trade with as they had been.

The rise of Brazilian and Cuban sugar was eating into the market, and there was a shift toward trade with Asia.[78] Alongside economic reconfiguration was a continued drive for political reform, and all of this under a new monarch, William IV, who took the throne in 1830.

The Reform Act of 1832 expanded the electorate by reducing the property qualification, bringing great changes to Parliament. Many abolitionist MPs were swept in, some taking seats from the West India lobby.[79] The violence of slave uprisings like the one in Jamaica—and social unrest in Britain in 1830–1832—suggested abolition would be a way for the Whig government to relieve some of the pressure on Parliament. By May 1832, a parliamentary select committee began investigating the possibility of abolition, and Reverend William Knibb, back from Jamaica, was one of the 32 people called to testify.[80]

All of these forces—social change in Britain, the persistence of the white abolitionist effort, the decline of the sugar colonies, and the massive revolt in Jamaica—converged in the spring of 1833. In May, when the Emancipation Bill was scheduled to be introduced in the House of Commons, the largest antislavery petition yet was brought to Parliament, with some 187,000 signatures.[81] Ultimately, petitions to end slavery garnered more than 1.3 million names. The West India lobby caved, not because its members had changed their minds about slavery but because of the understanding that they would receive some form of compensation for their human "property"—after negotiations the agreed payout was £20 million. Enslaved people across the West Indies would receive nothing—on the contrary, they would be required to work as "apprentices" without wages for up to six years, after which they would be free. Only children under the age of six would be freed immediately. Under these conditions, the Abolition of Slavery Act received royal assent in 1833 and came into effect on August 1, 1834.[82]

Freedom came to Bermuda, the Bahamas, Barbados, the Cayman Islands, Turks and Caicos, the Virgin Islands, Anguilla, Antigua, Barbuda, Montserrat, Saint Kitts, Saint Lucia, Nevis, Dominica, Saint Vincent, Grenada, Trinidad, Tobago, British Guiana, British Honduras, and, of course, Jamaica. Now some 800,000 people in the British West Indies faced six long years to "adjust" to it. But the apprenticeship idea immediately triggered protests by enslaved people in the British colonies, who knew this was an unfair deal. In Saint Kitts, enslaved people said they would strike on August 1, 1834, and only work for wages. Similar sentiments were expressed in other colonies, including Trinidad, British Guiana, and Jamaica.

Under the arrangement, "apprentices" had to work 45 hours a week for their former enslavers, with no compensation. There were two categories of apprentices, "praedials" (field workers) and "non-praedials" (skilled and domestic workers), with the former having to serve six years and the latter four. This distinction, inevitably, added another layer of contention on top of an already hated policy.[83] In addition, the long working hours meant the apprentices had less time to spend on their provision grounds. Since some planters were also cutting food rations, many apprentices were on a difficult footing from the beginning.

A system of appointed "stipendiary magistrates" was set up to adjudicate between former owners and slaves. The magistrates—not the former enslavers—were now permitted to administer corporal punishment.[84] Frequent castigations were meted out for a range of behaviors, as defined by the magistrates; for instance, "indolence" at work was punished with hours of forced labor, or a turn at the dreaded treadmill. Yet despite the unfairness of the new system and the unevenness of the apprenticeship period, the regime of slavery had been broken, with one observer writing, "The apprentice is daily becoming more heedless of and more disrespectful to his manager."[85] Now free to say what they pleased, without fear of being killed or sold, apprentices also filed hundreds of complaints with stipendiary magistrates to challenge bad treatment, overwork, and assaults in their workplaces.[86]

A provision in the Emancipation Bill allowed apprentices to buy out their contracts early, and manumit themselves, but the valuations were often set out of reach; still, thousands managed to find the money or were able to come to an arrangement with their former enslavers.[87] Some plantation owners seized the advantages of wage labor before the official apprenticeship period ended. Landowners could pay a pittance to desperate workers who had been left landless and homeless when they were freed. Freed people were bestowed with debt and poverty to start their new lives. Such moves proved effective in some places—indeed, sugar production rose in Barbados.[88]

The apprenticeship system had its share of critics among white abolitionists as well, who were aware of its abuses, many of which came to light in 1837 with *A Narrative of Events* as told by a Jamaican apprentice, James Williams, who was about 18 at the time. "When I was a slave I [was] never flogged," he explained. "But since the new law begin, I have been flogged seven times, and put in the house of correction four times." Williams—through an intermediary—told of his beatings and imprisonments. He also recalled details of the treadmill at the workhouse, a torturous punishment that involved hanging on to a rail while walking on a rotating, ridged cylinder that was around 6 feet in diameter.[89] As they were forced to "dance the treadmill," which made four to five rotations a minute, those who could not keep up were flogged, and even the ones who could had their legs whipped as they went.[90] Afterward, people were sent to work on different estates as part of penal gangs.

Williams was able to put the existing network of missionaries and abolitionists to use to bring this abuse to public attention, outraging Jamaican landowners and causing the Colonial Office to commission an investigation.[91] The anti-apprenticeship campaign in Britain held some 130 meetings, attracting thousands. In the end, the people forced to suffer under the apprenticeship system helped bring it to an end two years early, in 1838, and in doing so finally witnessed the full demise of the slavery system in the British Caribbean.

A memorial to Louis Delgrès who led the resistance to Napoleon Bonaparte's reinstitution of slavery in Guadeloupe, near where he was killed in the small town of Matouba.

Henry Christophe, one of the key generals of the Haitian Revolution, later became the ruler of the short-lived Kingdom of Haiti (1811–20) in the north of the island.

Alexandre Pétion was the first president of the Republic of Haiti, which was in the south of the island, from 1807–1820. The next president, Jean-Pierre Boyer, reunited the island after the deaths of Pétion and Christophe.

A sketch of a flag found on the rebels during a slave uprising in Barbados around Easter 1816, led by a man known as Bussa.

Robert Wedderburn was born in Jamaica to an enslaved woman, and his father was a white sugar planter and enslaver. Wedderburn was freed as a child and later moved to Britain, where he became active in radical politics, later writing an account of his life, *The Horrors of Slavery*, in 1824.

An etching depicting the mass slave uprising in 1823 in the British colony of Demerara (part of today's Guyana).

A monument in Hampton Park, Charleston, South Carolina, commemorating Denmark Vesey, a freedman who was executed in 1822 for allegedly plotting a slave revolt.

An eighteenth-century work known as a casta painting, which illustrates various "racial combinations" between adults and their resulting offspring in Mexico.

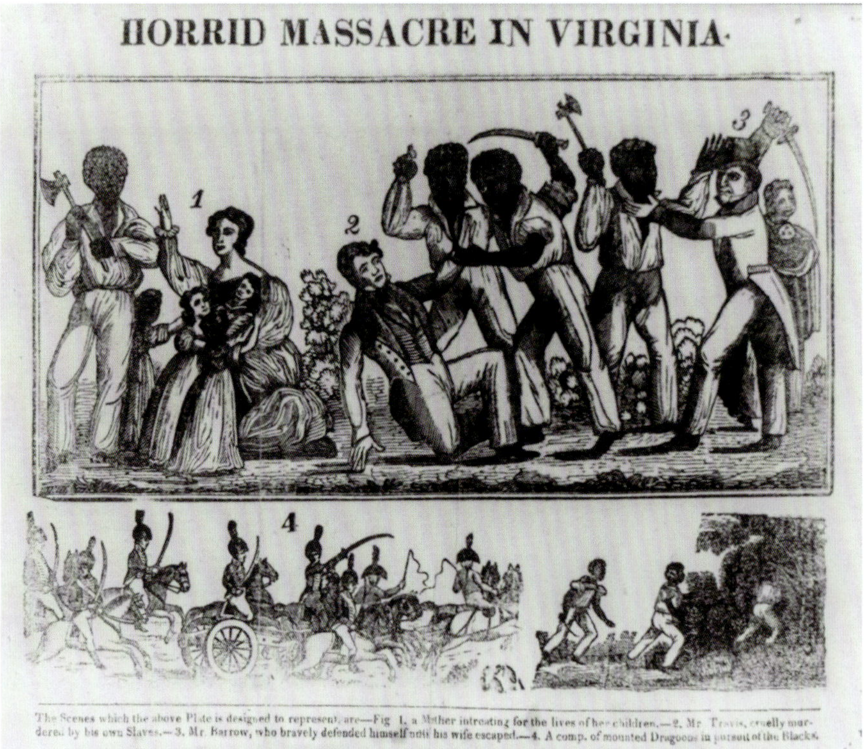

An illustration from a book about Nat Turner's 1831 revolt in Southampton County, Virginia.

The burning of the Roehampton Estate during the Baptist War in 1832 in Jamaica.

Benjamin Robert Haydon's painting of the World Anti-Slavery Convention held in London in June 1940.

A British steamer, *Rifleman*, pursues a Brazilian slave ship in 1850. Britain tried to intercept slave vessels in the Atlantic after ending its own participation in the slave trade in 1807.

Joseph Cinqué was the leader of the revolt of Africans on the Spanish slave ship *Amistad*, which ended up in New York. Its captives had to endure a lengthy legal battle to secure their freedom.

A workhouse "treadmill" in Jamaica in 1837, used as punishment during the "apprenticeship" period when people freed in 1833 were forced to continue working for no wages, which many resisted. The apprenticeship period ended in 1838.

An engraving in an 1869 edition of *Harper's Weekly* showing a battle during the independence struggle in Cuba against Spain, known as the Ten Years' War (1868–1878). Thousands of enslaved people obtained their freedom during the conflict.

The main house of a former sugar plantation, Hacienda la Esperanza, in Manatí, Puerto Rico.

A public celebration marking the abolition of slavery in Rio de Janeiro, Brazil, May 17, 1888. Brazil was the last nation in the Americas to abolish slavery.

Chapter 30

Liberation

THE FIRST THREE decades of the nineteenth century left Brazil transformed, but in very different ways from its neighbors. The earliest ripples of the waves to come reached Salvador de Bahia at the end of the 1700s. By then, the city had around 45,000 residents, with a large black population, as well as a significant number of free people of color, who had begun to chafe at the regime they were living under.[1] Word of the events in France, followed by the news from Saint-Domingue, had crossed the equator and reached eager listeners. Early in 1798, residents awoke to find that the gallows next to the *pelourinho*—the post for whipping slaves and issuing royal decrees in the city's main square—had been destroyed overnight. Lying at the damaged pole's base that morning were satirical pamphlets, later described as "seditious."[2] Nothing immediately came of it, but a few months later, on the morning of August 12 the city woke to a flurry of more pamphlets scattered around the city, including at three church sacristies, positioned to be picked up, read, and passed around.[3] One posted on a church door proclaimed: "Be encouraged people of Bahia because the time of our Liberty is approaching."[4] Another declared: "The happy time of our liberty is about to arrive; the time when all will be brothers, the time when all will be equal."[5]

Such talk was highly charged, especially since members of the public, like João de Deus Nascimento, were not happy with the existing order. Nascimento was a free Afro-European (mulatto) tailor, who understood the deeper significance of clothing and style, and how sumptuary laws might be used against people of color. He knew the meaning of a particular hat, or type of feather. He was also a corporal in the military, and was thus attuned to the importance of a uniform. Nascimento had become fond of French fashion, sporting tight breeches and pointed shoes—quite out of line for a man in his position.[6] He was even more enthusiastic about the political ideas that were coming from France. Style was rebellion, and at this juncture there was a wider fashion for all things French, even though Brazil actually had far more in common with Saint-Domingue: a large enslaved population, a significant free black community, and a white working class.

The tailors and their accomplices would have been aware of the events in Saint-Domingue, so they may have been using the language of "France" to describe the desire for equality that the free people on that island had expressed, but without directly invoking the specter of a full-on slave rebellion.[7] Ships brought news of events in both places. More locally, the satirical pamphlets appeared during a period of high food prices, and that, mixed with ongoing discontent, poverty, and discrimination, was sufficient cause for the events of that August morning.[8]

The authorities quickly pounced. Nearly 50 men were rounded up in this "conspiracy of the tailors" (*revolta dos alfaiates*), and 33 were put on trial.[9] The alleged authors were mainly free Afro-European tradesmen. As had been the case in pre-Revolutionary France and pre–*gracias al sacar* Spanish America, certain social and political roles were denied to free people of mixed heritage. In Brazil, for instance, that could mean being denied membership in artisans' guilds, something that would have mattered to tradesmen looking to improve their livelihood. Overall, in late 1790s Brazil, Afro-European people numbered 406,000, or 12 percent of the population.[10] In this conspiracy, there were five tailors, eleven slaves, six soldiers, three military officials, a businessman, two goldsmiths, an embroiderer, a bricklayer, a carpenter, a surgeon, and a teacher, and 22 of them were Afro-European *pardos* of varying descriptions ("dark," "clear," etc.), with one person described as black (*preto*), and 10 white. All of the men were locally born creoles.[11]

The tailors and the others arrested had not killed a single person and did not express any actual plans for a revolution. But four alleged plotters—all Afro-European, including João de Deus Nascimento—were to be made an example of. The four men were hanged, drawn, and quartered on November 8, 1799. One of the executed was former soldier Luís Gonzaga das Virgens e Veiga, whose hands were later

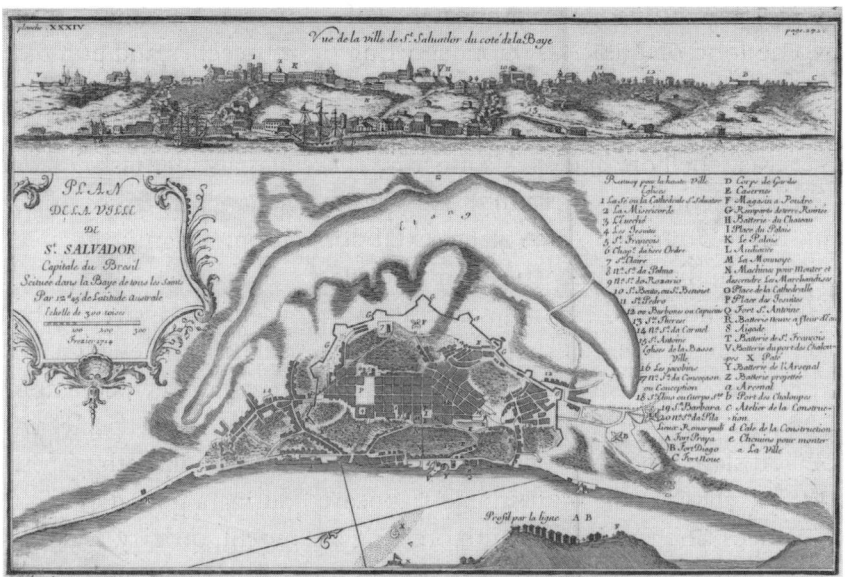

A French map of São Salvador de Bahia de Todos os Santos, Brazil, from 1716 by Amédée-François Frézier

nailed to the gallows as a warning to any would-be pamphleteer.[12] Upon being arrested, Nascimento is said to have declared: "All [Brazilians] would become Frenchmen, in order to live in equality and abundance . . . and reduce all to an entire revolution, so that all might be rich and taken out of poverty, and that the difference between white, black and brown would be extinguished."[13]

A few years later, France would have an even more dramatic impact on Brazil, as the entire Portuguese royal family under the Prince Regent Dom João fled to that colony after the French invaded Portugal during the Peninsular War in 1807.[14] This made them the first reigning monarchs of any European kingdom to come to a colony in the Americas.[15] The first stop of their flotilla, which carried 15,000 passengers, including members of the House of Braganza, along with assorted priests, administrators, and other elites, was Salvador, one of the engines of its empire. From there, they set up in the capital, Rio de Janeiro. Both cities were majority black, with large free populations. They were diverse, polyglot, African places—the product of the slave ships that sailed back and forth between Brazilian ports and the West African coast. Rio would be a dramatic new home, later called a "tropical Versailles" by historians, ringed by mountains. Beyond the city was the lush hinterland that provided riches of sugar, gold, and other commodities, which produced the customs duties that had long flowed into the royal family's coffers.

Britain was an ally of Portugal as well as a trade partner, and had been deeply involved in fighting France. Britain's help on that front and in providing protection for the royal flotilla meant that Prince Regent Dom João had little choice but to open up commerce between Britain and Brazil. Within a decade an English merchant community had become established in Rio.[16] Diplomats also began to pressure Portugal and Brazil over the slave trade by demanding that the Portuguese traffick humans only in their own dominions and promise to finally end the transatlantic trade, a pledge that would ultimately take decades to fulfil.[17] When the negotiations for the 1815 Congress of Vienna began, Portugal agreed to abolish its participation in the slave trade in the northern hemisphere starting in 1817, but managed to continue in the South Atlantic.[18] However, in an important additional convention to the treaty, the British navy was granted the right to search Portuguese vessels suspected of any involvement in illegal slaving north of the equator. If their suspicions were correct, the captured ship could be detained and the crew sent to an Anglo-Brazilian "mixed commission" in either Rio or Sierra Leone, depending on where it was apprehended.[19]

In 1821, the ongoing reconfiguration of politics on the Iberian Peninsula resulted in Dom João (who had become king in 1816) reluctantly returning to Portugal, leaving his son Dom Pedro as the prince regent of Brazil. The experience of the royal family living in Brazil had long-reaching ramifications, including its promotion to a "kingdom" equal to Portugal in 1815. Now Portugal's government wanted to put Brazil back under its direct control, an unpopular move with Brazilian elites, not least because some of them benefited from royal largesse, for instance in gaining land and titles of nobility. They did not want to see Brazil return to a subordinate status.[20]

Talk of independence grew—most of Spanish America had liberated itself from Spain, a process that people in Brazil could not fail to notice.[21] Dom Pedro was able to channel the burgeoning independence movement into a constitutional monarchy that was presented by its supporters as the only way to maintain Brazil's unity.[22] On September 7, 1822, he made a complete break, declaring Brazil's independence from Portugal. By the end of the year he was crowned Pedro I, Emperor of Brazil.[23]

Britain once again made itself indispensable to Portugal, and now to the Empire of Brazil, in the service of its own interests. It hammered out an agreement in 1825 in which Portugal would recognize Brazilian independence in exchange for £2 million in compensation. The price Britain extracted from Portugal for such diplomacy was a preferential trade deal and an agreement that the Brazilian slave trade would become illegal three years after the treaty was ratified, by March 1830.[24] The country's landowners remained a powerful force, and it was understood that more than a few blind eyes would be turned. The year 1830 came and went, but the slave trade carried on. Brazil passed a law in 1831 that, in theory, put penalties on anyone bringing slaves into the country, while also declaring any captives brought there to be free. But it was not well enforced and indeed was described as "a law for the English to see" or *uma lei para inglês ver*.[25] Between 1830 and 1850, some 550,000 Africans arrived in Brazil—now mainly on Brazilian ships travelling direct to and from West Africa—on top of the 1.1 million who had been trafficked between the French Revolution (1789) and Brazilian independence (1822), and the 450,000 taken between 1822 and 1830.[26]

A new era for Brazil had begun, but as the slavery numbers show, much of it would be built upon its old ways. No abolition measures would be introduced for some time, but there was a growing awareness that reliance on slave labor came at a price. The word *haitianismo* (Haitianism) crept into the popular vocabulary and the press in Brazil around this time, always in reference to any possibility of a Haitian-style uprising among people of color, free or slave. The term was also used as evidence by early opponents of the slave trade, who argued that the continued importation of Africans would similarly increase the risk of a revolt.[27]

Brazil, like Cuba, increased sugar production in the aftermath of Haiti's decline. By the time of Brazilian independence, 40 percent of its export earnings were from sugar.[28] Slavery permeated the entire country, but the majority of enslaved people could be found in a handful of provinces: Maranhão, Pernambuco, and Bahia in the sugar- and cotton-producing North; Minas Gerais, with its mines and cattle ranches; and Rio de Janeiro, both in the capital itself and on the coffee plantations around it, which eventually extended south to São Paulo. Enslavers forced the steady stream of Africans arriving in Brazil on to their sugar, cotton, and coffee plantations. The dangerous work of mining was also often reserved for captives who had no choice. It required a large workforce, and by 1819 Minas Gerais was the province with the largest enslaved population, at 170,000 people. Enslaved workers elsewhere in Brazil could also be found in all manner of other roles, from urban dockworkers to rural cattle hands to laborers on public works projects around the country.[29]

In 1831, Emperor Pedro I abdicated and left for Europe, after years of tensions with the Brazilian elite, who criticized what they considered to be his absolutist behavior. In addition, there had been a long-running conflict with the United Provinces of Rio de la Plata (today's Argentina) over a province called Cisplatina (also Banda Oriental). The result was a costly loss for both nations, as an independence movement eventually triumphed and led to the creation of Uruguay in 1825 (recognized by Brazil and Argentina in 1828). In 1830, Brazilians watched the French overthrow Charles X for Louis-Philippe, the so-called "Citizen King," and some began to agitate for change in Brazil. The criticism and calls for political reform within Brazil mounted, with regular public protest from both supporters of the emperor and those who wanted to see him go. In addition, a succession crisis within the House of Braganza—whose members ruled over both Portugal and Brazil—occurred in Portugal between Pedro I's daughter, Maria II, and his younger brother, Miguel. Opting to focus on matters in Portugal, Pedro I abdicated in favor of his five-year-old son, Pedro II, placing him under a regency until 1840, after which time he could take the throne as a creole emperor, born in Brazil like his subjects.[30]

In the middle of this period, a significant slave revolt broke out in Bahia in January 1835. In the decades leading up to this, there had been plenty of unrest in that region among enslaved communities. One rebellion, in February 1814, involved hundreds of enslaved people fleeing Bahia, gathering at a nearby runaway *quilombo*, and then going to a village on the coast. From there, they lured enslaved fishermen into their ranks and then attacked a village, killing around 50 people and burning down houses. The group then moved inland, to the Recôncavo sugar region, but officials stopped them before they could get any further.[31] Angry and fearful planters and merchants invoked Haiti in their criticism of the local government for not exerting enough control. One critic claimed,

> Blacks can be seen gathering in the streets at night, just as they did before [the February revolt], conversing about anything they please in their own language with constant whistling and other signs . . . They speak and know of the fatal success on the island of São Domingos [Saint-Domingue] . . . saying that by St John's Day [June 24], there will be no whites or mulattoes left alive.[32]

Throughout the 1820s at least 10 uprisings roiled the rolling green hills of the sugar-rich Recôncavo, almost all of them led and executed Africans, rather than creoles.[33] A steady stream of rumors forced officials to take action, clearing out nearby runaway *quilombos* and protecting local wells after claims that Muslim Hausa slaves from West Africa were going to poison the water.[34] All of this was on top of the ongoing political unrest in Bahia and other regions.

By 1835, more than three decades after the Tailors' Revolt of 1798, Salvador, the capital of the region, had grown to around 65,000 people, only 28 percent of whom were white, and the rest enslaved or free people of color. It was, therefore, a black city, in which free and slave lived in close quarters.[35] It was also a significantly African city, with 17,325 people (26 percent of the enslaved population) and another 4,615 free African people.[36] Within the city, enslaved people were often domestic workers or tradespeople, and a hiring-out system known as *escravos de ganho* (slaves for profit) employed wage-earning slaves. Under this system, enslaved people worked as artisans or market sellers and paid their enslavers part of their wages; some managed to earn and save enough to eventually buy themselves out of slavery.[37]

Although many of the prior revolts had been in the cane fields of the countryside, the uprising of 1835 was in the city. Despite the laws passed during the previous two decades, slave ships never stopped arriving. Ethnic identity mattered in many aspects of slave life. In Salvador people organized themselves socially around various "nations" (*nações*), both during holiday celebrations and in more formal associations like brotherhoods (*irmandades*) and mutual aid societies.[38] In addition, many of these Africans also became adherents of syncretic religious practices, like candomblé, or other forms of worship with roots in animist West African practices, in addition to Islam and Christianity. Through these networks some members of this broad community decided to organize something rather more dangerous than a social gathering: a revolt. The Yoruba-speaking people, known as Nagôs, were the main leaders, but they were joined by other West Africans, including some Hausa, Gege, and Tapa people, and the uprising was later known as the Malê (from the Yoruba word for Muslim, Ìmàle) Revolt.[39]

It was planned for the morning of Sunday, January 25, 1835, as Salvador was heading into summer. The streets were alive and animated as people looked forward to the annual festivities at the Church of Nosso Senhor do Bonfim, where they would honor Our Lady of Guidance (*Nossa Senhora da Guia*) as part of a cycle of events around the Bonfim church. At that time, the church sat in a village about five miles (eight kilometers) away, although today it has been absorbed into the city, perched on a hill, high above sprawling Salvador.[40]

In Salvador, sailors down on the docks had heard interesting gossip on Saturday afternoon: Apparently a group of slaves was coming in from the Recôncavo, led by an African named Ahuna. The news travelled along the city center's cobbled streets. A freed slave named Domingos Fortunato arrived home and told his wife, Guilhermina Rosa de Souza. They were both unsettled about this news, and Fortunato wanted his former enslaver, Fortunato José da Cunha, to know. While he was relaying that information to da Cunha, Rosa de Souza overheard from her window three Nâgo women talking about the plans: They would hear the call to battle as they went to fetch water from the public fountains at 5:00 a.m.—and they would know what to do. Rosa de Souza's unease grew after a conversation with a freed Nagô woman named Sabina da Cruz, who related that her partner was involved in the plot, and that she had been told she would not see him again until Africans were masters of the land.[41]

Rosa de Souza, now even more upset, went to a white neighbor and reported everything. The neighbor and others with him leapt into action to alert the authorities. The municipal guard was on the lookout by 10:30 p.m. that Saturday, with a ship in the bay keeping watch for any suspicious people trying to flee.[42]

The plotters, meanwhile, waited. Around 1:00 a.m., a patrol heard of a disturbance at the house of an Afro-European tailor, Domingos Marinho de Sá. When they asked him if any Africans were there, he replied that it was only his tenants. But minutes before, Marinho de Sá had been threatened with a knife when he went to investigate a noise in the basement of his building and found the plotters hiding. He tried to dissuade the patrol from going down there, but when they did, they saw a group of Muslim Africans waiting for the appointed time of 5:00 a.m. to start the uprising. As the patrol moved to look behind a door, another group of 50 to 60 Africans suddenly rushed out, waving swords and shouting, "Kill soldiers." From there, they dispersed into the city's hilly streets.[43]

One witness ran to his window and saw "a group of black Africans wearing white skullcaps and large smocks over their pants. They were armed with swords and heading toward the Praça do Palácio."[44] According to a later report, "different groups of armed blacks roamed the main streets of the city making noise and clamouring, beating on their cohorts' doors, entreating them to join in. The only opposition they encountered was from patrols who shot at them from time to time."[45] The rebels first went to the city hall to free an enslaved Muslim elder in the basement jail, but many ended up injured as they were shot at during the raid. Other Africans joined them as they moved through the city's streets. As dawn broke, battles erupted in bursts over the course of three hours. Eventually the cavalry arrived to help the troops put down the revolt, which had moved out of the city and was moving towards the barracks in Agua de Meninos, on the way to Bonfim. There, the final battle took place as the troops shot at the rebels. Some were killed or injured and taken prisoner, while others managed to flee.[46]

In the subsequent accounts of the fighting, the extent of the rebellion was never clarified. The total number of participants was estimated at between 200 and 600.[47] The plan was apparently not to take the city, but to disrupt it and then go into the Recôncavo to mobilize slaves on the plantations.[48] Some 70 people died in the fighting. Around one hundred were arrested, half of whom were free people of color. The participation of a large number of free people raises questions about what was at stake, beyond liberty for the enslaved; perhaps some of the rebels sought greater cultural or religious freedom, to live as African Muslims in Brazil without the constant surveillance and oppressive behavior of white Catholic authorities.[49] The constant grind of being a free black person in a slave society had driven Denmark Vesey to organize a revolt a decade earlier in South Carolina; such frustrations were inevitably shared with free people of color in Brazil and everywhere else in the slaveholding Americas.

Four men were executed; 45 more received a flogging, which could go up to 1,000 lashes; and dozens of others were jailed or deported to Africa.[50] Most of the punished defendants were Nagô, and all were Muslim.[51] Although it was one of the largest revolts of the time, the fact that so many people knew about it—including those willing to tell the authorities—meant the seeds of its failure were planted in advance. That it was organized along cultural lines and involved so many free people prompted the authorities to destroy the social and professional networks of those involved, sending Muslims out of Bahia, even out of Brazil.[52] But the only thing that would truly prevent slave conspiracies was a dismantling of the system—and that was still a long way off in Brazil.

By around 1850 Pedro II and successive governments had brought a greater degree of political stability to Brazil, and there was a growing public willingness to seriously consider abolishing the slave trade. The British now had a sizable community and delegation in Rio. Britain had continued to step up antislavery measures, for instance with the 1839 Palmerston Act, which gave Britain's navy the power to stop any suspected slave ship, whether or not any human cargo was on board.

This activity was intensified by another British act in 1845 that permitted the navy to treat Brazilian slavers as pirate ships and take their captains and crews before a vice-admiralty court.[53]

The demand for enslaved humans fluctuated throughout the 1830s and 1840s, in part because of the rise of the coffee industry. Although coffee plantations needed fewer workers than other crops, the number of estates increased in this period. This change is reflected in the numbers of captives being imported, with around 2,300 disembarking in 1832, rising to 57,000 in 1839, dropping to 15,000 in 1846, and going back up to 53,000 only three years later.[54] However, by the end of the 1840s, the Brazilian government had begun to consider alternative sources of workers and was encouraging more European immigration, which rose steadily from around 400 migrants in 1820 to more than 18,000 in 1836.[55]

By this point, the Brazilian legislature had decided to act against the Atlantic slave trade, passing a law punishing slave traders and making sure it was effectively enforced. The result was dramatic; in 1852 there were only two known landings of slave ships.[56] However, the internal trade of enslaved people was not affected, and this forced movement of people provided the necessary supply of labor for the booming coffee plantations, as it would do in a similar way for the cotton fields of the Southern United States.[57] People were taken from the sugar regions of the northeast and sent to the coffee areas further south, with an estimated 100,000 to 200,000 affected. The ending of the Atlantic trade forced up prices for slaves, inspiring many enslavers in sugar and cattle ranching areas to make a profit on their captives while they could, and replace them, gradually, with labor provided by free immigrants.[58]

―‹‹ • ››―

Somewhere between the Malê Revolt and the end of the slave trade in Brazil, another enslaved Muslim, Mahommah Gardo Baquaqua, arrived in the north of the country, in Pernambuco. He had been captured in Djougou, northern Dahomey (today's Benin), and had remained enslaved within Africa for a period before being put on a

Portuguese ship with hundreds of other captives to cross the Atlantic. He disembarked in Brazil in 1845 and was sold at a slave market, first to a slave trader and then to a baker. Although he was already on a journey through the hell of bondage, the twists and turns of his life would take him through and around the shifting, complicated world of Atlantic slavery, tracing a rare trail to freedom that intersected with many key developments of his time.[59]

Baquaqua's extraordinary story was published as a narrative in 1854, told through abolitionist intermediaries in New York after he arrived there. His initial enslavement to the baker was difficult, "hard labour, such as none but slaves and horses are put to," ferrying stones to build a house. He was later tasked with taking bread to the marketplace, and faced the lash if any loaves remained unsold. The situation was intolerable. He ran away but was caught. He later tried to drown himself in a river, but a nearby boat rescued him. After this he received a violent beating, "the scars from which savage treatment," he wrote, "are visible at this time, and will remain so as long as I live."

The baker sold Baquaqua, and he was sent to Rio de Janeiro and almost bought by a "colored man." Baquaqua makes a point of mentioning this, "to illustrate that slaveholding is generated in power, and anyone having the means of buying his fellow creature with the paltry dross, can become a slave owner, no matter his color, his creed or country." He ended up instead enslaved by a ship captain, working as a steward and enduring constant violence at the hands of his enslaver and other members of the crew.

In 1847, the captain was commissioned to take a shipment of coffee to New York. Baquaqua was aware that "at New York there was no slavery" and was therefore "most anxious to get there." The journey was arduous, with Baquaqua being tied to a cannon and whipped at one point. While recovering in the bow of the ship, he thought about "the first words of English that my two companions and myself ever learned . . . F-r-e-e; we were taught it by an Englishman on board, and oh! how many times did I repeat it." When they landed at the harbor in New York, "a great many colored persons came aboard the vessel, who inquired whether we were free." The captain had earlier instructed the slaves to lie about their status, but "we heeded not his wish." The captain, realizing his position, tried to tell the slaves that

New York was "a very bad place." To Baquaqua it couldn't be any worse than the ship.

He almost missed his chance, saying openly to the captain, after drinking too much wine, that he would not stay on board. The captain locked him in the bow, but Baquaqua broke down the door with an iron bar, left the ship, and ran, he said, "as if for my life." With no English, Baquaqua was unable to communicate at the port, and he was again locked up, and retrieved the next morning by the captain. However, New York abolitionists had been alerted, and told the captain that "all on board were free." The abolitionists took the slaves to the Brazilian consul, where Baquaqua declared, "I would rather die than return into slavery." Another of his enslaved shipmates, however, chose to stay with the captain. Baquaqua remained in custody as abolitionists worked on his case, and he was eventually sent to Boston. He was told that from there, he would be sent to either England or Haiti, the latter being his preferred option. "When I arrived at Hayti I felt myself free, as indeed I was. No slavery exists there." He met Haitian officials and secured employment with Reverend William Judd, a Baptist missionary, converting to Christianity.

He left Haiti around 1849 to avoid a military draft, and returned to New York, before eventually going to Canada, where he concluded the account of his life. He had ended up, he said, in a place "where every man acting as a man, no matter what his color, is regarded as a brother, and where all are equally free to do and to say." West Africa, Brazil, New York, Haiti, Canada—his journey was a voyage through this transitioning state of the mid-nineteenth-century Americas, where his freedom involved moving between slave and free places, though many remained unable to take similar leaps.

◂◂ • ▸▸

As this patchwork of slave and free places was emerging, a more liminal, undefined zone of freedom was being created in the wake of the West Africa Squadron (also known as the Preventive Squadron), a unit of the British navy that carried out a six-decade-long effort to suppress the slave trade. Starting soon after the British abolished their own participation in the slave trade in 1807, naval fleets patrolled the African coasts to enforce the British ban on the trade, attempting to capture ships still active in trafficking—a task doubtless made easier because of the knowledge acquired over the previous 150 years of supporting the slave trade. The seas were the same, even if the mission was now different.

The British went after Spanish, French, Dutch, Portuguese, and Brazilian slave ships on the grounds that these nations had agreed to give up the slave trade after 1815. Should any suspected vessels be spotted at sea, the British would intercept them and, if necessary, take the crew to a special court to determine if they were illegally trafficking humans.[60] This effort involved many often-changing treaties with these other European nations and, later, some of the republics of Latin America. With the latter, such agreements were usually part of Britain's condition for recognizing them; all of the new nations had already banned their own participation in the Atlantic slave trade.

This British search-and-seizure scheme in West Africa relied on the navy's continued presence in Sierra Leone, securing Britain's foothold along the coast. Abolition of the slave trade also gave the British a reason to attack when African leaders refused to go along with their demands to suppress their involvement, leading, for instance, to the naval bombardment of Lagos in 1851. The British used the cause of antislavery to open the door to later annexation and colonization. They also used it to pressure African leaders into giving them preferential trade deals and other benefits, such as protecting British property.[61]

Some nations considered this British desire to patrol the seas as an infringement on their sovereignty, as Brazil had; they saw Britain's actions as little more than a ruse by which they could serve their own diplomatic and commercial ends.[62] France, which had banned the slave trade by 1830, and the United States, which had quit the trade in 1807, pushed against the terms, finding it objectionable to have Britain's antislavery patrols harassing their vessels.[63] The US Navy also had a few of its own patrols in African waters, and cooperation with Britain increased over the years, culminating in the 1842 Webster-Ashburton Treaty, after which the US set up its own Africa Squadron to assist in the patrolling of the Atlantic. France, too, would send its vessels on antislavery patrols by the 1840s.[64]

Ultimately, this was a British enterprise: from 1808 until 1867, the West Africa Squadron was responsible for about 85 percent of overall captures.[65] The number of ships in Britain's squadron ranged from fewer than 10 early on to more than 30 by 1845. By midcentury, the 30 ships used on the patrols represented around 10 percent of Britain's total naval manpower, before declining going into the 1860s.[66]

The West Africa Squadron's success was limited. One in five slave ships of the estimated 7,600 sailing between 1808 and 1867 were intercepted, around 1,500 vessels.[67] To incentivize their humanitarian instinct, the sailors were also paid prizes, or "headmoney," for every slave "liberated." The years 1845 to 1850 were the most successful, with some 400 ships captured.[68] By 1867, at least 200,000 "liberated Africans," as they were called, were recorded. However, the total estimates of people taken out of slavery who ended up in apprenticeships or conscripted to the military apart from the squadron's activities by the 1890s go as high as 700,000.[69]

When the vessels were apprehended, the captives were released but the crew would face what were called mixed-commission courts, which would assess the legality of the cargo. These courts were bilateral, and agreed to under treaty between Britain and another power. They were staffed by officials from Britain and from whichever nation was party to the treaty. A guilty verdict would mean the loss of the ship by sale, with the proceeds going to both governments, but there was no punishment for the crew.

In addition to the courts established in Rio de Janeiro and Sierra Leone, there were a number of others, including Cuba (with Spain), New York (with the US), Suriname (with the Netherlands), and Cape Verde and Angola (with Portugal). There were also vice-admiralty courts run by the British to deal with its subjects or anyone who could be detained under British law. Those courts could be found in key areas, such as the Bahamas, Jamaica, and Lagos, as well as the South Atlantic island of Saint Helena, and other slaving points in Africa such as Mauritius and the Cape Colony, South Africa.[70] In addition to their work adjudicating the cases, officials in these courts also monitored and reported to London about the slave trade taking place around them.[71]

The "liberated Africans" freed by these courts had their details listed in a register and were given certificates of emancipation—but they had little liberty to decide where they would be "disposed of," to use the wording of the original 1807 Act for the Abolition of the Slave Trade.[72] None of the possibilities involved a return home. In Sierra Leone, 55,533 liberated Africans arrived between 1808 and 1833. Many were made "apprentices" for terms of up to 14 years—sometimes money also changed hands, blurring the boundary between apprenticeship and bondage.[73] The idea behind the apprenticeships was that the freed people would learn certain trades and live in one of the villages set up under the auspices of the Church Missionary Society. They were encouraged to join the other settlers, including Jamaican maroons and free black loyalists who had left Nova Scotia, in attending church on Sunday and receiving an education from the mission schools.[74] The missionaries' aim was to convert the now-free Africans to Christianity and have them settle in Sierra Leone, creating a sort of "civilized" peasantry.[75] However, for many "liberated Africans," such a prospect was distressing—they might have been freed, but they were still somewhere they did not want to be.

One British missionary in Sierra Leone in the early 1830s wrote in a letter home, "I . . . am told that the miseries the poor creatures suffer even after they are under British Protection . . . beggars all description; many, ignorant of what is become of them, when they are freed from their irons, throw themselves overboard in despair."[76] In some cases, people taken to Sierra Leone believed they were waiting to be sold or transported again, especially those taken to nearby Bunce Island, a former slaving port, where they were held in barracoons (an enclosure used to hold slaves prior to transport) while awaiting military conscription.[77] As the missionary observed, "When they arrive in this harbour, they have no means of being aware of what is wished to be done for them."[78]

Other "liberated" people were forced to go to the British West Indies to work as paid laborers on the plantations, a process that looked suspiciously similar to the slavery that had preceded it.[79] This was the fate for the thousands freed by the vice-admiralty court set up in 1840 in Jamestown, the capital of the rocky and remote island of Saint Helena. More than 1,000 miles (1,800 kilometers) separates Saint Helena from the Angolan coast, and Brazil is about double that distance away. However, the winds and currents brought an outsize number of ships to this tiny speck of land in the South Atlantic, which measures ten by five miles.

Over the next 28 years, 439 cases were adjudicated there, and at least 27,000 people were freed—if they survived. Saint Helena had a high mortality rate within the "depots" where the captives were held before and after the hearings.[80] Once the Africans were freed, they were forced to wait for a further passage, often to the Caribbean as a laborer: Some 17,148 liberated people were sent to the Caribbean, especially Guiana (5,359), Trinidad (4,039), and Jamaica (3,983).[81] A small number stayed in Saint Helena, reaching a total of 750 people by 1872, up from 391 in 1844, many of whom were made to labor on public works projects, such as churches and government buildings.[82]

Tens of thousands of people were thus spared a life of bondage by the courts—but were also never returned to their homelands, or even asked what sort of life they might actually want. British emancipators saw this as appropriate treatment for Africans, whom they considered, by and large, to be "uncivilized," and whom they aimed to convert to Christianity; or they considered such service a way to "pay" for the cost of their being freed.[83] However, some freed captives did not accept this situation and fled their apprenticeships.

Such treatment of freed captives was not limited to the British colonies. The French and Dutch had a similar system where they would contract with slave merchants in Africa and buy these supposedly free people, giving them an *engagé* work contract for around ten years. Under this system, 3,000 people were sent into military service in the East Indies for the Dutch, while another 54,000 were sent to the cane fields in the French Caribbean colonies of Martinique, Guadeloupe, and Guyane, as well as the African island of Réunion.[84] Until Britain's abolition of slavery 1833—and that of France and Holland later on—this meant that some "liberated Africans" sent to the Caribbean or other areas with slavery were forced to live in slave societies, putting their precarious freedom in jeopardy.

Thousands also found themselves conscripted into the British military. Between 1808 and 1816 alone, some 2,511 African men were enlisted in the Royal Navy and army, often ending up in one of the West India Regiments.[85] Some considered aspects of military service, especially in Sierra Leone, attractive, such as the pension or the social mobility offered though promotion into officer ranks.⁸⁶ For others, it was something to escape from.

On the evening of June 17, 1837, 280 black soldiers in the 1st West India Regiment mutinied at their barracks in the town of Saint Joseph, in northwestern Trinidad. Among them were liberated African soldiers, including a man named Dâaga, whom the British arrested as the leader. He was born somewhere in Togo or Benin and possibly had been involved in the slave trade, capturing Yoruba people, until he was tricked by Portuguese traders, who kidnapped him.⁸⁷ The ship carrying him was picked up by a British patrol, and he ended up a "liberated African" in the Caribbean, assigned to the 1st West India Regiment, where his officers renamed him Donald Stewart. After the commotion at the barracks, a small band of rebels divided up and fled, running into the forest toward the coast, but were soon caught or shot by the local militia. Six committed suicide in the forest; others faced courts-martial. Three, including Dâaga, were executed by a firing squad composed of black soldiers.⁸⁸ Dâaga's plan was never fully explained, but it seemed to have involved running for the shore, grabbing whatever boats he and his men could find, and sailing to somewhere they could be free from forced military service—and free to use whatever names they pleased.⁸⁹ Apparently, as Dâaga faced the firing squad, he pushed away his blindfold, turning a steely gaze to his executioner and declaring in his native language: "The curse of Holloloo on white men. Do they think that Dâaga fears to fix his eyeballs on death?"⁹⁰

Despite the efforts of the Atlantic slavery patrols, the number of people they managed to free between 1808 and 1867 was only a drop in the vast ocean of human misery: some 2.5 million Africans were trafficked over those six decades, with the squadron effort intercepting less than 10 percent.⁹¹ The slave trade, with the involvement of both legitimate shipping companies and criminal smugglers, was holding firm.

Once Brazil ended its participation in the slave trade, the remaining market was Cuba. People who had been involved in the trade from Brazil and other parts—including US merchants—continued trafficking humans in the shadows. One important operator was the Portuguese Company, set up in 1850s New York City and hiding in plain sight among all the other international trading companies. Shipowners and captains from the US were involved in the trade, dodging the British and US patrols.[92] In the final years of the slave trade, from 1850 to 1867, of the 310 voyages between Africa and Cuba, around 30 percent were in ships sailing under a US flag.[93]

Indeed, some of the anti-slavery trade measures indirectly aided the traffickers. For instance, the United States' refusal to allow vessels sailing under its flag to submit to searches by Britain—despite the cooperation regarding joint patrols—or any other foreign power gave slave traders an incentive to purchase US ships. In another case, one of the partners in the Portuguese Company, José da Silva Maia Ferreira, had earlier in his career served as a clerk on the Anglo-Portuguese Mixed Commission in Angola, where he learned firsthand exactly what was being done to suppress the trade.[94]

While slave ships continued to carry captives to Cuba, its neighboring British islands had to search for paid labor to replace the enslaved workforce after abolition in 1833. They turned to the East, looking to India, which was under Britain's control, and China, with which it had a trading relationship, including in opium. From there, East Indian and Chinese "coolie" workers began to be brought over on indenture contracts. One proponent of Indian labor was John Gladstone, the Demerara enslaver whose plantations were at the heart of the 1823 insurrection.[95] Talk of such schemes had begun before the ending of slavery in Britain's colonies, but by the 1830s the transition was deemed necessary because freed people refused to return to the cane fields. Gladstone's own early experiment with indentured labor ended in scandal as a commission investigated claims of physical abuse and financial extortion of the workers on his Demerara plantations. In 1838, the British governor-general of India prohibited any more emigration.[96] However, this policy was abandoned in 1845, and over the next six decades, nearly 500,000 people from South Asia would go to the British West Indies, along with some 17,000 Chinese. This practice was not limited to Britain's colonies: Starting in 1846, Chinese indentured workers made the voyage to Cuba, with around 125,000 going to the island by 1874.[97] Although technically free, these "coolie" laborers often survived in conditions little different from those endured by the slaves who had preceded them.

However, despite the introduction of paid foreign labor, the illicit slave trade continued, in part because it remained profitable, at times shockingly so. A Barcelona newspaper gloated in 1845 that where the slave trade was concerned, "no commercial activity leaves greater benefit."[98] Despite the trade being illegal and the Spanish government technically prohibiting it, slave ships continued to leave—mainly from Havana—for West Africa. Because the business was by now illegal, many of the records have been lost, but some historians have used existing ones to calculate that in 17 expeditions between Africa and Havana alone between 1815 and 1830, the average return on investment of a slaving voyage hovered around a staggering 100 percent.[99] With profits like that, it would take more than a scattered patrol of ships across the vast Atlantic to end the slave trade. It would require the end of the entire system of slavery, and that was still decades away.

Chapter 31

Lashings

In the hush of London's National Portrait Gallery hangs a large painting in a gilt frame. It depicts a sea of mostly white male faces, with some women seated around the edges. They are crammed into London's Freemasons' Hall, listening to a speaker who has his hand raised with a finger pointing to the sky.[1] This was the 1840 inaugural meeting of the World Anti-Slavery Convention, memorialized by the fashionable painter Benjamin Robert Haydon. An aged Thomas Clarkson is at the pulpit, giving the opening address at the event, which drew some 5,000 spectators over 10 days.[2] Although female delegates are depicted in the painting, they were not actually allowed to participate and were refused seating, fueling their determination to begin a campaign for women's rights.[3] The air of the portrait is grand, bordering on the self-congratulatory, but considering that this is an abolitionist society, very few non-white faces are visible.

One black man sits behind Clarkson, Louis Celeste Lecesne, who was born in Jamaica to parents from Saint-Domingue—a French father and an enslaved, later freed, African mother—in around 1798, as the Haitian Revolution was underway. He came to the attention of Jamaican authorities as he campaigned for equal rights for free people of color and was deported from the island in 1824 under the assertion that he had been born in Saint-Domingue and was therefore an alien. Lecesne rejected the charge and said he had been born in Jamaica, eventually travelling to England to pursue his case.[4] Across the auditorium, facing Clarkson, is Jean-Baptiste Symphor Linstant de Pradine, a Haitian lawyer and author of a multivolume series cataloguing the laws of Haiti's government.[5] Further back in the crowd is the light-brown face of another man from the Caribbean, Edward Barrett, who had been enslaved in Jamaica.[6]

Finally, in the front of the painting, in slight profile, is Henry Beckford, a black Jamaican who had obtained his freedom three years earlier and travelled to England with the abolitionist Reverend William Knibb, as Barrett had also done.[7] Beckford's back is mostly turned toward the viewer as he watches Clarkson. The darkness of his skin is almost subsumed by his surroundings: the dark wood of the seats, the men's somber clothing, and the low lighting. It is as if he is a shadow, present but scarcely seen. There is, however, no missing the man to Beckford's right, John Scoble, abolitionist and secretary of the British and Foreign Anti-Slavery Society, in full, recognizable profile, his skin a near-translucent white.

Because of the large number of people in the group portrait, Haydon needed some of the people in the painting to sit for him privately. When Scoble had his turn, the artist explained that he was planning to place Beckford near him, thinking "an abolitionist on thorough principle would have gloried in being so placed."[8] But that was not the case. Haydon later noted in his journal that he was surprised when Scoble seemed uncertain about the arrangement, suggesting there would be a "greater propriety of placing the Negro in the distance, as it would have much greater effect." After this exchange Haydon asked other sitters whether they would object to being placed next to Beckford, but in the final work, he painted Scoble and Beckford together. Haydon later told Clarkson that he was determined "to place the African in front of the picture on the same level as the Europeans." Haydon does so, but he places Beckford in an awkward position, his face mostly out of view.[9] He is not the center of the painting; Clarkson is. Two more abolitionists sit nearby, one looking toward Beckford, the other resting his hand in a protective gesture on Beckford's forearm. To the right of Scoble is Samuel Jackman Prescod, born to a free woman of color and a white father in Barbados. His countenance—with its intense gaze and his notably lighter skin—is shown in nearly full view. It is unknown whether anyone objected to his positioning.

The abolitionists had been on a mission to end slavery, not to introduce equality between black and white people. Instead of a story of equality, they created their own narrative, in which—ideally—black

Christian subjects were grateful to their white benefactors and willing to be "improved."[10] The "civilizing" mission of the nineteenth century was in full swing, now inextricable from abolition and Christian evangelism. Even the Catholics had caught up: In 1839 Pope Gregory XVI issued *In supremo apostolatus*, condemning the slave trade. Meanwhile, Protestant British abolitionists wanted to take their fight against bondage to all corners of the world, and along with it, their own ideas of civilization—including, especially, conversion to Christianity.

Beckford no doubt understood this. He was invited to speak briefly at the convention. He stood up and thanked the society, "which has been formed in this country," he said, "to deliver us from bondage," making no mention of the efforts of the enslaved in securing their own freedom. He appealed to the white abolitionists' sense of mission, saying that "slavery brought men down to the level of four-footed beasts," and asking for their assistance until the Africans could "become more thoroughly established in the blessings" they now enjoyed. He ended by invoking Christianity, closing the short address by saying, "It is good to be the servants of the Lord Jesus Christ, and to be engaged in promoting his cause."[11] His short speech contained all the correct words and sentiments. How Beckford felt about saying them remains unknown.

While abolitionists debated their next steps in elegant London halls, more direct action was taking place at sea. The 1840 World Anti-Slavery Convention fell between two significant shipboard slave revolts: the *Amistad* in 1839 and the *Creole* in 1841.

The story of the slave schooner *Amistad*—Spanish for "friendship"— actually began on a different ship, which was sailing somewhere it should not have been: Sierra Leone. Despite all the efforts of the British West Africa Squadron, the slave trade along the coast of West Africa proved impossible to eradicate. Spanish slave trader Pedro Blanco knew this: He maintained a profitable slave-trading enterprise along the Gallinas River, a low, swampy area south of Freetown and near the modern border with Liberia. His success depended on good relations with local leaders, which he maintained, especially with King Siaka (Shuckar), a Vai ruler in southern Sierra Leone.[12] Blanco had a sizable operation set up on a nearby island, including around 20 staff and a "harem" of some 50 women. Also on the site were barracoons that could hold up to 5,000 enslaved people, which the king helped procure.[13] Kidnapping and conflict along the coast and inland continued to produce a steady stream of captives for Blanco's slave ships.

Antislavery patrols eventually raided the site, but it was not soon enough for Cinqué, Faquorna, Moru, Kimbo, and hundreds of others who, in April 1839, were forced onto an illegal Portuguese or Brazilian slaver called *Teçora*, which sailed from Fort Lomboko on the shores of the Gallinas. The captives were of different ethnic groups but mostly from the area that corresponds to modern Sierra Leone, with almost half identified as Mende.[14] They were put in chains and sent below deck. The ship evaded antislavery patrols on its way to Cuba, and the captives were snuck into Havana late at night. They were held in barracoons for about 10 days, awaiting sale. An enslaver named José Ruiz purchased the four men and 45 others, who would need to be transported to the city of Puerto Príncipe (today's Camagüey), in another cane-growing region. The most expedient way to move them was by sea. Fellow enslaver Pedro Montes bought four children, who would join the forty-nine enslaved men on their voyage, this time on *Amistad*.[15]

In the dark, early hours of July 2, 1839, when the passage was underway, Cinqué, Faquorna, Moru, and Kimbo managed to remove a chain that held them together—possibly aided by two blacksmiths among the captives—and crept up onto the main deck. They took weapons they found on deck, killed most of the crew, and freed the other captives. Ruiz and Montes had also come on the journey—and now they were the Africans' prisoners.[16]

The Africans then decided to sail back to Sierra Leone, but they didn't know how. They were forced to enlist the surviving crew to steer the ship, demanding they go east, toward the rising sun, which had been to their backs on the outbound journey. Montes was an experienced sailor and took the helm, but did not head in the direction of Africa. He sailed east during the day, but kept the sails loose and went slowly. At night he turned west, hoping to hit another island or be captured by a patrol. Seven weeks later, they spotted some coastline. They thought it might be Africa. It was Long Island, New York. They had travelled thousands of miles in the wrong direction.[17]

The Africans did not know where they were, and so they dropped anchor about a mile offshore and sent a small delegation to find out their location. They discovered the following day that they were in a place without slavery—but it was not clear to them that they were in a place where their freedom could be secured. A short time later, a US Navy brig sailed in. At first the Africans thought it was a slave ship, while the navy crew thought the *Amistad* was a pirate vessel. While everything was being clarified, navy officials let the enslavers Ruiz and Montes go and held the captives as prisoners on board after hearing about the insurrection. From there the ship and its captives were taken to New London, Connecticut, on August 27. The Africans' struggle to escape slavery was now being discussed in terms of murder and piracy charges. They would have to fight for their lives again, and this time in a place where they were supposed to be free, in a language they did not speak, and under a legal system that was completely unfamiliar.[18]

News of this extraordinary story began to circulate while the captives were being questioned by a district judge. Cinqué, also referred to as Joseph Cinquez, was named as the instigator. The *New York Sun* described him as "calm and collected . . . he evinced no fear." The newspaper reported on the testimony of the various Spanish-speaking witnesses as translated through a naval officer, observing that the Africans could only guess at what was being said. According to one article, Cinquez "did not understand a word in either language, and stood a mute spectator."[19] The same paper also published heroic images of Cinqué, which became hugely popular as interest in the case grew.[20]

American abolitionists were involved from the beginning, in part because the antislavery activist Dwight Janes inspected the ship and spoke to witnesses, realizing that these Africans had committed no crime but rather, they had the right to fight for their freedom on an illegal slave ship. He alerted the abolitionist network while the Africans awaited their uncertain fate in a New Haven jail. For all they knew, they were about to be sent somewhere again. Or killed. Home was now an impossible distance away. Some who were already suffering the effects of the voyage and terrible conditions on board fell ill and died.[21]

Janes and other abolitionists also began a search for Africans who could speak a Mende language, a process hindered by the fact that they were unclear about where these Africans were from, confusing the captives' self-identification of "Kono" as "Congo" and "Mende" as "Mandingo."²² Finally, they stumbled on James Ferry, a cosmopolitan multilingual sailor who spoke an African language, as well as Spanish and English. Ferry had been kidnapped in Sierra Leone and claimed he was later liberated in Colombia by Simón Bolívar when he was around the age of 12, before ending up in the US. Even with his help, the process was tricky. Ferry was Kissi, not Mende, and spoke Vai, which only one captive, Bau, also did. But that was enough—the men could translate the questions and answers between English, Vai, and Mende, and so include Cinqué in the testimony. The process was cumbersome but crucial. The abolitionists were able to hear the full story, of both Bau's and Cinqué's lives in Africa, their capture, and subsequent events—but there was far more to translate.²³

One of the abolitionists was a linguist, and he quickly learned the numbers one to ten in Mende from the captives. He took this knowledge to New York City's waterfront, and walked around counting loudly. This eventually attracted the attention of two African sailors, Charles Pratt and James Covey. Both men were from Sierra Leone, having been kidnapped and later freed by the British West Africa patrols. The two men could speak many languages between them, most crucially Mende—and were curious as to why this white man was walking around counting in that language. They were quickly brought on board to help the imprisoned captives.²⁴

With the skills of Pratt and Covey, the Africans could now make a full case, including against their enslavers, Ruiz and Montes. It went to trial, and the public was gripped. The story of Cinqué and the mutiny for freedom ran for months, as the summer heat gave way to the biting New England cold. The charges of piracy and murder against Cinqué and the others had been dropped. The legal question now was whether their enslavement was lawful. Were they the property of Ruiz and Montes, or free people, illegally captured? The first verdict was that they were indeed free people of Africa, but the legal victory was short-lived—appeals were made all the way to the Supreme Court. By the time of that trial in February 1841, 18 months had elapsed since the Africans had landed on Long Island.²⁵

A good deal of the case against the now 36 surviving captives rested on Pinckney's Treaty of 1795 between the US and Spain, especially article 9: "All Ships and merchandise of what nature soever which shall be rescued out of the hands of any Pirates or Robbers on the high seas shall be brought into some Port of either State and shall be delivered to the custody of the Officers of that Port in order to be taken care of and restored entire to the true proprietor as soon as due and sufficient proof shall be made concerning the property thereof."[26]

The defense was taken up by the abolitionist Roger Baldwin and John Quincy Adams, the former US president (1825–1829), who was then a member of Congress. Baldwin spoke first, reminding the Supreme Court that the slave trade treaty in 1817 between Britain and Spain stipulated that "its victims shall be declared free" in the first port they reached; in the case of the *Amistad*, the captives "were placed in the custody of law, under process . . . against them *as property*."[27] This should have never happened to people "in the actual condition of freedom" when they arrived in New York, a state in which "all persons, except fugitives, &c, from a sister State, are declared to be free."[28] The entire process had worked against the Africans, Baldwin explained, from their initial treatment as property to the meddling from President Martin Van Buren, who was happy to comply with the Spanish minister's order to send the Africans to Cuba. The president wanted to be rid of this messy case, lest it rile up the Southern states.

When it came time for Adams to speak, his disgust at the behavior of the executive office was evident: "Is it possible that a President of the United States should be ignorant that the right of personal liberty is individual?" Adams asked the court. "That the right to it of every one, is *his own* – JUS SUUM; and that no greater violation of his official oath to protect and defend the Constitution of the United States, could be committed, than by an order to seize and deliver up at a foreign minister's demand, thirty-six persons, in a mass, under the general denomination of *all*, the negroes, late of the *Amistad*?"[29]

Both men made the existing freedom of the Africans central to their arguments. They said the Africans had to liberate themselves, and the core of their case was based on the testimony of Cinqué and the others. They tore up the Spanish argument based on the phrasing of article 9, with Adams asking, "Who were the merchandise and who were the robbers? . . . Is there anything more absurd than to say these forty Africans are robbers, out of whose hands they have themselves been rescued?"[30]

Adams also reminded the court that he had a particular knowledge of Spanish law, having negotiated the 1819 Adams-Onís Treaty for the cession of Florida when he was secretary of state. Regarding article 9, he said: "I am certain that neither of us [Adams and the minister of Spain] ever entertained an idea that this word *merchandise* was to apply to human beings."[31]

After the first day of Adams's testimony, the proceedings took an unexpected turn when one of the justices, Philip Barbour, died overnight, causing the hearing to be delayed for a few days.[32] When it resumed on March 1, Adams drove his case home. He reminded the court that until this point, sympathy for Ruiz and Montes, and not the Africans, had predominated and "justice had not been the motive of [the court's] proceedings."[33]

The Supreme Court agreed, deciding seven to one in the Africans' favor. They were now free to return to Sierra Leone, which they eventually did, in late November 1841.[34] It had been a painful, difficult two years, but in the uncertain waters of the partially free Atlantic, this group of Africans helped chart a path for others to follow.

That same November, as the former *Amistad* captives were preparing for their homeward voyage, prisoners on another ship, the *Creole*, tried to pilot their own way to freedom. The brig, carrying 135 people, was travelling between Norfolk, Virginia, and New Orleans as part of the internal slave trade permitted within the United States. But the enslaved people on board knew the route would take them near the Bahamas, a British colony that no longer had slavery.[35]

On board was Madison Washington, who had escaped to Canada once, but ended up re-enslaved after a failed attempt to rescue his wife from bondage. Washington was familiar with abolitionists in the northeastern United States, who had helped him on his first flight. He was also familiar with the story of the *Amistad*. Under his leadership—and taking advantage of the mobility afforded by his role as a cook for the slaves—he was able to organize a plan. He and 18 others staged a brief, successful uprising, during which John Hewell, a guard hired by a slave trader, was killed amid the tumult. The rebels took control of the ship and ordered the captured crew to set sail for Liberia. They were told that there were not enough provisions on hand for such a trip. Instead, they decided to go where "Mr Lumpkin's Negroes went last year," a reference to another slave ship, the *Hermosa*, which wrecked off the coast of the Abaco Islands in the Bahamas in October 1840, after which all the captives on board were freed.[36]

Some of the captives had sailing experience, and the crew would not be able to deceive them, as had happened with the *Amistad*. A couple of the rebels knew how to use a compass and so monitored the ship's path.[37] By the morning of November 9, 1841, they were approaching the harbor in Nassau. Despite the tales of ships like the *Hermosa*, it remained to be seen whether the British really would extend freedom to them. When the pilot boat pulled up, a black crew member told them that "he came out from Charleston, and that he got free by coming out there in that way." The people on board the *Creole* began to celebrate "and appeared much rejoiced."[38] The white survivors, meanwhile, went ashore and informed the US consul what had happened. The governor dispatched 24 members of the 2nd West India Regiment—all of them, bar the captain, were themselves "liberated Africans"—to guard the ship and keep the rebels on board while the matter was settled.[39]

News of the freedom-seekers waiting in the harbor did not sit well with the black community of Nassau, and crowds started to form in the harbor in solidarity with the captives. The US consul wanted to take the ringleaders from the ship and let the rest of the "cargo" reach New Orleans while they waited for the British to adjudicate.[40] The interests of the US and Britain were no longer mutual; they were rubbing up against each other, chafing at the proximity of slavery and abolition.[41] Only 40 years earlier, the entire hemisphere had been blanketed in slavery. Now, zones of freedom had emerged, though it remained unclear who was allowed to pass through them.

After four days in the harbor, everyone's patience was wearing thin. One rumor claimed that locals were going to attempt their own rescue mission. When the US consul went to the bay after hearing the news, he could see it had begun: A small flotilla of launches was heading out to the brig. Now the crowd of onlookers swelled to at least 2,000, waiting to see what the US and British officials would do, and what would become of the captives and the rescuers, especially given that the soldiers were still on board. The attorney general then went on board and decided that Washington and his men would be charged with mutiny and murder, but the rest could leave the vessel in the waiting launches and join the others as free people.[42]

Five captives, however, stayed on board the *Creole* and opted to go to New Orleans: Rachel Glover and her young son, Isah, Mary E. Scroggins, and two other unnamed women.[43] Perhaps they had kin in Louisiana, or remained suspicious of the British, or were wary of their prospects in the Bahamas. For a brief window, however, they had a choice, which they exercised. The *Creole* left on November 19. The rest of the people who had been on board stayed in the Bahamas, with a large party accepting an offer to go to Jamaica, where as "liberated" people they would likely be encouraged to work the land. Washington and the plotters were held for another six months, but the charges against them were eventually dropped. They walked off the pages of history and into their new lives.[44]

⋘ • ⋙

As the *Amistad* case made clear, the diplomatic waters around Cuba had turned choppy. Cuba was in the full throes of its "second slavery," sparked by the rise in sugar production in the aftermath of the Haitian Revolution, but with the pressure of both a large influx of illegally trafficked Africans and the antislavery officials trying to free them.[45] Cuban officials grudgingly acquiesced to the establishment of the Havana Slave Trade Commission in 1824. Like the "liberated Africans" elsewhere, the *emancipados* in Cuba were given a certificate proving their freedom and then more or less forced into apprenticeships—where their situation differed from many of the other regions with Mixed Commission courts is that the vast majority remained in Cuba, an island still dominated by slavery. While the court adjudicated the fate of 10,391 captives between 1824 and 1841, hundreds of thousands more were smuggled in. Puerto Rico was in a similar situation, albeit on a smaller scale. From the supposed end of Spain's slave trade in 1817 until 1840, Cuba saw some 390,000 Africans brought to the island, while the slave population of Puerto Rico doubled, from 21,730 in 1820 to nearly 42,000 by 1834.[46]

In addition, the newly freed people became their own category, set apart from the free black community and from the enslaved. The *emancipados* lived in a legal gray area, forced into unstable apprenticeships that could be changed through the buying, selling, or trading of their contract.[47] By the 1830s, they were being "apprenticed" to work on sugar plantations, with enslavers openly trading contracts or paying officials to "extend" them. Even worse, on some plantations, when a slave died, the planter would swap the dead person's identity with that of an *emancipado*, using the slave's death as a way to re-enslave the marginally free person.[48]

This continual importation of humans transformed Havana and the rest of Cuba into a diverse African space. One way of measuring this was in the diversity of "nation" (*nación*) names, which were Spanish terms grouping Africans together: *Congos,* from West Centra Africa; *Carabalís,* who had been enslaved in the Bight of Biafra; the Yoruba-speaking *Lucumís* from the Bight of Benin; the *Gangás* from Sierra Leone; *Mandingas* from the Upper Guinea coast; and the *Macúas,* from Mozambique, in East Africa.[49] However imprecise the terminology, the names became markers of identity and *nación* that enslaved and free people used in forming their social organizations (*cabildos de nación*) and religious confraternities—the exigencies of the slave trade caused new and old ethnic identities to overlap. At the same time, the Spanish government and Cuban officials, fearful of the island becoming too African, also encouraged white, ideally Catholic, European immigrants to come. Come they did, along with US investors, looking for steep profits.[50] In 1846, the white population of Cuba rose to 425,767, or 47 percent, with the enslaved population at 323,759, or 36 percent, and the free colored community making up the rest, crucially putting white people in the minority overall.[51]

Throughout this time, Cuba and Puerto Rico had also weathered the political upheavals of the Napoleonic period and the short-lived *Trienio Liberal* (1820–1823), during which Fernando VII was forced to accept the Cádiz constitution of 1812, until the Congress of Verona in 1822 allowed a French intervention to end the liberal government.

Both islands avoided independence movements, and Cuba especially was praised for remaining loyal. Having 20,000 Spanish troops on the island no doubt helped.[52] However, during the 1820s and '30s, both Cuba and Puerto Rico experienced a number of independence plots, such as the "Boricua" expedition to liberate Puerto Rico in 1822 and the Soles y Rayos de Bolívar in 1823 in Cuba, as well as rumors such as that Mexico and Colombia were going to invade and free the two islands.[53]

The imagined threat of Haiti also lingered. In Puerto Rico, it inspired a song that an enslaved man, José Joaquin, sang in July 1826. He used a "bomba" tune to spread his plan around the haciendas of Toa Baja and Bayamón in the north of the island. Joaquin did not want to lead a revolt—his plan was to raise money to procure a small launch to sail east to Haiti. But this modest scheme was soon betrayed, keeping Haiti's free soil just out of Joaquin's reach.[54]

Joaquin's actions came five years after a more serious conspiracy was uncovered in Puerto Rico, organized by Marcos Xiorro, whose enslaver was the captain of the island militia. That uprising was set to begin towards the end of July 1821, to coincide with the feastivities of Saint James's Day, taking place among the sugar *ingenios* around Bayamón. This area lies to the west of San Juan and had experienced a significant increase in sugar production between 1815 and 1820, and a doubling of the slave population by some 500 Africans.[55] Five days before the planned start, an enslaved Creole named Ambrosio divulged the plot. Officials arrested 61 people, and later captured Xiorro, who had been hiding in Mayagüez.[56]

Cuba, too, experienced a rising number of confrontations between the authorities and both enslaved and free people—including demonstrations and strikes, as well as more local rebellions around plantations, with at least 27 disruptions in the west-central part of the island from the 1820s to the 1840s.[57]

One particularly significant uprising took place in Guamacaro on the night of June 15, 1825, around Coliseo in the sugar-rich Matanzas region (*matanzas* also being the Spanish word for "massacre" or "slaughter"). It was led by three enslaved Africans, Pablo Gangá, Lorenzo Lucumí, and Federico Carabalí, all of whom may have had military experience in their homelands. This was the start of a series of slave revolts over the next few decades, led by Africans. Some of the Carabalís involved may have known each other in their homeland, and there were possible ties among the participants of the revolt. After the rebellion began, some 200 insurgents—around 20 percent of the enslaved population of that area—attacked two dozen estates for 12 hours before the authorities were able to suppress it. However, it took weeks to round up all the participants who fled in the aftermath, including Lorenzo Lucumí and Frederico Carabalí who were killed in June.[58]

The authorities had their hands full in this period, watching for potential subversives—white and black, free and slave—as well as reacting to growing abolitionist interventions from Britain. Cuba sat at an Atlantic crossroads, with pressure for independence coming from its fellow former Spanish colonies, and the attack on slavery and the slave trade coming from around the Caribbean.

By the 1830s, Cuba's sugar and coffee industries stretched out from Havana into Matanzas (tobacco was more common in Pinar del Rio, in the west of the island).[59] The backbreaking *zafra* (sugar harvest) started around December and lasted until the rainy season in May or June. It was dirty, deadly work, with workdays sometimes lasting up to 22 hours.[60] There had been some technical innovations that helped to boost output and efficiency, but sugar production still involved much of the same exhausting labor that had been required in the cane fields of seventeenth-century Barbados. Death stalked the plantations in Cuba, as disease and overwork cut lives short with an efficient brutality, sustaining the demand for the illicit slave trade, which showed little sign of slowing.[61]

By 1835 the British had pressured Spain to allow a superintendent in Cuba to oversee the treatment of *emancipados*; in 1840 that person was David Turnbull. He was a Scottish abolitionist—indeed, his visage is included in the portrait of the 1840 World Anti-Slavery Convention. He had already riled the Spanish authorities with his account of a trip to the island two years earlier, reporting on slavery and the contraband slave trade there.[62] His posting as both superintendent and the British consul was met with great consternation—Cuban authorities felt he might cause rebellions among the slaves, or among the supporters of independence. Turnbull did know people from both camps and, in fact, made contact with a small but significant group of influential white creoles in favor of independence or at the very least reform, like Domingo del Monte, whose parents came from two powerful slaveholding families.[63]

Turnbull's predecessor, Richard Robert Madden, had also moved in del Monte's circles, and had met Juan Francisco Manzano, an enslaved Afro-Cuban and talented poet who had written an autobiography. Madden presented Manzano's work to an English audience in 1840, with a translation of his poems and memoir.[64]

Manzano was born into slavery in Havana in 1797. His parents were domestic servants, and he was described as light-skinned (mulatto). Despite these relative advantages, he was still a slave and suffered because of this. He spent his childhood between Havana and an estate in Matanzas, where his parents were enslaved. By the age of 12, according to his autobiography, he was already creating poems. He "composed some verses in memory," he wrote, "because my godfather did not wish me to learn to write."[65] He went on to obtain some education, though he was mostly self-taught. When he was able to write, by the age of 18, he managed to buy "a handsome inkstand, a rule, and a good provision of pens, ink, and paper."[66]

He eventually fled to Havana, but by 1821 he was back in Matanzas and writing poetry, publishing a booklet that year, to be followed by another work, *Flores pasageras*, in 1830. The printing of both works may have involved someone paying for their publication, which was common at the time. In addition, although free people of color were active in the world of arts and letters in Cuba, Manzano, as a slave, would have needed special dispensation from colonial officials to publish his work. The details of the publication of these early works have been lost over time, as has any indication of their reach among readers.[67] However, by 1835 his work came to the attention of del Monte, and the following year Manzano read to del Monte's literary circle one of his most famous sonnets, "Treinta años" (Thirty Years), which included these lines:

> But 'tis nothing the past—or the pains,
> Hitherto I have struggled to bear,
> When I think, oh, my God! On the chains,
> That I know I'm yet destined to wear.[68]

Del Monte asked Manzano to write his autobiography, in part to give to Madden to publish abroad as part of the abolitionist effort. Manzano's autobiography recounts his many hardships—his domestic roles and literary talents did not buffer him from the stocks or whips or petty punishments of his enslavers. In one incident, Manzano was placed in stocks overnight in a makeshift morgue, an experience during which, he wrote, "my fancy saw the dead rising and walking about the room." His crime had been to absentmindedly pluck a leaf of a geranium while in the garden with his enslaver.[69]

Writing to del Monte, he said: "Remember, sir, when you read this letter, that I am a slave, and that a slave is nothing in the eyes of his master."[70] But his bondage was soon to end, and he obtained his manumission in 1836, paid for by del Monte and other admirers.[71]

Although Spanish authorities had their reasons to keep an eye on David Turnbull, the people cutting cane and enduring the hellish heat of the boiling houses on the plantations of the Matanzas province needed no outside agitators to convince them to rise up. Some 60 miles (100 kilometers) east of Havana, this region of rich red soil was the heart of the sugar belt, one that was quick to exploit—in all senses—the opportunity to implement the plantation economy. Between 1839 and 1842 alone, 200 mills were built in the region.[72]

It also became the center of the struggle against slavery. Although the region had been cleared for cane, there were still wild spaces, forests and hills, where people could gather in secret or steal away for a short respite from the grind of sugar production in the quiet hours of the night. Marronage was part of life in Cuba, and often the bane of officials who would periodically send out *rancheadores* (slave-hunters) to drive out the would-be self-emancipators from their *palenques* and get them back on the plantations.[73] In trying to control the growing population of enslaved people, Cuban officials mandated that the big estates create large barracks rather than allowing slaves to live in scattered huts, though many enslavers were slow to build them, as they questioned the wisdom of forcing an already angry workforce to live in hot, crowded confines.[74]

The first revolt of the turbulent year 1843 took place on Sunday, March 26. At some point that afternoon two men on the Trinidad plantation in eastern Matanzas alerted their enslaver to an uprising about to happen, and a man on the Alcancía estate in a neighboring district gave his enslaver the same warning. Officials investigated, but found little evidence. Then, at five thirty the following morning, a pile of cane trash was set alight at Alcancía, signaling the start of the revolt. Later testimony claimed the uprising was executed mostly by Lucumís, who made their way from Alcancía to the Trinidad estate that morning, entering the great house and later setting fire to its sugar processing mills, but leaving the owner unharmed. From there they continued their march, burning cane fields and outbuildings, gathering more people as they went toward the town of Soledad de Bemba, where they were to join forces with men laying railway lines near there. This would ultimately give the rebellion its name, the "Bemba uprising." By that point there were a reported 500 rebels, and the local infantry was mustered. After two days of battle, 132 slaves were dead. Others fled into the forests, and 123 were reported missing, with survivors taken into custody.[75]

By the late spring, Spanish authorities heard that Turnbull and his associates had been working with free people of color and slaves to plan an independence rebellion, aided by intellectuals such as del Monte. One rumor claimed Britain was offering protection for a free Cuba in exchange for full abolition.[76]

In the meantime, smaller incidents broke out on sugar estates throughout the summer and fall of 1843 until another eruption occurred, this time on Sunday evening, November 5.[77] It began on the Triunvirato estate, also in Matanzas, as workers were finishing up for the day. As later testimony described it, the enslaved workers were preparing to receive their evening meal when all of the sudden, they "saw the people in turmoil running from one side to the other."[78] It was a group of rebel slaves on the march, waving machetes and other weapons. Among them was a woman named Carlota Lucumí, thought to be one of the organizers. She and the others then left that plantation to make their way to Ácana, a nearby estate, where Fermina Lucumí was expecting them. Fermina had been involved in some earlier disturbances at Ácana in June and had been caught. She was beaten face-down and put into shackles, but she was not killed. Her shackles had come off only a few days before the November revolt.[79] But the punishment, far from dissuading Fermina, made her more determined.

A group of women in the Ácana infirmary heard the crowd coming, and the pulsing beat of the drums announcing their arrival. Soon they saw the rebels setting fires around the property, and telling the slaves there, "We are going to wage war and kill the whites."[80] Some quickly enlisted. Events turned violent, and the white people in that estate house were massacred. Carlota may have been involved in the attack on the overseer's daughter, along with two other rebels, who she told to kill the woman. White people tried to flee but found Fermina and other rebels on their heels. One witness recalled hearing Fermina shout, "Grab that fat white man and hit him with your machete, for he is the one who puts [us in] shackles."[81]

They moved from estate to estate, picking up rebels as they went, as well as collecting weapons, clothing, and money. By about two o'clock in the morning, with well over 100 people, they reached the San Rafael estate—and found this one ready for them. The cavalry and other troops attacked the rebels, and many fled. By the time the revolt was suppressed, at least 54 slaves were dead—including Carlota Lucumí—and 67 others taken prisoner, 13 of them women.[82] Others had used the chaos to flee, while many chose to hide, staying away from the violence. Eight of the alleged leaders—including Fermina—were imprisoned, interrogated, and executed, with their bodies burned.[83]

Anxiety reached a fever pitch. The planters panicked, asking for a special militia to be established.[84] The rebels didn't seem to have a primary leader, but instead—and perhaps more worrying to the authorities—these uprisings appeared to be local and, they thought, perhaps part of a larger conspiracy, the machinations of which were invisible.

To round off the year, in December 1843 an enslaved woman named Polonia Gangá, who lived on the 1,800-acre Santísima Trinidad estate, told her enslaver, the powerful planter Esteban Santa Cruz de Oviedo, that there was going to be a rebellion. This plantation was only a few miles from where the previous month's revolts had taken place, and Santa Cruz was clearly concerned about her news.[85] The authorities told him to investigate—and then they immediately executed 16 people and imprisoned more than 100 others.[86] Not long after, officials decided something more extensive was needed, and in January 1844 they began to sweep the plantations in the Matanzas area, arresting hundreds of people—including free people—and putting them in stocks until they could be interrogated. This was the beginning of a Cuban inquisition to unearth whatever truth could be procured with prison and torture about the revolts from earlier that year and the rumors that Turnbull was fomenting an independence war.

This episode in Cuban history was called *La Escalera*, the ladder, a reference to the device used to punish suspects. One enslaver described how he watched an interrogation where a slave was "stripped naked & lashed to a ladder on the ground with a rope around each wrist . . . while the ropes were secured to the top of the ladder, the feet and legs stretched in the same manner . . . in this position the poor negro was thought to be ready to commence his declaration! . . . Good God! Is it in the nineteenth Century that we live? Or the palmy days of the Inquisition once more returned?"[87] It was also called the Year of the Lash: one officer alone killed at least 42 free people of color and 54 enslaved by whipping them to death over the course of this brutal inquisition. In the Matanzas area alone, 78 people were executed, including one white person, 1,292 were imprisoned and 435 banished from the island.[88] The true toll of this reign of terror was incalculable.

The one person officials couldn't reach with their lash was David Turnbull. No doubt a thrashing would have caused a diplomatic row, but he had already been expelled from Cuba in 1842. Still, they believed he was the organizing force, and they found him guilty in absentia. Convincing themselves that outside agitators were causing this unrest was a necessary convenience. Only about 25 percent of the alleged plotters were enslaved—meaning the plot was largely blamed on free people of color.[89] The insurgents were within; the dreaded "race war" of Cuban colonial nightmares was looming, if there had ever really been a plan at all.

The other members of Turnbull's alleged plot were not so fortunate. Domingo del Monte went into exile in Spain, though the poet and former slave Juan Manzano was apprehended. However, he was freed after intervention from some of his supporters.[90] Another poet from that circle, the well-known free Afro-European Gabriel de la Concepción Valdés, known as Plácido, was also arrested, but earlier, in April 1843, when rumors of the British plot began to surface. He fared far worse than Manzano. He was imprisoned for months, and eventually testified that there had been a conspiracy but he was not involved in it. Some 32 witnesses named him as one of the principal organizers, despite his denials.[91] There was no escaping execution. In his final few seconds, on the morning of June 28, 1844, standing in front of a firing squad, he was said to have shouted "Fire!" and "Goodbye, world."[92]

Another suspect was Pablo Gangá—the organizer of the 1825 revolt. He had escaped death's noose the first time because he had allowed the wife of his enslaver to be hidden when the rebels arrived. He was able to use this to counter the other claims made against him. Instead of the gallows, he was sentenced to several years' hard labor, in irons. There is no record of how he spent the intervening years, except that his enslaver had changed. This time, however, 17 people accused him of being a ringleader and "sorcerer," or spiritual leader, in the more recent round of revolts. He too faced death by firing squad, on September 11, 1844, bringing to a symbolic end one cycle of African revolts in Cuba. The tactics would change after 1844, but the desire for freedom would remain undiminished.[93]

Chapter 32

Repeat

IN THE HEART of Fort-de-France, the capital of Martinique, there is a small square off the Rue Victor Schœlcher. Its gates are locked, and grass sprouts from cracks in the pavement. In the center is an empty plinth with plastic wrapped around the top and white, green, yellow, and purple paint splattered around its base. Hanging on one side of a perimeter fence is a handmade sign reading REPARATION—a reference to the ongoing debate about reparations for slavery. Victor Schœlcher, who once stood there, his arm protectively around one of the enslaved children his abolition legislation freed, is now gone. The statue was pulled down in the spring of 2020, as the protests of the Black Lives Matter movement spread around the world. Some observers were puzzled. Schœlcher was a committed abolitionist who was instrumental in the second French abolition of 1848. But he also represented a France that needed a second abolition, and a paternalistic nation that continued to adhere to racial hierarchies even after emancipation.

The enslaved people of France's West Indian colonies—now consisting of Martinique, Guadeloupe, Saint Martin, and Guyane (French Guiana)—saw their freedom actively taken away in 1802, when Napoleon Bonaparte reinstated slavery. When Bonaparte fell in 1815, slavery did not. France also stayed involved in the international slave trade, despite pledges to the contrary; around 18,500 Africans arrived in Martinique, 15,500 in Guadeloupe, and 6,400 in Guyane between the reinstatement of slavery in 1802 and its final abolition in 1848.[1]

The second dismantling of this system began in earnest deep in the green folds of Martinique's Carbet Mountains, on the coffee plantation of Nicolas Fizel. There, on the evening of Saturday, October 12, 1822, a group of around 30 enslaved people met in the hut of Jean-Louis. Their plan was to take nearby Saint-Pierre, the "Little Paris of the Antilles," a prosperous port city in the shadow of Mount Pelée situated along the black volcanic sands of the island's northwest coast.[2] From there they would fire a cannon to signal the start of the revolt. Then the slaves would rally, kill the whites, and retake the island.[3]

First, however, they needed weapons. They started at around 10:00 p.m., heading to a neighboring estate, or *habitation*, Canari cassé, killing the owner, taking arms, attracting recruits, and moving on to the next one, before returning to where they began. Their noise woke up Fizel, who ran out of his house to find out what was happening. The slaves killed him on the spot. His wife survived by locking herself in the bedroom. The military soon arrived, forcing the slaves to flee into the dense mountain forest, where they were pursued into the following month.[4] A reward was offered for the ringleaders, Jean-Louis and Pierre, who had a bounty of 200 gourdes each on their heads. The notice issued by the authorities described Jean-Louis as around being five foot three inches in height, with a "round face, light [*claire*] skin, ordinary eyes . . . hair not very frizzy [*crépus*]," and wearing "a small ring in each ear." He apparently had a scar on his chest, and injured legs, with one foot bigger than the other, and a bent back from falling off a horse. Pierre was said to be around the same height and "strongly built," with significant scarring, including on his scalp, which created a bald patch, and on both of his arms up to his elbows.[5]

The militia eventually located Pierre on November 10 and chased him to the edge of one of the island's many vertiginous cliffs, where he reportedly tried to hide under an escarpment but as he reached for some branches, he missed and instead fell into the sea. Or perhaps he chose to leap. As one official later wrote, "Pierre took his secret with him when he threw himself off a cliff into the sea."[6] Of those eventually arrested, seven—including Jean-Louis—were sentenced to a violent death on November 19 in Saint-Pierre. "Clothed in a red shirt and their heads covered by a black veil," they would have "their right fist cut off and their heads severed." This would be done by axe, as there was no guillotine on the island.[7] Another 14 would follow, their deaths by hanging.

After this revolt, white plantocracy paranoia soared. There were ongoing whispers of another island-wide conspiracy. And, some began to believe, the free people of color—who had helped suppress the rebels in Le Carbet—were secretly in league with the slaves, despite the fact that some *gens de couleur* were slave owners themselves.[8] According to an 1835 census, of the 78,076 slaves on the island, free people of color enslaved 13,585.[9]

This ongoing panic was compounded in 1823, when a free man of color, Cyrille Charles Auguste Bissette, distributed a pamphlet titled "De la situation des gens de couleur libres, aux Antilles françaises" (Regarding the Situation of Free People of Color in the French Antilles), calling for full and equal rights for free men of color. The population of free people of color was also rising, causing further white anxiety—by around 1831 there were 14,055 *gens de couleur* to 9,362 whites.[10] The authorities considered Bissette's pamphlet seditious and arrested him and two accomplices. As punishment, they were sentenced to be on their shoulders and to hard labor for life. Another 260 people were rounded up in connection with the case, with some deported to Senegal or France.[11] Bissette's labor sentence was overturned, though he was banned from Martinique for 10 years and imprisoned in France, where he pursued further legal remedies. During his trials, he used as evidence his involvement in putting down the 1822 revolt. By this point, his predicament was a cause célèbre, known as the *affaire Bissette*. Another verdict finally came in 1827, and the charges were dropped.[12]

Not long after, France ushered in its "July Monarchy" of 1830, a liberal constitutional regime under Louis Philippe I, which enacted some notable reforms. Among the government's anti-trafficking measures were imprisonment for slave traders and a bilateral treaty with Britain over the right to search vessels in the Atlantic, bringing France's illicit slave trade to an end. In 1831 full civil rights were granted to *gens de couleur*; this was followed in 1833 by the Colonial Charter, which gave full citizenship to *gens de couleur* in the overseas territories, though high tax and property requirements would curb political participation for most of them.[13] The following year, in 1834, a new abolition group was set up, the French Society for the Abolition of Slavery (Société française pour l'abolition de l'esclavage). Despite this initial enthusiasm, abolitionism in France never gained public traction the way it did in Britain.[14] However, there was growing public conversation about abolition, and how fast or slow that process should be.[15]

Two further significant uprisings occurred in Martinique around this time. The first occurred in February 1831, again near Saint-Pierre, right as the annual Carnival celebrations were to take place. It involved some 300 people attacking 11 plantations, with the rebels apparently singing the July Revolution theme *Parisienne*, but changing the lyrics to include phrases like "wash our furrows with the blood of whites."[16] The revolt was quickly suppressed, but the authorities spent the next six weeks interrogating more than 250 people and accusing 49, many of whom were *patronés*, also known as *libres de fait*.[17] This was a complex and informal category of formerly enslaved people who more or less had their freedom, but whose enslavers could not or did not want to pay the required tax on legal manumission. The people were free in practice, but not in law.[18] However, in this case, the ringleaders were two white men: Bernard Xavier Bosc, a plantation overseer who had a long-term relationship and a daughter with an enslaved woman, and Théodore LeChevalier, an apparently "wayward" son of an important family. Bosc was acquitted and LeChevalier fled to France—but 22 enslaved people were hanged in Saint-Pierre's main square.[19]

Relations continued to worsen between the plantocracy and the *gens de couleur* especially in light of the increased rights they had received since 1830. This culminated in the Grand'Anse Affair in 1833 on the east side of the island. The uprising was purportedly organized by *gens de couleur* who, frustrated by the prejudices of the white Creoles, encouraged enslaved people around Grand'Anse to revolt.[20] When news of this reached Paris, Bissette weighed in on the debate, claiming it wasn't a revolt, but rather a duel between some white colonists and *gens de couleur*.[21]

While the question of rights for free people had been Bissette's main preoccupation, by the mid-1830s he had turned his attention to slavery and was one of the earliest abolitionists in this period to call for full and immediate emancipation.[22] Other abolitionists, like Victor Schœlcher, later switched to a position of immediate abolition, as reflected in his 1842 work *Des colonies françaises. Abolition immédiate de l'esclavage*. However, Bissette and Schœlcher had a long-running feud throughout this period. They agreed about the need to end slavery—it was the aftermath that divided them. Part of this disagreement had to do with colonial rule and the plantocracy, which Bissette knew from experience to be oppressive. He also took issue with Schœlcher's depictions of the islands' black and mulatto communities, and his trust and admiration of white *"béké"* (white creole) planters.[23]

Another voice in the abolition debate was that of Alexis de Tocqueville, known in the United States for his earlier writings about democracy, and his condemnation of slavery there; in France he was a founding member of the Société française pour l'abolition de l'esclavage. However, in an 1843 essay, *The Emancipation of Slaves*, he curiously ignored the fact that France had abolished slavery between 1794 and 1802, and made no mention of Haiti. Rather, he wrote that slavery thus far had been abolished "not by the desperate effort of the slave, but by the enlightened will of the master."[24] In an earlier 1839 report on abolition, he did mention the island, referring to it by its colonial name of Saint-Domingue and saying that its version of emancipation was one of "bloody confrontations, where expulsion, and the massacre of whites must follow."[25] One of Tocqueville's main concerns about the transition from slavery to free labor in France's territories was how to do so while ensuring the larger stability and prosperity of French colonies, writing that emancipation, "if not a very dangerous enterprise, is at least a very considerable one."[26] Tocqueville did not come around to the views of Schœlcher and other abolitionists who wanted an immediate end to slavery, but rather sided with those who wanted a gradual transformation.[27]

There were no further significant changes on this matter until the upheaval of the 1848 February Revolution that ousted King Louis Philippe and established the Second French Republic, which lasted only four years. However, in that window, Schœlcher was appointed Undersecretary of State of the Colonies and convinced the government to abolish slavery, which was accomplished by decree on April 27, 1848, liberating 250,000 people across all of France's territories, though the government delayed the decree's publication and the dissemination of the news.[28] It travelled anyway, appearing in letters to the islands, and then spreading by word of mouth. Enslaved people began to slow down their work, or protest, even before the news was officially announced. One planter complained in mid-April, "There is general consternation. The slaves are already leaving their masters."[29]

Then, on the night of May 20, 1848, an enslaved man named Romain began to beat his drum. There was often drumming during the grinding of cassava (manioc) into flour, but for reasons unknown, the manager at the Duchamp plantation told him to stop. Romain would not, and so the manager had him arrested. News of the arrest spread as quickly as any revolt, with some people apparently blowing on conch shells to rally a crowd. Thousands of enslaved people and *gens de couleur* began to make their way to Saint-Pierre to demand that Romain be released. The deputy mayor, a free man of color, Pierre-Marie Pory-Papy, reading the crowd's mood, released him—and declared him free, though the April decree from Paris had not yet arrived—on May 22.[30]

That evening, Romain's relative freedom now secure, people began to make their way back to their plantations. In the village of Prêcheur, to the north of Saint-Pierre, some people returning from the earlier protests claimed they had been ambushed, and so decided to go back to Saint-Pierre. One rumor in the streets was that whites were going to attack the protesters, though many began to hide in their homes instead. At one point, gunfire shots were heard, and a house in the town was destroyed in a blaze, with other fires appearing that night in Prêcheur and Saint-Pierre. The situation seemed to be tipping into violent confrontation. The governor, who arrived that evening, sensed the tension and the following day, May 23, he declared emancipation on the island. The actual printed decree from Paris did not arrive until June 4.[31] The governor may have made the declaration—but enslaved people had taken action that put the law into effect.

Inevitably, in Martinique and all the other French territories, that freedom promised in the decree of 1848 was conditional. Formerly enslaved people faced struggles ahead to secure political participation, education, and land. Once again, the enslavers profited the most from abolition because they were financially compensated, with the French government providing a pot of 126 million francs.[32] And these same planters would soon bring in "coolie" laborers from India and China to keep wages low.

The Bissette-Schœlcher rivalry spilled into the aftermath of 1848, if anything becoming even more acrimonious. Bissette was victorious in one key battle, returning to the island after his exile to fight a bitter race against Schœlcher to be a National Assembly deputy for Martinique and Guadeloupe in 1849.[33] Schœlcher, however, outlived Bissette, who died in 1858, by 35 more years. He ended up as a deputy for those two islands during the Third Republic. Schœlcher also emerged the victor of the longer war and was remembered as the "liberator" of the West Indies, with Bissette's contributions relegated to the margins of history for more than a century.[34]

The French islands were not the only ones to see the arrival of emancipation in 1848. Denmark, like France, had been gripped by the wave of social revolution that washed through Europe in that year. In Denmark, this led to the end of absolute monarchy. The question of West Indian abolition also surfaced around this time, and Denmark enacted gradual abolition and "free womb" laws in 1847, with a 12-year transition period. However, as the Danish governor in the West Indies soon learned, the enslaved people living on those islands were not going to wait for their freedom.

Saint Croix was situated in the middle of a Caribbean transition zone. Although Puerto Rico and the Danish islands of Saint Thomas and Saint John lay to the west and north, Saint Croix's other neighbors included the now-free French Saint Martin (though not Dutch Sint Maarten) and many British colonies, including the Virgin Islands, Saint Kitts, and Antigua. The nearby Swedish colony of Saint Barthélemy also declared abolition for some 300 enslaved people on October 9, 1847.* Even before that point, at least 77 people on that island had taken freedom into their own hands and fled by canoe or boat to one of the nearby English colonies in the 15 years leading up to emancipation.[35]

Freedom was all around Saint Croix—and just out of reach. By July 1848, only months after the news of emancipation in the French Caribbean no doubt reached that island, the 20,000 enslaved people there decided they would wait no longer. Indeed, as had happened earlier in Martinique, many believed they had already been freed, but officials were keeping the news from them.[36]

---

* In 1878, Sweden sold the island back to France—which had occupied it from 1648 until 1784. Saint Bart's remains an overseas department of France.

On Sunday, July 2, fires were lit in the west of Saint Croix, accompanied by ringing estate bells and rallying calls blown on conch shells. By the following morning, some 8,000 enslaved people were gathered in front of the Frederiksted fort, in the far west of the island. The governor, who was returning from a visit to Saint Thomas, arrived later that afternoon. Stepping out of his coach, he took one look at the crowd and told them, "Now you are free, you are hereby emancipated."[37]

However, by Tuesday morning, a group of newly freed people were shot at—though it remains unclear by whom and for what reason—near the capital, Christiansted, about 15 miles (24 kilometers) east of Frederiksted. This prompted three days of riots and looting across the island, and a state of emergency was declared, with the governor stepping aside due to nervous exhaustion. By July 7, the military had instituted court-martial proceedings, and more than 100 people were brought in for interrogation, in a situation not unlike what they would have been subjected to as slaves only a few days earlier. Four were condemned to death on July 11: Decatur and Friday for rioting and theft, Augustus for "felonious wounding," and Adam for arson. Four more would join them.[38] Some of the witnesses—including the condemned—named Martin King and Gottlieb Bordeaux, also known as General Buddoe, as leaders, though both denied it. Augustus claimed that Buddoe's plan was for a work stoppage, with the newly freed telling their enslavers they were no longer slaves.[39] In the end, Buddoe was deported and eight people were executed in those first days of emancipation. In 1849, the Danish government brought in a complicated labor act that would ultimately keep the white elite in control of workers, who were forced to sign contracts, endure low pay and long working hours, and even have their freedom of movement and ability to seek other work curtailed, leaving them only a short distance from slavery.[40]

⋘ • ⋙

THE TRANSITION ZONES between slavery and freedom were not limited to the sea. They were also found along the border between the United States and Mexico. In 1820, the line divided territory that was part of the Louisiana Purchase from what was once Nueva España, although it would soon be redrawn.

Despite Mexico having had one of the largest enslaved and free black populations in the Americas two centuries earlier, slavery there had become marginal relative to free labor by the eve of the country's independence in 1821. In 1810, around 10,000 enslaved people lived among a population of 8 million.[41] However, slaves were considered "property" in Mexico as well, and because of this, abolishing slavery would occur, as it did elsewhere in the Americas, in stages to ensure the "rights" of slaveholders.

The years after Mexican independence was secured were unsteady as the nation found its footing, first as a short-lived empire. In the dying days of Spanish rule and early in Mexico's independence, a colonization plan proposed by an itinerant US businessman named Moses Austin was accepted for adoption in part of Tejas, a fertile area west of the Gulf of Mexico. After Moses's death, his son Stephen carried on the scheme, and by 1823 he had managed to secure a colonization agreement from the Mexican government, in which he would be an *empresario* (land agent), distributing thousands of acres of land to, initially, 300 settlers (Texians) in Tejas. For the moment, they were able to bring their enslaved workers with them, but the law would soon change.

In 1824, Mexico became a federal republic and crafted a new constitution granting its states power, including the newly formed Coahuila y Tejas. Slavery did not feature in that document, but other Mexican states began to implement "free womb" laws, and Mexico's Congress banned the importation of enslaved people in that same year: Anyone who entered Mexico was now free.[42] Such measures helped Mexico in its diplomatic relationship with Britain, and securing access to much-needed loans—though this was the very same Britain that would in a few years become an important market for slave-grown Texas cotton. However, it presented an obvious problem for the Tejas settlers. They received a reprieve from the ban on the condition that the enslaved people they brought with them were for personal use and not for sale, and that they treated them well. People from the US continued to arrive, bringing their enslaved workers with them, and cotton production was soon booming.

The settlers' problems were compounded in 1827 when Coahuila y Tejas legislators—many of whom were suspicious or hostile towards the Texians—issued a state constitution in which slavery was banned and the gradual abolition of existing enslaved people through "free womb" laws.[43] A few years later the issue of slavery returned to the national arena when President Vicente Guerrero, who was of partial African descent, abolished slavery throughout Mexico, on September 16, 1829, prompting an immediate outcry from enslavers, and especially those in Tejas. Guerrero was also fighting Spain's ill-fated attempt to take back its valuable colony. When Guerrero heard that US troop numbers were increasing at the border, near Nacogdoches, he was fearful of facing a conflict on a new front while still trying to push out Spain, so he relented and gave those in Tejas an exemption, allowing them to keep the slaves they already had. Nonetheless, Guerrero pursued other abolitionist channels. He dispatched an agent to Haiti to discuss with Jean-Pierre Boyer the possibility of a treaty—and to find a way to invade Cuba and liberate its slaves.[44]

The tensions between Mexicans and Anglos in Tejas continued to worsen. Guerrero, and his successor Anastasio Bustamante, who came to power in 1830, were also facing a war-weary, impoverished nation, and in Tejas and the north of Mexico there were constant attacks by Apache and other Native American groups. Bustamante was not popular with the Texians—now numbering around 30,000—and in October 1832 residents in Tejas met to discuss their grievances and contemplate their options. Some, including Stephen Austin, wanted Tejas to break away from Coahuila and be its own state, an idea that had little support among the 2,500 or so Mexican Tejanos living there and even less within the government. Undeterred, Austin went to Mexico City to meet with officials, but on his return to Coahuila y Tejas, he was arrested for inciting a revolt, though the charges were dropped.

President General Antonio López de Santa Anna, who took office in 1833, was having problems running Mexico, and in 1835 he announced that a new constitution would be drawn up, confirming fears within the nation that he was trying to centralize the system of government and consolidate his own power. Austin and the other Texians called for the reinstatement of the 1824 constitution because the federalism it had established was important to their case for having their own state.

By autumn 1835, skirmishes started taking place between Texians and Mexican troops. Plans continued to be debated within the Texian community, but Austin was clear on one thing: "Texas must be a slave country. It is no longer a matter of doubt."[45] The question now was how to make it happen. The military clashes intensified, with confrontations in Gonzales and at Presidio la Bahía, near Goliad, both in October 1835. The majority of Texians wanted independence from Mexico, and by 1836 they were using the language of the American Revolution, calling for "liberty or death."[46] Santa Anna decided to put an end to this troublesome behavior, marching into San Antonio de Béxar with 6,000 soldiers on February 23, 1836. The Texian rebel militia had been alerted to his arrival, but had had only enough time to retreat into a garrison housed in the former Spanish mission San Antonio de Valero, known locally as the Alamo. Santa Anna held the site under siege, trapping around 200 people inside, before an all-out assault on March 6, which left most of them dead.

While the fighting was raging at the Alamo, another group of Texians had gathered in the town of San Felipe de Austin to adopt a declaration of independence, which they did on March 2. It was followed two weeks later by a constitution of the Republic of Texas, which—inevitably—protected slavery. The document declared: "All persons of color who were slaves for life previous to their emigration to Texas, and who are now held in bondage, shall remain in the like state of servitude . . . Congress shall pass no laws to prohibit emigrants from the United States of America from bringing their slaves into the Republic."[47] The documents, however, could not undo the military defeat at the Alamo, and the battle against Mexico continued into the spring, by which point it was attracting much attention within the US.

The conflict reached its climax that April, as Santa Anna pursued Sam Houston and his troops, who had retreated east, catching him near today's Houston, where the San Jacinto River converges with Buffalo Bayou. There, on April 20, 1836, the rebels' fortunes turned, and with cries of "Remember the Alamo!" Houston and his men scored a decisive victory against Santa Anna, who was taken prisoner. A deal was arranged, though Mexico would never officially recognize the new Republic of Texas. Any plans to join the United States, however, were shelved, despite the Texians' enthusiasm for the idea. Texas would have joined the slaveholding South, tipping the existing balance of 12 slave and 12 free states, and provoking domestic unrest among abolitionists and the condemnation of Britain. For the moment, Texas would have to go it alone as a new republic.

Northern abolitionists like Benjamin Lundy, the editor of the *Genius of Universal Emancipation*, had understood what was truly taking place, namely that "the Texas rebellion was instigated, set on foot, and almost wholly sustained, by the exertions of those concerned in slave-holding, land-speculating, &c in the United States."[48] In his 1837 account, Lundy warned: "The great fundamental principles of universal liberty—the perpetuity of our free republican institutions—the prosperity, the welfare, and the happiness of future generations—are measurably connected with the prospective issue of this fierce and bloody conflict."[49] Lundy died in 1839 and so did not live to see the ascension of Texas to statehood by the end of 1845, nor the conflict between the United States and Mexico that would erupt the following year.

By 1845, the question of Texas had become a national issue, reignited by John Tyler, who became president after the death of William Henry Harrison in 1841. Tyler was born into a slaveholding Virginia family and had long wanted to bring Texas into the US slavery fold. Critics of annexation were worried that such a move, in addition to causing internal turmoil, would also trigger another conflict with Mexico. The matter was passed on to the next US president, James K. Polk, also a Southerner. He managed to push annexation through Congress in February 1845. That accomplished, he turned to his other plans to extend the United States to the Pacific, only to find that Mexico was in his way. The location of the boundary between the US and Mexico had become a source of tension between the two countries after the annexation of Texas, with US troops massed along the border. Diplomats were dispatched to offer to buy parts of Mexico, including Alta California, but to no avail. By late April 1846, what had started as a border skirmish had turned into the Mexican-American War, which would last for two years. In 1848, Mexico was forced, under the terms of the Treaty of Guadalupe Hidalgo that brought the war to an end, to cede 51 percent of its land to the US, making Polk's dream a reality. However, this enormous acquisition exacerbated the United States' growing division over slavery.

For enslaved people in Texas, Louisiana, and other parts of the South, Mexico presented something else entirely. For self-emancipators in some parts of the Deep South, it was a more viable option than the more distant Mason-Dixon Line or Canada. The number of enslaved people who fled to Mexico—between 3,000 and 5,000—is lower than the number of those who escaped via the Northern Underground Railroad—between 30,000 and 100,000—but it was an option for those who could get there.[50] It was not an easy life. Many of the people who escaped slavery in the US ended up living along the frontier and serving in the Mexican military, securing the border against Native American attacks; others found work, often poorly paid and in difficult, sometimes violent, conditions, on large haciendas or in domestic service.[51]

There was also the ongoing threat of slave-hunters willing to cross borders in pursuit of "property." However, some Mexicans were equally willing to protect the freedom of these new members of their communities. For instance, in 1852 in Guerrero, Coahuila, four town council members pursued an enslaver who had kidnapped a black man, inciting a brief shootout, in which the slave-hunter was killed.[52] Such communities were also concerned about possible abductions of fellow Mexican citizens—reports appeared that some were being kidnapped and sold into slavery in the US.[53]

Despite the intentions of the Mexican president Vicente Guerrero to liberate Cuba, nothing came of his plans. In fact, competing groups had designs to do the exact opposite: annex the island to the United States like a tropical Texas and spread slavery south. US control of Cuba had been a long-standing dream, and official government attempts were made to buy the island for $100 million in 1848, but Spain refused. That failure opened the door for a group of expansionists known as "filibusterers"—in this context, the word means a sort of land-grabbing pirate—who worked through other channels, including a Venezuelan named Narciso López.

López was not Cuban but ended up on the island after fighting in the Spanish military during the independence wars in South America. He was also in Cuba during the Escalera conspiracy in 1844, presiding over some of the earliest tribunals and passing death sentences on defendants.[54] López became friendly with Southern planters, with whom he plotted, as well with as Cuban elites receptive to the idea of the island's annexation. He led three expeditions between 1849 and 1851 to start an independence movement in Cuba that would ultimately lead to the island being annexed by the United States. Many of his men were veterans from the Mexican-American War. In the first attempt, they had to turn back after US federal agents were tipped off about their plans. The second saw them attacked by Spanish troops, with locals unwilling to come to their aid or join their campaign. And the third ended in their being routed again, López being garroted, and other captured members of the expedition being killed by firing squad.

In 1853, President Franklin Pierce tried once more to purchase Cuba, this time for $130 million, but Spain again refused. One final reprise of the Cuban annexation dream occurred during the "Ostend Manifesto" incident of 1854, when a communiqué between US diplomats was leaked from a conference in Ostend, Belgium, stating that the United States "ought, if practicable, to purchase Cuba with as little delay as possible." Nothing came of it beyond a diplomatic dispute.

Although the filibusters were connected to Cuba, some of them wanted to extend slavery to other regions south of the US, driven in part by the restrictions of the 1820 Missouri Compromise. If plantations and slavery were going to spread, it would have to be toward the south. In 1853 a Tennessean named William Walker made the first of a series of expeditions into Mexican territory in Baja and Sonora California. This was in complete defiance of Mexico's abolition of slavery and the slave trade. For the plan to work, Walker would have had to confront the Mexican military, but he did not have enough guns or men to make that happen. He then set his sights on the Central American republic of Nicaragua in 1855, managing to proclaim himself president briefly, before winding up in 1860 in Trujillo, Honduras, on the wrong side of a firing squad, sharing a fate with the Cuban filibusters who preceded him.

⋘ • ⋙

Full abolition in the rest of Spanish South America came unevenly throughout the 1850s. The process was hindered by the political machinations taking place in the new republics, with control oscillating between conservative and liberal. This was compounded by the reconfiguration of some of the nations: Uruguay was formed in 1825 in opposition to Juan Manuel de Rosas in Argentina (United Provinces of the Río de la Plata), avoiding annexation by Brazil; and Gran Colombia disintegrated in 1830 into the republics of Ecuador, Venezuela, and Nueva Granada (later Colombia). There was also a determined persistence on the part of enslavers to keep hold of what they considered to be their property.

Nevertheless, by the middle of the nineteenth century, over the course of eight years, these nations, plus Peru and Bolivia, would enlarge the zone of freedom in the Americas. For enslaved people, however, this period was filled with uncertainty, especially since some of the new laws and regulations concerning the status of enslaved people were disregarded. Freed people were forced to live in gray areas, unsure if their freedom might be taken from them, or if they might be forced to fight for it in a civil conflict. Policing of the slave trade remained uneven, and Africans were still being brought to some of these places long after it was deemed illegal.[55]

Uruguay enacted a semi-abolition in 1842, offering freedom to any slave who would enlist in the military during its long-running war, the Guerra Grande (Great War), which was both a civil war between liberals and conservatives and an international one that involved, at times, Argentine, British, French, and Brazilian interventions. Eventually this led to full abolition in 1846, before the conflict ended in 1851.[56] Argentina, from which Uruguay had separated, had a longer emancipation process. After Rosas was out of power in 1852, slavery was abolished in the country's 1853 constitution, though the province of Buenos Aires later rebelled and did not abide by the provision. It finally accepted the constitution in 1861.[57]

In Colombia, powerful landowning blocs in the Pacific southwest, an area of large agricultural haciendas and lowland gold mines, changed the laws in the 1840s to legalize the selling of enslaved people, first internally and then, between 1843 and 1847, to neighboring Peru where there was still demand.[58] From the 1820s onward, enslavers cited the need to get rid of "troublesome" slaves who were "enemies" of republicanism and a danger to the social "order."[59] In the years prior the law change, Colombia had endured a civil war (the War of the Supremes, 1839–1842), during which free black military leaders persuaded slaves to go into battle with promises of freedom in exchange for service.[60] Landowners in the southwest later pressed Colombia's Congress to export slaves who had supposedly betrayed the country—and also, more importantly to them, to "decrease the number of blacks."[61] At the same time, loopholes and gray areas surrounded the "service" of the children who were supposed to be born into freedom after the 1821 "free womb" legislation took effect, but who ended up in a situation akin to captivity.[62] For instance, a September 1846 shipment of 212 people to Peru included 159 supposedly free (*liberto*) people born after the free womb law.[63]

After a liberal regime came to power in 1849, abolition was once again in Colombia's sights. This prompted a counter-rebellion by angry elites in the Cauca Valley in April 1851. The government pressed ahead and issued an abolition law on May 21, 1851, that would go into effect on January 1 the following year. Enslavers started to campaign for compensation payments from the manumission juntas. By 1853, the new constitution enshrined abolition—and the enslavers continued to make their case to the juntas for payouts.[64] Neighbors Bolivia and Ecuador enacted full manumission around the same time, in 1851.

The years leading up to abolition in Venezuela were difficult for enslaved people, as the limits of freedom remained unclear. After Venezuela broke away from Gran Colombia and became an independent country, it revised its manumission laws in 1830 to keep children born to enslaved mothers working for the enslaver until the age of 21 instead of 18. This happened again in 1840, with the introduction of apprenticeship contracts that would keep them in service until the age of 25—despite having been born "free."[65] The 1840s saw a renewed legislative push for abolition, but the government claimed there was a lack of funds to compensate the enslavers. The money—eventually resulting in 190 pesos paid per former slave—was secured, and by 1854 Venezuela pushed abolition through, bringing freedom for 12,093 people, and freeing another 11,285 from the legal obligation to work for their former enslavers.[66]

Peru's journey to abolition was partially bound up with that of Colombia, though it finished later. Peruvian landowners blamed abolition measures for the country's poor economy, and in 1845 they were permitted to bring in more slaves in order to expand sugar plantations in the north.[67] This was facilitated by the resumption of the slave trade in Colombia, but came to an end in 1847, when Colombia cut off the supply.[68] Landowners then switched to indentured Chinese workers in 1849, bringing in 92,000 over the next 25 years.[69]

Peru experienced growing support for abolition in the 1850s—Harriet Beecher Stowe's *Uncle Tom's Cabin* (*La cabaña del tío Tom*) was published in Peru in 1853 and was popular enough to be staged as a drama.[70] A brief civil conflict between liberals and conservatives occurred that same year, with the former using promises of freedom to enlist slaves. The liberals won, and they delivered full emancipation on December 3, 1854, while enslavers received 300 pesos in compensation.[71]

Between the 1810s and the 1850s, enslaved people in all corners of these new republics reached for liberty as they could, navigating an endless set of contradictions, hypocrisies, and broken promises. Now, for the most part, they were free people and citizens—unlike in the United States, where the Supreme Court ruled in the 1857 *Dred Scott* decision that black people, slave or free, had no claim to citizenship.

The case *Dred Scott v. Sandford* had come before the Supreme Court in March 1857 after winding its way through the lower courts for years. Two decades earlier, Scott's enslaver had taken him from Missouri to the free state of Illinois and then to the free Wisconsin Territory while in the US Army. After returning to Missouri in the late 1840s, Scott went to court to make the case that, having lived in a free territory, he was now free. After many decisions and appeals, the Supreme Court was decisive, in a seven-to-two ruling against him. Chief Justice Roger B. Taney's now-infamous opinion had wider implications, beyond Scott's case. The decision clarified that black people could not be citizens of the United States, with Taney writing, "A free negro of the African race, whose ancestors were brought to this country and sold as slaves, is not a 'citizen' within the meaning of the Constitution of the United States."[72] Black people could be citizens of their states, but they had no recourse to federal protections and no ability to sue in federal court. Scott's status in Missouri was that of a slave, regardless of his time living in free areas. The ruling also claimed that the Missouri Compromise had been unconstitutional, and that the government had no power to prohibit the taking of human "property" into a federal territory.

Black people and white supporters of abolition were shocked and dismayed. The *New York Evening Post* thundered in the aftermath, "Hereafter, if this decision shall stand for law, slavery, instead of being what the people of the slave States have hitherto called it, their peculiar institution, is a federal institution, the common patrimony and shame of all the States . . . wherever our flag floats, it is the flag of slavery."[73] The United States stood increasingly alone in flying its "flag of slavery." Every attempt to resolve this question seemed to only further exacerbate the divisions between free and slave, making an already wide chasm even more unbridgeable.

Chapter 33

Reckoning

IN 1838, THE same year that enslaved people in the British Caribbean colonies welcomed final and full abolition, a young fugitive slave in the United States made it to the relative freedom of Massachusetts. His later account of this struggle, the *Narrative of the Life of Frederick Douglass*, published in 1845, propelled him into the abolitionist spotlight, where he would stay for the rest of his life. After the initial euphoria of securing his liberation upon his second attempt, Douglass wrote, "I was again seized with a feeling of great insecurity and loneliness. I was yet liable to be taken back, and subjected to all the tortures of slavery."[1] Although a group of supporters paid to secure his manumission a few years later, Douglass carried that memory with him into his work. And he no doubt watched with horror as those feelings resurfaced with passage of the Fugitive Slave Act of 1850, a federal law mandating the return of all enslaved people to their "owners," even if they had escaped to a free state.

This act was part of a larger body of legislation known as the Compromise of 1850, meant to settle a number of issues relating to the acquisition of the Mexican territory. The other measures that passed in September 1850 included accepting California into the Union as a free state, ending the internal slave trade in the District of Columbia, and permitting "popular sovereignty" to decide the question of slavery in the new territories of Utah and New Mexico. All of these, in one way or another, had the question of slavery at their core. But the Fugitive Slave Act sent chills up the spines of freedom-seekers throughout the nation. "We are, as a people, almost hopelessly unprotected," Douglass wrote in his newspaper, the *North Star*.[2] The abolitionists were also distraught by what *The Liberator* called an "indescribably cruel" bill. In an editorial, the newspaper said the act was unconstitutional—"in no aspect is it binding"—while reporting that many Bostonians "openly avow their readiness and fixed purpose to prevent its operation here, even though blood should flow like water."³

This was not the first act concerning runaways. Provisions had been made in the US Constitution (article 4, section 2, clause 3) regarding a "person held to service or labour" being returned if they escaped to another state, and this had been further strengthened by the Fugitive Slave Act of 1793, but these laws were loosely enforced in the North, where gradual abolition measures had either eliminated slavery or significantly reduced its presence.

When he drew up his original compromise of 1850, the Kentucky senator Henry Clay sought to satisfy both proslavery and antislavery factions by amending the existing fugitive slave provisions. Clay's compromise package failed after months of debate in 1850, but was revived later that year when Stephen Douglas, a senator from Illinois, introduced the measures of the compromise as individual bills that could be voted upon, which they were in September.⁴

The 1850 act now required state and federal law enforcement in any state or federal territory to arrest any alleged "fugitive" whose enslaver could prove, with two witnesses, that that person was his "property." In addition, anyone helping a runaway could be imprisoned for six months or fined $1,000. The act brought in federal oversight through the appointment of commissioners to adjudicate the cases. It was meant to close off any possibility of escape for enslaved people in the South, but it also raised the terrifying specter of re-enslavement—or even a first enslavement—for people who were freed or born free.

For black people, life in the free states had always come with challenges, and living north of the Mason-Dixon Line required constant vigilance. Recapture was legal, and it was not uncommon—nor was the outright kidnapping of a free black person. Indeed, this is what happened to Solomon Northup, sending him on a hellish journey deep into Louisiana cane country well before the Fugitive Slave Act of 1850.⁵

Northup's descent into slavery began in 1841, when he was offered work as a musician in Washington, DC. Until that time, he had been a free black man, living in Saratoga, New York, with his wife and children. He was a talented musician, and his violin-playing was often in demand. In March 1841, two men who claimed to work with a circus company offered him a temporary job playing in New York City at their performances, which he accepted, while his family stayed in Saratoga. When Northup decided to accompany the men to Washington, after a generous wage offer, the waters turned murky. First, they suggested that he procure his freedom papers as a precaution. "I thought at the time," he recalled, "that the papers were scarcely worth the cost of obtaining them." It was a clever ruse by the two men, and Northup had no concern about entering the District of Columbia, which still allowed slavery and the domestic slave trade. On the second day there, he was drugged and kidnapped, and woke up to find himself chained to a bench with his freedom papers missing. At first, he was disbelieving: "It could not be that a free citizen of New York, who had wronged no man, nor violated any law, should be dealt with thus inhumanly."

That was only the beginning. His brutal odyssey started in the infamous slave pens of the US capital before he was sent "down river" to New Orleans and into the bayous of Louisiana, along the way running a gauntlet of beatings, hunger, and difficult work, while also meeting people who had been born into slavery and suffered its cruelties for their entire lives. Northup was forced to take a new name, Platt, and hide his free status to survive, knowing, he wrote, "that I would be disposed of as a thief disposes of his stolen horse, if my right to freedom was even whispered." That simple elision of black and slave, *negro* and *esclavo*, made so long ago in the sixteenth-century records of Havana, had metamorphosed over time and through the slave societies of the New World into the very definition of unfreedom in the mid-nineteenth-century US South. To be black was to be a slave, unless proven otherwise.

Much of Northup's enslavement occurred around Bayou Boeuf, Louisiana, a remote area about 80 miles (130 kilometers) northwest of Baton Rouge, near the Red River. Eventually, in his twelfth year of enslavement, he made the acquaintance of a Canadian carpenter named Samuel Bass, to whom he confided his story. Bass tried to help him and sent letters to Northup's contacts in New York. After months of waiting, help arrived on January 3, 1853, in the form of family friends armed with the necessary evidence for his release, no easy matter after the new slave law of 1850. Asserting his freedom was not enough—it had to be proven.

By September, his account, *Twelve Years a Slave*, was published, with the assistance of David Wilson, a New York lawyer who edited Northup's story. Thus, soon after the passage of the Fugitive Slave Act of 1850, the public could read a full account of the journey from freedom to slavery and back, one that every free black person was now at risk of being forced into. In his final words, Northup reflected, "I doubt not hundreds have been as unfortunate as myself; that hundreds of free citizens have been kidnapped and sold into slavery." Frederick Douglass described the book as "a strange history; its truth is far greater than fiction."[6]

Public opinion in the United States had been turning in favor of abolition, though its activists remained a small group. The American Anti-Slavery Society was founded in Philadelphia in 1833, and by the end of the 1830s it had grown to 250,000 members, in a national population of 17 million, with around 2.5 million people enslaved.[7] The abolitionists were a broad church against slavery, but as the focus intensified on full abolition—the ending of slavery on US soil, rather than more general antislavery sentiment—so did the debate over whether it should be gradual or immediate, and whether it would lead some states to quit the Union.[8] Abolitionists and some members of the wider public might have harbored a dislike of slavery, but many also would have held unfavorable views about black people. Ideas about race buttressed by pseudoscientific notions of "superior" and "inferior" peoples gained traction throughout the nineteenth century. It was one thing to free the slaves, quite another to live among them as equals. Other segments of the public, especially slaveholding Southerners, thought abolitionists were fanatics.

However, there was no denying that the issue of slavery was now central to the direction of the growing nation, something the Compromise of 1850 had made clear. With the advent of the Fugitive Slave Act, abolition was even more pressing. "By that act, Mason and Dixon's line has been obliterated," Frederick Douglass told a packed audience in Rochester in 1852. "New York has become as Virginia; and the power to hold, hunt, and sell men, women and children, as slaves, remains no longer a mere state institution, but is now an institution of the whole United States."⁹

Douglass was speaking on July 5, the day after Independence Day, and the talk he gave, looking at the 600 faces gathered in the high-ceilinged elegance of the city's new Corinthian Hall, became one of his most famed. "What, to the American slave, is your 4th of July?" he asked the crowd.

> I answer; a day that reveals to him, more than all other days in the year, the gross injustice and cruelty to which he is the constant victim. To him, your celebration is a sham; your boasted liberty, an unholy license; your national greatness, swelling vanity; your sounds of rejoicing are empty and heartless; your denunciation of tyrants, brass fronted impudence; your shouts of liberty and equality, hollow mockery; your prayers and hymns, your sermons and thanksgivings, with all your religious parade and solemnity, are, to him, mere bombast, fraud, deception, impiety, and hypocrisy—a thin veil to cover up crimes which would disgrace a nation of savages. There is not a nation on the earth guilty of practices more shocking and bloody than are the people of the United States, at this very hour.

The shocking practices which Douglass evoked and under which free people like Solomon Northup were forced to live continued in the Southern states, which were having their own "second slavery" thanks to the rich alluvial soil of the Mississippi Delta.¹⁰ Cotton was in its full, painful bloom. Between 1836 and 1860, the United States produced 80 percent of the world's cotton, up from 0.16 percent in 1810, accelerated by Eli Whitney's cotton gin.¹¹ Britain was still a key market, despite the two nations' division over slavery, meaning the cotton picked by slaves was transformed into textiles woven in the "satanic mills" of England, often by the nimble fingers of children. Once again, the British proved capable of condemning slavery on the one hand and gobbling up its products on the other. Britain imported 30 percent of its cotton from the US in 1814; by the 1850s, this had risen to more than 80 percent.¹²

The cotton boom required a corresponding growing workforce, but unlike their counterparts in Cuba and Brazil, planters in the

South could not openly bring in Africans. Instead, a brutal internal slave trade proliferated, and after the passage of the Fugitive Slave Act, no black person was safe. Solomon Northup's experience was both a rallying call for white abolitionists and a horror story for free black people.

In addition, slave ships occasionally still dared to bring their illicit cargo to the Southern US, where the foreign slave trade had long been banned. The last known ship to do this was the *Clotilda*, which ran a voyage from Mobile, Alabama, to Dahomey (Benin) in 1860, organized by trafficker Timothy Meaher and captain William Foster. Once back in the United States with the "cargo" unloaded, the ship was scuttled and destroyed in a local bayou.[13] Meaher and Foster were not alone in their mission—other ships built in the US and sailing under its flag continued to traffick Africans, including to Cuba. Indeed, in the same year as the *Clotilda* expedition, the US Navy intercepted two more US-built vessels—*Wildfire* and *William*—near Key West. A third captured ship, the *Bogota*, was French-built, but connected to New York– and Havana-based slaving interests. In total, 1,432 captives were rescued from the three ships, though 294 died while in Key West.[14]

In the new Western territories of the United States, the extent of the division over slavery and the power of the Southern slaveholders in Congress were laid bare. Stephen Douglas had introduced a bill regarding the organization and development of the Nebraska Territory, which had been part of the Louisiana Purchase lands and subject to the restrictions of the Missouri Compromise. Douglas was a proponent of "popular sovereignty," allowing the people living in any federal territory to decide on the issue of permitting slavery or not. Although the Kansas-Nebraska Act passed Congress in 1854, it set off a maelstrom of protest in the North. The act allowed for the newly organized territories to decide for themselves through a vote on the question of slavery, in effect repealing the earlier provisions of the Missouri Compromise. It led to violent clashes in Kansas—a time known as Bleeding Kansas—between "free soil" and proslavery factions. A short time later, in response to the new act and the possibility that slavery might extend west, the Republican Party was formed, taking in many former Whigs. It fielded a candidate, John C. Frémont, in the 1856 presidential election, though the Democrat James Buchanan would win against him and former president Millard Fillmore (1850–1853) in a three-way race.

The nation's ongoing division intensified during Buchanan's presidency. The *Dred Scott* decision was handed down in 1857. Two years later, on October 16, 1859, the white abolitionist John Brown and 21 others attacked a federal armory in Harper's Ferry, Virginia (now West Virginia), a plot that he had been preparing for months. Brown's intention was to secure the weapons there and ignite a slave rebellion in the South. Frederick Douglass tried to dissuade him at the last minute, ultimately seeing his plan for the suicide mission it was, but Brown would not relent. The plotters and some of the hostages they took ended up trapped in the Harper's Ferry engine house, and the local militia and later US Marines attacked them, killing 16 of the raiders. Brown and six others were hanged. In the aftermath, Douglass was wrongly named as a participant after correspondence between the two men was discovered. Douglass fled to Canada and then England until the matter cooled down.[15] But the revolt left the nation unnerved and feverish, the heat further stoked by the divisive presidential election of 1860, which saw a former Congressman from Illinois nominated by the untested Republican Party.

A few weeks later, South Carolina delivered the new president-elect, Abraham Lincoln, an immediate crisis: On December 20, 1860, it voted to secede from the Union. In little more than a month—in time for Lincoln's taking office on March 4—Mississippi, Florida, Alabama, Georgia, Louisiana, and Texas followed, which would go on to form the Confederate States of America. By this point, according to the 1860 census, the US population of 31 million included 4 million enslaved people and 380,000 slaveholders.[16]

The opening shots of the brewing conflict were not far behind, coming on April 12, 1861, when Confederate forces attacked the military garrison at Fort Sumter in South Carolina. Soon after, Virginia, Arkansas, North Carolina, and Tennessee joined South Carolina and the Confederacy. However, Missouri, Kentucky, Maryland, and Delaware did not, and the western part of Virginia (today's West Virginia) chose to stay in the Union as well. The divisions were widening, and the drums of war growing louder.

WHILE THE US was about to go to war over slavery, the Netherlands was bringing its centuries of slavery to an end. The revolutions of 1848 in Europe had reconfigured the Dutch government into a constitutional monarchy. When it came to banning the slave trade, however, the Dutch were more than a decade behind their Danish and French counterparts, and 30 years behind the British. The Dutch had agreed to end the slave trade at the Congress of Vienna, which was reaffirmed by an Anglo-Dutch Slave Trade Treaty in 1818. Even though legal slave-trading ended, illicit trafficking between Dutch territories continued, and also trafficking to lucrative Spanish colonies, especially Cuba.[17]

Enslaved people in the Dutch Leeward Islands of Sint Eustatius, Saba, and Sint Maarten (shared with French Saint Martin), whose combined population in the 1840s was around 3,500, were quick to adapt to the changing circumstances. They knew the zone of freedom was widening, and lay within their reach.[18] Even before British abolition went into effect, enslaved people escaped to British colonies, especially Saint Kitts, which lay only a few hundred miles away to the southeast from Sint Eustatius.[19] As early as 1832, enslavers in Sint Eustatius complained to King Willem I that "very many" of their slaves "have been drawn away from this island to that of his Britannic majesty's of St. Christopher [Saint Kitts]."[20] After 1848, it was even more straightforward for enslaved people in Dutch Sint Maarten to run to freedom—they only had to cross an ill-defined frontier into French-controlled Saint Martin, with little enforcement of the border. The French governor in Saint Martin also declared that he would not send runaways back. The now-free Danish islands lay nearby as well. Some enslavers lost their entire enslaved workforce; the owner of the Diamond sugar plantation saw this with the mass flight on Sint Maarten of a group known later as the "Diamond 26."[21] Despite the proximity to freedom, other enslaved people remained in the Dutch territories, in part because they believed that abolition would come soon, or their enslavers—many of whom had begun to petition the government for compensation for loss of laborers—treated them as free, realizing the system was nearing its end.[22]

Suriname, the most profitable Dutch colony, was the main concern. Of the 48,000 enslaved people across the Dutch Caribbean, some 36,000 were in Suriname.[23] But Suriname, too, was pulled into this growing area of emancipation, flanked by now-free British and French colonies. It already had a long tradition of marronage, and in the years between 1848 and abolition, there were reports of riots, runaways, or strikes on at least 61 plantations. Some people even went to the capital to complain about their treatment, especially as colonial authorities were willing to castigate violent owners and enforce regulations to stave off further unrest.[24]

Interest in abolition in the Netherlands had been marginal, but British pressure in the nineteenth century made it a political and diplomatic issue, in part because of the Dutch Caribbean colonies' proximity to free British ones. However, by the 1850s the small Association to Promote the Abolition of Slavery was raising money to buy the freedom of "Christian" slaves in Suriname, and calling for abolition.[25] Plantation owners in Suriname could see the direction things were moving and began to push for compensation schemes to guarantee their economic security.[26] In the end, emancipation started in the Dutch East Indies with an 1859 abolition law and worked its way west, coming to the Caribbean colonies—Aruba, Curaçao, Bonaire, Saba, Sint Eustatius, Sint Maarten, and Suriname—in 1863. Indeed, the struggle in Suriname had been so protracted that when abolition finally arrived on July 1, 1863, many slaves were not convinced.[27] As a missionary there related to *The Liberator*, "They assembled, neatly dressed, in the church, and I tried to explain everything to them . . . they had previously heard, but refused to believe, the news, saying: 'The whites have deceived us so often!'" While this was not a full deception, what was being unveiled was only a partial emancipation, at best: they would still have a 10-year apprenticeship ahead.[28] This was followed by the Dutch parliament attempting to fill the labor gap by approving an indenture system in Suriname that led to the immigration of 34,000 East Indian and 33,000 Javanese people.[29]

Politicians in the Netherlands agreed to compensate enslavers and implement the apprenticeship system in Suriname, but not in the

Antilles.[30] However, other systems emerged there, such as the *paga tera* form of sharecropping in Curaçao, under which formerly enslaved people carried on living on a plantation and worked a few days unpaid every year in exchange for using the land.[31]

↤ • ↦

With Dutch abolition in 1863, the slaveholding zones of the Americas had been reduced to four: the United States, Puerto Rico, Cuba, and Brazil. In the early days of the Civil War, Abraham Lincoln was not initially focused on abolition. In 1861, he was still considering the war a revolt by the Southern states, though one for which he rallied 75,000 troops. But the Union defeat at the First Battle of Bull Run, outside Manassas, Virginia, in July 1861, brought the situation—and what it would require—into sharp focus. Lincoln, later called the "Great Emancipator," started as a reluctant one. He was ambivalent about the place of freed black people in the United States. Slavery itself he was clear about, claiming in 1858, "I have always hated slavery." But he believed living together in equality might not be possible because white people simply wouldn't tolerate it.[32]

However, Lincoln now had a war on his hands, and he was determined to preserve the Union. Frederick Douglass and other abolitionists watched as black people went to enlist in the Union Army and—as had been the case with the Continental Army almost a century earlier—were turned away. Douglass understood what needed to be done, and his frustration was evident: "The national edifice is on fire! Every man who can carry a bucket of water, or remove a brick, is wanted."[33]

The matter was even more urgent for enslaved people. The US Army might not want them, but Harry Jarvis thought it would have to take them anyway. In 1861, Jarvis, an enslaved man, fled to the Union's Fort Monroe, Virginia, on Chesapeake Bay. There, he asked commanding general Benjamin Butler to enlist but, as Jarvis later recalled, was told "it warn't a black man's war . . . I tol' him it would be a black man's war 'fore they got through."[34] Jarvis was correct, and he would later end up in the black infantry in the 55th Massachusetts Regiment.[35] In the earliest months of the war, some runaways were actually returned to their enslavers by Union soldiers under the Fugitive Slave Act.[36] But an important pivot happened in May 1861 when three slaves fled, also to Fort Monroe. Their enslaver, a Confederate colonel, demanded that General Butler return them. Instead, Butler turned the logic of the enslavers back on them: If slaves were property, and they were being used to aid an armed rebellion—in this case building fortifications—then under the "rules" of war, they could confiscate the humans as "contraband."[37] That August the Senate passed the Confiscation Act of 1861, turning this maneuver into policy.

Whether they were called contraband, self-emancipators, or rebels, enslaved people seized their opportunity by the thousand. Some historians have even argued that the Civil War was as much a strike, slave revolt, or collective marronage as it was a conflict between North and South.[38] Men, women, and children ran for the nearest Union lines. Once there, they did anything they could: cooked, cleaned, nursed, worked as laborers if they could not fight. In this way, they were also chipping away at the barrier that had been erected by the *Dred Scott* decision about citizenship.[39] The front lines of the Civil War also became the testing grounds for what would come after.

The numbers in these "contraband" camps soon swelled to at least 500,000, though other estimates go higher. These camps were described as dreadful places, with insufficient health care, crowded conditions, and limited government rations for the thousands who continued to arrive.[40] One in four people died in them, causing one volunteer to declare, "If the ostensible object was to kill [freed people], nothing could be more effective" than the camps.[41]

Other enslaved people, however, remained with the Confederates, and would do so throughout the entire conflict, feeling they had little choice, perhaps fearing the retribution should they back the wrong side in the conflict.[42] Others may not have wanted to leave family; some might have been offered a later freedom. Enslaved people in the South were put to work by the Confederate army as laborers, orderlies, and in other auxiliary roles—though not as soldiers, except for a few in the last days of the war.[43]

The many individual acts of bravery by black people continued to mount, well before they were considered for official Union enlistment. In May 1862, a 23-year-old enslaved sailor named Robert Smalls boarded a steamer in Charleston called the *Planter*, which was full of ammunition for the Confederates. Smalls had been trained as a river pilot and could use this training to execute his daring plan in the earliest hours of May 13. When the white captain and crew of the *Planter* had gone ashore, Smalls and his team snuck on board, stoked the fires in the engine room, and sailed out of the harbor, after stopping at a local wharf to pick up family members, including his wife and two children. He was able to glide out of the city because he knew what steam-whistle signals to give while passing Fort Sumter, and, in the dark of night, no one could see the crew. Smalls had the captain's hat on, just to be sure. They sailed into the Union blockade, looking for the first US Navy vessel they could find. When they spotted one, they hoisted a white flag and pulled up alongside it. Smalls's first words were "Good morning, sir! I've brought you some of the old United States guns, sir!"[44] He was also delivering himself and 16 others to freedom. Smalls was later named captain of that ship and became the first African American to command a US vessel. However, despite the willingness of free and self-emancipated people to serve, Lincoln continued to delay the conscription of black troops. Instead, he looked in a different direction.

On December 31, 1862, Lincoln was putting the final touches to the version of the Emancipation Proclamation that would be issued the following day. Earlier that day, Lincoln had approved the use of federal funds for a colonization effort for 5,000 black people on Île-à-Vache, a small island off the south coast of Haiti.[45] Earlier that year, in June 1862, Congress finally passed its official recognition of Haiti, as well as Liberia. Douglass wrote, "Justice has been done to those two nations . . . In after years men will marvel why this was not done by the United States as soon as it was done by other powers."[46] Black activists had been calling for official US recognition of Haiti since at least the 1830s. And despite the earlier lackluster results of emigration of black people from the US to Haiti, other plans resurfaced for discussion. Martin Delany, a free black newspaper editor who worked on Frederick Douglass's *North Star*, began to campaign for black emigration, but leaned toward Africa. In *The Condition, Elevation, Emigration, and Destiny of the Colored People of the United States* (1852), he had called for something separate from the paternalistic missionaries of the American Colonization Society. Indeed, Delany called that organization "one of the most arrant enemies of the colored man."[47] There were differing opinions on the ideal destination, but he and others were openly discussing the possibilities. In addition, in 1859 Haiti had seen a significant change in government and was now under the leadership of Fabre Geffrard, who ousted the unpopular Emperor Faustin I and returned the island to republican governance.

The Scottish abolitionist and journalist James Redpath joined the cause of Haitian emigration, travelling to Haiti in 1859, staying for two months, and watching the overthrow of Faustin I. He was impressed by Geffrard, and published *A Guide to Hayti* in 1861, bringing together a collection of articles to entice possible settlers from the US. In Boston, the Haytian Bureau of Emigration was founded in 1859 with a $20,000 donation from Geffrard.[48] The scheme initially proved a success, with some 2,000 black people leaving for the island by the end of 1861. Indeed, even Frederick Douglass was briefly swayed by the idea, but with the onset of the Civil War, he decided to stay in the United States, though he would serve as ambassador to the island from 1889 to 1891.[49] Critics of this and other schemes said that to emigrate was to leave their enslaved brethren in bondage and give up the fight to end slavery in the United States. Ultimately, the war shifted attention away from these ideas, though initially President Lincoln remained interested.[50]

Lincoln even mentioned his plans in his first message to Congress in December 1861, recommending "steps be taken for colonizing ['contraband'] at some place or places in a climate congenial to them. It might be well to consider, too, whether the free colored people already in the United States could not, so far as individuals may desire, be included."[51] Lincoln continued in this way for the rest of 1862, discussing colonization while also calculating whether emancipation was a political possibility.

A second Confiscation Act, passed by Congress on July 17, 1862, expanded the powers of the first. In section 9, it stipulated, "All slaves of such person found on [or] being within any place occupied by rebel forces and afterwards occupied by the forces of the United States, shall be deemed captives of war, and shall be forever free of their servitude, and not again held as slaves." This was followed by section 11, which said, "The President of the United States is authorized to employ as many persons of African descent as he may deem necessary and proper for the suppression of this rebellion."[52] These orders would become the basis of the Emancipation Proclamation, the draft of which Lincoln read to his cabinet on July 22.[53]

By the middle of 1862, Congress had appropriated some $600,000 for colonization efforts, and options were considered in Honduras, Costa Rica, and Panama, as well as Haiti and Liberia.[54] In July, Lincoln also met with representatives from the Union border states to discuss gradual emancipation and try to keep them on side, dangling in front of them the prospect of colonization, however impractical that would have been with a national black population of more than 4 million people. With his cabinet, he became increasingly open to the possibility of emancipation and enlisting black troops.[55]

Later that summer, on August 14, Lincoln gave a private address to five local black ministers regarding colonization, telling them about the possibilities in Central America and asking uncomfortable questions, like "Should the people of your race be colonized, and where?" Lincoln told the men: "Your race suffer very greatly, many of them by living among us"—in reference to the obvious racial prejudice in the nation—"while ours suffer from your presence," he added, referring to the war and sounding as if he were blaming black people for white secession.[56] Frederick Douglass was livid when he heard about the meeting. "Certainly the whole colonization scheme never appeared to us more detestable and wicked than at this moment," he wrote. "If the black man cannot find peace from the aggressions of the white race on this continent, he will not be likely to find it permanently on any part of the habitable globe. The same base and selfish lust for dominion which would drive us from this country would hunt us from the world."[57]

Lincoln was also facing pressure from white abolitionists. The following week, on August 22, 1862, Lincoln wrote a letter to the *New York Tribune* editor Horace Greeley, responding to criticism of his reluctance to enact emancipation. Lincoln wrote: "My paramount object in this struggle is to save the Union, and is not either to save or to destroy slavery. If I could save the Union without freeing any slave I would do it, and if I could save it by freeing all the slaves I would do it; and if I could save it by freeing some and leaving others alone, I would also do that."[58]

Lincoln pushed ahead with colonization and emancipation. His Preliminary Emancipation Proclamation of September 22, 1862, included the intention to continue "the effort to colonize persons of African descent with their consent, upon this continent, or elsewhere."[59] However, by the time of the final Emancipation Proclamation a few months later, any talk of colonization had disappeared. The Proclamation of January 1, 1863, was succinct: "All persons held as slaves within any State or designated part of a State, the people whereof shall then be in rebellion against the United States, shall be then, thenceforward, and forever free."[60]

The Confederacy ignored this proclamation, and its wording was designed to exempt the border states, technically keeping 450,000 in bondage there. But many of those enslaved people had already been fleeing to nearby states and sometimes claiming to be from a Confederate area to secure their freedom and be allowed to stay in "contraband" camps.[61] The proclamation also opened up enlistment, declaring that freed persons "of suitable condition, will be received into the armed service of the United States." Nearly 200,000 black men signed up, including two of Frederick Douglass's sons.[62] Even Martin Delaney abandoned his emigration plans to enlist, ending up a major in the Union Army.[63] Although the border states were exempted, enslaved people there often went to recruiting stations anyway and claimed to be free so they could enlist. Nobody asked for any proof. Women continued to work in auxiliary and support roles—though at least a dozen disguised themselves as men and went into battle.[64]

While thousands flocked to join the military, the 500 people who had signed up for the Haiti colonization effort departed for Île-à-Vache in April 1863. They did not stay long. Some died from tropical diseases, while others left the islet, finding it difficult to establish a livelihood. The plan was a disaster, and by March 1864, the 350 survivors returned to the US.[65] Congress withdrew funding for further colonization efforts. In 1863, it created the American Freedmen's Inquiry Commission, which dispatched agents through the Union-occupied parts of the South—including "contraband" camps—to report on conditions. They were also sent to Canada and Haiti to observe how black people lived as citizens in those countries.[66] The commission's final report would conclude: "We need the negro not only as a soldier to aid in quelling the rebellion, but as a loyal citizen to assist in reconstructing on a permanently peaceful and orderly basis the insurrectionary States."[67]

Black recruits continued to prove themselves in battle, despite being forced to accept the indignities of less pay ($10 a month, against $13 for white soldiers), worse medical care, and often racial abuse from fellow troops. They wrote to their commander-in-chief about these matters. One black soldier asked the president, "We have done a soldier's duty, why can't we have a soldier's pay?"[68]

After four long, bloody, devastating years, with the nation battered and bleeding, the leadership of the Confederacy surrendered on April 9, 1865. Five days later Lincoln was killed while attending a play at Ford's Theatre, in Washington. The next morning, Douglass paid tribute to Lincoln, whom he had befriended over the course of the war, despite their differences. "Though Abraham Lincoln dies," he told a memorial service at Rochester City Hall, "the Republic lives . . . I know that the nation is saved and liberty is established forever."[69]

The surrender and Lincoln's death were not quite the end of the war. Fighting continued in Texas into May. Once Confederate troops there surrendered, the Union general Gordon Granger moved in to administer the territory, and issued General Order No. 3 on June 19, 1865: "The people of Texas are informed that, in accordance with a proclamation from the Executive of the United States, all slaves are free."[70] This became known as Juneteenth, a day of celebration among the now-freed in Texas, and from 2021 a federal holiday in the US.

Slavery had ended in the United States, at the cost of at least 620,000 lives. The war was over, but many social and political battles lay ahead. The most immediate challenge was the ratification of the 13th Amendment to the Constitution, which legally abolished slavery, saying, "Neither slavery nor involuntary servitude, except as a punishment for crime whereof the party shall have been duly convicted, shall exist within the United States, or any place subject to their jurisdiction." It required ratification by two-thirds of the states, a process that took until the end of 1865. Indeed, some states took much longer. Delaware only ratified the 13th Amendment in 1901, Kentucky in 1976—and Mississippi in 2013.

The end of the war and the end of slavery in the United States would not be the end of the larger struggle. Although the 14th Amendment of 1868 overturned the *Dred Scott* decision and ensured that all black people born in the US were citizens, this citizenship would not open a smooth path to full freedom or equality. Racial prejudice permeated the nation. However, chattel slavery had died a dramatic death in the most violent fighting since the Haitian Revolution—due in no small part to the participation of the enslaved, who gave everything they had, including their lives, to secure that freedom.

A world that had accepted slavery had now mostly turned against it, except for Cuba, Puerto Rico, and Brazil. Their residents, slave and free, watched the events in the United States with a certainty that one of their countries would be next.

Chapter 34

Transformations

THE THIN WHITE tablecloth is laid out under protective glass. It comprises six sections stitched together, framed by an elegant *mundillo* lace border, with each part consisting of openwork lettering. They look like they might be beautifully stitched Bible verses, but upon closer inspection, one of them reads:

> The slaves José María Josefa Fernandez and Felipe Medina claim that they are woken up at midnight to collect bagasse [sugar cane residue], working in the mill without days off or time to make their own food.[1]

Another says:

> The slave Segundo Medina claims that the mayordomo [overseer] put him in stocks and the next day sent him to work with a collar around his neck, dragging an iron ball.

These are words based on *querellas* (legal disputes or lawsuits) from slaves in Puerto Rico. A group of six artisans from the island's lace-producing town of Moca committed them to cloth as a special commission for the hacienda La Esperanza.[2] These were not court cases selected at random—they were ones brought in the 1860s and '70s against the mostly absent owner of La Esperanza, José Ramón Fernández, the Marqués de la Esperanza, and his overseers. Today, the former plantation is a nature preserve and historical site, but in its final years under slavery, it was one of the most important estates on the island. Although enslaved people in the Spanish colonies already had recourse to the courts, legal changes starting in the 1860s, including the prohibition of severe punishments like whipping and beating, further emboldened slaves to put what few rights they had to use in reporting illegal mistreatment by enslavers and overseers. There were 29 complaints in Manatí district alone between 1868 and 1873.[3]

La Esperanza sits in that municipality, along the coastal plain of northern Puerto Rico, near the Manatí River and only a few miles from the sea, a palette of tropical greens and blues. The area west of San Juan along the coast was one of the most important sugarcane-growing zones, and La Esperanza was one of the largest estates, at more than 2,000 acres, though only about 300 acres were dedicated to cane, with the rest used for cattle and crops. In 1870, the hacienda had 152 enslaved workers, 53 of them African. Although the listed Africans were mostly over the age of 40, they may well have been some of the final captives transported to that island as the slave trade declined.[4]

This plantation was also one of the most technologically advanced, with a steam-powered trapiche installed in the 1860s to process the cane. Despite the technological innovations, the work—and life—remained hard. Another of the complaints now enshrined in cloth is Cecilio's. He had been unwell and was lying on the floor of the estate's infirmary when the overseer kicked him. The overseer was not punished, though he was told that he must "temper his behavior" in accordance with the current slavery law and regulations.[5] The word *esperanza* means hope in Spanish, another bitterly ironic plantation name. But by the late 1860s, enslaved people in Puerto Rico didn't need to hope—they knew abolition was on its way.

<+ • +>

THE FATES OF Puerto Rico and Cuba remained intertwined, but as neighbors and fellow Spanish colonies, the islands would ultimately turn in very different directions. Throughout the 1850s and early 1860s, slave ships continued to call into Cuba. From the end of the Escalera conspiracy in 1844 until 1866, another 220,000 Africans were taken to Cuba, and another 1,050 to Puerto Rico.[6] Slavery within Spain had ended in 1836, but the trade and practice in the Caribbean colonies continued. However, by the 1860s the situation was decidedly different: The British, Dutch, and French were out of the slave trade and no longer permitted slavery in their colonies. The United States had agreed to the Lyons-Seward Treaty of 1862, which allowed reciprocal searches of vessels and led to a dramatic decline in US ships going between Africa and Cuba.[7] By 1865, when the US Civil War was over, the isolation of the Spanish Caribbean colonies was clear. There would have to be a reckoning about slavery, and enslaved people on both islands were ready. Early on in in the US Civil War, enslaved people in Cuba were heard singing as they cut sugarcane, "Advance, Lincoln, advance / You are our deliverance."[8]

Metropolitan Spain had been gripped by many other problems, and was heading into another cycle (1872–76) of its Carlist Wars—a series of civil wars over claims to the Spanish throne. Limited interest in abolition had existed since the Cortes debates 50 years earlier, but by the 1860s the opposition to slavery had been re-energized—indeed eager Spanish readers were poring over translated copies of *Uncle Tom's Cabin*.[9] On April 2, 1865, the Sociedad Abolicionista Española (SAE) was established on the 54th anniversary of Agustín de Argüelles's historic speech on slavery to the Cortes of Cádiz in 1811, linking the two periods of abolitionist organization within Spain.[10]

In 1865, the Spanish government formed a commission to study the possibility of reforming its relationship with Cuba and Puerto Rico, including on the issue of slavery. During related hearings between October 1866 and late 1867, the Puerto Rican delegates to this committee submitted a shocking plan, calling for immediate emancipation with no restrictions on the slaves, but with compensation for the slaveholders.[11] Unlike Cuba's, Puerto Rico's sugar industry was not prospering, and the slave population had declined from a peak of 51,265 in 1846 to 43,348 by 1867, making enslaved people about 6 percent of the population.[12] Like other small Caribbean islands, Puerto Rico foresaw the end of slavery, and Puerto Rican planters wanted compensation to make the transition to a reformed, modernized economy.[13]

Cubans on the island and living in Spain were horrified by this proposal, with one writing that immediate abolition in Cuba "would be more than absurd and cruel; it would be a direct attack on the civilization and the homeland."[14] The Puerto Rican plan had island critics, too—among them the owner of La Esperanza, José Ramón Fernandez—with some invoking apocalyptic scenes of Haitian-style revolts and the collapse of sugar.[15]

In the meantime, the SAE grew to 700 members and began to organize public events, drawing attention to the continuation of the slave trade and demanding gradual abolition. In the Cortes, after the return of a liberal government, a bill for the Repression and Punishment of the Slave Trade passed in April 1866. The Spanish slave trade was over, after decades of noncompliance—Spain had signed its initial treaty with Britain nearly 50 years earlier. In 1867 the legislation was promulgated in Cuba, which by this point was the only destination for slave ships.[16] The slave trade to Cuba, under which more than 750,000 Africans had been trafficked since the island's Spanish colonization, was now officially over—but some 360,000 people remained in slavery.[17]

The following year, 1868, was a turning point. In mid-September, Queen Isabella II of Spain was forced into exile in the "Glorious Revolution," and was replaced by a provisional government. At around the same time, on September 23, a long-planned independence revolt began in Puerto Rico, deep in the lush coffee-growing hills in the northwest of the island, in a small town called Lares. The rebels—in this case a group of creole elites frustrated with the continued lack of local political autonomy on the island—issued their *grito*, or cry, for independence from Spain. They also called for the end of slavery and offered to free the slaves who joined them.[18] Some of the plotters included enslaved people on their estates in the plans, while other slaves spontaneously joined as the rebellion erupted and spread. However, it was quickly suppressed. In the aftermath, 46 enslaved people were arrested for participating and interrogated.[19] Hundreds of people were imprisoned, but under public pressure on the island and from Spain, the governor granted the prisoners amnesty and instead sent some of the ringleaders into exile.

Cuba, too, had its *grito*, on October 10, 1868, starting with the ringing of a plantation bell near the town of Yara, deep in the *oriente*, or east of the island. Yara may have been small, but it was near a sizable plantation, La Demajagua, belonging to Carlos Manuel de Céspedes. He and a group of men were frustrated with Spanish rule and had started to plan an independence revolt. Céspedes was an enslaver, and was thus well aware that other members of the elite might be too fearful of a Haitian-style uprising to support his actions, but it was a risk he was willing to take in the pursuit of independence.

He offered freedom to any enslaved person who fought with him, setting the tone of what was to come. "You are as free, as I am," he told the enslaved people on his plantation.[20] However, in his initial vision—he was a planter, after all—freedom would be gradual, and slaveholders would be compensated. By appearing gradualist, he won over some independence-leaning elites, and by offering freedom he won the collective muscle of the enslaved. However, the *oriente* had far fewer slaves than the west; in main jurisdictions such as Bayamo and Holguín they comprised less than 10 percent of the population.[21] Nevertheless, a door had opened. Enslaved people could join the fight to liberate the island and free themselves, though neither was going to be straightforward.

Céspedes clarified the situation in December. Any person enslaved by a pro-Spanish enemy of the independence movement was considered free (*liberto*); people enslaved by rebellion supporters could join up with permission, and the owners would be compensated; slaves could be "lent" to the cause, though they would be returned; and any maroon communities (*palenques*) that helped the rebellion would be considered free.[22] An assumption was made that men would join but women would carry on in the plantations; however, many firmly refused and instead went with their male companions and family members to the front lines.[23]

Céspedes soon had 12,000 soldiers, and they took the nearby city of Bayamo in October 1868. The conflict would continue for another decade from there, the duration giving it the name the Ten Years' War.[24] Calling themselves the Liberation Army, the rebels, known as *mambises*, fought a guerrilla war for national independence and bodily freedom. Thousands of Chinese laborers also joined them.[25] By 1869, the movement controlled much of the east, and issued its own constitution, which stipulated, "All inhabitants of the republic are entirely free."[26] Abolition and independence had become intertwined. A new language of racial equality was emerging, too, including proclamations such as "All men are our brothers, whatever the color of their skin."[27]

Much of the actual fighting involved guerrilla tactics across the eastern countryside. Fires were set to buildings, plantations were sabotaged, and enslaved people were recruited. Spanish troops held most of the cities, and by 1870 they were pushing hard with renewed offensives in the east. Insurgents, numbering between 10,000 and 20,000, were exhausted, with supplies running low, but they continued to fight. They failed to make much headway in the west; the white residents of Matanzas and Havana were far more fearful of the social and economic consequences of an independence revolt. In addition, there were desertions from Spanish troops to the rebels, and there were rebels who either quit fighting or switched their allegiance. This was not the same sort of battle Spain had fought against the other Latin American republics. The movements of the rebels at times appeared to range somewhere between war, banditry, and a slave revolt.[28]

In Spain, while the war in Cuba was raging, abolitionists like Emilio Castelar asked the Cortes, "How can a man of the nineteenth century continue to have property in slaves?"[29] Enough of his colleagues in the government agreed, and two years into the conflict with Cuba, on July 4, 1870, Spain passed the first gradual emancipation law, known as the *ley Moret* (Moret law, after the politician and abolitionist Segismundo Moret y Prendergast). It was intended as a "preparatory law" and applicable to both Cuba and Puerto Rico.[30] The legislation freed elderly slaves over the age of 60 and men who had served in the military without compensation to the owners. It also established "free womb" measures for newborns, who would have to stay in service to their mother's enslaver until the age of 18.[31] And, in a telling article 5, anyone who was an *"emancipado"*—that is, a person who had been freed by a West Africa Squadron patrol—was also to be immediately freed, even though in theory they should have been free already.[32]

In any case, anti-abolitionists on both islands dragged their feet and tried to delay the law's publication and implementation.[33] However, once news of the Moret Law arrived in Puerto Rico, it was immediately spread by the people it most affected. "It cannot be kept secret, and already bands of Negroes have seized horses, and, riding madly over the country, have proclaimed that all slaves are free," the British consul in San Juan reported at the time.[34] Demonstrations by slaves demanded the law be implemented. Some, like the 165 enslaved people on the hacienda Amelia, simply refused to work, claiming that they had been freed and that the authorities were hiding this news.[35] The execution of the Moret Law was uneven, and inevitable efforts were made to circumvent it. For instance, unscrupulous enslavers tried to change the birthdays of children and the elderly so that the measures could not be applied to them.[36] This resulted in older slaves going to the courts to contest their age. In one case, a man named Antonio was given permission to travel to a municipality where he no longer lived to obtain his baptismal record in order to prove that he was 60.[37]

These measures were unpopular with both abolitionists, because they did not go far enough, and with their opponents, who feared the Moret Law would wreak economic disruption. Both sides intensified their actions in Spain, holding public rallies and starting petition campaigns.[38] Around this time, Puerto Rico also began to push for more autonomy from Spain, while its abolitionists continued to press for a final end to slavery. The result was an abolition bill in Puerto Rico, passed in Madrid on March 22, 1873—but it did not bring immediate emancipation. Slaves would have to work under contract for another three years to "compensate" their former enslavers, or on public works. They would have to wait another two years beyond that, until 1878, for any political rights. As the island transitioned to free labor over those years, a number of issues and disputes emerged regarding *liberto* work contracts, with the authorities continuing to try to limit people's freedom of movement and control their labor.[39]

Enslaved people in Cuba who were not fighting in the independence war used the Moret Law to secure better treatment, change owners, and even bargain down the price for self-purchase.[40] At the same time, plantation owners struggled to keep their estates functioning, though much of the war was taking place in the east of the island, away from the sugar zone around Matanzas. However, with the arrival of the Moret measures and the lure of freedom in the independence struggle, enslavers increasingly had to accept what they could see coming. Plantations were forced to diversify, with more white and

Chinese paid workers brought in—some estates had as many as 40 percent free laborers. In the east of the island, the insurrection had destroyed much of the plantation infrastructure. Out of 100 *ingenios* around Santiago de Cuba before the conflict, only 39 were standing a decade later; only one remained in Puerto Príncipe.[41]

In 1873 a new general emerged in the Cuban Army of Independence, Antonio Maceo, known as "the Bronze Titan." He was born a free man of color, and joined the rebellion in 1868 as a 23-year-old, quickly rising through the ranks. The presence of a black man in this position confirmed what opponents of abolition wanted to believe—that Cuba would become another Haiti, a black republic with Maceo at the helm. There was concern about this even within the rebellion's leadership, causing white officers to shelve an 1873 plan to put Maceo in charge of an attack in the more slave-populated west.[42] Maceo knew about such talk, but thought it was coming from the Spanish. When he found out that the hostility was coming from within the independence movement, he spoke out in 1876, saying he had no designs other than "to shed his blood to see his country free and without slaves." He told his fellow rebels that he was "a part, and not an insignificant part, of this democratic Republic, which has established as its principal foundation liberty, equality, and fraternity, and which does not recognize hierarchies."[43]

The rebels were not faring well. The Spanish kept them contained in the east—literally—running a fortified ditch (*trocha*) across one of the narrower parts of the island, near Puerto Príncipe, where the distance from north to south is around 30 miles, to stop any westward advance. The Spanish also arrested anyone expressing support for the insurgency. Help from Cubans abroad was slow in arriving, and Céspedes's requests for the rebel government to be recognized by the US were rejected.[44] However, by 1875, another general, Máximo Gómez, managed to cross the *trocha* and attack plantations around the Sancti Spíritus area, burning 83 of them and freeing the enslaved people living there.[45] Overall, though, morale among the rebels was low as the conflict ground on.

By 1878 both sides were exhausted—the rebels were down to around 10,000 men, and Spain had sent some 100,000 troops to the island over the course of the conflict. The Spanish called for talks. The Cuban rebels and Spanish officials hammered out the Pact of Zanjón in February. It would not go in the rebels' favor, with Spain offering pardons for the insurgents but not independence for the island. It would, however, free 16,000 enslaved people who fought in the war and release Chinese indentured workers from their contracts.[46]

Maceo thought the rebel leaders' acceptance of the Zanjón deal was a humiliation and the terms dishonorable—there wasn't full emancipation, or any sort of move toward autonomy. Maceo met with the governor of Cuba in March 1878, telling him that the rebels under his command would surrender only once the slaves were freed, an objection known as the Protest of Baraguá, named for the town where the meeting was held.[47] After this meeting, there was an eight-day ceasefire before the fighting resumed with the rebels who were willing to go along with Maceo, but it did not last for long. The numbers of soldiers had dropped, and by May Maceo agreed to leave Cuba, going into exile in Jamaica—but he never made a formal surrender.[48]

Enslaved people continued to express their anger. Slaves in Santiago de Cuba refused to work and demanded their freedom, like the thousands who received it under the treaty, causing the governor to inform Madrid in 1879 that he had been forced to bring in troops to guard the estates because so many people were deserting. Similar reports of noncompliance came from across the island, including in the westernmost region, Pinar del Río.[49]

A small outburst occurred in 1879, the Little War, or *Guerra Chiquita*. Spanish authorities tried to play up the black participation in this conflict as a "race war," to dissuade white people from joining, presenting it as a rebellion rather than a new phase of the independence struggle.[50] Enslaved people continued to challenge the system, sometimes citing the Moret Law, sometimes simply walking away, while the number of freed people rose and a growing segment of the population—black and white—continued to fight for the republic that Maceo and Céspedes envisioned.

The Little War ended in defeat in June 1880, although that year brought a significant victory over slavery. Abolition would come to Cuba, but it would be gradual; there were 200,000 people still in slavery and enslavers were panicked about their financial futures. Slaveholders continued to invoke the specter of Haiti in relation to freeing the slaves, the fear of black rule ever present. But it was clear to Madrid that the situation on the island was untenable, and the Spanish Cortes voted to abolish slavery and replace it with the Patronato Law in 1880. In this Cuban version of apprenticeship, the former slaves would be given a *patronato*, an eight-year contract. They would be renamed *patrocinados* and their enslavers *patronos*. In addition, starting in 1885 enslavers had to free one-quarter of their slaves every year for the next four years, so that by 1888 everyone would be emancipated. More legal recourse for slaves was introduced in these eight transitional years, especially the possibility that a contract could be terminated over claims of mistreatment, including not being paid the required small stipend on time.[51] The endpoint was abolition, though the *patronato* scheme was devised to ensure a stable, secure labor supply. The new law also banned most of the brutal corporal punishments that had been heaped on slaves for centuries, but planters petitioned for the continued use of stocks and chains to maintain "order." They managed to convince officials for a while, and the use of those devices was permitted until 1883.[52]

As had been the case in the nearby Danish islands, the remaining enslaved people in Cuba did not wait for their freedom. Some just walked off the plantations, knowing their enslavers wouldn't pay to track them down; others bought out the end of their contracts; some denounced their owners for not abiding by the terms of the contract. From a starting point of 200,000 enslaved people, by 1883 the number of *patrocinados* was 100,000, and by 1886 there were only around 25,000. After discussions between the island's planters and Spanish officials, Spain's parliament voted to end the arrangement—and, finally, slavery—which was confirmed by royal decree on October 7, 1886, two years earlier than planned.[53]

A maroon named Esteban Montejo lived through this period. He had been surviving in the forest for years, but after hearing shouts of "We're free now," he returned to town to investigate. He was not initially convinced, as he explained many years later in his autobiography. "To my mind, it was a lie," he said.[54] Montejo was born in 1860 in the Las Villas region, east of Matanzas, but as a *"cimarrón* from birth," he ran away as soon as he could, after enduring a childhood of driving mules on a sugar plantation.[55] He was around 20 when he re-emerged, which would have been right at the beginning of the Patronato Law in 1880. "Even so," Montejo recalled, "many years passed in Cuba, and there were still slaves. It lasted longer than people believe."

However, the island had changed enough for him to safely quit maroon life and go to work, first at a sugar mill called Purio, where, he said, the difference was that "they didn't hit you like during slavery."[56] He continued working in the mills and saw the end of slavery. But the end of colonial rule would take a while longer.

Though he was too young to have fought in the Ten Years' War, Montejo volunteered in the next stage of the struggle, the independence war of 1895, joining a new generation of *mambises*. This conflict took a very different turn from its predecessors and ended up subsumed by the Spanish-American War of 1898. The United States triumphed, killing Puerto Rico's hope of independence, as it was ceded to the US in the aftermath. Cuba would be free, though its independence in the immediate aftermath was contingent on the demands and desires of the United States. Both islands lost one imperial power but found themselves under another. As in other post-emancipation societies, the stain of racial prejudice could not be scrubbed away, and free people on both islands would face further battles for their rights. But chattel slavery, after more than 350 years, was finally finished in Cuba and Puerto Rico.

Now, only one slave regime remained in the Western Hemisphere: Brazil.

Chapter 35

Flowering

THE BEACH AT Leblon is a dream, coming at the end of Rio de Janeiro's famed sandy stretches of Copacabana and Ipanema. To the west, it is hemmed in by the dramatic hills that ring the city. It's a place of wide sidewalks, luxury high-rise apartments, and relaxed beachgoers. Like much of Rio, it is built up, with little green space on the ground, so the only place to see the camellias is on a mural.

On a quiet, nondescript side street a 10-minute walk from the beach, where few tourists bother to venture, is a mural that spans the entire block, showing the neighborhood's history, from the Amerindian past to the present. One of the faces painted on the wall is of a white man with a bushy moustache, José de Seixas Magalhães. Next to him are three white flowers in full bloom: the camellias of abolition.

These flowers were rare in Brazil, but they became a symbol of the abolitionist movement, in part because they were recognizable; popping one in a buttonhole was an easy way to make a statement. They are delicate flowers, symbolizing the fragility of freedom—and they needed the hands of free workers, it was said, and not slaves, to make them grow.[1]

And grow they did in Leblon, on land purchased by Seixas in 1881, just as Brazil was reaching the end of slavery.[2] His Leblon *quilombo* became well-known for its flower production, and when fleeing slaves around Rio were looking for a place to go, they could seek out anyone wearing a camellia to guide them safely to Seixas's farm.[3]

⋘ • ⋙

Flowers and slavery were long woven together in Brazil and remain so today. Tiled into the sidewalks of the Largo de Santa Rita (Santa Rita Square) in Rio de Janeiro is an image of roses, one large one and many small ones, designed with black and white stone. These *rosas negras* are a permanent tribute to the unknown thousands who lie beneath the city's busy streets.[4] This area, across from the church after which it was named, was discovered in the twenty-first century to have been a dumping ground for the bodies of those who had not survived the Middle Passage three centuries earlier. Africans were buried there between 1722 and 1769—and possibly before and after, as the influx of captives was continual in this period—when Rio was the capital of Brazil.* An 1844 painting by the German artist Eduard Hildebrandt (1818–1869), *Chafariz e Igreja de Santa Rita no Largo de Santa Rita*, shows the area where the roses lie today. The fountain (*chafariz*) is gone, and a tram glides by where it once stood. In the painting, enslaved and possibly free people come to fetch water, while across from the busy fountain, a group of musicians plays. The church stands gleaming and white, a contrast to the dirt of the street, the afternoon shadows, and the dark skin of the subjects.[5]

A couple of decades after that painting was completed, the scene had changed. Slaves were still visible in public spaces, but the ships had stopped delivering African captives by the middle of the 1850s. Brazil and Portugal were out of the international slave trade, though an internal domestic trade persisted in Brazil, with at least 200,000 people being trafficked around the country over the next 30 years, mostly from the northeast to the coffee plantations of the central-south region around São Paulo.[6] The slave population in 1872 was around 1.5 million people, while free people of color numbered 4.2 million. Combined, they comprised 58 percent of the population of nearly 10 million.[7]

At this juncture, in the 1870s, Brazilians would have been watching the ongoing demise of slavery elsewhere in the Americas. Portugal, Brazil's former colonial ruler, was ending slavery in its other overseas territories. Despite its early legislation in 1761 declaring any slave brought to Portugal to be free, nearly a century passed before there was

---

* Brasilia became the country's capital in 1960.

any further emancipation in the Portuguese colonies. The Portuguese passed a number of gradual measures starting in 1856, with slavery and subsequent apprenticeship schemes finally abolished in 1875.[8]

The bloody end of slavery in the United States had a direct impact in Brazil, as some 20,000 white people from the defeated Confederate states moved there after the end of the war. They spread out across the vast country, north into Amazonia and further south into Rio de Janeiro. There was space, land, mineral wealth—and enslaved people to do the work. Some of the *confederados* went so far as to name one city Americana. It is located in the state of São Paulo, and has 240,000 residents today, some of whom are descendants of Alabama's Colonel William Hutchinson Norris and the band of Confederates he led there.[9]

While the issue of slavery did not result in a civil war in Brazil the way it did in the United States, another foreign conflict did have far-reaching ramifications for Brazil's enslaved people: the Paraguayan War, also known as the War of the Triple Alliance, from 1864 to 1870. This regional conflict over territorial boundaries pitted Brazil, Argentina, and Uruguay against Paraguay. It was an important conflict for Brazil for many reasons, including the large number of slaves who fought in it. Brazil's struggling army eventually had to rely on their conscription, with many of the soldiers taking the place of their enslavers who did not want to fight.

Brazilian generals, however, could not decide whether such soldier-slaves should receive their freedom for their service.[10] In some ways it was a moot point—by sending them at all, their enslavers had freed them, and it would be difficult to make them return to enslavement. In the aftermath of the war, the question of the treatment of black soldiers raised the specter of a full-on abolition debate.[11] Brazil, in fact, pressed for full abolition in Paraguay, after the latter's devastating loss. Louis Philippe Marie Ferdinand Gaston d'Orléans, the Conde d'Eu and husband of Brazil's Princess Isabel, was put in charge of the provisional Paraguayan government in 1869, where he oversaw the abolition of slavery.[12] The scale of slavery in Paraguay had been far smaller than in Brazil, with some 11,500 people classified as either slaves or free blacks (*pardos libres*) at the time of independence in 1811.[13] A "free womb" law was passed in 1843, with *liberto* children having to serve their *patronos* until the age of 25 for men and 24 for women.[14]

By the time of the Paraguayan War, the black population was around 20,000 enslaved and 25,000 free or *liberto*. Many would be pressed into military service during the conflict. Under the oversight of the Conde d'Eu, enslaved people were freed with no further obligations; however, the conflict had killed almost an entire generation of men in Paraguay, including the enslaved.[15]

For Brazil, the abolition process would be far more protracted and require two more decades. Enslavers, many of whom were prominent landowners and people of great wealth, were a powerful group, although significant smaller-scale urban slavery also existed. Brazil's Pedro II, while personally opposed to slavery, did not want to face the slave owners. But there was no ignoring the growing calls from abolitionists and the changing dynamics of the Americas, and Brazil's Chamber of Deputies set up a commission to examine the possibility of "free womb" legislation.[16]

A compromise was reached on September 28, 1871, known as the Rio Branco Law (Lei Rio Branco), which would bring in gradualist "free womb" measures. In Brazil, as elsewhere, the advantage to enslavers of such a system was not only the continued unpaid labor of the supposedly free-born children, but also that of the mother. As the committee examining the proposals explained it, "The enslaved woman can be considered in two aspects: as a tool of reproduction [and] as a tool of labor."[17] Enslavers could lose the womb, so to speak, but keep the slave. Freeing women—which was another proposal—would have meant a loss of half the slave population.

The Brazilian version of this law stipulated that anyone born after the date of enactment would be a free person, an *ingênuo*, though they would be subject to the enslaver's oversight for eight years. After that, they could work for the mother's enslaver until the age of 21, or live under the state's authority, in which case the master would receive financial compensation.[18] Only 113 children were given to the state, with most having little choice about staying in service.[19] In addition, the law established a slave register—anyone not on it would be freed, further angering the landowners because it put the onus on them to prove that they had enslaved a particular person. The act also set up a national emancipation fund to pay to free more people, giving priority to families. However, it also retained the status quo for at least eight years, as the new generation of "free" children were born. Many gray areas remained in the law and resulted in a number of court cases, involving, for instance, mothers trying to ensure their children were liberated.[20] Some women decided to flee instead, hoping to avoid familial separation or their child's forced labor.[21]

Anti-abolitionists expressed anger over the measures as well, fearful of the economic and social consequences. Once the bill was passed, however, they had to accept that slavery was coming to an end. At the same time, the demographics of Brazil had pushed the white population into a minority, at around 40 percent. The government began to pursue "whitening" policies, encouraging people from poor European countries, such as Italy, to fill the inevitable labor gap that the end of slavery would create and to populate the country with people who were not of African origin.[22]

Luís Gonzaga Pinto da Gama was one of the few people who had been working for abolition well before the passage of the Rio Branco Law. He was born to a free African woman, Luísa Mahin, in Bahia. She was a Nâgo and had been involved in the 1835 Malê Revolt, though she later left the city for Rio, abandoning Gama. His father was from a leading Portuguese Bahia family, but he sold the young Gama into slavery in 1840 to pay his gambling debts. At the age of 10, despite having been born free, Gama became a slave, first in Rio de Janeiro and then in São Paulo.[23] Over his difficult adolescence, the young man learned to read and write, and developed an interest in the law. He eventually secured his freedom, proving the illegality of his enslavement and ending his odyssey of eight years as a slave.

Gama joined the military and continued to study law, as well as to develop his wider literary writing and poetry.[24] He began to build a public profile, and in the late 1850s he was involved in legal battles to defend people who had been illegally enslaved. After the Rio Branco Law went into effect, Gama became known as the "Wretcheds' Advocate" and helped at least 500 people out of slavery, despite never having obtained formal legal training because of the prejudice and ridicule he experienced when he made an initial attempt to study at the Academy of Law.[25]

Gama was involved in the abolition movement at a time when the Brazilian public sphere was expanding, through avenues such as new newspapers and political groups, to include a wider range of non-elites.[26] Indeed, his writings in the newspapers *O Ipiranga* and *Radical Paulistano* were widely read and increasingly influential.[27] "I want to be as mad as John Brown, as Spartacus, as Lincoln," he once said.[28] However, illiteracy was high in Brazil in the 1870s, hovering at around 85 percent of free adults.[29] Still, even if many could not read the newspapers, they would have been familiar with the debates taking place in Brazil and have heard about the words of men like Gama, who were insisting that slavery had no place in their country. Some would liken abolition to a "second independence," placing freedom at the center of nation-building.[30]

But the inevitable divisions and differences existed within the movement. Gama was on one side, bringing black participation into the struggle and calling for an end to the monarchy and the implementation of a democratic form of government, later helping to found the Paulista Republican Party. On the other side was Joaquim Nabuco, a white politician from the Pernambuco sugar region, who had grown up with slaves and had his own personal conversion to abolition. Nabuco was one of the founders, in 1880, of the Brazilian Anti-Slavery Society (Sociedade Brasileira Contra a Escravidão), and represented the patrician arm of the movement, wanting to keep the monarchy in Brazil, and wary of direct black participation.[31] But the two men and their groups were by no means the only actors; another 23 antislavery societies were set up between 1868 and 1871—and eventually 359 civil groups were associated with abolition.[32]

In 1881 Gama instituted the Caixa Emancipadora Luís Gama (Luís Gama Emancipation Fund), followed by the Centro Abolicionista de São Paulo (Abolitionist Center of São Paulo), to facilitate the buying of freedom for enslaved people, for whom little had changed on the ground during these years. For instance, an 1881 request of a woman named Maria, sent to the Sociedade Nova Emancipadora in Recife, illustrated not only the brutality of the continuing slavery, but also the unwillingness of many enslavers to respect the terms of the 1871 law. Maria petitioned the abolitionist organization for a loan to buy her freedom, writing, "Sir, you cannot imagine how I live in this house, helplessly watching my master calling my three freed daughters slaves and beating them."[33]

Gama's work helping people like Maria came to a sudden end on August 24, 1882, when he died from complications of diabetes. São Paulo, where he lived, went into mourning as the news spread—flowers were placed around the city and along the funeral route. When the procession started, 4,000 people joined in, walking behind Gama's casket, representing his life's work: slaves and people he had helped free, lawyers, journalists, and grateful readers among them.[34]

Abolitionists continued to campaign, staging shows and musical spectacles with impassioned speeches to raise money and continue the fight for immediate abolition. Often, the climax of these rallies was a manumission ceremony. This involved an enslaved person selected by a drawing of lots coming onto the stage to formally receive his or her manumission certificate, purchased with the money raised by these public events. The audience would cheer and cry, showering the newly freed person with flowers, including, of course, camellias. Starting in Rio de Janeiro, these manumission ceremonies spread across Brazil to nearly every province, and more than 1,000 of them were staged between 1878 and 1884.[35]

Local and regional abolition groups were key in securing manumission, alongside the national fund, which had manumitted 20,000 people by 1885.[36] Traditional theaters also played a role in promoting abolition, allowing eager spectators to see performances of *Uncle Tom's Cabin* in the 1880s. They would have been familiar with the book, as it had been circulating throughout Brazil since the 1850s. But the work found a new generation of fans with the increased abolitionist activity of the 1870s.[37] These readers were composed of the black and white middle classes—lawyers, journalists, civil servants, university students, teachers. Women, too, took active roles in at least 36 abolitionist associations whose membership was either all or mostly female.[38]

By 1882, under a new moderate Liberal government, abolition was back on the agenda, with the prime minister João Lustosa da Cunha saying, "Every other State has abolished slavery, and Brazil is now the only Christian nation to preserve it."[39] However, a clear plan of action failed to materialize, and abolitionists pushed forward with their own schemes, now launching a "free soil" campaign, which involved working through an area door by door and asking people who had slaves to free them and pay them a wage, and in doing so create slavery-free zones.[40] Some regions even began to move toward abolition apart from the central government—in 1884, the provinces of Ceará and Amazonas were the first to abolish slavery, drawing from the free soil campaign. In the case of Ceará, a state in northeastern Brazil, north of Bahia and Pernambuco, opponents of slavery formed the Liberating Society of Ceará (SCL) in 1880. The group held parties and raised money to pay for manumissions. They also gained the support of dockworkers and fishermen, led by the pilot Francisco José do Nascimento, who had indigenous and African origins and was known as the Dragon of the Sea (*Dragão do Mar*). Nascimento and the SCL organized strikes and rallies from 1881 onward, including a gathering of 6,000 protesters in the main port city of Fortaleza to call for the end of the internal slave trade. Under Nascimento's leadership, port workers (*jangadeiros*) refused to ferry captives from the slave ships, and this strike quickly led to the end of the internal slave trade in Ceará, later reinforced by the state's law in 1884.[41]

In June 1884 Manuel Pinto de Souza Dantas came to office as prime minister, and set out a plan for a new law granting everyone over 60 their freedom, along with other reforms. This triggered a difficult, contentious fight with the proslavery brigade within parliament and outside. His tenure fell apart and he was replaced by Liberal statesman José Antônio Saraiva by the following spring. Saraiva weakened many of Dantas's proposed reforms, finding ways to slow down the process or compensate enslavers. A watered-down bill passed the Chamber of Deputies in August 1885. However, before it reached the Senate, Saraiva resigned and the emperor decided to appoint Conservative João Maurício Wanderley, baron of Cotegipe, as prime minister. It was under the Cotegipe regime that the Sexagenarian Law passed the Senate in September. It looked quite different from what Dantas had originally proposed. Slaves over the age of 60 would be freed, but as compensation they were required to do three more years of service; anyone who was aged 63 at the time of the bill would be released at

65. Adjustments also were made to the legislation over the issues of slave registration that resulted in fewer people being freed under this law. In the end, it would only apply to 107,331 out of the remaining 1.1 million enslaved people.[42]

The Cotegipe regime was hostile toward immediate abolition and wanted to keep the pace of change as slow as possible. The new prime minister sent out the military to hunt down runaway slaves and fined or imprisoned anyone who helped them, a Brazilian version of the US Fugitive Slave Act.[43] The abolitionists pressed on in the face of these challenges, reaching out to the public and continuing their grassroots efforts, while the government attempted to thwart their progress, even muscling in on the theatrical events. The air was often heavy with the threat of violence, and sometimes brawls broke out. Abolitionists also tried to prevent the recapture of slaves, intervening with the police, which also resulted in fights and the occasional exchange of gunfire.[44]

With their public events and conferences increasingly harassed, abolitionists pivoted to an active campaign of open civil disobedience, such as helping slaves to run away and form new *quilombos*, like the one in Leblon, or to go to the free provinces that had abolished slavery. Many enslaved people did not need encouragement—they were already fleeing, or demanding pay for their work, or rebelling on estates.

Leblon was not the only *quilombo abolicionista*.[45] These new *quilombos* were different from the ones of the former slavery era. Freedom-seekers were not being forced into marronage but instead invited to live on the land of abolitionists like Seixas. He was a successful Portuguese merchant who made and sold leather goods—though proslavery factions tried to encourage a boycott of his merchandise.[46] He also used his warehouse in the city as a meeting place for the abolitionists.[47] The Leblon *"camélias da liberdade"* were quickly becoming a symbol of these changes—even Princess Isabel caused a stir by wearing the flowers in public.[48]

What was out in the open was increasingly under attack by the repressive measures of the Cotegipe government, but the abolitionists were gaining ground. For instance, one *quilombo*, called Jabaquara, located south of São Paulo on the way to the port of Santos, eventually gave shelter to some 20,000 freedom-seekers who had gathered in these difficult years.[49]

By 1887, Brazil was boiling over with civil action against slavery, including revolts by enslaved people in the coffee-growing regions. The sitting government remained determined to repress it. In addition, Dom Pedro II fell ill and was unable to devote his attention to the growing crisis. On the long road to abolition, he had sided more with the landowning enslavers than with the slaves—understanding that the issue had to be resolved, while wanting to keep his liberal and conservative governments happy in turn. Now he was old, and ill.

Nor could Princess Isabel, who was out of the country, do anything. She returned in the summer, but her presence as regent while her father sought medical treatment in Europe did nothing to temper the government's growing repression. However, by the end of 1887 the army declared that it would no longer do the government's bidding. It was clear to military leadership that the government's policy of suppressing abolitionists was contributing to overall disorder—but their unwillingness to cooperate was also a reflection of the army's frustration with its poor treatment by the government, including low pay for soldiers and a declining military budget.[50]

The tide continued to turn in 1888. Planters in some areas freed their slaves and made arrangements to pay them for their work. São Paulo and other cities declared free soil, banning slavery. Abolitionist momentum continued to gain pace, requiring the regent to act. Isabel had been associated with abolitionism; since 1885, she had occasionally handed out manumission certificates at the official *Livro de Ouro* ceremonies paid for by Rio's local emancipation funds.[51] Now she had the opportunity to do that on a much larger scale. By February she was moving in that direction, and in March the Cotegipe government collapsed. The Conservatives stayed in power, but now with the more moderate João Alfredo Correia de Oliveira at the helm. More regions joined in declaring themselves free soil. Now, without the repressive measures of the previous government, the abolitionist parties and public events restarted in earnest. By the end of March, legislation was drafted for immediate abolition—without compensation for enslavers.[52]

In early May the legislation sped through parliament, with the final votes on Sunday, May 13. Outside, crowds gathered, celebrating the news from the Senate with a mixture of relief and exhaustion. The legislation, now passed, was taken to the royal palace. The abolitionists presented Isabel with gifts for her signing of the law, including a symbolic gold-and-ruby-encrusted pen—and two bouquets of camellias, one of which was harvested from the fields of Leblon.[53] At 3:00 p.m., she signed the "Lei Áurea" or Golden Law, immediately ending slavery. Rio de Janeiro erupted into days of celebration, with parties and parades, speeches, fireworks, and, of course, flowers. An official celebration took place on May 17, 1888, to commemorate the end of slavery and the freeing of the remaining 700,000 people in bondage. A photograph taken on that day shows officials and the princess on a stage where a Catholic mass of celebration was held, and a cheering crowd in front of them that stretches all the way to the horizon.[54]

After a struggle of more than 400 years, near the dawn of the twentieth century, the scourge of African slavery in the Americas was over. The following year, after 58 years as emperor, Pedro II was forced out in a coup, and a republic was established. Pedro II, who had come back to Brazil despite his ill health, now returned to Europe to live in exile. The republic of Brazil had shed its past, though what lay ahead for all people of color, newly freed or not, was far from clear.

Epilogue

Beginnings

Finally, by the last decade of the nineteenth century, after more than 400 years, the scourge of African slavery in the Americas had ended. That is not to say all slavery was over, or that murky areas of servitude did not persist. But it was the end of one era, but not yet the beginning of complete freedom. Slavery had forced everyone living under it, enslaver and enslaved, to make difficult moral choices. No one escaped its corruption, or its violence. The existence of that system was a poison, its toxins seeping through the societies of the Americas, the extent of the damage not fully understood when it ended. If anything, what lay ahead was a continual redefinition of the meaning of freedom. In the 1890s, black people in the Americas were no longer enslaved, but that did not mean they enjoyed the same freedoms as their white counterparts.

People of African descent would see their rights curtailed and the continuation of social prejudices going into the twentieth century, across all the nations in the Americas. Haiti would feel the humiliating sting of a US Marine occupation from 1915 to 1934, triggered by unrest that preceded the brutal killing of its president Guillaume Sam by a mob, arriving the same day as his death, July 28, 1915. The US showed up ostensibly to protect the business interests of US investors, which involved a raid on the island's treasury. The Marines did the same in the Dominican Republic in 1916.

African Americans in the Southern United States were forced to live under a segregated system, their hard-won rights slipping away as Reconstruction ended and was replaced with the racist laws of Jim Crow. Job opportunities in the South were limited, and sharecropping barely provided enough for survival; in addition, any prosperity could be taken away with impunity by white people who knew the law would protect them. Racialized violence became commonplace, with hundreds of lynchings all over the South, causing millions to leave for the North, only to find other forms of discrimination and struggle. The categories of "slave" and "free" turned into "black" and "white," racial labels that were—and remain—an expression of power rather than any biological reality.

Freedom in all post-emancipation societies may have been a legal reality, but much about it was also a fiction, perhaps even a fantasy. In Cuba and Brazil, black people, especially the recently liberated, struggled to move beyond poverty. Certain spaces became de facto whites-only—yacht clubs, bars, restaurants. There may not have been separate drinking fountain signs, as in the US, but who belonged where was deeply encoded. Domestic jobs continued to be held by black people, serving the needs of whites. Black people were denied good housing and forced to live in slums and favelas. Police harassment followed those who would not comply, with the old forms of discrimination underpinning the new order.

Elsewhere in Latin America, where smaller populations of Afro-descended people lived at the time of emancipation, they found themselves written out of history, or merged into other categories. In Mexico, for instance, they were swept up in the 1920s under the idea posited by the writer José Vasconcelos of a *"raza cosmica,"* a cosmic race, one that combined the diverse pasts of European, indigenous, and African, both celebrating difference and flattening it out, pushing the African story to the margins.

In Africa, the slaving relationship was replaced by another form of resource extraction. The Berlin West Africa Conference of 1884–1885 was the site of the carve-up known as the "scramble for Africa." Britain and other European powers claimed they needed to invade African nations because they wanted to stop what remained of the internal slave trade; however, their true intention was gaining access to natural resources, such as gold and diamonds, and later other valuable minerals and oil. Slavery was a convenient excuse. While African kingdoms had a role in the development of the Atlantic slave trade, its acceleration and manipulation were at the hands of Europeans—and now the same

Europeans were blaming Africans for that trade, and using it as justification to colonize their land. In 1926 the League of Nations issued a Convention to Suppress the Slave Trade and Slavery, but it had little to do with addressing the legacies of four centuries of Atlantic slavery.[1]

While it may have seemed easier or more convenient to try to forget this slave past, it was always simmering beneath the surface. When construction started in Rio de Janeiro in 2011 in preparation for the 2016 Olympics, a long-buried quay was uncovered. This was Valongo Wharf, once a main point of entry for ships—and for the nearly 1 million enslaved people brought aboard those ships between 1770 and 1830.[2] As one visitor in 1822 described it, Valongo was where "the slave-trade comes in all its horrors before one's eyes."[3] Its use as a slave port waned in the 1830s as the slave trade began to decline, but in the 1840s it was smartened up for the arrival of Teresa Cristina, princess of the Kingdom of the Two Sicilies, betrothed to Brazil's emperor Pedro II, who sailed into Rio's Guanabara Bay aboard the frigate *Constituição* in September 1843. However, as the city grew, some of the port area was filled in. Valongo was eventually submerged under a sea of concrete, destined to be neglected until work began for the Olympics. The only marker of its past was an Ionic column with a globe and cross on top to mark the occasion of the royal wedding. Valongo may have been overlooked for decades, but it was not forgotten by people in the local area, a neighborhood still called *Pequena África* (Little Africa).

Archaeologists got to work at the wharf, unearthing proof of its past, fragments of goods and fragments of people. In 2017 UNESCO made it a World Heritage Site.[4] Now it is uncovered, though the water no longer laps at it, and instead it is surrounded by the city. Some of the exposed stones bear rusted rings where ships' ropes would have been tied, silent witnesses to its nautical history, as cars drive past and curious pedestrians stop to see why this space has been marked out.

Another large mass burial site (*Cemitério dos pretos novos*), like the one in Santa Rita, was also found close to the Valongo Wharf. In this case, part of it was uncovered when the Guimaraes family started renovations on their home in the 1990s. Once the concrete of the nineteenth-century house came up, the bones were clear to see: There were thousands of fragments. Bits of skulls, of femurs, of teeth. It is believed that some 20,000 bodies may have been buried in the area, possibly making it the largest such African cemetery in the Americas.[5] Today the IPN Museu Memorial sits nearby, protecting the remains and educating the public about the history that was long entombed in the soil.[6]

Soil and concrete, skyscrapers and shantytowns—nothing will completely bury this history. It can be heard everywhere, a muffled lament from the underground graves in Brazil or a melancholy breeze that accompanies the gentle rustle of ripe sugarcane stalks in fields across the Caribbean. The past is there with the clink of every glass of rum, every bite of chocolate, and, certainly, every teaspoon of sugar. As Saidiya Hartman writes in her devastating work *Lose Your Mother*: "If the ghost of slavery still haunts our present, it is because we are still looking for an exit from the prison."[7]

Slavery, of course, continues to exist around the world. Now its shape has shifted into sex trafficking and the smuggling of desperate migrant workers. While millions are forced into modern bondage, the vestiges of the particular evil that plagued the Americas—the chains, the slave markets, the whips—are no longer visible. However, another pernicious residue can be found in the culture of violence that engulfs both North and South America. What started as the need for guns and militias to keep social order has turned into damning statistics showing that black people, in the United States, Brazil, and elsewhere, have for decades been more likely than whites to be on the receiving end of violence, whether from other citizens or from state actors such as the police or military. Without question, this can be traced back to the plantation and the slave ship. It took violence to keep the system in place. Once the system was gone, the weapons—and the mindset—remained.

⋘ • ⋙

"IF ANY WHITE man in the world says give me liberty or give me death, the entire white world applauds," the African American writer James Baldwin explained to the talk show host Dick Cavett in 1969. "When a black man says exactly the same thing—word for word—he is judged a criminal and treated like one."⁸ While Baldwin, with his trademark eloquence, was speaking in the context of the black power movement in the US, his words are applicable to the struggle against slavery, especially in the two centuries following the American Revolution.

The words "liberty" and "freedom" should be the opposite of "bondage" and "slavery." They fall short, however, when one is thinking about both emancipation and the afterlife of slavery. Even during slavery, "freedom" was not its mirror image. It was at once something worth dying for and a word that could be rendered meaningless, only as real as the paper it was written on—and paper can be destroyed.

Freedom, at its core, is simply a vessel. It is an idea. What the thousands of people who fought to escape slavery did was give it a particular meaning, adding layers of depth and form to a word that had carried a particular political resonance for a different group of people. The freedoms laid out in documents like the US Constitution took on new dimensions as people continued to fight for their emancipation. As much as this book has been an account of the long road to freedom, it has also been an illustration of the many embodiments of that word. From legal battles to maroon colonies to armed insurrections—and even to reporting a conspiracy to gain personal freedom—people used every possible route out of slavery. Their vision afterward was just as diverse. Leaping off a slave ship was freedom. Land was freedom. Autonomy was freedom. Reuniting with family was freedom. Writing was freedom. Ultimately, what became clear was that there was no one way to freedom, except that it could not be limited to a single group of people. Freedom had to be for everyone, otherwise it was a lie. The United States and Haiti in the 1800s embodied these very different visions of what it meant—and who was allowed—to be free.

Despite the complex journey to liberation, the state of affairs in 1890 would have scarcely been possible to imagine in 1750. Slavery had taken on a life of its own. This book has shown how the road to emancipation was long and difficult, pitted by violence, suppression, and hypocrisy. Many fine words have been said about the ending of slavery—often by the very people who benefited from the system in the first place. Yes, white abolitionists, politicians, and social campaigners played important roles in ending slavery, but they were constantly responding to crises. Every white abolitionist action cast a shadow: ending the slave trade, but with a 10-year transition window; bringing in emancipation, but only for children—who stayed enslaved until adulthood. The creation of Haiti brought with it the reality and possibility of universal emancipation—but Haitians paid a steep price in the aftermath.

Among the emancipators are the millions whose stories will never be known. The people who flung themselves from ships. The ones who perished during slave rebellions, whose heads ended up on pikes along dirt roads. Those who kept the flame of freedom from flickering out in Haiti. Those who were killed, but whose names were never recorded. Those who set up an alternative world in the forests of Brazil and Jamaica. Those who spoke truth to power and demanded the Vatican pay attention, or published pamphlets and newspapers making a ceaseless call for this practice to end. These people were the true instigators of liberty. They lived the struggle. They were the great resistance.

Acknowledgments

Writing is often depicted as a solitary pursuit, but it's actually the opposite—taking an idea and turning it into a book requires a large, enthusiastic team to cheer you on the entire way. That starts with the acquisition, and I'm deeply grateful to Morgan Entrekin at Grove Atlantic for once again choosing to publish my book. It has also been a pleasure to work on a second title with George Gibson, whose patient editing turns my rambling ideas into readable prose. The entire team at Grove Atlantic has been nothing but supportive, and it continues to be a joy to work with them. Alicia Burns's copyediting gave the manuscript the polish it needed, while Martin Lubikowski brought the geography alive with his wonderful maps. Many thanks also go to Basic Books UK, especially to Siam Hatzaw and Joe Zigmond, and to his predecessor Sarah Caro, for acquiring this book for the British market. And I'm always grateful for the help and support of my agent, Bill Hamilton.

Books like this are the result—first and foremost—of the work of dozens of scholars, whose research is indispensable in bringing together a large history like this one. Alongside this are countless conversations with people in the field, and I've been very fortunate in this regard. Special thanks go to Eduardo Posada-Carbó, Joanna Innes, and Mark Philp for including me in their "Re-imagining Democracy in Latin America and the Caribbean" project. The UCL Caribbean Seminar series is always a welcome home, and many thanks to Steve Cushion, Gad Heuman, and Kate Quinn for their ongoing interest in my work. Thanks are also due to Surekha Davies, who invited me to speak on panels at two conferences of the American Historical Association, in Philadelphia and New York City, about the challenges of writing history for the wider public.

This book took me to a lot of places and relied on the help and advice of a lot of people. Regarding Jamaica I'd like to thank: Jean Besson, Frances Botkin, Gad Heuman, and Tom Zoellner. A huge thank you goes to the wonderful Charles Town Maroon community, who were such generous hosts, including the late Colonel Marcia (Kim) Douglas, Rodney Rose, Claudia Brown, and Michael Lumsden. In the US, Sharron Grovner took me on a memorable tour of Sapelo Island. My conversation with John McCusker at Kid Ory House in LaPlace, Louisiana, helped me understand the events of 1811. And I'm grateful to Rick Francis in Southampton, Virginia, for sharing his vast resources. In Spain, it was a pleasure to chat with Antonio Moreno Ruiz, and I appreciate him putting me in contact with the Hermandad de Nuestra Señora de los Ángeles (los Negritos) in Seville, who were very generous in opening their doors to me. As always, the staff of the Archivo General de Indias helped me make the most of the time I had there. In Portugal, Naky Gaglo's African Lisbon Tour was eye-opening.

In Curaçao, Aidan Hermans was generous with his contacts, and it was truly enlightening to have conversations about the island's rich history with Dimitri Cloose, Jeanne Henriquez, and Charles do Rego. In Cartagena, Wendy Sánchez Guzmán walked me through the city's black history, and Travel Palenque provided a seamless visit to San Basilio de Palenque. David Knight generously took time to speak to me about Saint John. In Saint Vincent, it was a pleasure to talk about history with Prime Minister Ralph Gonsalves, and many thanks to him and his wife, Eloise, for their hospitality, and to Ginette Harris for the introduction. In Dominica, Polly Pattullo took me for a memorable swim, and is always the best guide to the island. I also appreciate Jacqueline Dupigny and Lowell Green taking the time to chat with me. And in Brazil, my final stop, the advice from Celso Castilho, Teresa Cribelli, and Yuko Miki was very helpful. Sayuri Koshima guided me through the rich past of Salvador de Bahia, and Damiana Silva's Rio Little Africa tour is a must-do in Rio de Janeiro. It has been an enormous inspiration to see how so many people are keeping this history alive in their communities.

Back home, my friends and family heard a lot about this book and their patience is appreciated far more than I can express. A special thank you goes to my writing-accountability group, Tamara J. Walker and Leah Redmond Chang, for reading the manuscript and providing such thoughtful feedback, as well as offering inspiration, support, and brilliant conversation during our regular check-ins.

Another big thanks goes to my travel buddies who took the time to join me on different legs of this trip, Crystal Paulk-Buchanan and Christina Proenza-Coles (who is also due a bonus thank-you for reading the manuscript!). May we find ourselves on the road again soon. Huge appreciation also goes to everyone who took time to read all or parts of the manuscript: Juan Cobo Betancourt, Matthew Cavazos, Michael Deibert, Rory Foster, Mariama Ifode-Blease, and Joshua Newton.

Others who deserve my ongoing gratitude include: Lisa Bachelor and Simon Hill, David Batty, Mark Berry, Victoria Burgher, Felipe Ceceña, Christine Cheung, Beth and Nick Gadd, David and Rebecca Ferguson, Vicky Frost and Anthony Pickles, Chloe Ireton, Jodie Adams Kirshner, Teague Paulk-Buchanan, Charlotte and Eric Rayburn, Anne-Isabelle Richard-Picchi and Alex Afonso, Diana Siclovan, Yvonne Singh, and Chloe Stockford.

The writing of this book sadly coincided with the deaths of my parents, James (2021) and Rose (2023). I appreciate my family's support during this difficult period, especially that of my brother, Michael Gibson, and his partner, Cassie Childs.

As always, my husband, Chris Stanford, remains the model of a supportive spouse—every writer should be so fortunate. Each book is an opportunity to remind myself how impossible it would be to do this work without his love and encouragement.

Timeline

1434 – Portuguese explorer Gil Eanes reaches the African coast around latitude 26° north and manages to return, opening the way to further European voyages to that region.

1444 – The first known market of enslaved Africans in Europe is established in Lagos, Portugal.

1482 – The Portuguese build the trading post of Elmina Castle on the Gold Coast (Ghana).

1492 – Genoese navigator Christopher Columbus lands on the Caribbean island he names Hispaniola (today's Dominican Republic and Haiti), signaling the start of European incursion in the Americas.

1500 – Queen Isabella declares indigenous enslavement illegal in Spain's colonies.

1502 – Enslaved Africans are taken to Hispaniola.

1521 – A group of 20 enslaved Africans rebel on Christmas day in Hispaniola, on the sugar plantation of Christopher Columbus's son, Diego.

1526 – Enslaved people set houses on fire in the short-lived Spanish colony of San Miguel de Gualdape (today's Georgia), hastening the colony's end.

1546–47 – Spanish attempts to suppress maroons on Hispaniola lead to the capture and execution of Sebastián Lemba.

1552 – A slave revolt occurs in a mining area of Venezuela, led by Miguel de Buría.

1572–73 – English pirate Francis Drake forms an alliance with maroons in Panama, under the leadership of *cimarrón* chief Pedro Mandinga, to attack and plunder the Spanish.

1575 – Portugal establishes a settlement in Luanda, on the coast of Angola.

1595 – Large-scale slave uprising takes place in São Tomé, led by an enslaved man named Amador, destroying sugar plantations.

1605 – A maroon *quilombo* in northern Brazil is established and becomes known as Palmares. Its population rises to around 10,000 by 1640.

1608–09 – Maroon leader Gaspar Yanga enters negotiations with the Spanish after years of fighting, leading to the establishment of the first free black town in Mexico.

1613 – The Spanish sign a treaty with a maroon settlement led by Benkos Biohó, in New Grenada (today's Colombia).

1619 – The first recorded enslaved Africans arrive at the English colony of Jamestown in Virginia.

1624 – The Dutch West India Company (WIC) establishes New Netherland in North America; the English claim Saint Christopher's (Saint Kitts) in the Caribbean, and the French later join them on that island. The Dutch WIC also attempts to take Brazilian territory and ends up in control of the Pernambuco area from 1630 to 1654.

1627 – The British claim the island of Barbados.

1635 – France claims the Caribbean islands of Martinique and Guadeloupe.

1654 – The Dutch are driven out of northern Brazil.

1655 – England takes Jamaica from Spain.

1661 – The Barbados Assembly adopts acts "for the better ordering and governing of Negroes," the first New World slave code.

1664 – France establishes the *Compagnie française des Indes occidentales* to trade between France, Africa, and the American colonies.

1671 – The Danish West India Company takes control of the Caribbean island of Saint Thomas.

1672 – England's Charles II grants a charter for the Royal African Company, which is given a monopoly over English trade to Africa, including in slavery.

1675 – Plans for a large-scale rebellion organized by "Coromantee" (Gold Coast) enslaved people are uncovered in Barbados.

1680 – The Virginia General Assembly passes an "Act for preventing Negroes Insurrections."

1684 – African noble Lourenço da Silva Mendonça arrives in Rome to take his case against slavery and the slave trade to the Vatican.

1685 – France's Code Noir (black code) is promulgated, regulating the treatment of enslaved people in its colonial territories.

1688 – Quakers in English North America issue their Germantown petition, criticizing the slave trade and slavery.

1693 – Spain's Carlos II offers liberty to any enslaved person who escapes to Spanish Florida from enemy English territory.

1694 – The Portuguese destroy the maroon settlement of Palmares after decades of failed attacks. The following year its leader, Zumbi, is executed.

1712 – A slave rebellion erupts in New York City. It is quickly put down, and 20 people are executed.

1713 – Britain is awarded the lucrative slave *asiento*, a contract to deliver African captives to Spain's American colonies.

1730 – The first Maroon War begins in Jamaica, between the British authorities and maroon communities on the island, lasting until 1739.

1733 – A slave rebellion takes place on the Danish Caribbean island of Saint John (Sankt Jan), under the leadership of "king" Claes, lasting more than six months.

1736 – Plans for an extensive rebellion organized by enslaved workers are uncovered in Antigua.

1739 – A group of enslaved workers in the Stono River area around Charleston, South Carolina, attempt to march to Florida, where they believe the Spanish king will grant them their freedom, but their rebellion is suppressed.

1741 – A slave conspiracy is uncovered in New York City, leading to the arrests of enslaved people, free people of color, and white participants. Thirty-four people are executed.

1760 – A large slave uprising, known as "Tacky's Rebellion," begins in Jamaica. It becomes a guerilla war with multiple leaders, lasting more than a year.

1761 – Portugal bans slavery in mainland Portugal and its Atlantic islands but not in Brazil.

1756–63 – The Seven Years' War causes conflict around the globe, including throughout North America and the Caribbean.

1763 – A serious slave revolt, under the leadership of an enslaved man named Coffij, erupts in the Dutch South American colony of Berbice, lasting months.

1769 – Relations between the British and the "Black Carib" (Afro-Kalinago) people in Saint Vincent break down, resulting in the First Carib War, which ends by treaty in 1773.

1770 – The Boston Massacre, in which British troops fire into a crowd of colonists, is the first in a series of events in a North American white colonial revolt, leading to a war of independence.

1772 – The *Somerset* decision effectively prohibits slavery in Britain, but this does not apply to British colonies.

1773 – Enslaved people in Massachusetts petition for freedom; others follow suit throughout New England.

1774 – Elizabeth Freeman's successful freedom suit helps pave the way for limited emancipation in Massachusetts.

1775 – The colonial governor of Virginia, Lord Dunmore, offers freedom to slaves who fight for the king's troops in the American Revolution.

1777 – Vermont outlaws slavery in its constitution, though emancipation is gradual: Children born to an enslaved mother after that date would be kept in bondage until the age of 21 for a man and 19 for a woman.

1780 – Pennsylvania passes a gradual emancipation law.

1783 – British society is horrified at the Zong massacre, in which more than 100 African captives were thrown off this ship in 1781 as part of an insurance fraud, bringing attention to the abolitionist cause.

1784 – Rhode Island and Connecticut adopt gradual emancipation laws.

1787 – African abolitionist Quobna Ottobah Cugoano publishes *Thoughts and Sentiments on the Evil and Wicked Traffic of the Slavery and Commerce of the Human Species*. The Society for Effecting the Abolition of the Slave Trade is set up in Britain.

1788 – The French abolitionist group *Société des Amis des Noir* is founded.

1789 – African abolitionist Olaudah Equiano publishes his *Interesting Narrative of the Life of Olaudah Equiano, or Gustavus Vassa, The African, Written by Himself.*

1790 – Free *homme de couleur* Vicente Ogé leads an uprising in the French colony of Saint-Domingue calling for greater rights for property-owning free people of color, but it fails and he is executed.

1791 – A revolt among enslaved people erupts in the northern region of Saint-Domingue, marking the beginning of the Haitian Revolution. In Britain, William Wilberforce introduces a motion to end the slave trade, which fails.

1792 – The Legislative Assembly in France grants equal rights to free people of color in its colonies. Another attempt to end the slave trade in the British parliament is blocked by the House of Lords. Denmark passes a law abolishing the slave trade, which would take effect by 1803.

1793 – French republican officials abolish slavery in Saint-Domingue, in the north in August and in the west and south by October. British troops invade southern and western Saint-Domingue.

1794 – The National Convention in France abolishes slavery in all French colonies. In Saint-Domingue, former slave and rebel leader Toussaint Louverture joins French Republican troops, after having left the colony in 1793 to command Spanish auxiliary forces in neighboring Santo Domingo. British forces invade

Guadeloupe and Martinique. Free black and enslaved inhabitants of Saint Lucia launch a guerrilla war against the British rulers, which runs until 1799.

1795 – Rebellions involving enslaved people occur in Grenada, led by Julien Fédon; Colihault, Dominica; Curaçao, led by Tula; Coro, Venezuela, led by José Leonardo Chirino; Puerto Príncipe and Bayamo, Cuba; and Aguadilla, Puerto Rico. A conspiracy among enslaved people is uncovered in Pointe Coupée, Louisiana. The second war between the Black Caribs and the British begins, ending the following year with the deportation of the Black Caribs to British Honduras (Belize). The Second Maroon War starts in Jamaica and ends with hundreds of maroons deported to Nova Scotia, Canada. Under the Peace of Basel, Spain cedes Santo Domingo to France, putting the whole island of Hispaniola under French control.

1798 – The British withdraw from Saint-Domingue. The "Tailors' Revolt" takes place in Salvador de Bahia, Brazil, involving a mix of enslaved and free people of color who were calling for improved rights.

1799 – The state of New York implements gradual emancipation.

1800 – A rebellion plan organized by enslaved blacksmith Gabriel Prosser in Richmond, Virginia, is uncovered.

1801 – Toussaint Louverture issues a new constitution for Saint-Domingue, appointing himself governor for life and reiterating the ban on slavery.

1802 – France's Napoleon Bonaparte sends an expedition to regain control of Saint-Domingue. Louverture is captured and imprisoned in France, where he dies the following year. Bonaparte reinstitutes slavery in all French colonies, triggering a final campaign in Saint-Domingue to drive out French forces.

1803 – France sells the Louisiana Territory to the United States for $15 million.

1804 – French forces are defeated in Saint-Domingue, and the independent nation of Haiti is established. The state of New Jersey enacts gradual emancipation.

1807 – British abolitionists win a victory in Parliament with the passing of the Abolition of the Slave Trade bill. The US passes an Act to Prohibit the Importation of Slaves. A British West Africa Squadron is established to patrol the Atlantic and capture illegal slaving vessels.

1808 – Bonaparte invades Spain, causing political unrest throughout Spanish America and opening the way for independence movements.

1810 – A priest named Miguel Hidalgo leads the charge for Mexico's independence from Spain with his "Grito de Dolores." He also calls for the immediate abolition of slavery.

1811 – Chile enacts a "free womb" law for the gradual emancipation of slaves. Under this law, children born to an enslaved mother would be free after reaching adulthood. The north of Haiti is declared a kingdom, with former general Henry Christophe proclaiming himself king; the south is a republic under the control of another general, Alexandre Pétion. A rebellion involving hundreds of slaves breaks out in the territory of Louisiana, in the German Coast plantation area, but it is suppressed within days.

1812 – A conspiracy is uncovered in Havana, and free black artist and carpenter José Antonio Aponte is blamed. The War of 1812 between Britain and the US begins, with the British offering some enslaved people freedom for their assistance in the conflict. A mass defection on plantations in Dominica triggers a maroon war that lasts until 1814.

1815 – Britain puts the abolition of the international slave trade on the agenda at the Congress of Vienna, held at the end of the Napoleonic Wars, pressuring France, Spain, Portugal, and Holland to stop their involvement. All agree to this measure, but illicit slaving continues for decades.

1816 – Barbados experiences its first slave rebellion in more than a century, though it is put down a few weeks later.

1817 – The American Colonization Society is established in the United States to encourage the emigration of free black people to Haiti and places in Africa.

1819 – Spain cedes Florida to the United States.

1821 – A "free womb" law is introduced in Peru; Colombia bans the slave trade, but emancipation is gradual.

1822 – A conspiracy organized by free blacksmith Denmark Vesey is uncovered in Charleston, South Carolina. Brazil becomes an independent empire, under the rule of Pedro I. Haiti is reunited under Jean-Pierre Boyer. Boyer occupies Spanish Santo Domingo (which had been returned to Spain in 1809) and bans slavery there. The American Colonization Society establishes a settlement called Monrovia, in West Africa, which will become the nation of Liberia.

1823 – A slave uprising involving thousands in the South American colony of Demerara shocks the British public and leads to increasing calls for the end of slavery. The Society of the Amelioration and Gradual Abolition of Slavery is founded in the UK. The republic of Chile abolishes slavery.

1825 – Haiti agrees to pay France an indemnity of 150 million francs in exchange for the recognition of its independence. A significant uprising erupts in the sugar-growing region of Matanzas, Cuba, followed by a number of rebellions over the next two decades.

1829 – Mexico's efforts to abolish slavery trigger unrest among white US settlers in the eastern part of the state of Coahuila y Tejas.

1830 – An enslaved man named Pompey leads a revolt on Exuma Island, Bahamas, after enslaved people refuse to be transferred to other islands by their enslavers.

1831 – In August, a revolt led by enslaved black carpenter Nat Turner, in Southampton, Virginia, leaves more than 50 dead. In Jamaica, a large rebellion breaks out around Christmas, led by an enslaved deacon, Samuel Sharpe, involving thousands and leading to the execution of more than 300 people. It further mobilizes British abolitionists to push for the end of slavery.

1833 – An Emancipation Bill is passed in Parliament abolishing slavery in the British colonies and freeing 800,000 people over the next five years. It compensates the enslavers some £20 million for their "losses," while requiring the formerly enslaved to serve unpopular "apprenticeships" for a number of years after being freed. In the US, the American Anti-Slavery Society is founded in Philadelphia.

1835 – In Salvador Bahia, Brazil, enslaved Malê Muslims organize an urban uprising.

1836 – The eastern part of Coahuila y Tejas breaks away from Mexico over the issue of slavery, establishing itself as the Republic of Texas, but is unable to join the US as a slave-holding state until 1845.

1837 – Black soldiers in the First West India Regiment in Trinidad mutiny under the leadership of an African man named Dâaga.

1839 – A rebellion aboard the *Amistad*, a ship taking captives from Havana to Puerto Príncipe, Cuba, results in the vessel arriving in the US. The subsequent trial and freeing of the captives grip public attention and increase abolitionist calls for the end of slavery.

1841 – Captives aboard the *Creole*, travelling from Virginia to New Orleans, stage a revolt and force the ship to sail to the Bahamas, where they claim their freedom in the British colony.

1843 – Gradual emancipation is enacted in Paraguay.

1844 – A period of slave revolts and conspiracy panics takes place in Cuba, known as *La Escalera* (the ladder), a reference to the punishment endured by many of being tied to a ladder and whipped.

1846 – Uruguay abolishes slavery.

1847 – Denmark abolishes slavery, but with a 12-year transition period. Sweden abolishes slavery in its Caribbean colony of Saint-Barthélemy.

1848 – Thousands of enslaved people in the Danish colony of Saint Croix protest to demand their immediate freedom, which they win. Under the Treaty of Guadeloupe Hidalgo, which ends the Mexican-American War, Mexico cedes 51 percent of its territory to the US. The land acquisition raises questions and tensions over the expansion of slavery into new states.

1848 – France abolishes slavery across its colonies, for the second time.

1850 – In the US, the Compromise of 1850 introduces the Fugitive Slave Act, under which any self-liberated person in a free state could be returned to slavery. This act puts free-born black people at risk of being kidnapped and sold into slavery.

1851 – Colombia, Bolivia, and Ecuador abolish slavery. Brazil bans the slave trade with other countries and enforces the law, ending illegal international trafficking, though a legal internal slave trade persists.

1853 – Argentina abolishes slavery.

1854 – Peru and Venezuela abolish slavery.

1857 – The Dred Scott trial in the US leads to a Supreme Court ruling that black people, free and enslaved, are not US citizens.

1859 – White abolitionist John Brown and 21 others raid a federal armory in Harpers Ferry, Virginia, in an attempt to trigger a slave rebellion. The attack fails, and Brown is hanged.

1860 – South Carolina votes to secede from the Union, and by early 1861 the Confederacy is formed with other Southern slave-holding states. By 1861, the American Civil War is underway.

1863 – US President Abraham Lincoln issues his Emancipation Proclamation, freeing those in bondage in the Confederate states. The Netherlands abolishes slavery in its colonies.

1864 –Paraguay goes to war against Brazil, Argentina, and Uruguay (until 1870) in the War of the Triple Alliance.

1865 – The US Civil War ends, and 13th Amendment to the Constitution permanently abolishes slavery in the United States (except as punishment for a crime). The Spanish Abolitionist Society (*Sociedad Abolicionista Española*) is established in Spain.

1866 – Spain finally and effectively abolishes the slave trade, after having agreed to do so 50 years earlier.

1868 – The 14th Amendment to the US Constitution reverses Dred Scott, and all black people, including the formerly enslaved, are granted citizenship.

1868 – In September, creole rebels in Puerto Rico issue the "Grito de Lares," a call for independence. In October, Cubans issue a similar cry, the "Grito de Yara." The rebellion is put down in Puerto Rico, but in Cuba it ignites a struggle known as the 10 Years' War.

1869 – Slavery is fully abolished in Paraguay, under pressure from Brazil, after the end of the War of the Triple Alliance.

1870 – Spain passes the Moret Law for Cuba and Puerto Rico, which frees enslaved people over the age of 60 and establishes a "free womb" law, which frees all children born to an enslaved mother after that date but requires them to work for their enslavers until the age of 18.

1871 – The Rio Branco Law is enacted in Brazil, bringing in "free womb" gradual abolition, freeing the children of enslaved mothers but requiring them to work for their enslavers until the age of 21.

1873 – Slavery is abolished in Puerto Rico, and enslavers are compensated with a payment and a concession that requires enslaved people to work for three more years.

1878 – The Pact of Zanjón ends the 10 Years' War between Cuba and Spain. It frees some of the enslaved people who fought in the conflict, but slavery in Cuba persists.

1884 – The Brazilian regions of Ceará and Amazonas abolish slavery.

1886 – Spain passes the Patronato Law in 1880, which abolishes slavery in Cuba and replaces it with an "apprenticeship" system, keeping enslaved people under contract to their enslavers. It is meant to last eight years but proves unenforceable, and the final abolition of slavery in Cuba is decreed two years earlier than planned.

1888 – Slavery is finally abolished in Brazil, the last nation in the Americas to end the practice.

Illustration Credits

Maps by Martin Lubikowski, ML Design, London.

In-text images

37. Courtesy of the Norman B. Leventhal Map & Education Center, Boston Public Library. https://collections.leventhalmap.org/search/commonwealth:6t053q88j
87. Courtesy of the Huntington Library Rare Book Maps Collection. https://hdl.huntington.org/digital/collection/p15150coll4/id/3299/
107. Courtesy of the John Carter Brown Map Collection. https://jcb.lunaimaging.com/luna/servlet/s/u286is
208. Courtesy of the Huntington Library Rare Book Maps Collection. https://hdl.huntington.org/digital/collection/p15150coll4/id/10171/rec/2
243. Courtesy of the Bibliothèque nationale de France. https://gallica.bnf.fr/ark:/12148/btv1b53216170d
350. Courtesy of the John Carter Brown Map Collection. https://jcb.lunaimaging.com/luna/servlet/s/mgtdt8
401. Courtesy of the John Carter Brown Map Collection. https://jcb.lunaimaging.com/luna/servlet/s/35g0hr

Insert

1. Courtesy of the Bibliothèque nationale de France. https://gallica.bnf.fr/ark:/12148/btv1b55002481n/f7.item
2. i) © The Berardo Collection, Lisbon.
2. ii) Courtesy of the Bibliothèque nationale de France. https://gallica.bnf.fr/ark:/12148/btv1b8458267s/f115.item#
3. i) Courtesy of the Statens Museum for Kunst, SMK Open. https://open.smk.dk/en/artwork/image/KMS7
3. ii) © Detroit Institute of Arts / Bridgeman Images.
4. i) https://commons.wikimedia.org/wiki/File:Zacharias_Wagner_-_Mercado_de_escravos_no_Recife.jpg
4. ii) Courtesy of the author.
5. i) Courtesy of the author.
5. ii) Courtesy of the Schomburg Center for Research in Black Culture, Manuscripts, Archives and Rare Books Division, The New York Public Library. https://digitalcollections.nypl.org/items/c375e810-c603-012f-616b-58d385a7bc34
5. iii) Courtesy of Antonia Graham.
6. i) Christie's Images / Bridgeman Images.
6. ii) Courtesy of the Schomburg Center for Research in Black Culture, Photographs and Prints Division, The New York Public Library. https://digitalcollections.nypl.org/items/d0cd5580-c5f4-012f-d378-58d385a7bc34

6. iii) Courtesy of the Art Institute of Chicago, purchased with funds provided by the Joseph and Helen Regenstein Foundation. https://www.artic.edu/artworks/44272/jean-baptiste-belley
7. i) Courtesy of the Schomburg Center for Research in Black Culture, Manuscripts, Archives and Rare Books Division, The New York Public Library. https://digitalcollections.nypl.org/items/4ab3f000-fe6d-0133-33b0-00505686a51c
7. ii) Courtesy of the Schomburg Center for Research in Black Culture, Manuscripts, Archives and Rare Books Division, The New York Public Library. https://digitalcollections.nypl.org/items/dec55be0-e8cd-013d-d13f-0242ac110003
7. iii) Courtesy of the John Carter Brown Archive of Early American Images. https://jcb.lunaimaging.com/luna/servlet/s/02uh65
8. i) Courtesy of the Library Company of Philadelphia. https://digital.librarycompany.org/islandora/object/Islandora%3A2706
8. ii) Courtesy of the Collection of the Massachusetts Historical Society.
8. iii) Courtesy of the author.
9. i) Courtesy of the author.
9. ii) Courtesy of the Aldridge Collection at the Charles Deering McCormick Library of Special Collections of Northwestern University Libraries. https://dc.library.northwestern.edu/items/9697405d-13d3-4fe6-947b-91e430b697f8
9. iii) Courtesy of the Schomburg Center for Research in Black Culture, Photographs and Prints Division, The New York Public Library. https://digitalcollections.nypl.org/items/5c0425d0-c60a-012f-af84-58d385a7bc34
10. i) The National Archives UK (MFQ 1/112(2).
10. ii) https://archive.org/details/horrors_of_slavery/mode/2up
11. i) Courtesy of the John Carter Brown Archive of Early American Images. https://jcb.lunaimaging.com/luna/servlet/s/1i6cp6
11. ii) Courtesy of the author.
12. i) Courtesy of the General Research Division, The New York Public Library. https://digitalcollections.nypl.org/items/9f61cf50-c605-012f-c9cb-58d385a7bc34
12. ii) Courtesy of the Library of Congress Rare Book and Special Collections Division. https://www.loc.gov/resource/cph.3a39248/
13. i) Christie's Images / Bridgeman Images.
13. ii) Bridgeman Images.
14. i) Courtesy of Slavery Images: A Visual Record of the African Slave Trade and Slave Life in the Early African Diaspora. https://www.slaveryimages.org/database/image-result.php?objectid=1136
14. ii) Courtesy of the Library of Congress Prints and Photographs Division. https://www.loc.gov/item/2018647801/
15. i) Courtesy of Slavery Images: A Visual Record of the African Slave Trade and Slave Life in the Early African Diaspora. https://www.slaveryimages.org/database/image-result.php?objectid=436
15. ii) Courtesy of the HathiTrust and the University of Michigan Humanities Text Initiative. https://babel.hathitrust.org/cgi/pt?id=mdp.39015014703279&seq=7
16. i) Courtesy of the author.
16. ii) https://commons.wikimedia.org/wiki/File:Missa_17_maio_1888.jpg

Selected Bibliography

I have included here more recent books and classic texts in English that might be of interest to the nonspecialist reader. For a full bibliography of primary and secondary works consulted, see carriegibson.co.uk.

Alonso, Angela. *The Last Abolition: The Brazilian Antislavery Movement, 1868–1888*. Cambridge University Press, 2022.
Andrews, George Reid. *Afro-Latin America, 1800–2000*. Oxford University Press, 2004.
Bagneris, Mia L. *Colouring the Caribbean: Race and the Art of Agostino Brunias*. Manchester University Press, 2018.
Bailyn, Bernard. *The Barbarous Years: The Peopling of British North America: The Conflict of Civilizations, 1600–1675*. Alfred A. Knopf, 2012.
Barcia, Manuel. *Seeds of Insurrection: Domination and Resistance on Western Cuban Plantations, 1808–1848*. Louisiana State University Press, 2008.
Barragan, Yesenia. *Freedom's Captives: Slavery and Gradual Emancipation on the Colombian Black Pacific*. Cambridge University Press, 2021.
Baumgartner, Alice L. *South to Freedom: Runaway Slaves to Mexico and the Road to the Civil War*. Basic Books, 2020.
Behn, Aphra. *Oroonoko*. Penguin Classics, 2003. Originally published in 1688.
Bergad, Laird W. *The Comparative Histories of Slavery in Brazil, Cuba, and the United States*. New Approaches to the Americas. Cambridge University Press, 2007.
Berlin, Ira. *Many Thousands Gone: The First Two Centuries of Slavery in North America*. Belknap Press, 1998.
Blackburn, Robin. *The Overthrow of Colonial Slavery, 1776–1848*. Verso, 1988.
Blanchard, Peter. *Slavery & Abolition in Early Republican Peru*. Scholarly Resources, 1992.
Blight, David W. *Frederick Douglass: Prophet of Freedom*. Simon & Schuster, 2018.
Bradley, Keith. *Slavery and Society at Rome*. Key Themes in Ancient History. Cambridge University Press, 1994.
Brown, Christopher Leslie. *Moral Capital: Foundations of British Abolitionism*. University of North Carolina Press, 2006.
Brown, Vincent. *Tacky's Revolt: The Story of an Atlantic Slave War*. Belknap Press, 2020.
Carretta, Vincent. *Phillis Wheatley: Biography of a Genius in Bondage*. University of Georgia Press, 2014.

Childs, Matt D. *The 1812 Aponte Rebellion in Cuba and the Struggle Against Atlantic Slavery.* University of North Carolina Press, 2006.

Clammer, Paul. *Black Crown: Henry Christophe, the Haitian Revolution and the Caribbean's Forgotten Kingdom.* Hurst, 2023.

Cowling, Camillia. *Conceiving Freedom: Women of Color, Gender, and the Abolition of Slavery in Havana and Rio de Janeiro.* University of North Carolina Press, 2013.

Craton, Michael. *Testing the Chains: Resistance to Slavery in the British West Indies.* Cornell University Press, 1982.

Cugoano, Quobna Ottobah. *Thoughts and Sentiments on the Evil of Slavery.* Edited by Vincent Carretta. Penguin Classics, 1999.

Curry, Christopher. *Freedom and Resistance: A Social History of Black Loyalists in the Bahamas.* University of Florida Press, 2017.

da Costa, Emília Viotti. *Crowns of Glory, Tears of Blood: The Demerara Slave Rebellion of 1823.* Oxford University Press, 1994.

Daut, Marlene L. *Awakening the Ashes: An Intellectual History of the Haitian Revolution.* University of North Carolina Press, 2023.

Davis, David Brion. *The Problem of Slavery in Western Culture.* Oxford University Press, 1988.

———. *The Problem of Slavery in the Age of Revolution, 1770–1823.* Oxford University Press, 1999.

———. *Inhuman Bondage: The Rise and Fall of Slavery in the New World.* Oxford University Press, 2006.

de Dijn, Annelien. *Freedom: An Unruly History.* Harvard University Press, 2020.

de la Fuente, Alejandro. *Havana and the Atlantic in the Sixteenth Century.* University of North Carolina Press, 2008.

Diouf, Sylviane. *Servants of Allah: African Muslims Enslaved in the Americas.* New York University Press, 2013.

———. *Slavery's Exiles: The Story of the American Maroons.* New York University Press, 2016.

Disney, A. R. *A History of Portugal and the Portuguese Empire: From the Beginnings to 1807.* Vol. 2, *The Portuguese Empire.* Cambridge University Press, 2009.

Douglass, Frederick. *Narrative of the Life of Frederick Douglass, an American Slave, Written by Himself.* Edited by Robert B. Stepto. Belknap Press, 1845.

Drescher, Seymour. *Abolition: A History of Slavery and Antislavery.* Cambridge University Press, 2009.

———. *Econocide: British Slavery in the Era of Abolition.* 2nd ed. University of North Carolina Press, 2010.

Du Bois, W. E. B. *Black Reconstruction in America.* Routledge, 2017. Originally published in 1935.

Dubois, Laurent. *A Colony of Citizens: Revolution & Slave Emancipation in the French Caribbean, 1787–1804.* University of North Carolina Press, 2004.

———. *Avengers of the New World: The Story of the Haitian Revolution.* Belknap Press, 2009.

Durkin, Hannah. *Survivors: The Lost Stories of the Last Captives of the Atlantic Slave Trade.* William Collins, 2024.

Egerton, Douglas. *He Shall Go Out Free: The Lives of Denmark Vesey.* Rowman & Littlefield, 2004.

Eltis, David. *Atlantic Cataclysm: Rethinking the Atlantic Slave Trades.* Cambridge University Press, 2025.

Equiano, Olaudah. *The Interesting Narrative of the Life of Olaudah Equiano.* Edited by Brycchan Carey. Oxford University Press, 2018. Originally published in 1789.

Ferrer, Ada. *Freedom's Mirror: Cuba and Haiti in the Age of Revolution.* Cambridge University Press, 2014.

———. *Cuba: An American History*. Scribner, 2021.
Fett, Sharla M. *Recaptured Africans: Surviving Slave Ships, Detention, and Dislocation in the Final Years of the Slave Trade*. University of North Carolina Press, 2017.
Fick, Carolyn E. *The Making of Haiti: The Saint Domingue Revolution from Below*. University of Tennessee Press, 1990.
Figueroa, Luis A. *Sugar, Slavery, and Freedom in Nineteenth-Century Puerto Rico*. University of North Carolina Press, 2005.
Foner, Eric. *The Fiery Trial: Abraham Lincoln and American Slavery*. W. W. Norton, 2011.
Forsdyke, Sara. *Slaves and Slavery in Ancient Greece*. Cambridge University Press, 2021.
Fracchia, Carmen. *"Black but Human": Slavery in Visual Art in Hapsburg Spain, 1480–1700*. Oxford University Press, 2019.
Fromont, Cécile. *The Art of Conversion: Christian Visual Culture in the Kingdom of Kongo*. Williamsburg, VA: Omohundro Institute of Early American History and Culture, 2014.
Fuentes, Marisa J. *Dispossessed Lives: Women, Violence, and the Archive*. University of Pennsylvania Press, 2016.
Gaffield, Julia. *Haitian Connections in the Atlantic World: Recognition after Revolution*. University of North Carolina Press, 2015.
Gaspar, David Barry. *Bondmen & Rebels: A Study of Master-Slave Relations in Antigua*. Johns Hopkins University Press, 1985.
Gaspar, David Barry, and David Patrick Geggus. *A Turbulent Time: The French Revolution and the Greater Caribbean*. Indiana University Press, 1997.
Geggus, David Patrick, ed. *The Impact of the Haitian Revolution in the Atlantic World*. University of South Carolina Press, 2001.
Geggus, David Patrick, and Norman Fiering, eds. *The World of the Haitian Revolution*. Indiana University Press, 2009.
Gerzina, Gretchen. *Black England: A Forgotten Georgian History*. John Murray, 2022.
Girard, Philippe R. *The Slaves Who Defeated Napoléon: Toussaint Louverture and the Haitian War of Independence, 1801–1804*. University of Alabama Press, 2011.
Gomez, Michael A. *Reversing Sail: A History of the African Diaspora*. 2nd ed. Cambridge University Press, 2020.
Gonzalez, Johnhenry. *Maroon Nation: A History of Revolutionary Haiti*. Yale University Press, 2019.
Goodfriend, Joyce D. *Before the Melting Pot: Society and Culture in Colonial New York City, 1664–1730*. Princeton University Press, 1992.
Gordon-Reed, Annette. *On Juneteenth*. Liveright, 2021.
Graubart, Karen B. *Republics of Difference: Religious and Racial Self-Governance in the Spanish Atlantic World*. Oxford University Press, 2022.
Gray, Thomas R. *The Confessions of Nat Turner*. Richmond, VA, 1832.
Green, Toby. *The Rise of the Trans-Atlantic Slave Trade in Western Africa, 1300–1589*. Cambridge University Press, 2011.
———. *A Fistful of Shells: West Africa from the Rise of the Slave Trade to the Age of Revolution*. Penguin, 2020.
Hahn, Steven. *The Political Worlds of Slavery and Freedom*. Harvard University Press, 2009.
Hall, Neville A. T. *Slave Society in the Danish West Indies: St. Thomas, St. John and St. Croix*. Edited by B. W. Higman. University of the West Indies Press, 1992.
Harris, John. *The Last Slave Ships: New York and the End of the Middle Passage*. Yale University Press, 2020.

Harris, Leslie M. *In the Shadow of Slavery: African Americans in New York City, 1626–1863*. University of Chicago Press, 2003.

Hartman, Saidiya. *Lose Your Mother: A Journey Along the Atlantic Slave Route*. London: Serpent's Tail, 2007.

Hazareesingh, Sudhir. *Black Spartacus: The Epic Life of Toussaint Louverture*. Allen Lane, 2020.

Hoffer, Peter Charles. *Cry Liberty: The Great Stono River Slave Rebellion of 1739*. Oxford University Press, 2010.

Honychurch, Lennox. *In the Forests of Freedom: The Fighting Maroons of Dominica*. Papillote Press, 2017.

Hurston, Zora Neale. *Barracoon: The Story of the Last "Black Cargo."* Edited by Deborah G. Plant. Amistad, 2018.

James, C. L. R. *Black Jacobins: Toussaint L'Ouverture and the San Domingo Revolution*. Penguin, 2001.

Kars, Marjoleine. *Blood on the River: A Chronicle of Mutiny and Freedom on the Wild Coast*. The New Press, 2020.

Landers, Jane G. *Atlantic Creoles in the Age of Revolutions*. Harvard University Press, 2010.

Lane, Kris. *Quito 1599: City and Colony in Transition*. University of New Mexico Press, 2002.

Lepore, Jill. *New York Burning: Liberty, Slavery, and Conspiracy in Eighteenth-Century Manhattan*. Vintage Books, 2005.

Lingna Nafafé, José. *Lourenço da Silva Mendonça and the Black Atlantic Abolitionist Movement in the Seventeenth Century*. Cambridge University Press, 2022.

Lugo-Ortiz, Agnes, and Angela Rosenthal. *Slave Portraiture in the Atlantic World*. Cambridge University Press, 2016.

Manjapra, Kris. *Black Ghost of Empire: The Long Death of Slavery and the Failure of Emancipation*. Scribner, 2022.

Martínez, María Elena. *Genealogical Fictions: Limpieza de Sangre, Religion, and Gender in Colonial Mexico*. Stanford University Press, 2008.

Matthews, Gelien. *Caribbean Slave Revolts and the British Abolitionist Movement*. Louisiana State University Press, 2006.

Morgan, Edmund S. *American Slavery, American Freedom: The Ordeal of Colonial Virginia*. W. W. Norton, 1975.

Morgan, Jennifer L. *Reckoning with Slavery: Gender, Kinship, and Capitalism in the Early Black Atlantic*. Duke University Press, 2021.

Murphy, Tessa. *The Creole Archipelago: Race and Borders in the Colonial Caribbean*. University of Pennsylvania Press, 2021.

Murray, David R. *Odious Commerce: Britain, Spain and the Abolition of the Cuban Slave Trade*. Cambridge Latin American Studies 37. Cambridge University Press, 1980.

Nash, Gary B. *Race and Revolution*. Rowman & Littlefield, 2001.

———. *The Forgotten Fifth: African Americans in the Age of Revolution*. Harvard University Press, 2006.

Needell, Jeffrey D. *The Sacred Cause: The Abolitionist Movement, Afro-Brazilian Mobilization, and Imperial Politics in Rio de Janeiro*. Stanford University Press, 2020.

Nessler, Graham T. *An Islandwide Struggle for Freedom: Revolution, Emancipation, and Reenslavement in Hispaniola, 1789–1809*. University of North Carolina Press, 2016.

Northup, Solomon. *Twelve Years a Slave*. Edited by Henry Louis Gates Jr. Penguin Books, 2012. Originally published in 1853.

Olusoga, David. *Black and British: A Forgotten History*. Pan Macmillan, 2016.

Otele, Olivette. *African Europeans: An Untold History*. Basic Books, 2020.
Paquette, Gabriel. *Imperial Portugal in the Age of Atlantic Revolutions: The Luso-Brazilian World, c. 1777–1850*. Cambridge University Press, 2013.
Paquette, Robert L. *Sugar Is Made with Blood: The Conspiracy of La Escalera and the Conflict between Empires over Slavery in Cuba*. Wesleyan University Press, 1988.
Patterson, Orlando. *Freedom*. Vol. 1, *Freedom in the Making of Western Culture*. Basic Books, 1991.
———. *Slavery and Social Death: A Comparative Study*. Harvard University Press, 2018.
Pattullo, Polly, ed. *Your Time Is Done Now: Slavery, Resistance, and Defeat: The Maroon Trials of Dominica (1813–1814)*. Papillote Press, 2015.
Peabody, Sue. *"There Are No Slaves in France": The Political Culture of Race and Slavery in the Ancien Régime*. Oxford University Press, 1996.
Pettigrew, William A. *Freedom's Debt: The Royal African Company and the Politics of the Atlantic Slave Trade, 1672–1752*. University of North Carolina Press, 2013.
Ponce Vázquez, Juan José. *Islanders and Empire: Smuggling and Political Defiance in Hispaniola, 1580–1690*. Cambridge University Press, 2020.
Posada-Carbó, Eduardo, Joanna Innes, and Mark Philip, eds. *Re-Imaging Democracy in Latin America and the Caribbean, 1780–1870*. Oxford University Press, 2023.
Price, Richard, ed. *Maroon Societies: Rebel Slave Communities in the Americas*. 3rd ed. Doubleday, 1996.
Prince, Mary. *The History of Mary Prince: A West Indian Slave*. Edited by Sara Salih. Penguin, 2004. Originally published in 1831.
Proenza-Coles, Christina. *American Founders: How People of African Descent Established Freedom in the New World*. NewSouth Books, 2018.
Rediker, Marcus. *The Slave Ship: A Human History*. Viking, 2007.
Restall, Matthew. *Seven Myths of the Spanish Conquest*. Oxford University Press, 2003.
Røge, Pernille. *Economistes and the Reinvention of Empire: France in the Americas and Africa, c. 1750–1802*. Cambridge University Press, 2019.
Scanlan, Padraic X. *Slave Empire: How Slavery Built Modern Britain*. Robinson, 2020.
Schloss, Rebecca Hartkopf. *Sweet Liberty: The Final Days of Slavery in Martinique*. University of Pennsylvania Press, 2009.
Schmidt-Nowara, Christopher. *Empire and Antislavery: Spain, Cuba, and Puerto Rico, 1833–1874*. University of Pittsburgh Press, 1999.
———. *Slavery, Freedom, and Abolition in Latin America and the Atlantic World*. University of New Mexico Press, 2011.
Schneider, Elena A. *The Occupation of Havana: War, Trade, and Slavery in the Atlantic World*. Williamsburg, VA: Omohundro Institute of Early American History and Culture, 2018.
Schwaller, Robert C. *African Maroons in Sixteenth-Century Panama: A History in Documents*. University of Oklahoma Press, 2021.
Schwarcz, Lilia M, and Heloisa M. Starling. *Brazil: A Biography*. Penguin, 2019.
Schwartz, Stuart B. *Sugar Plantations in the Formation of Brazilian Society, Bahia 1550–1835*. Cambridge University Press, 1985.
Scott, Julius S. *The Common Wind: Afro-American Currents in the Age of the Haitian Revolution*. Verso, 2018.
Sharples, Jason T. *The World That Fear Made: Slave Revolts and Conspiracy Scares in Early America*. University of Pennsylvania Press, 2020.
Sheridan, Richard B. *Sugar and Slavery: An Economic History of the British West Indies, 1623–1775*. Kingston, Jamaica: Canoe Press, 1994.

Sidbury, James. *Ploughshares into Swords: Race, Rebellion, and Identity in Gabriel's Virginia, 1730–1810*. Cambridge University Press, 1997.

Sinha, Manisha. *The Slave's Cause: A History of Abolition*. Yale University Press, 2016.

Smith, Clint. *How the Word Is Passed: A Reckoning with the History of Slavery Across America*. Little, Brown, 2021.

Stieber, Chelsea. *Haiti's Paper War: Post-Independence Writing, Civil War, and the Making of the Republic, 1804–1954*. New York University Press, 2020.

Stone, Erin Woodruff. *Captives of Conquest: Slavery in the Early Modern Spanish Caribbean*. University of Pennsylvania Press, 2021.

Stovall, Tyler. *White Freedom: The Racial History of an Idea*. Princeton University Press, 2021.

Taylor, Christopher. *The Black Carib Wars: Freedom, Survival, and the Making of the Garifuna*. University Press of Mississippi, 2012.

Taylor, Eric Robert. *If We Must Die: Shipboard Insurrections in the Era of the Atlantic Slave Trade*. Louisiana State University Press, 2006.

Taylor, Michael. *The Interest: How the British Establishment Resisted the Abolition of Slavery*. Vintage Books, 2020.

Thornton, John. *Africa and Africans in the Making of the Atlantic World, 1400–1800*. 2nd ed. Cambridge University Press, 1998.

Trouillot, Michel-Rolph. *Silencing the Past: Power and the Production of History*. Beacon Press, 1995.

Twinam, Ann. *Purchasing Whiteness: Pardos, Mulattos, and the Quest for Social Mobility in the Spanish Indies*. Stanford University Press, 2015.

Waldstreicher, David. *Slavery's Constitution: From Revolution to Ratification*. Hill and Wang, 2009.

Walker, David. *Appeal, In Four Articles; Together with A Preamble, to the Coloured Citizens of the World*. 3rd ed. Hill and Wang, 1965. Originally published in 1830.

Walvin, James. *Zong: A Massacre, the Law & the End of Slavery*. Yale University Press, 2017.

———. *Freedom: The Overthrow of the Slave Empires*. Robinson, 2019.

Wedderburn, Robert. *The Horrors of Slavery*. London, 1824.

Wheat, David. *Atlantic Africa and the Spanish Caribbean, 1570–1640*. University of North Carolina Press, 2016.

Wheatley, Phillis. *Poems on Various Subjects, Religious and Moral*. London, 1793. Originally published in 1773.

White, Ashli. *Encountering Revolution: Haiti and the Making of the Early Republic*. Johns Hopkins University Press, 2010.

Williams, Eric. *Capitalism and Slavery*. Penguin Modern Classics. Penguin, 2022.

Woo, Ilyon. *Master Slave Husband Wife: An Epic Journey from Slavery to Freedom*. Ithaka Books, 2023. Kindle.

Wood, Peter H. *Black Majority: Negroes in Colonial South Carolina from 1670 through the Stono Rebellion*. W. W. Norton, 1975.

Zoellner, Tom. *Island on Fire: The Revolt That Ended Slavery in the British Empire*. Harvard University Press, 2020.

Notes

Author's Note

1. Kris Manjapra, *Black Ghost of Empire: The Long Death of Slavery and the Failure of Emancipation* (Scribner, 2022), p. 9.
2. Carrie Gibson, *Empire's Crossroads: A History of the Caribbean from Columbus to the Present Day* (Grove Atlantic, 2014); and Carrie Gibson, *El Norte: The Epic and Forgotten Story of Hispanic North America* (Grove Atlantic, 2019).
3. This framing of emancipation as a larger war—often incorporating African military techniques—follows from the work of scholars like Vincent Brown and Manuel Barcia. See Brown, *Tacky's Revolt: The Story of an Atlantic Slave War* (Belknap Press, 2020); and Barcia, *The Great African Slave Revolt of 1825: Cuba and the Fight for Freedom in Matanzas* (Louisiana State University Press, 2012).
4. See for instance Seymour Drescher, *Abolition: A History of Slavery and Antislavery* (Cambridge University Press, 2009); Robin Blackburn, *The Overthrow of Colonial Slavery 1776–1848* (Verso, 1988); James Walvin, *Freedom: The Overthrow of the Slave Empires* (Pegasus, 2019); and David Brion Davis, *Inhuman Bondage: The Rise and Fall of Slavery in the New World* (Oxford University Press, 2006).
5. Keith Bradley, *Slavery and Society at Rome* (Cambridge University Press, 1994), p. 12.
6. See for instance Seymour Drescher and Pieter C. Emmer, eds. *Who Abolished Slavery? Slave Revolts and Abolitionism: A Debate with João Pedro Marques* (Berghahn Books, 2010).
7. Tyler Stovall, *White Freedom: The Racial History of an Idea* (Princeton University Press, 2021), p. 5.
8. Hilary McD. Beckles, "Caribbean Anti-Slavery: The Self-Liberation Ethos of Enslaved Blacks," *Journal of Caribbean History* 22, no. 1–2: p. 3.
9. Ibid., p. 11.
10. To cite just a few in English, see Barcia, *The Great African Slave Revolt*; Hilary McD. Beckles, *Black Rebellion in Barbados: The Struggle Against Slavery, 1627–1838* (Antilles Publications, 1984); Brown, *Tacky's Revolt*; Emília Viotti da Costa, *Crowns of Glory, Tears of Blood: The Demerara Slave Rebellion of 1823* (Oxford University Press, 1994); Douglas R. Egerton, *Gabriel's Rebellion: The Virginia Slave Conspiracies of 1800 and 1802* (University of North Carolina Press, 1993); Aisha K. Finch, *Rethinking Slave Rebellion in Cuba: La Escalera and the Insurgencies of 1841–1844* (University of North Carolina Press, 2015); Eugene D. Genovese, *From Rebellion to Revolution: Afro-American Slave Revolts in the Making of the Modern World* (Louisiana State University Press, 1992); Gad Heuman, *The Killing Time:*

The Morant Bay Rebellion in Jamaica (Macmillan Caribbean, 1994); Peter Charles Hoffer, *Cry Liberty: The Great Stono River Slave Rebellion of 1739* (Oxford University Press, 2010); Charles Do Rego and Lionel Janga, *Slavery and Resistance in Curaçao: The Rebellion of 1795* (Willemstad: Fundashon Parke Nashonal, 2009).

11 Orlando Patterson, *Freedom*, vol. 1, *Freedom in the Making of Western Culture* (Basic Books, 1991), p. xiii.

12 For more on archival and historical silences, see the classic work by Michel-Rolph Trouillot, *Silencing the Past: Power and the Production of History* (Beacon Press, 1995); Saidiya Hartman, "Venus in Two Acts," *Small Axe* 26, no. 2 (June 1, 2008): pp. 1–14.

13 Vincent Brown, "Social Death and Political Life in the Study of Slavery," *American Historical Review* 5, no. 114 (December 2009): p. 1249.

14 Earl Lovelace, *Salt* (Persea Books, 1996), p. 7.

Chapter 1

1 "Extract of a Letter from on board the Prince of Orange of Bristol . . . dated from St Christophers, 7 April, 1737," *Boston Weekly News-Letter*; also published in the *Virginia Gazette*, October 21–28, 1737; see Elizabeth Donnan, *Documents Illustrative of the History of the Slave Trade to America*, vol. 2 (Carnegie Institution of Washington, 1930), pp. 460–61; Eric Robert Taylor, *If We Must Die: Shipboard Insurrections in the Era of the Atlantic Slave Trade* (Louisiana State University Press, 2006), p. 12; Marcus Rediker, *The Slave Ship: A Human History* (Viking, 2007), chap. 9, EPUB. For more on the Price of Orange, see Voyage ID: 16873, SlaveVoyages: The Trans-Atlantic Slave Trade Database, accessed October 13, 2024, https://www.slavevoyages.org/voyages/MNpgNPJt.

2 Terri L. Snyder, "Suicide, Slavery, and Memory in North America," *Journal of American History* 97, no. 1 (2010): pp. 39–62; Toby Green, *A Fistful of Shells: West Africa from the Rise of the Slave Trade to the Age of Revolution* (Penguin, 2020), p. 86, Kindle; William D. Piersen, "White Cannibals, Black Martyrs: Fear, Depression, and Religious Faith as Causes of Suicide Among New Slaves," *Journal of Negro History* 62, no. 2 (1977): p. 147.

3 For more on cannibalism, consumption, and slavery, see Vincent Woodard, *The Delectable Negro: Human Consumption and Homoeroticism within US Slave Culture* (New York University Press, 2014).

4 Moses I. Finley and Brent D. Shaw, eds., *Ancient Slavery and Modern Ideology* (Princeton, NJ: Marcus Wiener Publishers, 1998), p. 136; Kostas Vlassopoulos argues that while the meaning of the term *andrapodon* does define a person as property, it does so in the context of prisoners captured in war, and so the idea of slaves as property is actually more limited than scholars have earlier argued. See Kostas Vlassopoulos, "Greek Slavery: From Domination to Property and Back Again," *Journal of Hellenic Studies* 131 (2011): p. 119.

5 For a detailed discussion of the (mis)use of the terms "chattel" and "chattel slavery," see Jennie Jeppesen, "In the Shadows between Slave and Free: A Case for Detangling the Word 'Slave' from the Word 'Chattel,'" *Atlantic Studies: Global Currents* 17, no. 3 (2020): pp. 399–418; and Davis, *Inhuman Bondage*, p. 30.

6 For more detail about the nuances of these ideas, see Sara Forsdyke, *Slaves and Slavery in Ancient Greece* (Cambridge University Press, 2021), chap. 4.

7   David Brion Davis, *Challenging the Boundaries of Slavery* (Harvard University Press, 2003), pp. 5–6; Orlando Patterson, *Slavery and Social Death: A Comparative Study* (Harvard University Press, 2018), chap. 2.
8   Forsdyke, *Slaves and Slavery in Ancient Greece*, pp. 83–84, 134–141.
9   Quoted in Peter Garnsey, *Ideas of Slavery from Aristotle to Augustine* (Cambridge University Press, 1996), p. 38.
10 Quoted in Giuseppe Cambiano, "Aristotle and the Anonymous Opponents of Slavery," in *Classical Slavery*, ed. M. I. Finley (Routledge, 1987), pp. 36–37.
11 Annelien De Dijn, *Freedom: An Unruly History* (Harvard University Press, 2020), p. 61; Keith Bradley, *Slavery and Society at Rome* (Cambridge University Press, 1994), p. 22.
12 K. R. Bradley, "On the Roman Slave Supply and Slavebreeding," in *Classical Slavery*, ed. M. I. Finley (Routledge, 1987), p. 53.
13 Garnsey, *Ideas of Slavery*, p. 97.
14 Orlando Patterson, *Freedom*, vol. 1, *Freedom in the Making of Western Culture* (Basic Books, 1991), pp. 228–29.
15 David Pelteret, "Slave Raiding and Slave Trading in Early England," *Anglo-Saxon England* 9 (1980): pp. 99–114; Patterson, *Freedom*, vol. 1, p. 349.
16 See Joseph Inikori, "The Struggle against the Transatlantic Slave Trade," in *Fighting the Slave Trade: West African Strategies*, ed. Sylviane Diouf (Ohio University Press, 2003), p. 175; see also Bradley, *Slavery and Society at Rome*, p. 172.
17 J. O. Hunwick, "Black Slaves in the Mediterranean World: Introduction to a Neglected Aspect of the African Diaspora," *Slavery & Abolition* 13, no. 1 (1992): p. 11; Michael McCormick, "New Light on the 'Dark Ages': How the Slave Trade Fuelled the Carolingian Economy," *Past & Present* 177 (November 2002): pp. 52–53.
18 Hunwick, "Black Slaves," p. 6. Davis, *Inhuman Bondage*, p. 60.
19 De Dijn, *Freedom*, pp. 134–35.
20 Davis, *Inhuman Bondage*, p. 49.
21 C. R. Whittaker, "Circe's Pigs: From Slavery to Serfdom in the Later Roman World," in *Classical Slavery*, ed. M. I. Finley (Routledge, 1987), p. 115; Davis, *Inhuman Bondage*, p. 82.
22 John Thornton, *Africa and Africans in the Making of the Atlantic World, 1400–1800*, 2nd ed. (Cambridge University Press, 1998), pp. 28–29; Felipe Fernández-Armesto, *Pathfinders: A Global History of Exploration* (W. W. Norton, 2006), chaps. 3 and 4, EPUB; Emily Berquist Soule, "From Africa to the Ocean Sea: Atlantic Slavery in the Origins of the Spanish Empire," *Atlantic Studies: Literary, Cultural and Historical Perspectives* 15, no. 1 (2018): pp. 16–39.
23 The Guanche communities were destroyed, but their DNA survives in modern Canarians; See Stefan Halikowski Smith, "The Mid-Atlantic Islands: A Theatre of Early Modern Ecocide?," *International Review of Social History* 55, supplement 18 (2010): p. 76.
24 A. R. Disney, *A History of Portugal and the Portuguese Empire: From the Beginning to 1807*, vol. 2, *The Portuguese Empire* (Cambridge University Press, 2009), p. 84.
25 Ibid., p. 85.
26 Ibid., pp. 86–87.
27 Benjamin Braude, "The Sons of Noah and the Construction of Ethnic and Geographical Identities in the Medieval and Early Modern Periods," *The William and Mary Quarterly* 54, no. 1 (1997): p. 126.
28 Disney, *A History of Portugal*, pp. 30, 43.

29 Green, *A Fistful of Shells*, p. 33.
30 G. Ugo Nwokeji, "Slavery in Non-Islamic West Africa, 1420–1820," in *The Cambridge World History of Slavery*, vol. 3, ed. David Eltis and Stanley L. Engerman (Cambridge University Press, 2011), p. 90.
31 Fernández-Armesto, *Pathfinders*, chap. 4.
32 Rediker, *The Slave Ship*, chap. 2.
33 Thornton, *Africa and Africans*, p. 30.
34 It's possible that he only reached Cape Juby, which is around 200 kilometers north of Cape Bojador, but it was still a significant breakthrough. See Disney, *A History of Portugal*, vol. 2, pp. 31–40.
35 Herman L. Bennett, *African Kings and Black Slaves: Sovereignty and Dispossession in the Early Modern Atlantic* (University of Pennsylvania Press, 2019), chap. 4. EPUB.
36 G. E. de Zurara, *The Chronicle of the Discovery and Conquest of Guinea*, translated from a 1452–53 original (Cambridge University Press, 2010), p. 36; see also P. Russell, *Prince Henry "the Navigator": A Life* (Yale University Press, 2000), pp. 130–34.
37 Zurara, *The Chronicle of the Discovery and Conquest of Guinea*, p. 81.
38 Zurara, *The Chronicle of the Discovery and Conquest of Guinea*, pp. 60–80; Russell, *Prince Henry*, chap. 10.
39 Zurara, *The Chronicle of the Discovery and Conquest of Guinea*, p. 79.
40 Ibid., p. 80.
41 Ibid., p. 81.
42 Ibid., p. 83.
43 Disney, *A History of Portugal*, pp. 45–46.
44 Quoted in José Lingna Nafafé, *Lourenço da Silva Mendonça and the Black Atlantic Abolitionist Movement in the Seventeenth Century* (Cambridge University Press, 2022), p. 344.
45 Bennett, *African Kings*, Chapter 4.
46 Hugh Thomas, *The Slave Trade: The History of Atlantic Slave Trade (1440–1870)* (Weidenfeld & Nicolson, 2015), pp. 88–89. Kindle.
47 Disney, *A History of Portugal*, pp. 47–48.
48 G. R. Crone, ed., *The Voyages of Cadamosto and Other Documents on Western Africa in the Second Half of the Fifteenth Century* (London: Hakluyt Society, 1937), pp. 58–60.
49 "Trans-Atlantic Slave Trade—Estimates," SlaveVoyages: The Trans-Atlantic Slave Trade Database, accessed October 13, 2024, https://www.slavevoyages.org/assessment/estimates.
50 Roquinaldo Ferreira, "Slaving and Resistance to Slaving in West Central Africa," in *The Cambridge World History of Slavery*, vol. 3, ed. David Eltis and Stanley L. Engerman (Cambridge University Press, 2011), p. 127.
51 For more on Mami Wata and water goddesses in Africa and the Caribbean, see Alex Van Stipriaan, "Watramama/Mami Wata: Three Centuries of Creolization of a Water Spirit in West Africa, Suriname, and Europe," *Matatu* 27–28 (2003): pp. 323–37; see also Kevin Dawson, *Undercurrents of Power: Aquatic Culture in the African Diaspora* (University of Pennsylvania Press, 2018), chap. 2.
52 See for instance the case of the *Hope*, in Taylor, *If We Must Die*, p. 1.
53 On the wide range of reasons for shipboard rebellions, see David Richardson, "Shipboard Revolts, African Authority, and the Atlantic Slave Trade," *William and Mary Quarterly* 58, no. 1 (2001): pp. 69–92.

54 Quoted in Ferreira, "Slaving and Resistance to Slaving," p. 125.
55 Disney, *A History of Portugal*, p. 240.
56 Rediker, *The Slave Ship*, p. 39.
57 From *A Description of the Coasts of North and South Guinea, and of Ethiopia Inferior, vulgarly Angola, being a new and accurate Account of the Western Maritime Countries of Africa*, by John Barbot, Agent-General of the Royal Company of Africa and Islands of America (1732), quoted in Elizabeth Donnan, *Documents Illustrative of the History of the Slave Trade to America*, vol. 1, no. 109 (Carnegie Institution of Washington, 1931), pp. 289–90.
58 Snyder, "Suicide, Slavery, and Memory in North America," p. 40.
59 Richardson, "Shipboard Revolts," pp. 73–74.
60 Royal Museums Greenwich, accessed October 13, 2024, https://www.rmg.co.uk/collections/objects/rmgc-object-254938; Thomas Clarkson took this diagram with him to Paris, where the Comte de Mirabeau had a model made, which he kept in his dining room, while around 3,700 copies of it were circulated in Philadelphia and beyond. Donnan, *Documents*, vol. 2, no. 280, pp. 592–593n1.
61 Currently, the most extensive biggest resource, the *SlaveVoyages: The Trans-Atlantic Slave Trade Database*, covers those years, though there were ships before 1514 and no doubt illegal ones after 1864, so a complete count will never be known. Overall, about 10 percent of voyages experienced a revolt. Davis, *Inhuman Bondage*, p. 93.
62 Stephanie E. Smallwood, *Saltwater Slavery: A Middle Passage from Africa to the American Diaspora*. (Harvard University Press, 2007), chap. 4.

Chapter 2

1 John L. Vogt, "The Lisbon Slave House and African Trade, 1486–1521," *Proceedings of the American Philosophical Society* 117, no. 1 (1973): p. 1, 8.
2 Stefan Halikowski Smith, "Lisbon in the Sixteenth Century: Decoding the Chafariz d'el Rei," *Race and Class* 60, no. 2 (2018): p. 69.
3 Ibid., p. 65.
4 David Brion Davis, *Inhuman Bondage: The Rise and Fall of Slavery in the New World* (Oxford University Press, 2006), p. 93; José Lingna Nafafé, *Lourenço da Silva Mendonça and the Black Atlantic Abolitionist Movement in the Seventeenth Century* (Cambridge University Press, 2022), p. 303.
5 Alejandro de la Fuente and Ariela J. Gross, *Becoming Free, Becoming Black: Race, Freedom, and Law in Cuba, Virginia, and Louisiana* (Cambridge University Press, 2020), p. 17.
6 James H. Sweet, "The Hidden Histories of African Lisbon," in *The Black Urban Atlantic in the Age of the Slave Trade*, ed. Jorge Cañizares-Esguerra et al. (University of Pennsylvania Press, 2013), p. 237.
7 Quoted in Sweet, "The Hidden Histories," p. 237.
8 Debra Blumenthal, *Enemies and Familiars: Slavery and Mastery in Fifteenth-Century Valencia* (Cornell University Press, 2009), chap. 1.
9 Carmen Fracchia, *"Black but Human": Slavery in Visual Art in Hapsburg Spain, 1480–1700* (Oxford University Press, 2019), pp. 128–129.
10 The story of Johana and the detail about Valencia come from Blumenthal, *Enemies and Familiars*, pp. 203–206.
11 Blumenthal, *Enemies and Familiars*, p. 1.

12 According to Blumenthal, one of the biggest slave-traders was Florentine Césaro de Barchi, who sent around 2,000 Africans to Valencia between 1489 and 1497; see Blumenthal, *Enemies and Familiars*, p. 19.
13 P. E. H. Hair, "Black African Slaves at Valencia, 1482–1516: An Onomastic Inquiry," *History in Africa* 7 (1980): p. 119.
14 Blumenthal, *Enemies and Familiars*, p. 4.
15 Ibid., pp. 20–21.
16 La Lonja de la Seda de Valencia is a UNESCO heritage site; see UNESCO website, https://whc.unesco.org/en/list/782/.
17 Ibid., pp. 194–96.
18 Ibid., p. 200.
19 Ibid., pp. 202–04.
20 Quoted in Blumenthal, *Enemies and Familiars*, p. 203.
21 Ibid., p. 204.
22 Ibid.
23 Ibid., pp. 204–205.
24 Quoted in Ibid., p. 206.
25 Ibid., pp. 220–221.
26 William D. Phillips Jr., "Africa and the Atlantic Islands Meet the Garden of Eden: Christopher Columbus's View of America," *Journal of World History* 3, no. 2 (1992): p. 154; see also William D. Phillips and Carla Rahn Phillips, *The Worlds of Christopher Columbus* (Cambridge University Press, 1992), pp. 93–94.
27 Phillips, "Africa and the Atlantic Islands," p. 150.
28 Ibid., p. 157.
29 Ibid., p. 162.
30 A. R. Disney, *A History of Portugal and the Portuguese Empire: From the Beginning to 1807*, vol. 2, *The Portuguese Empire* (Cambridge University Press, 2009), p. 88; Stefan Halikowski Smith, "The Mid-Atlantic Islands: A Theatre of Early Modern Ecocide?" *International Review of Social History* 55, supplement 18 (2010): p. 65.
31 Fracchia, *Black but Human*, p. 102.
32 Ibid., p. 14.
33 Ibid., p. 3.
34 See Nicolas R. Jones, *Staging Habla de Negros: Radical Performances of the African Diaspora in Early Modern Spain* (Penn State University Press, 2019).
35 For more on both marriages in the black community and their literary depiction, see A. M. Casares and M. G. Barranco, "Popular Literary Depictions of Black African Weddings in Early Modern Spain," *Renaissance and Reformation* 31, no. 2 (2008): pp. 107–21.
36 Fracchia, *Black but Human*, p. 76.
37 Ibid., pp. 48–49; on confraternities, see also Karen B. Graubart, *Republics of Difference: Religious and Racial Self-Governance in the Spanish Atlantic World* (Oxford University Press, 2022), pp. 186–91; for more on Seville's brotherhoods, see Isidoro Moreno, *La antigua hermandad de Los Negros de Sevilla: etnicidad, poder y sociedad en 600 años de historia* (Universidad de Sevilla, 1997).
38 Sue Peabody, "Slavery, Freedom, and the Law in the Atlantic World, 1420–1807," in *The Cambridge World History of Slavery*, vol. 3, ed. David Eltis and Stanley L. Engerman (Cambridge University Press, 2011), p. 600.
39 Quoted in Peabody, "Slavery, Freedom, and the Law," pp. 619–620.

40 Fracchia, *Black but Human*, p. 15.
41 De la Fuente and Gross, *Becoming Free, Becoming Black*, p. 1.

Chapter 3

1. This may be the first reference to black slaves in the new world according to Manuel Lucena Salmoral, *Regulación de la esclavitud negra en las colonias de América Española (1503–1886): Documentos para su estudio* (Universidad de Murcia, Universidad de Alcalá, 2005), p. 21; see also the excellent online resource *Los primeros negros en las Americas: La presencia africana en la República Dominicana*, Instituto de Estudios Dominicanos de CUNY, https://firstblacks.org/spn/.
2. Erin Woodruff Stone, *Captives of Conquest: Slavery in the Early Modern Spanish Caribbean* (University of Pennsylvania Press, 2021), p. 14.
3. Ibid., p. 45.
4. Toby Green, *The Rise of the Trans-Atlantic Slave Trade in Western Africa, 1300–1589* (Cambridge University Press, 2011), p. 186.
5. Stone, *Captives of Conquest*, pp. 5–7.
6. Ibid., p. 14.
7. Ibid., p. 5.
8. Green, *The Rise of the Trans-Atlantic Slave Trade*, p. 188.
9. Ibid.
10. Quoted in Lawrence Clayton, "Bartolomé de las Casas and the African Slave Trade," *History Compass* 7, no. 6 (2009): pp. 1537–38n13.
11. Ibid., p. 1529.
12. Laird W. Bergad, *The Comparative Histories of Slavery in Brazil, Cuba, and the United States* (Cambridge University Press, 2007), p. 2; Lilia M. Schwarcz and Heloisa M. Starling, *Brazil: A Biography* (Penguin, 2019), p. 9, Kindle.
13. Schwarcz and Starling, *Brazil*, p. 11.
14. Ibid., p. 12.
15. A. R. Disney, *A History of Portugal and the Portuguese Empire: From the Beginning to 1807*, vol. 2, *The Portuguese Empire* (Cambridge University Press, 2009), p. 212.
16. Daniel B. Domingues da Silva and Alexandre Vieira Ribeiro, "Amazonia and North-East Brazil in the Atlantic Slave Trade: An Assessment of the Brazilian Slave Trade North of Rio de Janeiro," *Atlantic Studies: Global Currents* 17, no. 4 (2020): p. 2.
17. According to Toby Green, the first known escapes of African captives from European slave traders on Cape Verde may date to 1463, based on a letter recounting a shipboard rebellion that ended with the rebels fleeing ashore on one of the islands. See Green, *The Rise of the Trans-Atlantic Slave Trade in Western Africa*, p. 106.
18. Disney, *A History of Portugal*, p. 102.
19. Ibid., pp. 102–103.
20. Ibid., pp. 103–104.
21. Quoted in Elizabeth Donnan, *Documents Illustrative of the History of the Slave Trade to America*, vol. 1, no. 109 (Carnegie Institution of Washington, 1930), p. 15.
22. For more on this, see chapters 3 and 4 in Green, *The Rise of the Trans-Atlantic Slave Trade*, p. 5.
23. Disney, *A History of Portugal*, p. 110.
24. Ibid., p. 111.

25 José Lingna Nafafé, *Lourenço da Silva Mendonça and the Black Atlantic Abolitionist Movement in the Seventeenth Century* (Cambridge University Press, 2022), p. 306.
26 Ibid., p. 304.
27 Disney, *A History of Portugal*, p. 112.
28 Toby Green, *A Fistful of Shells: West Africa from the Rise of the Slave Trade to the Age of Revolution* (Penguin, 2020), p. 170. Kindle.
29 Quoted in Green, *A Fistful of Shells*, p. 144.
30 Afonso I to João III, October 15, 1526, quoted in Green, *A Fistful of Shells*, p. 214.
31 Linda M. Heywood, "Slavery and Its Transformation in the Kingdom of Kongo: 1491–1800," *Journal of African History* 50, no. 1 (2009): p. 6.
32 Disney, *A History of Portugal*, p. 66; see also Cécile Fromont, *The Art of Conversion: Christian Visual Culture in the Kingdom of Kongo* (University of North Carolina Press, 2014); John Thornton, "The Development of an African Catholic Church in the Kingdom of Kongo, 1491–1750," *Journal of African History* 25, no. 2 (1984): pp. 147–67.
33 Roquinaldo Ferreira, "Slaving and Resistance to Slaving in West Central Africa," in *The Cambridge World History of Slavery*, vol. 3, ed. David Eltis and Stanley L. Engerman (Cambridge University Press, 2011), p. 123; see also Walter Rodney, "African Slavery and Other Forms of Social Oppression on the Upper Guinea Coast in the Context of the Atlantic Slave-Trade," *Journal of African History* 7, no. 3 (1966): pp. 431–43.
34 G. Ugo Nwokeji, "Slavery in Non-Islamic West Africa, 1420–1820," in *The Cambridge World History of Slavery*, vol. 3, ed. David Eltis and Stanley L. Engerman (Cambridge University Press, 2011), p. 83.
35 Thornton, *Africa and Africans*, pp. 87–88.
36 Ibid., p. 91.
37 Nwokeji, "Slavery in Non-Islamic West Africa," pp. 104–05.
38 Disney, *A History of Portugal*, p. 58.
39 Ibid., p. 49.
40 Thornton, *Africa and Africans*, pp. 38–39.
41 Green, *A Fistful of Shells*, pp. 90–96.
42 Disney, *A History of Portugal*, pp. 52–53.
43 Green, *A Fistful of Shells*, pp. 112–116.
44 Heywood, "Slavery and Its Transformation," p. 5.
45 Ibid.
46 Fromont, *The Art of Conversion*, pp. 143–44; Lingna Nafafé, *Lourenço da Silva Mendonça*, p. 65.
47 Quoted in Lingna Nafafé, *Lourenço da Silva Mendonça*, p. 65.
48 Davis, *Inhuman Bondage*, p. 94.
49 Green, *A Fistful of Shells*, p. 136.

Chapter 4

1 Erin Woodruff Stone, *Captives of Conquest: Slavery in the Early Modern Spanish Caribbean* (University of Pennsylvania Press, 2021), p. 140. For more on the details of Enrique's background, see I. Altman, "The Revolt of Enriquillo and the Historiography of Early Spanish America," *The Americas* 63, no. 4 (2007): pp. 587–614.
2 I. Altman, "The Revolt of Enriquillo," p. 596.

3 Stone, *Captives of Conquest*, p. 141.
4 Stone, *Captives of Conquest*, p. 141; English translation in A. Stevens-Acevedo, *The Santo Domingo Slave Revolt of 1521 and the Slave Laws of 1522: Black Slavery and Black Resistance in the Early Colonial Americas*, CUNY Dominican Studies Institute Research Monograph, 2019, p. 20, http://academicworks.cuny.edu/dsi_pubs/23/.
5 English translation in Stevens-Acevedo, *The Santo Domingo Slave Revolt of 1521*, p. 20.
6 Ibid., p. 21.
7 Stone, *Captives of Conquest*, p. 141.
8 It's possible that the first use of the word *cimarrón* in the context of runaways was in correspondence relating to these events. See Stone, *Captives of Conquest*, pp. 141, 213n66. Others have argued the word comes from other sources, such as *cima* (mountain top). For more on the debate in Spanish, see José Arrom, "Cimarrón: apuntes sobre sus primeras documentaciones y su probable origen," *Revista española de antropología americana* 8, (1983): pp. 47–57.
9 Manolo Florentino and Márcia Amantino, "Runaways and *Quilombolas* in the Americas," in *The Cambridge World History of Slavery*, vol. 3, ed. David Eltis and Stanley L. Engerman (Cambridge University Press, 2011), p. 710.
10 For an examination of the relationship between marronage and freedom in terms of political theory, see Neil Roberts, *Freedom as Marronage* (University of Chicago Press, 2015).
11 English translation in Stevens-Acevedo, *The Santo Domingo Slave Revolt of 1521*, p. 22.
12 Quoted in Stevens-Acevedo, *The Santo Domingo Slave Revolt of 1521*, pp. 23–24.
13 For English translation of the code, see Stevens-Acevedo, *The Santo Domingo Slave Revolt of 1521*, pp. 22–30.
14 Alejandro de la Fuente and Ariela J. Gross, *Becoming Free, Becoming Black: Race, Freedom, and Law in Cuba, Virginia, and Louisiana* (Cambridge University Press, 2020), pp. 22–23.
15 Stone, *Captives of Conquest*, p. 143.
16 Ibid., p. 144.
17 Letter to The Emperor (Carlos V) from Licenciados Zuazo and Espinosa, Santo Domingo, March 30, 1528, in Roberto Marte, ed., *Santo Domingo en los manuscritos de Juan Bautista Muñoz* (Santo Domingo: Ediciones Fundación García Arévalo, 1981), p. 331.
18 Stone, *Captives of Conquest*, p. 143.
19 Ibid., p. 144.
20 Erin Woodruff Stone, "America's First Slave Revolt: Indians and African Slaves in Española, 1500–1534," *Ethnohistory* 60, no. 2 (2013): p. 196.
21 "Letter to The Emperor," in Marte, *Santo Domingo*, p. 331.
22 Stone, *Captives of Conquest*, p. 146.
23 Karen B. Graubart, *Republics of Difference: Religious and Racial Self-Governance in the Spanish Atlantic World* (Oxford University Press, 2022), pp. 192–93.
24 Stone, *Captives of Conquest*, p. 151.
25 Gonzalo F. de Oviedo y Valdés, *Historia general y natural de las Indias*, ed. J. Amador de los Rios (Madrid, 1851), p. 629; see also J. Brent Morris, ed., *Yes, Lord, I Know the Road: A Documentary History of African Americans in South Carolina, 1526–2008* (University of South Carolina Press, 2017), pp. 38–39.
26 Paul E. Hoffman, *A New Andalucia and a Way to the Orient: The American Southeast During the Sixteenth Century* (Louisiana State University Press, 1990), pp. 60–63.

27 Stone, "America's First Slave Revolt," p. 202.
28 Hoffman, *A New Andalucia*, pp. 68–70.
29 Guy Cameron and Stephen Vermette, "The Role of Extreme Cold in the Failure of the San Miguel de Gualdape Colony," *Georgia Historical Quarterly* 96, no. 3 (2012): p. 296.
30 On the possibility that unforeseen cold levels led to the failure of the colony, see Cameron and Vermette, "The Role of Extreme Cold," pp. 291–307.
31 Hoffman, *A New Andalucia*, pp. 75–80; Morris, *Yes, Lord, I Know the Road*, pp. 38–39.
32 The Ayllón fiasco was included in the work by royal historiographer Gonzalo Fernández de Oviedo y Valdés, *Historia general y natural de las Indias* (Madrid, 1851–55, though parts of it were first published in 1535); however, Oviedo did interview Francisco Chicora when they were both in Spain.
33 Quoted in Charles La Roncière, *Histoire de la marine française*, vol. 3 (Paris, 1906), p. 300; Lilia M. Schwarcz and Heloisa M. Starling, *Brazil: A Biography* (Penguin, 2019), p. 12.
34 Annelien De Dijn, *Freedom: An Unruly History* (Harvard University Press, 2020), pp. 168–169.
35 Quoted in Jane Landers, *Black Society in Spanish Florida* (University of Illinois Press, 1999), p. 17.
36 See Carrie Gibson, *El Norte: The Epic and Forgotten Story of Hispanic North America* (Grove Press, 2019), chaps. 1–2.
37 A. R. Disney, *A History of Portugal and the Portuguese Empire: From the Beginning to 1807*, vol. 2, *The Portuguese Empire* (Cambridge University Press, 2009), p. 54.
38 Full text of Sublimis Deus is available at https://www.papalencyclicals.net/paulo3/p3subli.htm.
39 José Lingna Nafafé, *Lourenço da Silva Mendonça and the Black Atlantic Abolitionist Movement in the Seventeenth Century* (Cambridge University Press, 2022), pp. 47–48; Alejandro de la Fuente, *Havana and the Atlantic in the Sixteenth Century* (University of North Carolina Press, 2008), p. 164.
40 For a detailed examination of the Hani myth, see Benjamin Braude, "The Sons of Noah and the Construction of Ethnic and Geographical Identities in the Medieval and Early Modern Periods," *The William and Mary Quarterly* 54, no. 1 (1997): pp. 103–42. https://about.jstor.org/terms.
41 Quoted in Chloe Ireton, "'They Are Blacks of the Caste of Black Christians': Old Christian Black Blood in the Sixteenth- and Early Seventeenth-Century Iberian Atlantic," *Hispanic American Historical Review* 97, no. 4 (2017): pp. 579–612; see also Chloe Ireton, *Slavery and Freedom in Black Thought in the Early Spanish Atlantic* (Cambridge University Press, 2025).
42 See introduction and first part of M. E. Martínez, *Genealogical Fictions: Limpieza de Sangre, Religion, and Gender in Colonial Mexico* (Stanford University Press, 2008). See also Ireton, "'They Are Blacks of the Caste of Black Christians.'"
43 Martínez, *Genealogical Fictions*, pp. 158–160; James H. Sweet, "The Iberian Roots of American Racist Thought," *William and Mary Quarterly* 54, no. 1 (1997): 143–166.
44 "Trans-Atlantic Slave Trade—Estimates 1526–1600," SlaveVoyages: The Trans-Atlantic Slave Trade Database, accessed October 13, 2024, https://www.slavevoyages.org/voyages/xSqwfl4S and "Trans-Atlantic Slave Trade—Estimates 1575-1660," https://www.slavevoyages.org/voyages/yphADdBB.
45 Quotes from this section are from L. A. Clayton and D. M. Lantigua, *Bartolomé de las Casas and the Defense of Amerindian Rights: A Brief History with Documents* (University of Alabama Press, 2020), pp. 22–23.

Chapter 5

1. Letter of Oidor Grajeda, July 28, 1546, Archivo General de Indias, Santo Domingo, 49, in Fray Cipriano de Utrera, *Polemica de Enriquillo* (Santo Domingo: Academia Dominicana de la Historia, 1973), p. 482n57.
2. Quoted in Alonso López de Cerrato, "Lemba and the Maroons of Hispaniola," in *The Dominican Republic Reader: History, Culture, Politics*, ed. E. P. Roorda et al. (Duke University Press, 2014), p. 66.
3. Robert C. Schwaller, "Contested Conquests: African Maroons and the Incomplete Conquest of Hispaniola, 1519–1620," *The Americas* 75, no. 4 (2018): p. 620. Jane Landers, "The Central African Presence in Spanish Maroon Communities," in *Central Africans and Cultural Transformations in the American Diaspora*, ed. L. M. Heywood (Cambridge University Press, 2001), p. 234.
4. Schwaller, "Contested Conquests," p. 623; Roorda, Derby, and González, "Lemba and the Maroons," p. 66.
5. Letter to the Emperor (Carlos V) from Licenciado Cerrato, Santo Domingo, September 12, 1544, in Roberto Marte, ed., *Santo Domingo en los manuscritos de Juan Bautista Muñoz* (Santo Domingo: Ediciones Fundación García Arévalo, 1981), p. 404.
6. Landers, "The Central African Presence," p. 235.
7. Letter from the Oidores to the Emperor, October 16, 1547, Archivo General de Indias, Santo Domingo, 49, printed in Utrera, *Polemica de Enriquillo*, p. 483n57; Landers, "The Central African Presence," p. 234.
8. Landers, "The Central African Presence," p. 235.
9. Letter of Governor Cerrato to the Emperor, November 16, 1546, Archivo General de Indias, Santo Domingo, 49, printed in Utrera, *Polemica de Enriquillo*, p. 482n57.
10. Ibid., p. 483.
11. Letter from the Audiencia of Santo Domingo to the King, January 23, 1549, quoted in Schwaller, "Contested Conquests," p. 624.
12. Schwaller, "Contested Conquests," p. 625.
13. Stone, *Captives of Conquest*, p. 152.
14. Alejandro de la Fuente and Ariela J. Gross, *Becoming Free, Becoming Black: Race, Freedom, and Law in Cuba, Virginia, and Louisiana* (Cambridge University Press, 2020), p. 46.
15. Ibid., p. 13.
16. Molly A. Warsh, "Enslaved Pearl Divers in the Sixteenth Century Caribbean," *Slavery & Abolition* 31, no. 3 (2010): p. 346.
17. For more about the history of the Spanish empire and pearls, see Molly A. Warsh, *American Baroque: Pearls and the Nature of Empire, 1492–1700* (University of North Carolina Press, 2018).
18. Warsh "Enslaved Pearl Divers," p. 347; Alex Borucki, "Trans-Imperial History in the Making of the Slave Trade to Venezuela, 1526–1811," *Itinerario* 36, no. 2 (2012): p. 31.
19. Ricardo E. Alegría, "El rey Miguel: héroe puertorriqueño en la lucha por la libertad de los esclavos," *Revista de Historia de América*, no. 85 (1978): p. 13; Fray Pedro de Aguado, *Historia de Venezuela*, ed. Jerónimo Bécker (Madrid: La Real Academia de la Historia, 1918), p. 378, https://archive.org/details/historiadevenezuo1agua/page/378/mode/2up?q=MIguel.
20. Some accounts say this incident took place in 1552. At this point the Gregorian calendar was not in effect (that came in 1582), which may account for the discrepancy.

21 José de Oviedo y Baños, *The Conquest and Settlement of Venezuela* (1723), trans. Jeannette Johnson Varner (University of California Press, 1987), p. 96.
22 Alegría, "El rey Miguel," p. 15.
23 Karen B. Graubart, *Republics of Difference: Religious and Racial Self-Governance in the Spanish Atlantic World* (Oxford University Press, 2022), p. 194.
24 Aguado, *Historia de Venezuela*, p. 380.
25 Alegría, "El rey Miguel," p. 17.
26 Aguado, *Historia de Venezuela*, p. 382.
27 Oviedo y Baños, *The Conquest and Settlement of Venezuela*, p. 98.
28 Quoted in Miguel Acosta Saignes, *Vida de los esclavos negros en Venezuela* (Havana: Casa de América, 1978), p. 181.
29 Quoted in Acosta Saignes, *Vida de los esclavos negros*, p. 182.
30 Juan de Castellanos, "Elegia III, Canto IV," in *Elegías de Varones Ilustres de Indias*, ed. Carlos Aribau Buenaventura , 2nd ed. (Madrid, 1857), p. 245, https://archive.org/details/elegasdevaronesoocastg00g/page/n17/mode/2up.
31 Alexander von Humboldt, *Personal Narrative of Travels to the Equinoctial Regions of America, during the years 1799–1804*, vol. 2 (London, 1871), p. 66.
32 *Codex Telleriano-Remensis*, fol. 45 (recto), accessed October 15, 2024, https://gallica.bnf.fr/ark:/12148/btv1b8458267s/f115.item. My thanks to Felipe Ceceña for bringing this to my attention.
33 Elena FitzPatrick Sifford, "Mexican Manuscripts and the First Images of Africans in the Americas," *Ethnohistory* 66, no. 2 (2019): pp. 223–48.
34 Herman L. Bennett, *Africans in Colonial Mexico: Absolutism, Christianity, and Afro-Creole Consciousness, 1570–1640* (Indiana University Press, 2003), Introduction.
35 José Antonio Saco, *Historia de la esclavitud*, vol. 1 (Barcelona: Jaime Jepús, 1879), p. 172; English translations available at National Humanities Center, accessed October 12, 2023, https://nationalhumanitiescenter.org/pds/amerbegin/settlement/text6/text6read.htm. See also Colin A. Palmer, *Slaves of the White God: Blacks in Mexico, 1570–1650* (Harvard University Press, 1976), pp. 133–34.
36 Saco, *Historia de la esclavitud*, vol. 1, p. 172.
37 Ibid., p. 173.
38 Quoted in Palmer, *Slaves of the White God*, p. 135.
39 Jane Landers, "*Cimarrón* and Citizen: African Ethnicity, Corporate Identity, and the Evolution of Free Black Towns in the Spanish Circum-Caribbean," in *Slaves, Subjects, and Subversives: Blacks in Colonial Latin America*, ed. Jane Landers and Barry Robinson (University of New Mexico Press, 2006), pp. 121–24.
40 Ibid.; see also on Yanga, "'El primer libertador de las Americas' / The First Liberator of the Americas: The Editor's Notes," *Callaloo* 31, no. 1 (2008): pp. 1–11.
41 Padre Andres Pérez de Rivas, *Corónica y historia religiosa de la provincia de la Compañía de Jesús de México en Nueva España*, vol. 1 (Mexico: Imprenta del sagrado corazon de Jesus, 1896), p. 284.
42 Ibid., p. 285.
43 Ibid., p. 287; see also Juan Laurencio and Leonardo Pasquel, *Campaña contra Yanga en 1608* (Mexico City: Editorial Citlalteptl, 1974).
44 Pérez de Rivas, *Corónica y historia*, pp. 288–89.
45 Ibid., p. 285.
46 Ibid., p. 289.

47 Ibid., p. 290.
48 Landers, *"Cimarrón* and Citizen," p. 134.
49 Ibid., pp. 127–28.
50 Ibid., pp. 128–29.
51 Quoted in Tom Cummins, "Three Gentlemen from Esmeraldas: A Portrait Fit for a King," in *Slave Portraiture in the Atlantic World*, ed. Agnes Lugo-Ortiz and Angela Rosenthal (Cambridge University Press, 2016), p. 119. See the portrait at Museo del Prado website: https://www.museodelprado.es/coleccion/obra-de-arte/los-tres-mulatos-de-esmeraldas/1224cef3-e625-4ea6-9c27-2ae81d789e14.
52 Cummins, "Three Gentlemen from Esmeraldas," p. 123.
53 Charles Beatty-Medina, "Maroon Chief Alonso de Illescas' Letter to the Crown, 1586," in *Afro-Latino Voices: Translations of Early Modern Ibero-Atlantic Narratives*, ed. Kathryn McKnight and Leo J Garofalo (Indianapolis: Hackett, 2015), p. 20.
54 For this background, see Cummins, "Three Gentlemen from Esmeraldas," p. 123; Kris Lane, *Quito 1599: City and Colony in Transition* (University of New Mexico Press, 2002), pp. 28–29.
55 Karen B. Graubart, "'So color de una cofradía': Catholic Confraternities and the Development of Afro-Peruvian Ethnicities in Early Colonial Peru," *Slavery & Abolition* 33, no. 1 (2012): p. 46.
56 Cummins, "Three Gentlemen from Esmeraldas," pp. 123–25.
57 Ibid., p. 124.
58 Ibid., pp. 124–25.
59 According to Charles Beatty-Medina, the Spanish made more than 50 attempts to subjugate the Esmeraldas area between 1526 and 1603. See Beatty-Medina, "Maroon Chief Alonso de Illescas' Letter to the Crown," p. 20.
60 Lane, *Quito 1599*, pp. 44–46.
61 Cummins, "Three Gentlemen from Esmeraldas," p. 130; 137.

Chapter 6

1 Ruth Pike, "Black Rebels: The Cimarrones of Sixteenth-Century Panama," *The Americas* 64, no. 2 (2007): p. 245.
2 Information about 1575 taken from the Museo de la Plaza Mayor at the Patronato Panamá Viejo.
3 Pike, "Black Rebels," p. 247.
4 Ibid.; for more on Bayano, see Robert C. Schwaller, *African Maroons in Sixteenth-Century Panama: A History in Documents* (University of Oklahoma Press, 2021).
5 Richard Hakluyt, ed., *The Principal Navigations, Voyages, Traffiques, and Discoveries of the English Nation* (1589), vol. 10 (Cambridge University Press, 2014), pp. 65–66.
6 Ibid., p. 67.
7 For more on the far-reaching ramifications of smuggling in Spanish America, see Juan José Ponce Vázquez, *Islanders and Empire: Smuggling and Political Defiance in Hispaniola, 1580–1690* (Cambridge University Press, 2020).
8 Hakluyt, *The Principal Navigation*, pp. 67–73.
9 Irene A. Wright, ed., *Documents Concerning English Voyages to the Spanish Main, 1569–1580* (Farnham: Hakluyt Society, Ashgate, 1932), pp. xxxviii–xxxix.
10 Document 9, Interrogatory, May 15, 1571, in Wright, *Documents Concerning English Voyages to the Spanish Main*, p. 21.

11 Document 13, City of Panamá to the Crown, May 25, 1571, in Wright, *Documents Concerning English Voyages to the Spanish Main*, p. 33.
12 Document 4, Licenciado Carasa to the Crown, March 27, 1570, in Wright, *Documents Concerning English Voyages to the Spanish Main*, p. 10.
13 The remainder of this section, unless noted otherwise, comes from *Sir Francis Drake Revived*, in Wright, *Documents Concerning English Voyages to the Spanish Main*; this account comes from a retelling first published in 1626 by his nephew.
14 For more on Diego and how he ends up joining Drake, see Miranda Kaufmann, *Black Tudors: The Untold Story* (Oneworld, 2017), chap. 3.
15 Wright, *Documents Concerning English Voyages to the Spanish Main*, pp. xxxi–xl, 293.
16 Ibid., p. xln3.
17 Document 20, Pedro de Ortega de Valencia to the Crown, February 22, 1573, in Wright, *Documents Concerning English Voyages to the Spanish Main*, p. 46.
18 Document 21, Municipal Council of Panama to the Crown, February 24, 1573, in Wright, *Documents Concerning English Voyages to the Spanish Main*, pp. 48–50.
19 Ibid.
20 Ibid.
21 Pike, "Black Rebels," p. 258.
22 Ibid.
23 Ibid., p. 259; see also Document 24 in Schwaller, *African Maroons in Sixteenth-Century Panama*.
24 Document 52, Deposition of John Oxenham, October 20, 1577, in Wright, *Documents Concerning English Voyages to the Spanish Main*.
25 Ibid., p. 171.
26 Ibid., p. 176.
27 Sue Peabody, "Slavery, Freedom, and the Law in the Atlantic World, 1420–1807," in *The Cambridge World History of Slavery*, vol. 3, ed. David Eltis and Stanley L. Engerman (Cambridge University Press, 2011), p. 623.
28 Karen B. Graubart, *Republics of Difference: Religious and Racial Self-Governance in the Spanish Atlantic World* (Oxford University Press, 2022), pp. 193–95.
29 Document 71, Diego de Villanueva Zapata to the Crown, October 2, 1579, in Irene Wright, ed., *Further English Voyages to Spanish America, 1583–1594* (Farnham: Hakluyt Society, Ashgate, 1951), p. 235.
30 David Wheat, *Atlantic Africa and the Spanish Caribbean, 1570–1640* (University of North Carolina Press, 2016), p. 1.
31 Quoted in Wheat, *Atlantic Africa*, p. 2.
32 Pike, "Black Rebels," p. 265.
33 Ibid., p. 266.

Chapter 7

1 Gerhard Seibert, "São Tomé's Great Slave Revolt of 1595: Background, Consequences and Misperceptions of One of the Largest Slave Uprisings in Atlantic History," *Portuguese Studies Review* 18, no. 2 (2011): p. 37.
2 Arlindo Manuel Caldeira, "Learning the Ropes in the Tropics: Slavery and the Plantation System on the Island of São Tomé," *African Economic History* 39 (2011): p. 40.
3 Caldeira, "Learning the Ropes," p. 62; Seibert, "São Tomé's Great Slave Revolt of 1595," p. 34.

4 Luiz Felipe de Alencastro, *The Trade in the Living: The Formation of Brazil in the South Atlantic, Sixteenth to Seventeenth Centuries* (SUNY Press, 2018), pp. 58–61.
5 Seibert, "São Tomé's Great Slave Revolt of 1595," p. 35.
6 Ibid., pp. 37–38.
7 Ibid., p. 37; Alencastro, *The Trade in the Living*, p. 61.
8 Seibert, "São Tomé's Great Slave Revolt of 1595," pp. 38, 40.
9 Ibid., p. 38.
10 Ibid., p. 39.
11 Ibid.
12 Ibid., pp. 39–40.
13 Toby Green, *A Fistful of Shells: West Africa from the Rise of the Slave Trade to the Age of Revolution* (Penguin, 2020), pp. 143–45. Kindle.
14 Seibert, "São Tomé's Great Slave Revolt of 1595," p. 41.
15 Ibid., p. 42.
16 Geoffrey Parker, *The Dutch Revolt* (Penguin, 1985), pp. 194–95.
17 Ibid., p. 249.
18 Alencastro, *The Trade in the Living*, pp. 71–77.
19 Estimates of how many captives disembarked from 1520 to 1640 in SlaveVoyages: The Trans-Atlantic Slave Trade Database, accessed August 29, 2024, https://www.slavevoyages.org/voyages/cwuHmwTO.
20 Alencastro, *The Trade in the Living*, pp. 71–77.
21 Seymour Drescher, *Abolition: A History of Slavery and Antislavery* (Cambridge University Press, 2009), p. 23.
22 Sue Peabody and Keila Grinberg, *Slavery, Freedom, and the Law in the Atlantic World: A Brief History with Documents* (Bedford/St Martin's, 2007), chaps 1 and 2.
23 Quoted in Sue Peabody, "Slavery, Freedom, and the Law in the Atlantic World, 1420–1807," in *The Cambridge World History of Slavery*, vol. 3, ed. David Eltis and Stanley L. Engerman (Cambridge University Press, 2011), p. 602.
24 Quoted in Ibid.
25 Sue Peabody, *"There Are No Slaves in France": The Political Culture of Race and Slavery in the Ancien Régime* (Oxford University Press, 1996), p. 6.
26 See full text, "Open letter by Elizabeth I to the mayors of England, 11 July 1596" at the National Archives (online), accessed September 18, 2024, https://www.nationalarchives.gov.uk/education/resources/elizabeth-monarchy/open-letter-by-elizabeth-i/.
27 Gretchen Gerzina, *Black England: A Forgotten Georgian History* (John Murray, 2022), p. 4, Kindle.
28 Gerzina, *Black England*, p. 2; John C. Coombs, "'Others Not Christians in the Service of the English': Interpreting the Status of Africans and African Americans in Early Virginia," *Virginia Magazine of History and Biography* 127, no. 3 (2019): p. 221.
29 Imtiaz Habib, *Black Lives in the English Archives, 1500–1677: Imprints of the Invisible* (Routledge, 2008), pp. 109–10, 313–14.
30 Peabody, "Slavery, Freedom," p. 601.
31 Quoted in D. Hondius, "Access to the Netherlands of Enslaved and Free Black Africans: Exploring Legal and Social Historical Practices in the Sixteenth–Nineteenth Centuries," *Slavery & Abolition* 32, no. 3 (2011): p. 380.
32 Ibid.

Chapter 8

1. Archivo General de Indias, Indiferente General 2795, quoted in Engel Sluiter, "New Light on the '20 and Odd Negroes' Arriving in Virginia," *William and Mary Quarterly* 54, no. 2 (1997): pp. 395–98; Linda M. Heywood and John K. Thornton, "In Search of the 1619 African Arrivals," *Virginia Magazine of History and Biography* 127, no. 3 (2019): p. 205.
2. Heywood, "In Search of the 1619 African Arrivals," pp. 204–205.
3. That was for the fiscal years 1618 to 1622. See Sluiter, "New Light," p. 398.
4. Sluiter, "New Light," p. 396.
5. Quoted in Sluiter, "New Light," p. 396.
6. William Thorndale, "The Virginia Census of 1619," *Magazine of Virginia Genealogy* 33, no. 3 (1995): pp. 155–70; Jennifer L. Morgan, "Partus Sequitur Ventrem: Law, Race, and Reproduction in Colonial Slavery," *Small Axe* 22, no. 1 (2018): p. 8.
7. David J. Weber, *The Spanish Frontier in North America* (Yale University Press, 2009), p. 67; see also Jane Landers, *Black Society in Spanish Florida* (University of Illinois Press, 1999); Javier Cancio-Donlebún Ballvé, "The King of Spain's Slaves in St. Augustine, Florida (1580–1618)," *Estudios del Observatorio/Observatorio Studies* 74 (December 2021): pp. 1–81.
8. See Appendix 1, Table 14 in David Wheat, *Atlantic Africa and the Spanish Caribbean, 1570–1640* (University of North Carolina Press, 2016).
9. Heywood and Thornton, "In Search of the 1619 African Arrivals," p. 204.
10. Warren M. Billings, ed., *The Old Dominion in the Seventeenth Century: A Documentary History of Virginia, 1606–1700* (Chapel Hill, NC: Omohundro Institute of Early American History and Culture, 2007), p. 3.
11. Michael J. Jarvis, *In the Eye of All Trade: Bermuda, Bermudians, and the Maritime Atlantic World, 1680–1783* (Chapel Hill, NC: Omohundro Institute of Early American History and Culture, 2010), pp. 11–12.
12. King James I, *A Counterblaste to Tobacco [By James I]* (London, 1604).
13. Jarvis, *In the Eye of All Trade*, p. 27.
14. Imtiaz Habib, *Black Lives in the English Archives, 1500–1677: Imprints of the Invisible* (Routledge, 2008), p. 124.
15. Billings, *The Old Dominion in the Seventeenth Century*, p. 121.
16. Bernard Bailyn, *The Barbarous Years: The Peopling of British North America: The Conflict of Civilizations, 1600–1675* (Knopf, 2012), p. 65.
17. Ibid., p. 82.
18. Quoted in Bailyn, *The Barbarous Years*, p. 85.
19. Estimates of the number of captives disembarked in English North America 1520–1670 in SlaveVoyages: The Trans-Atlantic Slave Trade Database, accessed September 19, 2024, https://www.slavevoyages.org/voyages/PxJqc8Du.
20. Bailyn, *The Barbarous Years*, p. 182.
21. "A Rising on William Pierce's Plantation, 1640," in Billings, *The Old Dominion in the Seventeenth Century*, pp. 184–85.
22. See extracts from all three cases in Billings, *The Old Dominion in the Seventeenth Century*, p. 190.
23. John C. Coombs, "'Others Not Christians in the Service of the English': Interpreting the Status of Africans and African Americans in Early Virginia," *Virginia Magazine of History and Biography* 127, no. 3 (2019): p. 226.

24 Alejandro de la Fuente and Ariela J. Gross, *Becoming Free, Becoming Black: Race, Freedom, and Law in Cuba, Virginia, and Louisiana* (Cambridge University Press, 2020), pp. 14–15; Billings, *The Old Dominion in the Seventeenth Century*, pp. 180–81.
25 T. H. Breen and Stephen Innes, *Myne Owne Ground: Race and Freedom on Virginia's Eastern Shore, 1640–1676* (Oxford University Press, 2005), pp. 11–12, 68.
26 "Deposition of Anthony Johnson's Servant, 1655," in Billings, *The Old Dominion in the Seventeenth Century*, pp. 180–81.
27 Ibid. For more details of the case, see Breen and Innes, *Myne Owne Ground*, pp. 14–15.
28 Quoted in De la Fuente and Gross, *Becoming Free, Becoming Black*, p. 15.
29 Breen and Innes, *Myne Owne Ground*, p. xx.
30 Bailyn, *The Barbarous Years*, pp. 190–91.
31 Estimates of the number of captives disembarked in English North America 1670–1700 in SlaveVoyages: The Trans-Atlantic Slave Trade Database, accessed September 19, 2024, https://www.slavevoyages.org/voyages/rMCsQf3B.
32 US Department of Commerce, *Historical Statistics of the United States: Colonial Times to 1970, Part 2* (Washington, DC: Bureau of the Census, 1975), p. 1168.
33 Russell R. Menard, "Making a 'Popular Slave Society' in Colonial British America," *Journal of Interdisciplinary History* 43, no 3 (Winter 2013): p. 379.
34 Quoted in De la Fuente and Gross, *Becoming Free, Becoming Black*, pp. 30–31.
35 Billings, *The Old Dominion in the Seventeenth Century*, p. 133.
36 Coombs, "'Others Not Christians in the Service of the English,'" pp. 228–29.
37 "Fernando Appeals His Suit to the General Court, 1667," in Billings, *The Old Dominion in the Seventeenth Century*, p. 200.
38 This section on Fabulé comes from Lucien Peytraud, *L'esclavage aux Antilles Françaises avant 1789* (Paris: Librairie Hachette, 1897), p. 346; Adrien Dessalles, *Histoire générale des Antilles* (Paris: Libraire-Éditeur, 1847), pp. 109–16; Philip B. Boucher, *France and the American Tropics to 1700: Tropics of Discontent?* (Johns Hopkins University Press, 2008), pp. 183, 297–98; Gabriel Debien, "Marronage in the French Caribbean," in *Maroon Societies: Rebel Slave Communities in the Americas*, ed. Richard Price (Doubleday, 1996, 3rd edition), chap. 7.
39 Anne-Clair Faucquez, "Corporate Slavery in Seventeenth-Century New York," in *The Many Faces of Slavery: New Perspectives on Slave Ownership and Experiences in the Americas*, ed. Lawrence Aje and Catherine Armstrong (Bloomsbury Academic, 2020), p. 91.
40 Ibid., p. 92.
41 Ibid.
42 Ira Berlin, *Many Thousands Gone: The First Two Centuries of Slavery in North America* (Belknap Press, 1998), pp. 51–52.
43 Ibid., p. 51; Andrea Mosterman, *Spaces of Enslavement: A History of Slavery and Resistance in Dutch New York* (Cornell University Press, 2021), p. 20.
44 Berlin, *Many Thousands Gone*, pp. 51–52.
45 Ibid., p. 52.
46 Kathleen DuVal and John DuVal, eds., *Interpreting a Continent: Voices from Colonial America* (Rowman & Littlefield, 2009), pp. 157–58.
47 Estimates of the number of captives transported under a Danish flag 1514–1866 in SlaveVoyages: The Trans-Atlantic Slave Trade Database, accessed September 19, 2024, https://www.slavevoyages.org/voyages/gipq3Liq.

48 Neville A. T. Hall, *Slave Society in the Danish West Indies: St. Thomas, St. John and St. Croix*, ed. B. W. Higman (University of the West Indies Press, 1992), pp. 6–7.

Chapter 9

1 See Frans Post, *View of the Jesuit Church at Olinda*, 1665, Detroit Institute of Arts, accessed October 16, 2024, https://dia.org/collection/view-jesuit-church-olinda-brazil-57483.
2 This section on Frans Post comes from chapter 1 of Bia Corrêa do Lago, *Frans Post e o Brasil Holandês na Coleção do Instituto Ricardo Brennand* (Recife: Instituto Ricardo Brennand, 2010), pp. 13–23.
3 Stuart B. Schwartz, "The Commonwealth within Itself: The Early Brazilian Sugar Industry, 1550–1670," in *Tropical Babylons: Sugar and the Making of the Atlantic World, 1450–1680*, ed. Stuart B. Schwartz (University of North Carolina Press, 2004), p. 159.
4 Ibid., p. 160.
5 Ibid., p. 161; Stuart B. Schwartz, *Sugar Plantations in the Formation of Brazilian Society, Bahia 1550–1835* (Cambridge University Press, 1985), p. 165.
6 Schwartz, *Sugar Plantations*, p. 168.
7 Schwartz, "The Commonwealth within Itself," p. 167.
8 Stephanie Archangel, "João: Caught in the Crossfire in Dutch Brazil," in Eveline Sint Nicolaas and Valika Smeulders, eds., *Slavery (Rijksmuseum Exhibition Catalogue)* (Atlas Contact, 2021), p. 71.
9 Schwartz, "The Commonwealth within Itself," pp. 162–163.
10 David Brion Davis, *Inhuman Bondage: The Rise and Fall of Slavery in the New World* (Oxford University Press, 2006), pp. 107–08.
11 Archangel, "João," pp. 66–69. See the image online at Zacharias Wagener, *Mercado de escravos no Recife*, 1637–1644, Wikimedia Commons, https://commons.wikimedia.org/wiki/File:Zacharias_Wagner_-_Mercado_de_escravos_no_Recife.jpg.
12 Quoted in José Lingna Nafafé, *Lourenço da Silva Mendonça and the Black Atlantic Abolitionist Movement in the Seventeenth Century* (Cambridge University Press, 2022), p. 341.
13 Disney, *A History of Portugal*, p. 73.
14 Toby Green, *A Fistful of Shells: West Africa from the Rise of the Slave Trade to the Age of Revolution* (Penguin, 2020), pp. 1–10.
15 Cécile Fromont, *The Art of Conversion: Christian Visual Culture in the Kingdom of Kongo* (University of North Carolina Press, 2014), pp. 115; 121.
16 Ibid., p. 165.
17 The portraits are in the Statens Museum for Kunst in Copenhagen, Denmark, and can be seen here: Jaspar Beckx, "Dom Miguel de Castro," 1643, SMK.open, https://open.smk.dk/artwork/image/KMS7; Jaspar Beckx, "Pedro Sunda," 1641–1645, SMK.open, https://open.smk.dk/artwork/image/KMS8; Jaspar Beckx, "Diego Bemba," 1641–1645, SMK.open, https://open.smk.dk/artwork/image/KMS9.
18 Fromont, *The Art of Conversion*, pp. 165–67. There are records of one portrait of him in Kongo dress, but it has been lost; see P. J. P. Whitehead and M. Boeseman, *A Portrait of Dutch 17th Century Brazil: Animals, Plants and People by the Artists of Johan Maurits of Nassau* (Amsterdam: North-Holland, 1989), pp. 173–74, note d.
19 Fromont, *The Art of Conversion*, pp. 165–67.
20 Lingna Nafafé, *Lourenço da Silva Mendonça*, p. 12; see chapter 1 for a more detailed explanation of the workings of the tax.

21 Estimates of the number of captives transported from West Central Africa under a Portuguese flag, 1513–1626, SlaveVoyages: The Trans-Atlantic Slave Trade Database, accessed October 13, 2024, https://www.slavevoyages.org/voyages/PQHq2kz9.
22 Linda W. Heywood, *Njinga of Angola: Africa's Warrior Queen* (Harvard University Press, 2017), pp. 133–40.
23 Ibid., p. 151.
24 Ibid., pp. 155–56.
25 Quoted in Lingna Nafafé, *Lourenço da Silva Mendonça*, pp. 342–343.
26 Estimates of the number of journeys under a Dutch flag from Luanda, 1641–1626, SlaveVoyages: The Trans-Atlantic Slave Trade Database, accessed November 6, 2023, https://www.slavevoyages.org/voyages/s1KgrkVd.
27 Hendrik Kraay, "Arming Slaves in Brazil from the Seventeenth Century to the Nineteenth Century," in *Arming Slaves: From Classical Times to the Modern Age*, ed. Christopher Leslie Brown and Philip D. Morgan (Yale University Press, 2006), pp. 155–156.
28 R. K. Kent, "Palmares: An African State in Brazil," in *Maroon Societies: Rebel Slave Communities in the Americas*, ed. Richard (Doubleday, 1996, 3rd edition), chapter 11.
29 Ibid., pp. 176–177.
30 Quoted in Kent, "Palmares: An African State in Brazil," pp. 177–178
31 Sebastião da Rocha Pitta, *Historia da America Portugueza* (Lisboa, 1730), p. 472, https://palmares.ifch.unicamp.br/); Kent, "Palmares: An African State in Brazil," pp. 173–175."
32 Kent, "Palmares: An African State in Brazil," p. 176.
33 Lingna Nafafé, *Lourenço da Silva Mendonça*, pp. 241, 271.
34 Kent, "Palmares: An African State in Brazil," p. 172.
35 Quoted in Kent, "Palmares: An African State in Brazil," p. 178.
36 See Robert Nelson Anderson, "The Quilombo of Palmares: A New Overview of a Maroon State in Seventeenth-Century Brazil," *Journal of Latin American Studies* 28, no. 3 (1996): pp. 545–65.
37 Rocha Pitta, *Historia da America Portugueza*, p. 471.
38 Lingna Nafafé, *Lourenço da Silva Mendonça*, p. 243.
39 Rocha Pitta, *Historia da America Portugueza*, p. 476.
40 Lingna Nafafé, *Lourenço da Silva Mendonça*, pp. 256, 258.
41 Estimates of the number of captives transported to Cartagena, 1533–1700, SlaveVoyages: The Trans-Atlantic Slave Trade Database, accessed November 8, 2023, https://www.slavevoyages.org/voyages/dKrDiA7R; Estimates of the number of captives transported to Mainland North America, 1533–1700, SlaveVoyages: The Trans-Atlantic Slave Trade Database, accessed April 10, 2025, https://www.slavevoyages.org/voyages/7vY0R3Nv.
42 Quoted in Chloe L. Ireton, "Black Africans' Freedom Litigation Suits to Define Just War and Just Slavery in the Early Spanish Empire," *Renaissance Quarterly* 73, no. 4 (2020): p. 22.
43 Quoted in Ireton, "Black Africans' Freedom Litigation," p. 22.
44 Jane Landers, "The African Landscape of Seventeenth-Century Cartagena and Its Hinterlands," in *The Black Urban Atlantic in the Age of the Slave Trade*, ed. Jorge Cañizares-Esguerra et al. (University of Pennsylvania Press, 2013), p. 149.
45 Landers, "The African Landscape," p. 151.
46 Ibid., p. 150.
47 Sara Vicuña Guengerich, "The Witchcraft Trials of Paula de Eguiluz, a Black Woman, in Cartagena de Indias, 1620–1636," in *Afro-Latino Voices: Translations of Early Modern*

Ibero-Atlantic Narratives, ed. Kathryn Joy McKnight and Leo J. Garofalo (Indianapolis: Hackett, 2015), p. 117.
48 The section and sources for this case come from Vicuña Guengerich, "The Witchcraft Trials of Paula de Eguiluz," pp. 116–26.
49 Landers, "The African Landscape," p. 152.
50 Omar H. Ali, "Benkos Biohó: African Maroon Leadership in New Grenada," *Atlantic Biographies: Individuals and Peoples in the Atlantic World (Vol 27)*, Jeffrey A. Fortin and Mark Meuwese, eds. (Brill, 2014), p. 279.
51 On heritage, see Maria Fernanda Escallón, *Becoming Heritage: Recognition, Exclusion, and the Politics of Black Cultural Heritage in Colombia* (University of Cambridge Press, 2023); Blanca Camargo and Alain Lawo-Sukam, "San Basilio de Palenque (Re)Visited: African Heritage, Tourism, and Development in Colombia," *Afro-Hispanic Review* 34, no. 1 (2015): pp. 25–45.
52 For more on Matudere, see Landers, "The African Landscape," pp. 155–59; see also Kathryn Joy McKnight, "Confronted Rituals: Spanish Colonial and Angolan 'Maroon' Executions in Cartagena de Indias (1634)," *Journal of Colonialism and Colonial History* 5, no. 3 (2004).
53 Ali, "Benkos Biohó," p. 264.
54 Ibid., p. 286.
55 Ibid., p. 288.

Chapter 10

1 *A topographicall [Description and] Admeasurement [of the yland of] Barbados in t[he West Indyaes] with the Mrs. [Names of the Seuerall plantacons]* (London, Humphrey Moseley, 1657); John Carter Brown Library online collection, accessed August 5, 2022, https://jcb.lunaimaging.com/luna/servlet/detail/JCBMAPS~1~1~1486~101320001:A-topographicall--Description-and--?qvq=q:barbados&mi=1&trs=138.
2 For more on the political implications of this in Barbados, see Edward B. Rugemer, *Slave Law and the Politics of Resistance in the Early Atlantic World* (Harvard University Press, 2018), chap. 1.
3 Richard Ligon, *A True and Exact History of the Island of Barbados*, ed. David Smith (digital edition, 2014), p. 135.
4 Ibid.
5 Stuart B. Schwartz, ed., *Tropical Babylons: Sugar and the Making of the Atlantic World, 1450–1680* (University of North Carolina Press, 2004), p. 2.
6 Ligon, *A True and Exact History*, p. 75.
7 Jerome S. Handler and Matthew C. Reilly, "Contesting 'White Slavery' in the Caribbean," *New West India Guide / Nieuwe West-Indische Gids* 91, no. 1 (2017): p. 33.
8 Jerome Handler, "Slave Revolts and Conspiracies in Seventeenth-Century Barbados," *New West India Guide / Nieuwe West-Indische Gids* 56, no. 1/2 (1982): p. 7.
9 Hilary Beckles, *Black Rebellion in Barbados: The Struggle Against Slavery, 1627–1838* (Bridgetown: Antilles Publications, 1984), pp. 41–42; Rugemer, *Slave Law*, p. 26.
10 The Slave Voyages database records only go back to 1641 for Barbados, though undoubtedly hundreds were brought between 1627 and 1641. Estimates of the number of enslaved people taken to Barbados, 1627–1700, SlaveVoyages: The Trans-Atlantic Slave

Trade Database, accessed November 11, 2023, https://www.slavevoyages.org/voyages/dcbD8g1P.
11 Ligon, *A True and Exact History*, p. 196.
12 Ibid., p. 160.
13 Ibid., p. 81.
14 Stuart B. Schwartz, "The Commonwealth within Itself: The Early Brazilian Sugar Industry, 1550–1670," in *Tropical Babylons: Sugar and the Making of the Atlantic World, 1450–1680*, ed. Stuart B. Schwartz (University of North Carolina Press, 2004), p. 166.
15 Robin Blackburn, *The American Crucible: Slavery, Emancipation and Human Rights* (Verso, 2011), p. 54.
16 Handler, "Slave Revolts and Conspiracies," pp. 8–9.
17 The section on the 1676 conspiracy comes from Handler, "Slave Revolts and Conspiracies," pp. 14–17; Michael Craton, *Testing the Chains: Resistance to Slavery in the British West Indies* (Cornell University Press, 1982), p. 109; *Great Newes from the Barbados. Or, a True and Faithful Account of the Grand Conspiracy of the Negroes against the English* (L Curtis, 1676), pp. 11–12.
18 Much of the following comes from *Great Newes*, pp. 9–13.
19 Handler, "Slave Revolts and Conspiracies," pp. 14–15.
20 *Great Newes*, pp. 9–10.
21 November 25, 1675, No. 712, "America and West Indies: November 1675," in *Calendar of State Papers Colonial, America and West Indies: Volume 9, 1675–1676 and Addenda 1574–1674*, ed. W. Noel Sainsbury (London, 1893), pp. 300–05, British History Online, accessed August 5, 2022, http://www.british-history.ac.uk/cal-state-papers/colonial/america-west-indies/vol9/pp300-305.
22 Craton, *Testing the Chains*, pp. 100–11, 357n14; December 18, 1683, No. 1475, "America and West Indies: December 1683," in *Calendar of State Papers Colonial, America and West Indies: Volume 11, 1681–1685*, ed. J. W. Fortescue (London: 1898), pp. 557–73, British History Online, accessed November 10, 2023, http://www.british-history.ac.uk/cal-state-papers/colonial/america-west-indies/vol11/pp557-573.
23 Quoted in Handler, "Slave Revolts and Conspiracies," p. 20.
24 Ibid., p. 21.
25 Handler, "Slave Revolts and Conspiracies," p. 23.
26 November 3, 1693, No. 2,599, "America and West Indies: November 1692," in *Calendar of State Papers Colonial, America and West Indies: Volume 13, 1689–1692*, ed. J. W. Fortescue (London, 1901), pp. 731–42, British History Online, accessed November 10, 2023, http://www.british-history.ac.uk/cal-state-papers/colonial/america-west-indies/vol13/pp731-742.
27 Handler, "Slave Revolts and Conspiracies," pp. 24–26.
28 Quoted in Handler, "Slave Revolts and Conspiracies," p. 27.
29 Ibid.
30 November 3, 1693, No. 2,599, "America and West Indies: November 1692," in *Calendar of State Papers Colonial, America and West Indies: Volume 13, 1689–1692*, ed. J. W. Fortescue (London, 1901), pp. 731–42, British History Online, accessed November 10, 2023, http://www.british-history.ac.uk/cal-state-papers/colonial/america-west-indies/vol13/pp731-742.
31 Craton, *Testing the Chains*, p. 114.
32 Beckles, *Black Rebellion in Barbados*, p. 46.
33 Handler, "Slave Revolts and Conspiracies," p. 28.

34 Beckles, *Black Rebellion in Barbados*, p. 43.
35 November 3, 1693, No 2,599, "America and West Indies: November 1692," pp. 731–42, British History Online, accessed November 10, 2023, http://www.british-history.ac.uk/cal-state-papers/colonial/america-west-indies/vol13/pp731-742.
36 William A. Pettigrew, *Freedom's Debt: The Royal African Company and the Politics of the Atlantic Slave Trade, 1672–1752* (University of North Carolina Press, 2013), p. 4.
37 Ibid., p. 11.
38 Ibid., p. 31.
39 Quoted in Elizabeth Donnan, *Documents Illustrative of the History of the Slave Trade to America*, vol. 1, pp. 290–91.
40 See Carla Gardina Pestana, *The English Conquest of Jamaica: Oliver Cromwell's Bid for Empire* (Harvard University Press, 2017), chap. 3.
41 Gardina Pestana, *The English Conquest of Jamaica*, p. 119.
42 Gardina Pestana, *The English Conquest of Jamaica*, pp. 120–24.
43 Ibid., pp. 127–28.
44 Rugemer, *Slave Law*, p. 37.
45 Craton, *Testing the Chains*, p. 70.
46 Ibid.
47 Gardina Pestana, *The English Conquest of Jamaica*, p. 198.
48 Ibid., pp. 233–34.
49 Ibid., p. 239.
50 Craton, *Testing the Chains*, pp. 70–71; see also "Proclamation of Sir Chas. Lyttelton," February 1, 1663, No. 412, in *Calendar of State Papers Colonial, America and West Indies: Volume 5, 1661–1668* (London, 1889), British History Online, accessed April 8, 2022, https://www.british-history.ac.uk/cal-state-papers/colonial/america-west-indies/vol5/pp122-124.
51 Craton, *Testing the Chains*, pp. 71–72.
52 Ibid., p. 74; "Orders of the Governor and Council of War in Jamaica," no. 1049, September 1, 2022, *Calendar of State Papers Colonial, America and West Indies: Volume 5, 1661–1668* (London, 1889), British History Online, accessed April 8, 2022, https://www.british-history.ac.uk/cal-state-papers/colonial/america-west-indies/vol5/pp321-323.
53 Estimates of the number of captives transported to Jamaica, 1659–1670, SlaveVoyages: The Trans-Atlantic Slave Trade Database, accessed November 11, 2023, https://www.slavevoyages.org/voyages/N9OvYFyN and during the Spanish period, 1514–1659, https://www.slavevoyages.org/voyages/sZhmOTzW.
54 Gardina Pestana, *The English Conquest of Jamaica*, pp. 146–147.
55 Craton, *Testing the Chains*, pp. 71–72; "Minutes of the Council of Jamaica," May 2, 1670, No. 179, *Calendar of State Papers Colonial, America and West Indies: Volume 7, 1669–1674* (London, 1889), British History Online, accessed April 8, 2022, https://www.british-history.ac.uk/cal-state-papers/colonial/america-west-indies/vol7/pp64-68.
56 Craton, *Testing the Chains*, pp. 67.
57 Ibid., p. 75.
58 Ibid., pp. 75–76; see no. 339, "Lieutenant-Governor Molesworth to William Blathwayt," *Calendar of State Papers Colonial, America and West Indies: Volume 12 1685–1688 and Addenda 1653–1687*, ed. J. W. Fortescue (London, 1899), British History Online, accessed April 8, 2022, https://www.british-history.ac.uk/cal-state-papers/colonial/america-west-indies/vol12/pp71-86.

NOTES TO PAGES 120–125 545

59 Craton, *Testing the Chains*, pp. 75–76; see "Minutes of the Council of Jamaica," November 5, 1685. No. 445, *Calendar of State Papers Colonial, America and West Indies: Volume 12 1685–1688 and Addenda 1653–1687* (London, 1899), British History Online, accessed April 8, 2022, https://www.british-history.ac.uk/cal-state-papers/colonial/america-west-indies/vol12/pp114-123.
60 Craton, *Testing the Chains*, pp. 75–76; see "Minutes of the Council of Jamaica," April 8, 1686. No. 623, *Calendar of State Papers Colonial, America and West Indies: Volume 12 1685–1688 and Addenda 1653–1687* (London, 1899), British History Online, accessed April 8, 2022, https://www.british-history.ac.uk/cal-state-papers/colonial/america-west-indies/vol12/pp168-182.
61 Craton, *Testing the Chains*, p. 75; see also Orlando Patterson, "Slavery and Slave Revolt: A Sociohistorical Analysis of the First Maroon War," in *Maroon Societies: Rebel Slave Communities in the Americas*, ed. Richard Price (Doubleday, 1996, 3rd edition), chapter 15
62 Craton, *Testing the Chains*, pp. 76–77n24, pp. 353–54; see also "Earl of Inchiquin to Lords of Trade and Plantations," August 31, 1690, No. 1041, *Calendar of State Papers Colonial, America and West Indies: Volume 13, 1689–1692* (London, 1889), British History Online, accessed April 12, 2022, https://www.british-history.ac.uk/cal-state-papers/colonial/america-west-indies/vol13/pp301-317.

Chapter 11

1 The account of the *Dorothy* comes from Elizabeth Donnan, *Documents Illustrative of the History of the Slave Trade to America*, vol. 2 (Carnegie Institution of Washington, 1930), pp. 312–317.
2 Ibid., p. 311; the *Dorothy*, voyage ID, 21556, SlaveVoyages: The Trans-Atlantic Slave Trade Database, accessed October 16, 2024, https://www.slavevoyages.org/voyages/H2BHTZox.
3 Jennifer L. Morgan, "Accounting for 'The Most Excruciating Torment': Gender, Slavery, and Trans-Atlantic Passages," *History of the Present* 6, no. 2 (2016): pp. 201–02.
4 For a full account of Mendonça, his world, and the case he brought against the Vatican, see José Lingna Nafafé's excellent *Lourenço da Silva Mendonça and the Black Atlantic Abolitionist Movement in the Seventeenth Century* (Cambridge University Press, 2022). The section that follows is indebted to that work.
5 Lingna Nafafé, *Lourenço da Silva Mendonça*, pp. 1–2.
6 Ibid., p. 213.
7 Ibid., pp. 188–89.
8 Ibid., p. 14.
9 Estimates of the number of captives transported to Brazil, 1600–1700, SlaveVoyages: The Trans-Atlantic Slave Trade Database, accessed November 13, 2023, https://www.slavevoyages.org/voyages/CXC9CQBX.
10 Hendrik Kraay, "Arming Slaves in Brazil from the Seventeenth Century to the Nineteenth Century," in *Arming Slaves: From Classical Times to the Modern Age*, ed. Christopher Leslie Brown and Philip D. Morgan (Yale University Press, 2006), pp. 147, 155.
11 Lingna Nafafé, *Lourenço da Silva Mendonça*, p. 147.
12 Ibid., p. 216.
13 Ibid., p. 208.
14 Quoted in Lingna Nafafé, *Lourenço da Silva Mendonça*, pp. 237–238.

15 Lingna Nafafé, *Lourenço da Silva* Mendonça, p. 199.
16 A. J. R. Russell-Wood, "Black and Mulatto Brotherhoods in Colonial Brazil: A Study in Collective Behavior," *Hispanic American Historical Review* 54, no. 4 (1974): p. 576.
17 Lingna Nafafé, *Lourenço da Silva Mendonça*, pp. 296–97.
18 Ibid., p. 20; Lingna Nafafé also notes that the name Mendonça, or Mendoza in Spanish, was considered to be a Jewish surname, and could potentially have linked him with the Jewish "conversos" or "New Christians," who converted to Christianity in Iberia under threat of the Inquisition, some of whom would end up living throughout Spanish and Portuguese territories, including in Africa; see pp. 20–21.
19 Ibid., pp. 304–08.
20 Ibid., p. 310.
21 On the nuances of the word *pardo*, see Lingna Nafafé, *Lourenço da Silva Mendonça*, p. 22.
22 Lingna Nafafé, *Lourenço da Silva Mendonça*, p. 317.
23 Ibid., pp. 329–30.
24 Ibid., p. 346.
25 Quoted in Lingna Nafafé, *Lourenço da Silva Mendonça*, p. 351.
26 For a more detailed discussion of these types of laws and Mendonça's argument, see Lingna Nafafé, *Lourenço da Silva Mendonça*, pp. 369–71.
27 Lingna Nafafé, *Lourenço da Silva Mendonça*, pp. 371–72.
28 Ibid., p. 40.
29 Ibid., pp. 40–41.
30 Ibid., p. 360.
31 Ibid., pp. 41–42; 460.
32 Ibid., p. 356.
33 Ibid., p. 43.
34 Richard Gray, "The Papacy and the Atlantic Slave Trade: Lourenço da Silva, the Capuchins and the Decisions of the Holy Office," *Past & Present* 115 (May 1987): p. 61.
35 Lingna Nafafé, *Lourenço da Silva Mendonça*, p. 385.
36 Ibid., p. 44.

Chapter 12

1 José Lingna Nafafé, *Lourenço da Silva Mendonça and the Black Atlantic Abolitionist Movement in the Seventeenth Century* (Cambridge University Press, 2022), p. 374.
2 The "Tannenbaum thesis" explored the differences between the systems of slavery that developed from Iberian and Protestant Europe; see Frank Tannenbaum, *Slave and Citizen: The Classic Comparative Study of Race Relations in the Americas* (Beacon Press, 1992).
3 Estimate of the number of captives taken from Africa to the Americas under a French flag, 1670–1685, SlaveVoyages: The Trans-Atlantic Slave Trade Database, accessed November 14, 2023, https://www.slavevoyages.org/voyages/AbO1sftw.
4 The code would be adapted for use in French Louisiana in 1724.
5 For an English translation of key articles of the code, see Exploring the French Revolution, accessed November 15, 2023. https://revolution.chnm.org/d/335/.
6 See full text at UNB Libraries, accessed November 15, 2023, https://slaveryandfreedomlaws.lib.unb.ca/laws/barbados-1661. See also Jerome S. Handler, "Custom and Law: The Status of Enslaved Africans in Seventeenth-Century Barbados," *Slavery & Abolition* 37, no. 2 (2016): pp. 233–55.

7 Jerome Handler, "Slave Revolts and Conspiracies in Seventeenth-Century Barbados," *New West India Guide / Nieuwe West-Indische Gids* 56, no. 1/2 (1982): p. 9.
8 Quoted in Handler, "Slave Revolts and Conspiracies," p. 17.
9 "An Act for the Governing of Negroes (1688)," UNB Libraries, accessed November 15, 2023, https://slaveryandfreedomlaws.lib.unb.ca/laws/barbados-1688.
10 John C. Coombs, "'Others Not Christians in the Service of the English': Interpreting the Status of Africans and African Americans in Early Virginia," *Virginia Magazine of History and Biography* 127, no. 3 (2019): p. 215.
11 Quoted in Warren M. Billings, *The Old Dominion in the Seventeenth Century: A Documentary History of Virginia, 1606–1700* (Chapel Hill, NC: Omohundro Institute of Early American History and Culture, 2007), p. 204.
12 Alejandro de la Fuente and Ariela J. Gross, *Becoming Free, Becoming Black: Race, Freedom, and Law in Cuba, Virginia, and Louisiana* (Cambridge University Press, 2020), p. 36; on Bacon's rebellion, see Edmund S. Morgan, *American Slavery, American Freedom: The Ordeal of Colonial Virginia* (W. W. Norton, 1975), chap. 13.
13 Act quoted in Billings, *The Old Dominion in the Seventeenth Century*, p. 205.
14 Sue Peabody, "Slavery, Freedom, and the Law in the Atlantic World, 1420–1807," in *The Cambridge World History of Slavery*, vol. 3, ed. David Eltis and Stanley L. Engerman (Cambridge University Press, 2011), p. 601.
15 Michael Craton, *Testing the Chains: Resistance to Slavery in the British West Indies* (Cornell University Press, 1982), p. 31.
16 Manisha Sinha, *The Slave's Cause: A History of Abolition* (Yale University Press, 2016), pp. 12–13.
17 "An Act to Prevent the People called Quakers, from bringing Negroes to their Meeting (1676)," UNB Libraries, accessed November 15, 2023, https://slaveryandfreedomlaws.lib.unb.ca/laws/barbados-1676.
18 Germantown Petition full text at Library of Congress, accessed April 11, 2025, https://www.loc.gov/resource/rbpe.14000200/?st=text.
19 Sinha, *The Slave's Cause*, p. 12.
20 R. K. Kent, "Palmares: An African State in Brazil," in *Maroon Societies: Rebel Slave Communities in the Americas*, ed. Richard Price (Doubleday, 1996, 3rd edition), p. 178.
21 Kent, "Palmares: An African State in Brazil," p. 178.
22 On the meaning of names and titles, see Stuart B. Schwartz, *Slaves, Peasants, and Rebels: Reconsidering Brazilian Slavery* (University of Illinois Press, 1992), p. 127.
23 Quoted in Kent, "Palmares: An African State in Brazil," p. 179. See also Mary Karasch, "Zumbi of Palmares. Challenging the Portuguese Colonial Order," *The Human Tradition in Colonial Latin America* (2nd ed), Kenneth J. Andrien (ed) (Lanham, MD: Rowman & Littlefield, 2013), chapter 7.
24 Quoted in Kent, "Palmares: An African State in Brazil," p. 179.
25 Ibid., p. 180.
26 Ibid., p. 184.
27 Quoted in Robert Nelson Anderson, "The Quilombo of Palmares : A New Overview of a Maroon State in Seventeenth-Century Brazil," *Journal of Latin American Studies* 28, no. 3 (1996): p. 560.
28 Kent, "Palmares: An African State in Brazil," pp. 185–186.
29 Lingna Nafafé, *Lourenço da Silva Mendonça*, pp. 260–261.
30 Kent, "Palmares: An African State in Brazil," pp. 185–187.
31 Quoted in Kent, "Palmares: An African State in Brazil," p. 187.

32 Quoted in Terri L. Snyder, "Suicide, Slavery, and Memory in North America," *Journal of American History* 97, no. 1 (2010): p. 51; John Locke, *Two Treatises of Government*, ed. Peter Laslett (Cambridge University Press, 1988), pp. 284–85.
33 For more on the influence of Locke in North America, see Holly Brewer, "Slavery, Sovereignty, and 'Inheritable Blood': Reconsidering John Locke and the Origins of American Slavery," *American Historical Review* 122, no. 4 (2017): pp. 1038–78; see also Wayne Glausser, "Three Approaches to Locke and the Slave Trade," *Journal of the History of Ideas* 51, no. 2 (1990): pp. 199–216; full text of the Carolina Charter of 1665 is available at Lillian Goldman Law Library, accessed November 16, 2023, https://avalon.law.yale.edu/17th_century/nc04.asp.
34 Sinha, *The Slave's Cause*, p. 35.
35 Richard Ligon, *A True and Exact History of the Island of Barbados*, ed. David Smith (digital edition, 2014), p. 35.

Chapter 13

1 William Gilmore Simms, *The History of South Carolina from Its First European Discovery to Its Erection into a Republic* (Redfield, New York, 1860), pp. 111–112; inflation calculations done at CPI Inflation Calculator, https://www.in2013dollars.com/.
2 Robin Blackburn, *The American Crucible: Slavery, Emancipation and Human Rights* (Verso, 2011), chap. 4.
3 José Lingna Nafafé, *Lourenço da Silva Mendonça and the Black Atlantic Abolitionist Movement in the Seventeenth Century* (Cambridge University Press, 2022), pp. 218–19.
4 Richard B. Sheridan, *Sugar and Slavery: An Economic History of the British West Indies, 1623–1775* (Kingston, Jamaica: Canoe Press, 1994), p. 11.
5 For a discussion of different profit calculations, see Robin Blackburn, *The Making of New World Slavery: From the Baroque to the Modern, 1492–1800* (Verso, 2010), pp. 532–537.
6 For more on the lobby, see Andrew J. O'Shaughnessy, "The Formation of a Commercial Lobby: The West India Interest, British Colonial Policy and the American Revolution," *Historical Journal* 40, no. 1 (1997): pp. 71–95.
7 Estimates of the number of captives transported by the South Sea Company, 1714–1750, SlaveVoyages: The Trans-Atlantic Slave Trade Database, accessed October 22, 2024, https://www.slavevoyages.org/voyages/ozGzOa9K.
8 Estimates of the number of captives transported by the Royal African Company, 1714–1750, SlaveVoyages: The Trans-Atlantic Slave Trade Database, https://www.slavevoyages.org/voyages/EACoPIZA; and estimates of the number of captives transported under a British flag, 1714–1750, SlaveVoyages: The Trans-Atlantic Slave Trade Database, accessed October 22, 2024, https://www.slavevoyages.org/voyages/yuKM3RKI.
9 Eric Williams, *Capitalism and Slavery* (Penguin Modern Classics, 2020), p. 31, Kindle.
10 An online collection, Underwriting Souls, offers a detailed explanation of the connection between slavery and insurance and includes many digitized documents, including from the archives of Lloyd's of London: https://underwritingsouls.org/about/.
11 From the *Country Journal*, August 2, (1729, September); *The Weekly News-Letter* (Boston), 1–2, in Elizabeth Donnan, *Documents Illustrative of the History of the Slave Trade to America*, vol. 4, p. 274; see also M. Rediker, *The Slave Ship: A Human History* (Viking, 2007), p. 298.
12 David Eltis, *Atlantic Cataclysm: Rethinking the Atlantic Slave Trades* (Cambridge University Press, 2025), pp. 275–278.

13 Estimates of the number of voyages in 1729, SlaveVoyages: The Trans-Atlantic Slave Trade Database, accessed October 22, 2024, https://www.slavevoyages.org/voyages/P3lJGfgv.
14 David Richardson, "Shipboard Revolts, African Authority, and the Atlantic Slave Trade," *William and Mary Quarterly* 58, no. 1 (2001): pp. 79–80.
15 Ibid., p. 72.
16 As Richardson puts it: "Africans who died resisting slave traders as well as those who resisted unsuccessfully . . . saved perhaps 600,000 other Africans from being shipped to America in the long eighteenth century and 1,000,000 during the whole history of the trade." Richardson, "Shipboard Revolts," pp. 74–75.
17 Rediker, *The Slave Ship*; see also W. Jeffrey Bolster, *Black Jacks: African American Seamen in the Age of Sail* (Havard University Press, 1997).
18 Kevin Dawson, "The Cultural Geography of Enslaved Ship Pilots," in *The Black Urban Atlantic in the Age of the Slave Trade*, ed. Jorge Cañizares-Esguerra et al. (University of Pennsylvania Press, 2013), pp. 163–64.
19 Dawson, "The Cultural Geography," p. 169.
20 See for instance Matthew Restall, "Black Conquistadors: Armed Africans in Early Spanish America," *The Americas*, Vol. 57, No 2, October 2000: pp. 171–205.
21 Peter Linebaugh and Marcus Rediker, *The Many-Headed Hydra: Sailors, Slaves, Commoners and the Hidden History of the Revolutionary Atlantic* (Beacon Press, 2000), pp. 165–166.
22 For more on Quoshey, see Simon P. Newman, *Freedom Seekers: Escaping from Slavery in Restoration London* (University of London Press, 2022), p. 133.
23 Estimated number of enslaved people disembarked in New York, 1600–1700, SlaveVoyages: The Trans-Atlantic Slave Trade Database, https://www.slavevoyages.org/voyages/od78CtiR; estimated number of enslaved people disembarked in New York, 1700–1800; SlaveVoyages: The Trans-Atlantic Slave Trade Database, accessed October 22, 2024, https://www.slavevoyages.org/voyages/wBKWjCoH; estimated number of enslaved people disembarked in New York, 1700–1800 from within the Americas, SlaveVoyages: The Intra-American Slave Trade Database, accessed October 22, 2024, https://www.slavevoyages.org/voyages/lONhTbW5.
24 Joyce D. Goodfriend, *Before the Melting Pot: Society and Culture in Colonial New York City, 1664–1730* (Princeton University Press, 1992), p. 113; Kenneth Scott, "The Slave Insurrection in New York in 1712," *New-York Historical Society Quarterly* 45 (January 1961): p. 44.
25 Quoted in Goodfriend, *Before the Melting Pot*, p. 114; Leslie M. Harris, *In the Shadow of Slavery: African-Americans in New York City, 1626–1863* (University of Chicago Press, 2003), p. 28.
26 Scott, "The Slave Insurrection in New York," p. 44.
27 Harris, *In the Shadow of Slavery*, p. 28.
28 For more on the events on Long Island, see Ben Hughes, *When I Die, I Shall Return to My Own Land: The New York City Slave Revolt of 1712* (Yardley, PA: Westholme Publishing, 2021), chap. 5, EPUB; See also Scott "The Slave Insurrection," p. 45.
29 Hughes, *When I Die*, chap. 12.
30 Quoted in Goodfriend, *Before the Melting Pot*, pp. 123–24.
31 *Boston News-Letter*, April 14, quoted in Hughes, *When I Die*, chap. 12.

32 Ibid. Today the African Burial Ground National Monument sits on part of this site in lower Manhattan; see National Park Service, "African Burial Ground," https://www.nps.gov/afbg/index.htm.
33 Harris, *In the Shadow of Slavery*, pp. 37–38.
34 Hughes, *When I Die*, chap. 14.
35 Harris, *In the Shadow of Slavery*, pp. 37–38.
36 Governor Robert Hunter to the Lords of Trade, June 23, 1712, in John Romeyn Brodhead, *Documents Relative to the Colonial History of the State of New York* (Albany: Weed, Parsons, 1855), p. 341.
37 Hughes, *When I Die*, chap. 13.
38 Scott, "The Slave Insurrection in New York in 1712," pp. 62–66.
39 Hughes, *When I Die*, chap. 14; Governor Robert Hunter to Secretary Popple, September 10, 1713, in Brodhead, *Documents Relative to the Colonial History of the State of New York*, p. 371.
40 Harris, *In the Shadow of Slavery*, p. 39.

Chapter 14

1 Governor Hunter to the Council of Trade and Plantations, May 10, 1730, No. 225: "America and West Indies: May 1730, 1–15," in *Calendar of State Papers Colonial, America and West Indies: Volume 37, 1730*, ed. Cecil Headlam and Arthur Percival Newton (London, 1937), pp. 97–113, British History Online, accessed November 22, 2023, http://www.british-history.ac.uk/cal-state-papers/colonial/america-west-indies/vol37/pp97-113.
2 Governor Hunter to the Council of Trade and Plantations, May 10, 1730, No. 311 (xii): "America and West Indies: July 1730, 1–5," in *Calendar of State Papers Colonial, America and West Indies: Volume 37, 1730*, pp. 155–65, British History Online, accessed November 22, 2023, http://www.british-history.ac.uk/cal-state-papers/colonial/america-west-indies/vol37/pp155-165.
3 Governor Hunter to the Council of Trade and Plantations, July 4, 1730, No. 311 (ix): "America and West Indies: July 1730, 1–5," in *Calendar of State Papers Colonial, America and West Indies: Volume 37, 1730*, pp. 155–165, British History Online, accessed November 22, 2023, http://www.british-history.ac.uk/cal-state-papers/colonial/america-west-indies/vol37/pp155-165.
4 Governor Hunter to the Duke of Newcastle, February 11, 1731, No. 15, "America and West Indies: February 1731," in *Calendar of State Papers Colonial, America and West Indies: Volume 38, 1731*, ed. Cecil Headlam and Arthur Percival Newton (London, 1938), pp. 31–51, British History Online, accessed November 22, 2023, http://www.british-history.ac.uk/cal-state-papers/colonial/america-west-indies/vol38/pp31-51.
5 Estimate of the number of enslaved people taken to Jamaica, 1655–1730, SlaveVoyages: The Trans-Atlantic Slave Trade Database, accessed October 22, 2024, https://www.slavevoyages.org/voyages/HbjztxDn; Orlando Patterson, "Slavery and Slave Revolts: A Socio-Historical Analysis of the First Maroon War Jamaica, 1655–1740," *Social and Economic Studies* 19, no. 3, (1970): p. 303.
6 Patterson, "Slavery and Slave Revolts," p. 300.
7 Michael Craton, *Testing the Chains: Resistance to Slavery in the British West Indies* (Cornell University Press, 1982), p. 77.
8 Quoted in Patterson, "Slavery and Slave Revolts, p. 301.

9   Ibid., p. 302.
10 Craton, *Testing the Chains*, pp. 77–78.
11 Ibid., p. 78.
12 Ibid., p. 83.
13 Ibid., p. 78.
14 Ibid., pp. 83–84.
15 Ibid., pp. 81–82; p. 345n2.
16 $500JMD is about $3USD, https://boj.org.jm/core-functions/currency/bank-notes/. Nanny was put in her current prominent place in the 1970s; see Karla Gottlieb, *The Mother of Us All: A History of Queen Nanny* (London: Africa World Press, 2000).
17 Gottlieb, *The Mother of Us All*, p. xv; Jenny Sharpe, *Ghosts of Slavery: A Literary Archaeology of Black Women's Lives* (University of Minnesota Press, 2003), p. 2.
18 Gottlieb, *The Mother of Us All*, p. 24; see Sharpe, *Ghosts of Slavery*, chap. 1.
19 Patterson, "Slavery and Slave Revolts," p. 302.
20 Craton, *Testing the Chains*, p. 81; Gottlieb, *The Mother of Us All*, p. 24.
21 Gottlieb, *The Mother of Us All*, pp. 26–27.
22 Patterson, Slavery and Slave Revolts," p. 302n52.
23 Ibid., pp. 304–305.
24 Ibid., pp. 306–307.
25 Craton, *Testing the Chains*, pp. 81–82; Governor Hunter to the Council of Trade and Plantations, October 13, 1733, no. 358, vii, "America and West Indies: October 1733, 1–15," in *Calendar of State Papers Colonial, America and West Indies: Volume 40*, British History Online, accessed April 12, 2022, https://www.british-history.ac.uk/cal-state-papers/colonial/america-west-indies/vol40/pp197-216.
26 Craton, *Testing the Chains*, p. 85.
27 Quoted in Patterson, "Slavery and Slave Revolts," p. 309.
28 Ibid., p. 310.
29 Gov Edward Trelawny to Duke of Newcastle, No. 86, March 5, 1739, "America and West Indies: March 1739," in *Calendar of State Papers Colonial, America and West Indies: Volume 45, 1739*, ed. K. G. Davies (London, 1994), pp. 50–72, British History Online, accessed April 12, 2022, http://www.british-history.ac.uk/cal-state-papers/colonial/america-west-indies/vol45/pp50-72.
30 Extract of letter from Col John Gutherie to Governor Trelawny, Feb 17, 1739, No. 86i in "America and West Indies: March 1739," in *Calendar of State Papers Colonial, America and West Indies*, pp. 50–72. British History Online, accessed November 30, 2023, http://www.british-history.ac.uk/cal-state-papers/colonial/america-west-indies/vol45/pp50-72.
31 Quoted in Patterson, "Slavery and Slave Revolts," p. 311.
32 See R. C. Dallas, *The History of the Maroons* (London, 1801).
33 See full text at No. 116 March 30, 1739, "America and West Indies: March 1739," in *Calendar of State Papers Colonial, America and West Indies*, pp. 50–72. British History Online, accessed November 30, 2022, http://www.british-history.ac.uk/cal-state-papers/colonial/america-west-indies/vol45/pp50-72; Patterson, "Slavery and Slave Revolts," p. 311.
34 Governor Edward Trelawny to Duke of Newcastle, No. 243, June 30, 1739, "America and West Indies: June 1739," in *Calendar of State Papers Colonial, America and West Indies: Volume 45, 1739*, pp. 112–130, British History Online, accessed April 12, 2022, http://www.british-history.ac.uk/cal-state-papers/colonial/america-west-indies/vol45/pp112-130.
35 Patterson, "Slavery and Slave Revolts," pp. 312–313.

36 Ibid.
37 Ibid.
38 Gottlieb, *The Mother of Us All*, pp. 36–37.
39 Full text of Windward Treaty, June 30, 1739, in Gottlieb, *The Mother of Us All*, pp. 99–101.
40 Governor Edward Trelawny to the Duke of Newcastle, June 30, 1739, No. 243 in "America and West Indies: June 1739," in *Calendar of State Papers Colonial, America and West Indies: Volume 45, 1739*, pp. 112–130, British History Online, accessed November 30, 2023, http://www.british-history.ac.uk/cal-state-papers/colonial/america-west-indies/vol45/pp112-130; Craton, *Testing the Chains*, pp. 91–92.
41 Gottlieb, *The Mother of Us All*, pp. 28–31.
42 Ibid., p. 95 (appendix 1).
43 Patterson, "Slavery and Slave Revolts," p. 313.
44 Craton, *Testing the Chains*, pp. 93–94.
45 Holly Kathryn Norton, "Estate by Estate: The Landscape of the 1733 St. Jan Slave Rebellion," PhD diss., Syracuse University, 2013, p. 68.
46 Louise Sebro, "The 1733 Slave Revolt on the Island of St. John: Continuity and Change from Africa to the Americas," in *Scandinavian Colonialism and the Rise of Modernity: Small Time Agents in a Global Arena*, ed. Magdalena Naum and Jonas M. Nordin (Springer, 2013), p. 261.
47 Sebro, "The 1733 Slave Revolt on the Island of St John," p. 263; Neville A. T. Hall, *Slave Society in the Danish West Indies: St.Thomas, St. John and St.Croix*, BW Higman (ed.). (University of the West Indies Press, 1992), p. 40; Norton, "Estate by Estate," p. 52.
48 Holger Weiss, "The Danish Gold Coast as Multinational and Entangled Space, c. 1700–1850," in *Scandinavian Colonialism and the Rise of Modernity: Small Time Agents in a Global Arena*, ed. Magdalena Naum and Jonas M. Nordin (Springer, 2013), p. 245.
49 David W. Knight, in discussion with the author, January 30, 2023.
50 Estimates of the number of captives transported to Danish West Indies, 1700–1733, SlaveVoyages: The Trans-Atlantic Slave Trade Database, accessed November 4, 2024, https://www.slavevoyages.org/voyages/V2mXWOfH.
51 William Mathew to the Council of Trade and Plantations, March 19, 1734, No. 83, "America and West Indies: March 1734, 16–31," in *Calendar of State Papers Colonial, America and West Indies: Volume 41, 1734–1735* (London, 1953), pp. 55–67, British History Online, accessed December 2, 2023, http://www.british-history.ac.uk/cal-state-papers/colonial/america-west-indies/vol41/pp55-67.
52 Norton, "Estate by Estate," p. 78.
53 Ibid., p. 56.
54 Sebro, "The 1733 Slave Revolt," p. 266.
55 Ibid., p. 270.
56 Ibid., p. 269.
57 See for instance Pierre J. Pannet, *Report on the Execrable Conspiracy Carried Out by the Amina Negroes on the Danish Island of St. Jan in America, 1733* (Christiansted, St Croix: Antilles Press, 1984).
58 Norton, "Estate by Estate," p. 80.
59 Quoted in Ruth Hull Low and Rafael Valls, eds., *St. John Backtime: Eyewitness Accounts from 1780 to 1956* (Saint John, USVI: Eden Hill Press, n.d.), p. 11.
60 Norton, "Estate by Estate," p. 90.

61 Craton, *Testing the Chains*, p. 121.
62 Ibid., pp. 122–123.
63 David Barry Gaspar, *Bondmen and Rebels: A Study of Master-Slave Relations in Antigua* (Johns Hopkins University Press, 1985), p. 66.
64 Craton, *Testing the Chains*, p. 115.
65 Ibid., p. 118; Mr Gamble to Governor Codrington, December 30, 1701, No. 1132.11., "America and West Indies: December 1701, 27–31," in *Calendar of State Papers Colonial, America and West Indies: Volume 19, 1701*, ed. Cecil Headlam (London, 1910), pp. 696–729, British History Online, accessed April 15, 2022, http://www.british-history.ac.uk/cal-state-papers/colonial/america-west-indies/vol19/pp696-729.
66 Craton, *Testing the Chains*, p. 118; Governor Codrington to the Council of Trade and Plantations, December 30, 1701, No. 1132, "America and West Indies: December 1701, 27–31," in *Calendar of State Papers Colonial, America and West Indies: Volume 19, 1701*, British History Online, accessed April 15, 2022, http://www.british-history.ac.uk/cal-state-papers/colonial/america-west-indies/vol19/pp696-729.
67 Craton, *Testing the Chains*, p. 118.
68 Ibid., p. 119.
69 Ibid., p. 120.
70 Quoted in Jason T. Sharples, *The World That Fear Made: Slave Revolts and Conspiracy Scares in Early America* (University of Pennsylvania Press, 2020), p. 109.
71 Craton, *Testing the Chains*, pp. 121, 358n13.
72 Ibid., pp. 120–121.
73 Ibid., p. 121.
74 Ibid., pp. 124, 359n23.
75 Ibid., p. 121.
76 Ibid., p. 122.
77 Quoted in Gaspar, *Bondmen & Rebels*, p. 28.
78 Sharples, *The World That Fear Made*, p. 98.
79 Craton, *Testing the Chains*, p. 122.
80 Gaspar, *Bondmen and Rebels*, p. 83.

Chapter 15

1 P. C. Hoffer, *Cry Liberty: The Great Stono River Slave Rebellion of 1739* (Oxford University Press, 2010), p. 13n.
2 James Edward Oglethorpe, "An Account of the Negroe Insurrection in South Carolina (1740)," in *Publications of James Edward Oglethorpe*, ed. Rodney M. Baine (University of Georgia Press, 2014), pp. 252–55.
3 See Irene A. Wright, "Dispatches of Spanish Officials Bearing on the Free Negro Settlement of Gracia Real de Santa Teresa de Mose, Florida," *Journal of Negro History* 9, no 2 (1924): pp. 144–95.
4 Jane Landers, "Gracia Real de Santa Teresa de Mose: A Free Black Town in Spanish Colonial Florida," *American Historical Review* 95, no. 1 (1990): p. 14.
5 Journal of the Commons House of Assembly, June 20, 1711, quoted in Timothy James Lockley, *Maroon Communities in South Carolina: A Documentary Record* (University of South Carolina Press, 2009), p. 9.

6. Ibid.
7. Landers, "Gracia Real de Santa Teresa de Mose," pp. 10, 15–18.
8. Oglethorpe, "An Account of the Negroe Insurrection," p. 253.
9. P. H. Wood, *Black Majority: Negroes in Colonial South Carolina from 1670 through the Stono Rebellion* (W. W. Norton, 1975), pp. 309–13.
10. Hoffer, *Cry Liberty*, pp. 62–65; Mark M. Smith, ed., *Stono: Documenting and Interpreting a Southern Slave Revolt* (University of South Carolina Press, 2005).
11. E. A. Pearson, "'A Countryside Full of Flames': A Reconsideration of the Stono Rebellion and Slave Rebelliousness in the Early Eighteenth Century South Carolina Lowcountry," in *The Slavery Reader*, ed. Gad Heuman and James Walvin (Routledge, 2003), p. 580.
12. Elizabeth Donnan, *Documents Illustrative of the History of the Slave Trade to America*, vol. 4, no. 139, p. 256; Wood, *Black Majority*, p. 302.
13. Pearson, "A Countryside Full of Flames," p. 576.
14. John K. Thornton, "African Dimensions of the Stono Rebellion," *American Historical Review*, 96, no. 4 (1991): pp. 1102–04, 1109.
15. Oglethorpe, "An Account of the Negroe Insurrection," p. 253; Thornton, "African Dimensions," p. 1102. For possible Catholic connections, see M. M. Smith, "Remembering Mary, Shaping Revolt: Reconsidering the Stono Rebellion," *Journal of Southern History* 67, no. 3 (August 2001): pp. 513–34.
16. Oglethorpe, "An Account of the Negroe Insurrection in South Carolina (1740)," p. 253.
17. Ibid., p. 254.
18. Wood, *Black Majority*, p. 315.
19. Oglethorpe, "An Account of the Negroe Insurrection in South Carolina (1740)," p. 254.
20. Thornton, "African Dimensions," p. 1112.
21. Oglethorpe, "An Account of the Negroe Insurrection in South Carolina (1740)," p. 255; see also introduction in Smith, *Stono: Documenting and Interpreting a Southern Slave Revolt*.
22. Document 2, A Ranger's Report of Travels with Gen Oglethorpe, 1739–1742, in Smith, *Stono: Documenting and Interpreting a Southern Slave Revolt*, pp. 7–8.
23. *South Carolina Gazette*, December 27, 1742, quoted in Lockley, *Maroon Communities in South Carolina*, p. 13.
24. "Act for the Better Ordering and Governing of Negroes and Other Slaves in this Province," May 1740, excerpts at https://wisc.pb.unizin.org/ls261/chapter/ch-1-1-the-slave-code-of-south-carolina-1740/
25. Smith, *Stono: Documenting and Interpreting a Southern Slave Revolt*, xiv.
26. Landers, "Gracia Real de Santa Teresa de Mose," pp. 26, 29.
27. Oglethorpe, "An Account of the Negroe Insurrection in South Carolina (1740)," p. 252.
28. Quoted in Betty Wood, "Thomas Stephens and the Introduction of Black Slavery in Georgia," *Georgia Historical Quarterly* 58, no. 1 (1974): p. 32.
29. See Wood, "Thomas Stephens"; and for a summary, see Betty Wood, "Slavery in Colonial Georgia," *New Georgia Encyclopedia*, September 19, 2002, accessed November 5, 2024, https://www.georgiaencyclopedia.org/articles/history-archaeology/slavery-in-colonial-georgia/; see also Betty Wood, *Slavery in Colonial Georgia, 1730–1775* (University of Georgia Press, 1984), chap. 4.
30. William A. Pettigrew, *Freedom's Debt: The Royal African Company and the Politics of the Atlantic Slave Trade, 1672–1752* (University of North Carolina Press, 2013), pp. 192–93.
31. Marcia Pointon, "Slavery and the Possibility of Portraiture," in *Slave Portraiture in the Atlantic World*, ed. Agnes Lugo-Ortiz and Angela Rosenthal (Cambridge University Press,

2016), pp. 44–46; see the portrait at: William Hoare, "Ayuba Suleiman Diallo," oil on canvas, 1733, National Portrait Gallery, accessed November 12, 2024, https://www.npg.org.uk/collections/search/portrait/mw202604/Ayuba-Suleiman-Diallo

32 This section is from Thomas Bluett, *Some Memoirs of the Life of Job, the Son of Solomon, the High Priest of Boonda in Africa* (London, 1734), unless otherwise indicated.

33 Pettigrew, *Freedom's Debt*, p. 194.

34 Jason T. Sharples, *The World That Fear Made: Slave Revolts and Conspiracy Scares in Early America* (University of Pennsylvania Press, 2020), p. 110; Daniel Horsmanden, *The New-York Conspiracy, or a History of the Negro Plot* (New York: Southwick & Pelsue, 1810), pp. 24–25; Jill Lepore, *New York Burning: Liberty, Slavery, and Conspiracy in Eighteenth-Century Manhattan* (Vintage Books, 2005), chap. 2, EPUB.

35 On the persistent fear of slave revolts, see Sharples, *The World That Fear Made*.

36 Horsmanden, *The New-York Conspiracy*, p. 29.

37 The main surviving account was a collation of transcripts published in 1744 by Daniel Horsmanden, who was also the lead investigator and a justice on the Supreme Court of Judicature, titled *The New-York Conspiracy, or a History of the Negro Plot, with the Journal of the Proceedings Against the Conspirators at New-York in the Years 1741–42*. Other documents were lost in a fire, almost no letters remain, and the city's newspapers either are missing for those dates or have only short reports. See Lepore, *New York Burning*, chap. 4.

38 Sharples, *The World That Fear Made*, p. 106; Horsmanden, *The New-York Conspiracy*, p. 274.

39 Sharples, *The World That Fear Made*, pp. 107–08.

40 Horsmanden, *The New-York Conspiracy*, p. 15.

41 Sharples, *The World That Fear Made*, p. 111.

42 Horsmanden, *The New-York Conspiracy*, pp. 16–18.

43 Ibid., pp. 37–39.

44 Lepore, *New York Burning*, chap. 3.

45 Sharples, *The World That Fear Made*, pp. 115–16; Ben Hughes, *When I Die, I Shall Return to My Own Land: The New York City Slave Revolt of 1712* (Yardley, PA: Westholme Publishing, 2021), p. 181.

46 Lepore, *New York Burning*, chap. 6.

47 Sharples, *The World That Fear Made* p. 117; Horsmanden, *The New-York Conspiracy*, pp. 99–100.

48 Sharples, *The World That Fear Made*, p. 108.

49 Lepore, *New York Burning*, preface.

50 Leslie M. Harris, *In the Shadow of Slavery: African-Americans in New York City, 1626–1863* (University of Chicago Press, 2003), p. 46.

Chapter 16

1 David Geggus, ed., *The Haitian Revolution: A Documentary History* (Indianapolis: Hackett, 2014), pp. 19–20. See also Médéric-Louis-Élie Moreau de Saint-Méry, *Description topographique . . . de Saint-Domingue*, Philadelphia, 1797–1798, vol. 1, pp. 651–53, accessible at https://gallica.bnf.fr/ark:/12148/bpt6k111179t/f674.item.

2 Marlene L. Daut, *Awakening the Ashes: An Intellectual History of the Haitian Revolution* (University of North Carolina Press, 2023), p. 103, Kindle; *Relation d'une conspiration tramée par les Negres dans l'Isle de San Domingue* (Paris?, 1758), p. 5, Library of Congress,

https://tile.loc.gov/storage-services/service/gdc/gdcwdl/wd/l_/14/72/0/wdl_14720/wdl_14720.pdf.
3. Estimates of the number of captives transported to French Saint-Domingue, 1697–1797, SlaveVoyages: The Trans-Atlantic Slave Trade Database, accessed October 23, 2024, https://www.slavevoyages.org/voyages/IEtd37SQ.
4. Trevor Burnard and John Garrigus. *The Plantation Machine: Atlantic Capitalism in French Saint-Domingue and British Jamaica* (University of Pennsylvania Press, 2016), p. 43.
5. Carolyn E. Fick, *The Making of Haiti: The Saint Domingue Revolution from Below* (University of Tennessee Press, 1990), p. 52.
6. Laurent Dubois, *Avengers of the New World: The Story of the Haitian Revolution* (Belknap Press, 2004), pp. 54–55.
7. "Judge Courtin's Reflection on Macandal's Interrogation," translated in Laurent Dubois and John D. Garrigus, eds., *Slave Revolution in the Caribbean, 1789–1804: A Brief History with Documents* (Bedford/St Martin's, 2006), p. 41.
8. Fick, *The Making of Haiti*, p. 60.
9. Translated in Geggus, *The Haitian Revolution*, pp. 19–20; also in Médéric Louis Élie Moreau de Saint-Méry, *Description topographique . . . de Saint-Domingue*, vol. 1 (Philadelphia, 1797–1798), pp. 651–53, https://gallica.bnf.fr/ark:/12148/bpt6k111179t/f674.item.
10. Monique Allewaert, "Super Fly: François Makandal's Colonial Semiotics," *American Literature* 91, no. 3 (2019): p. 465.
11. Ibid., pp. 468–70.
12. M. de C., "Makandal, histoire veritable," *Mercure de France*, September 15, 1787, p. 106.
13. Translated in Geggus, *The Haitian Revolution*, pp. 19–20.
14. Geggus, *The Haitian Revolution*, p. 19.
15. Fick, *The Making of Haiti*, p. 60.
16. Ibid., p. 61; Daut, *Awakening the Ashes*, p. 102.
17. Sylviane A. Diouf, *Servants of Allah: African Muslims Enslaved in the Americas* (New York University Press, 2013), pp. 216–17.
18. Fick, *The Making of Haiti*, p. 63.
19. Moreau de Saint-Méry, *Description topographique*, p. 652.
20. Ibid.
21. *Relation d'une conspiration*, p. 5.
22. "Judge Courtin's Reflection," p. 41.
23. Dubois, *Avengers of the New World*, p. 51.
24. Geggus, *The Haitian Revolution*, pp. 19–20.
25. Ibid.
26. Ibid.
27. *Relation d'une conspiration*, pp. 2, 4.
28. Fick, *The Making of Haiti*, p. 62.
29. *Relation d'une conspiration*, p. 5.
30. Fick, *The Making of Haiti*, p. 62.
31. For more on the afterlife of Makandal, see Daut, *Awakening the Ashes*, pp. 109–12.
32. "Planters' Account of Médor's Confession (1757)," translated in Dubois and Garrigus, *Slave Revolution in the Caribbean*, p. 40.
33. Waldemar Westergaard, "Account of the Negro Rebellion on St. Croix, Danish West Indies, 1759," *Journal of Negro History* 11, no. 1 (1926): pp. 53–54.

34 Ibid., p. 54.
35 Ibid.
36 Ibid., p. 55.
37 Ibid.
38 Ibid.; Michael Craton, *Testing the Chains: Resistance to Slavery in the British West Indies* (Cornell University Press, 1982), p. 124.
39 Westergaard, "Account of the Negro Rebellion on St. Croix," pp. 56–57.
40 Quoted in Ibid., pp. 59–61.
41 Ibid., p. 58.
42 Ibid., p. 52.
43 Ibid., pp. 51–52.
44 Vincent Brown, *Tacky's Revolt: The Story of an Atlantic Slave War* (Belknap Press, 2020), p. 130; Craton, *Testing the Chains*, p. 129.
45 Quoted in Brown, *Tacky's Revolt*, p. 130.
46 The excellent *Tacky's Revolt* by Vincent Brown is indicative of this scholarship, and this section on Jamaican revolts 1760–61 is indebted to that work.
47 Brown, *Tacky's Revolt*, p. 7.
48 Ibid., p. 138.
49 Ibid., p. 145.
50 Ibid., p. 147.
51 Craton, *Testing the Chains*, p. 136.
52 Brown, *Tacky's Revolt*, pp. 151–52; 157
53 Ibid., p. 164.
54 Ibid., p. 169.
55 Ibid., p. 1.
56 Ibid., p. 174.
57 Ibid., pp. 63–65.
58 Ibid., pp. 185–187; see also Trevor Burnard, *Jamaica in the Age of Revolution* (University of Pennsylvania Press, 2020), chap. 4.
59 Ibid, pp. 198–99.
60 Craton, *Testing the Chains*, p. 138.
61 Craton, *Testing the Chains*, p. 139; Brown, *Tacky's Revolt*, pp. 222–23.
62 Elena A. Schneider, "A Narrative of Escape: Self Liberation by Sea and the Mental Worlds of the Enslaved," *Slavery & Abolition* 42, no. 3 (2021): p. 488.
63 Brown, *Tacky's Revolt*, pp. 213–214.
64 Quoted in Craton, *Testing the Chains*, p. 138; Brown, *Tacky's Revolt*, pp. 216–219.
65 Craton, *Testing the Chains*, pp. 138–139.
66 Aphra Behn, *Oroonoko* (Penguin Classics, 2003), p. 13.
67 Ibid., p. 63.
68 Ibid., p. 67.
69 Ibid., p. 76.
70 Ibid., pp. xx–xxi.
71 Ibid., p. xxxi.
72 The following section on Coffij and the events of 1763 Berbice is indebted to the excellent *Blood on the River: A Chronicle of Mutiny and Freedom on the West Coast*, by Marjoleine Kars (London: Profile Books, 2022).
73 Kars, *Blood on the River*, p. 16.

74 Quoted in Ibid., p. 22.
75 Ibid., p. 75.
76 Ibid., pp. 86–87.
77 Ibid., p. 79.
78 Quoted in Kars, *Blood on the River*, p. 110.
79 Ibid., pp. 135–136.
80 Ibid., pp. 142–146.
81 Quoted in Ibid., p. 161
82 Kars, *Blood on the River*, p. 167.
83 Ibid., pp. 226–227; 240.
84 Ibid., pp. 243; 254.
85 Estimates of the number of captives transported to the Americas, 1700–1763, SlaveVoyages: The Trans-Atlantic Slave Trade Database, accessed October 23, 2024, https://www.slavevoyages.org/voyages/RdqUkRkr.
86 Sue Peabody, "Slavery, Freedom, and the Law in the Atlantic World, 1420–1807," in *The Cambridge World History of Slavery*, vol. 3, ed. David Eltis and Stanley L. Engerman (Cambridge University Press, 2011), p. 623.
87 Seymour Drescher, *Abolition: A History of Slavery and Antislavery* (Cambridge University Press, 2009), p. 94.
88 Alejandro de la Fuente and Ariela J. Gross, *Becoming Free, Becoming Black: Race, Freedom, and Law in Cuba, Virginia, and Louisiana* (Cambridge University Press, 2020), p. 50.
89 Quoted in Sue Peabody, *"There Are No Slaves in France": The Political Culture of Race and Slavery in the Ancien Régime* (Oxford University Press, 1996), pp. 119–120.
90 Pierre H. Boulle, "Racial Purity or Legal Clarity? The Status of Black Residents in Eighteenth-Century France," *Journal of The Historical Society* 6, no. 1 (2006): pp. 31–39.
91 Drescher, *Abolition*, p. 104.
92 Cristina Nogueira da Silva and Keila Grinburg, "Soil Free from Slaves: Slave Law in Late Eighteenth- and Early Nineteenth-Century Portugal," *Slavery & Abolition* 32, no. 3 (September 2011): p. 433; see also Gabriel Paquette, *Imperial Portugal in the Age of Atlantic Revolutions: The Luso-Brazilian World, c. 1777–1850* (Cambridge University Press, 2013), chap. 1.
93 Quoted in Nogueira da Silva and Grinburg, "Soil Free from Slaves," pp. 434–36.
94 Ibid., p. 432.
95 Peabody, "Slavery, Freedom, and the Law," p. 625.
96 Quobna Ottobah Cugoano, *Thoughts and Sentiments on the Evil of Slavery*, ed. Vincent Carretta (Penguin Classics, 1999), p. x.
97 Robin Blackburn, *The Overthrow of Colonial Slavery 1776–1848* (Verso, 1988), p. 80.
98 Stephen Mullen et al., "Black Runaways in Eighteenth-Century Britain," in *Britain's Black Past*, ed. Gretchen H. Gerzina (Liverpool University Press, 2020), p. 81; see also the online database Runaway Slaves in Britain: Bondage, Freedom and Race in the Eighteenth Century, accessed November 6, 2024, https://www.runaways.gla.ac.uk/.
99 Granville Sharp, *Extract from A Representation of the Injustice and Dangerous Tendency of Tolerating Slavery, or Admitting the Least Claim of Private Property in the Persons of Men in England* (London, 1769), pp. 6–7.
100 *Runaway Slaves in Britain: Bondage, Freedom and Race in the Eighteenth Century*, accessed November 6, 2024, https://www.runaways.gla.ac.uk/database/display/?rid=33.

Chapter 17

1. Bible, Acts 8:26–40, AV.
2. The church of Saint James's Piccadilly held a number of events in 2023 to mark the 250th anniversary of Cugoano's baptism; see Saint James's Piccadilly website, https://www.sjp.org.uk/about-music-arts-ideas/cugoano/.
3. Quobna Ottobah Cugoano, *Thoughts and Sentiments on the Evil of Slavery*, ed. Vincent Carretta (Penguin Classics, 1999), pp. ix–xi.
4. Quoted in William M. Wiecek, "Somerset: Lord Mansfield and the Legitimacy of Slavery in the Anglo-American World," *Law Review* 42, no. 1 (Autumn 1974): pp. 86–87.
5. Quoted in Vincent Carretta, *Phillis Wheatley: Biography of a Genius in Bondage* (University of Georgia Press, 2014), chap. 5, EPUB.
6. See Paula Byrne, *Belle: The True Story of Dido Belle* (William Collins, 2014).
7. Wiecek, "Somerset," p. 87.
8. Charles R. Foy, "'Unkle Sommerset's' Freedom: Liberty in England for Black Sailors," *Journal of Maritime Research* 13, no. 1 (2011): p. 22.
9. Cugoano, *Thoughts and Sentiments*, p. 7.
10. Ibid., p. xviii.
11. Ibid., p. xix.
12. Ibid., p. 10.
13. Ibid., p. 23.
14. James Albert Ukawsaw Gronniosaw, *Narrative of the Most Remarkable Particulars in the Life of James Albert Ukawsaw Gronniosaw, an African Prince, as Related by Himself* (third edition published in 1790 in Leeds as *Wonderous Grace Display'd in the Life and Conversion of James Albert Ukawsaw Gronniosaw, an African Prince*, 3rd ed.), p. 9.
15. Ibid., p. 14.
16. Ibid., p. 24.
17. Ibid., pp. 25–30.
18. Carretta, *Phillis Wheatley*, chap. 2.
19. Gronniosaw, *Wonderous Grace*, p. 46.
20. Carretta, *Phillis Wheatley*, chap. 1.
21. Ibid., chap. 3.
22. Ibid., chaps. 2–3.
23. "Review of New Publications," *The London Magazine, or Gentleman's Monthly Intelligencer*, September 1773, p. 456, https://babel.hathitrust.org/cgi/pt?id=mdp.39015021278604&view=1up&seq=524.
24. Carretta, *Phillis Wheatley*, chaps. 4–5.
25. Ibid., chap. 4.
26. Quoted in Ibid., chap. 3.
27. Cugoano, *Thoughts and Sentiments*, p. 17.
28. Gretchen Gerzina, *Black England: A Forgotten Georgian History* (John Murray, 2022), chap. 2.
29. Much of Sancho's early life has proved difficult for historians to verify; see Brycchan Carey, "'The Extraordinary Negro': Ignatius Sancho, Joseph Jekyll, and the Problem of Biography," *British Journal for Eighteenth-Century Studies* 26, no. 1 (2003): pp. 1–13.
30. Ignatius Sancho, *Letters of the Late Ignatius Sancho, an African*, vol. 1 (London: J. Nichols, 1782), pp. v–ix.

31 Carretta, *Phillis Wheatley*, chap. 5.
32 Sancho, *Letters of the Late Ignatius Sancho*, p. 176.
33 Ibid., pp. 123–25.
34 Vincent Carretta, "Three West Indian Writers of the 1780s Revisited and Revised," *Research in African Literatures* 29, no. 4 (1998): p. 75.
35 There is also the possibility that they briefly had the same enslaver, Alexander Campbell. He brought Cugoano to England, but he may have earlier lived in Virginia when Equiano was sold there. See Carretta, "Three West Indian Writers," p. 76.
36 Olaudah Equiano, *The Interesting Narrative of the Life of Olaudah Equiano*, ed. Brycchan Carey (Oxford University Press, 2018), introduction, EPUB.
37 Ibid., chap. 4.
38 Ibid., chap. 5.
39 Ibid., chap. 7. It's possible that Equiano misremembers and actually heard Whitefield the previous year, in Savannah, Georgia. See endnote 110.
40 Ibid.
41 Ibid.
42 Ibid., chap. 8.
43 Ibid.
44 Ibid.
45 Ibid.
46 Ibid., chap. 9.
47 Ibid., chap. 10.

Chapter 18

1 The Kalinago name for Saint Vincent was Yourourmaÿn; see Christopher Taylor, *The Black Carib Wars: Freedom, Survival, and the Making of the Garifuna* (University Press of Mississippi, 2012), p. 9.
2 Lennox Honychurch, *In the Forests of Freedom: The Fighting Maroons of Dominica* (London: Papillote Press, 2017), p. 25.
3 Ibid., pp. 25, 30.
4 Ibid., chap. 5.
5 Tessa Murphy, *The Creole Archipelago: Race and Borders in the Colonial Caribbean* (University of Pennsylvania Press, 2021), pp. 43–45.
6 Ibid., p. 50.
7 Ibid., p. 153.
8 Michael Craton, *Testing the Chains: Resistance to Slavery in the British West Indies* (Cornell University Press, 1982), pp. 153–155.
9 Ibid.
10 William Young, *An Account of the Black Charaibs in the Island of St. Vincent's; with the Charaib Treaty of 1779, and Other Original Documents* (London, 1795), https://archive.org/details/accountofblackch00youn.
11 Ibid., p. 9; Craton, *Testing the Chains*, pp. 146–147.
12 This point is made by Julie Chun Kim, "The Caribs of St. Vincent and Indigenous Resistance during the Age of Revolutions," *Early American Studies* 11, no. 1 (2013): p. 123.
13 Murphy, *The Creole Archipelago*, p. 163.
14 Young, *An Account of the Black Charaibs*, pp. 1–2.

15 Craton, *Testing the Chains*, pp. 146–47.
16 Quoted in Taylor, *The Black Carib Wars*, pp. 57–58.
17 Quoted in Ibid., p. 67.
18 Ibid.
19 Taylor, *The Black Carib Wars*, p. 68.
20 Ibid., p. 72.
21 Quoted in Taylor, *The Black Carib Wars*, p. 70.
22 Taylor, *The Black Carib Wars*, pp. 71–72.
23 Murphy, *The Creole Archipelago*, p. 161; Taylor, *The Black Carib Wars*, p. 74.
24 Craton, *Testing the Chains*, p. 151.
25 Ibid.
26 Taylor, *The Black Carib Wars*, p. 75.
27 Quoted in Murphy, *The Creole Archipelago*, p. 166.
28 Sarah Thomas, "Envisaging a Future for Slavery: Agostino Brunias and the Imperial Politics of Labor and Reproduction," *Eighteenth-Century Studies* 52, no. 1 (2018): pp. 117–18.
29 Ibid., pp. 118–19.
30 Ibid., p. 116.
31 Ibid., p. 124.
32 Cugoano, *Thoughts and Sentiments*, p. 16.
33 Mia L. Bagneris, *Colouring the Caribbean: Race and the Art of Agostino Brunias* (Manchester University Press, 2018), pp. 40–45.
34 Ibid., pp. 40–41.
35 Quoted in F. Nwabueze Okoye, "Chattel Slavery as the Nightmare of the American Revolutionaries," *William and Mary Quarterly* 37, no. 1 (1980): p. 3.
36 Samuel Johnson, *Taxation no Tyranny; an Answer to the Resolutions and Address of the American Congress* (London, 1775), p. 89; Samuel Johnson employed a black manservant named Francis Barber, who may have known other prominent black Britons like Ignatius Sancho; see Gerzina, *Black England*, chap. 2.
37 Quoted in Drescher, *Abolition*, pp. 124–25; available at National Archives, Founders Online, accessed November 9, 2024, https://founders.archives.gov/documents/Jefferson/01-01-02-0176-0004.
38 Manisha Sinha, *The Slave's Cause: A History of Abolition* (Yale University Press, 2016), p. 40.
39 Cugoano, *Thoughts and Sentiments*, xi.
40 Mary Turner, "Slave Worker Rebellions and Revolution in the Americas to 1804," in *The Cambridge World History of Slavery*, vol. 3, ed. David Eltis and Stanley L. Engerman (Cambridge University Press, 2011), p. 679.
41 Sinha, *The Slave's Cause*, p. 48; Jason T. Sharples, *The World That Fear Made: Slave Revolts and Conspiracy Scares in Early America* (University of Pennsylvania Press, 2020), p. 214. For the impact of the American Revolution on black mariners and the Royal Navy, see Charles R. Foy, "'Unkle Sommerset's' Freedom: Liberty in England for Black Sailors," *Journal of Maritime Research* 13, no. 1 (2011): pp. 21–36.
42 Craton, *Testing the Chains*, pp. 174, 364n7; Richard B. Sheridan, "The Jamaican Slave Insurrection Scare of 1776 and the American Revolution," *Journal of Negro History* 61, no. 3 (1976): p. 295.
43 Craton, *Testing the Chains*, p. 177; Vincent Brown, *Tacky's Revolt: The Story of an Atlantic Slave War* (Belknap Press, 2020), pp. 238–239.
44 Quoted in Craton, *Testing the Chains*, p. 174.

45 Sheridan, "The Jamaican Slave Insurrection Scare of 1776," pp. 290–308.
46 Craton, *Testing the Chains*, p. 175.
47 Sinha, *The Slave's Cause*, p. 51; for more specific troop numbers, see Alan Gilbert, *Black Patriots and Loyalists: Fighting for Emancipation in the War for Independence* (University of Chicago Press, 2012), chap. 5, EPUB.
48 Judith Van Buskirk, *Standing in Their Own Light: African American Patriots in the American Revolution* (University of Oklahoma Press, 2017), pp. 9–10, 102–06.
49 Sinha, *The Slave's Cause*, p. 47; Van Buskirk, *Standing in Their Own Light*, p. 61.
50 Gilbert, *Black Patriots and Loyalists*, chap. 6.
51 Van Buskirk, *Standing in Their Own Light*, pp. 3–4.
52 Gary B. Nash, *The Forgotten Fifth: African Americans in the Age of Revolution* (Harvard University Press, 2006), p. 15.
53 Quoted in Gilbert, *Black Patriots and Loyalists*, chap. 5.
54 Philip D. Morgan and Andrew Jackson O'Shaughnessy, "Arming Slaves in the American Revolution," in *Arming Slaves: From Classical Times to the Modern Age*, ed. Christopher Leslie Brown and Philip D. Morgan (Yale University Press, 2006), p. 180.
55 Maria Alessandra Bollettino, "'Of Equal or of More Service': Black Soldiers and the British Empire in the Mid-Eighteenth-Century Caribbean," *Slavery & Abolition* 38, no. 3 (2017): pp. 510–11.
56 David Lambert, *Soldiers of Uncertain Rank: The West India Regiments in British Imperial Culture* (Cambridge University Press, 2024), p. 9.
57 Alejandro de la Fuente and Ariela J. Gross, *Becoming Free, Becoming Black: Race, Freedom, and Law in Cuba, Virginia, and Louisiana* (Cambridge University Press, 2020), p. 76.
58 Paul Clammer, *Black Crown: Henry Christophe, the Haitian Revolution and the Caribbean's Forgotten Kingdom.* (Hurst & Company, 2023), pp. 22–29.
59 Nash, *The Forgotten Fifth*, p. 23.
60 Quoted in Thomas J. Davis, "Emancipation Rhetoric, Natural Rights, and Revolutionary New England: A Note on Four Black Petitions in Massachusetts, 1773–1777," *New England Quarterly* 62, no. 2 (1989): pp. 251–254.
61 Ibid., p. 252.
62 Ibid., p. 253.
63 Ibid., p. 255.
64 Quoted in Sinha, *The Slave's Cause*, p. 43.
65 Ibid., p. 75.
66 Jeffery A. Fortin, "Paul Cuffe's Journey from 'Musta' to Atlantic-African, in *Atlantic Biographies: Individuals and Peoples in the Atlantic World (Vol 27).* Jeffrey A. Fortin and Mark Meuwese, eds. (Brill, 2014), p. 324.
67 Quoted in Ibid., pp. 330–331.
68 Sari Edelstein, "'Good Mother, Farewell': Elizabeth Freeman's Silence and the Stories of Mumbet," *New England Quarterly* 92, no. 4 (2019): pp. 585–87.
69 Ibid., p. 587.
70 Catherine Sedgwick, "Slavery in New England," *Bentley's Miscellany* 34 (1853): p. 421. For a critical reading of the Sedgwick essay, see Edelstein, "Good Mother, Farewell."
71 Estimates of the number of voyages beginning in Rhode Island, 1701–1820, SlaveVoyages: The Trans-Atlantic Slave Trade Database, accessed November 10, 2024, https://www.slavevoyages.org/voyages/bTRT4G3C; Anne Farrow et al., *Complicity: How the North Promoted, Prolonged, and Profited from Slavery* (Ballantine, 2005), chap. 5, EPUB.

72 Farrow et al., *Complicity*, chap. 2; Williams, *Capitalism and Slavery*, p. 74.
73 On this point, see Sean Wilentz, "The Radicalism of Northern Abolition," *New England Quarterly* 96, no. 1 (2023): pp. 8–26.
74 Sinha, *The Slave's Cause*, p. 70.
75 Manjapra, *Black Ghost of Empire*, pp. 20-23.

Chapter 19

1 Seymour Drescher, *Abolition: A History of Slavery and Antislavery* (Cambridge University Press, 2009), p. 131; David Waldstreicher, *Slavery's Constitution: From Revolution to Ratification* (Hill and Wang, 2009), prologue, EPUB.
2 Federalist No. 54, *The Avalon Project*, accessed November 10, 2024, https://avalon.law.yale.edu/18th_century/fed54.asp. On the "legal fiction" of the three-fifths clause, see Malick W. Ghachem, "The Slave's Two Bodies: The Life of an American Legal Fiction," *William and Mary Quarterly* 60, no. 4 (2003): pp. 809–42.
3 Full text online at Constitution Annotated, accessed November 10, 2024, https://constitution.congress.gov/constitution/article-1/#article-1-section-9.
4 For more detail of the debates, see Waldstreicher, *Slavery's Constitution*, chap. 2.
5 Full text at National Archives, https://www.archives.gov/founding-docs/constitution-transcript.
6 Manisha Sinha, *The Slave's Cause: A History of Abolition* (Yale University Press, 2016), p. 51.
7 For the remarkable story of Harry Washington, see Cassandra Pybus, *Epic Journeys of Freedom: Runaway Slaves of the American Revolution and Their Global Quest for Liberty* (Beacon Press, 2006).
8 Maya Jasanoff, "The Other Side of Revolution: Loyalists in the British Empire," *William and Mary Quarterly* 65, no. 2 (2008): p. 208; see also Maya Jasanoff, *Liberty's Exiles: American Loyalists in the Revolutionary World* (Knopf, 2011). For background on the "black loyalist" terminology debate, see the introduction in Christopher Curry, *Freedom and Resistance: A Social History of Black Loyalists in the Bahamas* (University of Florida Press, 2017), Introduction. Kindle.
9 Quoted in Pybus, *Epic Journeys*, p. 148.
10 Harvey Amani Whitfield, "The African Diaspora in Atlantic Canada: History, Historians, and Historiography," *Acadiensis* 46, no. 1 (2017): pp. 213–32.
11 Text of the act is at the Canadian Encyclopedia, https://www.thecanadianencyclopedia.ca/en/article/1793-act-to-limit-slavery-in-upper-canada.
12 Curry, *Freedom and Resistance*, pp. 9–10.
13 Ibid., p. 76.
14 Ibid., p. 71.
15 Ibid., p. 80.
16 Ibid., pp. 80–81.
17 Quoted in Curry, *Freedom and Resistance*, p. 82.
18 Pybus, *Epic Journeys*, p. 83.
19 Ibid., pp. 77–78.
20 Ibid., p. 103.
21 Ibid., p. 107; see also Gerzina, *Black England*, chap. 5.
22 Pybus, *Epic Journeys of Freedom*, p. 108.

23. Estimates of the number of captives embarked in Africa, 1780–1790, SlaveVoyages: The Trans-Atlantic Slave Trade Database, accessed October 24, 2024, https://www.slavevoyages.org/voyages/xlSUrYJM.
24. Quoted in Pybus, *Epic Journeys*, p. 109.
25. Ibid., p. 117.
26. Equiano, *Interesting Narrative*, chap. 12.
27. Pybus, *Epic Journeys*, p. 140.
28. James Walvin, *Zong: A Massacre, the Law and the End of Slavery* (Yale University Press, 2017), p. 92.
29. Quoted in Ibid., pp. 97–98.
30. Ibid., pp. 97, 99; the *Zong*, voyage ID: 84106, in SlaveVoyages: The Trans-Atlantic Slave Trade Database, accessed October 24, 2024, https://www.slavevoyages.org/voyages/eKkQ5K3b.
31. Henry Roscoe, *Reports of Cases Argued and Determined in the Court of King's Bench*, vol. 3 (London, 1831), pp. 232–35.
32. Walvin, *Zong*, p. 106.
33. Ibid., pp. 140–42.
34. Quoted in Ibid., p. 146.
35. Quoted in Ibid., p. 153.
36. Ibid., p. 144.
37. Ibid., pp. 154–155.
38. Elizabeth Donnan, *Documents Illustrative of the History of the Slave Trade to America*, vol. 2, no. 267, pp. 555–57.
39. Walvin, *Zong*, pp. 148–49.
40. Christopher Leslie Brown, *Moral Capital: Foundations of British Abolitionism* (University of North Carolina Press, 2006), p. 284.
41. Quobna Ottobah Cugoano, *Thoughts and Sentiments on the Evil of Slavery*, ed. Vincent Carretta (Penguin Classics, 1999), p. 85.
42. Ibid., p. 10.
43. Brown, *Moral Capital*, p. 1.
44. Gerzina, *Black England*, p. 216.
45. Brown, *Moral Capital*, pp. 27–29.
46. Cugoano, *Thoughts and Sentiments*, p. 98.
47. Ibid., p. 24.
48. Drescher, *Abolition*, p. 211.
49. Robin Blackburn, *The Making of New World Slavery*, pp. 433, 435; for more detail on these numbers, see Seymour Drescher, *Econocide: British Slavery in the Era of Abolition*, 2nd ed. (University of North Carolina Press, 2010), chap. 3.
50. Eric Williams, *Capitalism and Slavery* (Penguin Modern Classics, 2022), pp. 137–38.
51. Drescher, *Abolition*, pp. 214–215.
52. Anne K. Mellor, "Sex, Violence, and Slavery: Blake and Wollstonecraft," *Huntington Library Quarterly* 58, no. 3 (1995): pp. 345–70.
53. Equiano, *Interesting Narrative*, introduction.
54. Paul Clammer, *Black Crown: Henry Christophe, the Haitian Revolution and the Caribbean's Forgotten Kingdom* (C. Hurst, 2023), p. 44.
55. Drescher, *Abolition*, pp. 151–52.

56 See Pernille Røge, *Economistes and the Reinvention of Empire: France in the Americas and Africa, c. 1750–1802* (Cambridge University Press), 2019.
57 Henry Louis Gates Jr. and Andrew S. Curran, *Who's Black and Why? A Hidden Chapter from the Eighteenth-Century Invention of Race* (Belknap Press, 2022), pp. ix; 6.
58 Estimates of the number of captives transported to Saint-Domingue, 1763–1789, Slave-Voyages: The Trans-Atlantic Slave Trade Database, accessed October 24, 2024, https://www.slavevoyages.org/voyages/QQCBtPxu.
59 Røge, *Economistes and the Reinvention of Empire*, p. 73.
60 David Geggus, *The Haitian Revolution: A Documentary History* (Indianapolis: Hackett, 2014), chap. 21.
61 John D. Garrigus, *Before Haiti: Race and Citizenship in French Saint-Domingue* (Palgrave Macmillan, 2006), pp. 171, 190.
62 Quoted in Garrigus, *Before Haiti*, p. 167; see also John D. Garrigus, "Vincent Ogé 'Jeune' (1757–91): Social Class and Free Colored Mobilization on the Eve of the Haitian Revolution," *The Americas* 68, no. 1 (2011): p. 33.
63 Garrigus, "Vincent Ogé 'Jeune,'" p. 47.
64 Both letters quoted in Laurent Dubois and John D. Garrigus, *Slave Revolution in the Caribbean, 1789–1804: A Brief History with Documents* (Bedford/St Martin's, 2006), pp. 50–53.
65 Ibid., p. 54.
66 Geggus, *The Haitian Revolution*, chap. 23; Garrigus, "Vincent Ogé 'Jeune,'" pp. 48–49.
67 Garrigus, "Vincent Ogé 'Jeune,'" p. 50.
68 Ibid., p. 53.
69 Quoted in Geggus, *The Haitian Revolution*, chap. 27.
70 Chavannes was at the Battle of Savannah; see Garrigus, "Vincent Ogé 'Jeune,'" p. 54.
71 Garrigus, "Vincent Ogé 'Jeune,'" p. 56.
72 John D. Garrigus, "'Thy Coming Fame, Ogé! Is Sure': New Evidence on Ogé's 1790 Revolt and the Beginnings of the Haitian Revolution," in *Assumed Identities: The Meaning of Race in the Atlantic World*, ed. John D. Garrigus and Christopher Morris (Texas A&M Press, 2010), p. 21.
73 Garrigus, "Thy coming fame, Ogé! Is sure," pp. 32–34.
74 Ibid., pp. 33; 35–36.
75 Graham T. Nessler, *An Islandwide Struggle for Freedom: Revolution, Emancipation, and Reenslavement in Hispaniola, 1789–1809* (University of North Carolina Press, 2016), p. 31.
76 Garrigus, "Thy coming fame, Ogé! Is Sure," p. 21.
77 Ibid., p. 32.
78 Geggus, *The Haitian Revolution*, chap. 29.
79 Garrigus, "Vincent Ogé 'Jeune,'" p. 61.

Chapter 20

1 Vincent Brown, *Tacky's Revolt: The Story of an Atlantic Slave War* (Belknap Press, 2020), p. 239.
2 Laurent Dubois, *Avengers of the New World: The Story of the Haitian Revolution* (Belknap Press, 2004), pp. 99–100. See also the classic work on the Haitian Revolution, C. L. R. James, *The Black Jacobins* (Penguin, 2001).

3. Some consider this moment an integral part of the history and development of Haitian voudou; see Dubois, *Avengers*, p. 102.
4. Paul Clammer, *Black Crown: Henry Christophe, the Haitian Revolution and the Caribbean's Forgotten Kingdom* (C. Hurst, 2023), p. 31.
5. Ibid., p. 46.
6. Carolyn E. Fick, *The Making of Haiti: The Saint Domingue Revolution from Below* (University of Tennessee Press, 1990), p. 106; Sudhir Hazareesingh, *Black Spartacus: The Epic Life of Toussaint Louverture* (Allen Lane, 2020), p. 48.
7. Dubois, *Avengers*, p. 109.
8. Ibid., pp. 105–06.
9. Quoted in Laurent Dubois and John D. Garrigus, *Slave Revolution in the Caribbean, 1789–1804: A Brief History with Documents* (Bedford/St Martin's, 2006), p. 82.
10. Graham T. Nessler, *An Islandwide Struggle for Freedom: Revolution, Emancipation, and Reenslavement in Hispaniola, 1789–1809* (University of North Carolina Press, 2016), p. 36; Fick, *The Making of Haiti*, p. 113.
11. Fick, *The Making of Haiti*, p. 113; Hazareesingh, *Black Spartacus*, p. 50; Jane G. Landers, *Atlantic Creoles in the Age of Revolutions* (Harvard University Press, 2010), p. 58.
12. Fick, *The Making of Haiti*, p. 113.
13. Dubois, *Avengers*, p. 120.
14. Ibid., p. 123.
15. Quoted in Dubois and Garrigus, *Slave Revolution in the Caribbean*, p. 88.
16. Nessler, *An Islandwide Struggle*, pp. 36–37.
17. Dubois, *Avengers*, p. 129; Landers, *Atlantic Creoles*, p. 58.
18. Hazareesingh, *Black Spartacus*, p. 53.
19. Quoted in Nessler, *An Islandwide Struggle*, p. 38.
20. Dubois, *Avengers*, pp. 134–136.
21. Ibid., p. 130.
22. Landers, *Atlantic Creoles*, p. 67.
23. Dubois, *Avengers*, p. 142.
24. James, *The Black Jacobins*, p. 122.
25. Dubois, *Avengers*, p. 146.
26. Nessler, *An Islandwide Struggle*, pp. 33–34.
27. Ibid., p. 41.
28. Hazareesingh, *Black Spartacus*, p. 58
29. Quoted in Landers, *Atlantic Creoles*, p. 68.
30. Nessler, *An Islandwide Struggle*, p. 42.
31. Quoted in Hazareesingh, *Black Spartacus*, p. 41.
32. Hazareesingh, *Black Spartacus*, pp. 25–26.
33. Ibid., p. 30.
34. Ibid., p. 38.
35. Clammer, *Black Crown*, p. 55; Dubois, *Avengers*, p. 163.
36. Hazareesingh, *Black Spartacus*, p. 59.
37. Dubois, *Avengers*, p. 153.
38. Ibid.
39. Seymour Drescher, *Abolition: A History of Slavery and Antislavery* (Cambridge University Press, 2009), p. 219.
40. Ibid., p. 222.

41 Thomas Clarkson, *The True State of the Case, Respecting the Insurrection at St. Domingo* (Ipswich: J Bush, 1792), p. 3.
42 Drescher, *Abolition*, p. 220.
43 William Fox, *An Address to the People of Great Britain, on the Propriety of Abstaining from West India Sugar and Rum* (London, 1791), pp. 1, 7–8.
44 *Debate on a Motion for the Abolition of the Slave-Trade in the House of Commons* (London, 1792), p. 102.
45 Ibid., p. 127.
46 Ibid., p. 139.
47 Quoted in David Geggus, "The British Government and the Saint Domingue Slave Revolt, 1791–1793," *English Historical Review* 96, no. 379 (April 1981): p. 286.
48 Quoted in Dubois, *Avengers*, p. 166.
49 Geggus, "The British Government," p. 285.
50 Quoted in Dubois, *Avengers*, p. 167.
51 Dubois and Garrigus, *Slave Revolution in the Caribbean, 1789–1804*, p. 112.
52 Dubois, *Avengers*, p. 169. For more on Belley, see Christine Levecq, *Black Cosmopolitans: Race, Religion, and Republicanism in an Age of Revolution* (University of Virginia Press, 2019).
53 For more on their trials and tribulations in Paris, see Jeremy D. Popkin, *You Are All Free: The Haitian Revolution and the Abolition of Slavery* (Cambridge University Press, 2010), chap. 10.
54 Quoted in Dubois, *Avengers*, p. 170.
55 Dubois, *Avengers*, pp. 177–79.
56 Hazareesingh, *Black Spartacus*, pp. 36–37.

Chapter 21

1 Gwendolyn Midlo Hall, "The 1795 Slave Conspiracy in Pointe Coupée: Impact of the French Revolution," *Proceedings of the Annual Meeting of the French Colonial Historical Society* 15 (1992): p. 138.
2 Ulysses S. Ricard, "The Pointe Coupée Slave Conspiracy of 1791," *Proceedings of the Meeting of the French Colonial Historical Society* 15 (1992): p. 118.
3 Hall, "The 1795 Slave Conspiracy," p. 133.
4 Ricard, "The Pointe Coupée Slave Conspiracy of 1791," p. 119.
5 Ibid.
6 Ibid., p. 127.
7 For an overview and digitized sources, see "1795: Pointe Coupée, Louisiana," Louisiana Slave Conspiracies, accessed February 16, 2025, https://lsc.berkeley.edu.
8 Jack D. L. Holmes, "The Abortive Slave Revolt at Pointe Coupée, Lousiana, 1795," *Louisiana History: The Journal of the Louisiana Historical Association* 11, no. 4 (1970): p. 348.
9 Ibid., p. 345.
10 "Declaration of Jean Baptiste Riché, April 25, 1795," Louisiana Slave Conspiracies, accessed February 16, 2025, https://lsc.berkeley.edu/node/230/viewer.
11 "Statement of Françoise, May 6, 1795," Louisiana Slave Conspiracies, accessed February 16, 2025, https://lsc.berkeley.edu/node/247/viewer?page=1.
12 Holmes, "The Abortive Slave Revolt at Pointe Coupée," p. 347.
13 "Declaration of Antoine Sarrasin, May 11, 1795," Louisiana Slave Conspiracies, accessed February 16, 2025, https://lsc.berkeley.edu/node/292/viewer?page=2.

14 "Declaration of Antonio Cofi Mina, May 17, 1795," Louisiana Slave Conspiracies, accessed February 16, 2025, https://lsc.berkeley.edu/node/9769/viewer.
15 Hall, "The 1795 Slave Conspiracy," p. 135; Holmes, "The Abortive Slave Revolt at Pointe Coupée," p. 353.
16 Holmes, "The Abortive Slave Revolt at Pointe Coupée," p. 352.
17 Hall, "The 1795 Slave Conspiracy," p. 137.
18 Holmes, "The Abortive Slave Revolt at Pointe Coupée," pp. 325–53.
19 Ibid., p. 355.
20 Ramón Aizpurua, "Revolution and Politics in Venezuela and Curaçao," in *Curaçao in the Age of Revolutions, 1795–1800*, ed. Wim Klooster and Gert Oostindie (Leiden: KITLV Press, 2011), p. 98.
21 Ibid., p. 99.
22 Ibid.
23 Ibid., p. 100.
24 Ibid.
25 Ibid., p. 101.
26 David Patrick Geggus, "Slave Resistance in the Spanish Caribbean in the Mid-1700s," in *A Turbulent Time: The French Revolution and the Greater Caribbean*, ed. David Barry Gaspar and David Patrick Geggus (Indiana University Press, 1997), p. 133; Adriana Chira, *Patchwork Freedoms: Law, Slavery, and Race beyond Cuba's Plantation* (Cambridge University Press, 2022), pp. 60; 93–96. For more on the *cobrero* community, see María Elena Díaz, *The Virgin, the King, and the Royal Slaves of El Cobre: Negotiating Freedom in Colonial Cuba, 1670–1780* (Stanford University Press, 2000).
27 Quoted in Geggus, "Slave Resistance in the Spanish Caribbean," p. 134.
28 Ann Twinam, *Purchasing Whiteness: Pardos, Mulattos, and the Quest for Social Mobility in the Spanish Indies* (Stanford University Press, 2015), p. 13.
29 Chira, *Patchwork Freedoms*, pp. 93–96.
30 Guillermo A. Baralt, *Esclavos rebeldes: conspiraciones y sublevaciones de esclavos en Puerto Rico (1795–1873)*, 2nd ed. (Río Piedras: Ediciones Huracán, 1982), p. 16.
31 Quoted in Jane G. Landers, *Atlantic Creoles in the Age of Revolutions* (Harvard University Press, 2010), p. 77.
32 Gert Oostindie, "Slave Resistance, Colour Lines, and the Impact of the French and Haitian Revolutions in Curaçao," in *Curaçao in the Age of Revolutions, 1795–1800*, ed. Wim Klooster and Gert Oostindie (Leiden: KITLV Press, 2011), p. 5.
33 Charles do Rego and Lionel Janga, *Slavery and Resistance in Curaçao: The Rebellion of 1795* (Willemstad: Fundashon Parke Nashonal, 2009), pp. 46–47.
34 Ibid., p. 47.
35 Ibid., p. 48.
36 Oostindie, "Slave Resistance," p. 8.
37 David Geggus, "Slave Rebellion during the Age of Revolution," in *Curaçao in the Age of Revolutions, 1795–1800*, ed. Wim Klooster and Gert Oostindie (Leiden: KITLV Press, 2011), p. 33; Julius S. Scott, *The Common Wind: Afro-American Currents in the Age of the Haitian Revolution* (Verso, 2018), p. 180.
38 Quoted in Oostindie, "Slave Resistance," p. 8.
39 Ibid., p. 9.
40 Rego and Janga, *Slavery and Resistance in Curaçao*, p. 54.
41 Ibid., p. 58.

42 Ibid., p. 62.
43 Ibid., p. 61.
44 Christopher Taylor, *The Black Carib Wars: Freedom, Survival, and the Making of the Garifuna* (University Press of Mississippi, 2012), p. 114.
45 Ibid., p. 115.
46 Quoted in Michael Craton, *Testing the Chains: Resistance to Slavery in the British West Indies* (Cornell University Press, 1982), p. 190.
47 Ibid., pp. 190–91.
48 Quoted in Taylor, *The Black Carib Wars*, p. 119.
49 Ibid., p. 191.
50 Ibid., p. 120.
51 Ibid.
52 Ibid., pp. 120–121.
53 Ibid., pp. 122–23.
54 Ibid., pp. 124–125.
55 Craton, *Testing the Chains*, p. 194.
56 David Barry Gaspar, "La Guerre des Bois: Revolution, War, and Slavery in Saint Lucia, 1793–1838," in *A Turbulent Time: The French Revolution and the Greater Caribbean*, ed. David Barry Gaspar and David Patrick Geggus (Indiana University Press, 1997), p. 103.
57 Ibid., pp. 103, 121.
58 Ibid., p. 104.
59 Ibid., p. 106.
60 Craton, *Testing the Chains*, p. 200.
61 Gaspar, "La Guerre des Bois," p. 107.
62 Craton, *Testing the Chains*, p. 195.
63 Gaspar, "La Guerre des Bois," pp. 114–116.
64 Craton, *Testing the Chains*, p. 200.
65 Gaspar, "La Guerre des Bois," p. 113.
66 Quoted in Gaspar, "La Guerre des Bois," p. 115.
67 Ibid., p. 116.
68 Craton, *Testing the Chains*, p. 201.
69 Craton, *Testing the Chains*, p. 201; Gaspar, "La Guerre des Bois," p. 121.
70 Craton, *Testing the Chains*, p. 202; Gaspar, "La Guerre des Bois," p. 121.
71 Taylor, *The Black Carib Wars*, pp. 127–28, 135; Craton, *Testing the Chains*, pp. 193–94, 204.
72 Taylor, *The Black Carib Wars*, p. 135.
73 Ibid., p. 136.
74 Ibid., pp. 136–137.
75 Quoted in Taylor, *The Black Carib Wars*, p. 137.
76 Ibid., p. 138.
77 Ibid.
78 Taylor, *The Black Carib Wars*, p. 138.
79 The National Archives (TNA), London, UK WO 1/82/491 (Miscellaneous. Despatches on the capture of various West Indies Islands and Guiana from the French and Dutch, 1793–1797), Governor Seton to the Duke of Portland, November 16, 1796.
80 TNA, WO 1/82/648 (Miscellaneous. Despatches on the capture of various West Indies Islands and Guiana from the French and Dutch, 1793-1797), "Return of Black Charibs

landed at Baliseau from July 1796 to the 2nd February 1797," March 3, 1797; TNA, WO /1/82/649.
81. TNA, WO 1/82/583 (Miscellaneous. Despatches on the capture of various West Indies Islands and Guiana from the French and Dutch, 1793–1797), Governor Seton to the Duke of Portland, November 16, 1796. Samaná is a peninsula, not an island.
82. TNA, WO 1/82/651 (Miscellaneous. Despatches on the capture of various West Indies Islands and Guiana from the French and Dutch, 1793–1797), "Return of Black Caribs landed at Rattan," April 12, 1797.
83. Craton, *Testing the Chains*, p. 225.
84. Ibid., p. 226. See also Tessa Murphy, *The Creole Archipelago: Race and Borders in the Colonial Caribbean* (University of Pennsylvania Press, 2021), chap. 7.
85. Craton, *Testing the Chains*, p. 227.
86. Ibid.
87. Ibid.
88. Ibid., p. 183.
89. Ibid.
90. Ibid., p. 185.
91. Kit Candlin, "The Role of the Enslaved in the 'Fedon Rebellion' of 1795," in *Slavery & Abolition* 39, no. 4 (2018): p. 692.
92. Ibid., p. 693.
93. Craton, *Testing the Chains*, p. 185; Candlin, "The Role of the Enslaved," p. 694; Murphy, *Creole Archipelago*, pp. 210–216.
94. Candlin, "The Role of the Enslaved," p. 694.
95. Craton, *Testing the Chains*, p. 186; Candlin, "The Role of the Enslaved," p. 694.
96. Craton, *Testing the Chains*, pp. 186–88; Candlin, "The Role of the Enslaved," p. 695.
97. Joel Montague et al., "The Island of Grenada in 1795," *The Americas* 40, no. 4 (1984): p. 535; Candlin, "The Role of the Enslaved," p. 696.
98. Candlin, "The Role of the Enslaved," p. 698.
99. Craton, *Testing the Chains*, pp. 186–87.
100. Murphy, *The Creole Archipelago*, p. 214.
101. Craton, *Testing the Chains*, p. 188.
102. Ibid.
103. Ibid., p. 189.
104. Ibid., p. 190.
105. Ibid., pp. 207–208.
106. Candlin, "The Role of the Enslaved," p. 685.
107. Craton, *Testing the Chains*, p. 210.
108. Ibid., p. 211. See also Bryan Edwards, *The Proceedings of the Governor and Assembly of Jamaica, in Regard to the Maroon Negroes* (London, 1796).
109. Craton, *Testing the Chains*, p. 212.
110. David Geggus, "The Enigma of Jamaica in the 1790s: New Light on the Causes of Slave Rebellions," *William and Mary Quarterly* 44, no. 2 (1987): p. 283.
111. Craton, *Testing the Chains*, p. 213.
112. Ibid., p. 214.
113. Geggus, "The Enigma of Jamaica," p. 280.
114. Ibid.
115. Craton, *Testing the Chains*, p. 214.

116 Ibid.
117 Ibid., p. 215.
118 Ibid., p. 217.
119 Ibid., p. 218.
120 Quoted in Craton, *Testing the Chains*, pp. 217–218.
121 Ibid., 219–20.
122 Ibid., p. 221.
123 Ibid., p. 222.

Chapter 22

1 Quoted in Sudhir Hazareesingh, *Black Spartacus: The Epic Life of Toussaint Louverture* (Allen Lane, 2020), p. 104.
2 Quoted in Laurent Dubois, *Avengers of the New World: The Story of the Haitian Revolution* (Belknap Press, 2004), p. 203.
3 Dubois, *Avengers of the New World*, p. 179.
4 Ibid., p. 182.
5 Ibid., pp. 183–184.
6 Johnhenry Gonzalez, *Maroon Nation: A History of Revolutionary Haiti* (Yale University Press, 2019), p. 66.
7 Quoted in "The Plantation Policies of Étienne Polverel, 1794," in Dubois and Garrigus, *Slave Revolution in the Caribbean*, pp. 131–135.
8 Proclamation, March 22, 1795, in Nick Nesbitt, ed., *Toussaint L'Ouverture: The Haitian Revolution*, pp. 14–15.
9 Gonzalez, *Maroon Nation*, p. 69.
10 Dubois, *Avengers*, p. 196.
11 C. L. R. James, *The Black Jacobins* (Penguin, 2001), p. 180.
12 Quoted in James, *The Black Jacobins*, p. 180; Dubois, *Avengers*, p. 206.
13 Quoted in Hazareesingh, *Black Spartacus*, p. 111.
14 Quoted in Dubois, *Avengers*, p. 206.
15 Letter to the Directory, November 1797, quoted in Nesbitt, *Toussaint L'Ouverture*, pp. 32–35.
16 Dubois, *Avengers*, p. 216.
17 David Geggus, "The Cost of Pitt's Caribbean Campaigns, 1793–1798," *Historical Journal* 26, no. 3 (1983): p. 699.
18 Dubois, *Avengers*, p. 217.
19 Quoted in Hazareesingh, *Black Spartacus*, p. 136.
20 Hazareesingh, *Black Sparactus*, p. 137; Dubois, *Avengers*, p. 218.
21 Dubois, *Avengers*, p. 223.
22 "Friday's Mail, London, November 29," *The Derby Mercury*, December 6, 1798, p. 1.
23 Quoted in Dubois, *Avengers*, pp. 218–219.
24 Dubois, *Avengers*, pp. 220–222.
25 "Selections," *The Observer*, November 11, 1798, p. 4.
26 Dubois, *Avengers*, pp. 198–200.
27 See Dubois, *Avengers*, pp. 232–33, for a discussion about whether this conflict was a "race war" between black and "mulatto" factions.
28 Ibid., pp. 234–236.

29. For a detailed account of this moment, see Ronald Angelo Johnson, *Diplomacy in Black and White: John Adams, Toussaint Louverture, and Their Atlantic World Alliance* (University of Georgia Press, 2014).
30. Quoted in Johnson, *Diplomacy*, chap. 2, EPUB.
31. Hazareesingh, *Black Spartacus*, p. 191; Johnson, *Diplomacy*, chap. 2.
32. Arthur Scherr, "Arms and Men: The Diplomacy of US Weapons Traffic with Saint-Domingue under Adams and Jefferson," *International History Review* 35, no. 3 (2013): p. 603; Dubois, *Avengers*, p. 224.
33. Johnson, *Diplomacy*, chaps. 1 and 2.
34. Quoted in Hazareesingh, *Black Spartacus*, p. 191; Johnson, *Diplomacy*, chap. 2.
35. Quoted in Graham T. Nessler, *An Islandwide Struggle for Freedom: Revolution, Emancipation, and Reenslavement in Hispaniola, 1789–1809* (University of North Carolina Press, 2016), p. 104.
36. Quoted in Nessler, *An Islandwide Struggle*, p. 109.
37. Hazareesingh, *Black Spartacus*, pp. 228–29; Nessler, *An Islandwide Struggle*, pp. 102–10.
38. Hazareesingh, *Black Spartacus*, p. 230.
39. Dubois, *Avengers*, p. 241.
40. Ibid., p. 242.
41. Saint-Domingue Constitution 1801, in Nesbitt, *Toussaint L'Ouverture*, pp. 48–49.
42. Dubois, *Avengers*, pp. 239–40.
43. Ibid., p. 249.
44. Saint-Domingue Constitution 1801, in Nesbitt, *Toussaint L'Ouverture*, pp. 48–49.
45. Ibid.
46. Saint-Domingue Constitution 1801, in Nesbitt, *Toussaint L'Ouverture*, p. 51.
47. Dubois, *Avengers*, p. 246.
48. Ibid., p. 247.
49. Dubois, *Avengers*, pp. 246–47; Gonzales, *Maroon Nation*, pp. 69–70.
50. Quoted in Dubois, *Avengers*, pp. 247–48.
51. Ibid., p. 254.
52. Dubois, *Avengers*, p. 254.
53. Hazareesingh, *Black Spartacus*, pp. 298–99.
54. Quoted in Dubois, *Avengers*, p. 255.
55. Ibid., p. 256.
56. Dubois, *Avengers*, p. 262.
57. Scherr, "Arms and Men," p. 633.
58. Dubois, *Avengers*, p. 247.
59. Letter from Napoleon to Toussaint, November 18, 1801, in Nesbitt, *Toussaint L'Ouverture*, p. 63.
60. Ibid., p. 264.
61. Quoted in Dubois, *Avengers*, p. 266.
62. Letter to Dessalines, February 8, 1802, in Nesbitt, *Toussaint L'Ouverture*, p. 76.
63. Dubois, *Avengers*, p. 267.
64. Ibid., p. 268.
65. Ibid., pp. 269–70.
66. Quoted in Paul Clammer, *Black Crown: Henry Christophe, the Haitian Revolution and the Caribbean's Forgotten Kingdom* (C. Hurst, 2023), p. 101.
67. Ibid., p. 103.

68   Dubois, *Avengers*, p. 275.
69   Hazareesingh, *Black Spartacus*, p. 315.
70   Dubois, *Avengers*, p. 276.
71   Hazareesingh, *Black Spartacus*, p. 316.
72   Dubois, *Avengers*, p. 277.
73   Quoted in Dubois, *Avengers*, p. 278.
74   Acts quoted in Nesler, *An Islandwide Struggle*, pp. 139–40.
75   Dubois, *Avengers*, pp. 284–85.
76   Quoted in Dubois, *Avengers*, pp. 291–92.
77   Ibid., p. 251.
78   Ibid., p. 297.
79   Quoted in Dubois and Garrigus, *Slave Revolution in the Caribbean*, p. 178.
80   Ibid., p. 182.
81   Philippe R. Girard, *The Slaves Who Defeated Napoléon: Toussaint Louverture and the Haitian War of Independence, 1801–1804* (University of Alabama Press, 2011), p. 317.
82   "A Survivor of Dessalines's Massacre," in Jeremy D. Popkin, *Facing Racial Revolution: Eyewitness Accounts of the Haitian Insurrection* (University of Chicago Press, 2007), pp. 356–57.
83   Girard, *The Slaves Who Defeated Napoléon*, p. 321.
84   "Extract from the Secret Deliberations of the Government of the Island of Hayti," *Caledonian Mercury*, July 5, 1804.
85   Marlene L. Daut, *Awakening the Ashes: An Intellectual History of the Haitian Revolution* (University of North Carolina Press, 2023), pp. 103, 214; *Caledonian Mercury*, July 21, 1804, p. 2.
86   Full text of April 28, 1804, proclamation available at Haiti and the Atlantic World, accessed April 28, 1804, https://haitidoi.com/2015/10/30/dessalines-reader-28-april-1804/.
87   This section is indebted to Laurent Dubois, *A Colony of Citizens: Revolution & Slave Emancipation in the French Caribbean, 1787–1804* (University of North Carolina Press, 2004).
88   Dubois, *A Colony of Citizens*, pp. 208–09.
89   Quoted in Dubois, *A Colony of Citizens*, p. 309.
90   Ibid., p. 327.
91   Ibid., pp. 374–75.
92   Quoted in Dubois, *A Colony of Citizens*, p. 349.
93   Ibid., p. 354.
94   Quoted in Dubois, *A Colony of Citizens*, p. 357.
95   Ibid., pp. 360–362.
96   Ibid., pp. 379–81.
97   Ibid., p. 382.
98   Quoted in Dubois, *A Colony of Citizens*, pp. 389–91.
99   Ibid., pp. 393–94.
100 Ibid., p. 394.
101 Auguste Lacour, *Histoire de la Guadeloupe*, vol. 3, *1798–1803* (Basse-Terre, Guadeloupe, 1858), p. 311.
102 Quoted in Lacour, *Histoire de la Guadeloupe*, p. 311; Dubois, *Colony of Citizens*, p. 396.
103 Lacour, *Histoire de la Guadeloupe*, p. 311.
104 Dubois, *Colony of Citizens*, p. 398.
105 Ibid., p. 400.

106 Ibid., p. 404.
107 Ibid., p. 419. See also Miranda Frances Spieler, "The Destruction of Liberty in French Guiana: Law, Identity and the Meaning of Legal Space, 1794–1830," *Social History* 36, no. 3 (2011): pp. 260–79.
108 Estimates of the number of captives transported to the French Caribbean 1802–1835, SlaveVoyages: The Trans-Atlantic Slave Trade Database, accessed November 23, 2024, https://www.slavevoyages.org/voyages/MZ9WdCok.
109 Michel-Rolph Trouillot, *Silencing the Past: Power and the Production of History* (Beacon Press, 2015), p. 73.

Chapter 23

1 Quoted in Thomas Hallock, "Space, Time, and Purpose in Early American Texts: Starting from Igbo Landing," *Early American Literature* 54, no. 1 (2019): p. 26.
2 Lorna McDaniel, "The Flying Africans: Extent and Strength of the Myth in the Americas," *Nieuwe West* 64, no. 1/2 (1990): p. 33. See also Gay Wilentz, "If You Surrender to the Air: Folk Legends of Flight and Resistance in African American Literature," *Melus* 16, no. 1 (Spring 1989–Spring 1990): pp. 21–32; Ramenda Cyrus, "The Fight to Remember the Black Rebellion at Igbo Landing," *Mother Jones*, January/February 2022, accessed March 28, 2024, https://www.motherjones.com/media/2021/12/igbo-landing-georgia-dunbar-creek-toni-morrison-flying-african/.
3 Timothy B. Powell, "Ebos Landing," *New Georgia Encyclopedia*, July 16, 2020, accessed November 26, 2024, https://www.georgiaencyclopedia.org/articles/history-archaeology/ebos-landing/.
4 "Testimony in the Trial of Gabriel," October 6, 1800, Library of Virginia, accessed April 15, 2024, https://www.lva.virginia.gov/exhibits/deathliberty/gabriel/gabtrial17.htm.
5 Douglas R. Egerton, "Gabriel's Conspiracy and the Election of 1800," *Journal of Southern History* 56, no. 2 (1990): p. 192; Michael L. Nicholls, *Whispers of Rebellion: Narrating Gabriel's Conspiracy* (University of Virginia Press, 2012), chap. 1, EPUB; see also testimony at The Library of Virginia, https://www.lva.virginia.gov/exhibits/deathliberty/alldocs.htm#gabriel; and Encyclopedia Virginia, https://encyclopediavirginia.org/entries/testimony-in-the-trial-of-gabriel-october-6-1800/.
6 J. Sidbury, *Ploughshares into Swords: Race, Rebellion, and Identity in Gabriel's Virginia, 1730–1810* (Cambridge University Press, 1997), p. 58.
7 Ibid., p. 80.
8 Egerton, "Gabriel's Conspiracy," p. 193n6.
9 Ibid., p. 194.
10 Ibid., p. 195.
11 Quoted in Nicholls, *Whispers of Rebellion*, chap. 1.
12 Egerton, "Gabriel's Conspiracy," pp. 192, 196.
13 Nicholls, *Whispers of Rebellion*, chap. 1.
14 "To Thomas Jefferson from James Thomson Callender, 13 September 1800," Founders Online, National Archives, https://founders.archives.gov/documents/Jefferson/01-32-02-0090 (original source: Barbara B. Oberg, ed., *The Papers of Thomas Jefferson*, vol. 32, 1 June 1800–16 February 1801 (Princeton University Press, 2005), pp. 136–38.
15 See for instance Sidbury, *Ploughshares into Swords*, chap. 1; A. White, *Encountering Revolution: Haiti and the Making of the Early Republic* (Johns Hopkins University Press, 2010);

J. A. Dun, *Dangerous Neighbors: Making the Haitian Revolution in Early America* (University of Pennsylvania Press, 2016); Julius S. Scott, *The Common Wind: Afro-American Currents in the Age of the Haitian Revolution* (Verso, 2018).
16 Nicholls, *Whispers of Rebellion*, chap. 2.
17 Egerton, "Gabriel's Conspiracy," p. 196; Nicholls, *Whispers of Rebellion*, chap. 1; Sidbury, *Ploughshares into Swords*, p. 67.
18 Court testimony quoted in Egerton, "Gabriel's Conspiracy," p. 196.
19 "Gabriel's Conspiracy," p. 197.
20 Sidbury, *Ploughshares into Swords*, p. 68.
21 Nicholls, *Whispers of Rebellion*, chaps. 1 and 2.
22 Egerton, "Gabriel's Conspiracy," pp. 199–201.
23 Quoted in Nicholls, *Whispers of Rebellion*, chap. 2.
24 Egerton, "Gabriel's Conspiracy," p. 204.
25 Ibid., p. 203; Nicholls, *Whispers of Rebellion*, chap. 2.
26 Nicholls, *Whispers of Rebellion*, introduction.
27 This is how James Monroe described the rain in his later address to the Virginia Assembly; see "Governor James Monroe's Annual Address to the Virginia Assembly," James Monroe Highland, accessed April 15, 2024, https://highland.org/teacher-resources/gabriels-rebellion/ (original source: Virginia General Assembly, House, Office of the Speaker, December 5, 1800, Executive Communications 1800–1802, Access 3691, Miscellaneous Reel 5382); Nicholls, *Whispers of Rebellion*, chap. 3.
28 James Sidbury argues that they had at some point been involved; see Sidbury, *Ploughshares into Swords*, pp. 106–11.
29 "Testimony of Daniel," in *Evidence adduced against Solomon the property of Thomas Henry Prosser in his trial on the 11th September 1800*, Library of Virginia, accessed April 15, 2024, https://www.lva.virginia.gov/exhibits/deathliberty/gabriel/evidence.htm.
30 Nicholls, *Whispers of Rebellion*, chap. 3.
31 "To Thomas Jefferson from James Monroe, 9 September 1800," Founders Online, National Archives, https://founders.archives.gov/documents/Jefferson/01-32-02-0086 (original source: *The Papers of Thomas Jefferson*, vol. 32, 1 June 1800-16 February 1801, Oberg (ed.), pp. 131–132).
32 Nicholls, *Whispers of Rebellion*, chap. 4.
33 Ibid., appendix B.
34 Ibid., chap. 4.
35 "Confession of Solomon," September 15, 1800, James Monroe Highland, accessed April 15, 2024, https://highland.org/teacher-resources/gabriels-rebellion/.
36 "To Thomas Jefferson from James Monroe, 15 September 1800," Founders Online, National Archives, https://founders.archives.gov/documents/Jefferson/01-32-02-0094 (original source: *The Papers of Thomas Jefferson*, vol. 32, 1 June 1800-16 February 1801, Oberg (ed.), pp. 144–45).
37 "To James Monroe from Thomas Jefferson, 20 September 1800," Founders Online, National Archives, https://founders.archives.gov/documents/Jefferson/01-32-02-0097 (original source: *The Papers of Thomas Jefferson*, vol. 32, 1 June 1800–16 February 1801, Oberg (ed.), pp. 160–61).
38 Nicholls, *Whispers of Rebellion*, chap. 4.
39 Quoted in Egerton, "Gabriel's Conspiracy," p. 212.
40 Nicholls, *Whispers of Rebellion*, chap. 5.

41 Quoted in Nicholls, *Whispers of Rebellion*, chap. 5.
42 Ibid., chap. 5.
43 "Testimony in the Trial of Gabriel," October 6, 1800, Library of Virginia, accessed April 15, 2024, https://www.lva.virginia.gov/exhibits/deathliberty/gabriel/gabtrial17.htm.
44 Nicholls, *Whispers of Rebellion*, chap. 6.
45 Thomas D. Morris, *Southern Slavery and the Law: 1619–1860* (University of North Carolina Press, 1996), pp. 253–55.
46 As Nicholls points out, it had been decades since Virginia had granted manumission for revealing a conspiracy; *Whispers of Rebellion*, chap. 6.
47 "Governor James Monroe's Annual Address to the Virginia Assembly," accessed April 15, 2024, https://highland.org/teacher-resources/gabriels-rebellion/ (original source: Virginia General Assembly, House, Office of the Speaker, December 5, 1800, Executive Communications 1800–1802, Access 3691, Miscellaneous Reel 5382).
48 Ibid.
49 Quoted in Nicholls, *Whispers of Rebellion*, chap. 6.
50 Michael Taylor, *The Interest: How the British Establishment Resisted the Abolition of Slavery* (Vintage, 2020), chap. 1, EPUB.
51 Seymour Drescher, *Abolition: A History of Slavery and Antislavery* (Cambridge University Press, 2009), p. 170.
52 Ibid., pp. 208–09.
53 For more on the roots of the moral aspect, see Christopher Leslie Brown, *Moral Capital: Foundations of British Abolitionism* (University of North Carolina Press, 2006).
54 Drescher, *Abolition*, pp. 226–227.
55 Taylor, *The Interest*, chap. 1.
56 An Act to Prohibit the Importation of Slaves into Any Port or Place within the Jurisdiction of the United States, accessed November 25, 2024, https://maint.loc.gov/law/help/statutes-at-large/9th-congress/session-2/c9s2ch22.pdf.
57 Manisha Sinha, *The Slave's Cause: A History of Abolition* (Yale University Press, 2016), pp. 82–84.
58 Estimates of the number of captives transported to US ports, 1783–1807, SlaveVoyages: The Trans-Atlantic Slave Trade Database, accessed November 24, 2024, https://www.slavevoyages.org/voyages/xorCCCzn.
59 Pernille Røge, "Why the Danes Got There First – A Trans-Imperial Study of the Abolition of the Danish Slave Trade in 1792," *Slavery & Abolition* 35, no. 4 (2014): 576–592. Estimates of the number of captives transported from Africa under a Danish flag, 1792–1803, SlaveVoyages: The Trans-Atlantic Slave Trade Database, accessed November 26, 2024, https://www.slavevoyages.org/voyages/ScwDgidh.
60 Estimates of the number of captives transported from Africa, 1808–1818: SlaveVoyages: The Trans-Atlantic Slave Trade Database, accessed November 26, 2024, https://www.slavevoyages.org/voyages/Gfjx7Fu4; estimates of the number of captives transported from Africa, 1818–1866: SlaveVoyages: The Trans-Atlantic Slave Trade Database, accessed November 26, 2024, https://www.slavevoyages.org/voyages/GeiFOiHS.
61 Absalom Jones, *A Thanksgiving Sermon Preached January 1, 1808 in St. Thomas's, or the African Episcopal Church, Philadelphia, on Account of the Abolition of the African Slave Trade on That Day at the Congress of the United States* (Philadelphia, 1808), pp. 14–17.

Chapter 24

1. Arturo Morales Carrión, ed., *El proceso abolicionista en Puerto Rico*, vol. 1, *La institución de la esclavitud y su crisis, 1823–1873* (San Juan: Instituto de Cultura Puertorriqueña, 1975), pp. 125–26; Guillermo A. Baralt, *Esclavos rebeldes: conspiraciones y sublevaciones de esclavos en Puerto Rico (1795–1873)*, 2nd ed. (Ediciones Huracán, 1982), p. 23. This letter also appears in Christopher Schmidt-Nowara, *Slavery, Freedom, and Abolition in Latin America and the Atlantic World* (University of New Mexico Press, 2011), pp. 90–91.
2. For a useful historiographic review of a very complicated period, see Gabriel Paquette, "The Dissolution of the Spanish Atlantic Monarchy," *The Historical Journal* 52, no. 1 (2009): pp. 175–212.
3. Brian R. Hamnett, *The End of Iberian Rule on the American Continent, 1770–1830* (Cambridge University Press, 2017), pp. 110–12.
4. Ibid.
5. *Diario de sesiones de las Córtes Generales y Extraordinarias*, vol. 1 (Madrid: J. A. García, 1870), pp. 327–28; Jesús Sanjurjo, *In the Blood of Our Brothers: Abolitionism and the End of the Slave Trade in Spain's Atlantic Empire, 1800–1870* (University of Alabama Press, 2021), chap. 1, EPUB; see also Emily Berquist, "Early Anti-Slavery Sentiment in the Spanish Atlantic World, 1765–1817," *Slavery & Abolition* 31, no. 2 (2010): pp. 181–205. Esteban Palacios was also the uncle of Simón Bolívar. See https://historia-hispanica.rah.es/biografias/35132-esteban-de-palacios-y-blanco.
6. Ada Ferrer, *Freedom's Mirror: Cuba and Haiti in the Age of Revolution* (Cambridge University Press, 2014), p. 265.
7. *Diario de sesiones de las Córtes*, p. 753; see also Ferrer, *Freedom's Mirror*, p. 265.
8. *Documentos de que hasta ahora se compone el expediente que principiaron las Cortes Extraordinarias sobre el trafico y esclavitud de los negros* (Imprenta de Repulles, 1814), pp. 87–89.
9. For more on Agustín de Argüelles, see Sanjurjo, *In the Blood of Our Brothers*, chap. 1.
10. *Diario de sesiones de las Córtes Generales y Extraordinarias*, vol. 2 (Madrid: J. A. García, 1870), pp. 809–10.
11. Sanjurjo, *In the Blood of Our Brothers*, introduction.
12. Ibid., chap. 1. For more on the Anglo-Spanish alliance and the Peninsular War, see Charles Esdaile, *The Peninsular War: A New History* (Palgrave Macmillan, 2003).
13. *Diario de sesiones de las Córtes*, vol. 2, pp. 811–12.
14. Ibid., pp. 811–13.
15. Ferrer, *Freedom's Mirror*, p. 266.
16. Jaime E. Rodríguez O., "The Emancipation of America," *American Historical Review* 105 (2000): pp. 144–45. For the full text in English of the Spanish Constitution of 1812, see Biblioteca Virtual Miguel de Cervantes, accessed November 27, 2024, https://www.cervantesvirtual.com/obra-visor/the-political-constitution-of-the-spanish-monarchy-promulgated-in-cadiz-the-nineteenth-day-of-march--0/html/ffd04084-82b1-11df-acc7-002185ce6064_1.html.
17. Morales Carrión, *El proceso abolicionista en Puerto Rico*, p. 122.
18. Morales Carrión, *El proceso abolicionista en Puerto Rico*, p. 122; Antonio J. Pinto, "Negro Sobre Blanco: La Conspiración Esclava de 1812 en Puerto Rico," *Caribbean Studies* 40, no. 1 (2012): p. 123.

19 Morales Carrión, *El proceso abolicionista en Puerto Rico*, p. 124.
20 Ibid., p. 127.
21 Ibid., pp. 122–23.
22 Baralt, *Esclavos rebeldes*, p. 27; Schmidt-Nowara, *Slavery, Freedom, and Abolition*, p. 92.
23 Morales Carrión, *El proceso abolicionista en Puerto Rico*, p. 123.
24 Ibid., p. 131.
25 Ibid., p. 117.
26 Ferrer, *Freedom's Mirror*, p. 271.
27 Matt D. Childs, *The 1812 Aponte Rebellion in Cuba and the Struggle against Atlantic Slavery* (University of North Carolina Press, 2006), p. 93; Ferrer, *Freedom's Mirror*, p. 271.
28 See Dale Tomich, "The Wealth of Empire: Francisco Arango y Parreno, Political Economy, and the Second Slavery in Cuba," in *Interpreting Spanish Colonialism: Empires, Nations, and Legends*, ed. Christopher Schmidt-Nowara and John M. Nieto-Phillips (University of New Mexico Press, 2005).
29 Childs, *The 1812 Aponte Rebellion*, p. 55.
30 *Documentos de que hasta ahora se compone el expediente que principiaron las Cortes Extraordinarias*, p. 102.
31 For more detail on what was read out and its unclear meanings, see Ferrer, *Freedom's Mirror*, pp. 271–273.
32 The rebels may have also started fires on the plantation Soledad, owned by Andrés de Jaúregui, but this, too, is mostly shrouded in mystery, in part because it may have been only a rumor. See Ferrer, *Freedom's Mirror*, pp. 284–85.
33 For more detail about the March revolts, see Childs, *The 1812 Aponte Rebellion*, chap. 4.
34 Elena A. Schneider, *The Occupation of Havana: War, Trade, and Slavery in the Atlantic World* (University of North Carolina Press, 2018), p. 304, Kindle.
35 Quoted in Ferrer, *Freedom's Mirror*, p. 285.
36 Ibid., pp. 293–296.
37 Jorge Pavez O, trans., "Lámina XXVI," in *Expediente sobre José Antonio Aponte y el sentido de las pinturas que se hayan en el libro que se le aprehendió en su casa 1812*, p. 730, accessed November 27, 2024, http://aponte.hosting.nyu.edu/wp-content/uploads/2017/10/Aponte-Trial-Transcript-Jorge-Pavez-Ojeda.pdf; Sibylle Fischer, *Modernity Disavowed: Haiti and the Cultures of Slavery in the Age of Revolution* (Duke University Press, 2004), p. 46.
38 Schneider, *The Occupation of Havana*, p. 306.
39 Pavez O, *Expediente*, p. 720; Ferrer, *Freedom's Mirror*, pp. 314–315.
40 Quoted in Fischer, *Modernity Disavowed*, p. 49. See also Ferrer, *Freedom's Mirror*, p. 278; Jose Luciano Franco, *Las conspiracies en Cuba de 1810 y 1812* (Barcelona: Linkgua, 2013). On the circulation of images, see Julius S. Scott, *The Common Wind: Afro-American Currents in the Age of the Haitian Revolution* (Verso, 2018).
41 Quoted in João José Reis and Flávio dos Santos Gomes, "Repercussion of the Haitian Revolution in Brazil, 1791–1850," in *The World of the Haitian Revolution*, ed. David P. Geggus and Norman Fiering (Indiana University Press, 2009), p. 287.
42 Pavez O, *Expediente*, pp. 758–59.
43 See Digital Aponte, láminas 24 and 25, accessed May 10, 2024, https://aponte.hosting.nyu.edu/transcript/laminas-24-25/; Schneider, *The Occupation of Havana*, p. 304.
44 Ferrer, *Freedom's Mirror*, p. 301.
45 Ibid., p. 319.

46 Pavez O, *Expediente*, p. 736; Ferrer, *Freedom's Mirror*, p. 303.
47 Ferrer, *Freedom's Mirror*, p. 325.
48 Fischer, *Modernity Disavowed*, p. 50; Ferrer, *Freedom's Mirror*, p. 278.
49 Laurent Dubois, *Haiti: The Aftershocks of History* (Picador, 2013), p. 54, Kindle.
50 Clammer, *Black Crown*, pp. 156–57.
51 Quoted in Clammer, *Black Crown*, p. 157.
52 Dubois, *Haiti*, p. 57.
53 Clammer, *Black Crown*, pp. 181–182.
54 Dubois, *Haiti*, p. 86.
55 Clammer, *Black Crown*, pp. 197–198. The Code Henry can be found online at https://archive.org/details/codehenry00hait/codehenry00hait/page/vi/mode/2up.
56 Ibid., p. 7.
57 Earl Leslie Griggs and Clifford H. Prator, eds., *Henry Christophe and Thomas Clarkson: A Correspondence* (University of California Press, 1952), p. 104.
58 Clammer, *Black Crown*, p. 250.
59 See the introduction in Clammer, *Black Crown*.
60 See Rosalie McCrea, "Portrait Mythology? Representing the 'Black Jacobin': Henri Christophe in the British Grand Manner," *British Art Journal* 6, no. 2 (2005): pp. 66–70; Tabitha McIntosh and Grégory Pierrot, "Capturing the Likeness of Henry I of Haiti (1805–1822)," *Atlantic Studies* 14, no. 2 (2016): pp. 127–51.
61 Marlene Daut has done extensive work on Vastey. See Marlene L. Daut, *Baron de Vastey and the Origins of Black Atlantic Humanism* (Palgrave Macmillan, 2017); and Marlene L. Daut, *Awakening the Ashes: An Intellectual History of the Haitian Revolution* (University of North Carolina Press, 2023).
62 Baron de Vastey, *Reflexions on the Blacks and Whites* (London: J. Hatchard, 1817), pp. 65–72. For a detailed examination of the differences between the print culture of north and south Haiti, see chapters 2 and 3 in Chelsea Stieber, *Haiti's Paper War: Post-Independence Writing, Civil War, and the Making of the Republic, 1804–1954* (New York University Press, 2020).
63 Prince Sanders, *Haytian Papers: A Collection of the Very Interesting Proclamations and Other Official Documents; Together with Some Account of the Rise, Progress, and Present State of the Kingdom of Hayti* (London, 1816).
64 Clammer, *Black Crown*, p. 231; Arthur O. White, "Prince Saunders: An Instance of Social Mobility Among Antebellum New England Blacks," *Journal of Negro History* 60, no. 4 (1975): pp. 526–35.
65 See Article 142 in "Révision de la Constitution Haïtienne de 1806 (1816)," Haiti and the Atlantic World, accessed November 27, 2024, https://haitidoi.com/constitutions/1816-2/.
66 Baron de Vastey, *Essai sur les causes de la révolution et des guerres civiles d'Hayti* (Sans-Souci, l'Imprimerie Royal, 1819), p. 368.
67 Simón Bolívar to Alexandre Pétion, January 21, 1816, *Escritos del Libertador*, vol. 9 (Caracas: Sociedad Bolivariana de Venezuela, 1973), p. 7.
68 Alexandre Pétion to Simón Bolívar, February 18, 1816 quoted in Paul Verna, *Pétion y Bolívar*, Caracas, 1969, p. 170.
69 For more on the "counter-plantation" model, see J. Casimir, *The Haitians: A Decolonial History*, trans. Laurent Dubois (University of North Carolina Press, 2020).
70 Johnhenry Gonzalez, *Maroon Nation: A History of Revolutionary Haiti* (Yale University Press, 2019), p. 11.
71 Dubois, *Haiti*, p. 84.

72 Quoted in Fredrik Thomasson, "Sweden and Haiti, 1791–1825," *Journal of Haitian Studies* 24, no. 2 (2018): p. 19. Sweden was not the only nation interested in commerce with Haiti; see also Julia Gaffield, *Haitian Connections in the Atlantic World: Recognition after Revolution* (University of North Carolina Press, 2015).

Chapter 25

1 Ashli White, "The Limits of Fear: The Saint Dominguan Challenge to Slave Trade Abolition in the United States," *Early American Studies* 2, no. 2 (2004): pp. 363–64. See also Ashli White, *Encountering Revolution: Haiti and the Making of the Early Republic* (Johns Hopkins University Press, 2010); and James Alexander Dun, *Dangerous Neighbors: Making the Haitian Revolution in Early America* (University of Pennsylvania Press, 2016).
2 White, "The Limits of Fear," pp. 363–64.
3 Ibid., p. 374.
4 Rebecca Scott, "Paper Thin: Freedom and Re-Enslavement in the Diaspora of the Haitian Revolution," *Law and History Review* 29, no. 4 (2011): p. 1063.
5 Ibid., pp. 1072–73.
6 Sue Peabody, "'Free Upon Higher Ground': Saint-Domingue Slaves' Suits for Freedom in US Courts, 1792–1830," in *The World of the Haitian Revolution*, ed. David P. Geggus and Norman Fiering (Indiana University Press, 2009), pp. 262–63.
7 "Runaway Negro" in *Le Courrier de la Louisiane*, September 4, 1809, quoted in Albert Thrasher, *"On to New Orleans!" Louisiana's Heroic 1811 Slave Revolt* (Cypress Press, 1996), p. 49.
8 Robert L. Paquette, "'A Horde of Brigands?' The Great Louisiana Slave Revolt of 1811 Reconsidered," *Historical Reflections / Réflexions Historiques* 35, no. 1 (2009): p. 80.
9 Daniel Rasmussen, *American Uprising: The Untold Story of America's Largest Slave Revolt* (HarperCollins, 2011), chap. 6, EPUB. For more on the development of the slave "driver" system, see Randy M. Browne, *The Driver's Story: Labor and Power in the World of Atlantic Slavery* (University of Pennsylvania Press), 2024.
10 Some historians think Charles Deslondes had direct connections to Saint-Domingue, maybe having been born there, but there is no clear paper trail. It could be that he was brought to the Deslondes plantation in 1793, as the fighting was intensifying in Saint-Domingue; Rasmussen, *American Uprising*, chap. 6; Paquette, "A Horde of Brigands?," p. 80.
11 Rasmussen, *American Uprising*, chapter 8.
12 Ibid.
13 Ibid.; Paquette, "A Horde of Brigands?," p. 83.
14 *New York Evening Post*, February 19, 1811, p. 3; also quoted in Paquette, "A Hoard of Brigands?" p. 74.
15 Rasmussen, *American Uprising*, chap. 9.
16 Ibid., chap. 10.
17 Paquette, "A Horde of Brigands?," p. 80.
18 1811 Census of New Orleans, quoted in Thrasher, *"On to New Orleans!"* p. 210.
19 As Paquette points out, in Saint-Domingue "brigand" was used to describe the rebel slaves, though the British called any non-white opponent a brigand. See Paquette, "A Horde of Brigands?," p. 85.
20 Rasmussen, *American Uprising*, chap. 11.

21 Ibid.
22 Rasmussen, *American Uprising*, chap. 12.
23 Paquette, "A Horde of Brigands?," pp. 73; 77.
24 Rasmussen, *American Uprising*, chap. 13.
25 "Louisiana Plantation Where Historic Slave Revolt Started Now under Black Ownership," NPR, July 9, 2024, accessed July 22, 2024, https://www.npr.org/2024/07/09/nx-s1-4893179/louisiana-woodland-plantation-slave-revolt-black-ownership; see also The Descendants Project, https://www.thedescendantsproject.org/about-4.
26 "The Next Generation," Destrehan Plantation website, accessed May 16, 2024, https://www.destrehanplantation.org/history/remodeling.html.
27 "First Slavery, Then a Chemical Plant and Cancer Deaths: One Town's Brutal History," *Guardian*, May 6, 2019, accessed November 28, 2024, https://www.theguardian.com/us-news/2019/may/06/cancertown-louisiana-reserve-history-slavery.
28 Lennox Honychurch, *In the Forests of Freedom: The Fighting Maroons of Dominica* (London: Papillote Press, 2017), pp. 142–46.
29 Ibid., p. 146.
30 Ibid., p. 154.
31 Ibid., pp. 156, 160; Polly Pattullo, ed., *Your Time Is Done Now: Slavery, Resistance, and Defeat: The Maroon Trials of Dominica (1813–1814)* (London: Papillote Press, 2015), p. 8.
32 Honychurch, *In the Forests of Freedom*, p. 160.
33 Rebecca Hall, "Not Killing Me Softly: African American Women, Slave Revolts, and Historical Constructions of Racialized Gender," *Freedom Center Journal* 2 (2007): pp. 1–2, https://papers.ssrn.com/sol3/papers.cfm?abstract_id=1874927; H. W. Flournoy, ed., *Calendar of Virginia State Papers and Other Manuscripts*, vol. 10 (Richmond, 1892), p. 120.
34 Flournoy, *Calendar*, p. 121.
35 Ibid., p. 122.
36 Ibid., p. 121.
37 Ibid., p. 122.
38 Ibid., p. 123.
39 Honychurch, *In the Forests of Freedom*, p. 163.
40 Ibid., pp. 165–66.
41 Ibid., p. 166.
42 Ibid., p. 167.
43 Ibid., p. 171.
44 Pattullo, *Your Time Is Done Now*, p. 40.
45 Quoted in Pattullo, *Your Time Is Done Now*, pp. 85–86.
46 Honychurch, *In the Forests of Freedom*, p. 176.
47 Ibid., pp. 177–78.
48 Pattullo, *Your Time Is Done Now*, p. 38.
49 The following section comes from Pattullo, *Your Time Is Done Now*, pp. 43–52, 55–61; see also TNA CO 71/51.
50 Honychurch, *In the Forests of Freedom*, p. 184.
51 Ibid., p. 185.
52 Quoted in Pattullo, *Your Time Is Done Now*, pp. 5; 89.
53 Frank A. Cassell, "Slaves of the Chesapeake Bay Area and the War of 1812," *Journal of Negro History* 57, no. 2 (1972): p. 144.

54 Ibid., p. 154.
55 Flournoy, *Calendar*, p. 217.
56 Ibid., p. 283.
57 Ibid., p. 309.
58 Cassell, "Slaves of the Chesapeake Bay Area," p. 147.
59 Ibid.
60 From *National Intelligencer* reports quoted in Cassell, "Slaves of the Chesapeake Bay Area," p. 145.
61 Flournoy, *Calendar*, p. 339.
62 Cassell, "Slaves of the Chesapeake Bay Area," p. 150.
63 Manisha Sinha, *The Slave's Cause: A History of Abolition* (Yale University Press, 2016), p. 154.
64 Cassell, "Slaves of the Chesapeake Bay Area," p. 151.
65 Flournoy, *Calendar*, p. 333.
66 Cassell, "Slaves of the Chesapeake Bay Area," p. 153.
67 Ibid., p. 152.
68 Ibid., pp. 153–154.
69 K. O. Laurence, "The Settlement of Free Negroes in Trinidad Before Emancipation," *Caribbean Quarterly* 9, no. 1/2 (March/June 1963): pp. 26–52.
70 Justin Iverson, "Fugitives on the Front," *Florida Historical Quarterly* 98, no. 2 (Fall 2019): p. 105; Nathaniel Millett, "Defining Freedom in the Atlantic Borderlands of the Revolutionary Southeast," *Early American Studies* 5, no. 2 (2007): p. 381.
71 Millett, "Defining Freedom," pp. 382, 386.
72 For more on these men, see Millett, "Defining Freedom," pp. 390–91.
73 Sinha, *The Slave's Cause*, p. 154.
74 Quoted in Carrie Gibson, *El Norte: The Epic and Forgotten Story of Hispanic North America* (Grove Press, 2019), p. 170. See Andrew Jackson to Mauricio de Zuñiga, April 23, 1816, *The Papers of Andrew Jackson Digital Edition*, accessed August 8, 2016, http://rotunda.upress.virginia.edu/founders/JKSN-01-04-02-0013.
75 Jane G. Landers, *Atlantic Creoles in the Age of Revolutions* (Harvard University Press, 2010), pp. 179–85.
76 Iverson, "Fugitives on the Front," p. 123.
77 Ibid., p. 125.
78 Landers, *Atlantic Creoles*, p. 193.
79 Iverson, "Fugitives on the Front," p. 126; Landers, *Atlantic Creoles*, p. 196.

Chapter 26

1 "Confession of Robert," in Barbados House of Assembly, *A Report from A Select Committee of the House of Assembly Appointed to Inquire into the Origin, Causes, and Progress of the Late Insurrection* (London, 1818), p. 29.
2 Ibid.
3 On Portugal and Spain, see Fernanda Bretones Lane et al., "The Congress of Vienna and the Making of Second Slavery," *Journal of Global Slavery* 4, no. 2 (2019): pp. 162–95.
4 For more on the Cage and late eighteenth-century Bridgetown and the enslaved women who lived there, see Marisa J. Fuentes, *Dispossessed Lives: Women, Violence, and the Archive*

(University of Pennsylvania Press, 2016), especially chapter 1. Complaints about the Cage eventually led to its being moved, in 1818, to a less populated site, across the Careenage (today's Constitution River).
5 Fuentes, *Dispossessed Lives*, p. 42; Hilary McD. Beckles, "The Slave-Drivers' War: Bussa and the 1816 Barbados Slave Rebellion," *Boletín de Estudios Latinoamericanos y del Caribe* 39 (December 1985): p. 106.
6 For more on marronage in Barbados, see Jerome S. Handler, "Escaping Slavery in a Caribbean Plantation Society: Marronage in Barbados, 1650s–1830s," *New West Indian Guide / Nieuwe West-Indische Gids* 71, no. 3/4 (1997): pp. 183–225.
7 "Examination of Daniel," *A Report from A Select Committee*, p. 26.
8 "Examination of Thomas Stoute, Esq.," *A Report from A Select Committee*, p. 52.
9 "Examination of Daniel," *A Report from A Select Committee*, p. 26.
10 Michael Craton, *Testing the Chains: Resistance to Slavery in the British West Indies* (Cornell University Press, 1982), pp. 256–257.
11 Ibid., p. 257.
12 Ibid., p. 261.
13 Beckles, "The Slave-Drivers' War," p. 91.
14 This is attributed to oral tradition, see Beckles, "The Slave-Drivers' War," p. 90.
15 "Confession and Deposition of James Bowland, slave belonging to the Plantation called 'The River,'" *A Report from A Select Committee*, p. 33.
16 Craton, *Testing the Chains*, p. 261.
17 Ibid., p. 263.
18 Quoted in David Lambert, *Soldiers of Uncertain Rank: The West India Regiments in British Imperial Culture* (Cambridge University Press, 2024), pp. 50–51.
19 Col Codd's letter also mentions a flag with a "rude drawing" showing a black man with a white woman, though no other evidence of it was mentioned, nor was it sent to London, unlike the other one. "Col Edward Codd to James Leith, April 25, 1816," National Archives (UK), CO 28/85, fol 14. See sketches of the flag at TNA, ADM 1/377 or online: https://www.nationalarchives.gov.uk/wp-content/uploads/2021/09/MFQ-1_112-_2_1816-smaller-size.jpg.
20 By this point, George III was very unwell, and since 1811 the Crown had been under the control of the prince regent, who would go on to become George IV in 1820.
21 Craton, *Testing the Chains*, p. 264.
22 "A Proclamation," April 18, 1816, TNA, CO 28/85, fol 14.
23 Craton, *Testing the Chains*, p. 264; Beckles, "The Slave-Drivers' War," p. 87.
24 "Col Edward Codd to James Leith, April, 25, 1816," TNA, CO 28/85, fols 14–15.
25 Ibid.
26 "Extract of a Letter from Barbados," June 6, 1816, TNA, CO 28/85, fol. 139.
27 *The Barbados Mercury and Bridgetown Gazette*, December 28, 1816, p. 1, accessed May 30, 2024, https://eap.bl.uk/archive-file/EAP1086-1-15-12-8.
28 *The Barbados Mercury and Bridgetown Gazette*, December 17, 1816, p. 1, accessed May 30, 2024, https://eap.bl.uk/archive-file/EAP1086-1-15-12-5#.
29 Richard Huzzey, "The Politics of Slave-Trade Suppression," in *The Suppression of the Atlantic Slave Trade: British Policies, Practices, and Representations of Naval Coercion*, ed. Robert Burroughs and Richard Huzzey (Manchester University Press, 2015), p. 19.
30 Robert Wedderburn, *The Horrors of Slavery* (London, 1824), p. 5.

31 Katey Castellano, "Provision Grounds Against the Plantation: Robert Wedderburn's *The Axe Laid to the Root*," *Small Axe* 25, no. 1 (2021): p. 15.
32 Wedderburn, *The Horrors of Slavery*, p. 8.
33 Ibid., p. 13.
34 Ibid., p. 10; Peter Linebaugh and Marcus Rediker, *The Many-Headed Hydra: Sailors, Slaves, Commoners and the Hidden History of the Revolutionary Atlantic* (Beacon Press, 2000), chap. 9.
35 Wedderburn, *The Horrors of Slavery*, pp. 10–11.
36 Quoted in Ryan Hanley, *Beyond Slavery and Abolition: Black British Writing c. 1770–1830* (Cambridge University Press, 2019), p. 210; Linebaugh and Rediker, *The Many-Headed Hydra*, p. 285.
37 Quoted in Linebaugh and Rediker, *The Many-Headed Hydra*, p. 314.
38 On the role of provision grounds in Wedderburn's thought, see Castellano, "Provision Grounds," pp. 15–27.
39 Linebaugh and Rediker, *The Many-Headed Hydra*, chap. 9.
40 Ibid., pp. 290–298.
41 Ibid.
42 Quoted in Castellano, "Provision Grounds," p. 16.
43 Linebaugh and Rediker accept the correspondence as genuine, and write that officials in Jamaica offered a reward for confiscated copies of *The Axe Laid to the Root*, while Ryan Hanley has argued that Wedderburn wrote both sides of the correspondence, and that such a technique was in line with the broader style of some of his other writings. Additionally, he says there is no evidence that the newspaper ever reached Jamaica. See Hanley, *Beyond Slavery and Abolition*, p. 211.
44 Robert Wedderburn, *The Axe Laid to the Root*, no. 4 (1817), reprinted in *From Enlightenment to Romanticism: Anthology I*, ed. Ian Donnachie and Carmen Lavin (Manchester University Press, 2003), p. 180.
45 Hanley, *Beyond Slavery and Abolition*, p. 212.
46 Ibid., p. 213.
47 Quoted in Raphel Hoermann, "'Fermentation will be universal': Intersections of Race and Class in Robert Wedderburn's Black Atlantic Discourse of Transatlantic Revolution," in Gretchen H. Gerzina (ed), *Britain's Black Past* (Liverpool University Press, 2020), pp. 304–305.
48 Craton, *Testing the Chains*, pp. 267, 373n2; Emília Viotti da Costa, *Crowns of Glory, Tears of Blood: The Demerara Slave Rebellion of 1823* (Oxford University Press, 1994), p. xiii.
49 From 1824 numbers cited in Craton, *Testing the Chains*, p. 373n6.
50 Craton, *Testing the Chains*, p. 247. The first London Missionary Society members arrived in Demerara in 1808; da Costa, *Crowns of Glory*, p. 19.
51 da Costa, *Crowns of Glory*, p. 10.
52 Ibid., p. 101.
53 Ibid., pp. 174–76.
54 See Gelien Matthews, *Caribbean Slave Revolts and the British Abolitionist Movement* (Louisiana State University Press, 2006), chap. 4.
55 da Costa, *Crowns of Glory*, pp. 180, 182.
56 Ibid., p. 145.
57 Ibid., p. 183.

58 Ibid., pp. 184–85.
59 Craton, *Testing the Chains*, p. 278.
60 da Costa, *Crowns of Glory*, p. 179.
61 Testimony reprinted as "Jack's defense," in Joshua Bryant, *Account of an Insurrection of the Negro Slaves in the Colony of Demerara* (Georgetown: A. Stevenson, 1824), p. 74.
62 Craton, *Testing the Chains*, p. 280.
63 da Costa, *Crowns of Glory*, p. 186.
64 Ibid., p. 196.
65 Ibid., p. 197.
66 Ibid., p. 209.
67 Quoted in da Costa, *Crowns of Glory*, p. 211.
68 Craton, *Testing the Chains*, p. 283.
69 Quoted in da Costa, *Crowns of Glory*, pp. 216–17.
70 Ibid., p. 217.
71 Ibid., pp. 203, 217.
72 Ibid., pp. 220–21.
73 Ibid., pp. 221–22.
74 Ibid., pp. 224–229.
75 Craton, *Testing the Chains*, p. 277.
76 Ibid.
77 da Costa, *Crowns of Glory*, p. 172.
78 Ibid., p. 173.
79 Craton, *Testing the Chains*, p. 288.
80 "Jack's defense," pp. 74–76.
81 Ibid., pp. 78–79.
82 da Costa, *Crowns of Glory*, p. 244.
83 Ibid., p. 241.
84 Ibid., p. 274.
85 Craton, *Testing the Chains*, pp. 288–89.
86 Matthews, *Caribbean Slave Revolts*, chap. 1.
87 Elizabeth Heyrick, *Immediate, Not Gradual Abolition* (1824) (Boston: Isaac Knapp, 1838), pp. 9, 17–18. For more on Heyrick, see Clare Midgley, *Women Against Slavery: The British Campaigns 1780–1870* (Routledge, 1992).
88 Hanley, *Beyond Slavery and Abolition*, pp. 218–20.
89 Ryan Hanley, "A Radical Change of Heart: Robert Wedderburn's Last Word on Slavery," *Slavery & Abolition* 37, no. 2 (2016): p. 424.
90 Wedderburn, *The Horrors of Slavery*, p. 3.
91 Hanley, "A Radical Change of Heart," p. 425.
92 Wedderburn, *The Horrors of Slavery*, p. 22.
93 For more on the discovery of this text and a closer analysis of it, see Hanley, "A Radical Change of Heart."
94 Hanley, "A Radical Change of Heart," pp. 430–31.
95 This section uses the full reproduction of the text found in Hanley, "A Radical Change of Heart," pp. 433–41.
96 Castellano, "Provision Grounds," p. 27.
97 Wedderburn, *The Horrors of Slavery*, p. 24.

Chapter 27

1. Douglas R, Egerton and Robert L. Paquette, eds., *The Denmark Vesey Affair: A Documentary History* (University Press of Florida, 2017), p. 184; italics in original.
2. On Denmark Vesey's family, see chapter 4 in Douglas R. Egerton, *He Shall Go Out Free: The Lives of Denmark Vesey* (Rowman & Littlefield, 2004), EPUB.
3. This brief biographical sketch is based on Egerton, *He Shall Go Out Free*, chap. 1.
4. Egerton, *He Shall Go Out Free*, chap. 6.
5. Ibid., chap. 4.
6. For more on Denmark Vesey's familial life, see chapter 4 in Egerton, *He Shall Go Out Free*.
7. See US census data for 1800 at United States Census Bureau, accessed November 30, 2024, https://www.census.gov/library/publications/1801/dec/return.html; and for 1820, https://www.census.gov/library/publications/1821/dec/1820a.html.
8. Egerton, *He Shall Go Out Free*, chap. 5.
9. *Washington (DC) Gazette*, February 24, 1821, quoted in Egerton and Paquette, *The Denmark Vesey Affair*, p. 14.
10. Quoted in Michael P. Johnson, "Denmark Vesey and His Co-Conspirators," *William and Mary Quarterly*, 58, no. 4 (2001): pp. 962–63.
11. Egerton and Paquette, *The Denmark Vesey Affair*, p. 163.
12. Ibid., pp. 86–88.
13. Ibid., p. 176.
14. Ibid., p. 88.
15. Ibid.
16. Ibid., pp. 73; 165; 289–90.
17. Egerton, *He Shall Go Out Free*, chaps. 6 and 8.
18. In the *Official Report*, "Legislature" was changed to "Congress," one of the many inconsistencies and mysteries of these hearing transcripts. See Johnson, "Denmark Vesey and His Co-Conspirators," p. 961; Egerton and Paquette, *The Denmark Vesey Affair*, pp. 162–64; 287.
19. Egerton and Paquette, *The Denmark Vesey Affair*, p. 164.
20. The full official report is included in Egerton and Paquette, *The Denmark Vesey Affair*, chap. 3.
21. Ibid., p. 161n12.
22. Ibid., p. 172.
23. Johnson, "Denmark Vesey and His Co-Conspirators," p. 956.
24. Ibid., p. 958.
25. Egerton and Paquette, *The Denmark Vesey Affair*, p. 167.
26. Ibid., p. 181.
27. Ibid., p. 182.
28. Ibid., p. 184.
29. Egerton, *He Shall Go Out Free*, chap. 8.
30. According to Douglas Egerton, there is a local tradition that says Vesey and the others were killed at the "hanging tree" that was near present-day Ashley Avenue and Fishburn Street, but no such tree has appeared in the official sources. See Egerton and Paquette, *The Denmark Vesey Affair*, p. 168n12.
31. Egerton, *He Shall Go Out Free*, chap. 8.
32. Egerton and Paquette, *The Denmark Vesey Affair*, p. 86.

33 Johnson, "Denmark Vesey and His Co-Conspirators," p. 937.
34 Egerton and Paquette, *The Denmark Vesey Affair*, p. xxi. The church was rebuilt in 1865, and architect Robert Vesey, son of Denmark, was involved in its construction. The AME Church in Charleston, known as "Mother Emanuel," was the scene of a horrific white supremacist shooting that left nine people dead on June 17, 2005. https://motheremanuel.com/our-story.
35 For more on the debates, see the introduction to Egerton and Paquette, *The Denmark Vesey Affair*; and Johnson, "Denmark Vesey and His Co-Conspirators." There are a number of articles dedicated to this question in the January 2002 issue of *The William and Mary Quarterly*, volume 59, number 1; James O'Neil Spady, "Power and Confession: On the Credibility of the Earliest Reports of the Denmark Vesey Slave Conspiracy," *William and Mary Quarterly* 68, no. 2 (2011): pp. 287–304; Richard C. Wade, "The Vesey Plot: A Reconsideration," *Journal of Southern History* 30, no. 2 (1964): pp. 143–61.
36 Linebaugh and Rediker, *The Many-Headed Hydra*, chap. 9; Egerton and Paquette, *The Denmark Vesey Affair*, p. xxi.
37 Douglas R. Egerton, "Abolitionist or Terrorist?," *New York Times*, February 25, 2015, accessed June 21, 2024, https://www.nytimes.com/2014/02/26/opinion/abolitionist-or-terrorist.html.

Chapter 28

1 Quoted in Andrew Walker, "All Spirits Are Roused: The 1822 Antislavery Revolution in Haitian Santo Domingo," *Slavery & Abolition* 40, no. 3 (2019): p. 586; see also Chelsea Stieber, *Haiti's Paper War: Post-Independence Writing, Civil War, and the Making of the Republic, 1804–1954* (New York University Press, 2020), p. 128, Kindle.
2 See Article 44 of the Haitian constitution, accessed June 21, 2024, https://haitidoi.com/constitutions/1816-2/.
3 Johnhenry Gonzalez, "Defiant Haiti: Free-Soil Runaways, Ship Seizures and the Politics of Diplomatic Non-Recognition in the Early Nineteenth Century," *Slavery & Abolition* 36, no. 1 (2015): pp. 128–129.
4 Walker, "All Spirits Are Roused," p. 596; see also the epilogue in Ada Ferrer, *Freedom's Mirror: Cuba and Haiti in the Age of Revolution* (Cambridge University Press, 2014).
5 Leslie M. Alexander, "Black Utopia: Haiti and Black Transnational Consciousness in the Early Nineteenth Century," *William and Mary Quarterly* 78, no. 2 (2021): p. 220.
6 "Thomas Jefferson to James Monroe, November 24, 1801," Founders Online, National Archives, https://founders.archives.gov/documents/Jefferson/01-35-02-0550; original source: *The Papers of Thomas Jefferson*, vol. 35, *1 August–30 November 1801*, ed. Barbara B. Oberg (Princeton University Press, 2008), pp. 718–22; "Thomas Jefferson to Jared Sparks, February 4, 1824," Founders Online, National Archives, https://founders.archives.gov/documents/Jefferson/98-01-02-4020; Marlene L. Daut, *Tropics of Haiti: Race and the Literary History of the Haitian Revolution in the Atlantic World, 1789–1865* (Liverpool University Press, 2015), p. 507.
7 Quoted in Sara Fanning, *Caribbean Crossing: African Americans and the Haitian Emigration Movement* (New York University Press, 2015), p. 65.
8 On the relationship between Sierra Leone and Liberia, see Bronwen Everill, *Abolition and Empire in Sierra Leone and Liberia* (Palgrave Macmillan), 2013.
9 Ibid., pp. 65–66.

10 Douglas R. Egerton and Robert L. Paquette, *The Denmark Vesey Affair: A Documentary History* (University Press of Florida, 2017), pp. 12, 710–11.
11 Fanning, *Caribbean Crossing*, pp. 69–71.
12 Quoted in Leon D. Pamphile, *Haitians and African Americans: A Heritage of Tragedy and Hope* (University Press of Florida, 2001), p. 42.
13 Pamphile, *Haitians and African Americans*, p. 42.
14 Loring Daniel Dewey, *Correspondence Relative to the Immigration to Hayti of the Free People of Colour, in the United States* (New York, 1824), p. 7; see also chapter 2 in Pamphile, *Haitians and African Americans*.
15 Fanning, *Caribbean Crossing*, p. 18.
16 Dewey, *Correspondence*, p. 34; originally published in the *Columbian Sentinel*, July 3, 1824.
17 Alexander, "Black Utopia," p. 221; *Daily National Intelligencer*, July 24, 1824, page 2.
18 Pamphile, *Haitians and African Americans*, p. 44.
19 For more on Boyer and US recognition, see chapters 3 and 4 in Fanning, *Caribbean Crossing*.
20 See also Lazaro Gamio et al., "The Ransom: Haiti's Lost Billions," *New York Times*, May 20, 2022, accessed June 21, 2024, https://www.nytimes.com/interactive/2022/05/20/world/americas/enslaved-haiti-debt-timeline.html. For more on the indemnity, see Marlene L. Daut, *Awakening the Ashes: An Intellectual History of the Haitian Revolution* (University of North Carolina Press, 2023), chap. 8.
21 Stieber, *Haiti's Paper War*, p. 131.
22 On the counter-plantation system, see J. Casimir, *The Haitians: A Decolonial History*, trans. Laurent Dubois (University of North Carolina Press, 2020), chap. 5; see also Johnhenry Gonzalez, *Maroon Nation: A History of Revolutionary Haiti* (Yale University Press, 2019), chap. 1.
23 Christopher Schmidt-Nowara, *Slavery, Freedom, and Abolition in Latin America and the Atlantic World* (University of New Mexico Press, 2011), pp. 112–113.
24 *Mundum del bando de Miguel Hidalgo aboliendo la esclavitud*, Valladolid, 18 de octubre de 1810, accessed June 24, 2024, https://bagn.archivos.gob.mx/index.php/legajos/article/download/706/694/; Robin Blackburn, *The Overthrow of Colonial Slavery 1776–1848* (Verso, 1988), pp. 369, 371.
25 Thomas Mareite, "Slavery, Resistance(s) and Abolition in Early Nineteenth-Century Chile," *Journal of Global Slavery* 4, no. 3 (2019): p. 376. For the texts of these laws, see The Free Womb Project, accessed June 25, 2024, https://thefreewombproject.com/.
26 Peter Blanchard, *Under the Flags of Freedom: Slave Soldiers and the Wars of Independence in Spanish South America* (University of Pittsburgh Press, 2008), pp. 7–8.
27 Blanchard, *Under the Flags of Freedom*, pp. 45–46; Blackburn, *The Overthrow of Colonial Slavery*, p. 351.
28 Quoted in Daut, *Awakening the Ashes*, p. 232; Schmidt-Nowara, *Slavery, Freedom, and Abolition*, p. 109.
29 Quoted in John Lynch, *Simón Bolívar: A Life* (Yale University Press, 2006), p. 151.
30 Ibid.
31 Aline Helg, *Liberty & Equality in Caribbean Colombia, 1770–1835* (University of North Carolina Press, 2004), p. 165.
32 Jane Landers, "Africans and Their Descendants in the Spanish Empire in the Age of Revolutions," in *The Cambridge History of the Age of Atlantic Revolutions*, ed. Wim Klooster (Cambridge University Press, 2023), p. 318; Helg, *Liberty & Equality in Caribbean Colombia*, p. 163.

33 Helg, *Liberty & Equality in Caribbean Colombia*, pp. 170–71.
34 Sibylle Fischer, "Bolívar in Haiti: Republicanism in the Revolutionary Atlantic," in *Haiti and the Americas*, ed. Carla Calargé (University Press of Mississippi, 2013), pp. 27, 33, 43; Bolivia Constitución de 1826, accessed February 17, 2021, https://www.ensayistas.org/antologia/XIXA/bolivar/bolivia.htm.
35 Quoted in Blackburn, *The Overthrow of Colonial Slavery*, p. 361.
36 Quoted in Daut, *Awakening the Ashes*, p. 238.
37 Christine Hünefeldt, *Paying the Price of Freedom: Family and Labor among Lima's Slaves, 1800–1854* (University of California Press, 1994), pp. 9, 23.
38 Lynch, *Simón Bolívar*, p. 174.
39 Carlos Aguirre, *Agentes de su proprio libertad* (Lima: Pontifica Universidad Católica del Peru, 1993), p. 189.
40 Blanchard, *Under the Flags of Freedom*, p. 62.
41 See for instance, Marcela Echeverri Muñoz, *Indian and Slave Royalists in the Age of Revolution: Reform, Revolution, and Royalism in the Northern Andes, 1780–1825* (Cambridge University Press, 2016); Blanchard, *Under the Flags of Freedom*, chap. 2.
42 Blanchard, *Under the Flags of Freedom*, pp. 80–82.
43 Ibid., pp. 37–40.
44 Blanchard, *Under the Flags of Freedom*, pp. 59–62; Laurence Blair, *Patria: Lost Countries of South America* (Bodley Head, 2024), chap. 6.
45 Blackburn, *The Overthrow of Colonial Slavery*, p. 355.
46 Ibid., p. 357.
47 The cases and quotes from Juliana García and Josefa Tenorio come from chapter 7 in Blanchard, *Under the Flags of Freedom*.
48 Nancy P. Appelbaum, "From Caste to Race," in *Re-imagining Democracy in Latin America and the Caribbean, 1780–1870*, ed. Eduardo Posada-Carbó et al. (Oxford University Press, 2023), pp. 135–36, 144.
49 See, for instance, Aline Helg, "Simón Bolívar and the Spectre of 'Pardocracia': José Padilla in Post-Independence Cartagena," *Journal of Latin American Studies* 35, no. 3 (2003): pp. 447–71; Sibylle Fischer, "Specters of The Republic: The Case of Manuel Piar," *Journal of Latin American Cultural Studies* 27, no. 3 (2018): pp. 295–311.
50 Helg, *Liberty and Equality*, pp. 165–67.
51 For more detail on the case and trial, see Fischer, "Specters of The Republic."
52 Helg, *Liberty and Equality*, pp. 195–199.
53 Quoted in Ibid., p. 195.
54 Ibid., p. 196.
55 Ibid., pp. 200–201.
56 Ibid., pp. 203–209.
57 Quoted in Mareite, "Slavery, Resistance(s) and Abolition," pp. 384–385; Blackburn, *The Overthrow of Colonial Slavery*, pp. 358–59.
58 Blackburn, *The Overthrow of Colonial Slavery*, p. 372.
59 Quoted in Blanchard, *Under the Flags of Freedom*, p. 112.

Chapter 29

1 "Spartacus" in Clement Foust, *The Life and Dramatic Works of Robert Montgomery Bird* (New York: Knickerbocker Press, 1919), pp. 297–440.

2. Quoted in Richard Harris, "A Young Dramatist's Diary: The Secret Records of R. M. Bird," *Library Chronicle* 25, no. 1 (1959), pp. 16–17.
3. Harris, "A Young Dramatist's Diary," pp. 16–19. For more on the genesis of the play and Bird's views on abolition and race, see Jenna M. Gibbs, *Performing the Temple of Liberty* (Johns Hopkins University Press, 2014), pp. 181–94.
4. David F. Allmendinger, *Nat Turner and the Rising in Southampton County* (Johns Hopkins University Press, 2014), p. 24.
5. Ibid., p. 99.
6. Ibid., p. 14.
7. Thomas R. Gray, *The Confessions of Nat Turner* (Baltimore, 1831), pp. 11–23.
8. Patrick H. Breen, *The Land Shall Be Deluged in Blood: A New History of the Nat Turner Revolt* (Oxford University Press, 2015), p. 32.
9. Gray, *The Confessions of Nat Turner*, p. 14.
10. Allmendinger, *Nat Turner*, pp. 167–70.
11. Ibid., p. 179.
12. Ibid., p. 1.
13. Ibid., p. 1; see roster of insurgents, p. 281.
14. Ibid., p. 8.
15. Allmendinger, *Nat Turner*, p. 230; Breen, *The Land Shall Be Deluged in Blood*, chapter 6.
16. Sylviane Diouf, *Slavery's Exiles: The Story of the American Maroons* (New York University Press, 2016), pp. 279–282.
17. Allmendinger, *Nat Turner*, p. 4.
18. Allmendinger, *Nat Turner*, p. 203; see also chapter 4 in Breen, *The Land Shall Be Deluged in Blood*.
19. Quoted in Breen, *The Land Shall Be Deluged in Blood*, p. 85.
20. Allmendinger, *Nat Turner*, pp. 4–5.
21. Ibid., p. 242.
22. Allmendinger, *Nat Turner*, p. 7; for more on Thomas R. Gray, see, pp. 216–20.
23. Ibid., pp. 253–254.
24. Breen, *The Land Shall Be Deluged in Blood*, p. 17.
25. Gray, *The Confessions of Nat Turner*, p. 19.
26. Ibid., p. 7
27. Ibid., p. 8.
28. Ibid., p. 9.
29. Ibid., p. 9.
30. Gray, *The Confessions of Nat Turner*, p. 10; Allmendinger, *Nat Turner*, pp. 16; 20.
31. Gray, *The Confessions of Nat Turner*, pp. 10–11.
32. Gray, *The Confessions of Nat Turner*, p. 11; Allmendinger, *Nat Turner*, p. 22.
33. Gray, *The Confessions of Nat Turner*, p. 12.
34. Douglas R. Egerton, *He Shall Go Out Free: The Lives of Denmark Vesey* (Rowman & Littlefield, 2004), chap. 5, EPUB.
35. David Walker, *Appeal, In Four Articles; Together with A Preamble, to the Coloured Citizens of the World*, 3rd ed. (Boston, 1830), p. 3.
36. Ibid., p. 49.
37. Ibid., pp. 62; 77.
38. Cynthia G. Hawkins-León, "Walker, David (1795/6/7–1830)," in *Encyclopaedia of American Civil Liberties*, ed. Paul Finkleman (Routledge, 2013), p. 1734.

39 "To the public," *Genius of Universal Emancipation*, September 2, 1829, p. 6, Yale University Library website, accessed June 26, 2024, https://collections.library.yale.edu/catalog/17479549.
40 Breen, *The Land Shall Be Deluged in Blood*, p. 2.
41 Gray, *The Confessions of Nat Turner*, p. 5.
42 Breen, *The Land Shall Be Deluged in Blood*, p. 2.
43 This also triggered unrest on Cat Island, Bahamas. See Allan Meyers, "Striking for Freedom: The 1831 Uprising at Golden Grove Plantation, Cat Island," *International Journal of Bahamian Studies* 21, no. 1 (2015): pp. 74–90.
44 Tom Zoellner, *Island on Fire: The Revolt That Ended Slavery in the British Empire* (Harvard University Press, 2020), pp. 106–07; Michael Craton, *Testing the Chains: Resistance to Slavery in the British West Indies* (Cornell University Press, 1982), p. 293.
45 Craton, *Testing the Chains*, p. 296.
46 Michael Craton, "We Shall Not Be Moved: Pompey's Slave Revolt in Exuma Island, Bahamas, 1830," *New West Indian Guide / Nieuwe West-Indische Gids* 57, no. 1/2 (1983): pp. 23–24.
47 Ibid., p. 26.
48 Ibid., p. 27.
49 Ibid., p. 28.
50 Craton, *Testing the Chains*, p. 299.
51 Henry Bleby, *Death Struggles of Slavery: Being A Narrative of Facts and Incidents, Which Occurred in a British Colony, During the Two Years Immediately Preceding Negro Emancipation* (London: Hamilton, Adams, 1853), p. 115; Craton, *Testing the Chains*, p. 299.
52 Testimony of Colonel Gardner and Captain Dove, in *Facts and Documents Connected with the Late Insurrection in Jamaica*, 1837 (Cambridge University Press, 2012 reprint), p. 10.
53 "Evidence of the Rev William Knibb, House of Commons," in *Report from the Select Committee on the Extinction of Slavery Throughout the British Dominions* (London, 1833), p. 229, HathiTrust, accessed June 28, 2024, https://babel.hathitrust.org/cgi/pt?id=nyp.33433075913339&se%20q=9&q1=sharpe.
54 Zoellner, *Island on Fire*, pp. 103; 107–108.
55 "Testimony of Edward Hilton," in *Facts and Documents Connected with the Late Insurrection in Jamaica*, p. 12.
56 Zoellner, *Island on Fire*, p. 108.
57 Quoted in Zoellner, *Island on Fire*, p. 109.
58 Ibid., p. 110.
59 Craton, *Testing the Chains*, p. 303.
60 Zoellner, *Island on Fire*, p. 2.
61 Ibid., p. 124.
62 Ibid., p. 125.
63 Ibid., p. 132.
64 Ibid., pp. 135–36.
65 Craton, *Testing the Chains*, p. 311.
66 Zoellner, *Island on Fire*, p. 155.
67 Bleby, *Death Struggles of Slavery*, p. 26.
68 Craton, *Testing the Chains*, p. 315; Bleby, *Death Struggles of Slavery*, p. 117.
69 Bleby, *Death Struggles of Slavery*, pp. 113–114.

70 Ibid., p. 116.
71 Craton, *Testing the Chains*, p. 312.
72 Bleby, *Death Struggles of Slavery*, p. 199.
73 Craton, *Testing the Chains*, pp. 317–18.
74 Mary Prince, *The History of Mary Prince: A West Indian Slave* (1831), ed. Sara Salih (Penguin, 2004), EPUB.
75 The book also spawned two court hearings—one by Thomas Pringle against claims in *Blackwood Magazine* that expressed doubts about the authenticity of the story, and one by Prince's former enslaver, John Wood, who brought a libel suit against Pringle, which he won. Mary Prince had to testify in the second case. See the introduction in *The History of Mary Prince*.
76 Prince, *The History of Mary Prince*.
77 Gelien Matthews, *Caribbean Slave Revolts and the British Abolitionist Movement* (Louisiana State University Press, 2006), chap. 5.
78 Robin Blackburn, *The Overthrow of Colonial Slavery 1776–1848* (Verso, 1988), p. 434; see also Eric Williams, *Capitalism and Slavery* (Penguin Modern Classics, 2022), chap. 8.
79 James Walvin, *Freedom: The Overthrow of the Slave Empires* (Pegasus, 2019), p. 135, Kindle.
80 Zoellner, *Island on Fire*, p. 232.
81 Seymour Drescher, *Abolition: A History of Slavery and Antislavery* (Cambridge University Press, 2009), p. 250.
82 Walvin, *Freedom*, loc 1979, Kindle, p. 137.
83 Gad Heuman, "The Apprenticeship System in the Caribbean: The World of the Apprentices," *New West Indian Guide / Nieuwe West-Indische Gids* 97, no. 3/4 (2023): p. 230.
84 Ibid.
85 Quoted in Heuman, "The Apprenticeship System in the Caribbean," pp. 236–237.
86 Heuman, "The Apprenticeship System in the Caribbean," p. 238.
87 Ibid., pp. 244–45.
88 Craton, "We Shall Not Be Moved," p. 30.
89 James Williams, *A Narrative of Events, since the First of August, 1834, by James Williams, An Apprenticed Labourer in Jamaica* (1837), ed. Diana Paton (Duke University Press, 2001), pp. 5; 31n36.
90 Ibid., pp. 10–11.
91 Ibid., pp. xxxviii; xl.

Chapter 30

1 Donald Ramos, "Social Revolution Frustrated: The Conspiracy of the Tailors in Bahia, 1798," *Luso-Brazilian Review* 13, no. 1 (1976): p. 74.
2 Lilia M. Schwarcz and Heloisa M. Starling, *Brazil: A Biography* (Penguin, 2019), p. 148. Kindle.
3 Ibid.
4 Quoted in Ramos, "Social Revolution Frustrated," p. 74.
5 Quoted in Kenneth Maxwell, *Conflicts and Conspiracies: Brazil and Portugal, 1750–1808* (Routledge, 2004), p. 186. For transcriptions, also see L. H. Dias Tavares, *Sedição intentada na Bahia em 1798*, 2nd ed. (Editora da Universidade Federal da Bahia, 2016), pp. 34–40.
6 Schwarcz and Starling, *Brazil*, p. 150.

7   João José Reis and Flávio dos Santos Gomes, "Repercussion of the Haitian Revolution in Brazil, 1791–1850," in *The World of the Haitian Revolution*, ed. David P. Geggus and Norman Fiering (Indiana University Press, 2009), p. 286.
8   See Stuart B. Schwartz, *Sugar Plantations in the Formation of Brazilian Society, Bahia 1550–1835* (Cambridge University Press, 1985), p. 477. On high food prices, see chapter 8 in Maxwell, *Conflicts and Conspiracies*.
9   Dias Tavares, *Sedição Intentada na Bahia em 1798*, p. 21.
10 Reis and Santos Gomes, "Repercussion of the Haitian Revolution in Brazil," p. 285.
11 Dias Tavares, *Sedição Intentada na Bahia em 1798*, pp. 21–22; Ramos, "Social Revolution Frustrated," p. 74; Maxwell, *Conflicts and Conspiracies*, p. 187.
12 Schwarcz and Starling, *Brazil*, p. 152.
13 Quoted in Maxwell, *Conflicts and Conspiracies*, p. 185.
14 Laird W. Bergad, *The Comparative Histories of Slavery in Brazil, Cuba, and the United States* (Cambridge University Press, 2007), p. 7.
15 Schwarcz and Starling, *Brazil*, p. 179.
16 Leslie Bethell, *The Cambridge History of Latin America*, vol. 3 (Cambridge University Press, 1985), p. 172.
17 Ibid., p. 174.
18 For more detail on the Congress of Vienna, Cuba, and Brazil, see Fernanda Bretones Lane et al., "The Congress of Vienna and the Making of Second Slavery," *Journal of Global Slavery* 4, no. 2 (2019): pp. 162–95.
19 Bethell, *The Cambridge History of Latin America*, p. 178.
20 Bergad, *The Comparative Histories of Slavery*, p. 8.
21 For more on the independence movement, see chapter 2 in Gabriel Paquette, *Imperial Portugal in the Age of Atlantic Revolutions: The Luso-Brazilian World, c. 1777–1850* (Cambridge University Press, 2013).
22 Bethell, *The Cambridge History of Latin America*, p. 186.
23 Bergad, *The Comparative Histories of Slavery*, p. 8; Bethell, *The Cambridge History of Latin America*, p. 187.
24 Bethell, *The Cambridge History of Latin America*, pp. 193–194.
25 Ibid., p. 696.
26 Estimates of the number of captives transported to Brazil, 1830–1850, SlaveVoyages: The Trans-Atlantic Slave Trade Database, accessed December 7, 2024, https://www.slavevoyages.org/voyages/tK9C5mLH; estimates of the number of captives transported to Brazil, 1789–1822, SlaveVoyages: The Trans-Atlantic Slave Trade Database, accessed December 7, 2024, https://www.slavevoyages.org/voyages/VJOTwnMn; estimates of the number of captives transported to Brazil, 1822–1830, SlaveVoyages: The Trans-Atlantic Slave Trade Database, accessed April 30, 2025, https://www.slavevoyages.org/voyages/2YS9BD7H.
27 Reis and Santos Gomes, "Repercussions of the Haitian Revolution in Brazil," p. 284.
28 Bethell, *The Cambridge History of Latin America*, pp. 680–81.
29 Ibid., pp. 679–80.
30 Paquette, *Imperial Portugal*, chap. 4; Schwarcz and Starling, *Brazil*, chap. 9.
31 Reis and Santos Gomes, "Repercussions of the Haitian Revolution in Brazil," p. 287.
32 Quoted in Reis and Santos Gomes, "Repercussions of the Haitian Revolution in Brazil," p. 288; see also Washington Santos Nascimento, "'São Domingos, o grande São Domingos': Repercussões e representações da Revolução Haitiana no Brasil escravista

(1791–1840)," *125 Dimensões* 21 (2008): pp. 125–42; Luiz R. B. Mott, "A Revolução dos negros Do Haiti e do Brasil," *Historia: Questões & Debates* 3, no. 4 (1982): pp. 55–65.
33   See Schwartz, *Sugar Plantations in the Formation of Brazilian Society*, pp. 486–87; Manuel Barcia, "'An Islamic Atlantic Revolution': Dan Fodio's Jihād and Slave Rebellion in Bahia and Cuba, 1804–1844," *Journal of African Diaspora Archaeology and Heritage* 2, no. 1 (2013): pp. 12–14; see also João José Reis, *Rebelião escrava no Brasil: A história do levante dos Malês (1835)* (São Paulo: Editora Brasiliense, 1986), pp. 64–83; and Sylviane A. Diouf, *Servants of Allah: African Muslims Enslaved in the Americas* (New York University Press, 2013), chap. 1.
34   Schwartz, *Sugar Plantations in the Formation of Brazilian Society*, pp. 479–80.
35   Mieko Nishida, "Manumission and Ethnicity in Urban Slavery: Salvador, Brazil, 1808–1888," *Hispanic American Historical Review* 73, no. 3 (1993): p. 365.
36   Reis, *Rebelião escrava no Brasil*, p. 16.
37   Nishida, "Manumission and Ethnicity," p. 369.
38   Ibid., pp. 372–73.
39   Reis, *Rebelião escrava no Brasil*, pp. 115–116; C. Moura, *Dicionário da escravidnao negra no Brasil* (Editora da Universidade de São Paulo, 2004), pp. 254–59; Barcia, "An Islamic Atlantic Revolution," pp. 6–17.
40   Ibid., p. 87.
41   Ibid., pp. 88–89.
42   Ibid., p. 89.
43   Ibid., pp. 91–93.
44   Quoted in Reis, *Rebelião escrava no Brasil*, p. 94.
45   Ibid., p. 96.
46   Ibid., p. 101.
47   Ibid., p. 107.
48   Ibid., p. 104.
49   Diouf, *Servants of Allah*, chap. 5, EPUB.
50   Reis, *Rebelião escrava no Brasil*, p. 255.
51   Diouf, *Servants of Allah*, chap. 5.
52   Ibid.
53   Bethell, *The Cambridge History of Latin America*, p. 735.
54   Estimates of the number of captives transported to Brazil, 1830–1850, SlaveVoyages: The Trans-Atlantic Slave Trade Database: accessed December 6, 2024, https://www.slavevoyages.org/voyages/tK9C5mLH.
55   Bethell, *Cambridge History of Latin America*, pp. 732–33.
56   Estimates of the number of voyages to Brazil, 1850–1855, SlaveVoyages: The Trans-Atlantic Slave Trade Database: accessed December 6, 2024, https://www.slavevoyages.org/voyages/tqbvLGoy.
57   Bethell, *The Cambridge History of Latin America*, p. 744.
58   Herbert S. Klein and Francisco Vidal Luna, *Slavery in Brazil* (Cambridge University Press, 2010), pp. 101, 173.
59   The quotes in this section come from Mahommah G. Baquaqua, *Biography of Mahommah G. Baquaqua, A Native of Zoogoo, in the Interior of Africa* (Detroit: Geo. E. Pomeroy, 1854), accessed July 3, 2024, https://docsouth.unc.edu/neh/baquaqua/baquaqua.html. See also Bergad, *The Comparative Histories of Slavery in Brazil, Cuba, and the United States*, pp. 83–95.

60 Richard Huzzey, *Freedom Burning: Anti-Slavery and Empire in Victorian Britain* (Cornell University Press, 2012), p. 46.
61 Huzzey, *Freedom Burning*, pp. 146–47; Eltis, *Economic Growth*, p. 88; Everill, *Abolition and Empire*, chapter 7.
62 For more on Britain's objectives, see Andrew Lambert, "Slavery, Free Trade and Naval Strategy, 1840–1860, in *Slavery, Diplomacy, and Empire: Britain and the Suppression of the Slave Trade, 1807–1975*. Keith Hamilton and Patrick Salmon (eds.) (University of Liverpool Press, 2013), chap. 3.
63 Huzzey, *Freedom Burning*, p. 52; David Eltis, *Economic Growth and the Ending of the Transatlantic Slave Trade* (Oxford University Press, 1987), pp. 86–87.
64 On Britain and France, see Paul Michael Kielstra, *The Politics of Slave Trade Suppression in Britain and France, 1814–48: Diplomacy, Morality and Economics* (Palgrave Macmillan 2000).
65 Huzzey, *Freedom Burning*, p. 46.
66 Eltis, *Economic Growth*, p. 92.
67 Huzzey, *Freedom Burning*, p. 46.
68 Bethell, *The Cambridge History of Latin America*, p. 736.
69 The higher estimate of 700,000 is from the Liberated Africans website (University of Colorado Boulder), https://liberatedafricans.org/about/essays.php. The site contains digitized documentation, including a Register of Liberated Africans.
70 Huzzey, *Freedom Burning*, pp. 46–49.
71 For more detail on the composition and workings of the courts, see Farida Shaikh, "Judicial Diplomacy: British Officials and the Mixed Commission Courts," in *Slavery, Diplomacy, and Empire: Britain and the Suppression of the Slave Trade, 1807–1975*, Keith Hamilton and Patrick Salmon (eds.) (University of Liverpool Press, 2013), chap. 2.
72 Farida Shaikh, "Judicial Diplomacy," p. 48.
73 Everill, *Abolition and Empire*, p. 21; Emma Christopher, "'Tis enough that we give them liberty'? Liberated Africans at Sierra Leone in the Early Era of Slave-Trade Suppression," in *The Suppression of the Atlantic Slave Trade: British Policies, Practices and Representations of Naval Coercion*, ed. Robert Burroughs and Richard Huzzey (Manchester University Press, 2015), pp. 57–58. See also Padraic X. Scanlon, *Freedom's Debtors: British Antislavery in Sierra Leone in the Age of Revolution* (Yale University Press, 2017).
74 Everill, *Abolition and Empire*, pp. 20–22.
75 Christopher, "'Tis enough that we give them liberty'?," p. 57.
76 Mary Church, *Sierra Leone; or The Liberated Africans, in a Series of Letters from a Young Lady to Her Sister in 1833 & 34* (London: Longman & Co, 1835), p. 29.
77 Christopher, "'Tis enough that we give them liberty'?," pp. 59–60.
78 Church, *Sierra Leone*, p. 29.
79 Huzzey, *Freedom Burning*, p. 183.
80 Anderson and Lovejoy, *Liberated Africans*, p. 11, chap. 15; Andrew Pearson, "Liberated African Settlers on St. Helena," in *Liberated Africans and the Abolition of the Slave Trade 1807–1896*, ed. Richard Anderson and Henry B. Lovejoy (Boydell & Brewer, 2020), p. 313.
81 Pearson, "Liberated African Settlers on St. Helena," p. 314.
82 Ibid., pp. 315–17.
83 David Eltis, *Atlantic Cataclysm: Rethinking the Slave Trades* (University of Cambridge Press, 2025), pp. 347–348.
84 Eltis, *Atlantic Cataclysm*, p. 297.

85 Suzanne Schwarz, "The Impact of Liberated African 'Disposal' Policies in Early Nineteenth-Century Sierra Leone," in *Liberated Africans and the Abolition of the Slave Trade, 1807–1896*, ed. Richard Anderson and Henry B. Lovejoy (Boydell & Brewer, 2020), p. 54.
86 Everill. *Abolition and Empire*, pp. 120–123.
87 John Saillant, "Dâaga the Rebel on Land and at Sea," *CLR James Journal* 25, no. 1/2 (Fall 2019): p. 175; see also E. L. Joseph, *History of Trinidad* (London, 1838), pp. 260–72.
88 Saillant, "Dâaga the Rebel," pp. 166–67, 174.
89 Ibid., p. 177.
90 Ibid., p. 176; also quoted in Joseph, *History of Trinidad*, p. 271.
91 Estimates of the number captives transported from Africa, 1808–1866, SlaveVoyages: The Trans-Atlantic Slave Trade Database, accessed December 7, 2024, https://www.slavevoyages.org/voyages/xzEoQX3Y.
92 John Harris, *The Last Slave Ships: New York and the End of the Middle Passage* (Yale University Press, 2020), introduction, EPUB.
93 Estimates of the number of captives transported from Africa, 1850–1867, SlaveVoyages: The Trans-Atlantic Slave Trade Database, accessed April 20, 2025, https://www.slavevoyages.org/voyages/okeS7Cf8
94 John Harris, *The Last Slave Ships*, chap. 1.
95 Huzzey, *Freedom Burning*, p. 180.
96 Moon-Ho Jung, *Coolies and Cane: Race, Labor, and Sugar in the Age of Emancipation* (Johns Hopkins University Press, 2006), p. 14.
97 Ibid., p. 17.
98 Quoted in Jose Miguel Sanjuan-Marroquin and Martin Rodrigo-Alharilla, "'No Commercial Activity Leaves Greater Benefit': The Profitability of the Cuban-Based Slave Trade during the First Half of the Nineteenth Century," *Economic History Review* 77, no. 1 (February 2024): pp. 268–87.
99 Ibid., p. 269.

Chapter 31

1 See Benjamin Robert Haydon, "The Anti-Slavery Society Convention, 1840," oil on canvas, 1841, National Portrait Gallery, https://www.npg.org.uk/collections/search/portrait/mw00028/The-Anti-Slavery-Society-Convention-1840.
2 Seymour Drescher, *Abolition: A History of Slavery and Antislavery* (Cambridge University Press, 2009), p. 267.
3 Kathryn Kish Sklar, "'Women Who Speak for an Entire Nation': American and British Women Compared at the World Anti-Slavery Convention, London 1840," *Pacific Historical Review* 59, no. 4 (1990): pp. 453–99.
4 A brief sketch of Louis Celeste Lecesne's life can be found on the UCL Centre for the Study of the Legacies of British Slavery site: https://www.ucl.ac.uk/lbs/person/view/44760
5 Marlene L. Daut, *Awakening the Ashes: An Intellectual History of the Haitian Revolution* (University of North Carolina Press, 2023), p. xvi.
6 Catherine Hall, "The Lords of Humankind Re-Visited," *Bulletin of the School of Oriental and African Studies* 66, no. 3 (2003): pp. 472–85.
7 Ibid., p. 477.
8 Quoted in Paul O'Keeffe, *A Genius for Failure: The Life of Benjamin Robert Haydon* (Bodley Head, 2009), pp. 407–09. See also David Olusoga, *Black and British: A Forgotten History*

(Pan Macmillan, 2016), pp. 257–59; and Hall, "The Lords of Humankind Re-Visited," pp. 472–85.
9 Quoted in Hall, "The Lords of Humankind Re-Visited," p. 480.
10 Ibid., p. 478. See also Richard Huzzey, *Freedom Burning: Anti-Slavery and Empire in Victorian Britain* (Cornell University Press, 2012).
11 *The British and Foreign Anti-Slavery Reporter*, June 17, 1840, p. 135.
12 Hugh Thomas, *The Slave Trade: A History of the Atlantic Slave Trade, 1440–1870* (Simon & Schuster, 1997), pp. 1024–1027. Kindle.
13 Ibid.
14 This section relies on Marcus Rediker's detailed and excellent *The Amistad Rebellion: An Atlantic Odyssey of Slavery and Freedom* (Viking, 2012), chap. 1. EPUB.
15 Ibid., chap. 2.
16 Ibid.
17 Ibid.
18 Ibid.
19 "Judicial Investigation" (*New York Sun*), published in the *Hartford Courant*, August 29, 1839, page 2.
20 Rediker, *The Amistad Rebellion*, chap. 3.
21 Ibid.
22 Ibid.
23 Ibid.
24 Ibid., chap. 4.
25 Ibid.
26 "Treaty of Friendship, Limits, and Navigation Between Spain and The United States, October 27, 1795," The Avalon Project, accessed July 7, 2024, https://avalon.law.yale.edu/18th_century/sp1795.asp#art9.
27 "Argument of Roger S. Baldwin, of New Haven, Before the Supreme Court of the United States in the Case of the United States, Appellants, vs Cinque, and Others, Africans of the Amistad" (New York, 1841), pp. 5–6. Access online at https://archive.org/details/argumentofrogers00bald/page/n11/mode/2up.
28 Ibid., p. 14.
29 "Argument of John Quincy Adams, before the Supreme Court of the United States, in the Case of the United States, Appellants, v. Cinque, and Others, Africans," New York, 1841, p. 82. Access online at https://archive.org/details/argumentofjohnqu1841adam/page/n3/mode/2up.
30 Ibid., p. 23.
31 Ibid., p. 21.
32 Ibid., p. 53.
33 Ibid., pp. 54–55.
34 Their return was not exactly straightforward, and they had to raise money as well. See Rediker, *The Amistad Rebellion*, chap. 6.
35 Anita Rupprecht, "'All We Have Done, We Have Done for Freedom': The Creole Slave-Ship Revolt (1841) and the Revolutionary Atlantic," *International Review of Social History* 58, no. 21 (2013): p. 253.
36 Rediker, *The Amistad Rebellion*, conclusion; Rupprecht, "All We Have Done," p. 265; see also Jeffrey Kerr-Ritchie, *Rebellious Passage: The Creole Revolt and America's Coastal Slave Trade* (Cambridge University Press, 2019), chap. 5.

37 Rupprecht, "All We Have Done," p. 265.
38 Quoted in Rupprecht, "All We Have Done," p. 267.
39 Rupprecht, "All We Have Done," p. 267.
40 Ibid., p. 269.
41 See Kerr-Ritchie, *Rebellious Passage*, chap. 1.
42 Rupprecht, "All We Have Done," p. 274.
43 Kerr-Ritchie, *Rebellious Passage*, p. 154.
44 Rupprecht, "All We Have Done," p. 276. The story of the *Creole* inspired Frederick Douglass's only work of fiction, *The Heroic Slave*, published in 1852.
45 On "second slavery," see Dale Tomich, "The Wealth of Empire: Francisco Arango y Parreno, Political Economy, and the Second Slavery in Cuba," in *Interpreting Spanish Colonialism: Empires, Nations, and Legends*, ed. Christopher Schmidt-Nowara and John M. Nieto-Phillips (University of New Mexico Press, 2005).
46 Inés Roldán de Montaud, "The Misfortune of Liberated Africans in Colonial Cuba, 1824–76," in *Liberated Africans and the Abolition of the Slave Trade 1807–1896*, ed. Richard Anderson and Henry B. Lovejoy (Boydell & Brewer, 2020), pp 153–159; Schmidt-Nowara, *Empire and Antislavery*, pp. 38–39; Estimates of the number of captives transported from Africa to Cuba 1817–1840, SlaveVoyages: The Trans-Atlantic Slave Trade Database, accessed December 8, 2024, https://www.slavevoyages.org/voyages/gUzzGc1r.
47 Roldán de Montaud, "The Misfortune of Liberated Africans," p. 154.
48 Ibid., pp. 164–165.
49 Aisha K. Finch, *Rethinking Slave Rebellion in Cuba: La Escalera and the Insurgencies of 1841–1844* (University of North Carolina Press, 2015), pp. 27–28.
50 Manuel Barcia, *The Great African Slave Revolt of 1825: Cuba and the Fight for Freedom in Matanzas* (Louisiana State University Press, 2012), pp. 77–81.
51 Schmidt-Nowara, *Empire and Antislavery*, p. 16.
52 Finch, *Rethinking Slave Rebellion in Cuba*, p. 46; see also chapter 1 in Schmidt-Nowara, *Empire and Antislavery*.
53 See Vanessa Mongey, *Rogue Revolutionaries: The Fight for Legitimacy in the Greater Caribbean* (University of Pennsylvania Press, 2020), chap. 4; Guillermo A. Baralt, *Esclavos Rebeldes: conspiraciones y sublevaciones de esclavos en Puerto Rico (1795–1873)*, 2nd ed. (Ediciones Huracán, 1982), chap. 7; Barcia, *The Great African Slave Revolt of 1825*, pp. 1, 122.
54 Baralt, *Esclavos Rebeldes*, pp. 44–45.
55 Ibid., p. 32.
56 Ibid., p. 39.
57 Finch, *Rethinking Slave Rebellion in Cuba*, p. 48.
58 For a detailed account of the revolt and its aftermath, see Barcia, *The Great African Slave Revolt of 1825*, chaps. 4 and 5.
59 On Cuban tobacco see Jean Stubbs, *Tobacco on the Periphery: A Case Study in Cuban Labour History, 1860–1958* (Cambridge University Press, 1985).
60 Finch, *Rethinking Slave Rebellion in Cuba*, pp. 35–36.
61 Ibid., p. 38.
62 See Robert L. Paquette, *Sugar Is Made with Blood: The Conspiracy of La Escalera and the Conflict between Empires over Slavery in Cuba* (Wesleyan University Press, 1988), chap. 5; see also David Turnbull, *Travels in the West: Cuba; with Notices of Porto Rico and the Slave Trade* (London, 1840).

63 Finch, *Rethinking Slave Rebellion in Cuba*, p. 118; Schmidt-Nowara, *Empire and Antislavery*, p. 33.
64 A complete printed edition did not come out in Spanish until 1937. Manzano's autobiography was one of only two narratives written by an Afro-descended person, Cuba not having a tradition of "slave narratives" similar to that in the US. Juan Francisco Manzano, *The Life and Poems of a Cuban Slave: Juan Francisco Manzano 1797–1854*, ed. Edward J. Mullen (Palgrave Macmillan, 2014), pp. 3, 14. See pp. 25–30 for more on Richard Robert Madden and the translation of Manzano's work.
65 Quoted in Manzano, *The Life and Poems of a Cuban Slave*, p. 80.
66 Ibid., p. 92.
67 Ibid., p. 6.
68 Quoted in Ibid., p. 8.
69 Ibid., pp. 84–85.
70 Quoted in Ibid., p. 8.
71 Sylvia Molloy, "From Serf to Self: The Autobiography of Juan," *MLN* 104, no. 2 (1989): p. 395.
72 Finch, *Rethinking Slave Rebellion in Cuba*, p. 75.
73 See chapter 3 in Barcia, *Seeds of Insurrection*.
74 Finch, *Rethinking Slave Rebellion in Cuba*, p. 69.
75 Ibid., pp. 81–85.
76 Finch, *Rethinking Slave Rebellion in Cuba*, pp. 115–26; Paquette, *Sugar Is Made with Blood*, chap. 6.
77 Finch, *Rethinking Slave Rebellion in Cuba*, p. 87.
78 Ibid., p. 88.
79 Ibid., pp. 107–108.
80 Quoted in Finch, *Rethinking Slave Rebellion in Cuba*, p. 89.
81 Ibid., p. 147.
82 Finch, *Rethinking Slave Rebellion in Cuba*, pp. 90–93, 100, see chap. 5 for more on the women rebels. Paquette, *Sugar Is Made with Blood*, p. 210.
83 Finch, *Rethinking Slave Rebellion in Cuba*, p. 101.
84 Paquette, *Sugar Is Made with Blood*, p. 211.
85 Finch, *Rethinking Slave Rebellion in Cuba*, p. 141.
86 Paquette, *Sugar Is Made with Blood*, p. 215.
87 Quoted in Ibid., p. 226.
88 Ibid., pp. 221; 229.
89 Barcia, *Seeds of Insurrection*, p. 46.
90 Schmidt-Nowara, *Empire and Antislavery*, pp. 32–33.
91 Finch, *Rethinking Slave Rebellion in Cuba*, pp. 119–122; on Plácido, see chapter 8 in Ada Ferrer, *Cuba: An American History* (Scribner, 2021).
92 Quoted in Ferrer, *Cuba*, p. 104.
93 Barcia, *The Great African Slave Revolt of 1825*, p. 146.

Chapter 32

1 Estimates of the number of captives transported from Africa to the French Caribbean, 1802–1848, SlaveVoyages: The Trans-Atlantic Slave Trade Database, accessed July 10, 2024, https://www.slavevoyages.org/voyages/E7EfpEsr.

2. Lorelle Semley, *To Be Free and French: Citizenship in France's Atlantic Empire* (Cambridge University Press, 2017), p. 116.
3. Françoise Thésée, "La révolte des esclaves du Carbet à la Martinique (Octobre-Novembre 1822)," *Revue Française d'histoire d'outre-Mer* 80, no. 301 (1993): pp. 569–570.
4. Ibid., pp. 560–61.
5. Quoted in Thésée, "La révolte des esclaves," p. 566.
6. Ibid., p. 567.
7. Thésée, "La révolte des esclaves," pp. 571–74.
8. Melvin D. Kennedy, "The Bissette Affair and the French Colonial Question," *Journal of Negro History* 45, no. 1 (1960): p. 2.
9. *Notices statistiques sur les colonies françaises*, Paris, 1837, pp. 49–50.
10. Lawrence C. Jennings, "Cyrille Bissette, Radical Black French Abolitionist," *French History* 9, no. 1 (1995): p. 51; Kennedy, "The Bissette Affair," p. 1; Rebecca Hartkopf Schloss, *Sweet Liberty: The Final Days of Slavery in Martinique* (University of Pennsylvania Press, 2009), p. 135.
11. Kennedy, "The Bissette Affair," p. 3; Semley, *To Be Free and French*, p. 115.
12. Cyrille Bissette was also related via illegitimacy to the Pagerie family of Josephine Bonaparte. Chris Bongie, "'C'est du papier ou de l'histoire en marche?': The Revolutionary Compromises of a Martiniquan Homme de Couleur, Cyrille-Charles-Auguste Bissette," *Nineteenth-Century Contexts* 23, no. 4 (2002): pp. 439–40; Jennings, "Cyrille Bissette," pp. 48–66; Semley, *To Be Free and French*, p. 118.
13. Bongie, "C'est du papier ou de l'histoire en marche?," p. 440; Semley, *To Be Free and French*, p. 140.
14. Jennings, "Cyrille Bissette," p. 50.
15. On the proslavery debate, see Naomi J. Andrews, "'How Should Slaves Disappear?': Defending Slavery in France, 1834–1848," *Slavery & Abolition* 41, no. 3 (2020): pp. 643–68.
16. Quoted in Schloss, *Sweet Liberty*, p. 135; Semley, *To Be Free and French*, p. 116.
17. Schloss, *Sweet Liberty*, pp. 135–36.
18. Ibid., p. 11.
19. Ibid., pp. 135–37; see also chapter 3 in Semley, *To Be Free and French*.
20. Schloss, *Sweet Liberty*, p. 155.
21. Ibid., p. 159.
22. Jennings, "Cyrille Bissette," p. 50.
23. Bongie, "C'est du papier ou de l'histoire en marche?," p. 456.
24. Alexis de Tocqueville, "The Emancipation of Slaves (1843)," in *Writings on Empire and Slavery*, ed. Jennifer Pitts (Johns Hopkins University Press, 2000), p. 200. For a more detailed discussion about Tocqueville's thought and writings on abolition in terms of property rights and French imperialism, see chapter 2 in Nick Nesbitt, *Caribbean Critique: Antillean Critical Theory from Toussaint to Glissant* (Liverpool University Press, 2013), pp. 66–85.
25. Quoted in Nesbitt, *Caribbean Critique*, p. 85.
26. Alexis de Tocqueville, "The Emancipation of Slaves (1843)," pp. 201, 207.
27. For more on Tocqueville's views on slavery and abolition, see Sally Gershman, "Alexis de Tocqueville and Slavery," *French Historical Studies* 9, no. 3 (1976): 467–483.
28. Françoise Vergès, "The Slave Trade, Slavery, and Abolitionism: The Unfinished Debate in France," in *A Global History of Anti-Slavery Politics in the Nineteenth Century*, ed. William Mulligan and Maurice Bric (Palgrave Macmillan, 2013), p. 203; Jennings, "Cyrille Bissette," p. 49.

29 Pierre Dessalles, *Sugar and Slavery, Family and Race: The Letters and Diary of Pierre Dessalles, Planter in Martinique, 1808–1865*, ed. Elborg Forster and Robert Forster (Johns Hopkins University Press, 1996), p. 209.
30 Semley, *To Be Free and French*, pp. 141–143.
31 However, May 22 is the day that is celebrated as Emancipation Day in Martinique. Semley, *To Be Free and French*, pp. 143–144; 148.
32 Vergès, "The Slave Trade, Slavery, and Abolitionism," p. 202. For more on the compensation, see https://www.portail-esclavage-reunion.fr/en/compensation-paid-out-to-slave-owners-recorded-in-a-database/ (accessed April 21, 2025).
33 Bongie, "C'est du papier ou de l'histoire en marche?," p. 441; Jennings, "Cyrille Bissette," p. 65.
34 Semley, *To Be Free and French*, pp. 147–48.
35 Yolande Lavoie et al., "A Particular Study of Slavery in the Caribbean Island of Saint Barthelemy: 1648–1846," *Caribbean Studies* 28, no. 2 (1995): p. 399; François Nault and Francine M. Mayer, "L'abolition de l'esclavage à Saint–Barthélemy vue à travers l'étude de quatre listes nominatives de sa population rurale de 1840 à 1854," *Revue Française d'histoire d'outre–Mer* 79, no. 296 (1992): pp. 305–40.
36 See chapter 12 in Neville A. T. Hall, *Slave Society in the Danish West Indies: St. Thomas, St. John and St. Croix*, ed. B. W. Higman (University of the West Indies Press, 1992).
37 Quoted in Hall, *Slave Society in the Danish West Indies*, p. 208.
38 Hall, *Slave Society in the Danish West Indies*, p. 212.
39 Ibid., pp. 216–217.
40 Lomarsh Roopnarine, "Contract Labor Migration as an Agent of Revolutionary Change in the Danish West Indies," *Labor History* 61, no. 5/6 (2020): pp. 692–705.
41 Alice L. Baumgartner, *South to Freedom: Runaway Slaves to Mexico and the Road to the Civil War* (Basic Books, 2020), p. 5.
42 Ibid., pp. 49–53; see also chapter 11 in William H. Beezley and Michael C. Meyer, eds., *The Oxford History of Mexico* (Oxford University Press, 2010).
43 Baumgartner, *South to Freedom*, pp. 55–58, 62.
44 Ibid., pp. 67–69; see chapter 4 for more on the plan to liberate Cuba.
45 Quoted in Carrie Gibson, *El Norte: The Epic and Forgotten Story of Hispanic North America* (Grove Atlantic, 2019), p. 194.
46 Gibson, *El Norte*, p. 196.
47 See the full text of the Texas Constitution of 1836 at Tarlton Law Library, Jamail Center for Legal Research, accessed July 13, 2024, https://tarlton.law.utexas.edu/c.php?g=815580&p=5820518. For more on Texas and Mexico, see chapter 9 in Gibson, *El Norte*.
48 Benjamin Lundy, *The War in Texas: A Review of Facts and Circumstances, Showing That This Contest Is A Crusade Against Mexico, Set on Foot and Supported by Slaveholders, Land-Speculators, &c. in Order to Re-Establish, Extend, and Perpetuate the System of Slavery and the Slave Trade* (Philadelphia: Merrihew and Gunn, 1837), p. 46.
49 Ibid., p. 3.
50 Baumgartner, *South to Freedom*, p. 4; see also Scott Shane, "How the Underground Railroad Got Its Name," *New York Times*, September 11, 2023, https://www.nytimes.com/2023/09/11/opinion/man-who-named-underground-railroad.html.
51 Baumgartner, *South to Freedom*, p. 3.
52 Ibid., pp. 178–79.

53 Ibid., pp. 180–81.
54 For more on Narciso López and his annexation plots, see chapter 9 in Ada Ferrer, *Cuba: An American History* (Scribner, 2021).
55 Natalia Sobrevilla Perea, "The Abolition of Slavery in the South American Republics," *Slavery & Abolition* 44, no. 1 (2023): p. 95.
56 Sobrevilla Perea, "The Abolition of Slavery in the South American Republics," pp. 95, 101; Alex Borucki, *From Shipmates to Soldiers: Emerging Black Identities in the Río de La Plata* (University of New Mexico Press, 2015), chap. 4; James E. Sanders, *The Vanguard of the Atlantic World: Creating Modernity, Nation, and Democracy in Nineteenth-Century Latin America* (Duke University Press, 2014), chap. 1.
57 Sobrevilla Perea, "The Abolition of Slavery in the South American Republics," p. 102.
58 For more detail on this, see Marcela Echeverri, "Slave Exports and the Politics of Slave Punishment during Colombia's Abolition Process (1820s–1840s)," *Journal of Global Slavery* 7, no. 1/2 (2022): pp. 73–102.
59 Echeverri, "Slave Exports and the Politics of Slave Punishment," pp. 84–86.
60 Ibid., pp. 88–89.
61 Quoted in Ibid., p. 92.
62 Yesenia Barragan, *Freedom's Captives: Slavery and Gradual Emancipation on the Colombian Black Pacific* (Cambridge University Press, 2021), p. 10.
63 Echeverri, "Slave Exports and the Politics of Slave Punishment," p. 92.
64 Sobrevilla Perea, "The Abolition of Slavery in the South American Republics," p. 101.
65 Sarah Washbrook, "Independence for Those without Freedom: Slavery and Manumission in Mérida, Venezuela, 1810–1854," *Slavery & Abolition* 39, no. 4 (2018): p. 716.
66 Sobrevilla Perea, "The Abolition of Slavery in the South American Republics," p. 102.
67 Echeverri, "Slave Exports and the Politics of Slave Punishment," pp. 92–93; Peter Blanchard, *Slavery & Abolition in Early Republican Peru* (Wilmington, DE: Scholarly Resources, 1992), chap. 3.
68 Blanchard, *Slavery & Abolition in Early Republican Peru*, p. 182.
69 Benjamin N. Narváez, "Abolition, Chinese Indentured Labor, and the State: Cuba, Peru, and the United States during the Mid Nineteenth Century." *The Americas* 76, no. 1 (2019): pp. 5, 10.
70 Blanchard, *Slavery & Abolition in Early Republican Peru*, pp. 166–167.
71 Sobrevilla Perea, "The Abolition of Slavery in the South American Republics," p. 103. See also Blanchard, *Slavery & Abolition and Early Republican Peru*; Carlos Aguirre, *Agentes de su proprio libertad* (Lima: Pontifica Universidad Católica del Peru, 1993).
72 Full text at the US National Archives: accessed December 8, 2024, https://www.archives.gov/milestone-documents/dred-scott-v-sandford.https://www.archives.gov/milestone-documents/dred-scott-v-sandford.
73 *New York Evening Post*, quoted in *The Liberator*, March 20, 1857, p. 1.

Chapter 33

1 Frederick Douglass, *Narrative of the Life of Frederick Douglass, an American Slave, Written by Himself* (Belknap Press, 1845), p. 106.
2 "The First Victim Under the New Fugitive Slave Bill," *North Star*, October 3, 1850, p. 2.
3 "The Slave-Catching Law," *The Liberator*, October 4, 1850, p. 2.

4 For the full text, see National Archives, accessed December 9, 2024, https://www.archives.gov/milestone-documents/compromise-of-1850.
5 This section is based on his account of these 12 years; see Solomon Northup, *Twelve Years a Slave (1853)* (Penguin, 2012).
6 "Twelve Years a Slave!" *The Liberator*, August 26, 1853, p. 3.
7 Andrew Delbanco, ed., *The Abolitionist Imagination* (Harvard University Press, 2012), pp. 3–4.
8 On the question of abolition versus antislavery, see Manisha Sinha, "Did the Abolitionists Cause the Civil War?" in *The Abolitionist Imagination*, ed. Andrew Delbanco (Harvard University Press, 2012), p. 88.
9 Frederick Douglass, "The Meaning of July Fourth for the Negro," July 5, 1852; Mass Humanities, accessed July 15, 2024, https://masshumanities.org/wp-content/uploads/2024/03/Reading-Frederick-Douglass-Together_speech_full.pdf; David W. Blight, *Frederick Douglass: Prophet of Freedom* (Simon & Schuster, 2018), chap. 13, EPUB.
10 Sinha, "Did the Abolitionists Cause the Civil War?," p. 91.
11 James Walvin, *Freedom: The Overthrow of the Slave Empires* (Pegasus, 2019), p. 144, Kindle.
12 Seymour Drescher, *Abolition: A History of Slavery and Antislavery* (Cambridge University Press, 2009), p. 245.
13 Remains of the ship were found in 2018; see Ben Raines, "History Demands We Preserve the Wreck of America's Last Slave Ship," *Time*, February 18, 2022, accessed July 16, 2024, https://time.com/6148417/clotilda-preserve-americas-last-slaveship/. See also Hannah Durkin, *Survivors: The Lost Stories of the Last Captives of the Atlantic Slave Trade* (London: William Collins, 2024); Zora Neale Hurston, *Barracoon: The Story of the Last "Black Cargo,"* ed. Deborah G. Plant (Amistad, 2018).
14 For more on the captured US ships, see Sharla M. Fett, *Recaptured Africans: Surviving Slave Ships, Detention, and Dislocation in the Final Years of the Slave Trade* (University of North Carolina Press, 2017).
15 Manisha Sinha, *The Slave's Cause: A History of Abolition* (Yale University Press, 2016), pp. 551–52; James Oakes, *The Radical and the Republican: Frederick Douglass, Abraham Lincoln, and the Triumph of Antislavery Politics* (W. W. Norton, 2007), chap. 3, EPUB.
16 See the 1860 census, accessed July 16, 2024, https://www.census.gov/library/publications/1864/dec/1860a.html.
17 Jessica Vance Roitman, "Land of Hope and Dreams: Slavery & Abolition in the Dutch Leeward Islands, 1825–1865," *Slavery & Abolition* 37, no. 2 (2016): p. 387.
18 Ibid., p. 383.
19 Ibid., p. 375.
20 Quoted in Roitman, "Land of Hope and Dreams," p. 379.
21 Roitman, "Land of Hope and Dreams," p. 381; Valika Smeulders, "Lokhey," in Eveline Sint Nicolaas and Valika Smeulders, eds., *Slavery* (Rijksmuseum Exhibition Catalogue) (Atlas Contact, 2021), p. 280.
22 Roitman, "Land of Hope and Dreams," p. 381.
23 Alex van Stipriaan, "Suriname and the Abolition of Slavery," in *Fifty Years Later: Antislavery, Capitalism and Modernity in the Dutch Orbit*, ed. Gert Oostindie (University of Pittsburgh Press, 1996), p. 118.
24 Ibid., pp. 132–33.
25 The society's full name was Vereeniging ter bevordering van de afschaffing der slavernij. See Maarten Kuitenbrouwer, "The Dutch Case of Antislavery: Late and Elitist

Abolitionism," in *Fifty Years Later: Antislavery, Capitalism and Modernity in the Dutch Orbit*, ed. Gert Oostindie (University of Pittsburgh Press, 1996), p. 74.
26 Kuitenbrouwer, "The Dutch Case of Antislavery," p. 73.
27 Van Stipriaan, "Suriname and the Abolition of Slavery," p. 139.
28 "Emancipation in Surinam," *The Liberator*, August 21, 1863, p. 1.
29 Kuitenbrouwer, "The Dutch Case of Antislavery," p. 77.
30 Ibid.
31 Eveline Sint Nicolaas, "Dutch Colonial Slavery," in Eveline Sint Nicolaas and Valika Smeulders, eds., *Slavery* (Rijksmuseum Exhibition Catalogue) (Atlas Contact, 2021), p. 55.
32 Oakes, *The Radical and the Republican*, chap. 2.
33 Quoted in Oakes, *The Radical and the Republican*, p. 203.
34 Quoted in David Williams, *I Freed Myself! African American Self-Emancipation in the Civil War Era* (Cambridge University Press, 2014), p. 63.
35 Ibid., p. 63, note 115.
36 Ibram X. Kendi, *Stamped from the Beginning: The Definitive History of Racist Ideas in America* (Bodley Head, 2017), p. 215, Kindle.
37 Chandra Manning, "Working for Citizenship in Civil War Contraband Camps," *Journal of the Civil War Era* 4, no. 2 (2014): p. 178.
38 Steven Hahn, *The Political Worlds of Slavery and Freedom* (Harvard University Press, 2009), chap. 2.
39 Manning, "Working for Citizenship," pp. 172–204.
40 Ibid., p. 190.
41 Quoted in Manning, "Working for Citizenship," p. 190; Kendi, *Stamped from the Beginning*, p. 216.
42 Kevin M. Levin, *Searching for Black Confederates: The Civil War's Most Persistent Myth* (University of North Carolina Press, 2019).
43 Ibid., introduction.
44 Quoted in Williams, *I Freed Myself!*, chap. 2.
45 Michael Vorenberg, "Abraham Lincoln and the Politics of Black Colonization," *Journal of the Abraham Lincoln Association* 14, no. 2 (1993): p. 23. See also chapter 4 in Eric Foner, *The Fiery Trial: Abraham Lincoln and American Slavery* (W. W. Norton, 2011).
46 "Recognized at Last," *Douglass' Monthly*, July 1, 1862, p. 685. See also chapter 9, Leslie Alexander, *Fear of a Black Republic: Haiti and the Birth of Black Internationalism in the United States* (University of Illinois Press, 2023).
47 Martin Robinson Delany, *The Condition, Elevation, and Destiny of the Colored People of the United States* (Philadelphia, 1823), p. 31.
48 Alexander, *Fear of a Black Republic*, chap. 7.
49 Ibid.
50 For more on the debate around Haiti and emigration schemes, see chapter 7 in Alexander, *Fear of a Black Republic*.
51 First Annual Message to Congress, December 3, 1861, UVA Miller Center website, accessed July 17, 2024, https://millercenter.org/the-presidency/presidential-speeches/december-3-1861-first-annual-message; Vorenberg, "Abraham Lincoln and the Politics of Black Colonization," p. 28.
52 The Second Confiscation Act, Freedmen and Southern Society Project, accessed July 17, 2024, https://freedmen.umd.edu/conact2.htm.
53 Foner, *The Fiery Trial*, p. 218.

54 Vorenberg, "Abraham Lincoln and the Politics of Black Colonization," pp. 29–33.
55 Ibid., p. 31.
56 Quoted in Oakes, *The Radical and the Republican*, chap. 5.
57 *Douglass' Monthly*, September 1862, pp. 705–706.
58 Abraham Lincoln to Horace Greeley, August 22, 1862, Library of Congress, accessed July 17, 2024, https://www.loc.gov/resource/mal.4233400. See also James McPherson, "Who Freed the Slaves?" *Proceedings of the American Philosophical Society* 139, no. 1 (1995): pp. 1–10.
59 Preliminary Emancipation Proclamation, September 22, 1862, National Archives and Records Administration, accessed July 17, 2024, https://www.archives.gov/exhibits/american_originals_iv/sections/transcript_preliminary_emancipation.html; Vorenberg, "Abraham Lincoln and the Politics of Black Colonization," p. 36.
60 Emancipation Proclamation, January 1, 1863. National Archives, accessed July 18, 2024, https://www.archives.gov/milestone-documents/emancipation-proclamation#transcript.
61 Williams, *I Freed Myself!*, chap. 2.
62 Ibid.
63 Sinha, *The Slave's Cause*, p. 580.
64 Williams, *I Freed Myself!*, chap. 2.
65 Vorenberg, "Abraham Lincoln and the Politics of Black Colonization," p. 44.
66 Manning, "Working for Citizenship," pp. 180–181.
67 Quoted in Ibid., p. 192.
68 Quoted in Williams, *I Freed Myself!*, chap. 3.
69 Quoted in Oakes, *The Radical and the Republican*, chap. 6.
70 General Order Number 3, June 19, 1865, National Archives Catalog, accessed July 18, 2024, https://catalog.archives.gov/id/182778372.

Chapter 34

1 The full text reads: "Los esclavos José Mariá Josefa Fernandez y Felipe Medina reclaman que los levantan a medianoche a recoger bagazo, trabajando en la molienda sin días libres ni tempo para hacer su comida." Another says: "El esclavo Segundo Medina reclama que el mayordomo lo puso en el cepo y al día siguiente lo mando a trabajar con argolla al cuello, arrastrando un pilón de hierro."
2 For more information on the current site, see the Hacienda la Esperanza website, https://mascerca.paralanaturaleza.org/centros/hacienda-la-esperanza.
3 Astrid Cubano Iguina, "Freedom in the Making: The Slaves of Hacienda La Esperanza, Manatí, Puerto Rico, on the Eve of Abolition, 1868–76," *Social History* 36, no. 3 (2011): p. 287.
4 Ibid., pp. 280–84.
5 On Cecilio's case, see Cubano Iguina, "Freedom in the Making," pp. 280–81; 290.
6 Estimates of the number of captives transported to Cuba and Puerto Rico, 1844–1866, SlaveVoyages: The Trans-Atlantic Slave Trade Database, accessed December 9, 2024, https://www.slavevoyages.org/voyages/ucEYBWjR.
7 Jesús Sanjurjo, *In the Blood of Our Brothers: Abolitionism and the End of the Slave Trade in Spain's Atlantic Empire, 1800–1870* (University of Alabama Press, 2021), chap. 5, EPUB.
8 Quoted in Matt Childs, "Cuba, the Atlantic Crisis of the 1860s, and the Road to Abolition," in *American Civil Wars: The United States, Latin America, Europe, and the Crisis of the 1860s*, ed. Don H. Doyle (University of North Carolina Press, 2017), p. 213.

9 Christopher Schmidt-Nowara, "Anti-Slavery in Spain and Its Colonies, 1808–06," in *A Global History of Anti-Slavery Politics in the Nineteenth Century*, ed. William Mulligan and Maurice Bric (Palgrave Macmillan, 2013), p. 143.
10 Sanjurjo, *In the Blood of Our Brothers*, chap. 5.
11 Luis A. Figueroa, *Sugar, Slavery, and Freedom in Nineteenth-Century Puerto Rico* (University of North Carolina Press, 2005), p. 108; Luis Diaz Soler, *Historia de la esclavitud negra en Puerto Rico* (Editorial Universitaria, Universidad de Puerto Rico, 1970), chap. 11.
12 Schmidt-Nowara, "Anti-Slavery in Spain and Its Colonies," p. 143; Figueroa, *Sugar, Slavery, and Freedom*, p. 48.
13 Schmidt-Nowara, "Anti-Slavery in Spain and Its Colonies," pp. 143–44.
14 Quoted in Ibid., p. 144.
15 Figueroa, *Sugar, Slavery, and Freedom*, p. 111; Cubano Iguina, "Freedom in the Making," p. 286.
16 Sanjurjo, *In the Blood of Our Brothers*, chap. 5.
17 Ibid.
18 Figueroa, *Sugar, Slavery, and Freedom*, p. 112.
19 Guillermo A. Baralt, *Esclavos rebeldes: Conspiraciones y sublevaciones de esclavos en Puerto Rico (1795–1873)*, 2nd ed. (Río Piedras: Ediciones Huracán, 1982), p. 169–70.
20 Quoted Ada Ferrer, *Insurgent Cuba: Race, Nation, and Revolution, 1868–1898* (University of North Carolina Press, 1999), p. 15.
21 Ibid., pp. 21–22.
22 Childs, "Cuba, the Atlantic Crisis of the 1860s, and the Road to Abolition," p. 214.
23 Rebecca J. Scott, "Gradual Abolition and the Dynamics of Slave Emancipation in Cuba, 1868–86," *Hispanic American Historical Review* 63, no. 3 (1983): pp. 450–451. See also Rebecca J. Scott, *Slave Emancipation in Cuba: The Transition to Free Labor, 1860–1899* (University of Pittsburgh Press, 1985).
24 Hugh Thomas, *Cuba: A History* (Penguin, 2010), chap. 16.
25 Benjamín N. Narváez, "Subaltern Unity? Chinese and Afro-Cubans in Nineteenth-Century Cuba," *Journal of Social History* 51, no. 4 (2018): pp. 886–88.
26 Quoted in Ferrer, *Cuba*, p. 132.
27 Ibid.
28 Hugh Thomas calls it "less a war than a breakdown of order"; see Thomas, *Cuba*, chap. 17; Ferrer, *Insurgent Cuba*, pp. 43–44.
29 Quoted in Arthur F. Corwin, *Spain and the Abolition of Slavery in Cuba, 1817–1886* (University of Texas Press, 1967), p. 249.
30 Figueroa, *Sugar, Slavery, and Freedom*, pp. 113–114.
31 Schmidt-Nowara, "Anti-Slavery in Spain and Its Colonies," pp. 144–145; see also chapter 13 in Corwin, *Spain and the Abolition of Slavery in Cuba*.
32 Inés Roldán de Montaud, "The Misfortune of Liberated Africans in Colonial Cuba, 1824–76," in *Liberated Africans and the Abolition of the Slave Trade 1807–1896*, ed. Richard Anderson and Henry B. Lovejoy (Boydell & Brewer, 2020), p. 170.
33 Figueroa, *Sugar, Slavery, and Freedom*, p. 115.
34 Quoted in Figueroa, *Sugar, Slavery, and Freedom*, p. 115.
35 Ibid., p. 116.
36 Ibid.
37 Cubano Iguina, "Freedom in the Making," p. 289.
38 Schmidt-Nowara, "Anti-Slavery in Spain and Its Colonies," p. 145.

39 Figueroa, *Sugar, Slavery, and Freedom*, pp. 117–119.
40 Scott, "Gradual Abolition and the Dynamics of Slave Emancipation in Cuba," p. 454.
41 Scott, "Gradual Abolition and the Dynamics of Slave Emancipation in Cuba," p. 456; Corwin, *Spain and the Abolition of Slavery in Cuba*, p. 295.
42 Ferrer, *Insurgent Cuba*, pp. 58–59.
43 Quoted in Ibid., pp. 59–60.
44 Thomas, *Cuba*, chap. 17.
45 Ibid., chap. 18.
46 Childs, "Cuba, the Atlantic Crisis of the 1860s, and the Road to Abolition," p. 215; Ferrer, *Insurgent Cuba*, p. 63.
47 Ferrer, *Insurgent Cuba*, p. 64.
48 Ibid., pp. 66–67.
49 Scott, "Gradual Abolition and the Dynamics of Slave Emancipation in Cuba," pp. 456–457.
50 Ferrer, *Insurgent Cuba*, pp. 71–73.
51 Scott, "Gradual Abolition and the Dynamics of Slave Emancipation in Cuba," pp. 457–458.
52 Ibid., pp. 460–461.
53 Ibid., p. 473.
54 Esteban Montejo's story is one of the few surviving accounts from enslaved people and is all the more extraordinary for being recounted in the twentieth century—in 1963, when Montejo was 103 years old, to anthropologist Miguel Barnet. See the preface in Miguel Barnet, *Biography of a Runaway Slave*, trans. W. Nick Hill (Curbstone Press, 1994); see also pp. 56–57.
55 Barnet, *Biography of a Runaway Slave*, pp. 22, 45.
56 Ibid., p. 61.

Chapter 35

1 Lilia M. Schwarcz and Heloisa M. Starling, *Brazil: A Biography* (Penguin, 2019), p. 345.
2 Eduardo Silva, *As camélias do Leblon e a abolição da escravatura: uma investigação de história cultura* (São Paulo: Companhia das letras, 2003), p. 79.
3 Schwarcz and Starling, *Brazil*, p. 345.
4 I was shown the *rosas negras* while on the Little Africa Tour, Rio de Janeiro, July 2023. For more information, see Florenciostour, https://www.instagram.com/florenciostour/.
5 See Eduard Hildebrandt, "Chafariz e Igreja de Santa Rita no Largo de Santa Rita," 1844, Wikimedia Commons, https://commons.wikimedia.org/wiki/File:Eduard_Hildebrandt_Largo_de_Santa_Rita_1844.jpg.
6 Kim D. Butler, "Slavery in the Age of Emancipation: Victims and Rebels in Brazil's Late 19th-Century Domestic Trade," *Journal of Black Studies* 42, no. 6 (2011): p. 972.
7 Laird W. Bergad, *The Comparative Histories of Slavery in Brazil, Cuba, and the United States* (Cambridge University Press, 2007), pp. 120–21.
8 Cristina Nogueira da Silva and Keila Grinburg, "Soil Free from Slaves: Slave Law in Late Eighteenth- and Early Nineteenth-Century Portugal," *Slavery & Abolition* 32, no. 3 (September 2011): p. 437.
9 Beatriz Balanta, "Tropical Dreams: Promoting Brazil in Nineteenth-Century US Media," in *Envisioning Others: Race, Color, and the Visual in Iberia and Latin America*, ed. P. A. Patton (Brill, 2015), p. 241. See also Lloyd Belton, "'She Refused to Be Left Behind': The Sinews of Modern Day Trafficking in the Late Illegal US-Brazil Slave Trade, ca. 1860s–1880s,"

Slavery and Abolition 44, no. 3 (2023): pp. 496–518. On the present day legacy, see "The Brazilian Town Where the American Confederacy Lives On," *Vice*, February 5, 2015, https://www.vice.com/en/article/gq8ae9/welcome-to-americana-brazil-0000580-v22n2.
10 Schwarcz and Starling, *Brazil*, p. 329.
11 Ibid., p. 331.
12 Angela Alonso, *The Last Abolition: The Brazilian Antislavery Movement, 1868–1888* (Cambridge University Press, 2022), p. 45.
13 Jerry W. Cooney, "Abolition in the Republic of Paraguay: 1840–1870," *Jahrbuch für die Geschichte Lateinamerikas* 1 (1974): p. 150.
14 Ibid., p. 152.
15 Ibid., pp. 154, 159, 162–163.
16 Alonso, *The Last Abolition*, p. 47.
17 Quoted in Margarita Rosa, "Filial Freedoms, Ambiguous Wombs: Partus Sequitur Ventrem and the 1871 Brazilian Free Womb Law," *Slavery & Abolition* 41, no. 2 (2020): p. 383; Camillia Cowling, *Conceiving Freedom: Women of Color, Gender, and the Abolition of Slavery in Havana and Rio de Janeiro* (University of North Carolina Press, 2013), pp. 55–59.
18 Rosa, "Filial Freedoms, Ambiguous Wombs," p. 384.
19 Cowling, *Conceiving Freedom*, p. 56.
20 See chapter 3 in Cowling, *Conceiving Freedom*.
21 Rosa, "Filial Freedoms, Ambiguous Wombs," p. 384.
22 Schwarcz and Starling, *Brazil*, p. 304.
23 Alonso, *The Last Abolition*, pp. 85–86; James H. Kennedy, "Luiz Gama: Pioneer of Abolition in Brazil," *Journal of Negro History* 59, no. 3 (1974): pp. 255–67.
24 Kennedy, "Luiz Gama," p. 258.
25 Alonso, *The Last Abolition*, pp. 101–06; Kennedy, "Luiz Gama," pp. 260–63.
26 Alonso, *The Last Abolition*, p. 90.
27 Kennedy, "Luiz Gama," p. 262.
28 Quoted in Alonso, *The Last Abolition*, p. 105.
29 Alonso, *The Last Abolition*, p. 121. See also Sandra L. Graham, "Writing from the Margins: Brazilian Slaves and Written Culture," *Comparative Studies in Society and History* 49, no. 3 (2007): 611–36.
30 Alonso, *The Last Abolition*, p. 99.
31 Kennedy, "Luiz Gama," p. 263.
32 Alonso, *The Last Abolition*, pp. 17, 363.
33 Quoted in C. Castilho and C. Cowling, "Funding Freedom, Popularizing Politics: Abolitionism and Local Emancipation Funds in 1880s Brazil," *Luso-Brazilian Review*, 47, no. 1 (2010): pp. 89–90.
34 Kennedy, "Luiz Gama," pp. 265–266.
35 Alonso, *The Last Abolition*, pp. 18, 131–133.
36 Castilho and Cowling, "Funding Freedom," pp. 94–99; Bergad, *The Comparative Histories of Slavery in Brazil, Cuba, and the United States*, p. 286.
37 Alonso, *The Last Abolition*, pp. 136–137; see also Celso Thomas Castilho, "The Press and Brazilian Narratives of Uncle Tom's Cabin: Slavery and the Public Sphere in Rio de Janeiro, ca. 1855," *Americas* 76, no. 1 (2019): pp. 77–106.
38 Alonso, *The Last Abolition*, pp. 139–141.
39 Quoted in Ibid., p. 178.
40 Ibid., p. 184.

41 Ibid., pp. 163–65.
42 Ibid., pp. 230–232; 273.
43 Ibid., pp. 281–82.
44 Ibid., pp. 286; 293.
45 Silva, *As camélias do Leblon*, p. 11.
46 Ibid., p. 25.
47 Schwarcz and Starling, *Brazil*, p. 343.
48 Silva, *As camélias do Leblon*, pp. 35–36.
49 Alonso, *The Last Abolition*, pp. 296, 302; Bergad, *The Comparative Histories of Slavery in Brazil, Cuba, and the United States*, p. 287.
50 Alonso, *The Last Abolition*, pp. 311–12, 320; Robin Blackburn, *The Reckoning: From the Second Slavery to Abolition, 1776–1888* (Verso, 2024), chap. 10, EPUB.
51 Castilho and Cowling, "Funding Freedom, Popularizing Politics," p. 99.
52 Alonso, *The Last Abolition*, p. 331.
53 Silva, *As camélias do Leblon*, p. 8.
54 See the image at "Brazil: Five Centuries of Change," Brown University Library, accessed December 10, 2024, https://library.brown.edu/create/fivecenturiesofchange/chapters/chapter-4/abolition/.

Epilogue

1 Seymour Drescher, *Abolition: A History of Slavery and Antislavery* (Cambridge University Press, 2009), pp. 410–411.
2 See reports of the discovery, for instance "Brazil's Hidden Slavery Past Uncovered at Valongo Wharf," BBC News, December 25, 2014, accessed December 12, 2024, https://www.bbc.com/news/world-latin-america-30413525.
3 Maria Graham, *Voyage to Brazil and Residence There, during Part of the Years 1821, 1822, 1823* (London: Longman & Co, 1824), p. 170.
4 See "Valongo Wharf Archaeological Site," UNESCO World Heritage Convention, accessed March 18, 2024, https://whc.unesco.org/en/list/1548/.
5 "Slaves' Mass Grave Is Grim Reminder of Brazil's Racist Legacy," December 30, 2005, *Guardian*, accessed March 18, 2023, https://www.theguardian.com/world/2005/dec/30/brazil.mainsection.
6 For more on the IPN Museu Memorial, see IPN Museu Memorial website, https://pretosnovos.com.br/museu-memorial/.
7 Saidiya Hartman, *Lose Your Mother: A Journey Along the Atlantic Slave Route* (London: Serpent's Tail, 2007), p. 133.
8 See James Baldwin's 1969 interview with Dick Cavett, "James Baldwin Discusses Racism," The Dick Cavett Show, May 16, 1969, YouTube, 17:08, https://www.youtube.com/watch?v=WWwOi17WHpE.

Index

Abercromby, Ralph, 262, 263, 264, 265–66
Abolition of Slavery Act (1834 U.K.), 396–397
abolitionists/abolition. See also *specific individuals*
  in Argentina, 375
  Bird and, 382
  Bonaparte and, 281
  in Brazil, 484, 487–94
  in Britain, 199, 231–34, 247–48, 302, 338–39, 343–44, 355–56, 394, 395, 396–98, 419
  in Canada, 226
  in Central America, 381
  in Chile, 374, 380–81
  Christophe and, 317
  in Colombia, 452–53
  in Cuba, 428, 429, 476–78, 479–82
  in Danish colonies, 444–45
  in Dutch colonies, 463–65
  in France, 234–35, 438, 440–42
  in French colonies, 250–51, 283, 286, 443
  in Mexico, 374, 447
  in New England, 223
  Paraguay and, 486–87
  in Peru, 453–54
  Portugal and, 486, 493–94
  in Puerto Rico, 476, 478–79
  Quakers, 201, 232
  in Saint-Domingue, 247
  in South America, 452–53
  in Spain, 475, 476, 478
  in Suriname, 464–65
  in U.S., 302–3, 423–26, 456, 459–60, 462, 465, 467–70, 471–72
  use of *Zong* trial by, 231–32
  in Venezuela, 375, 377, 453
  views about black people, 420–21, 459
  women and, 490
  works by/about enslaved, 189, 199–203, 204, 234, 394–95, 456
Abruco, 187
Accara, 191
Account of the Negroe Insurrection in South Carolina, 163–64, 165, 166–67, 169
Act to Prohibit the Importation of Slaves (1807 U.S.), 303
Adams, John Quincy, 425–26
Address to Lord Brougham and Vaux (Wedderburn), 357–58
Afonso I (king of Kongo), 30–31, 33
Africa. See also *specific nations*
  colonization of, 370–71, 496–97
  European contest for control in, 42
  exploration of, 6–8
  gold in, 6, 33, 115–16
  inhabitants as descendants of Ham, 43
  leaders in, as sellers in slave trade, 4, 171
  national companies for trading with Africa, 115–16
  Portuguese tax, 96–97, 123, 128
African Methodist Episcopal (AME) Church, 361, 363, 366
Aguado, Padre Pedro, 51
Aguilar, Estanislao, 311–12
Ailhaud, Jean-Antoine, 245
Ainslie, George Robert, 329–30, 332
Alfonso X (king of Spain), 21–22
Álvares Cabral, Pedro, 27
Amador, 72, 73
Amarroco, Duarte, 74
American Colonization Society (ACS), 370–71, 468
Amistad, 421–26, 428
Andry, Manuel, 322, 324
Ansa, Kwamena (African king), 33
Antigua, 158–62, 182
Anti-Slavery Society (Britain), 395
Apinda, 155
Aponte y Ulabarra, Jose Antonio, 312–15
Appeal to the Coloured Citizens of the World (D. Walker), 388
Arbuthnot, Robert, 159, 161
Archer, Edward, 142–43
Argentina, 374–75, 377, 452
Argüelles, Agustín de, 307–8
Aristotle, 3
Arobe, Don Francisco de and family, 57–58
Ashley, John, 222
asientos de negros, 75, 80
Atta, 192–93
Attucks, Crispus, 216
Austin, Stephen, 446, 447
The Axe Laid to the Root (Wedderburn), 345, 346, 347
Ayllón, Lucas Vázquez de, 39–40, 41
Azores, 5, 10

Bacon's Rebellion (1676), 134
Bahamas, 24, 226–28, 390–91, 427–28
Bailey, Dick, 340
Balboa, Vasco Núñez de, 62

INDEX 611

Balcarres, Earl of, 270–71
Baldwin, James, 498–99
Baldwin, Roger, 425–26
Baliceaux, 265
Baptise, 265
Baptist War, 392–94
Baquaqua, Mahommah Gardo, 409–11
Barbados, 107
  agriculture on, 107, 108
  badges of freedom, 138
  basic facts about, 107
  Carolina colony and, 115
  enslaved in, 108, 340
  Jews in, 108
  revolts on, 110–14, 340–43
  runaways on, 106, 109, 339
  slave laws, 132–33
  sugar on, 109, 110
Barbados Gazette, 243
Barbot, John, 116
Barbour, Philip, 426
Barrett, Edward, 419–20
Barrio y Sepúlveda, Juan de, 57, 59–60
Bass, Samuel, 458
Batteau, 364, 366
Bayano, 62
Beckford, Henry, 420, 421
Beckles, Sir Hilary, xv
Beckx, Jaspar, 96
Behn, Aphra, 188–89
Belle, Dido Elizabeth, 198–99
Belleforest, François de, 76
Belley, Jean-Baptiste, 250–51
Ben (slave), 297, 298–99, 300
Benavides, Alonso de, 54–55
Benavides, Antonio de, 165
Bennett, Ned, 364, 366
Bennett, Rolla, 363, 364, 366
Bennett, Thomas, 364
Ben (Son of) Solomon, Job, 170–72
Berbice, 189–93
Berlin West Africa Conference (1884-85), 496
Bermuda, 81, 82
Biassou, Georges, 242, 243–44, 246
Biohó, Benkos (Domingo), 104, 105
Bird, Japhet, 1
Bird, Robert Montgomery, 382–83
Bissette, Cyrille Charles Auguste, 440, 441–42, 443–44
Black Caribs/Black Charaibs, 207, 210–13, 215, 260, 264–66

black confraternities
  in Brazil, 98, 125, 126, 128
  on Cape Verde islands, 29
  in Portugal, 195
  on São Tomé, 30
  in Spain, 17, 18, 21
Black Ghost of Empire (Manjapra), xiii
"black king Bayano," 62
black people
  abolitionists' views about, 420–21, 459
  in colonial New York, 143–44
  in colonial Virginia, 84–85
  deportation of, from Britain, 76–77
  in Portugal, 14–15
  in Spain, 15, 21
  witchcraft accusations against, 103–4
black people, free
  during American Civil War, 466–67, 470–71
  during American Revolution, 219
  in Bahamas, 226–27
  in Brazil, 496
  in Cartagena, 102
  in Cuba, 48, 311, 429, 434, 436, 496
  as enslavers, 85, 209, 236–37
  in Florida, 168, 335–37
  in former Spanish colonies, 378–80
  in France, 194
  in French army, 220
  Fugitive Slave Act and, 457
  Haiti as destination for, 369–70, 371–72, 467–68, 470
  on Jamaica, 147, 187
  laws to distinguish slaves from, 130–31
  on Martinique, 440
  on Saint-Domingue, 234, 236–37, 238–40, 243, 244, 249, 273–75
  segregation and Jim Crow in U.S., 495–96
  in Spain, 43
  in Spanish army, 71, 220
Blackwall (Abruco), 187
Blackwood, Jesse, 366
Blanchelande, Philibert François Rouxel de, 245
Blanco, Pedro, 421–22
Bleby, Henry, 394
Bluett, Thomas, 170–72

Bolívar, Simón, 318–19, 368, 375, 376–77, 378, 379–80, 381
Bolivia, 376, 453
Bonaparte, Napoleon, 281, 282–83, 284, 305–9, 438
Bosc, Bernard Xavier, 441
Boukman, 241, 242, 243
Bouyaval, Joseph, 254–55
Boyer, Jean-Pierre, 319, 362, 368, 369, 371, 372–73
Brazil, 401
  abolition in, 484, 487–94
  African imprint in, 98
  black confraternities in, 98, 125, 126, 128
  Britain and, 402, 403
  Dutch in, 107
  free black people in, 496
  free soil campaign in, 491
  gold in, 136, 139
  Holland and, 93–94, 95, 98, 99
  Jewish people in, 93–94
  land for runaways, 100
  maroon communities in, 99–101, 125, 135–37
  as monarchy, 401, 402–9
  Paraguayan War, 486
  population of, 399, 400, 401–2, 404, 405, 485
  Portugal and, 27
  revolts in, 405–8, 493
  slave trade and, 95, 409, 485, 497
  sugar in, 93, 109, 404
  WIC and, 93
Bredà, Toussaint. *See* Louverture, Toussaint
Breffu, 157–58
Bremner, William, 330, 331
Brissot, Jacques Pierre, 235
Britain. See also *specific colonies*
  abolition in, 199, 231–34, 247–48, 302, 338–39, 343–44, 355–56, 394, 395, 396–98, 419
  American cotton and, 460
  attack on Hispaniola, 117
  attack on Jamaica, 117–18
  Black Caribs and, 211–13, 260, 264–66
  black people deported from, 76–77, 229, 379
  black population in, 143, 195, 228–29
  Bonaparte and, 305, 308
  Brazil and, 402, 403
  Caribbean colonies, 90

Britain (*continued*)
  Ceded Islands, 207, 210, 260
  Christophe and, 317
  Florida and, 164–65, 168, 335
  free soil principle, 75
  in Guadeloupe, 260, 289
  land reform in, 344, 345–46, 347, 357, 358
  Martinique and, 283–84
  Maryland colony, 83
  mutiny in British Army, 416
  Navigation Act (1651), 109–10
  New Netherland and, 90
  news of Caribbean revolts in, 187
  removal of enslaved from, 198, 199
  runaways in, 195, 196
  on Saint-Domingue, 249, 273, 275, 276
  in Saint Lucia, 262–64
  Seven Years' War and, 193
  slavery abolished in, 199, 396–98
  slave trade and, 233, 248–49, 302, 408–9, 411–13
  slave trade monopoly of, 140
  Spenceans, 344, 345, 346, 347
  Suriname ceded to Dutch by, 90, 189
  Treaty of Madrid and, 114, 118
  War of 1812, 328, 333, 334, 335
  works by/about enslaved in, 189, 199–203, 204, 234, 394–95
British North American colonies, 83, 115, 134, 216–20. See also *specific colonies*
British West Indies, 139, 414. See also *specific islands*
Brooks, 12
Brougham, Henry, 357
Brown, John, 462
Brown, Vincent, xvii
Brunias, Agostino, 213
Buchanan, James, 461–62
Buddoe/Bordeaux, Gottlieb, 445
Bull, William, 167
Burton, Mary, 174–75
Bussa, 340–42
Bustamante, Anastasio, 447
Butler, Benjamin, 465, 466
Byrd, Sam, Jr., 296

Cabello de Balboa, Miguel, 59
Cadamosto, Alvise, 10

Caledonian Mercury, 288
Calixtus III (pope), 10
Campbell, Alexander, 198
Campbell, Elizabeth, 346–47
Canada, 226, 229
Canary Islands, 4–5, 7, 10, 16, 19, 20
Candace (queen of Ethiopia), 197–98
cannibals, 1–2, 10, 25
Cape Verde Islands, 28–29
Carabalí, Federico, 430–31
Caribbean Sea, *x*, 42
Caribs (Kalinago), 23, 209–10, 211, 212–13
Carleton, Sir Guy, 226
Carlos I (king of Spain), 26
Carondelet, Baron de, 253, 254, 255
Carpata, Bazjan/Bastiaan, 258–59
Cartagena, Colombia, 48, 62, 101–2, 103, 104
Cary, Samuel, 268
Casa de Contratación (Seville, Spain), 20
Casa dos Escravos de Lisboa, 14
Casor, John, 85
caste in Spanish America, 43–44
Castellanos, Juan de, 51–52
Castellanos, Miguel de, 51
Castilla del Oro, 61, 62
Castro, Dom Miguel de, 95, 96
Castro, Rámon de, 257
Catholics/Catholicism
  conversion in African kingdoms to, 31
  indigenous people and, 24, 42
  infidels as "just" slaves, 5, 16, 23–24
  Jewish *conversos* and, 103
  legality of slave system and, 9, 123, 126–29
  in maroon communities, 54, 55, 136
  marriage among black people, 21
  Protestant Reformation and break with, 41–42
  "purity of blood," 43
  slave trade and, 421
  sugar and, 25–26
  Treaty of Tordesillas and, 19, 26
Ceded Islands, 207, 210, 260. See also *specific islands*

Céspedes, Carlos Manuel de, 477
Chacón, Clemente, 312
Chafariz e Igreja de Santa Rita no Largo de Santa Rita (Hildebrandt), 485
Charboniel, Antonio, 309, 310
Charles II (king of England), 114, 115
Chatoyer, Joseph, 207, 210, 212, 213, 214–15, 261
Chatoyer the Chief of the Black Charaibes in St. Vincent with His Five Wives (Brunias), 215
Chavannes, Jean-Baptiste, 239, 240
Chicora, Francisco de, 39–40
Chile, 374, 380–81
Chirino, José Leonardo, 255
Christians/Christianity. See *also* Catholics/Catholicism
  acceptance of, and being "fit" for freedom, 395
  enslavement of, 42, 86, 133
  enslavement of non-Christians by, 5, 16, 23–24
  Ethiopian history of, 42
  missionaries, 391, 394, 414
  in narratives by formerly enslaved, 201, 203, 205, 206
  slavery in Bible, 42–43
Christmas rebellion (1521), 34–35
Christophe, Henry, 251, 284, 285, 286, 315–19, 320, 369
Cinqué (Cinquez), Joseph, 422–26
Claes, King, 155, 156
Clarkson, Thomas, 233, 234, 248, 419, 420
Clay, Henry, 457
Clerveaux, Augustin, 286
Clinton, Henry, 220
Clodoré, Robert de, 88
Clotilda, 461
Cochrane, Alexander, 334
Cochrane-Johnstone, Andrew, 327
Codd, Edward, 241, 242–43
Codrington, Christopher, 159–60
Coffij, 190, 191–92
Collingwood, Luke, 229–30
Colombia
  abolition and, 452–53
  Cartagena, 101–2
  dissolution of Gran Colombia, 452
  free black people in, 102

INDEX 613

Jewish *conversos* in, 103
revolts in, 48
slave trade in, 62, 102, 104, 375–76, 453
Columbian Sentinel, 371
Columbus, Christopher, 18–19, 20, 23
Columbus, Diego, 34, 36
Colvile, Andrew, 356
Compromise of 1850, 456, 457
The Condition, Elevation ... Colored People of the United States (Delany), 467–68
The Confessions of Nat Turner (Gray), 385–87, 389
Connecticut, 223
Cooper, Anthony Ashley, 137
Cooper, Johnny, 340
Corpus Juris Civilis (Roman law), 21
Correspondence Relative to the Emigration to Hayti ... United States (Dewey), 370, 371
Cosway, Maria, 199
Cosway, Richard, 199
Cotegipe, baron of, 491–92
cotton, 29, 361, 460–61
Council of Westminster, 3
Couper, John, 294
Court (slave), 161–62
Covey, James, 424
Creole, 426–28
Cromwell, Oliver, 107, 108, 117
Crump, Nathaniel, 160
Cuba
 abolition and independence in, 428, 429, 430, 476–78, 479–82
 as destination for runaways, 187, 256, 311
 free black people in, 48, 311, 434, 436, 496
 indigenous people on, 48
 as last market for slave trade, 416–17, 418, 474, 476
 map of (1870), xi
 Mexico and, 447, 450
 revolts on, 256–57, 311–12, 430–31, 433–37, 481
 runaways fighting Spanish with indigenous people, 48
 "second slavery," 311, 428
 slave population, 80
 Spain and, 429–30
 sugar on, 93, 311, 431
 U.S. and, 450–51, 483

Cudjoe, 218
Cuffee, 145, 146, 148–49, 150
Cuffee, John, 221–22
Cuffee, Paul, 221–22
Cugoano, Quobna Ottobah, 197–98, 199–200, 214, 232, 233
Cunha, João Lustosa da, 490–91
Curaçao, 258–59, 464, 465

Dâaga, 416
da Gama, Vasco, 26
Dallas, Robert Charles, 152
Dalrymple, William, 212, 213
Davis, Cain, 340
Davis, Caleb, 165
Davis, Hugh, 84
Davis, William, 182
Decrès, Denis, 286
Delany, Martin, 467–68, 470
Delgrès, Louis, 290–91, 292
del Monte, Domingo, 432, 433, 436
Demane, Harry, 199
Demerara-Essequibo, 348–49, 350, 351–56, 358, 391
Denmark
 colonies, 91, 155–58, 182–84, 444–45
 monopoly trading company for Africa, 115, 116
 slave trade and, 303–4
Desfon, 265
Desfourneaux, Edme Étienne Borne, 289
Deslondes, Charles, 322–25
Dessalines, Jean-Jacques, 247, 251, 285, 286, 287, 288, 315
Dewey, Loring Daniel, 369–70, 371
Diallo, Ayuba Suleiman, 170–72
Diana, mother of Georges Biassou, 244
Dias, Bartolomeu, 26
Dias, Henrique, 99
Dias, Paschoal, 128
Dickinson, John, 216
diseases and deaths of indigenous populations, 25, 26
Dominica
 ceded to Britain, 207
 as destination for runaways, 159, 209
 French settlement of, 88, 209
 maroon communities on, 266–69, 327, 329–30, 332–33

as "neutral island," 209
 revolts on, 266, 326–27, 328, 330–32
 sugar on, 209, 327
Doran, James, 205
Douglas, Peter, 393
Douglas, Stephen, 457, 461
Douglass, Frederick, 456, 459–60, 462, 465, 467, 468, 469
Drake, Francis, 63, 64–69, 70, 71
Drake, John, 64, 65
Drake, Joseph, 64, 65
Drummond, James, 264
Dundas, Henry, 248, 249
Dunmore, Lord, 227

Eanes, Gil, 7
Eckhout, Albert, 96
Ecuador, 57, 58–59, 452, 453
Edinburgh Advertiser, 196
Edwards, Nelson, 383
Eguiluz, Paula de, 103–4
"El Chicorano," 39–40
Elegía (Castellanos), 51–52
Elfrith, Daniel, 80, 81
Elizabeth I (queen of England), 76–77
The Emancipation of Slaves (Tocqueville), 442
Emancipation Proclamation (U.S.), 470
encomienda system, 24, 25
Enrique (cacique), 34, 36, 38–39
enslaved people. *See* slavery/enslaved people
Equiano, Olaudah, 204–6, 229, 231, 232, 234
Ethiop(ian)s, 15, 31, 42

Fabulé, Francisque, 87–88
Faquorna, 422–26
Fédon, Jean, 268
Fédon, Julien, 267, 268, 269
Felipillo, 62
Ferguson, Frank, 365
Fermin, 305, 309, 310
Fernández, José Ramón, 473–74
Fernando V (king of Spain), 23, 25
Ferry, James, 424
filibusterers, 450–51
Fizel, Nicolas, 439
Florida, 164–65, 168, 335–37
Foot, George, 182, 183
Fortunato, Domingos, 406–7
Foster, William, 461

Fox, George, 134
Fox, William, 248
France. *See also specific colonies*
  abolition in, 234–35, 438, 440–42
  Bonaparte, 281, 282–83, 284, 305–9, 438
  Code Noir, 130, 131–32, 194
  free black people in, 194
  free black people in army of, 220
  free soil principle, 75, 76, 194
  Holland occupied by, 258
  Kalinagos and, 209, 211
  monopoly trading company for Africa, 115, 116
  North American colony, 88–89
  pirates in Caribbean, 42
  recognition of Haiti by, 372
  revolt on Saint John (1733) and, 157
  Revolution in, 241, 245, 275, 293
  Santo Domingo ceded to, 257
  Seven Years' War and, 193, 235–36
  slave trade and, 131, 440
  Treaty of Rijswijk and, 177
Francés, Joseph el, 256
Francis, Sam, 383
Francis, Will, 383, 384, 387
François I (king of France), 41
freedom. *See also* abolitionists/abolition; maroons/maroon communities; runaway slaves
  acceptance of Christianity and, 395
  for Africans liberated by European navies, 413–16
  during American Revolution, 218, 219, 220
  badges of, 138
  black loyalists after American Revolution, 225–26
  in Brazil, 99
  during Civil War, 465–66, 468–70
  on Cuba, 428, 429
  by drawing lots, 490
  Dutch "half-freedom," 89–90
  economic havoc caused by, 51
  for enslaved women under French law, 132
  by escaping to Cuba, 187
  by escaping to Florida, 164–65
  exile requirement in Virginia, 300
  fight for equality and, 236–37
  free soil principle and, 75–76, 77–78, 194, 491
  free "womb" measures, 374, 375, 444, 446, 447, 453, 478, 486, 487
  in French Caribbean colonies, 438
  Haiti as beacon of, 317, 369–70
  for helping colonial governments, 118, 330
  for helping quash revolts, 48
  as human's natural state, 21
  under Islamic rule, 4
  knowledge of French Revolution and, 241
  lawsuits for, 48, 322, 488
  meanings of, 499
  for maroon communities on Jamaica, 153
  in northern U.S., 303
  for not helping pirates, 71
  overview of routes to, xvi–xvii
  petitions for, 195, 221–22
  purchasing, 17, 18, 124, 205
  Quakers and, 134–35
  racialization of concept of, xv
  routes to, in Africa, 32
  routes to, in Spain, 21–22
  routes to, in Valencia, 17–18
  by setting foot on France, 194
  for slave catchers, 38, 56, 153–54, 187, 347
  for some enslaved brought from Saint-Domingue, 322
  suicide as, 1, 109, 137, 157–58
  during War of 1812, 333
Freeman, Elizabeth "Mum Bett"/"Mumbet," 222
free soil principle, 75–76, 77–78, 194, 491
Frelinghuysen, Theodorus Jacobus, 200
Frémont, John C., 461
French Caribbean colonies. *See also* Dominica; Grenada; Guadeloupe; Martinique; Saint-Domingue
  abolition in, 250–51, 283, 286, 443
  Bonaparte and freedom in, 438
  return of slavery in, 292–93
  slave trade in, 438
Fugitive Slave Act (U.S., 1793), 457
Fugitive Slave Act (U.S., 1850), 456

Gabriel (slave), 301
Gabriel, John, 155
Gainsborough, Thomas, 204
Gama, Luís Gonzaga Pinto da, 488–90
Gangá, Pablo, 430–31, 437
Gangá, Polonia, 435
Ganga Zumba, 135–36
García, Joaquín, 245–46
García, Juliana, 378
Garcia, Miguel, 310
García de Solís, Fulgencio, 168
Garcia II (king of Kongo), 95, 97
García Quintana, Domingo, 306–7
Garrison, William Lloyd, 388–89
Genius of Universal Emancipation (Garrison), 388–89
Georgia, 40–41, 169–70
Gilbert, Thomas, 230–31
Ginés Doncel, 39, 40, 41
Girodet de Roussy-Trioson, Anne-Louis, 250–51
The Gladiator (Bird), 382–83
Gladstone, Jack, 349, 351, 352, 353, 354, 355
Gladstone, John, 348, 417
Gladstone, Quamina, 349, 351, 352, 353
Glover, Isah, 428
Glover, Rachel, 428
gold
  in Africa, 6, 9, 33, 115–16
  in Brazil, 136, 139
  Castilla del Oro (Panama) and, 61–62
  in South America, 49
Gómez, Máximo, 480
Gonçalves Baldaia, Afonso, 7
Gonçalves Zarco, João, 5
González, Francisco, 43
González, José Caridad, 255–56
González de Herrera, Pedro, 55
Gordillo, Francisco, 39
Gordon, Jack, 265

INDEX 615

Gran Colombia, 368–69, 380, 452, 453
Gray, Thomas R., 385–87, 389
Great Newes from the Barbados, 110–12
Greece, slavery in ancient, 2, 3
Greeley, Horace, 468
Green, William, 199
Gregory XVI (pope), 421
Gregson, William, 230–31
Grenada, 88, 198, 266–69
Griggs, Nancy, 338
Grignon, William, 389–90
Gronniosaw, Ukawsaw, 200–201
Guadeloupe
    abolition in, 289
    British in, 260, 289
    as French territory, 88
    revolts on, 289, 290–92
Guales, 40
Guanches, 5, 7, 16, 20
Guerrero, Vicente, 447, 450
A Guide to Hayti (Redpath), 468
Guridi y Alcocer, José Miguel, 307
Guthrie, John, 151–52
Guyana (Berbice), 189–93. *See also* Demerara-Essequibo
Guy's Town (Jamaica), 151

Haiti, 243.
    Christophe vs. Pétion, 316, 318–19
    under Dessalines, 287
    as destination for free black people, 369–70, 371–72, 467–68, 470
    as destination for runaways, 362
    French recognition of, 372
    Gran Colombia and, 369
    as republic, 315
    revolt on, 287–88
    U.S. Marines in, 495
Hallett, William, 144
Hamilton, John, 351
Hanway, Jonas, 228–29
Harth, Mingo, 363, 365
Hartman, Saidiya, 498
Hastings, Selina, 202
Hawkins, John, 63, 77
Hawkins, Richard, 59
Haydon, Benjamin Robert, 419, 420
Hector, Sam, 182–83
Hédouville, Gabriel-Marie-Théodore-Joseph d', 276–78

Henry ('navigator' prince of Portugal), 6, 8–9
Herrera, Juan Bautista, 253
Hesselberg, Engelbret, 182–83, 184
Hewell, John, 426
Heyrick, Elizabeth, 355–56
Hidalgo, Father Miguel, 306, 374
Hildebrandt, Eduard, 485
Hispaniola, French. *See* Saint-Domingue
Hispaniola, Spanish
    arrivals of slaves directly from Africa, 25, 26
    attempts to eradicate maroon communities, 46
    British attack on, 117
    domination by rebels on, 36, 38
    enslavement of indigenous population, 23–24
    maps of, xii, 37
    maroons in, 23, 35, 38, 39
    racialization of slavery on, 36
    revolts on, 34–36
    slave code (1522), 36
    slave population, 80
    slave trade and, 29
    sugar on, 46–47, 48, 93
Historia General y Natural de las Indias (Oviedo), 34, 35–36
The History of Mary Prince (Prince), 394–95
History of the Indies (las Casas), 45
Hoare, William, 170, 172
Hogeboom, Pieter, 222
Hogg, Robert, 174
Holland. *See also specific colonies*
    in Africa, 95, 97
    Berbice and, 190
    in Brazil, 93–94, 95, 98, 99
    Caribbean colonies, 90, 189, 463–65
    free soil principle in, 75, 77–78
    French occupation of, 258
    "half-freedom," 89–90
    revolt against Spain, 74–75, 98
    slave laws, 134
    Suriname and, 90, 188–89, 190, 464–65
    Sweden and, 91
Home, Ninian, 267, 268

Honduras, 48
The Horrors of Slavery (Wedderburn), 344–45, 356, 357, 358
Hughson, John, 174, 175
Hughson, Sarah, 174, 175
Hugues, Victor, 260, 289, 292
Hunter, Robert, 146–48, 149, 150, 151

Iberian Union, 75
Immediate, Not Gradual Abolition (Heyrick), 355–56
indentured servants
    in Bahamas, 226–27
    in Barbados, 108
    in British North American colonies, 83–84, 85, 115, 134
    from China, 417, 443, 454, 477, 480
    in French law, 128
    from India, 417, 443, 464
indigenous people. *See also* specific groups
    on Berbice, 190
    on Cuba, 48
    diseases and deaths of, 25, 26
    enslavement of, 24–25, 39, 42, 86
    fighting Spanish with maroons, 48
    in Florida, 337
    maroon communities and, 58, 99, 117–18
    in Virginia, 82
Innocent XI (pope), 127, 128, 129, 136
The Interesting Narrative of the Life of Olaudah Equiano (Equiano), 204–6, 234
Isabella (queen of Spain), 24, 25
Islam, 3–4, 15

Jacinto, 305, 309, 310
Jackey, 340–41
Jackson, Andrew, 335, 336–37
Jamaica
    British attack on, 117–18
    escape to Cuba from, 187
    free black people in, 147, 187
    landscape, 148, 149
    Leeward maroons, 148–49
    map of (1750), xi
    maroon communities on, 117–19, 148–53

INDEX

Jamaica *(continued)*
  population of, 118, 119, 147, 148
  provision grounds in, 346
  revolts on, 119–21, 148–54, 184–87, 218–19, 269–71, 389–90, 392–94
  sugar on, 184, 186, 390
  Windward maroons, 119, 149–150, 153, 154, 269, 271
James, Daniel, 395
James I (king of England), 81, 82
Janes, Dwight, 423–24
Jarvis, Harry, 465
Jaúregui, Andrés de, 307, 308, 309, 310
Jean-François, 310, 311–12
Jefferson, Thomas, 216–17, 299, 370
Jewish people
  in Barbados, 108
  in Brazil, 93–94
  in Cartagena, 103
  children sent to São Tomé, 29–30
  in *Code Noir*, 131
  as slaves, 15
João II (king of Portugal), 6, 29, 33
João III (king of Portugal), 33
Joaquin, José, 430
Johan, Anthoni, 18
Johana, 15–18
Johnson, Anthony, 85
Johnson, Samuel, 216
Jones, Absalom, 304
Jope, John, 80, 81
Juni, 155
Justinian (Roman emperor), 21

Kalinago (Caribs), 209–10, 211, 212–13
Kansas-Nebraska Act (U.S., 1854), 461
Kanta, 155
Kelsall, James, 231
Kendall, James, 114
Kenner, Henry, 322–25
Kerby, Thomas, 161
Kerry, Peggy, 174, 175
Kimbo, 422–26
King, Robert, 205
Kishee, 150
Knibb, William, 392, 396, 420
Komina, 322–25
Kongo, Kingdom of
  as Catholic, 31
  civil wars in, 166

Dutch and, 95
Portugal and, 31, 33, 42, 95, 97
Saint-Domingue revolt and, 242
slave trade and, 33, 166

Lacrosse, Jean-Baptiste Raymond de, 290
La Escalera, 436
Land of the True Cross, 27
La Roche, Joe, 363, 364
las Casas, Bartolomé de, 25–26, 44–45
Laurencio, Juan, 55, 56
Laveaux, Étienne, 273, 275
Laws of Burgos (Spain, 1512), 25
Lecesne, Louis Celeste, 419
LeChevalier, Théodore, 441
Leclerc, Charles, 283, 284–85, 286
Lemba, Sebastián, 46, 47–48
Le Testu, Guillaume, 68
Leyton, John, 122
The Liberator, 389, 457, 464
Ligon, Richard, 108, 109, 138
Lincoln, Abraham, 462, 465, 468, 469–70, 471
Lindsay, Alexander, 270–71
Lintz, Bartholomeus, 99
Lisundia, Juan Bautista, 311–12
Locke, John, 137
The London Magazine, 201, 202
Lonja de la Seda (Valencia, Spain), 17
López, Narciso, 450–51
López de Cerrato, Alonso, 46, 47
Losada, Diego de, 51
Lose Your Mother (Hartman), 498
Louisiana, 252–55, 322–25
Louis X (king of France), 76
Louis XIV (king of France), 76
Louverture, Moïse, 277–78, 281, 282
Louverture, Toussaint
  basic facts about, 246–47
  Bonaparte and, 281, 282–83, 284
  British and, 273, 275, 276
  economic reforms of, 281–82
  exile of, 285–86
  free black people on Saint Domingue and, 274–75
  French abolition of slavery and, 251
  Hédouville and, 277–78

Raimond and, 276
Rigaud and, 278–79
Saint-Domingue revolt and, 242–43, 244, 247
Santo Domingo and, 280–81
Sonthonax and, 275–76
Lovelace, Earl, xvii
Lowry-Corry, Somerset, 389
Lucumí, Carlota, 434, 435
Lucumí, Fermina, 434–35
Lucumí, Lorenzo, 430–31
Lundy, Benjamin, 449
Luyola, Juan (Juan de Bolas/ Juan Lubolo), 118

Maceo, Antonio, 480, 481
Madden, Richard Robert, 432
Madeira, 5–6, 10, 19–20, 93
Madison, James, 224–25
Maitland, Thomas, 276–77
Makandal (Mackandal/Macandal), François, 177, 178–81
Mandinga, Pedro, 65–66
Mangache, Andrés, 58, 59
Manjapra, Kris, xiii
Mansa Musa, 6
Mansfield, Lord, 198–99, 230, 231
Manuel I (king of Portugal), 15, 33
Manzano, Juan Francisco, 432–33
María Luisa, 253
Maroons / maroon communities, 35.
  in Brazil, 99–101, 125, 135–37
  Catholicism and, 54, 55, 136
  in Colombia, 104–5
  in Demerara, 348
  in Dominica, 266–69, 327, 329–30, 332–33
  in Florida, 165
  in Hispaniola, 38, 39
  with indigenous people, 58, 99, 117–18
  in Jamaica, 117–19, 148–53, 185, 269–71
  in Martinique, 87–88
  in Mexico, 54, 55
  in Panama, 62–64, 66, 71
  peace with Spain, 70
  in Peru, 56, 57, 58–59
  in Saint-Domingue, 178, 179, 278
  in São Tomé, 72–73
  in Suriname, 190
Martinique
  under Britain, 283–84

under France, 88
free black people on, 440
map (circa 1680), 87
revolts on, 237–38, 438–39, 441
maroon communities on, 87–88
Maryland colony, 83, 139
Massachusetts, 221–223
Mathew, William, 156
Matiza, Francisco de la, 55–56
Maurits, Johan, 93, 95
McKenzie, Kenneth, 268
Meaher, Timothy, 461
Médor, 181
Meléndez, Salvador, 310
Mendonça, Lourenço da Silva, 123–29
Mendoza, Antonio de, 53–54
Mexico, 53, 54–56, 374, 446–50
Miguel de Buría, 49–52
Mills, Nathaniel, 122
Mina, Antonio Cofi, 253, 254
Missouri Compromise (U.S., 1820), 361, 454
Mocambo Quarter (Lisbon, Portugal), 15
Molesworth, Hender, 120
Monroe, James, 298, 299
Montejo, Esteban, 482–83
Montes, Pedro, 422, 423
Montiano, Manuel de, 165
Moore, Hark, 383
Moore, John, 263, 264
Moors, 15
Moreau de Saint-Méry, Médéric Louis Élie, 177, 178, 179, 180
Morgan, Henry, 61
Morning Chronicle, 198
Moru, 422–26
Murray, John, 218, 352, 353, 354–55

Nabuco, Joaquim, 489
Nanny/Nanny Town, 149–50, 151, 153, 154
A Narrative of Events (James Williams), 398
Narrative of the... Life of ... an African Prince, as Related by Himself (Gronniosaw), 200–201
Narrative of the Life of Frederick Douglass (Douglass), 456
Nascimento, Francisco José do, 491
Nascimento, João de Deus, 399–401

National Intelligencer, 371–72
Natural History (Pliny the Elder), 4–5
Nava, Juan Bautista, 51
Nelson, Red, 385
Netherlands. *See* Holland
New Hampshire, 223
New Netherland, 89–90
New York, 143–46, 173–76
New York Evening Post, 455
Nicholas V (pope), 9
Njinga/Nzinga (African queen), 96–97
Nobo, Francisco & Antonio, 309
North Star, 456
Northup, Solomon, 457–59
Northwest Ordinance (U.S., 1787), 361–62
Nossa Senhora do Rosário, 29, 30
Novimies, Hector, 77

Ocampo, Diego de, 46
Ogé, Vincent, 234, 236–37, 238, 239–40, 241
Oglethorpe, James, 169, 170, 172
O'Higgins, Bernardo, 378
"On Being Brought from Africa to America" (P. Wheatley), 203
Orde, James, 266
Ordenanzas de los negros (1522), 26
Oroonoko ... Royal Slave (Behn), 188–89
Ovando, Nicolás de, 23, 25
Oviedo, Esteban Santa Cruz de, 435
Oviedo, Gonzalo Fernández de, 34, 35–36
Oxenham, John, 69–70

Padilla, José, 379–80
Palmares, Brazil, 99–101, 125, 135–37
Panama
gold in, 61
pirates and, 64–65
revolts in, 61–62
maroon communities in, 66, 71
runaways, 62–64
slave population, 80
Papillon, Jean-François, 242, 243–44, 273
Paraguay, 486–87
Pascal, Henry, 205

Patterson, Orlando, xvi
Paul, Thomas, 371
Paul, William, 363, 365
Pedre, Jean-Louis Marin, 263
Pélage, Magloire, 290, 291
Pennsylvania, 135 (colony), 223
Peru
abolition in, 453–54
independence of, 376–77
maroon communities in, 38, 56, 57, 58–59
revolts in, 48
slave trade and, 453
Peter the Doctor, 145
Pétion, Alexandre, 286, 315, 316, 318–19, 376
Philipse, Cuffee, 173, 175
Philipse, Frederick, 173
Piar, Manuel, 379
Pierce, Franklin, 451
Pike, Robert, 66–67
pirates. *See also specific individuals*
black sailors as, 142
enslaved and, 64, 65, 67
runaways and, 68–70, 71
slave trade and, 75
Pitt, William, the Younger, 233, 248–49
Pliny the Elder, 4–5
Plymouth, Massachusetts, 83
Poems on Various Subjects, Religious and Moral (P. Wheatley), 202
Pointe Coupée (Louisiana), 252–55
poisonings, 179–80, 181
Polk, James K., 449
Polverel, Étienne, 245, 249, 273–75
Pompey, 390–91
Porter, Henry, 383, 384
Portrait of Citizen Jean-Baptiste Belley (Girodet de Roussy-Trioson), 250–51
Portugal. *See also specific colonies*
abolition and, 486, 493–94
black confraternities in, 195
black people in, 14–15
Brazil and, 27
European slave trade begun by, 8–9
first encounter with sub-Saharan Africans, 7
freedom in, 194–95
gold and, 9
Iberian Union and, 75
Kongo and, 31, 33, 42, 95, 97

Portugal (continued)
  new slaves prohibited in North Atlantic colonies and in, 194
  papal grant of monopoly over all African lands to Portugal, 10
  as port of entry for Africans, 14
  tax on slaves and African leaders, 95, 96, 123, 128
  trade with Africans, 9, 31, 32–33
  Treaty of Tordesillas and, 19, 26
Pory-Papy, Pierre-Marie, 443
Post, Frans, 92, 94
Power y Giralt, Don Ramón, 305
Poyas, Peter, 363, 365, 366
Poydras, Julien, 254
Pradine, Jean-Baptiste Symphor Linstant de, 419
Pratt, Charles, 424
Prescod, Samuel Jackman, 420
Prester John, 6
Preto, Domingos, 73–74
Preto, Lázaro, 73–74
Prevost, George, 264
Price, Arthur, 175
Prince (slave), 155
Prince, Mary, 394–95
Prince of Orange, 1, 2
Pringle, Thomas, 395
Prioleau, Peter, 363
Propaganda Fide, 123, 130
Prosser, Gabriel, 295–301, 386
Protestant Reformation, 41–42
"pueblos de Indios," 38
Puerto Rico
  abolition and independence on, 430, 476, 478–79
  lawsuits brought by slaves in, 473–74
  revolts in, 257, 309–10
  runaways fighting Spanish with indigenous people, 48
  slave trade and, 429, 474
  sugar on, 93, 475
  U.S. and, 483

Quaco/Quawcoo, 158
Quakers, 134–35, 201, 232
Quamina, 182, 183
Quao, 148–49, 150, 153, 154
Quejo, Pedro de, 39
Quick, Jacobus, 173
Quoshey/Quashey, 142–43

racialization of slavery
  Africans as descendants of Ham, 43
  in Britain, 76–77
  in British colonies, 86
  devolution into racialized violence, 496
  on Hispaniola, 36
  ideas associated with word "black," 44
  during seventeenth century, 84
  in Spain, 15
Raimond, Julien, 234, 236–37, 238, 275, 276, 281
Recio y Miranda, Don Serapio, 256
redemption and freedom, 17
Redpath, James, 468
Reform Act (1832 U.K.), 396
Reese, Jack, 383
Reijmbach, Jurgens, 99, 100
Religious Society of Friends. *See* Quakers
"A Representation of the Injustice and Dangerous Tendency of Tolerating Slavery ... in England" (Sharp), 195–96
Resistance to enslavement
  about, 11
  during Civil War, 465–67
  conditions affecting ability for, 110
  poisonings, 179–80, 181
  slave ships destroyed, 122–23
  sugar fields burned by slaves, 46–47, 48
  suicides, 1, 109, 137, 157–58
  uprisings on slave ships, 141–42
  work-related, 144, 339, 391–92, 442–43, 478, 481
revolts
  on *Amistad*, 421–26, 428
  in Antigua, 158–62, 182
  in Bahamas, 227–28, 390–91
  in Barbados, 110–14, 340–43
  in Berbice, 190–93
  in Brazil, 405–8, 493
  in British Army, 416
  in Cartagena, 48
  on *Creole*, 426–28
  in Cuba, 256–57, 311–12, 430–31, 433–37, 481
  in Curaçao, 258–59
  in Demerara, 348, 351–56
  in Dominica, 266, 326–27, 328, 330–32

  estimated number of, 13
  first in North America, 40–41
  in Grenada, 266–69
  in Guadeloupe, 289, 290–92
  in Haiti, 287–88
  in Hispaniola, 34–36
  in Honduras, 48
  in Jamaica, 119–21, 148–54, 184–87, 218–19, 269–71, 389–90, 392–94
  in Louisiana, 253–55, 322–25
  as making system untenable, xvi
  map of key, ix
  in Martinique, 237–38, 438–39
  in Mexico, 53
  in New York, 144–46, 173–76
  in Panama, 61–62
  in Peru, 48
  in Puerto Rico, 257, 309–10
  records of, 11–12
  in Saint Croix, 182–84, 445
  in Saint-Domingue, 241–48, 252, 274–75, 279, 282, 286
  in Saint John, 155, 156–58
  in Saint Lucia, 262–64
  in Saint Vincent, 260–62, 264–66
  in Santo Domingo, 34
  in São Tomé, 72, 73
  in South Carolina, 163–64, 165–68, 363–67
  in Tobago, 210
  in Venezuela, 48–52, 255–56
  in Virginia, 134, 295–301, 333–34
Rhode Island, 223
rice, 139, 166
Riché, Jean Baptiste, 254
Richepanse, Antoine, 291
Rigaud, Andre, 259, 273, 278–79
Rigaud, Tula, 258–59
Roanoke colony, 70–71, 81
Roatán, 265–66
Rockemborgh/Roquemborg, George, 254–55
Rodriguez, Juana, 43
Rolfe, John, 80
Rolle, Jeannot, 209
Rolle, John, 390
Rome, slavery in ancient, 3, 21
Romualdo, 256, 309
Rosa de Souza, Guilhermina, 406–7
Rosario, Juan Agapito del, 309
Roume de Saint-Laurent, Philippe Rose, 275, 280–81

INDEX   619

Royal African Company (RAC), 115–16, 140, 170, 172
Ruiz, José, 422, 423
runaway slaves
  aiding British Army, 333, 334, 335
  during American Civil War, 465–66, 470–71
  from Antigua, 159
  on Barbados, 106, 109, 339
  in Britain, 195, 196
  on Cuba, 482–83
  Dominica as destination for, 159, 209
  enslaved from Saint-Domingue, 322
  fighting Spanish with indigenous people, 48
  Florida as destination for, 164–65
  freedom in exchange for not helping pirates, 71
  Fugitive Slave Acts and, 456, 457
  Haiti as destination for, 362, 470
  helping colonial governments, 118, 393
  in Hispaniola, 23, 35, 38
  in Mexico, 54–56
  Mexico as destination for, 450
  in Panama, 62–64
  in Peru, 56, 57
  pirates and, 68–70
  raiding by, 54–55, 88
  on Saint Vincent, 211
  on São Tomé, 30
  as slave catchers, 38, 56, 153–54, 187, 347
  terms used for, 35
  in U.S. Constitution, 457
  variants of "running away," 35
  in Venezuela, 49

Saint Augustine, Florida, 80
Saint Barthélemy, 444
Saint Croix, 182–84, 444–45
Saint-Domingue. *See also* Haiti; Louverture, Toussaint
  abolition in, 247, 250–51
  Britain and, 249, 273, 275, 276
  enslaved population on, 177–78, 236
  escape to Cuba from, 256, 311
  free black people on, 234, 236–37, 238–40, 243, 244, 273–75
  French control after Louverture, 286–87
  maroon communities on, 178, 180, 278
  poisonings on, 179–80, 181
  refugees in South Carolina, 362
  revolts on, 241–48, 252, 274–75, 279, 282, 286
  trade with U.S., 279–80, 284
Saint Helena, 413, 414–15
Saint John, 155, 156–58
Saint Lucia, 262–64
Saint Thomas, 91, 155
Saint Vincent, 208
  Black Caribs on, 260–62
  ceded to Britain, 207
  Kalinago and, 211
  map of (1776), 208
  as "neutral island," 209
  revolt on, 260–62, 264–66
  runaways on, 211
  sugar and, 212
Salt (Lovelace), xvii
Sánchez Galque, Andrés, 57–58, 60
Sancho, Ignatius, 203–4
San Lorenzo de los Negros/San Lorenzo de Cerralvo (Mexico), 56
San Martín, José de, 376, 378
Santa Anna, Antonio López de, 448–49
Santa Catarina (Lisbon, Portugal), 15
Santo Domingo
  ceded to France, 257
  enslaved population of, 280
  incorporated into Haiti, 369
  Louverture and, 280–81
  revolt in, 34
  revolt in Saint-Domingue and, 245–46
São Tomé, 29–30, 72–74, 93
Sarrasin/Sarazin, Antoine, 254
Sartine, Antoine de, 194
Schoelcher, Victor, 438, 441–42, 444
Scoble, John, 420
Scots Magazine, 332–33
Scott, Dred, 454–55, 462
Scroggins, Mary E., 428
Sedgwick, Catharine Maria, 222
Sedgwick, Theodore, 222
segregation by race, 15, 495–96
Seixas Magalhães, José de, 484, 492
Serras, Juan de, 118
Seton, James, 262
Seven Years' War, 193, 235–36
Seville, Spain, 20–21
Sharp, Granville, 195–96, 198, 231–32
Sharpe, Samuel, 391–92, 393, 394
Sierra Leone, 229, 370, 412, 414
Siete Partidas (Spanish law), 21–22
silver, 58
Sir William Young Conducting a Treaty ... St Vincent (Brunias), 214–15
slavery/enslaved people
  ability of, to earn wages, 124
  during American Revolution, 219
  among Africans, 31–32
  in ancient world, 2–3, 21
  Barbados's population of, 108
  white society's belief in good treatment of, 137–38, 214
  in Bible, 42–43
  Brazil's population of, 404, 405, 485
  in British colonies, 80, 217
  in Canada, 226
  in Cape Verde Islands, 29
  of Christians, 24, 42, 133
  codes, 36, 130, 131–32, 168, 194
  enslavers compensation for murdered, 300
  in Curaçao, 258
  current forms of, 498
  by Dutch, 89–90
  in France, 76
  French Enlightenment intellectuals and, 235
  Fugitive Slave Acts (U.S., 1793 and 1850), 456, 457
  ghost of, in present, 497–98
  of Guanches in Canary Islands, 5, 7, 16, 20
  independence wars of Spanish colonies and, 377–78
  of indigenous people, 24–25, 39, 86
  indigenous people replaced by Africans, 25–26, 44

INDEX

slavery/enslaved people (*continued*)
  internal tensions among, 156–57
  introduction of, into Georgia, 169–70
  Islam and, 3–4
  Jamaica's population of, 119
  Kansas-Nebraska Act (U.S., 1854), 461
  laws to control, 130–34
  lawsuits brought in Puerto Rico by, 473–74
  legality of system court case, 123, 126–29
  as metaphor for white oppression, 236
  Missouri Compromise and, 361, 454
  in New York, 144–46
  of non-Christians by Christians, 5, 16, 23–24
  number of, transported to America by Spain, 44
  owned by free black people, 85, 209, 236–37
  pirates and, 64, 65, 67
  Portuguese in sub-Saharan Africa, 8–9
  power as basis of, 2
  profits from, in New England, 222–23
  reasons for, 15
  religious instruction of, 361
  removal from Britain of, 198, 199
  returned to French Caribbean colonies, 292–93
  Saint Croix's population of, 183
  Saint-Domingue's population of, 177–78, 236
  Santo Domingo's population of, 280
  on São Tomé, 30
  Slavic people as, 4
  in Spain, 15, 20
  in Spanish army, 220
  in Spanish colonies during Bonaparte, 306–9
  supposed affections of, for captors, 160
  in Tejas/Texas, 446, 448–49
  as temporary condition, 21
  in Virginia colonies, 86, 217
  working on slave trade ships, 142
slave societies, xiv–xv

slave trade
  abolished in Europe, 339
  abolition and increase in, 303–4
  Africans as sellers, 4, 171
  among British colonies, 390–91
  in Argentina, 375
  arrivals directly from Africa to Caribbean islands, 25, 26
  beginning of European, 8–9
  Brazil and, 95, 403, 409, 485, 497
  Britain and abolition of, 232–33, 248–49, 302, 408–9, 411–13
  British monopoly for South American, 140
  Cape Verde Islands and, 28
  captives jumping overboard during voyages, 1
  captives working on ships, 142
  Cartagena and, 62, 102, 104
  Catholicism and, 421
  in Colombia, 375–76, 453
  Columbus and, 23
  Council of Westminster and, 3
  Cuba as last market, 416–17, 418, 474, 476
  Cuba's "second slavery" and, 428
  deaths due to illness, 79
  Denmark and, 91
  despair of captives, 12
  estimated number of voyages, 13
  formalization and industrialization of, 12
  France and, 131, 440
  in French Caribbean colonies, 438
  Hispaniola and, 29
  Holland and, 463
  Iberian Union and, 75
  insurance and, 230–31
  kidnappings by privateers, 79–80
  Kongo and, 33, 166
  Muslims and, 3–4
  number of Africans crossing Atlantic, 11
  in Peru after abolition, 453
  pirates in, 75
  Portuguese tax and, 96–97, 123, 128

  Prince Henry and, 8–9
  Puerto Rico and, 429, 474
  RAC and, 115–16
  relinquished by Spain in West Africa, 75
  Richmond in, 295
  routes, 14
  Royal African Company and, 115–16, 140, 170, 172
  ships destroyed, 122–23
  Spain and, 20, 25, 26, 310, 373
  sugar and expansion of, 97
  system finances, 140–41
  uprisings on ships, 141–42
slave trade and U.S.
  abolition of international, 302–3
  Constitution and, 225
  illegal, 417
  internal, 461
  Lyons-Seward Treaty and, 475
  Portuguese Company, 416–17
  profits from, in New England, 222
Smalls, Robert, 466–67
Smeathman, Henry, 229
Smith, John, 349, 351, 352, 353, 354–55
Smith, Thomas, 228
Société des Amis des Noirs, 234–35, 236
Society for Effecting the Abolition of the Slave Trade (SEAST), 232, 233
Solitude, 291–92
Some Memoirs of the Life of Job ... in Africa (Bluett), 170–72
Somerset, James, 198
Sonthonax, Léger-Félicité, 245, 247, 249–50, 273–76
Sorrell, Bernat, 16, 17, 18
Sorubiero, Margaret, 174
South Carolina
  Barbados and, 115
  Charleston, 360
  cotton in, 361
  enslaved population in, 217
  population in, 168
  revolts in, 163–64, 165–68, 363–67
  rice, 139, 166
  Saint-Domingue refugees in, 362
  slave code amended, 168
  slave trade in, 303

Spanish expedition to, 39–40
South Carolina Gazette, 167–68
South Sea Company, 140
Spain. See also *specific colonies*
  abolition and, 475, 476, 478
  black community in, 15, 21
  black confraternities in, 17, 18, 21
  under Bonaparte, 305–9
  Dutch revolt and, 74–75, 98
  enslaved in army of, 220
  enslavement of indigenous populations, 24–25
  European nations contesting control of, in Africa, 42
  expeditions to South Carolina and Georgia, 39–41
  Florida and, 164, 168
  free black people in, 43
  free black people in army of, 71, 220
  Iberian Union and, 75
  Louisiana and, 252–55
  Muslim states in, 15
  negotiations with maroon communities, 38, 59–60
  number of Africans transported to America by, 44
  peace with maroon communities, 70
  positions for persons of mixed racial heritage, 256–57
  "purity of blood" and "new Christians," 43
  Seven Years' War and, 193
  slavery in, 15–18, 20
  slave trade and, 20, 25, 26, 310, 373
  Treaty of Madrid and, 114, 118
  Treaty of Rijswijk and, 177
  Treaty of Tordesillas and, 19
Spalding, Thomas, 294
Stewart, Charles, 198
Stono Rebellion (1793), 163–64, 165–68
Stovall, Tyler, xv
Strickland, Susanna, 394
Stubbs, Robert, 231
sugar(cane)
  on Antigua, 159, 160
  on Barbados, 108, 109, 110
  in Brazil, 93, 109, 404
  in British West Indies, 139

Columbus and, 20
on Cuba, 311, 431
on Dominica, 209, 327
Dominican priests and, 25–26
expansion of slave trade and, 97
fields burned by slaves, 46–47, 48
growing and processing of, 94
on Hispaniola, 46–47, 48, 93
on Jamaica, 184, 186, 390
on Madeira, 5, 19–20, 93
as multinational project, 93
on Puerto Rico, 93, 475
on Saint John, 158
on Saint Vincent, 212
on São Tomé, 30, 74, 93
on St. Thomas, 91
WIC and, 92–93
suicides, 1, 109, 137, 157–58
Suriname
  abolition in, 464–65
  ceded to Dutch, 90, 189
  in fiction, 188–89
  maroon communities on, 190
Swedish colonies, 90–91

Tacky and Tacky's Revolt, 184–87
Taínos, 23–24, 25, 36, 38
Talleyrand-Périgord, Charles Maurice de, 283
Taney, Roger B., 454
Tejas/Texas, 446, 448–49, 471
Tellería, José, 255
Tenorio, Josefa, 378
Thoma, 155
Thomas, Ben, 173
Thoughts and Sentiments on the Evil and Wicked Traffic of Human Species (Cugoano), 199–200, 232
The Times of London, 330
tobacco, 81–83, 139
Tobago, 207, 210
Tocqueville, Alexis de, 442
Tomboy (slave), 161, 162
trade between Europeans and Africans, 31, 32–33, 92
Travis, Joseph, 383–84
Treaty of Alcáçovas (1479), 10
Treaty of Breda (1667), 90
Treaty of Madrid (1670), 114, 118
Treaty of Rijswijk (1697), 177

Treaty of Tordesillas (1494), 19, 26
"Treinta anos" (Thirty Years, Manzano), 432
Trelawny, Edward, 151, 153
Trépagnier, François, 324
Tupís, 27
Turnbull, David, 431–32, 433, 434, 436
Turner, Nat, 383–87
Twelve Years a Slave (Northrup), 459
Two Treatises of Government (Locke), 137
Tyler, John, 449

Uncle Tom's Cabin (Stowe), 490
United Provinces, 74–75
United States. See also slave trade and U.S.
  abolition in, 423–26, 456, 459–60, 462, 469–70
  Amistad and, 423–26
  Civil War, 462, 465–71
  Creole and, 427–28
  Cuba and, 450–51, 483
  Dred Scott decision, 454–55, 462
  escape to, from Saint-Domingue, 321–22
  Florida as territory of, 337
  Fugitive Slave Acts, 456, 457
  Kansas-Nebraska Act, 461
  Louverture and trade with, 279–80, 284
  Marines in Haiti, 495
  Missouri Compromise (1820), 361, 454
  Northwest Ordinance, 361–62
  post-Civil War amendments, 471–72
  profits in New England from slavery, 222–23
  Puerto Rico and, 483
  "second slavery" in, 460–61
  segregation and Jim Crow in, 495–96
  slave trade's end, 302–3
  Texas and, 449
  War of 1812, 328, 333, 334, 335
Uruguay, 452
Ury, John, 175

Valdés, Gabriel de la Concepción, 436–37
Valencia, Spain, 15–18, 20

Vallano, Panama, 63–64
Van Buren, Martin, 425
van der Hagen, Pieter, 77–78
van Hoogenheim, Wolfert Simon, 191, 192
van Juff, Printz, 155
Vantilborough, Peter, 145
van Uytrecht, Caspar, 258
Vaquero, Juan, 69–70
Vassa, Gustavus, 205
Vastey, Pompée Valentin, 318
Vaz Teixeira, Tristão, 5
Velasco, Luis de, 54–55
Venezuela
    abolition in, 375, 377, 379, 453
    dissolution of Gran Colombia, 452
    revolts in, 49–52, 255–56
    runaways in, 49
Vermahaly Negroes, 118–19
Vermont, 224
Vesey, Denmark, 359–62, 364–67
Vesey, Joseph, 359–60
Vieira, Antonio, 136
Vimeur, Donatien Marie Joseph de Rochambeau de, 286–87
Virgens e Veiga, Luís Gonzaga das, 400–401
Virginia
    exile requirement of freedom in, 300
    revolts in, 295–301, 333–34, 383–87
    runaways during War of 1812, 333, 334, 335
    slave trade and, 295
Virginia colonies
    black people during seventeenth century, 84–85

early workers, 83
enslaved population in, 217
first slaves in, 80
growth of slavery in, 86
indentured servants in, 83–84, 85
Jamestown, 80, 81
Roanoke, 70–71, 81
slave laws, 133
tobacco and, 81–82, 139
Treaty of Madrid and, 114
von Humboldt, Alexander, 52

Wagener, Zacharias, 95
Wager (Apongo), 186
Walker, David, 388
Walker, William, 451
Wanderley, João Maurício, 491–92
Warner, John, 86
War of 1812, 328, 333, 334, 335
Warren, Peter, 173
Washington, Madison, 426
Washington Gazette, 362
Watts, William, 84
Wedderburn, Robert, 344–48, 356–58
Wellesley, Arthur, 308
Wellesley, Henry, 308
Wellington, Duke of, 308
West India Company (WIC)
    in Africa, 97
    Brazil and, 93
    New Netherland and, 89–90
    and maroon communities, 99
    sugar and, 92–93
Wheatley, John, 201–2
Wheatley, Nathaniel, 202
Wheatley, Phillis, 201–3

Whitefield, George, 201, 205
White Freedom (Stovall), xv
Widow Grey's plantation revolt, 119–20
Wilberforce, William, 233, 247, 248, 249, 301, 302, 356, 357–58
Williams, James, 398
Williams, John, 393
Williamson, Mary, 84
Wilson, George, 363
Wiltshire, King, 240 340
witchcraft, 103–4
Wolof people, 15–16
women
    in abolitionist associations, 490
    freedom for enslaved, under French law, 132
    as leaders of maroon communities, 149–50, 153
    as participants in revolts, 291–92
    in Union Army, 470
    witchcraft accusations, 103–4
Woolfolk, Ben, 297
World Anti-Slavery Convention (1840), 419–421

Xiorro, Marcos, 430

Yanga, Gaspar, 54–56
Yllescas, 58, 59
Young, Sir William, 210–11, 212, 213

Zong trial, 230–32
Zumbi, 136, 137
Zurara, Gomes Eanes de, 7, 8–9